TEN HEADS OF RAVANA

A Critique of Hinduphobic Scholars

Edited by
Rajiv Malhotra & Divya Reddy

Published by
Garuda Prakashan Private Limited
Gurugram, Bharat

www.garudabooks.com

First published in India 2023

Copyright © 2023
Infinity Foundation India 2021 – 2023

Edited By: Rajiv Malhotra & Divya Reddy

All rights reserved. No part of this publication may be reproduced or transmitted in any form or by any means, electronic or mechanical, including photocopying, recording, or any information storage or retrieval system, without prior permission in writing from the publishers.

No responsibility for loss caused to any individual or organisation acting on or refraining from action as a result of the material in this publication can be accepted by Garuda Prakashan or the author.

The content of this book is the sole expression and opinion of its author, and not of the publisher. The publisher in no manner is liable for any opinion or views expressed by the author. While best efforts have been made in preparing this book, the publisher makes no representations or warranties of any kind and assumes no liabilities of any kind with respect to the accuracy or completeness of the content and specifically disclaims any implied warranties of merchantability or fitness of use for a particular purpose.

The publisher believes that the content of this book does not violate any existing copyright/intellectual property of others in any manner whatsoever. However, in case any source has not been duly attributed, the publisher may be notified in writing for necessary action.

ISBN: 979-8-8857-5066-0

Printed in India

Dedicated to all Intellectual Kshatriyas

Contents

Introduction
    Rajiv Malhotra   vii

1. **Romila Thapar**
   Pushpaka Vimana and the Flights of Her Historical Imagination
   Anurag Sharma   15

2. **Sheldon Pollock**
   Propaganda and Prevarication
   K.S. Kannan   57

3. **Michael Witzel**
   Flights of Fantasy
   Manogna Sastry   87

4. **Devdutt Pattanaik**
   Deconstructing Devduttology
   Subhodeep Mukhopadhyay   112

5. **Irfan Habib**
   Hoodwinking History
   Manogna Sastry   164

6. **Shashi Tharoor**
   The Quintessential Macaulay Putra
   Divya Reddy   189

7. **Audrey Truschke**
   Truschke-nāma or The Tales of Truschke
   Subhodeep Mukhopadhyay & Manogna Sastry   223

8. **Ramachandra Guha**
   Anarchic #FiberalDistorian
   T.N. Sudarshan and Divya Reddy   267

9. **Kancha Ilaiah**
   Bharat Vikhander
   Sharda Narayanan & Subhodeep Mukhopadhyay   295

10. **Wendy Doniger**
    Quest for Eroticism
    H.R. Meera   341

Acknowledgments   369

About the Authors   370

Introduction

Rajiv Malhotra

Infinity Foundation India (IFI) has, for the past several years, been at the forefront in the field of civilizational studies, applying the lens of Dharma to examine a broad range of topics. As a leading think tank, it has published game-changing original research that has been widely disseminated through books, blogs, social media, e-learning courses and videos. The themes it has worked on have included the history of Indian science and technology, impact of modern technologies such as Artificial Intelligence, consciousness studies, cultural and spiritual history, comparative studies of civilizations, education, ecology, ethics and human rights. Since the past two centuries, Indology has been controlled by Western scholars and institutions, who have applied Western methods to study Indian civilization. Infinity Foundation India has been a pioneer in exposing this stranglehold and providing responses from the Indian point of view. It coined the term *Swadeshi Indology* to refer to this new approach to disrupt Western Indology and construct its own traditional interpretations. The present book – *Ten Heads of Ravana* – is the latest offering from our team of brilliant scholars.

The idea of *Ten Heads of Ravana* was born during an Infinity Foundation India retreat in 2019, to commemorate and reflect on its work thus far and plan ahead for the changing nature of the kurukṣetra. Nestled in the beautiful surroundings of Rishikesh, the retreat was a memorable time for the team to reconsider its work through Dharmic frameworks and paradigms. As they contemplated the current dynamics of Indology, there emerged a need for an anthology that would inform the general reader of the thoughts of some well-known scholars of the field. I am delighted to see that discussion bear fruit through this book.

The title of this anthology—*Ten Heads of Ravana*—has been chosen with care. The use of 'Ravana' is intended as a parody and not literally. The metaphorical resemblences are clear: The historical Ravana disrupted society's Hindu structures, and the 'heads' chosen for this book are considered by Hindus today to be individuals doing something similar but intellectually and not with physical violence. The historical Ravana was very intelligent, a great scholar, hard working and with immense power at his disposal. The ten scholars featured in this book are powerful in the current academic discourse, have worked diligently most of their lives to develop their intellectual "weapons", and their impact is not to be trivialized.

The scholars chosen as the intellectual heads of the metaphorical Ravana are being taken seriously in this book. There is no intention on the part of the authors to attack the individuals at a personal level, but rather to cast their work in the framework from the perspective of Dharma. The essays consider the major themes and arguments from each individual's ouvre and showcase why they misrepresent and distort studies related to Bhārata and Dharma and why the typical reader needs to be mindful of the narratives being pushed due to the powerful influence of the ecosystem they have built over several decades. The authors have taken care to not engage in any ad hominem attacks or unprofessional takedown of the individual scholars.

The *Ramayana*, one of the greatest mahakavya-s of Bhārata, shows us the nature of Ravana as the king of Lanka and the main antagonist of the epic. He is believed to have learnt the *Arthashastra* from Shukracharya, adept at the use of maya and won boons from Brahma and Siva. Ravana's use of tactics—from the manner in which he abducted Sita to his battle with Srirama and his army, trying to trick Sita by showing the severed head of Srirama, to using psychological warfare tactics during Sita's captivity at the Asokavana—hold many lessons. These are not merely instances from an epic story but hold equivalents even in today's world. In the arena of Indological studies, such tactics have presented themselves in the works of scholars we consider in this current volume, to create some of the most disempowering narratives for Dharma and Bhārata.

The ten contemporary scholars in this book have been chosen because their work includes aspects that many Hindus today consider adharmic, just as the historical Ravana was perceived in his time. And just as the historical Ravana defended his positions, so also the ten scholars featured have an aggressive presence on the world stage of Hinduism studies with their own points of view. The authors of this book respect the opponents' right to intellectual freedom and merely wish to offer rebuttals so the readers can decide for themselves.

Each essay establishes the importance of engaging with a specific "intellectual Ravana's" work in terms of contemporary influence, expands on the major positions of the protagonist, and shows how the arguments are rooted in weak and disingenuous foundations, while having disproportionate impact due to the intellectual and popular ecosystems they control. Matters such as the use of diacritics have been left to the discretion of each author for their respective articles.

Consider for example, the article on Romila Thapar. She has been one of India's foremost historians, having held control of premier national educational and research institutions to influence academic discourse and government policies over decades. Anurag Sharma, in his brilliant essay, refutes Thapar's historiographical assumptions by providing strong counterexamples from Indian history. In the first section, he critically examines her views on the Islamic period of Indian history; in the second, her theories related to Hindu Dharma and the sacred texts such as *Ramayana, Mahabharata* and the *Puranas*; and in the third, her views on India as a nation and Hindu nationalism. Using evidence from fields of numismatics, archaeology, epigraphy, art and traditional texts to debunk many of the claims, Sharma makes a compelling case as to why Thapar's work is unreliable and cannot be assumed as the mainstream narrative if we wish to return to scientific, objective and fact-based representations of history.

The Sanskrit scholar, Sheldon Pollock, has been the subject of my book *The Battle for Sanskrit*. Several volumes were published from the series of Swadeshi Indology conferences held in Chennai and New Delhi by Infinity Foundation India. The editor of these volumes, Professor K.S. Kannan, presents a powerful essay on Pollock's major arguments and modus operandi. Kannan shows that despite being a scholar making his living from Sanskrit, Pollock denies the very nativity of Sanskrit to India, and calls the language dead despite many proofs to the contrary. Pollock's work is analyzed for the major characteristics of his method, including how he uses a narrow definition to determine the vitality of a tradition, selects data to fit a theory and intentionally uses various terms/frameworks of social science, modern psychology, anthropology, Biblical Studies etc., in order to superimpose them on traditional Indian thought to discredit the latter. The major themes of Pollock's work, including his devious quest to find linkages between Sanskrit and Nazism, trying to find racism in cāturvarṇya system, imagining connections and patterns of power in Sanskrit grammar are all considered by Kannan, while also highlighting the many rebuttals of Pollock's work from several scholars.

Michael Witzel is an important scholar discussed in this anthology of essays and Manogna Sastry analyzes his work in her cogent essay. Sastry discusses one of the major themes of Witzel's academic work, consisting of his championing the Aryan Invasion/Migration into India theories, to the point of disregarding evidence and denigrating through ad hominem attacks, the works which challenge and have negated several of his central points. His proof and methodology have included "creating" evidence when none exists, through mistranslations and grammatical errors, to the point of distorting verses to suit his whims. When his claims have been discredited by others, Witzel has gone on to offer farcical explanations, even as the lack of academic ethics in his work stands tall. The essay highlights how such instances demonstrate the poor scholarship that accompanies Witzel's work in a theme as crucial as the Aryan issue, for it has direct implications on the temporal and spatial origins of the *Vedas* and Sanskrit heritage. Witzel has been a vociferous critic of Indians wherever they are fighting for a fair and just representation of their history. He played a role, along with Marxist historians such as Romila Thapar, in trying to thwart the attempts made by Hindus in North America to correct the history textbooks of Grade VI taught in California Public Schools. Witzel's writings, laden under the garb of trying to protect "historical accuracy", lays bare much of what is fallacious about his scholarship. The essay considers several such instances of Witzel's work to demonstrate why his work qualifies him as one of today's Intellectual Ravanas.

Devdutt Pattanaik is a prolific writer who has produced a vast amount of literature on various religious and social issues especially pertaining to India and Hinduism. He has authored over fifty books, many of which are bestsellers, and written over a thousand columns for various websites, centered around the relevance of what he calls "mythology" in today's times, and how it impacts management, governance and leadership. Pattanaik's book *Indian Culture, Art and Heritage*, is even recommended as reading material for civil service aspirants in India. Subhodeep Mukhopadhyay shows in his excellent analysis of Pattanaik's work, the protagonist's major positions—from equating Hindutva to militant Brahmanism, reading bizarre meanings into texts such as Krsna apparently having accepted and endorsed infidelity, to praising the brilliance and simplicity of Aryan Invasion/Migration Theories despite them being repeatedly discredited with evidence—which, far from being rooted in tradition, are riddled with willful misinterpretations, distortions and divisive narratives. Mukhopadhyay builds a compelling picture of why Pattanaik, far from being considered an authority on Dharma related matters and texts, should be replaced by returning to the numerous accurate commentaries and interpretations from within the tradition which are grounded in pramana sastra.

Irfan Habib, the Marxist scholar from Aligarh Muslim University, is the subject of Manogna Sastry's essay. Habib has the distinction of being amongst the most vocal and unrelenting voices opposing the archaeological results of the excavations at Ayodhya against the backdrop of the dispute for the land demolished at the erstwhile Babri Masjid. Sastry analyzes his notorious role as a witness and 'expert' in the Ram

Janmabhoomi issue at Ayodhya, as well as his and his coterie's hold over the country's premier historical research institutes and universities. Sastry's lucid essay highlights several such points and key observations on a range of issues, drawing from original readings of Habib's works and others. She traces the significant contributions of Irfan Habib to the disfiguring of Indian history and his role in creating a hegemony in academic institutions that perpetuate divisive and false historical accounts.

Shashi Tharoor, a serving Member of Parliament (Indian National Congress) of the Lok Sabha from Thiruvananthapuram, Kerala and the former under-secretary general of the United Nations, forms the subject of Divya Reddy's article. In popular media and for most aspirational urban Indians, Tharoor is seen as a slick and eloquent interpreter of Hinduism for the twenty-first century. Reddy shows that Tharoor's work on Hinduism consists of an assortment of theories drawn from colonial Indologists and historians. These historians have been rejected because they used the colonized lens to conjure a history of India. They denied the indigenous origin of the country's mainstream culture, instead giving credit to foreign 'invaders' while devaluing India's cultural heritage by portraying it as less ancient than its true accounts. Considering Tharoor's work on Hinduism and religious conversions, Reddy shows how he has distorted and misinterpreted the notion of 'liberalism' and 'pluralism' inherent in Hinduism to convince an average 'Macaulaiyzed' English speaking Hindu youth, who has no deep moorings in Hindu thinking. Tharoor's eloquence, public persona and good use of English have catapulted him as a world spokesman on Indian cuture, but Reddy exposes his inauthenticity.

In their analysis of Audrey Truschke's work, Subhodeep Mukhopadhyay and Manogna Sastry explicate the key themes of her research. Truschke's positions on Hinduism and Hindutva, her whitewashing of the temple destructions that took place under Aurangzeb's rule, her blatant misrepresentations of incidents from the Rāmāyaṇa through mistranslations and other important aspects are studied through a careful analysis of her writings. Mukhopadhyay and Sastry show how Truschke's work is riddled with poor data and sloppy reasoning, and the use of her academic affiliations to make bizarre charges against those who do not share her Hinduphobic ideologies.

Ramachandra Guha's work forms the subject of T.N. Sudarshan and Divya Reddy's study in the current volume. Guha, known for his elaborations on "Nehru, Gandhi, cricket history, environment, politics and economics" is the recipient of the Padma Bhushan in 2009, India's third-highest civilian award. Analyzing Guha's work, the authors deconstruct several major themes, such as Gandhi's relationship with Hinduism, and comparison of Nehru with Subhash Chandra Bose and Sardar Patel. The threads of subalternism, colonialism, nationalism, Marxism and the blatant hatred for Hindutva seen in Guha's work are unpacked by the authors for the general reader.

Kancha Ilaiah Shepherd's work is analyzed by Sharda Narayanan and Subhodeep Mukhopadhyay. Ilaiah, who has been hoisted as one of India's foremost social thinkers, is instrumental in internationalizing Dalit issues and bringing them to the attention of global institutions. In a written testimony submitted to the UK Parliament, the Christian Solidarity Network cited Ilaiah's testimony at a US Congress hearing, on how anti-conversion laws in India perpetuate Dalit slavery by obstructing their freedom to leave the Hindu religion. Ilaiah has cast Hinduism as a "cult" which ostensibly encourages vegetarianism, nudity and sexual perversion, in stark contrast to Christianity which he feels has an ethic of sacrifice and civility. Narayanan and Mukhopadhyay analyze critically the major themes of Ilaiah's work, expose his research methodology and caliber, including his use of superficial similarities in name endings to establish a fantastic linkage between the Harappan civilization and the Bible!

The American Indologist Wendy Doniger, whose academic activity has spanned over forty years with several tomes in different genres, including interpretive works on religion, translations and edited volumes, forms the subject of Dr. H.R. Meera's essay. The author, through a meta-analysis of Doniger's methods and frameworks of study, shows how Doniger's understanding of Indian chronology leads to several wrong interpretations of the historical timelines of important texts of the

Sanskrit canon, while highlighting her derision for Indian thinkers such as Manu, Kauṭalya and Vātsyāyana. Kannan shows the various mistranslations of Sanskrit words in Doniger's works and how this is an important tool in the latter's work for propaganda writing and building misinterpretations of several important Dharma texts. The desacralization project of scholars such as Doniger is also analyzed by Kannan, especially how the former uses psychoanalytic techniques on dhārmic vidyā-s, as seen in the case of studies on Tantra, which forms the core of Tibetan Buddhism as well as Hinduism. Kannan highlights how while the former is left alone, the Tantra related to Hinduism is targeted by Doniger.

We hope the collection of essays in this book accomplish dual aims: The first is to introduce the general reader to the major themes in the works of each "head of the intellectual Ravana", and the second, is the larger framework for understanding the contemporary studies about Bharata. The second aim is especially important in helping one understand and build a pūrvapakṣa of some of the most important narratives of India.

It is important to reiterate that this book is an engagement with the works of the chosen scholars and not an ad hominem attack on anyone. Infinity Foundation India has always given those with opposing views the basic courtesy of fair engagement despite the background of most Western scholars ignoring native Indological scholarship. The hope is that this volume will stimulate healthy discussions and debates that will expand our minds and our understanding of India's vast cultural history.

ONE

Romila Thapar
Pushpaka Vimana and the Flights of Her Historical Imagination

Anurag Sharma

Introduction

The fundamental object of writing history must be the eternal quest for truth. Moral judgment as well as various interpretations and inferences are welcome but only when the facts are established with a scrupulous regard for the truth alone, without any influence of preconceived judgment and theories. Kalhana (c. twelfth century CE), the great historian of ancient India from Kashmir, held that a true historian must keep a detached mind and like a judge should recount events after having discarded all bias and prejudice.[1] A true historian must not tailor history to a pattern or subject it to a formula or a master concept. However, this wise counsel of a medieval Hindu historian is ignored by the Marxist historians of India, who consider history as a political tool to advance certain narratives. They understand history through the prism of class struggle and bring in new interpretations of history to redefine the grand narrative of our country.

Romila Thapar is one of the most well known contemporary historians of India and is held in high academic esteem both nationally and internationally. She is foremost among the historians of India who have meticulously worked at new interpretations of incidents and personalities in Indian history, based on the application of Marxist principles. Historians like her, over the years, have also used their control of educational institutions to influence public discourse and government policies. Her writings consistently strike at the very heart of Indian culture and civilization by making claims such as the non-existence of India or Hinduism before the modern era or by denunciation of sacred Hindu texts and ancient Indian social system as narrow-minded and oppressive for the general population. Hence, it becomes imperative to closely examine her works and test the veracity of her claims. It is also essential to refute the theories and claims that are found to be in disagreement with the facts. Rajiv Malhotra, in a video lecture series, has carried out an excellent critical analysis of Romila Thapar's methodology and responded to her "colonized" approach towards history writing.[2] My analysis in this essay is largely based on the themes selected by Rajiv Malhotra for this video series. My aim is to refute the historiographical assumptions of Romila Thapar by providing strong counterexamples from Indian history. This essay is divided into three sections. In the first section, I try to critically examine her views on the Islamic period of Indian history. In the second section, Thapar's theories related to Hindu dharma and sacred Hindu texts such as *Ramayana*, *Mahabharata* and the *Purana-s* are examined. Finally, in the third section I critically analyze her views on the Indian nation and Hindu nationalism.

1. Islamic Rule in India

Romila Thapar and other Marxist historians have produced numerous monographs and papers to show that the medieval foreign rulers of India were not actually motivated by religious considerations, but all their actions vis-à-vis the non-Muslims of this country were prompted mainly by political or economic considerations. Strangely enough, any criticism of a medieval Muslim ruler is considered by them as "un-secular" and an "attack" on contemporary Muslims. By the same logic, any criticism of a British administrator in pre-independence days should also be treated as a blow against the secular ideal of the Indian state, since there are many Indians today who profess Christianity, the religion of the old British administrators. Despite this, some historians believe that history must not call to memory the dastardly crimes and atrocities of India's past Islamic rulers because such recollections give rise to unhealthy trends which militate against the secular fabric of this country.

The afore-mentioned attitude drives Thapar to gloss over the iconoclasm of Mahmud Ghazni (c. 971-1030 CE) by suggesting that he was not primarily motivated by religious fanaticism in attacking major temple towns like Mathura, Vrindavana, Thanesar, Kanauj and Somanatha. She says that the concentration of wealth in the temples at these places made him attack them as his "greed for gold was insatiable".[3] She states that since Somanatha temple (attacked in c. 1025 CE) was renowned for its wealth, it was inevitable that greedy Mahmud would have attacked it. However, Ibnu'l-Athir, in his account of Sultan Mahmud written around 1230 CE and generally regarded as very authentic and trustworthy by historians,[4] says:

> "When Yaminu'd-Dawlah (i.e. Sultan Mahmud) was gaining victories and demolishing temples in India, the Hindus said that Somnath was displeased with these idols, and that if it had been satisfied with them no one could have destroyed or injured them. When Yaminu'd-Dawlah heard this, he resolved upon making a campaign to destroy this idol". (Nazim 1931:115)

Thapar tries to suggest that Mahmud's raid on the Somanatha temple was not very agonizing for the Hindus. It did not leave any lasting-impression on their memory and they were soon back to business as usual. While discussing a land grant inscription that mentions transfer of land to one Nur-ud-din, an Arab owner of a shipping company, for the construction of a mosque in Somanatha in 1264 CE under the reign of a Chalukya-Vaghela king, she states:

> "The inscriptions raise a number of questions. The raid of Mahmud could not have been forgotten 200 years after the event if it had been as traumatic as it is currently said to be...Did the transaction recorded in Nur-ud-din's inscription not interfere with the memory of Mahmud's raid on Somanatha or the threats of the Turkish Sultans if they were as frequent as is claimed in Persian sources, in the minds of the rajas, the priests and the 'big men' who were all party to the decision to permit the building of the mosque on the estates of the temple and in its vicinity?" (Thapar 2004:99-100)

However, a large number of Arabs involved in the profession of trade and commerce had already settled in the coastal areas of Kutch, Saurashtra and Gujarat by the tenth century CE, which is nearly four hundred years before the said event of mosque construction and around one hundred years before the Somanatha attack.[5] Their settlements in Gujarat acted as the chief intermediaries of trade between the Middle East and the Far East. Hence, a land grant given by some local king to an Arab merchant for some reason not known to us, nearly 250 years after the disaster, does not imply that the attack on Somanatha by the Turks was a minor incident. The intensity of Mahmud's raid can be gauged from the fact that more than 50,000 Hindus sacrificed their lives in front of the temple gate in a single day in order to defend the honor of their deity. Mahmud captured vast wealth from the temple amounting to 20,000,000 *dirhams*.[6]

Thapar claims that the silence of the Hindu or Jain sources about the Somanatha raid implies that the destruction of the temple was highly exaggerated in later times. While discussing inscriptions granting land to Brahmins and Jain temples from twelfth century Gujarat, she states:

> "That no mention is made of Mahmud's attack on the Somantha temple is strange, given the statement that the temple had deteriorated and needed renovation. This is puzzling as there are occasional references to the breaking of temples...Or was the looting of temple not such an extraordinary event, given that some Hindu rulers also attacked the temples of those they had conquered, or in order to confiscate the wealth of the temple". (Thapar 2004:86-87)

However, the record of the attack on Somanatha in the indigenous historical sources is not completely absent. References to Mahmud's raid are found in the Jain texts. For example, in a nearly contemporaneous account, the poet Dhanapala in his *Apabhramsha* poem, *Satyapuriya Sri Mahavira Utsaha,* states that Anahlivada, Soratha and Someshvara (or Somanatha) were looted by the Turks. Similarly, the fourteenth century Jain text *Vividhatirtha-kalpa* written by Jinaprabha Suri refers to the looting of Gurjara country by *Gajjanavi* (i.e. Mahmud Ghazni) in 1025 CE.[7]

Thapar accuses "Hindutva ideologues" of bias by saying that "history" for them only means victimization of Hindus under Muslim tyranny in the medieval period. However, Mahmud Ghazni, mentioned earlier, is not the only Islamic invader that perpetrated horrible crimes against the Hindus. The bloody saga of atrocities and temple destruction continued almost throughout the medieval period, wherever the Islamic invaders went. For example, Muhammad bin Tughluq, even after capturing the Kakatiya capital Warangal in 1323 CE and sending off King Pratapa Rudra to his capital in Delhi, destroyed the great and beautiful Svayambhu Shiva temple and constructed a congregational mosque at the site of the temple. He desecrated the *Svayambhu Shiva Linga* of the temple by getting it uprooted and broken into two pieces so that it could not be installed for worship in future.[8] Similarly, Firuz Shah Tughluq, after the siege of Jajnagar (in present-day Odisha) and the conclusion of peace with the Rai of Jajnagar, marched to Puri and attacked the beautiful temple of Jagannatha in 1361 even though there could be no political purpose to do this after the Rai's surrender. If anyone would like to give him the benefit of doubt, *Sirat-i-Firuz Shahi*, a text written at the dictates of Firuz Shah himself, states that two objectives of the Sultan in undertaking the expedition against Jajnagar were massacring the unbelievers and demolishing their temples.[9] Firuz also invaded Nagarkot and desecrated the famous temple of Jvalamukhi.[10] In another instance, a Brahmin of Delhi, who was charged with publicly performing the worship of idols in his house, was burnt alive by this Sultan when he refused his offer to accept Islam.[11]

Two centuries later, Akbar (r. 1556-1605 CE), who is considered to be a great hero by "secular" historians and an exemplar of religious tolerance, says in a letter to his official Abdullah Khan in 1586 CE that the territories which had never been captured ever since the rise of Islam in India have now become the dwelling places and homes of the faithful (i.e. Muslims).[12] He says that the temples of heretics and infidels have become mosques and *kufr* (infidelity) has been eliminated. He further asserts that he has accomplished what he wished.[13] The religious fanaticism of Aurangzeb (r. 1658-1707 CE) is well known to every informed Indian and we shall not delve into it for lack of space.

Thapar not only denies the horrible crimes of Islamic rulers but also resorts to their unwarranted eulogization and glorification. She says that some of the most notable achievements in knowledge of various kinds, from literature to mathematics, can be ascribed to Hindu scholars that were patronized during the medieval period by the Turks and the Mughals. She further adds:

> "Far from being victimized, Hindu culture flourished along with other cultures in these centuries and this is demonstrated in texts such as Madhava's *Sarva-darshana-sangraha* on the prevailing schools of philosophy, Samayasundara's *Artharatnāvali* on linguistic explorations and Sayana's renowned exposition of the Rigveda in the fourteenth century." (*Reflections on Nationalism and History in* [Thapar, Noorani, and Menon 2016; Thapar 2004])

According to her, the medieval period brought about an intermingling of cultures, as is evident in the new kinds of classical music that was composed and sung at the courts of this period. Best known among these was the creation and evolution of Dhrupad, regarded by many as the finest form of Hindustani classical music.[14] The Mughal court also became the most impressive patron of the translation of many Sanskrit religious texts into Persian. Among these the *Mahabharata* (translated as the *Razmnamah*) and the *Bhagavad Gita* hold pride of place. Brahmin priests worked together with Persian scholars on these translations, encouraged by Hindu and Muslim noblemen at the Muslim courts. Likewise, she further states:

> "The *bhajans* of Mira and Suradasa and the poetry of Kabir and Tukaram, as well as the many renderings of the *Ramayana*, such as by Tulsidasa and by Krittivasa, were all composed in this period. Their popularity was so immense among various communities of people that phrases and verses from these compositions became idioms in the languages of their composition such as Hindi, Bengali and Marathi. This experience was paralleled in other languages of the subcontinent". (*Reflections on Nationalism and History in* [Thapar, Noorani, and Menon 2016])

However, in her desire to shower praises on the Islamic rulers, Thapar forgets that most of the scholars and saints she mentions had nothing to do with them. Most of them either worked independently or under the patronage of independent Hindu kingdoms beyond the influence of Islamic rulers. For example, just because Surdas was a contemporary of Akbar, it does not imply that the bhajan-s he composed can be credited to Akbar in any way. Surdas had nothing to do with Akbar and hagiographical stories of the saints of the Vallabha *sampradāya* (called *Vārtās*), to which Surdas belonged, state that it was just once when Akbar met Surdas and the meeting was anything but cordial. It is said that when Akbar asked Surdas to give him a command to follow, Surdas replied,

> "From now on, never again summon me and never try to meet me again." (Barz 1992:122)

Moreover, the Vaishnava Vārtā literature unequivocally views the Turks and Mughals as foreigners who have occupied India. They are deemed to be barbaric and opposed to Hindu dharma. Govind Svami, who is among the eight great saints (*Ashta Chhāp*) of the Vallabha sampradāya, initially refused to take the legendary musician Tansen as his student because he had become a *Mlechha* by serving Akbar. It is only when Tansen renounced his Mlechha identity and became a member of Vallabha sampradāya that he relented and took him on as his student.[15]

Mirabai was born in 1498 CE in a Hindu Rajput royal family of Marwar and was brought up at Merta. She was married to Prince Bhojaraja, the eldest son of Rana Sanga of Mewar in 1516 CE where she spent her later life. Both Marwar and Mewar were independent Hindu kingdoms at this time of history and so there is absolutely no reason to include Muslim rulers while discussing her contribution to Bhakti literature.

Much as Romila Thapar would like to credit Akbar and other Muslim rulers for the literary activity of Bhakti saints in medieval India, the fact remains that all these saints and poets composed their works under very adverse circumstances by keeping away from the vicious reach of these rulers. That Hindu saints and scholars continued with their literary activity despite the turmoil caused by Islamic invasions can be seen from the fact that the famous Maharashtrian saint, Jnaneshwar wrote his magnum opus work *Jnaneshwari*, the commentary on the *Bhagavad Gita*, in c. 1296 CE, which is the very year of Alauddin Khalji's raid on the Deccan.[16] Likewise, Vedanta Desika, the great saint and scholar of the Sri Vaishnava sampradāya, wrote many of his philosophical and literary works during his exile in Melkote forced as a result of the Islamic invasion of Srirangam in the early fourteenth century. Venkatadhvarin, a south Indian Sanskrit scholar of the mid-seventeenth century, aptly describes the predicament of most Hindus who were serving in the Muslim courts at that time in his work *Vishvagunaadarshachampu*. He says that Brahmins who serve the Turks and Mughals are only doing so out of helplessness and in order to save whatever can be saved of the ancient Hindu dharma. He adds that if they do not do so then the world would be engulfed by the "*Yavanas*" i.e. Mlecchas.[17]

Another great Bhakti saint and the founder of Sikhism, Guru Nanak Dev, describes in the following words, the pathetic condition of the people in general and Hindu women in particular, and the barbarity in vogue at the time of Babur's invasion of India when the Lodi dynasty ruled over north India. He says:

"They who wore beautiful tresses

and the partings of whose hair were dyed with vermillion

Have their locks now shorn with scissors,

And dust is now thrown upon their heads.

....Eating coconuts and dates they sported on their couches,

But now chains are on their necks and broken are their

String of pearls.

The wealth and beauty which afforded them pleasure

have now become their bane.

The order was given to Soldiers to take and dishonour them". (Ahuja N.A.:66)

Contrary to Thapar's claims, the Muslim rulers, instead of patronizing Hindu scholarship in Sanskrit or other vernacular Indian languages, made Persian the language of literary culture. Thus, Persian poets and scholars received major patronage to the near exclusion of Sanskrit and all other indigenous languages of the country. Amir Khusrau (c. 1253-1325 CE), the noted Indo-Persian poet during the Khalji and Tughluq rule and a close associate of six successive Sultans, proudly reveals the attitude of Muslim rulers to Indian languages in the following remark in his work *Nuh Sipihr* (1318 CE):

> "Arabic is knowledge and learning, Turki is art, Persian is sweet, all other languages are bad and worth nothing". (Orsini and Sheikh 2014:131fn)

The neglect of Indian languages by Muslim rulers only grew in later centuries of the Muslim rule. Among the Muslim rulers of India, Akbar was the first to formally institute a position of *Malik-ush-shu'ara'* or poet laureate at the court which was to be awarded to a Persian poet only.[18] Akbar was also the first among the Indo-Islamic kings to declare Persian to be the language of administration at all levels. Learning, knowledge and high culture began to be associated with Persian in the Mughal Indian society due to this bias of the Mughal rulers. Thus, to give credit to the Muslim rulers for the literary activity of the Bhakti saints or scholars of the vernacular languages is not well supported by the facts of history. The translations of some Sanskrit texts to Persian that Thapar mentions, were only done to digest within the Islamic tradition, the timeless knowledge and wisdom contained in the texts in Sanskrit language.[19]

Sayanacharya, mentioned by Thapar, was a Sanskrit scholar in the Hindu Vijayanagar kingdom, who completed the stupendous task of writing commentaries on the *Samhita-s* of all the four *Vedas* and many of the *Brahmana-s* and *Aranyaka-s* with the patronage of Vijayanagar kings Bukka I (r. 1356-1377 CE) and Harihara II (r. 1377-1404 CE).[20] In the introduction to various sections of his commentaries, Sayana often identifies himself as King Bukka's minister. For example, in the preamble to his *Rigsamhita bhashya* 7.3, he refers to himself as Sayana, the king's minister and one of unimpeded understanding.[21] Madhva, the author of *Sarva-darshana-sangraha*, mentioned by Thapar, was Sayana's brother. Similarly, Samayasundara (sixteenth-seventeenth century CE) was a distinguished scholar of Jainism who carried on his literary activities in different parts of Rajasthan. He composed his works in Sanskrit and Rajasthani languages and all of them were written at places in Rajasthan like Bikaner, Merta and Jalor, far away from the influence of the Mughal king in Delhi.[22] In his work *Artharatnāvali* (also called *Ashtalakshi*), he gives eight lakh interpretations of a sentence containing eight letters. This work was merely presented in the royal court of Akbar by someone and he was astonished at the erudition of the scholar.[23] Hence, there is no reason whatsoever to attribute the production of this literary work to the patronage of any Mughal ruler in Delhi.

Thapar considers the creation of Dhrupad music as one of the achievements of Mughal rule. However, Dhrupad is a very ancient genre of Hindustani music and not something created through the intermingling of Hindu and Islamic cultures. The term Dhrupad is derived from a combination of *Dhruva* (immutable or fixed) and *Pada* (hymn or verse) and refers to a genre of raga-based music dealing with various attributes and praises of God. Dhrupad was a successor of *Prabandha Gāṇa* genre which enjoyed great popularity between the eleventh and the thirteenth century CE.[24] It was during Alauddin Khalji's (r. 1296-1316 CE) time that Nayak Gopal, a great musician of the time and a native of the Braj region, translated ancient Dhrupad songs into Braj Bhasha from the original Sanskrit verses. From the fourteenth century onwards, Dhrupad replaced Prabandha Gāṇa, reaching peak status and popularity between the fifteenth and the eighteenth centuries. Raja Man Singh Tomar (r. 1486-1516 CE), who ruled Gwalior, was a notable connoisseur and is held in great esteem in Dhrupad history for his patronage of this music. The raja himself was an excellent musician and regularly met the most accomplished musicians of the time to formulate the rules and requirements of Dhrupad singing. His musical advisers, called *nayakas*, included well known musicians as Bhanoo, Charju, Bakshu and Dhundhi. The raja was instrumental in the compilation of a Hindi book titled *Mān*

Kutuhal which explained the latest theories on music.[25] The legendary musician Tansen once embellished his court. In fact, the title "Tansen" was given to him by Raja Man Singh's son Vikramjeet.[26] When Akbar brought Tansen to his imperial court, he was already a famous and accomplished musician. In medieval times, the holy town of Vrindavana was the well known seat of learning for Dhrupad music. Many great Vaishnava saints like Shrila Jiva Gosvami, Raghunathdas and others were the famous exponents of the genre.[27] Tansen was also sent to Vrindavana and spent a decade there to learn music from his guru, Swami Haridas who was an acknowledged master of the Dhrupad style. Swami Haridas, born in late fifteenth century CE, was a *sannyasi* of the Vaishnava Nimbarka sampradāya. He also holds the distinction of being the guru of a large number of famous musicians of his time like Baiju Bavra, Ramdas, Manadali, Raja Sanmukhan Singh of Ajmer (who accompanied Tansen on the veena) and Rani Mrignaini of Gwalior (wife of Raja Man Singh Tomar).[28] With such a great and well-established tradition of Dhrupad already in existence within Hinduism, it is absolutely wrong to claim that Dhrupad was created through the intermingling of Hindu and Islamic cultures under the Mughals.

Thapar would like us to believe that the bulk of the conversion to Islam in the medieval period was not by brute force of arms but under the benign influence of Sufis.[29] This assertion also reveals her underlying assumption that the Sufis were always peaceful and never resorted to any kind of violence for conversions. However, Sufi hagiographic biographies called *Tazkira* portray many of them as heroes who waged *Jihad* and slew countless infidels against overwhelming odds. The Sufis, who were the first to carry Islamic culture into an area, often acted as mercenaries of the invading Muslim armies. For example, the biographical account of Shaikh Sufi Sarmast (d. 1281 CE) of Deccan, belonging to the Chishti order, mentions that he came to Deccan from Arabia at a time when the Deccan was a land of unbelievers with no sign of Islam and in a bitter war that followed with a local Hindu ruler Kumaram, countless Hindus were killed.[30] Another Sufi, Pir Ma'bari Khandayat, accompanied Alauddin Khalji's general Malik Kafur in his military campaign in the Tamil country in 1311 CE. His biography adds that later on, the "saint" went to

Bijapur, waged Jihad against the Hindu rajas, broke their heads and necks with his iron bar and defeated them. After all this, by the will of God, many idolators repented for their unbelief and accepted Islam.[31] It should also be remembered that many Sufis were very often called *ghazi* (holy warrior) and so in Islam it was not unusual to find militant and mystical traditions converging in the same individual.

Thapar says that the "Hindutva ideologues" speak of Hindus being enslaved for a thousand years by Islamic rule, but do not give thought to the fact that caste Hindus victimized the lower castes, Dalits and *Adivasis* for two thousand or more years, and most caste Hindus, with a few exceptions, regarded it as quite legitimate. But this assertion is again a result of her Marxist approach to history which views everything through the lens of class struggle. Indian history repeatedly saw the rise of *Shudra-s* to the position of kings and even emperors. The Nanda dynasty, which ruled northern India in the fourth century BCE is unanimously regarded as shudra in origin by Hindu, Jaina and Buddhist sources. Thus, Mahapadma Nanda, who would be considered the first historical emperor of northern India by Thapar, was a Shudra. Similarly, the next great emperor of India, Chandragupta Maurya (c. 321-297 BCE) was also a Shudra according to the Hindu and Jain sources. Even in medieval India, the Kakatiya dynasty monarchs (c. 1163-1323 CE) who ruled from Warangal in the Telugu-speaking Andhra region were Shudra-s. That the Shudra kings considered themselves as Hindus and were not opposed to 'Brahmanism' or Vedic culture could be seen from the Sanskrit inscription of Andhra chief Prolaya Nayaka (1330 CE). He, along with his cousin Kapaya Nayaka, was the leader of the movement of liberation of the Deccan from the Muslims in 1329 CE. While describing the ravages caused by the "Yavana" soldiers in the "Tailanga" country after the defeat of the Kakatiya ruler Pratap Rudra II by Muhammad bin Tughlaq, the inscription says:

> "Then arose chief Prolaya of the Musumuri family of Shudra caste. Unable to resist his might, the Yavanas abandoned their forts and fled to unknown places. He restored the agrahara lands to the Brahmins and revived the performance of Vedic sacrifices. He cleansed the

Andhra Pradesha of the pollution caused by the movements of the Turushkas, by means of the butter smoke arising out of the sacrificial fire pits". (Ray 2003:98)

Apart from denying the brutal conquests of the Islamic invaders, Thapar also believes that they should not be equated with the colonial Britishers, as Arabs and Turks had a long history of commercial and political relations with India. According to her, the British came from distant lands, spoke languages and had a religion, customs and rituals which were alien.[32] Due to these differences, Britishers could be considered colonizers but the interventions in India of the West Asian and central Asian Muslims after the eighth century CE should not be similarly perceived. However, she forgets that British colonization of India also began with commercial relations and merely having trade relations with people doesn't make them any less foreign. Arabs and Turks were considered to be "Mlecchas" by the Indians and after their conversion to Islam their customs and religion became even more alien to the Indians of that time.

2. Hinduism and Hindu Epics

Hinduism is an inherently inclusive, tolerant and pluralist religion. However, Romila Thapar makes a multi-pronged attack on Hinduism and its sacred texts by interpreting them on the basis of the theories of class-struggle. She has theorized that Hinduism, as reflected in the *Purana*-s, should be called Puranic Hinduism to differentiate it from 'Vedic Brahmanism', a term she uses to refer to the religion apparently of "upper" caste Hindus. Vedic Brahmanism, in her view, propagated the use of Sanskrit through elaborate rituals and had to compromise with local indigenous cults, and in this process of acculturation between Brahmanic "high-culture" and the "low-culture" of indigenous local cults, the more popular Puranic Hinduism emerged. Thapar believes that deities like Vishnu and Shiva were earlier marginal but later came to be worshipped as pre-eminent deities in Puranic Hinduism through assimilation. This transformation happened between the Gupta period (c. 400-600 CE) and the end of first millennium CE.[33]

Contrary to Thapar's theory, deities like Vishnu and Shiva are accorded a higher place than other *devata-s* in the *Vedas* themselves, even though fewer hymns may be addressed to them. The larger number of hymns to a deity in the *Vedas* does not necessarily imply that the deity is more important. The *Vedas* themselves state that Agni is the lowest of all the deities and Vishnu is the highest.[34] *Taittiriya Aranyaka* (1.8) of the *Krishna Yajur Veda* states explicitly that Vishnu upholds both the universe and the higher region. Similarly, in the *Purusha Sukta* of the *Rig Veda*, *Purusha* or the Supreme Being is equated with Vishnu (*Rig Veda* 10.90.1).[35] The *Shvetashvatara Upanishad* belonging to the *Yajur Veda* equates the Highest reality with Rudra or Shiva (3.2, 3.4, 4.12).

Besides textual evidence, we also have numismatic and archaeological evidences to show the importance of Vishnu and Shiva in ancient India much before the first millennium CE. Even prior to the Gupta period, the Indo-Scythian ruler Maues who ruled the north-western part of India in first century BCE, paid homage to Shiva by issuing several coins with His image.[36] Similarly, in the pre-Gupta period, Shaka and Kushana rulers of India also issued coins where Shiva is shown holding a trident and accompanied by Nandi.[37] For example, the Kushana ruler Wima Kadphises (r. 64-78 CE) who ruled the north-western part of India, was connected to Shaiva faith and used the title of *"Maheshvara"* (devotee of Shiva belonging to the *Pashupata* sect) on all his coins to describe himself. Shiva, with his long trident and sometimes accompanied by His bull Nandi, is invariably seen on his coins.[38] The gold coins of the later Kushana ruler Huvishka (first half of second century CE) show Shiva along with His consort Uma and their son Karttikeya.[39] Apart from the Kushanas, the Indo-Parthian ruler Gondophares of the 1st century CE was also a Shaiva by faith and issued numerous coins with the image of Shiva on them.[40] *Shiva Linga* of 1.5m height, belonging to the Shunga period (first century BCE) and with a full figure of Shiva carved onto its shaft, is still under worship in the Parashurameshvara temple at Gudimallam in Andhra Pradesh.[41] Even a sculpture of Shiva belonging to the first Century CE was discovered as far as Kunduz in Afghanistan.[42]

Again, there is archaeological and numismatic evidence to show that Vishnu worship was so popular in India before the Gupta period that even foreigners were attracted to it. The inscription on Besnagar pillar (c. 120-100 BCE) at the ancient site of Vidisha in Madhya Pradesh states that the pillar is a *Garuda-dhvaja* constructed by the Greek ambassador Heliodorus in honour of *Vāsudeva*, the God of gods. The inscription describes Heliodorus as a *bhāgavata* i.e. worshipper of Krishna or Vāsudeva. Garuda is the vehicle of Vishnu and the now missing crowning element of the pillar represented it. Garuda-dhvaja-s were often placed near a Vishnu temple and excavations around the temple did reveal the foundations of such a Vishnu temple.[43] Similarly, a torso of Lord Vishnu belonging to the Shunga (second century BCE) or the Kushana period (first to second century CE), was discovered in excavations around the site of Fatehpur Sikri in Uttar Pradesh.[44] The British archaeologist Alexander Cunningham (1814-93) discovered a nicolo seal attributed to the Kushana ruler Huvishka (early half of second century CE). The seal shows the four-armed God Vishnu typically holding His *Gada* (club), *Chakra* (discus), *Shankha* (conch) and *Padma* (lotus). Huvishka is shown on the seal standing in a suppliant attitude before Vishnu. Huvishka is indisputably recognized from the typical head-dress that he wears on several coins issued by him.[45]

Thapar further suggests that the Varaha incarnation of Vishnu was appropriated into "Puranic Hinduism" from the forest tribes of Central India in the sixth century CE after their conquest and conversion. She says Varaha incarnation represents a compromise between tribal cults of Central India and Puranic religion.[46] However, this claim is falsified by the various references to Varaha in not only the *Purana*-s but also the Vedic texts, which are thousands of years older than sixth century CE. *Taittiriya Aranyaka* (1.10.8), which is a part of *Yajur Veda*, mentions that the earth was lifted from water by a black boar. Other references to the Varaha incarnation story, where He is mentioned to have rescued the earth from deep water, are found in *Satapatha Brahmana* (14.1.2.11) and the *Taittiriya Brahmana*.[47] In addition to textual evidence, there is also archaeological evidence to support the popularity of Varaha incarnation much earlier than the sixth century CE. A sculpture belonging to the second century BCE discovered at Bhita shows Varaha, the boar form of Vishnu along with the Narasimha or the lion form. Both the incarnations are represented in theriomorphic form.[48] Another image of Varaha was discovered in Mathura. This image is sculpted on a stone slab with an inscription in the Kushana script, which assigns the sculpture to the Kushana period of first-second century CE. In this image, Varaha is depicted in anthropomorphic form and wears thick drapery, necklace, armlets and anklets besides the *Srivatsa* symbol. A female figure representing Bhumi Devi is seated on His shoulder and holds a lotus in her hand. A devotee with folded hands and wearing a typical Indo-Scythian dress is also shown.[49] This sculpture conclusively proves that the Varaha incarnation and the story of His rescuing the earth was popular in India even during the Kushana period. If Varaha incarnation was appropriated into Hinduism from the tribes of Central India around the sixth century CE, then how do we explain this sculpture, depicting the story of Varaha, in the northern part of India nearly five hundred years before the supposed "conquest" and "conversion" of forest tribes. Even the famous Varaha cave of central India at Udayagiri in Madhya Pradesh was excavated around c. 401 CE during the reign of Chandragupta II.[50] This is nearly a century before its alleged appropriation into Hinduism in the sixth century CE. The presence of more Varaha sculptures in Central India is simply because they were saved from destruction by the invaders due to their interior and remote location.

Numerous seals and gold coins issued by the imperial Chalukyas of Vatapi (present day Badami in Karnataka), who rose to power in the sixth century CE, carry the image of Varaha, which was their royal emblem.[51] Even the kings of ancient Assam like that of the Varman dynasty (fourth-seventh century CE) traced their descent from the Varaha incarnation of Vishnu and their inscriptions refer to the story of Varaha.[52] The prevalence of worship of Varaha *Avatara* throughout India, since ancient times, is further substantiated by the presence of the Adi-Varaha cave temple at Mahabalipuram (in Tamil Nadu) built around sixth-seventh century CE under the auspices of the Pallava dynasty. Thus, the worship of Varaha incarnation, during the concerned period, was not something exclusive and original to the 'forest tribes' of Central India as Thapar imagines.

Thapar claims that during the Kushana period (first-second century CE) Indians began to worship foreign deities and some of them entered the Indian pantheon, such as the goddess Ardochsho in the form of Shree.[53] This claim is completely unfounded and ignores the strong contrary evidence from the ancient Hindu sacred texts. Shree or Lakshmi has been revered in India since time immemorial and *Shree Suktam,* found in the Rig Veda, is the most ancient invocation to the Goddess. Similarly, in Satapatha Brahmana (11.4.3.1) of the *Shukla Yajur Veda*, Shree is mentioned as the Goddess of fortune and beauty. The Vedas are thousands of years older than the Kushana period even according to conservative estimates of Western scholars and thus, to ascribe worship of Shree or Lakshmi in India to foreign influence is unacceptable. Moreover, there is archaeological and numismatic evidences to prove that Shree or Lakshmi was worshipped in India as the Goddess of wealth and prosperity prior to the Kushana period. The medallion from a railing post of the stupa at Bharhut in Madhya Pradesh shows Lakshmi as the lotus Goddess, being bathed by elephants holding upturned pots in their trunks. The Bharhut stupa belongs to the Shunga period of second century BCE.[54] Similarly, there are coins from the second century BCE bearing the image of *Gaja-Lakshmi* (Lakshmi being bathed by two elephants) and also the city name Ujeni (present day Ujjain in Madhya Pradesh). These coins were used in the ancient Avanti region.[55]

In order to discredit the sacred texts of Hinduism, Thapar posits that Purana-s claim their evolution from the Vedas largely to ensure status and acceptability. They contain much that is marginal to the Vedas and even non-Vedic.[56] This claim is again baseless because the Vedas themselves mention about Purana-s at various instances and call them the fifth Veda. For example, *Itihasa* and Purana are mentioned in the *Atharva-Veda Samhita* (15.6.4) along with other currently less-known classes of compositions like *Gāthās* and *Nārāśaṁsīs*.[57] Similarly, *Chandogya Upanishad* (VII.1.2) declares them to be the fifth Veda.

The immortal Itihasa work Ramayana is very significant for Indian culture and almost everyone in India is familiar with the story of Ramayana in some form. The Indian mind as well as those in the neighboring countries has always cherished the values nurtured in the epic. Indian tradition holds Valmiki as the first poet (*Adi-Kavi*) and Ramayana as the first poem (*Adi-Kavya*). According to Thapar, however, Valmiki Ramayana is a hegemonic text and she creates doubts over its authenticity by raising unwarranted controversies on the historicity and authorship of the text.[58]

Thapar says that Valmiki perhaps composed a single text of Ramayana from a floating bardic tradition of fragmentary stories dealing with Rama. Since she considers the text to be interpolated at various times, it cannot be dated to a particular period. Fragmentary narratives from the oral tradition were probably selected and recomposed and compiled as an epic poem by Valmiki. She theorizes that the books (or *Kanda-s*) 1 and 7 are extraneous to the story and have been added mainly for didactic purposes. I could not find any instance in her works where she offers evidence to substantiate this view. According to her, Valmiki Ramayana evolved in five stages. The initial version of the story was the narration in the books 2-6, complied in c. 500-400 BCE and revised with periodic interpolations from c. 300 BCE-100 CE. In the subsequent two centuries, books 1 and 7 were added and from c. 400-1200 CE, small passages were incorporated. She says that the first and the last books present major evidence for the 'Brahmanization' of the text in the form of frequent references to the four varnas, the importance of dharma and *danda* to the functioning of the king, Rama as an Avatara of Vishnu, and Rama-bhakti being as important, if not more so, as the performance of the *yajna-s*.

It is indeed strange and difficult to understand why the 1st book '*Bala Kanda*' should be regarded as a later addition. This is because Ramayana is the story of Rama and it is only logical for the text to deal with the birth, early life and marriage of its protagonist. If Bala Kanda is regarded as a later addition, then, according to Thapar, the original Ramayana must have begun with the *Ayodhya Kanda*. However, it would be absurd to regard the first *shloka* of Ayodhya Kanda, which talks about Bharata going to his maternal grandmother's house along with Shatrughna, as the first shloka of the entire epic. Ayodhya Kanda nowhere introduces readers to Ayodhya, Dasharatha or his four sons. How can any author suddenly begin writing about the characters of his story without introducing them? Besides, Valmiki Ramayana has been studied and analyzed by traditional scholars and *acharya-s* for the past hundreds of years and numerous commentaries have been written on it. For instance, the Sri Vaishnava acharya Udali wrote a commentary on Ramayana in the thirteenth century. Similarly, *Ramabhirami tika* by Nagesh Bhatta was written in the eighteenth century.[59] No traditional acharya has ever suggested that books 1 and 7 of Ramayana are later additions. Valmiki Ramayana (1.3.38) itself proclaims that Valmiki is the author of events in the *Uttara Kanda* as well. The evidence to support the fact that books 1 and 7 were very much a part of the original Valmiki Ramayana, exists not only in the Hindu sources but also the Buddhist canon, considered to be very authentic by Thapar herself. Ashvaghosha, the Buddhist philosopher from the first century CE and author of the epic *Buddhacharita*, shows knowledge of the opening canto of book 1 of Valmiki Ramayana. He also refers to Valmiki having performed all the *samskara-s* for the two sons of Devi Sita.[60] If Uttara Kanda, which deals with the story of Luv and Kush, the two sons of Devi Sita, was an interpolation, added only in the third century CE as Thapar claims, how could Ashvaghosha have mentioned the events within it a century or two earlier? In fact, Thapar herself accepts that the narrative of Buddhacharita parallels that of Valmiki Ramayana and that Ashvaghosha was familiar with Valmiki's text.[61] So the claim of interpolation made by Thapar holds no ground.

Further, Thapar says that Rama's role as an incarnation of Vishnu is highlighted particularly in the interpolated first and the seventh books of Ramayana to convert the epic into a Bhāgavata text. However, if the addition of the 1st and 7th book is an outcome of the 'Brahmanization' of the text and done only to deify Rama as an incarnation of Vishnu, then there should be no references to the connection between Rama and Vishnu in the so called 'earlier' and 'un-Brahmanized' books 2 to 6. However, these books contain numerous shloka-s which refer to Rama as an incarnation of Vishnu. For example, book 2 states that Shree Rama, who is the eternal Purusha and Lord Vishnu Himself, descended on earth on the entreaty of the devata-s to slay Ravana, the enemy of the whole world (Valmiki Ramayana 2.1.7). Similarly, shloka-s in the other Kanda-s, which directly state Rama to be the Supreme Reality or Bhagavan include 2.44.15, 2.44.16, 3.37.13, 3.37.18, 3.64.54, 3.62.64, 3.64.71, 4.24.31, 4.42.4, 5.51.104, 6.111.9, 6.119.17, 6.119.28.[62] The list of such shloka-s is unending and if all of them are also regarded as later interpolations, then the whole text of Valmiki Ramayana might as well be regarded as one big work of interpolation. It is difficult to believe that the neglect of so many shloka-s referring to Rama as an incarnation of Vishnu could be unintentional; else it becomes clear that Thapar has not cared to examine the complete text in original Sanskrit.

Thapar also sees class-struggle in Ramayana and believes it to be a confrontation between two types of societies: the kingdom of Kosala and the more 'diffused society' of the *rakshasa-s*. According to her, Ramayana symbolizes the triumph of kingship-based order over the society of rakshasa-s closer in form and spirit to chiefships. The kingdom of Rama is an exemplar of early kingship. She tries to suggest that rakshasa-s were actually forest dwellers and their association with magic and supernatural powers were poetic ways to portray them in a negative light. This is nothing but another way to present the discredited Aryan invasion theory in a new garb. According to this theory, it could be suggested that Ramayana figuratively represents the expansion of Aryan civilization among the indigenous forest dwellers in the southern part of India. There is absolutely no evidence in the Valmiki Ramayana to support this theory and Ravana himself is repeatedly called as '*Rakshasendra*' or the king of the rakshasa-s in the text. To believe that Lanka represents a 'diffused society', whatever this ambiguous term means, with no actual king, is only a figment of Thaper's imagination.

Thapar again makes a completely unfounded claim that the Buddhist *Dasaratha Jataka* was dated earlier than Valmiki Ramayana and that Valmiki utilized it to write his Ramayana.[63] She offers no proof to establish the veracity of her statement. It is natural to wonder why

Dasaratha Jataka cannot, in fact, be regarded as a distorted version of the Ramayana. Dasaratha Jataka is a short story meant only for didactic purpose and does not claim anywhere to be the authentic story of Bhagavan Shree Rama. It was narrated by Buddha to a householder in Jetavana to prevent him from renouncing his family duties on the death of his father. Buddha wanted him to learn from the fortitude shown by Rama on the death of Dasharatha. It is natural that a popular text like Ramayana would be used by other heterodox sects with modifications to teach their own doctrines. All Hindu texts are unanimous in regarding Valmiki as a contemporary of Rama and thus Valmiki Ramayana is actually a first-hand account of the history of the age. Thapar further laments that the telecast of the Hindu version of Rama-katha would drive out versions of the story like Dasaratha Jataka which do not conform to the renderings of Valmiki and Tulsidasa.[64] However, why should anyone in India care for this obscure story called Dasaratha Jataka? It holds no significance for the Hindus and is certainly not essential to Buddhism as well.

Similar to Ramayana, Thapar builds an imaginary chronology for the development of the other great Itihasa viz. Mahabharata. According to her, Mahabharata in its present form evolved in phases. The earliest version may have been called *Jaya* with 8800 verses, then came *Bharata*, attributed to Vyasa, comprising 24,000 verses and this was later inflated to 100,000 verses and came to be called Mahabharata. Also, Bhagavad Gita was interpolated into Mahabharata to give the Gita both antiquity and currency.[65] I could not find in her works neither any details regarding the time when this interpolation was done nor any evidence that supports her claim. She wonders why Vyasa chose to make Krishna an incarnation of Vishnu given his ambiguity in relation to ethical norms.[66] The answer to her question is because Krishna *is* an incarnation of Vishnu. Vyasa did not choose anyone randomly as an incarnation of Vishnu because he was not writing a fictional tale but only recounting actual historical events. In this context, it is important to point out that her imaginary theory, that it was only in the last one thousand years that the 'cult' of Krishna (or Rama) became popular with its own mythologies, rituals, literatures and circuits of pilgrimage, holds no weight.[67] Reference to Krishna as God is found even in Panini's *Ashtadhayi* which belongs to fifth-fourth century BCE according to the conservative esimates of modern historians. In one of the *sutra-s* (IV.3.98), Vāsudeva and Arjuna are mentioned together in connection with the rules for the derivation of the words denoting their devotees. Patanjali (second century BCE), in commenting on this sutra in his *Mahabhashya*, clearly states that Vāsudeva here is the name of the worshipful one, God.[68] That Bhagavata Vaishnavism and worship of Krishna was extant as far as Afghanistan during the mid-second century BCE is also proven by the coins of Indo-Greek king Agathocles (early second century BCE) which depict Krishna along with His elder brother Balarama.[69]

Thapar says that some modern ideologies of nationalism in their more extreme forms insist on the historicity of epic events and persons and in order to construct a historical narrative from these. They attempt to authenticate the contents of the epics by searching for archaeological counterparts but this has yielded no viable results as was expected because epic compositions like Ramayana and Mahabharata are mostly fantasies. However, much as Thapar would like to label the Itihasa-s like Ramayana and Mahabharata as fantasies, archaeological evidences do not support her. The discovery of the ancient sea-submerged city of Dwarka and *Rama-setu* and their scientific study bear testimony to the fact that events mentioned in the epics are historical.

Coming to later times, Thapar says that Bhakti tradition belonged to Puranic Hinduism and not Vedic Brahmanism. Like Buddhism and Jainism, early Bhakti sects were opposed to Vedic Brahmanism and were the inheritors of these Shramanic religions. She says that the feeling of human inadequacy that became an important facet of the Bhakti devotional sects would have owed more to Buddhist ancestry than to Vedic.[70] However, Bhakti is a significant element in the doctrines of the Vedas or 'Vedic Brahmanism' as she calls it. Vedic hymns are imbued with feelings of intense love and veneration for *Brahman* and teach the path of love as the surest means of gaining ultimate liberation. They definitely show the consciousness of love and reverence to the deity as the only way for upliftment. In a hymn of the Rig Veda (10.7.3) Brahman is called the father, mother and every other relation of a person. Again, Brahman is metaphorically described as a well-oared divine-ship, boarding on which, each and every one can cross the vast ocean of *samsara* (Rig Veda 10.63.10). Even the seeds of Bhakti mysticism and *Madhurya Bhakti* which is so important in Bhakti sampradāyas can be clearly traced to the hymns of the Rig Veda (10.43.1).[71]

Highlighting human inadequacy in the attainment of *moksha*, *Mundaka Upanishad* (3.2.3) states:

> "Paramatma is not attained through mere rumination, nor through mere meditation, nor through much hearing. He is attainable by that individual self whom this Paramatman chooses. This Supreme Self reveals His own form to such a one". (Rangacharya 2003:156)

The same teaching is reiterated in *Katha Upanishad* 1.2.23. Similarly, *Shvetashvatara Upanishad* states:

> "Subtler than the subtle, greater than the great is the Self that is set in the cave of the (heart) of the creature. One beholds Him as being actionless and becomes freed from sorrow, when through the grace of the Creator he sees the Lord and His majesty". (Radhakrishnan 2010:730)

It is clear from these examples that feeling of human inadequacy in attaining moksha and the doctrine of the surrender to the Divine, which are so characteristic of the Bhakti tradition, have their roots in the Upanishads themselves. Moreover, even a cursory look at the Buddhist philosophy would reveal that it is basically nihilistic and atheistic in its approach. Buddhism does not believe in the existence of any permanent ultimate reality at all, be it individual self (*jivatman*) or the Universal Self (*Paramatman* or Bhagavan). In the viewpoint of all the four major schools of Buddhist philosophy, all entities are impermanent and in a continuous state of change. The Buddhist doctrine of *kshanikavada* states that apart from the flow of cognitions there is no permanent self or *atman* as the seat of consciousness. Hence, with their denial of reality to both Bhagavan and jivatman, Buddhism is fundamentally opposed to any form of bhakti for the attainment of moksha. Therefore, it is incorrect to say that bhakti sects in Tamil Nadu or elsewhere owed to Buddhism for their emergence and for the development of their spiritual practices.

Further, Thapar says that the concept of compassionate deity among the Tamil bhakti saints reflected the Buddhist notion of the compassionate *Bodhisattva*.[72] It will be worthwhile to examine some historical facts in order to appreciate the fallacious nature of this claim. Bodhisattva icon worship constitutes a characteristic feature of Mahayana Buddhism. Anthropomorphic representation of Buddha was forbidden due to age-old injunctions in Buddhism and early Buddhist monuments of the Shunga and post-Shunga period (c. 200 BCE-100 CE) do not usually represent Buddha in the iconic form. It was Mahayana Buddhism, which for the first time, incorporated the conception of countless Buddhas and Bodhisattva-s and also advocated the worship of numerous gods and goddesses. It is generally accepted by modern historians that Mahayana Buddhism became prominent only in the first or second century CE. However, as we have seen, temples of Hindu deities existed much before first century CE and their images very frequently appeared on the coins issued by various kings. In light of these facts, it is not hard to arrive at the conclusion that the concept of image worship of a deity was adopted into Buddhism from Hinduism. This happened at a time when Mahayana Buddhism substituted Bhakti to the person of Buddha for the original Buddhist idea of Buddha as a human teacher. It is well-known that the idea of Bhakti is a central theme of the Bhagavad Gita and even if we go by Thapar's chronology, Bhagavad Gita is centuries older than the Mahayana sect of Buddhism. Hence, it is more logical to conclude that the idea of Bhakti was also adopted into Mahayana Buddhism from Hinduism.

Coming now to the subject of compassionate Bodhisattva. In the developed Mahayana pantheon, Bodhisattva Avalokiteshvara occupies a very prominent position. The earliest known image of Avalokiteshvara appears in the Ajanta caves in the latter half of the fifth century CE during the Gupta period. One of the names of Avalokiteshvara is

Mahakarunika or the great compassionate. Contrary to what Thapar claims, Mahayana Buddhists themselves equate Avalokiteshvara with Shiva and also call him Shiva-Lokeshvara. He is often depicted with matted locks and wearing a lion skin just like Shiva.[73] Around c. 400-500 CE, goddess Tara also appeared as a significant member of the Mahayana Buddhist pantheon as the consort of Avalokiteshvara. With the appearance of Avalokiteshvara and Tara in the Buddhist pantheon, many legends and metaphysical ideas woven around Shiva and Durga were transferred to them. Thus, it should be clear from this brief discussion that the idea of the deification of the Buddha and all the Bodhisattva-s, as well as the concept of their Bhakti and image worship were all appropriated into Buddhism from Hindusim. The compassionate and merciful nature of God is highlighted even in the hymns of the Rig Veda and is not an idea propounded by the Buddhists for the first time.[74] In light of this, it is absurd to claim that the Tamil Bhakti saints copied the idea of the compassionate deity from the Buddhist idea of a compassionate Bodhisattva. Clearly contradicting Thapar's claim that early Bhakti saints were influenced by Shramanic religions like Buddhism and Jainism, the great Tamil Shaiva saint Appar declares that he remained alienated from devotion to the Ultimate Reality during his earlier life as a Jain ascetic.[75] Nambiyandar Nambi, the eleventh century Shaiva scholar and compiler of the sacred *Tirumurai-s*, in his work *Tiruttontar Tiruvantati*, praises the Tamil Shaiva saint Sambandhar by stating that he restored Shaivism to its past glory by defeating the Jains in debates.[76]

Again, Thapar claims that Tamil bhakti saints either denied or ignored the 'Vedic gods'.[77] However, Vishnu and Shiva worshipped by the Tamil saints, *Alvar-s* and *Nayanar-s,* are referred to in the Vedas numerous times and are nothing but 'Vedic'. Vaishnavism and Shaivism, according to her, were an expression of local sentiment questioning the attempts at homogenization made by Vedic Brahmanism with its insistence on orthodox practices and social inequality. Bhakti saints, she suggests, resisted the Sanskritic culture and opposed the Vedas and the Brahmins.[78] However, this is refuted by what the saints themselves have written. Tamil Bhakti saints, in their hymns, often eulogize places where the Brahmins lived and performed Vedic yajna-s. Appar, mentioned above and one of the Nayanars, praises Shiva as the One who is the message of the great metrical Vedas.[79] He further says that Shiva is both Sanskrit and Tamil; He is the one who gave the four Vedas to the world.[80] Sambandhar, another celebrated Shaiva Nayanar, praises Shiva as the Brahmin who knows the four Vedas and the six *Vedanga-s*.[81] Similarly, the great Alvar Vaishnava saint Nammalvar, in his work *Thiruvoimozhi*, sings that the ocean-hued Krishna resides in Tiruvanvandur amid the echoes of Vedic chants.[82] In another verse from the same work, he sings that his only refuge is Krishna's abode in high-mansioned Tirucchengunrur (name of the place) where fragrant smoke of the Vedic yajna-s clouds the sky.[83] Sekkizhar is his work *Periya Puranam*, mentions that '*upanayanam*' (ceremony for investiture of sacred thread) of saint Sambandhar was duly performed according to the Vedic rites when he attained the seventh year of his age.[84] To further get a glimpse of the attitude of Bhakti saints in later times towards Brahmins and the Vedas, it would be worthwhile to briefly look at a few incidents from the life of the great Maharashtrian saint Tukaram (1608-50 CE) who was a Shudra by birth and hence cannot be blamed for any undue bias towards Brahmins. Tukaram in his message to Chhatrapati Shivaji says:

> "Now listen while I tell you the duties of a kshatriya. He must conquer his enemies and protect his own faith; reverence the brahmins; see the supreme in all creatures; oppress none; delight in worship; speak no falsehood; feed the hungry; and remember God continually". (Fraser and Edwards 1922:101)

He even goes to the extent of saying that a Brahmin is superior in the three worlds though he may sometimes fail in his duty.[85] In another instance, Tukaram helped a Brahmin debtor and fed his family. Tukaram was also generally honored by the Brahmins. It is clear from this that Bhakti saints of India did not subscribe to Thapar's views on Vedas and Brahmins.

Thapar claims that the great Dvaita philosopher and saint, Madhvacharya was familiar with the teachings of the Christian church of Malabar and that some his ideas were inspired by Christianity.[86] She specifically states that the idea of bestowal of 'moksha' through the intercession of Vayu believed in the Madhva sampradāya is alien to Brahmanical and Puranic beliefs but parallels that of holy spirit in Christianity. Professsor B.N.K. Sharma, the foremost scholar of Dvaita Vedanta in recent times, refutes this baseless allegation through unassailable evidences.[87] The special place given to Vayu in Madhva's system is rooted in the Upanishad-s, Purana-s and Itihasa-s. For example, Chandogya Upanishad (4.15.5) states that Vayu leads the souls eligible for *mukti* to Brahman. Similarly, the *Isha Upanishad* (4) states that Vayu (Matarishva) gives the accounts of doings of a Jivatman to Bhagavan. According to western scholars and Thapar, herself, the Upanishad-s mentioned above are centuries older than the emergence of Christianity and hence, if borrowing did happen, the more likely possibility would be that the idea went from Upanishad-s to Christianity and not vice versa.

Similarly, she vaguely tries to suggest that the notion among the followers of Ramanujacharya of the Vishishtadvaita school that the deity selects those who are to be liberated could have been inspired by the Calvinist Christians.[88] However, the possibility of realization of Brahman and achieving moksha through Divine grace is present in the Upanishad-s themselves. Katha Upanishad (1.2.23) states that Brahman cannot be attained by instruction, nor even by intellectual power, nor even through much hearing. He is to be attained only by the one whom He chooses. To such a one He reveals His own nature.

3. Indian Nation and Hindu Nationalism

As pointed out earlier, Romila Thapar employs the colonized lens of Western social theories and models to interpret the facts of Indian history. She believes that nationalism and the idea of nation is a modern phenomenon that did not exist in pre-modern societies in general and India in particular, emerging only in the post-Enlightenment period of Europe. It coincided with a major change, i.e the emergence of societies from the earlier feudal systems and was the result of industrialization, growth of capitalism and resulting economy. As a universalizing concept, it lent itself to asserting political power and that became the direction taken by most nationalisms. However, it is interesting to note that this modernist view of the nation is debatable in the West itself and is challenged by the traditionalist view of the nation, held by many Western sociologists, who believe that nationhood, as a reality and a sentiment, is much older. It existed even before modernity, perhaps as far back as antiquity, and not only in Europe but throughout the world.[89]

Thapar goes further and says that one often faces questions if Indian nationalism existed in pre-modern times. She answers this question by asserting that historians, by which she means herself and her peers, think not. She says that it was British colonial scholarship that defined Indian civilization as located in the territory of British India with its language to be Sanskrit and its religion Hinduism. This definition was later dutifully appropriated by Indians, without giving attention to other significant features that went into the making of the civilization, or questioning whether this was all that was required for even defining a civilization. Thapar further states that the culture of the dominant elite went into defining Indian civilization and non-elites and their cultural patterns, especially in rural areas, were hardly recognized. To further support her theory of non-existence of Indian nation, she goes on to say that even within the very limited definition of Indian civilization, geographical boundaries and languages changed, religions mutated, as did the cultural identity and what was recorded as history.

Thus, according to Thapar, the idea of nationalism began to emerge in India in the late nineteenth century among the upper-caste and middle-class people who worked as administrators for the colonial economy. She says that renowned historians of the early twentieth century like R.C. Majumdar, K.A.N. Sastri, H.C. Raychaudhuri etc. were either participants in the national movement for independence or influenced by it. She calls such historians as 'nationalistic' and claims that their interpretations of Indian history were biased by nationalistic sentiments.[90] They popularized the view that Aryan Vedic culture was the foundation of Indian civilization and also forcibly took its antiquity back to second millennium BCE. These historians put a premium on Sanskrit language and its sources and deliberately ignored Pali, Prakrit and other regional languages. They regarded languages other than

Sanskrit as lesser languages used by people of lesser status. She says that the nationalist historians gave priority to Valmiki's Ramayana and neglected other versions of the story of Shree Rama because they were in Pali and Prakrit. Thus, she believes that Indian nationalism was an expression of 'class-interest' of the middle-class people. However, what Thapar forgets is that nationalism is a theory of political legitimacy which essentially demands, among other things, that the ruler should belong to the same nation as the ruled. The classic definition of nationalism considers it primarily to be a political principle (or a sentiment or movement associated with it), which holds that the state and the nation should be congruent.[91] The existence of nationalistic sentiment in India in the nineteenth century can be simply explained as the result of the violation of this basic principle, as the Britishers, belonging to a foreign nation, were ruling the Indians. As we have seen in earlier sections, the same nationalistic sentiment existed, even in medieval times, against the Turks and the Mughals who were also foreigners and called Mlecchas on that account. Hence, there is no necessity to imagine this new theory of class-interest to explain the 'emergence' of Indian nationalism in the nineteenth century. Also, her argument that nationalism appeared suddenly out of thin air due to popularization of the Aryan Vedic culture and the Sanskrit language by a few 'nationalistic' historians is very weak. A powerful emotion like nationalism, which profoundly stirs people's souls and motivates them to sacrifice even their lives, cannot suddenly cystallize *ex-nihilo*. Even Marxist British historian Eric Hobsbawm, who was one of prominent proponents of this modernist theory of origin of nationalism, admits that a proto-national base may be desirable, perhaps even essential, for the formation of serious state-aspiring national movements.[92]

Moreover, in all her arguments and theories, Thapar is fixated on the European idea of nation and fails to recognize that there can be other notions of collective identity where people living in a certain geographical region can identify themselves as belonging to it. Common religion and common language are not the only criteria to regard a community of people as a nation. Even the modern definition of a nation doesn't strictly regard them as the only criteria and a united unit of population which is full of emotional, spiritual and psychological bonds can also be considered a nation. Nations are not necessarily homogeneous cultures. Thapar also seems to mix up the idea of a state with the idea of a nation when she says that the geographical boundaries of Indian civilization changed in the past. This is because a nation is a more stable entity and can continue to exist even when the political boundaries of a state (or states) associated with it may change. Moreover, the Indian ideas of *Desha*, *Rashtra* and *Sanskriti* are alternatives to the European idea of nation and state which she never uses to study the case of India.[93] It will be incorrect to assume that our ancient Indian ancestors were unaware of the idea of territorial character of a state. The term rashtra, which occurs many times in the Vedas, and *durga* (fortified capital) which occurs in the Mahabharata and *Arthashastra,* stress the territorial aspect of a state. Both were regarded as important elements of the ancient Indian state, just as they are in the modern definition of a nation state.[94] In a hymn (10.173.1-2) of the Rig Veda, the king is asked to maintain the territorial integrity of rashtra. It is true that the Indian subcontinent was not always politically integrated as one state in ancient times. However, even according the modern concept of nation, it is perfectly possible for a nation to live in a multiplicity of political states. The Kurdish nation which spans across sections of states like Iran, Iraq, Turkey and Syria is a good example from the present times. Thus, it cannot be said that people of the Indian subcontinent did not comprise a nation merely because it was split into a number of kingdoms.

Moreover, it cannot be denied that there was always a cultural, spiritual and psychological unity in India. Ramayana and Mahabharata were known all over the region while the cow, Vedas, Purana-s and other scriptures were respected throughout the Indian subcontinent. Immortality of soul, reincarnation, karma and moksha were doctrines believed in, and followed by, majority of the people living in the entire subcontinent. Indians had a sense of the sacredness for all life and realised the importance of charity and mutual respect. Hindus, Jains and Buddhists and others had and continue to have their sacred places all over the country. Puri in the east, Rameshwaram in the south, Dwarka in the west and Badrinath in the north were the unifying *tirtha-s* of

Hindus and bear testimony to India being regarded as one land in ancient times. There was a basic unity of literary ideas, philosophy and outlook upon life throughout the country—the cultural unity of India is still reflected in the similar social ceremonies, various samskara-s and religious rites, festivals and other modes of life throughout the expanse of the country. *Kumbh Mela,* which has been celebrated since time immemorial, at Haridwar, Prayag, Ujjain and Nashik, attracted, like in the present times, people from all over the country. If there had been no sense of unity then Adi Shankaracharya would not have gone as far as Kashmir in the north to debate with people.

Also, the Purana-s identify the Indian subcontinent as one land and repeatedly call it as *Bharatavarsha*. *Vayu Purana* (45.75-76) mentions that Bharatavarsha lies to the south of Himalayas and north of the Indian ocean and is so named for here dwell the descendants of Bharata. Further, the Purana also states (45.86) that the king who rules complete Bharatavarsha is a *Samraat*. It lists the auspicious rivers of Bharatavarsha (45.94-107) which includes Indus in the north to Kaveri in the south. That the Indian subcontinent was the sphere of influence of an Indian imperial ruler is also clear from Kautilya's Arthashastra which states that the land that extends from Himalayas in the north to Indian Ocean in the south is the sphere of influence (kshetra) of a *Chakravartin*. Similarly, Rajashekhara's *Kavyamimamsa* also asserts the same.[95] The aspiration of every Hindu king was to become a Chakravartin or Samraat which, as mentioned, meant the extension of his rule from Himalayas in the north to Rameshwaram in the south. Rajashekhara in his Kavyamimamsa discusses the theme of *desha-vibhaga* (division of desha or 'country') after a thorough discussion of the terms *Jagat* (universe) and *Bhuvana* (world).[96] It is in the context of the discourse on desha that he deals with Bharatavarsha, clearly signifying the unitary character of Indian subcontinent.

Apart from the textual, we also have epigraphic evidences to suggest that the Indian subcontinent was recognized as one land by the people living here since millennia. The Hathigumpha inscription of Kharavela, the king of Kalinga in the first century BC, mentions that in the tenth year of his reign he undertook an expedition to conquer the whole of Bharatavarsha. Moreover, it was not just the Indians but even the foreigners who identified India as one land. For example, the Greek envoy Megasthenes in c. 302 BCE used the term 'India' for the entire country and says that it is in the shape of a quadrilateral and surrounded by sea on its eastern and western side and by the Himalayas in the north. Similarly, Alberuni referred to the entire Indian subcontinent as Hindustan.

From the brief survey above, it should be clear to anyone that in ancient times there was a definitely a sense of national identity among the people residing in the Indian subcontinent. Vishnu Purana even expresses patriotic sentiment towards this land of Bharatavarsha when it says that it is only after thousands of births and the accumulation of much merit (*punya*) that living beings are sometimes born in Bharatavarsha as humans (2.3.23). It was this concept of Bharatavarsha which made the leaders of this country formalize in the solemn declaration of our Constitution: 'India, that is Bharat, shall be a union of States'. However, historians like Thapar overlook all these facts. One can evaluate Thapar's affinity to India from a statement in her book, describing it as a country that is poor, violent, corrupt, overpopulated, misogynistic, unequal, and prone to sectarian violence, terrorism and environmental disasters.[97]

Similar to her denial of Indian nation, Thapar denies the existence of Hindu identity in the past. She says that the notion of Hindu community does not have a long ancestry and the need for postulating it became a requirement for political mobilization in the nineteenth century, when representation by religious community became a key to power and where such representation gave access to economic resources. The competition for middle class employment and the argument that the size of the community should be taken into consideration for such purpose made some people with vested interests propagate the idea of Hindu community. She strongly suggests that the notion of existence of Hindu identity in the ancient past was merely 'imagined' in the last two centuries and hence it is a purely modern construction.[98] What we call Hindu community today was in fact, a variety of communities determined by location, caste, occupation etc. and none of them were necessarily bound together by a common religious identity.

However, her fanciful claim is refuted by numerous instances in the history of medieval India where kings and people clearly identify themselves as Hindu. Thus, in an inscription from 1352 CE, Bukka I, the founder of the great Vijaynagara kingdom, who also later became its ruler, refers to himself as Hindu. Similarly, Rana Kumbha of Mewar and Krishna Deva Raya of Vijaynagara assumed the title of Hindu emperor for themselves in 1438 CE and 1513 CE respectively.[99] *Prithviraja Raso*, a Hindi ballad narrating the encounter between Prithviraja Chauhan and Muhammad Ghori and written by Chand Bardai, court poet and friend of Prithviraja, calls Prithviraja a Hindu king and frequently refers to those who fought against the Turkish invaders as 'Hindus'.[100] It states, while referring to the battle of Tarain, that the two (Hindus and *Turak-s*) played a bloody game of Holi.[101] At another place, while describing the battle between Prithviraja and Ghori, the text states:

> "The Hindus catching the mlechchas by their hands, whirled them round, just as Bhima did to the elephants; but the comparison does not do justice to the fight". (Eaton 2006:42)

Similarly, another epic poem *Prithviraja Vijaya* composed by the Kashmiri author Jayanaka between 1178 and 1200 CE and the fifteenth century work *Hammira Mahakavya* written by a Jain Nayachandra Suri, use the word 'Hindu' to refer to the natives of India. In the latter work Muhammad Ghori is accused of burning Hindu cities and defiling Hindu women.[102] Even before the emergence of any influential middle class in India, to whom Thapar attributes the concoction of Hindu identity, the famous military general of the Maratha empire, Peshwa Baji Rao I (r. 1720-1740 CE), declared that his aim was to establish a *Hindupad Padshahi* or a Hindu empire.[103] The ideal of Hindupad Padshahi helped him to secure the support of Hindu chiefs by evoking their sympathy. Apart from this, all the Persian chronicles, right from the beginning of Islam's encounter with India, unambiguously denoted the people of this country as Hindus in the religious sense of pagans or infidels. Thapar says that the idea of two distinctive, segregated civilizations, the Hindu and the Muslim, in conflict with each other was assumed in British colonial scholarship and did not exist earlier. However, even a cursory look at any of the Persian chronicles of medieval India would belie her assertion, as the formula through which interaction between the natives and invaders was defined in them was always Hindu versus Muslim.

Thapar says that the concepts of nations based on a single exclusive identity—religious, linguistic, ethnic and similar single identities—are actually pseudo-nationalisms and should be precluded from being called a 'nationalism'. She adds that Hindu Nationalism dominates the thinking of those that regard themselves as defending all things Indian, by which they often mean Hindu, or else defending the religion they support and oppose the minority community from which non-compliance is feared. However, Thapar fails to realize that in every country when there is a revival of consciousness of national identity, people invariably turn back to what they regard as their classical age and seek to derive new inspiration from that heritage. It would be highly unjustified that in order to emphasize the composite character of Indian society and cultural heritage, we neglect the exploration of India's ancient Hindu past. There is no justification to label such an endeavor as pseudo-nationalism, Hindu revivalism or fascism. We cannot simply ignore the palpable fact that for the majority of Indians who follow religions other than Hinduism today, the classical age is the same as that for Hindus. A change of religion does not alter the fact that the epics, literature, philosophy and the entire culture of ancient India constitute the common heritage of all Indians irrespective of their religious differences today. Moreover, Hinduism with its open architecture does not fear non-compliance from any other religious community but only demands mutual respect.[104]

Conclusion

My objective in this essay has been to show that most of the theories propagated by Romila Thapar are merely speculations riddled with factual errors. Evidences from fields of numismatics, archaeology, epigraphy, art and also from our traditional texts have been presented to debunk many of the claims, made by Thapar in her various works over the years. Marxist historiography tends to work with unilinear Western historical models focusing on class stratification and economic and social structures. However, history cannot be squeezed within the moulds of pre-determined ideological frameworks as it inevitably results into its crude distortion. One must honestly understand the limitations of ideological and theoretical frameworks in order to make advances in history writing. It is mentioned in Ramayana that the *asura* Ravana had a *Pushpaka-Vimana* in which he could fly instantly to any place he thought of in his mind. The title of this essay tries to caution that history writing should not be reduced to such flights of one's mental imaginations by disregarding facts. The tradition and culture of our Bharatavarsha cannot be sidelined in any interpretation of historical facts.

Bibliography

Ahuja, N.D. N.A. *The Great Guru Nanak and the Muslims*. Chandigarh: Kirti Publishing House.

Banerjee, Jamini M. 1967. *History of Firuzshah Tughluq*. Delhi: Munshiram Manoharlal.

Baruah, S.L. 2013. *A Comprehensive History of Assam*. New Delhi: Munshiram Manoharlal Publishers.

Barz, Richard. 1992. *The Bhakti Sect of Vallabhacharya*. New Delhi: Munishiram Manoharlal.

Beveridge, H. 1939. *Akbarnama Volume 3*. Kolkata: The Asiatic Society.

Bharati, Srirama. 2000. *The Sacred Book of Four Thousand*. Chennai: Sri Sadagopan Tirunarayanaswami Divyaprabandha Pathashala.

Bhargava, Meena. 2010. *Exploring Medieval India II*. New Delhi: Orient Blackswan.

Chattopadhyaya, Brajadulal. 1998. *Representing the Other? Sanskrit Sources and the Muslims*. New Delhi: Manohar Publishers.

Chattopadhyaya, Brajadulal. 2015. *Essays in Ancient Indian Economic History 2nd Edition*. New Delhi: Primus Books.

Chaudhuri, Roma. 2012. *Ten Schools of Vedanta*. Kolkata: Rabindra Bharati University.

Choudhary, Dr. G.C. 1954. *Political History of Northern India from Jain Sources*. Amritsar: Sohanlal Jaindharma Pracharak Samiti.

Dalal, C.D., Pandit R.A. Sastry, and Siromani K.S.R. Sastri. 1934. *Kavyamimamsa of Rajasekhara*. Baroda: Oriental Institute.

Dalmia, Vasudha. 2014. *Religious Interactions in Mughal India*. New Delhi: Oxford University Press.

Eaton, Richard. 2006. *India's Islamic Traditions*. New Delhi: Oxford University Press.

Eaton, Richard. 2013. *Sufis of Bijapur*. New Delhi: Munshiram Manoharlal Publishers.

Eaton, Richard M. and Phillip B. Wagoner. 2014. *Power, Memory and Architecture: Contested Sites on India's Deccan Plateau, 1300-1600*. New Delhi: Oxford University Press.

Evans, Sir J. 1893. *The Numismatic Chronicle and Journal of the Numismatic Society 3rd Series Vol. XIII*. London: N.A.

Fraser, Nelson and J.F. Edwards. 1922. *The Life and Teaching of Tukaram*. N.A.: The Christian Literature Society for India.

Galewicz, Cezary. 2009. *A Commentator in the Service of Empire*. Vienna: De Nobili Research Library.

Gat, Azar and Alexander Yakobson. 2013. *Nations: The Long History and Deep Roots of Political Ethnicity and Nationalism*. New York: Cambridge University Press.

Gellner, Ernest. 1983. *Nations and Nationalism*. New York: Cornell University Press.

Harle, J.C. 1994. *The Art and Architecture of the Indian Subcontinent*. London: Yale University Press.

Hobsbawm, E.J. 2013. *Nations and Nationalism Since 1780*. New York: Cambridge University Press.

Huntington, Susan L. 2016. *The Art of Ancient India*. New Delhi: Motilal Banarsidass.

Jain, Kailash C. 1963. *Jainism in Rajasthan*. Sholapur: Gulabchand Hirachand Doshi Publishers.

Jain, Rekha. 1995. *Ancient Indian Coinage*. New Delhi: D.K. Printworld Pvt. Ltd.

Jain, K.C. 1999. *History of Jainism Vol. 2*. New Delhi: D.K. Printworld (P) Ltd.

Karpatri, Swami M. 2001. *Ramayana Mimamsa*. Vrindavana: Radhakrishna Dhanuka Prakashan Sansthan.

Majumdar, A.K. 1965. *Bhakti Renaissance*. Bombay: Bharatiya Vidya Bhavan.

Majumdar, R.C. 2001. *The Struggle For Empire*. Mumbai: Bharatiya Vidya Bhavan.

Majumdar, R.C. 2006. *The Delhi Sultanate*. Mumbai: Bharatiya Vidya Bhavan.

Malhotra, Rajiv. 2011. *Being Different*. New Delhi: Harper Collins.

Malhotra, Rajiv and Satyanarayana D. Babaji. 2020. *Sanskrit Non-Translatables: The Importance of Sanskritizing English*. New Delhi: Amaryllis.

Massey, Reginald and Massey Jamila. 1996. *The Music of India*. New Delhi: Abhinav Publications.

Michell, George. 2000. *Hindu Art and Architecture*. London: Thames & Hudson.

Mittal, Prabhudayal. 1960. *Sangeet Samraat Tansen: Jeevani aur Rachnayein*. Mathura: Sahitya Sansthan.

Nagar, Shanti L. 1993. *Varaha in Indian Art*. New Delhi: Aryan Books International.

Nazim, Muhammad. 1931. *The Life and Times of Sultan Mahmud of Ghazna*. Cambridge: Cambridge University Press.

Orsini, Francesca and Samira Sheikh. 2014. *After Taimur Left*. New Delhi: Oxford University Press.

Quintanilla, Sonya R. 2007. *History of the Early Stone Sculpture at Mathura*. Leiden: Brill Publishers.

Radhakrishnan, S. 2010. *The Principal Upanishads*. Noida: HarperCollins Publishers.

Raghavan, V. 2009. *Studies on Ramayana*. Chennai: Dr. V. Raghavan Centre for Performing Arts.

Rajiv Malhotra Official. 2019. "Rajya is Strong, Where is the Rashtra?" YouTube. Retrieved October 18, 2021 (https://www.youtube.com/watch?v=SnkbmERdyBg).

Ramachandran, T.N. 1995. *Tirumurai The Sixth, Eng. Translation*. Mayiladuthurai: Dharmapuram Aadheenam.

Rangacharya, Anantha N.S. 2003. *Principal Upanishads Vol. 1*. Bangalore: N.A.

Rangaswamy, Dorai M.A. 1990. *The Religion and Philosophy of Tevaram 2nd Edition Vol. 3*. Madras: University of Madras.

Rao, Nagaraja M.S. 1978. *The Chalukyas of Badami*. Bangalore: The Mythic Society.

Ray, Rajat K. 2003. *The Felt Community*. New Delhi: Oxford University Press.

Rezavi, Syed A.N. 2013. *Fathpur Sikri Revisited*. New Delhi: Oxford University Press.

Sastri, K.A.N. 1987. *A Comprehensive History of India Vol. 2*. New Delhi: People's Publishing House.

Sen, Surendra N. 1958. *The Military System of the Marathas*. New Delhi: Orient Longmans.

Sharma, R.S. 1992. *A Comprehensive History of India Volume 4 Part 1*. New Delhi: People's Publishing House.

Sharma, B.N.K. 2000. *History of Dvaita School of Vedanta 3rd Revised Edition*. New Delhi: Motilal Banarsidass.

Sharma, Ram S. 2012. *Aspects of Political Ideas and Institutions in Ancient India*. New Delhi: Motilal Banarsidass.

Stein, M.A. 1961. *Rajatarangini Volume 1*. New Delhi: Motilal Banarasidass.

Stoker, Valerie. 2016. *Polemics and Patronage in the City of Victory*. California: California University Press.

Talbot, Cynthia. 2016. *The Last Hindu Emperor: Prithviraj Chauhan and the Indian Past 1200-2000*. Cambridge: Cambridge University Press.

Thapar, Romila. 2002. *The Penguin History of Early India*. New Delhi: Penguin Books.

Thapar, Romila. 2003. *Early India*. New Delhi: Penguin India.

Thapar, Romila. 2004. *Cultural Pasts*. New Delhi: Oxford University Press.

Thapar, Romila. 2004. *Somanatha—The Many Voices of History*. New Delhi: Penguin Books.

Thapar, Romila. 2012. *Ancient Indian Social History 2nd Edition*. New Delhi: Orient BlackSwan.

Thapar, Romila. 2013. *The Past Before Us*. New Delhi: Permanent Black.

Thapar, Romila, A.G. Noorani, and Sadananda Menon. 2016. *On Nationalism*. New Delhi: Aleph Book Company.

Vanmikanathan, G. 1985. *Periya Puranam by Sekkizhar*. Madras: Sri Ramakrishna Math.

Various. 1970. *India's Contribution to World Thought and Culture*. Madras: Vivekananda Rock Memorial Commitee.

Vatsyayan, Kapila. 2006. *The Cultural Heritage of India Volume 7 Part 2*. Kolkata: Ramakrishna Mission Institute of Culture.

Whitney, William D. 1905. *The Atharva-Veda Samhita English Translation 2nd Volume*. Cambridge Massachusetts: Harvard University Press.

Notes

1. (Stein 1961:2)
2. (Rajiv Malhotra Official 2019)
3. (Thapar 2003:428)
4. (Sharma 1992:359)
5. (Chattopadhyaya 2015:155)
6. (Majumdar 2001:20)
7. (Choudhary 1954:238)
8. (Eaton and Wagoner 2014:52)
9. (Banerjee 1967:58)
10. (Majumdar 2006:105-106)

11. (Majumdar 2006:104)
12. (Beveridge 1939:757)
13. (Beveridge 1939:757)
14. Reflections on Nationalism and History in (Thapar, Noorani, and Menon 2016).
15. (Dalmia 2014:329)
16. (Eaton 2006:68)
17. (Dalmia 2014:106)
18. (Bhargava 2010:46)
19. (Malhotra and Babaji 2020:5-9)
20. (Galewicz 2009:34)
21. (Stoker 2016:50)
22. (Jain 1963:157)
23. (Jain 1999:716)
24. (Massey and Jamila 1996:44)
25. (Massey and Jamila 1996:46)
26. (Mittal 1960:2)
27. (Vatsyayan 2006:507)
28. (Massey and Jamila 1996:51)
29. (Thapar 2004:1102)
30. (Eaton 2013:22)
31. (Eaton 2013:30)
32. (Thapar 2004:994)
33. (Thapar 2003:270) and (Thapar 2004:969)
34. See Aitreya Brahmana 1.1.1 and Taittiriya Samhita 5.5.1
35. Also See *Satapatha Brahmana* (13.6.1.1)
36. (Various 1970:140)
37. (Various 1970:143)
38. (Sastri 1987:232)
39. (Jain 1995:100)
40. (Various 1970:221)
41. (Michell 2000:40-42)

42. (Michell 2000:218)
43. (Huntington 2016:58)
44. (Rezavi 2013:10)
45. (Evans 1893:126-127)
46. (Thapar 2003:294)
47. (Nagar 1993:4)
48. (Nagar 1993:118-120)
49. (Nagar 1993:79-80)
50. (Huntington 2016:192)
51. (Rao 1978:186)
52. (Baruah 2013:159)
53. (Thapar 2003:223)
54. (Michell 2000:39)
55. (Various 1970:138)
56. (Thapar 2013:266)
57. (Whitney 1905:780)
58. (Thapar 2013:209)
59. (Raghavan 2009:79)
60. (Raghavan 2009:343)
61. (Thapar 2013:447)
62. (Karpatri 2001:200-204)
63. (Thapar 2013:209)
64. (Thapar 2004:1089)
65. (Thapar 2004:1030)
66. (Thapar 2013:156)
67. (Thapar 2004:1035)
68. (Sastri 1987:381-382)
69. (Quintanilla 2007:92)
70. (Thapar 2002:356)
71. (Majumdar 1965:1)
72. (Thapar 2002:356)
73. (Harle 1994:454)

74. See for instance Rig Veda VII.87.7
75. (Ramachandran 1995:0-29)
76. (Rangaswamy 1990:984)
77. (Thapar 2002:352)
78. (Thapar 2002:355)
79. (Ramachandran 1995:187)
80. (Chaudhuri 2012:66)
81. (Chaudhuri 2012:66)
82. (Bharati 2000:526)
83. (Bharati 2000:571)
84. (Vanmikanathan 1985:182)
85. (Fraser and Edwards 1922:267)
86. (Thapar 2003:401)
87. (Sharma 2000:609)
88. (Thapar 2003:401)
89. (Gat and Yakobson 2013:1)
90. (Thapar 2012:10)
91. (Gellner 1983:1)
92. (Hobsbawm 2013:78)
93. (Rajiv Malhotra Official 2019)
94. (Sharma 2012:156,197)
95. (Dalal, Sastry, and Sastri 1934:92,148)
96. (Dalal, Sastry, and Sastri 1934:242-244)
97. (Thapar, Noorani, and Menon 2016:Foreword)
98. (Thapar 2004:984-985)
99. (Chattopadhyaya 1998:54)
100. (Talbot 2016:154,168)
101. (Ray 2003:88)
102. (Eaton 2006:42)
103. (Sen 1958:57)
104. (Malhotra 2011:Chapter 1)

TWO

Sheldon Pollock
Propaganda and Prevarication

K.S. Kannan

In the following pages, an assessment of the contribution of Prof. Sheldon Pollock to the anti-India, anti-Hindu, anti-Sanskrit genre of literature is made. Even though I have edited seven volumes (all published by Infinity Foundation India) that closely examined the writings of Pollock on about half a dozen issues, it is fair to say that many more issues remain unexamined. The volumes were a result of the series of conferences held in Chennai and Delhi with participants from all walks of life, from India and abroad, and run to around 1500 pages. In the brief essay, of just a score of pages to follow, I have tried to note only a few key points that go to show the hollowness and specious nature of the arguments of Pollock. I have also cited frequently, though from just a few of the numerous scholars that participated in the conferences and presented papers on specific topics after a detailed study.

Who is Pollock?

Sheldon Pollock holds a high academic position. He joined Richard Gombrich (a British Indologist) in 2008 as editor of *Clay Sanskrit Series* (modelled after Loeb Classics, and named after its sponsor John Clay, and closed in 2014). In 2015, Pollock became the Founding Editor of *Murty Classical Library of India* (MCLI), published from Harvard University Press; it was made possible by a donation of $4.5 million given by Rohan Murthy. The MCLI publishes books of languages and religions of South Asia not excluding Islam.

The MCLI aims to make available "the greatest literary works of India from the past two millennia."[1] The project is launched with this objective: "Many classic Indic texts have never reached a global audience, while others are becoming increasingly inaccessible even to Indian readers."[2] India has the single most complex and continuous multilingual tradition of literature in the world, which MCLI seeks to reintroduce to a new generation of readers. So far 29 books are out in the series as per its website.

In his academic career starting around 1965, Pollock has written on a variety of topics that pertain to a wide variety of vistas on Indian literature—poetry and poetics, religion and philosophy, sociology and politics. As interventionalism is a matter of right for the West, Westerners take their positions on every issue of India's past, present, and future; they have high stakes in the current trends in Indian politics. Accordingly, Pollock poked his nose into the Ram Janmabhoomi issue for this very reason, and also in respect of denying a visa to Narendra Modi, the then Chief Minister of Gujarat (and the current Prime Minister of India).

Pollock is the Arvind Raghunathan Professor of South Asian Studies at the Department of Middle Eastern South Asian and African Studies at Columbia University, New York. He has also been awarded the Padma Shri Award by the Government of India earlier. He was a professor at the University of Iowa, and also the George V. Bobrinsky Professor of Sanskrit and Indic Studies at the University of Chicago. He is also famous for directing the Project SKSEC (Sanskrit Knowledge Systems on the Eve of Colonialism), and is editing a series of historical source books in classical Indian thought.

Educated at Harvard, he received his Bachelor in Arts in Classical Greek and PhD in Sanskrit and Indian Studies. His work *The Language of Gods in the World of Men* (2006) won, ironically, the Coomaraswamy Award. Pollock has also received the Distinguished Achievement Award from the Andrew W. Mellon Foundation. He has also received a Presidential Certificate of Honor. He is a Fellow of the American Academy of Arts and Sciences.

Overt Political Tones: Hindutva and the "Dead" Sanskrit

A Sanskrit scholar making his living out of Sanskrit, Pollock denies the very nativity of Sanskrit to India, and even calls it dead, despite many proofs to the contrary. Deeply worried about the ascent of BJP to power, he makes a declaration that Hindutva propagandists have *sought to show that* Sanskrit is indigenous to India. An avowed Leftist, he is totally averse to the idea that Sanskrit can be the source and preserver of world culture. The root of the problem appears to him to be the inclusion of Sanskrit amongst the Scheduled Languages of India.

One of the theses he loves to peddle is, as we noted, that Sanskrit is "dead"; how "timely" that the very year next to the "Sanskrit Year", declared by the Central Government in India (viz. 2000), he wrote an article entitled "The Death of Sanskrit"![3] For him, nothing worthwhile in Kashmir was written after Maṅkha: Śrīvara's *Subhāṣitāvalī*, an anthology, notes no literature of substantial significance between 12th and 15th centuries. In the Vijayanagar Empire, the sacredness of Sanskrit was well acknowledged, and if King Kṛṣṇadevarāya still composed in Sanskrit, it was because "Sanskrit *kāvya* is profoundly historicist political." Warranted or unwarranted, Pollock uses his "power"—glasses everywhere: "*all for power; everything from power*"—seems to be the sole motto he pursues in anything dealing with Sanskrit.

Speaking of Jagannātha Paṇḍita, he speaks in contradiction: for all his brilliance, Jagannātha had, we are told, the same assumptions, procedures, and goals as his predecessors; yet he had a modern subjectivity (Pollock 2001:404-405). Pollock wants to see some autobiographical element in some of Jagannātha's "last" poems; whereas in actual fact, many of these poems are already cited as examples in his magnum opus *Rasagaṅgādhara*, written much earlier; he imagines that Jagannātha composed some of these verses after the "death of his Muslim wife"!

Hinduphobia and Islamophilia

If Kavīndrācārya Sarasvatī had a big manuscript library, it must have been on account of a pension from the Mughal Emperor, says Pollock (2001: 408), whose Islamophilia is matched only by his Hinduphobia.

Never does Pollock miss an opportunity to speak spitefully of Sanskrit: be it Tanjore or Jaipur or Mysore, the patronized productions never left the Court, and the Court-produced literature ceased to make history. For him, Sanskrit literature became "a practice of repetition and not renewal" (2003a: 100).

The central values of Sanskrit literature can only be appreciated by those who have the necessary cultural training. The death of Sanskrit tradition is a given for him, and what remains to be figured out is only the how and the why of it. He wants to emphasize that Sanskrit is, like Latin, ever more exclusively associated with narrow forms of religion and priestcraft. He refuses to note that whereas Latin faded into the background, Sanskrit continued to be studied by the very people who promoted the vernaculars.

For him, it was the barbarous invader who was *trying to revive Sanskrit*, whereas indigenous cultural, social, and political changes caused its death. Pollock wants to exonerate Islamists everywhere, and accuses Indian kings of *sabotaging Sanskrit*. Making the accusation that Sanskrit tradition has only been recycling things, and nothing new came to be established, while at the same time taking note of the development of 'Navya Nyāya' as a new mode of presentation—are mutually contradictory. Despite the massive and extensive commentaries on the Vedas produced in the period, "nothing new was produced in Sanskrit in the Vijayanagar period." His terming Jagannātha as "the last Sanskrit poet" is indeed ludicrous—as ludicrous as some of his *chela*-s calling him "the last Sanskrit Pandit." Hanneder (2002: 309) has shown examples of many eminent Sanskrit poets after Jagannātha.

Nothing matches Pollock's labelling of Islamists' library-burning, planned and systematic though it regularly was, as a mere fire accident. To quote Pollock (2001: 398): "Important creative texts may have disappeared in one of the fires that periodically engulfed the capital of Kashmir": by the same yardstick the 9/11 attacks could as well be buildings disappearing from periodic plane crashes that engulfed New York. To speak in this tone despite the evidence even in contemporary chronicles such as the *Rājataraṅgiṇī* of Śrīvara viz:

> *sekandhara-dharānātho yavanaiḥ preritaḥ purā |*
> *pustakāni ca sarvāṇi tṛṇāny agnir ivādahat ||* (1.5.75)

"Instigated by Muslims, Sikandar, the Sultan, burnt down all the books, just as fire would burn down grass" holds a mirror to his brazenness.

Pollock has no occasion—amidst his ever-present and ever-ready Islamophilical concerns—to make even a passing allusion to the devastation wrought by Muslims on the Vijayanagar Empire as the fallen capital was ruthlessly pillaged and destroyed for a full five months as noted by Sewell (1962: 207). Pollock would only say "In fact, it was often the barbarous invader who sought to revive Sanskrit" (Pollock 2001: 416).

Techniques of Prevarication

In Kannan and Meera (2017: 225-226) it has been shown with examples how Pollock employs certain tricks in his writings to disparage/understate/misinform/misinterpret the material (i.e. ideas, concepts etc.) in Sanskrit. To cite some:

(a) choosing a narrow definition to determine the vitality of a tradition/language

(b) selecting data to fit a theory

(c) selective playing up and playing down

(d) intentional usage of various terms/frameworks of social science, modern psychology, anthropology, Biblical Studies etc., in order to superimpose them on traditional Indian thought to the disadvantage of the latter,

(e) list-and-dismiss technique; and last but not the least,

(f) *divide et impera.*

Pollock's "writings betray many internal contradictions." For example, he calls Śrīvara as "clerical" at one place, but also as "the most interesting intellectual at the court of Zain-ul-'abedin" at another place, as pointed out by Hanneder (2002: 302).

Pollock charges that the cause of Sanskrit is championed merely by promoters of Hindutva, while on the other hand, there was a large-scale high regard for Sanskrit prior to Independence, and even subsequent to the same for a few decades, until the most anti-Hindu political party, viz, that of the Nehru dynasty, did everything to kill and destroy Sanskrit. The P.V. Narasimha Rao government (1991-96) sought to remove Sanskrit from the CBSE syllabus, and it was only with the intervention of the Supreme Court that the Government withdrew its foolish endeavor.

It must be noted that several individuals and organizations—that are unconnected to Hindutva, or perhaps have not even heard of the Hindutva movement—have lent their voluntary support and encouragement to Sanskrit at a personal level, and even through some small local organizations. For Pollock, all attempts to promote Sanskrit are a politically based or politically biased exercise in nostalgia.

It is another example of Pollock's routine fallacies that he establishes no rigorous conditions in order to declare a language to be dead. The major lacunae in his arbitrary analysis is shown by Manogna Sastry as two-fold: "(a) his exclusive focus on the general genre of *kāvya* (excluding even *stotra*-s) as the only measure of the vitality of the language, and (b) his very small set of four instances spread over a millennium across the country during which the language declined" (Sastry 2017: 236).

Hanneder (2002: 308) makes out how Pollock has "interpreted the evidence to fit his thesis without considering other options." And turning the arguments of Pollock against himself, Sastry (2017: 248) shows, with his own examples, "the resilience and indomitability of Sanskrit language—to have withstood shocks, assault, negligence, and attempts to actively destroy it for over a millennium", and what is more, Sanskrit "continues to survive, and rediscover itself even in our own day and age."

Sanskrit and Nazism

Among the various charges made against Sanskrit, nothing can be more sinister than linking it with Nazism. Some of the best persons to tackle this issue are Dr. Koenraad Elst, the Flemish Indologist, and Prof. K. Gopinath, an eminent scientist at the Indian Institute of Science, Bangalore. Elst very well points out how the allegation by Pollock of the National Socialist connection of Sanskrit is "heavily over-interpreted and emphatically taken to be causal, as if the interest in Sanskrit has caused the Holocaust" (2017: 93). Elst also characterizes some of the claims made by or relied upon by Pollock as surprisingly weak or simply wrong.

It should not be very difficult to realize the puerile nature of Pollock's statements in this regard. As Elst indicates, even non-specialists could easily have checked that Adolf Hitler held Hinduism in utter contempt. While it is the Aryan Invasion Theory that forms the cornerstone and perfect illustration of the narcissistic Nazi world-view, Pollock is prepared to concede to the Out-of-India Theory (OIT)—in order merely to link Sanskrit and Nazism, even though he is otherwise opposed to OIT! And worse: the American academe raises no objection against this otherwise unpardonable hypothesis; and why? That is because of their "general animus against Hinduism and Indo-European indigenism" (Elst 2017: 93). The patent hypocrisy of both Pollock and his American peers stands out here.

Pollock indicts German Indology of the National Socialist Era for fostering "the ultimate Orientalist project, the legitimation of genocide" (Pollock 1993: 96); and yet he is not able to quote even a single instance of any of the German Indologists as actually declaring that they wanted genocide. The deliberate design of Pollock in respect of his claims about Indology and National Socialism was to direct it against the Sanskrit tradition. Instances of genocide in the Biblical or Islamic traditions would never be cited by Pollock. But when it comes to Hinduism, he would seize every opportunity or the mildest hint to bend facts to his line of interpretation. Thus, if Vedic literature indeed enjoined genocide, Pollock would "gleefully quote it", as Elst couches it well. No proof whatsoever on such or similar lines exists, and thus Pollock is an expert in constructing a superstructure without foundations. There is nothing in the entire and vast Vedic literature that can suggest anti-Semitism even in the mildest manner. While Vedic literature is just unaware of the Jews, the Jews were actually accorded hospitality on the Malabar Coast—quite in keeping with the never-forsaken pluralism of the Hindu heritage.

All of Pollock's quotations from National Socialist Indologists pertain, Elst notes, to the Buddha. To Pollock, Nazis needed inspiration as it were from the Mīmāṁsā thinkers who molded Hindu law, for justifying societal hierarchy. Yet, Pollock could lay hand on not a single Nazi quote to that effect, even by implication, straight or contrived! The Buddha is presented by Pollock as an antidote to Vedic inequality, yet it is the Buddha, Elst points out, who is very popular among the Nazis. And the Nazis never considered India as their homeland either!

Proposal to Theorem to Truism: Trajectories of Mendacity

Speaking of the wild imagination of racism in the *cāturvarṇya* system, Elst remarks that "none of the interesting musings about Indian society played any role whatsoever in NS policies" (Elst 2017: 108). What is the modality to which [the ilks of] Pollock resort(s) in this zeal for disinformation? None can better Elst in presenting it succinctly and effectively: "...an idea is first launched and argued in highbrow papers like the *New York Review* or the *Economic & Political Weekly*; subsequently it is presented as the received wisdom in more general media like *The Washington Post* or *The Times of India*; but the final stage is when the idea is presented as a matter of course, and conveyed through popular media, women's magazines etc. That is what completes the instilling of false ideas in the popular mind." (Elst 2017: 109).

Elst (2017: 109) lays bare the Pollockian paradigm very well. "Similarly, to promote an idea intended to become a fixture in our world view, it is useful to repeat it, first as a topical proposal to be proven, then as a theorem deemed to have been proven, finally as a truism on which other proposals can be usefully and safely built."

For all the widespread revulsion of the West against the caste system, there is no evidence textual or historical, of any genocide whatsoever as related to it, directly or indirectly. But then, goaded by the fancy notion of the "symmetry fallacy", Westerners presume that Hinduism is quite like their own religions of the Abrahamic faith. As the Abrahamic faiths routinely indulge in terrorism of one sort or the other, Hinduism must have a similar strain of terrorism too. Pollock is only determined to read genocide into the texts.

Well has it been said: "not failure, but low aim is crime", and it applies to Pollock aptly. He has made extraordinary allegations against Hinduism. "Sling mud; even if the mud does not stick, the stain remains", so goes another saying. And again, "he who fails to substantiate his allegations is verily guilty of slander." On these counts, Pollock is patently guilty of slander, even though he has no feeling whatsoever of any guilt; and is the worse for it. And the deeper tragedy is that Pollock, the guilty, is by no means overcome by remorse or regret; and one is only reminded of hardened criminals. The question that should then be asked is: "should the Sanskrit tradition be given in care to a professor of Sanskrit who stands by such a grave though false allegation against it?" (Elst 2017: 110)

Proficiency in Propagandism

Prof. Gopinath has very well analyzed the *modus operandi* adopted by Pollock. It is instructive, Gopinath says, "how certain questions are posed, extraneous elements subtly brought in, and selected evidence then marshalled to deduce or suggest certain desired conclusion", which is in essence how propagandist systems work.

Three classic examples of racism can be provided:

(a) Jews and Christians not being permitted to eat together;

(b) prohibition of intermarriage and of sexual intercourse between Christians and Jews;

(c) Jews not permitted to show themselves in the streets during Passion Week

(Gopinath 2017: 30-31).

The scale of genocide practiced by the West is mind-boggling: between 1846 and 1870, California's Native American population plunged from around 150,000 to 30,000. By 1880, it was barely 16,000. Homicides, battles, massacres, and diseases, dislocation and starvation—all willfully enforced resulted in such decimation of population (cf. Gopinath 2017: 37). India has never had racism or genocide of the above kind, or of any kind for that matter—till, of course, such cruelties were inflicted upon them by Muslims and Christians, the invading plunderers.

We see the irony of facts—in that, Columbus was praised as "the discoverer of the Americas", whereas the actual natives were decimated ruthlessly till recently. Rajiv Malhotra refers to these as the "greatest episodes of ethnic cleansing and genocide", of Native Americans, who were regularly represented as innately inferior. The physical genocide, where prevented, was made up by cultural genocide; and they were all explained as "the native's inability to adapt to civilization." As Gopinath describes in regard to issues such as this, "the sentiment of Pollock seems insubstantial or frivolous", as he has never experienced any oppression as such.

Sense of "Responsibility"

Mocking Pollock's fancy idea of the link between Sanskrit's "deep structure" and Nazi genocide, Gopinath invokes the concepts of "butterfly effect" and *Kākatālīya nyāya* which best expose the naïve causality of Pollock's concoctions. Pollock could more easily have conceived of the Church as his model nonpareil for genocide. The two-millennia old church has digested paganism (in its several hues), and many native cultures (Native American, Ethiopian, Indian etc.). "The victim is victimized in Pollock's analysis,"—as Gopinath (2017: 43) remarks perceptively.

Well has it been said that when a politician wants to commit an act of crime, he first declares it as his duty. So it is with Pollock: he first declares that Hindutva is responsible for many ills that afflict India, and, as a concerned person, it is of course his duty to fight against such tendencies. Islamic forces, the Leftist forces, and the Christian forces in India and US—all joined the chorus demanding denial of a visa to the US for Mr. Narendra Modi, the then Chief Minister of Gujarat—despite the fact that not even a single FIR (First Information Report) had been filed against him till then (or even subsequently). And Pollock was a signatory to the petition demanding the denial of a US visa to Mr. Modi. And such high political "non-partisanship" characterizes Pollock, the American mentor of Indology!

Solid Counter-evidence

Refuting with plain facts Pollock's characterization of Sanskrit as "dead", Satyanarayana Dasa shows (2017: 153) an actual increase in the number of philosophical authors—by 6970, from the 17th century to the 18th century; and by 69% from the 19th century to the 20th century (Dasa 2017: 152). And again, statistics provided by the Sahitya Akademi (in the context of awards) provides a strong pointer – to the fact that literary production in Sanskrit has all along been vying more or less on an equal terms and footing with other languages (Dasa 2017: 150). Dasa also produces abundant evidence – of the large mass of literary production of various genres – in the self-same period that Pollock would portray as a period of great decline.

"Feeding Tubes and Oxygen Tanks"?

Pollock's statement viz., "Government feeding tubes and oxygen tanks may try to preserve the language in a state of quasi-animation, but most observers would agree that in some crucial way, Sanskrit is dead" – has been severely attacked by Dr. Jayaraman Mahadevan, citing the *Sanskrit Commission Report* instituted by the Government of India: the 1957 Report shows clearly how the British Raj had downgraded the facilities extended to the traditional schools; and post-Independence, the attitude of the ruling party has been such that "Sanskrit has not been allowed to enjoy even the status and facilities it had under the British Raj" (Mahadevan 2017: 185).

Mahadevan speaks of "the step-motherly attitude of the [Congress] Government" towards Sanskrit – which is not reflective of the feelings of the people at large: "...during the British period, the salary of Sanskrit teachers was half the salary of the teachers of other subjects due to which

Sanskrit was looked down upon for long", and the tradition continues to this day (Cf. *Vision and Road Map for the Development of Sanskrit Report*, 2016: 5 as cited by Mahadevan)

Quite contrary to the fabrications of Pollock, Sanskrit was associated with the cultural consciousness of the country, and the love for Sanskrit was "next only to that of patriotism towards Mother India" (*Sanskrit Commission of India Report* 1957: 65), as Mahadevan cites.

Various non-governmental players made their contributions to the constant and steady growth and efflorescence of Sanskrit. This is all quite contrary to Pollock's baseless assertions. Players and contributors included the Maharajas of the princely states, Hindu religious institutions, non-brahmins, individual pandits, and voluntary organizations. Over a dozen palace libraries were great storehouses of Sanskrit and traditional knowledge. Inspired by the princes, many zamindars and merchants also founded Sanskrit colleges. Many maṭha-s and temples funded, or founded, Sanskrit colleges as did many affluent leaders and public leaders (Mahadevan 2017: 188).

In Andhra and Kerala, entire non-brahmin classes were imbued with Sanskrit. In Kerala, Izhavas, Thiyas, Moplas and Christians too studied Sanskrit. Evidence form other places is provided by the Sanskrit Commission Report. Cutting across religions, caste and gender, love and loyalty towards Sanskrit is evident all over; and is further evidenced by even literary contribution similarly. There have been numerous instances where Pandits wrote poems and plays in Sanskrit, and many could employ Sanskrit with eloquence and oratorical effect (*Sanskrit Commission of India Report* 1957: 45).

Further, modern scholars like Prof. George Cardona can converse well in Sanskrit (as well as Prof. Paul Deussen in the past, who, ignorant of the many Indian languages, did have free access of dialogue with many scholars, who were only too glad to meet a Western scholar in Sanskrit – as far back as 1878 – over a century and quarter ago).[4] Many replies to the Commission were in Sanskrit, and so were many interviews too! Despite abundant evidence to the contrary, well-chronicled at that, Pollock has the cheek to say Sanskrit died – funnily assigning different dates each time to the death of Sanskrit as a language! How many deaths did Sanskrit die, then!

It is not difficult to discern why Pollock loves to hate Sanskrit so much: it is because Sanskrit is the only pan-Indian language that can unite, and strengthen the solidarity of, India, which particularly is most hateable to most leftists. Quite contrary to his imagination, more than 750 voluntary Sanskrit institutions working for the cause of Sanskrit have received financial assistance from the government in the year 2009-10 (Mahadevan 2017: 194).

Grammar and Politics of Power

Obsessed with "power" as he is – obsessed, in fact, as much as is Wendy Doniger with sex – Pollock views/perceives/interprets everything in the framework of power – immaterial of whether it is valid or invalid, warranted or unwarranted. The scale of this overbearing obsession can only be imagined when he goes to the extent of connecting grammar and politics! (Of course, this is not on lines of, or has anything to do with, *The Grammar of Politics* (by Harold Laski 1925)).

What puzzles Pollock is the "widely shared, largely uniform cosmopolitan style of Sanskrit inscriptional discourse", reaching even up to the farthest corner of the Far East, which is to say "the Sanskrit Cosmopolis", to adopt his own expression. The style of the inscriptional literature that obtains there bears immense kinship with that of standard Sanskrit poetry. For this to come about, there must necessarily have been a "precedent broadcasting of the philological instruments." Daṇḍin's *Kāvyādarśa* was, Pollock says, "the most influential work on literary scene in world history after Aristotle's *Poetics*." It is indisputable, after all, that nowhere else in the world was the study of language so highly developed, and at so early an age – so much so that Western linguistics owes immensely to Sanskrit linguistics. This fact is openly acknowledged by many eminent linguists such as Bloomfield and Emeneau (though nominally, or even hardly, acknowledged in many recent writings of linguists, given the generally prevalent Eurocentrism – hypocrisy of a high order, no doubt).

Grammar and politics are "mutually constituted" – asserts Pollock, and with "evidence" in the form of half a dozen inscriptions. Probing every "evidence" proffered by Pollock, Dr. Sowmya Krishnapur has shown in Kannan (2018:23) how every evidence Pollock provides falls short of his tall claims, as he speaks of "the spread of a widely shared, largely uniform cosmopolitan style of Sanskrit inscriptional discourse: with the texts of literary art, metrics, lexicography etc. accorded the status of precious cultural commodities." For him, grammar carried cultural and political association in premodern South Asia far more potent than any other form of knowledge (Pollock 2006: 164); and "understanding the Indian care for language also depends... on understanding the place of language care in the Indian social-moral order, and *that in part means grasping the relationship of political power*" (Pollock 2006: 165) (*italics ours*).

He goes to the extent of asserting that rulership and Sanskrit grammaticality were mutually constitutive.

Miracles of Metonymy

Pollock seeks to demonstrate this, notes Krishnapur, by selecting three features viz. kings celebrating grammatical learning; patronizing it; and encouraging it in a competitive fashion. Presenting her own case very logically, Krishnapur shows that such celebration, patronage, or encouragement of grammatical learning was not without exceptions, nor did it not figure with respect to other *śāstra*-s. If grammatical learning mattered, thus, in no way significantly different from other *śāstra*-s, the claims of Pollock will all fall flat.

But Pollock would not relent, a master of sleight of tongue that he is. He extends the very scope of the word "grammar" by saying "grammar is often found to be used *metonymically standing for knowledge of lexicology, prosody and the like, including literature*" (Pollock 2009: 166) (*italics ours*). One could as well say biology is what all scientists are unanimous in admiring about or work upon – as it may be said to be metonymically standing for all of chemistry and physics, and even further, of ethology, sociology and anthropology and culture studies. What branch of knowledge would then be left out, if one holds on to such tricks?

Prescriptions "based on Inscriptions"

Pollock refers to the famed Rudradaman Inscription (150 CE) which has the expression *śabdārtha-gāndharva-nyāyādyānāṁ*, but he picks upon the word *śabdārtha* alone, and says it refers to grammar—even though music (*gāndharva*) and logic (*nyāya*) followed by "*etcetera*" (*ādya*) are explicitly stated—in a coplanar manner. Such blatant and brazen cherry-picking and twisting is a very usual feature with Pollock.

The Samudragupta Inscription (4th century CE) that he offers as a second proof, "makes no reference to grammar, either explicit or implicit," as Krishnapur points out very clearly (Krishnapur 2017: 27). Pollock translates the expression *śāstra-sūkṣmārtha-vedī* as "one who knows the subtleties of grammar"! The word *śāstra* stands for *any discipline*, and to translate it as "grammar" is utterly unacceptable. No traditional *kośa* of Sanskrit, or a modern dictionary of Sanskrit, signifies or renders *śāstra* as grammar! But the fancies of Pollock are unfettered.

In another inscription (Angkor 1002 CE), the word *bhāṣya* occurs, and Pollock jumps to render it as the [Great] Commentary [on Pāṇini]! Again, why should *bhāṣya* mean only *Mahābhāṣya*? Are there not *bhāṣya*-s on so many *sūtra* texts that have nothing to do with grammar? Pollock proposes a fantastic theory—of "political correctness *deriving from* grammatical correctness"—which can be encountered nowhere in Sanskrit literature, grammatical or other. His reasoning is weird. Says he: "it stands to reason that power should have actively cared for grammar by sponsoring the production of grammatical texts and ensuring their continued study" (Pollock 2006: 167)!

The Lure of Theory in Lieu of Facts

Taking note of the presence and role of numerous Sanskrit books on lexicon and grammar, Pollock seems to assume that among the ways and means employed by the British to expand their regime, engendering and encouragement of the production of numerous types of English dictionaries and books on English grammar and usage, must have played their role; what worked in the close past must have worked exactly the same way in the distant past as well! While English was imposed from the higher-ups in the echelons of power, nothing even remotely comparable ever happened with respect to Sanskrit.

Apparently disagreeing with Hartmut Scharfe that the impetus to grammatical studies came as three spurts at different points of time viz the 5th, 11th and 17th centuries (so fancifully and neatly equally spaced as to lend some stamp of periodicity and uniformity and continuity!), Pollock comments that it was "not just episodic", and proceeds to make a strong assertion that royal power seemed to have "provided the essential precondition for the flourishing of the post-liturgical philological tradition – as philology likewise provided a precondition for power – from the birth of the Sanskrit Cosmopolitan order throughout its lifetime."

If Scharfe failed to provide any historical *evidence*, Pollock seems to think he can compensate proffering of evidence by some grand-looking *theory* – one that could be applied from birth and "throughout its lifetime." If strong theories are founded on well-founded facts in abundance where theory emerges on its own, or at least with very little imposition of any colorful hypothesis, Pollock seems to think contrarily: facts are, after all, an avoidable luxury when a charming theory couched in linguistic flourish can work equally well or strongly enough – without any need of even a shred of evidence!

Thin Data Compensated by Thick Theory

Pollock's generosity in admitting his own weak position is also very illuminating; and very disarming. He indeed speaks of "the *historical data which are too thin* to demonstrate the mutual constitutive relationship of grammar and power with much cogency."(Pollock 2009: 168). Right in the face of it nevertheless, he doggedly holds on to his fanciful theories.

All that Pollock could muster is a legend mentioned by Xuang Zang, a Chinese pilgrim (7th century CE) – a veritable cock-and-bull story that finds not a single mention, even a most indirect one at that, or even mildly suggestive an allusion – in the thousands of pages of grammatical literature that followed Pāṇini, mostly by way of commentary. Even

Patañjali makes a mention of but one or two kings, but makes no such reference as can as much as faintly resemble the projections of Pollock thereupon.

The grandeur of patently ambiguous statements supported by flimsiest of historical data – is illustrated by statements such as these of Pollock (2006: 171) "whether it was Śarvavarman or Kumāralāta who composed the original Kātantra, *there is little doubt that* the author was closely associated with a ruling power. Whether in the South or in the North" [*italics ours*]. We cannot of course fathom why Pollock did not have the patience or the zeal to add "or in the East or in the West" to make the circuit complete. The climactic part of the sentence is, of course, "*there is little doubt that...*" - such as would not issue from the lips of even a man of Dutch courage.

Grammatical Tradition: Frequently Orphaned!

While Pollock asserts that "it was a royal obligation to ensure the stability and continuation of the grammatical order" (Pollock 2006: 173), we find that already in *Vākyapadīya*, 5th century CE), Bhartṛhari grieves that the tradition of grammar had been totally lost! Bhartṛhari is so sorry that the massive work *Saṅgraha* of Vyāḍi was lost too "*saṅgrahe'stam upāgate*" (*Vākyapadīya* 2.478)! It was so completely lost in the North that the grammatical tradition had at last to be retrieved from the South. There are references to the loss of the grammatical tradition more than once even!

Pollock *begins his work by* claiming an inalienable link between royalty and grammar, and *ends with* stating that one may have to *bring in even rhetorical works* in order to "perceive a vast field of scholarly poetic texts on kings and literary culture." It is amusing that Pollock thinks that providing long lists of poets or rhetoricians who had some kind or the other of royal patronage suffices to demonstrate the strong bonds between kings and grammarians! Nothing truer than the maxim "the sinking man catches hold of a straw"!

Out of the three inscriptional evidences he offers, that is, of royal patronage to grammar, only one has some content, but it is a tragedy that

Pollock is so weary of actual historical references that he adopts a bold strain to cover his weak spots, saying "further amassing data would only be redundant." It is so easy for a giant scholar to condone one's own self! What a sweet escape route!

Krishnapur indeed promises to tackle in another article, the other claim of Pollock (2006:165), that there was "competitive zeal among rulers everywhere to encourage grammatical creativity, and adorn their courts with scholars who could exemplify it." We only hope that there will be another opportunity to do the same so that the fantastic theory of grammar and royalty buttressing each other is laid to permanent rest.

"Theory and Practice": The Cart and the Horse

Another vital paper of Pollock is "Theory of Practice and Practice of Theory in Indian Intellectual History" written in 1985. He translates *śāstra* and *prayoga* as "theory" and "practical activity". Pollock developed a full-fledged program – of blaming *śāstra*-s for all the ills of India. In this great "enterprise", he is, as it were, at one with Wendy Doniger: both seem to have labored hard to discover what things precisely hurt Hindus.

Hinduism values *brahmacarya*, and Doniger is *therefore* bent upon showing our *purāṇa*-s to be grossly violating that norm; Hinduism values *ahiṁsā*, and she and her clout are *therefore* out to show that the *Bhagavad Gītā* justifies war, and so is essentially a dishonest work. And Hindus respect the Veda-s and *śāstra*-s a great deal: every *ācārya* of Vedānta has, after all, proclaimed *vedāḥ pramāṇam*; the *Bhagavad Gītā* clearly states that one who leads a wanton life throwing into winds the injunctions of the *śāstra*-s will find happiness neither here nor hereafter:

> *yaḥ śāstra-vidhim utsṛjya vartate kāmakārataḥ |*
> *na sa siddhim avāpnoti na sukhaṁ na parāṁ gatim ||*
> (*Bhagavadgītā* 16.23):

And it is *therefore* that the railing and ranting by Pollock against the *śāstra* in general is so intense and so repetitive. And again, it is Mīmāṁsā, "the king of *śāstra*-s", that enunciates the key principles of interpretation of the Vedic literature, and it is exactly *therefore* that it becomes a key target of Pollock's attacks. His vitriol against the Vedic is very caustic. Of course, the Buddhists and the Jains, whose contribution to śāstric literature is by no means small, accorded no regard for the Veda-s, after all, but all blame should nevertheless be put on the Veda-s: as we know, the Buddhists and Jains made their own contributions to even *śāstra*-s such as mathematics and medicine. Whatever be the case, blame the Veda-s.

Unfailing *astra*

The strong and unfailing weapons in the armor of Pollock which he regularly deploys are: ignoring facts, bypassing them, trivializing them. "Theory is derived from practice in the West", he says, "but as with many other things, it is the reverse, the "diametrically opposed" in India", he asserts; which is to say, Hindu intellectuals invariably derived and deduced *prayoga* from *śāstra*, practice from theory. To quote Pollock's fanciful statements (1985: 502): *śāstra* refers more specifically to Veda, as when, for example, Brahma is described as *śāstrayoni* – "that is, the source of our knowledge of which is *śāstra*."

Vedas are the fountainhead of all knowledge, and the belief in their eternality, Pollock posits, "constrains the production of new knowledge, as *śāstra*-s only reformulate what the Veda-s have already stated. Theory is held to always and necessarily precede and govern practice. All knowledge is already pre-existent and what best may be accomplished is a regressive reappropriation of the past." The consequence of this is that experience, experiment, invention, discovery, and innovation are all "logically excluded from epistemological meaningfulness." There is no question of "progress as a forward movement from worse to better", which is what kills all innovation (Pollock 1985: 515).

Mischievous Extrapolations

In his diatribe against the śāstric tradition, and especially against the high value accorded to the *śāstra*-s, the theory of *satkāryavāda* comes in very handy for Pollock – of course by recourse, again, to his wanton and brazen misinterpretation. This pre-eminently Sāṅkhyan theory states that "what is only issues from what was; nothing, in other words, comes out of nothing. "A pot, for example, must pre-exist in the clay (since otherwise it could never be brought into existence, or could be brought into existence from some other material e.g. threads."

While a faithful statement of the Sāṅkhyan theory could never be easily opposed, Pollock's extrapolation is mischievous, to say the least. He extends it thus: "so knowledge must pre-exist in something in order that we may derive it thence... we ourselves do not 'create' knowledge, but merely bring it to manifestation from the (***textual***) materials in which it lies concealed from us" (Pollock 1985: 517) [*emphasis ours*].

The mischievous insertion within brackets of "textual" tells it all. One could argue as well in regard to law, invoking statements like "The promulgation of most legal rules is based on common sense judgements about the world" and level "*a priori*" charges here too.

In which *śāstra*, one could indeed ask, has it been stated that the knowledge contained in the *śāstra* has *all* been nothing but a deduction straight from and only from the Vedic?

For one thing, a great deal of Vedic literature has been lost – lost already by the time of Patañjali (BCE)! We cannot even form an idea of how much of precious literature was lost even subsequently – just on account of Muslim vandalism – in the burning of libraries they indulged in in various parts of the country, where libraries burnt for months! And there yet are millions of manuscripts yet to see the light of day. Many *smṛti*-s refer to "lost Vedic prescriptions." Many ideas could indeed have their seed form in the Vedic, but elucidated and expatiated upon, and enhanced and expanded in later times.

There indeed are many foundational principles obtained in the Veda-s that did serve as sprouts of vast and burgeoning disciplines. Dr. Ananda K. Coomaraswamy has traced, for example, many motifs or representations in Buddhist art, to their Vedic roots. Taking hints and clues from the Vedic, numerous fields and disciplines would surely have developed—precisely owing to the creative abilities of the particular masters who drew ideas and inspiration from the vast and divinely inspired literature.

One or two fields may suffice to illustrate: the *Vyākaraṇa śāstra* of Pāṇini, and the *Chandaśśāstra* of Piṅgala and the *Nāṭyaśāstra* of Bharata (and even the *Arthaśāstra* of Kauṭalya)—could be premier examples, with all the authors cited actually referred to as *muni*-s, showing thereby their essential continuity with the Vedic/ascetic tradition—all, interestingly, of the pre-Christian era. None can indeed doubt the highly creative abilities of the said authors. Each of these has high veneration towards the Vedic, but in no way has that hampered their essentially creative outputs – all of extraordinary standards, undoubtedly. The grammatical system of Pāṇini, the binary system that issued out of Piṅgala, and the essential concepts of dramaturgy outlined by Bharata or the comprehensive scheme of administration set forth in Kauṭalya – are all unparalleled to this day, and will likely never lose their relevance and application. Bloomfield in fact, referred to Pāṇini's work as "a monument of *human* intelligence" and note, not just Indian/ [South] Asian/Eastern intelligence.

To speak then of "the crippling of the innovative spirit of Indian intellectuals" can only be described as coming nowhere near even the shadow of any truth, but issuing only from imagination – bordering, well, on insanity. The countless examples and analogies that our *kavi*-s and *śāstra-kāra*-s supply in profusion are all drawn from Nature, and not derived from some prior "textual" material. The inferiority complex of the West shows itself in myriad manners, verily.

Debunking "Divine" Origins?

All the same, there is perhaps no discipline in India which does not claim a divine origin. A very typical representation is in the *Viṣṇu-sahasranāman* where it says

> *yogo jñānaṁ tathā sāṅkhyaṁ vidyāś śilpādi-karma ca |*
> *vedāś śāstrāṇi vijñānam etat sarvaṁ janārdanāt ||*
> (*Mahābhārata* 13.149.139).

It is not only a text like the *Mahābhārata* which makes this claim, but even individual texts do so. Oftentimes, the very *maṅgala-śloka* mentions some or the other divinity as the source of inspiration.

Tantric texts are all thus fashioned as conversations between Śiva and Pārvatī. It is Viṣṇu and Lakṣmī in many Āgamic texts. This, however, is not in religious/philosophical texts alone. The tendency is so prominent, prevalent, and evident that even the great mathematician of the last century claimed that his discoveries were inspired by a certain divinity (viz. Nāmagiri Mahālakṣmī Nāmakkaḷ) – who used to appear in his dreams.

Did this "superstition" kill his creativity? On the contrary! We have ample evidence, however, of the utter originality of Ramanujan's papers and calculations. It is even said he was rather ahead of his times. "Ramanujan had more creativity than most of us do" says Bruce Brendt—adding that a remarkable feature of this Indian mathematical genius was "his ability to take small strands of knowledge and expand them into long highways"; the American mathematician who is quoted here is himself an outstanding authority on Ramanujan.[5]

Search for Truth Never Hindered

The world has perhaps not witnessed such wondrous variety of lexica and works on grammar as were produced in India, leave alone millions of poetical works. Hundreds of *Rāmāyaṇa*-s have been written in dozens of languages, yet none is a mere replica of any previous work. The number of works produced on mathematics and medicine alone are mind-boggling. Meulenbeld and Wujastyk, contemporary scholars of Ayurvedic history, can attest to this.

Had Indian scriptures replicated the roles of their Western counterparts, hundreds of Galileos could have been incarcerated, dozens of Brunos burnt here. India surely cannot boast of a democracy that made Socrates drink hemlock. "*Asabeia*" = "not believing in the god of the State" – was never a crime in India – be it noted! On the contrary, Galileo was forced at the peril of his life, to recant his statement, which none of the scientists here in India had ever had to face: not a single instance of it do we encounter this in India's long history! To this day, the Abrahamic faiths are, on the other hand, opposed to the theory of evolution and endeavoring to overthrow it by hook or by crook. The heliocentric theory too was only recently, and nominally, accepted by the Vatican—centuries later.

Conflation – in Order to Cause Confusion:

(Ayur)Vedic "Understanding"

Wilful conflation of concepts by our beloved master of sleight of tongue can also be illustrated. The word *āgama* or *āptavākya* is used in two senses in Sanskrit. Kālidāsa himself uses the word *āgama* with both senses but clearly distinctly: in the opening canto of *Raghuvaṁśa* (1.15), he uses it in the sense of *śāstra jñāna*, or *śāstra-paricaya*, mastery over the *śāstra*-s; whereas in the same work, a little later (at 10.26), he refers by the same word to the Veda-s.

Caraka says there are three ways of knowing, that is, by *āptopadeśa* "Instructions of [=imparted by] the Adepts"; and then *pratyakṣa* and *anumāna* (Perception and Inference) (*Caraka-saṁhitā* 3.4.5). Caraka defines *āpta*-s as persons (*note the plural* used in the original, 3.4.4) *āptā hy avitarka-smṛti-vibhāga-vidaḥ*... They are ones whose knowledge is not beset with doubts, and is not based on mere memory or on partial information. Nor is their understanding tinged by prejudicial love or hatred, bias towards or repulsion against some pet notion or theory.[6]

Clearly stating that novices cannot all start from scratch – which is to say, depending even upon mere *pratyakṣa* and *anumāna* alone – Caraka emphasizes the need for training under experts, the *āpta*-s, whose teachings constitute *āptopadeśa*. (*Caraka-saṁhitā* 3.4.5) What is it that one [a novice] can learn, after all, via *pratyakṣa* and *anumāna* [alone]—without, that is, *upadeśa*?—so asks Caraka. Others texts like those of Ḍalhaṇa or Vātsyāyana corroborate this idea of Caraka.

Empirical Knowledge Sacrificed at the Altar of "The Book"?

The importance given to *pratyakṣa* in Ayurvedic texts in the examination of a patient has been very high.[7] The doctor should diagnose making use of *all of the sense organs*. These have been detailed in Tables 220-224 in Kannan (2011:320-322). This involves five auditory perceptions, seven visual perceptions, seven tactile perceptions, one olfactory perception, and one gustatory perception. The doctor is also cautioned against any direct gustatory perception as this can be problematic. Suśruta has given these in detail in *Suśruta-saṁhitā* 1.10.4-5.[8] Empirical knowledge was thus encouraged, not discouraged; and was not substituted by knowledge derived from "the Book."

A detailed discussion upon the details of inferential knowledge as detailed in Ayurvedic texts can be obtained in Kannan (2011: 323-364). Inference in general, Caraka says, is based on perception "*pratyakṣa-pūrva*" (*Caraka-saṁhitā* 1.11.21) (which is to say, he does **not** say it is based on earlier **textual** material, not on some "the Book"—some "Scripture", to wit). If typical dedicated texts on logic speak of a Five-membered Syllogism, Caraka speaks of an Eight-membered one! Caraka speaks of three types of non-reason (*ahetu*).[9] There is also a detailed analysis of logical fallacies (Kannan 2011:350), valid and invalid analogies set forth in Ayurvedic texts (Kannan 2011: 360). Caraka notes where *pratyakṣa* could be risky, and hence *anumāna* can don that role, and serve the actual purpose (*Caraka-saṁhitā* 3.4.7). He shows 42 items of knowledge deduced inferentially (CS 3.4.8), listed in Kannan (2011: 363-364)! Such meticulousness and such exhaustiveness!

Caraka deals also with other modes of valid knowledge (apart from and along with perception and inference) viz. *upamāna, yukti, arthāpatti* etc. all detailed in Kannan (2011: 365-376).[10] Investigation of causality in Āyurveda has also been dealt with in Kannan (2011: 382-398).

In sections on Perception and Inference, no *āgama* texts have been invoked by Caraka, or his commentators, or their successors. To accuse them then as relying on *āgama* solely or essentially is nothing but willful misleading; plain mischievous misinterpretation.

No "Forward" Movement?

That the *forward movement* of medical history in India (and of other fields as well, too) has been *from good to better,* is very much borne out by the tradition. This fact is too strong to be refuted, even if it had been claimed in some traditional text that *prayoga* issued only from *śāstra*.

There has, however, been no text making such absurd claims, and so the assertions and allegations of regressive movement generally made by Pollock are, to say the least, utterly preposterous, and betray no hint of a responsible scholar.

Another technique adopted by Pollock is: to present counter-evidence or counter-arguments himself – so as to be pre-emptive with respect to others who may present them and direct them against him; and to pretend that he is making his assertions being fully aware of what all there is against his own (pro)position. But the truth is that, he offers not a shred of evidence or a semblance of an argument nullifying what goes against his concocted (hypo)thesis! He may just(ly) be asked: If you have not been able to shoot down the arguments of the opponent, how do you convince even your own self, first of all, that you are probably, or even by mistake, right?

If the Socratic theory of amnesia postulates something no different from what our *śāstra*-s have said, why criticize the *śāstra* alone as regressive? Did Caraka or Kauṭalya or Pāṇini or Bharata theorize first, and only subsequently begin to look for illustrative or corroborative instances? Did not Kauṭalya say

sarva-śāstrāṇyanukramya prayogam upalabhya ca? (*Arthaśāstra* 1.8.25)

Where in India did he, Pollock, find theorization first and practice constrained to conform to it – except in his own unfounded theorizations issuing out his own wild cerebrations and lucubrations?

Description = Verdict?

Pollock is wont to give sometimes certain graphic descriptions, and can spin theories out of the same. Westerners, he says, find Hindu rules of etiquette rather peculiar; and by describing some Hindu rules of etiquette, he feels he has actually proven that they are peculiar, and thinks others are bound to be convinced by the same. The frog in the well may as well claim everything outside its own little domain is exotic and erratic.

Look at this man in a country which is not even 250 years old, passing his stentorian evaluations and peremptory judgments and offhand proclamations on a 5000-year-old civilization, saying "Oh a Westerner finds all this peculiar and curious, alien and strange, and just incomprehensible after all – and presto! They *are* indeed so, QED!" (*Quod Erat Demonstrandum*! – or rather, "Quite Easily Done!) A veritable Daniel come to judgment, to whom the whole world should listen indeed! Is it then a case of the pot calling the marble black?

How They Begin and How They End!

An extraordinarily long tradition of scholarship that Hindus have had, some of the greatest masters – whether Daṇḍin or Amarasiṁha or other – have *commenced their śāstra work* with the statement—that they have looked into the precedent works in the field – which is to say done their literature survey first – to use a modern phrase; and have summarized and/or elaborated (as the case may be), and more particularly *improved upon* (*saṁkṣiptaiḥ pratisaṁskṛtaiḥ*) (*Amara-kośa* 1.0.2) the earlier productions, [obviously going by practical considerations etc.]; and again, *concluded their śāstra-work* with the statement that, all said, there remains much more to be said, and that what is left unstated must be made up—by looking into what is actually in practice *śeṣaṁ tu jñeyaṁ śiṣṭā-prayogataḥ*! (*Amara-kośa* 3.6.45)

They thus take all care and responsibility to do a good job first of all, and all care and responsibility to caution the reader that the last word has not been said after all, and all has not been said, of course, and what remains to be added is to be gathered from *actual usages/practices* in the world! What more can one ask for or want? Can a modern lexicographer or grammarian beat or better these archetypal masters?

As stated at the outset, there are numerous other issues – of Pollock's views on the *Rāmāyaṇa*, on *rasa*, on Mimāṁsā, on chronology and so on – the criticism of each of which has occupied a full volume, an average of over 200 pages in the series of the Conference Proceedings of Swadeshi Indology, all published by IFI (all edited by myself). Readers are requested to look into those volumes for further detailed treatment of issues and full textual references.

The following verse of Mathew Arnold typifies the Eastern attitude to the Western onslaughts:

> The East bowed low before the blast
> In patient, deep disdain;
> She let the legions thunder past
> And plunged in thought again.
>
> —*Obermann Once More* (Arnold (1897: 442))

The truth of the poem is of course well taken, but when intellectual atrocities and cultural genocide gain momentum, as they have done now, it is time for reparatory action if not retribution. When there comes about *dharma-glāni* (*dharma* getting blighted), even the Lord descends to act! It is time to administer these Western doctors a taste of their own medicine.

Bibliography

Acharya, J.T., and Acharya, N.R. (Ed.s) (1938). *Suśrutasaṁhitā of Suśruta with Nibandhasaṅgraha of Ḍalhaṇa*. Bombay: Nirnaya Sagar Press.

Amarakośa. See Sivadatta.

Arthaśāstra. See Kangle.

Arnold, Matthew. (1897). *The Poetical Works of Matthew Arnold*. Boston: Thomas Y. Crowell & Company.

Bhagavadgītā. See Radhakrishnan.

Breckenridge, Carol A., van der Veer, Peter. (Eds.) (1993). *Orientalism and the Postcolonial Predicament*. Philadelphia: University of Pennsylvania Press.

Carakasaṁhitā. See Sharma.

Dasa, Satyanarayana. (2017). "Sanskrit is not Dead." In Kannan (2017). pp 147-180.

Deussen, Paul. (1893). *My Indian Reminiscences*. Madras: G.A. Natesan and Co.

Elst, Koenraad. (2017). "Pollock's Idea of a "National-Socialist Indology." In Kannan (2017). pp 93-113.

Gopinath, K. (2017). "German Indology, Sanskrit and Nazi Ideology." In Kannan (2017). pp 21-63.

Hanneder, J. (2002). "On "The Death of Sanskrit." *Indo-Iranian Journal*. Vol. 45. No. 4. pp. 293-310.

Hindu, The. (2011). "Ramanujan had more creativity than most of us do." <https://www.thehindu.com/news/national/tamil-nadu/ramanujan-had-more-creativity-than-most-of-us-do/article2046255.ece#>. Accessed on 31 August 2020.

Iyer, K.A. Subramania. (Ed.) (1977). *The Vākyapadīya of Bhartṛhari. Kāṇḍa II*. Poona: Deccan College.

Joglekar, K.M. (1916). *Raghuvaṁśa of Kālidāsa (with Sañjīvanī of Mallinātha)*. Bombay: Nirnaya Sagar Press.

Kangle, R.P. (1960). *The Kautilīya Arthaśāstra (Critical Edition with Glossary)*. Bombay: University of Bombay.

Kannan, K.S. (2011). *The Theoretical Foundations of Āyurveda*. Bangalore: Foundation for Revitalising Local Health Traditions.

Kannan K.S. (2017). *Western Indology and Its Quest for Power*. Chennai: Infinity Foundation of India.

Kannan, K.S. (2018). *Śāstra-s Through the Lens of Western Indology*. Chennai: Infinity Foundation India.

Kannan, K.S. and Meera, H.R. (2017). "Sanskrit: The Phoenix Phenomenon." In Kannan (2017). pp 203-231.

Kaul, Srikanth (Ed.) (1966). *Rājataraṅgiṇī of Śrīvara and Śuka*. Hoshiarpur: Vishveshvaranand Institute.

Krishnapur, Sowmya. (2018). "On Grammar and Royal Power." In Kannan (2018). pp 23-45.

Mahābhārata. (1958). Gorakhpur: Gita Press.

Mahadevan, Jayaraman. (2017). "On "Feeding Tubes and Oxygen Tanks" for Sanskrit." In Kannan (2017). pp 181-202.

Malhotra, Rajiv. (2016). *The Battle for Sanskrit*. New Delhi: HarperCollins Publishers.

Meera, H.R. (2015). "*Arthāpatti* and Non-literal Usage of Language." *The Quarterly Journal of the Mythic Society* (Vol 1. Issue 1, April 2015). pp. 114-128.

Pollock, Sheldon. (1985). "The Theory of Practice and the Practice of Theory." *Journal of American Oriental Society.* Vol.105. No.3. pp 499-519.

Pollock, Sheldon. (1993). "Deep Orientalism? Notes on Sanskrit and Power Beyond the Raj." In Breckenridge and van der Veer. pp. 76-133.

Pollock, Sheldon. (2001). "The Death of Sanskrit." *Comparative Studies in Society and History.* Vol. 43. No. 2. pp 392-426.

Pollock, Sheldon. (2003a). "Sanskrit Literary Culture from the Inside Out." In Pollock (2003b). pp 39-130.

Pollock, Sheldon. (Ed.) (2003b). *Literary Cultures in History.* Berkeley: University of California Press.

Pollock, Sheldon. (2006). *The Language of Gods in the World of Men.* California: University of California Press.

Radhakrishnan, S. (Ed.) (Tr.) (1948). *The Bhagavadgītā.* London: George Allen and Unwin Ltd.

Raghuvaṁśa. See Joglekar.

Rājataraṅgiṇī. See Kaul.

Sanskrit Commission Report. (1956-57). Information Repository of Education in India. <http://cslrepository.nvli.in//handle/123456789/1961>. Accessed on 31 August 2020.

Sastry, Manogna. (2017). "On "Death of Sanskrit." In Kannan (2017). pp 233-252.

Sewell, Robert. (2000, 19001). *A Forgotten Empire: Vijayanagar.* New Delhi: Asian Educational Services.

Sharma, Yadav. (Ed.) (1941). *Carakasaṁhitā of Caraka (with Āyurvedadīpikā of Cakrapāṇi).* Bombay: Nirnaya Sagar Press.

Sivadatta. (Ed.) (1929). *Amarakośa of Amarasiṁha (with Vyākhyāsudhā of Bhānujidīkṣita).* Bombay: Nirnaya Sagar Press.

Suśrutasaṁhitā. See Acharya and Acharya.

Vākyapadīya. See Iyer.

Notes

1. See https://murtylibrary.com/

2. "Why a Classical Library of India?" The Murty Classical Library of India. <https://murtylibrary.com/why-a-classical-library-of-india.php>. Accessed on 16-Oct-2021.

3. The reference is to the points Pollock makes that have been listed in the following paragraphs, and refer to Pollock (2001).

4. This has been duly recorded in his travelogue, Deussen (1893).

5. "Ramanujan had more creativity than most of us do." The Hindu <https://www.thehindu.com/news/national/tamil-nadu/ramanujan-had-more-creativity-than-most-of-us-do/article2046255.ece>. Accessed on 16-Oct-2021

6. See Kannan (2011: 247)

7. See Kannan (2011: 210-322)

8. See also *Caraka-saṁhitā* 3.4.7

9. See Kannan (2011: 342-344)

10. For a detailed treatment of *arthāpatti*, see Meera (2015).

THREE

Michael Witzel
Flights of Fantasy

Manogna Sastry

Introduction

Academic and intellectual discussions at institutions, with a monopolistic stronghold over discourses on Indian history and culture, have since long become grounds for some of the most disempowering and disingenuous narratives created for Bhārata. The players involved, include those who profess their love of Sanskrit and the accompanying heritage, most of them occupying high seats of influence and power, to synthesize and direct narratives at prestigious universities of the world. As the center of dominance, in many spheres, moved from Europe to the United States of America post the Second World War, so too has been the case in Indology. Michael Witzel, the Wales Professor of Sanskrit at the Department of Sanskrit and Indian Studies, Harvard University (the first endowed chair for Sanskrit studies in the United States, established in 1903; Witzel is only the fourth chair of this position), promulgates through his scholarship, specious and fallacious accounts of India's past and present, with deep consequences for the Indian identity.

Witzel's work spans decades and as the editor of the *Harvard Oriental Series* (volumes 50-80), he has edited important volumes under this series including Patrick Olivelle's *The Law Code of Visnu* and Iravatham Mahadevan's *Early Tamil Epigraphy from the Earliest Times to the Sixth Century A.D*, while authoring volume 65, i.e *Katha Aranyaka*. One of the major themes Witzel champions in his academic work, also considered in this essay, is the now unambiguously discredited Aryan Invasion/Migration (AI/M) into India theories, to the point of disregarding evidence and denigrating through ad hominem attacks, the works which have successfully challenged and negated several of his central points. This indicates his dangerous tendency to normalize and legitimize affronts in academic discourse, as a means of garnering support for his ideas, or worse still, to 'prove' them right. It thus lowers, wholesale, the standards of intellectual engagement on important issues. His suspect repertoire of 'proof' and methodology have included fabricating evidence when none exist, through mistranslations and grammatical falsities, to the point of distorting verses to suit his agenda, as will be shown in this essay. When his claims have been discredited by the Indological domain, Witzel has gone on to offer farcical explanations, even as the lack of academic ethics in his work stands stark. This article highlights how such instances demonstrate the poor scholarship that accompanies Witzel's work in a theme as crucial as the Aryan issue, for it has direct implications for many on the temporal and spatial origins of the Veda-s and Sanskrit heritage of Bhārata.

Witzel has been a vociferous critic of Indians, both at home and abroad, who have been fighting for a fair and just representation of their history. This article considers his role, along with many Marxist historians of India such as Romila Thapar, in trying to destabilize and thwart the attempts made by Hindus in North America seeking accuracy and changes in the history textbooks of Grade VI taught at California Public Schools. Witzel's opposition, laden under the garb of trying to protect 'historical accuracy', a self-inflicted irony, lays bare much of what is fallacious about his scholarship. One of the corrections recommended by the Ad Hoc Committee (AHC) and Content Review Panel (CRP) of California, has been the rectification of the incorrect statement in the textbook that the Indian epic *Mahābhārata* was written before the *Rāmāyaṇa*. Witzel, Stanley Wolpert and team have responded to this correction with, "Who in sixth grade cares which epic was "written" first?"[1] Scholarly indeed!

The present article considers several such instances of Witzel's scholarship to demonstrate why his work is a prime example of intellectual misdirection and falsity to understand his presence in this collection of Intellectual Rāvaṇa-s. It may also serve as a warning exposition, of the sly and dangerous assortment of techniques frequently employed by such "scholars" to cast traps for those with a sincere intent to pursue civilizational studies and then co-opt them into a school of thought with deception, falsification, fabrication as its pillars.

Witzel and AI/MT

Archaeological Evidence

Witzel's work on AI/MT now spans decades and there have been comprehensive rebuttals to several of his core points, such as those by Vishal Aggarwal, Nicolas Kazanas and S. Kalyanaraman. This article considers a few salient points from Witzel's recent 2019 article *Beyond the Flight of the Falcon: Early 'Aryans' Within and Outside India,* for it provides a good overview of many of Witzel's core arguments. While beginning the essay with a call for multi-disciplinary approaches to the problem of the AI/MT, Witzel then pulls out of thin air, with no references or sources, the following: "The title refers to the Vedic and Avestan designation of the Hindu Kush mountains: *upariśyena/upari.saēna*. It suggests the path of migration of some Indo-Iranian tribes into Eastern Iran and subsequently into Northern India."[2] *Upariśyena* literally means "beyond the reach/scope of the eagle" in Sanskrit and is the designation of the Hindu Kush mountains – how and why this would refer to migration of Indo-Iranians *into* India, is a leap beyond any rational mind, considering the absence of a single textual source to support this interpretation.

Witzel's explanation of the term 'Aryan' includes the admission that the term itself is neither a racial one, nor a linguistic one; what he fails to mention and thus conceals though, when he says it is a term used by 'linguists'[3] is that it is a term used by European linguists through centuries of Indology packed entirely through the lens of colonial explorations and understandings.[4] Witzel's arguments in the Archaeology section read more like a litany one has seen since the 1990s that hold water only in an echo chamber of fellow AI/MT proponents. The complete absence of any mention, even in 2019, of the archaeological research on the Sarasvati river paleo-channels and their impact on the chronology of the region under consideration by Witzel does not come across as an innocuous omission but another instance of the long history of using only selective data (sometimes even the absence of data) and non-Indic sources for framing hypotheses.[5] With no reference at all, Witzel ascribes 1300 BC to the Rig Vedic period, when in fact, 1900 BC could be seen as the *terminus ante quem* for the timelines of the Mahabhārata.[6] Having not considered a single instance of the recent findings, Witzel instead accuses "revisionist/Hindutva writers" of "exploring disagreements between individual scholars" and pushing "alternative facts" about the chronologies,[7] when he himself is a revisionist advancing alternative lies.

Witzel's major argument in the archaeological section, boils down to one which has been flogged for decades by AI/MTheorists – the contention that the domesticated horse (and the IE language) was introduced into the Indus Valley Civilization by those who invaded/migrated from the Steppes. The argument is crucial to Witzel's decades of work simply because, to cite Laurie Patton from *The Indo-Aryan Controversy*, "...if the horse is ever discovered contemporaneous with early Indus Valley culture, or pre-Vedic South Asian civilization, the migrationist theories would have to change dramatically."[8] While most AI/MT proponents have conveniently chosen not to engage with a wealth of evidence that has shown the presence of terracotta horse figurines and bones and other faunal remains excavated,[9] the case of the remains discovered at Surkotada is noteworthy of mention. Excavations carried out under J.P. Joshi of the Harappan site Surkotada, in Kutch, led to the discovery of the faunal remains of the *equus cabalus linn* i.e. the true horse, during all three phases of the settlements (IA: 2100 BC-1950 BC, IB: 1950-1800 BC, IC:1800-1700 BC).[10] When the findings of the Indian archaeologists were challenged, the results were examined by the Hungarian archaeologist Sándor Bökönyi, who confirmed that the remains were indeed that of the true horse, at all three phases.[11] Further, Sanjay Manjul's 2018 excavations at Sanauli in western Uttar Pradesh, have unearthed chariots dating to 2100 BC – 1900 BC – a chariot with solid wheels reinforced even with copper, but Witzel has challenged the identification of the discovery as a chariot and instead believes that the find points to "...the survival of an extra-Harappan organized society,"[12] whatever the vague phrase means. Despite all contrary evidence, Witzel maintains that proto-chariots were invented in the Ural region and imported into India by mid-second millennium BC.

Linguistic Evidence

While the archaeological arguments presented by Witzel raise more questions about his dubious lines of reasoning than the substance itself, he uses linguistic arguments to try and explain away the gaping loopholes in his AI/M model. Comparative historical linguistics has, rightly, come under heavy scrutiny for its shaky fundamentals but Witzel's take on this is revealing. Calling comparative and historical linguistics a "natural science", Witzel admits that "establishing comparative meanings is more complex" but, to have it on a secure base, one would need "a large-scale database and input using artificial intelligence."[13] Failing to establish any clear basis except, naming a range of language families associated with India, Witzel examines the "Indo-Aryan migration path" by making a series of declarative statements sans sources or evidence. Speakers of Proto-Indo-Iranian language apparently lived in Russia/Steppes and came to Bactria, Afghanistan and finally, present-day India and left behind loan words in their trail. Even if one were to accept Witzel's linguistic examples which show the 'trail', he gives no explanation as to *how the arrow of direction of this trail can be established through linguistic evidence alone.* The truth of the matter is that, in the absence of archaeological evidence, or evidence from any other independently verifiable domain, comparative linguistics is trapped in circular fallacy.

Witzel's paper, *Early Indian history: Linguistic and textual parameters* (1995) presents some of the other important arguments he has made concerning linguistics. Witzel dates the *Mahābhārata* to 1200 BC and, in fact, has a cavalier approach to the text, especially its historicity. Considering several examples, Witzel shows that while many English and American places show traces of the original names. As he does not find a similar pattern for Indo-Aryan names in South Asia, especially in northern India, Witzel suggests instead that the towns themselves are of later period and hence there is an absence of such names.[14] Studying hydronomy next, Witzel notes that rivers of northern India have Sanskrit names from the earliest Vedic period. Instead of drawing the most natural conclusion from this fact, that there has been no influence from the very beginning of any non-local or foreign forces, Witzel comes up with a groundless and spurious argument by comparing the Indian river names with their possible equivalent ones in Iranian and, having decided, with no evidence, that the latter is "closer to the older, Rgvedic home of the Vedic tribes", "the Iranians simply changed the old Indo-Iranian names into their respective Iranian forms when they moved into the area, while the Vedic, Indo-Aryan speakers took some of these names with them eastwards, up to Bihar, in the typical fashion of people on the move."[15]

Further losing himself in a baseless web, Witzel tries to explain that "there has been an almost complete Indo-Aryanisation"[16] of the river-names in northern India, despite not a single piece of evidence suggesting this. Witzel continues more incredulously, to suggest that this complete lack of evidence for his hypothesis is, in fact, evidence for the collapse of the local population. Despite this claim too not being backed by a single piece of evidence—literary or archaeological, Witzel remarks—"The Indo-Aryan influence, whether due to actual settlement, acculturation, or, if one prefers, the substitution of Indo-Aryan names for local ones, was powerful enough from early on to replace local names, *in spite of the well-known conservatism of river-names. This is especially surprising in the area once occupied by the Indus civilization, where one would have expected the survival of earlier names, as has been the case in Europe and the Near East...* The failure to preserve old hydronomes, even in the Indus Valley (with a few exceptions noted above), indicates the extent of the social and political collapse experienced by the local population."[17]

Indeed, Witzel's fixation with Iran as the origin/source/predecessor of the most significant elements of IVC and Hinduism is a characteristic present across most of his work. Speaking about the 'Agnihotra' ritual for instance, Witzel introduces it as a "sun spell" with the association between the sun and the fire, attributed first to the Zoroastrians. "Its original purpose was as a sun spell:5 in the evening, the power of the sun enters into the embers of the fire, from where it has to be rekindled the following morning. The underlying identification of sun and fire is very old, in any case already Indo-Iranian, as shown by the fire worship of the Zoroastrians. This is already seen in the *Yasna Haptaŋhāiti*, composed in quasi-Zarathustrian Old Avestan."[18] While it is true that several ancient cultures have associated worship with the Sun and Fire, Witzel's attribution of roots of a fundamental Vedic ritual to the Zoroastrians in such a casual manner with any lack of evidence is startling, and yet an unsurprising fixture of his prejudice.

Finally, Witzel's model, incredulous and convenient at once, for the invasion/migration of the Indo-Europeans into India proceeds along the following lines: "...we may regard the "importation" of Indo-Aryan into the Sub continent as the outcome of the influx of a group of clans, tribes or people who spoke early Vedic and had an Indo-Iranian, or rather Indo-Aryan, civilisation with exogamous groups of patrilineal descent, practised pastoralism and fought with horse-drawn chariots. By the time they reached the Subcontinent they were already racially mixed: emerging from the lower Volga region, and passing through Central Asia, they may have had the typical somatic characteristics of the ancient populations of the Turanian/Iranian/Afghan areas, and may not have looked very different from the modern inhabitants of the Indo-Iranian Borderlands. Their genetic impact would have been negligible and, as was the case with the Normans in England, would have been "lost" in a few generations in the much larger gene pool of the Indus people. One should not, therefore, be surprised that "Aryan bones" have not been found so far (Kennedy, this volume; Hemphill, Lukacs and Kennedy 1991)... the immigrant group was politically dominant because of its new military technology and tactics, especially the horse-drawn chariot which was quickly taken over by all major states in Egypt, Mesopotamia and China (Mair 1990: 44), although *without taking over the language of the chariot drivers.* The first appearance of thundering chariots must have stricken the local population with a terror similar to that experienced by the Aztecs and Incas upon the arrival of the iron-clad, horse-riding Spaniards."[19] Witzel further, helpfully, adds to the picture, "Something of this fear of the horse and of the thundering chariot, the "tank" of the 2nd millennium B.C. is transparent in the famous horse 'Dadhikra' of the Puru king Trasadasya ("Tremble enemy" in RV 4.38.8) ...The first appearance of thundering chariots must have stricken the local population with terror similar to that experienced by the Aztecs and the Incas upon the arrival of the iron-clad, horse riding Spaniards."[20] One wonders if Witzel's 2nd millennium BC "tank" would have been helpful to those nations that have unsuccessfully faced the terrain and climate of the Hindu Kush Mountains in this century alone.

Witzel's AI/MT essentially amounts to a group of pastoral tribes, from the Steppes, already a part of an Aryan civilization, riding through the mountainous terrains of Iran, Afghanistan and present day north India, on horse-chariots and arriving to terrorize the local population. Throughout this journey, they mixed with local populations and became racially mixed, over a few generations and finally reached modern north India, perhaps with such huge collective amnesia that they left not a single trace of their journey or their history, in neither the trail nor in the final destination, in some form or the other. Despite "thundering" through the journey and establishing themselves in the new place, they seem to have settled into the river-fed plains of the IVC, which were as fertile as Witzel's colorful imagination, while neither naming the places nor rivers or any other geographical markers of their final destination in connection with their supposed place of origin. Meanwhile, the local population, which presumably had "collapsed" also had collective amnesia so as to not leave behind a single trace of such an invasion or migration in its history! And since, this entire process is based on intermingling of several orders and theorizations based on sources entirely foreign to the actual place under consideration, no trace of physical or literary evidence will be found, making it a highly convenient explanation. With a model such as this, no amount of horse remains ever excavated from any IVC site will be sufficient to counter the claims, because the model has in-built protection against any physical or other evidence. Further, Witzel claims that the language of the Harappans of the IVC was a hypothetical "Para-Munda/Kubhā-Vipāś substrate," which the invading/migrating Indo-Aryans encountered when they first came to the region.[21]

In the absence of any textual evidence for his theories, what Witzel did was mistranslate a verse from *Baudhāyana Śrauta Sūtra*, related to the two sons of Purūravas and Ūrvaśi—Āyu and Amāvasu—to make it appear that, indeed, there was a reference to the migration he desperately tries to find in all Indian texts. Writing in *Rgvedic History: Poets, Chieftains and Politics*, Witzel translates the sutra 18.44:397.9,

> "Taking a look at the data relating to the immigration of the Indo-Aryans into South Asia, one is stuck by the number of vague reminiscences of foreign localities and tribes in the Rgveda, in spite repeated assertions to the contrary in the secondary literature. Then, there is the following direct statement contained in (the admittedly much later) BSS (=Baudhayana Shrauta Sutra) 18.44:397.9 sqq which has once again been overlooked, not having been translated yet: 'Ayu went eastwards. His (people) are the Kuru Panchala and the Kasi-Videha. This is the Ayava (migration). (His other people) stayed at home. His people are the Gandhari, Parsu and Aratta. This is the Amavasava (group)'".[22]

Koenraad Elst pointed the mistake in the manner in which Witzel had split the verse and interpreted it and showed that, in fact, the verse shows a movement from India to west of the Sarasvati River and not any migration into India,

> "This passage consists of two halves in parallel, and it is unlikely that in such a construction, the subject of the second half would remain unexpressed, and that terms containing contrastive information (like 'migration' as opposed to the alleged non-migration of the other group) would remain unexpressed, all left for future scholars to fill in. It is more likely that a non-contrastive term representing a subject indicated in both statements, is left unexpressed in the second: that exactly is the case with the verb pravavrâja 'he went', meaning 'Ayu went' and 'Amavasu went'. Amavasu is the subject of the second

statement, but Witzel spirits the subject away, leaving the statement subject-less, and turns it into a verb, 'amâ vasu', 'stayed at home'. In fact, the meaning of the sentence is really quite straightforward, and doesn't require supposing a lot of unexpressed subjects: 'Ayu went east, his is the Yamuna-Ganga region', while 'Amavasu went west, his is Afghanistan, Parshu and West Panjab'. Though the then location of 'Parshu' (Persia?) is hard to decide, it is definitely a western country, along with the two others named, western from the viewpoint of a people settled near the Saraswati river in what is now Haryana. Far from attesting an eastward movement into India, this text actually speaks of a westward movement towards Central Asia, coupled with a symmetrical eastward movement from India's demographic centre around the Saraswati basin towards the Ganga basin".[23]

With Witzel offering no response to the scholar Vishal Aggarwal when he raised the matter of the mistranslation, Kalyanaraman sought the expert opinion of George Cardona on the same, and he too agreed that Witzel's interpretation was wrong.[24] Instead of admitting the mistranslation in a straightforward manner, of the sole direct evidence he has tried to find related to migration from the entire Indian canon throughout his career, Witzel resorted to patronizing statements against Elst, "I have read Elst's criticism of my 1995 BSS translation. This is one of the "very" few cases where he is right indeed in his stringent immigration/trickling in stance (who speaks of "invasion" these days?) My translation, as it reads, is wrong in the "translations" of "amaavasus." (Interpretation is quite another thing, see below. The whole passage plays with names and their Nirukta-like interpretation as verbs). My paper in Erdosy, Ancient Indo-Aryans, where this was published, is full of printing and some other mistakes; I did not see the proof and could not correct it before it was published. The BSS translation as printed is a mixture of translation and interpretation. I have already corrected it in a paper (still in press) which has been given to some friends long ago."[25]

Witzel's AI/MT model, as droll as it seems to any rational mind, shares its fundamentals with those of many others, including Romila Thapar et al, with the primary consequences focussed on the following[26]:
1) Sanskrit and the Rig Veda are not a purely Indian intellectual property

and inheritance; 2) the ancestors of Bhārata are invaders/those who migrated from outside and hence, an involute basis is laid for future invaders being a part of the Bhāratīya identity; 3) relegation of Sanskrit sources, commentaries and historical records of the land that have existed as the corpus since millennia to oblivion even after the political end to the European colonization project in India – what Bhārata's own written and oral records have consistently maintained since 3000 BC is inconsequential as primacy must be accorded to specious and uncritical Iranian or/and Greek records and associations which are barely subject to any serious scrutiny. With such dubious basis, Witzel's model is riddled with chronologically weak points, that necessitate further unreasonable hypotheses to create a fuller picture, such as that seen in his chronology and understanding of the Rig Veda or when Witzel remarks on the connection between understanding ritual and the chronology of the text being considered[27] or in Witzel's scheme of first urbanization of ancient India.[28] Examining the complete chronology of ancient India in Witzel's work is a paper in itself and beyond the scope of the current essay.

Witzel's Vedic Hinduism

In the current section, some significant arguments from Witzel's work on Hinduism are considered, from the point of view of understanding some of the major themes which emerge in his huge body of work as a Sanskritist studying some of the most profound and significant texts and principles of Hinduism. Witzel's 1992 work with S.W. Jamison captures many of the salient features of the former's core body of work on Vedic Hinduism. Witzel and Jamison date the Vedic period to "1500-500 BCE" with the lower limit directed by Bechert's influential work on dating Gautama Buddha.[29] In defining Vedic Hinduism, Witzel sets out his first premise – "It may also be added that to call this period "Vedic Hinduism" is a contradiction *in terminis* since Vedic religion is very different from what we generally call "Hindu religion",—at least as much Old Hebrew religion is from medieval and modern Christian religion. However, Vedic religion is treatable as a predecessor of Hinduism." The note inline leads to "There are, of course, many surprising continuities (see Gonda 1965).

On the other hand, one can certainly not speak of an "eternal India" that always followed a form of the parâtana dharma that differed only slightly from the later Epic and Purânic religion: see below on such gods as Vishnu and Śiva."[30]

Witzel is one amongst several non-practitioners of Hinduism, such as David White, David Anthony, Christopher Beckwhit, and so on, who have held onto the discredited AI/MT to define what they consider as Hinduism within the academic domain. It is one thing to speak of various influences and morphology of the religion over centuries but the comparison used by Witzel and Jamison itself betrays their stark lack of understanding of the fundamentals of the former, for the sheer differences between a dharmic religion and an Abrahamic one are not mere superficial comparisons in timescales of evolution or chronology, but fundamental shifts in approach to the very principles.[31]

Having defined in his view what is Vedic literature, Witzel says that the names and titles of the works in the Vedic framework "misrepresent" the content within (pp. 5) and further speculates that the Rig Veda, at least parts of it, may have been composed in the Avestan region, "Possible between c. 1900 BC. and c. 1100 BCE, see above, n.1. This time frame includes only the period of possible immigration and settlement in Northern and North-West India; parts of the RV may have been composed already in Afghanistan (on the Sarasvatī = Avest. Haraxvatī, etc.)" (pp.6, footnote 8). Witzel's basis for the above statement is, again, his AI/MT model of "thundering" Indo-Europeans riding in horse-drawn chariots through the treacherous terrain of the Hindu Kush mountains, while also staying along the way long enough to become racially mixed, and bringing with them proto-Sanskrit and the *Rig Veda* from Iran into India, and doing so in a way that has left no trace in neither the archaeological nor literary nor inscriptional nor any other form of records since 3000 BC except in AI/M Theorists' models.

Witzel and Jamison further, make a series of assertions in the paper regarding some crucial elements of Hinduism. Considering the *Pravargya* ritual of the *Āraṇyaka*, they argue that contrary to what "medieval Hindu tradition" asserts about the type of textual material that the Āraṇyaka constitutes falling in the *Vānaprastha* stage, and maintain instead that the Āranyaka texts "deal, quite in the fashion of other Brāhmaṇa type texts, with a particular ritual."[32] Calling the texts "dangerous" again, Witzel and Jamison attribute to P. Theime, the "first" correct understanding of the structure of the *Bṛhadāraṇyaka Upaniṣad* text,[33] making one wonder if all the Indian commentaries in the canon, until the arrival of the white man, were for complete nought. Witzel further teaches one how Ādi Śaṅkarācāryaḥ's approach to the Upaniṣad-s was "wrong ... from the point of view of the development of Indian thought"[34] and tries to explain away the lack of a single mention of the AI/M event in the literature of the land to many texts not being translated because of the "difficulty of the Vedic language and expression" and consequent suffering of research into Vedic and Hindu religion.[35]

Witzel's fixation on Iran is a major hallmark throughout his works and results in a series of equivalences and associations in *Vedic Hinduism* that are labored and convoluted. While considering rituals associated with rites of passage, such as the upanayanam, he mentions about equivalent ones found amongst the Iranian people, but does so without mentioning any details of the latter to establish the comparison.[36] Rites of passage are present in most cultures across the world, but one fails to understand what the specific connection is between the *upanayanam*, which is a unique *saṃskāra*, and some vague equivalent ritual found in Iran. Despite Iranian practices having undergone significant changes in its turn to Zoroastrianism, Witzel, *sans* subjecting them to any critical examination, continues to use the Iranian works as standard to which Indian practices are compared, to establish an older historicity for the Iranian and a consequent and subsequent influence and timeline for the ancient Indian. A typical ploy reminiscent of many an imperialistic pronouncement by colonizers with scarce comprehension of a civilization overwhelmingly varied from their own.

Witzel and Jamison further "discover" in the texts amazing characteristics of young men who had chosen to study the Vedas. Drawing on the works of Heesterman, Falk and Bollée, they remark that the young students of Veda "live an independent life, away from home and trying to collect a starting capital of cattle by threat and extraction from their neighbors,"[37] making the young disciples sound like they are embarking on a life of larceny and peculation when they set out to learn the Veda! Witzel and Jamison remark further that the role of women in Vedic Hinduism, especially the Upaniṣad-s is "usually overstated. The role played by women in the Upaniṣads is usually overstated. It should be noted that women (Gārgī, Maitreyī) -- just like Kṣatriya-s and kings, or even the son of a god, Bhṛgu, -- are inserted into the Brahmanical dialogues at critical points or when a special proposition has to be made, e.g. when introducing a particular new or striking theory."[38]

Witzel and Jamison's understanding of the fundamentals of Hinduism and the Veda-s is brought into question when one reads their work on *naivedya* and *prasāda*: "As such, transubstantiated food can travel towards the gods in the form of smoke and aroma (medha) and is consumed by them. What remains here on earth is a gift by the gods who have tasted the offering while sitting at the sacred fire, soiled it by their spittle and rendered it consumable only to their socially inferior relations, the human beings: this is the remnant (*ucchiṣṭa*). It is not useless or thrown away as "soiled" food is apt to be. Instead, as especially AV extols in great detail, the "remnant" has enormous potential (cf. Malamoud 1972, Wezler 1978) in the peculiar social hierarchy that exists between men and god (*deva*), just as between wife and husband (*deva*), or between the people (prajā) and the king (*deva*). "Food remnants" of the deva are "palatable" to members of "lower" social rank: i.e. men, wives, subjects."[39]

In addition to his academic work as a Sanskritist and Indologist, Michael Witzel has raked up an impressive set of ad hominem attacks against scholars who disagree with his work, or point to the mistakes he has made despite claiming to be an expert Sanskritist. V. Swaminathan, the former Principal of Guruvayur Sanskrit Vidyapeeth, for instance, has been at the receiving end of disparaging remarks from Witzel for calling him out on the latter's remarks that the *ācārya*-s Pāṇini and Sāyaṇa were not aware of the injunctive, which Witzel had made in critiquing David Frawley's interpretation of the term *samudra* in the Rig Veda. In his rebuttal to Witzel, Swaminathan details how Pāṇini was aware of the injunctive used by European Orientalists and even refers to a verse "P VIII.3.50 wherein Panini notices the injunctive, subjunctive and the imperative forms of the root kri- *kah, karat, karati, kridhi* and *kritam*"[40] and similarly demonstrates Sāyaṇācārya's awareness of the same. Witzel's response, instead of a mature and objective addressal of the points raised by Swaminathan, is an emotionally charged tirade.[41] Shrikant Talageri, Nicholas Kazanas, David Frawley, S. Kalyanaraman, Vishal Aggarwal are a few of the notable names who have faced ad hominem attacks, slander, taunts, jibes on Indology listings online, by Witzel in response to their scholarly critiques of his work.[42] Witzel, and his assistant Steve Farmer have the choicest of words for their critiques, despite the standards of Witzel's own scholarship considered thus far, "The historical fantasies of writers like Rajaram must be exposed for what they are: propaganda issuing from the ugliest corners of the pre-scientific mind. The fact that many of the most unbelievable of these fantasies, are the product of highly trained engineers should give Indian educational planners deep concern."[43] In reality, it is the academic world and affected communities which should be deeply concerned that professors such as Witzel occupy positions and chairs in universities where young minds are shaped.

Witzel's Petition

Apart from entertaining the academic world with his many remarks and name-calling, Witzel has also donned the role of being the lead petitioner under the guise of saving Indian history from inaccuracies. The California State Board of Education (CSBE) evaluates the material it uses as recommended text books and resource material for its schools every six years and in the process, gives an opportunity for members of various communities to present views on matters which represent their heritage and history. In 2005, during one such review cycle, members of the Hindu community in the United States, as well as other Indian Americans, presented their review of the content in the grade VI textbooks that carried material on Ancient India. Some of the content included in the material taught to students about India until then included shockingly false and racist calumny such as the following:[44]

1. Page 148 of *Ancient Civilization* by Holt Basic Reading Series: *"Though they are mostly religious, some of the Vedas describe Aryan victories during their invasion of India"* – which is a factually wrong statement.

2. Page 169 of *Ancient Civilization* by Holt Basic Reading Series claims: *"The Ramayana, written later than the Mahabharata,..."* – since this is written for Grade VI students, one can safely assume they are not referring to any discussion on any particular version of the *Rāmāyaṇa* being written later than *Mahābhārata*; instead this seems to be referring to the actual historical events themselves, making it a shockingly ignorant statement.

3. Page 364 of *Ancient Civilization* by Harcourt School Publishers claims: *"Hindi is written with the Arabic alphabet, which uses 18 letters that stand for sounds"*—factually wrong, as Hindi is written in Devanāgarī script.

4. Page 81 of the *The Ancient South Asian World* by Jonathan Mark Kenoyer: *"The Vedic peoples discriminated against the Dasa, a group of people who spoke a different language that did not sound at all like Sanskrit. The Brahmins sometimes made fun of the Dasa and said that they spoke as if they had no noses. (Pinch your nose and see what you would sound like.) The Dasa had wide flat noses and long curly black hair, and the Brahmins claimed that they had darker skin and called them uncivilized barbarians, who didn't know how to behave...."The Dasa had, in reality lived in the region for hundreds of years. Their ancestors in the Indus Valley were the Harappans who had named the rivers and mountains, and had built the cities that now lay abandoned."* – It is not surprising that Witzel would wish to see such nonsensical text continue to be taught.

5. Page 87 of the *The Ancient South Asian World* by Jonathan Mark Kenoyer: *"The monkey king Hanuman loved Rama so much that it is said that he is present every time the Ramayana is told. So look around—see any monkeys?"* – is the text asking the students to look around and potentially call Hindu students, who believe in Hanumān, monkeys?

Having collated and reviewed all such offensive and inaccurate statements found in the books being taught to students, members of the Hindu American and Indian American communities submitted their feedback and inputs to the CSBE, which accepted them for review. Michael Witzel 'thundered' into situation at this juncture, along with Romila Thapar, D.N. Jha and et al, calling those who were fighting for the changes as "religious fundamentalists"[45] and being driven by Hindutva ideology. In Witzel's own words, "Approximately 150 scholars, specialists on South Asia from UCLA, Stanford, UC Berkeley, Columbia, Princeton, Yale, Harvard, The University of Florida, Cornell, Smith College, Massachusetts Institute of Technology, and dozens of other well-respected schools, sent a letter to Dr. Ruth Green, the president of the California State Board of Education." What Witzel omits when he mentions these "specialists" that he had led in his petition, is that, even those specializing in Road Transportation, such as S. Palaniappan, were amongst the signatories. The CSBE then asked Witzel, amongst four of the signatories of the petition, to present his views on the revisions sought by the members of the Hindu American and Indian American community and further invited to discuss the edits with the Curriculum Committee expert S. Bajpai. Further, the Curriculum Commission comprised members such as the biologist Stan Metzenberg and the physicist Charles Munger, Jr. It is interesting to read reports of the details of the Commission's discussion, which show that only Munger campaigned to have Witzel's edits retained.[46] Commissioner Metzenberg's remarks include the understandable thought that Hindus should at least "recognize their own religion when they read these textbooks", calling out Witzel's group's following remark on *Rāmāyaṇa* and the *Mahābhārata*—"Who in sixth grade cares which epic was 'written' first?" to which Metzenberg observed, "It obviously matters to Hindus" and on Witzel's pet AI/M Theory, Metzenberg unequivocally said, "I've read the DNA research, and there was no Aryan migration. I believe the hard evidence of DNA more than I believe historians."[47]

The recommendations Witzel's group campaigned for include, for instance, that the mūrti-s of Hindu gods should be called "statues" instead of deities as requested by the Hindu community and using the lowercase g (as in god) to refer to the Hindus' view of the Supreme Self/ Īśwara/Paramātma instead of using the uppercase (as in God) as recommended by the community. Dr. Heitzman, advocating on behalf of Witzel's group is said to have remarked, "I advise you to err on the side of conservatism and be very careful about adopting any of these changes." Commissioner Metzenberg replied pointedly, "On the contrary, to err on the side of conservatism, we should err on the side of Hindus. After all, it's their religion." The changes recommended and resisted by Witzel's group are a true representation of their sense of entitlement to be seen as having the *adhikāra* to speak for Hindu views and beliefs than practising Hindus themselves, while working off an academic ecosystem which has operated since two centuries of Western Indology, in a manner which ignores the repeated errors and rebuttals of their views highlighted by the Sanskritists and scholars of the country who are not biased by colonial dogmas.

Conclusion

While this essay captures a few brief features that have characterized Witzel's scholarship and academic oeuvre of the last few decades, much remains to be done in the years ahead in analyzing the works that have become authoritative in the field of Indology due to the ever expanding influence of Western echo chambers perpetuated by scholars such as Witzel. The systematic and scholarly rebuttals of several of Witzel's works by scholars mentioned in this article, and those such as Bhagwan Singh, the author of *The Vedic Harappans*, who has shown how little Witzel knows of the material he claims to be an expert in, while challenged in a live discussion, are all examples of necessary and welcome interventions in academic debate.[48] Future directions of research can include dissecting Witzel's works through the lens of Sanskrit Non-Translatables to analyze how the impact on his interpretations of various important Dharma texts. Witzel's work in Mythology[49], which is an unscientific, illogical and racist attempt at constructing a grand mythological narrative based on two races, "Gondwana" and "Laurasian", deserves a separate review by itself and similar analysis for several of his long list of works.

Special attention also needs to be paid to Witzel's several disconcerting works, including his role in the SARVA project led by the Department of Sanskrit and Indian Studies at Harvard University and the project 'Simulating the Evolution of Political-Religious Extremism: Implication for International Policy Decisions', led by Witzel and Farmer. It goes beyond an academic exercise and aims to research the impact of technology use by Hindu movements and provide policy advice; as Rajiv Malhotra and Aravind Neelakandan explain in *Breaking India*, "Steve Farmer explains on his webpage that its goal is to 'allow policy analysts and historians to build cultural simulations without any formal programming'. [30] The term 'cultural simulations' means the ability to simulate 'what if' the USA were to collaborate with group X against group Y, and various permutations and combinations of scenarios for such 'cultural interventions' in India. One can see similar theoretical interventions actually being implemented in Afghanistan, Pakistan, Iraq and Yemen."[50] Scholars such as Witzel, have since long, used academia to perpetuate agendas rather than unbiased research and it thus, becomes more important for us, with every generation, who bear the brunt of such dangerous games of identity politics, to be vigilant and ensure our history is presented from decolonized and scientific lenses. Cultivating a greater and deeper education on our own civilization through our own native lens, while engaging in meaningful, respectful, and evidence-led dialogue with dominant centers of Western Indology, is the most effective inoculation against the weaponization of academia, the brink of which scholars such as Witzel are only too keen to advance.

Bibliography

Agarwal, Vishal. 2003. *A Reply to Michael Witzel's 'Ein Fremdling im Rgveda'*, Journal of Indo-European Studies, Vol. 31, No.1-2: pp.107-185

Agarwal, Vishal. 2005-2006. *Misrepresentation of Ancient India and Hinduism*

in American School Textbooks. History Today (Journal of the Indian History and Culture Society, New Delhi), Vol. VII, 2005-2006, pp. 72-89

Anthony, David .W. 2010. *The Horse, the Wheel, and Language*: *How Bronze-Age Riders from the Eurasian Steppes Shaped the Modern World*. Princeton University Press.

Bökönyi, Sándor.1997. *Horse Remains From the Prehistoric Site of Surkotada, Kutch, Late 3rd Millennium B.C.*, South Asian Studies, 13:1

Bollée, W.B. 1981. *The Indo-European sodalities in Ancient India* ZDMG 131, 172-191

Bryant, Edwin and Patton, Laurie. (Eds.) 2005. *The Indo-Aryan Controversy: Evidence and Inference in Indian History.* Routledge.

Cardona, George and Jain, Dhanesh (Eds.). 2003. *The Indo-Aryan Languages.* Routledge .

Heesterman, J.C. 1981. *Householder and wanderer* Fs. L. Dumont (ed. T. N. Madan). New Delhi. pp. 251-71.

Danino, Michael. 2006. *The Horse and the Aryan Debate.* Retrieved on 3 December 2021. (https://www.researchgate.net/publication/237413669_THE_HORSE_AND_THE_ARYAN_DEBATE)

Elst, Koenrad. 2007. *Asterisk in Bhāropīyasthān: Minor Writings on the Aryan Invasion Debate.* Aditya Prakashan, New Delhi.

Elst, Koenrad. 2018. *Still No Trace of Aryan Invasion: A Collection of Indo-European Origins. Aryan Books International.*

Jamison, Stephanie & Witzel, Michael. 1992. *Vedic Hinduism*

Joshi, J.P. (with contributions from A.K. Sharma). 1990. *Excavation at Surkotada 1971-72 and Exploration in Kutch*, Memoirs of the Archaeological Survey of India 87, New Delhi

Kazanas, Nicholas. 2001. *The AIT and Scholarship.* Retrieved on 3 December 2021. (http://omilosmeleton.gr/wp-content/uploads/2018/01/AITandscholarship.pdf)

Kazanas, Nicholas. 2011. *Indo-Aryan Origins and Other Vedic Issues.* Aditya Prakashan.

Kazanas, Nicholas. 2015. *Vedic and Indo-European Studies.* Aditya Prakashan.

Lal, B.B. 2015. *The Rigvedic People: Invaders, Immigrants or Indigenous.* Aryan books International.

Olivelle, Patrick. 2009. *The law code of Viṣṇu - A Critical edition and Annotated*

Translation of the Vaiṣṇava-Dharmaśāstra. Harvard Oriental Series 73. Department of Sanskrit and Indian Studies, Harvard University

Mahadevan, Iravatham. 2003. *Early Tamil Epigraphy from the Earliest Times to the Sixth Century A.D.* Harvard Oriental Series 62. Harvard University Press.

Malhotra, Rajiv and Neelakandan, Aravindan. 2011. *Breaking India: Western Interventions in Dravidian and Dalit Faultlines.* Amaryllis.

Malhotra, Rajiv. 2011. *Being Different: An Indian Challenge to Western Universalism.* Harper Collins

Manjul, Sanjay Kumar & Manjul, Arvin. 2018. *Recent Excavation at Sanauli, District Bagpat, UP: A Landmark in Indian Archaeology.* Purātattva 48: 220–225 & pl. 1–12

Sastry, Manogna & Megh Kalyansundaram. 2019a. *The A of ABC of Indian chronology: Dimensions of the Aryan problem revisited in 2017.* Proceedings from the Swadeshi Indology Conference Series Studies in Tamil Civilisation (Land of Dharma):87-130

Sastry, Manogna & Kalyanasundaram, Megh. 2019b. *The B of ABC of Indian chronology: Dating Buddha's Parinirvāṇa, A critique of Heinz Bechert's echo chamber.* Retrieved on 3 December, 2021. (https://www.academia.edu/38794701/The_B_of_ABC_of_Indian_chronology_Dating_Buddhas_Parinirvāṇa_A_critique_of_Heinz_Becherts_echo_chamber.)

Sastry, Manogna & Kalyanasundaram, Megh. 2019c. *Sarasvatī in the Mahābhārata—A Study.* Presented at Third International Conference on Sarasvati River (Feb. 8-9, 2019) at Panjab University, Chandigarh, India. Retrieved on 3 December, 2021.

(https://www.academia.edu/38369132/Sarasvatī_in_the_Mahābhārata_A_Study_Sastry_and_Kalyanasundaram_2019_pdf)

Singh, Bhagwan. 1998. *The Vedic Harappans.* Aditya Prakashan.

Witzel, Michael. 1995a. *Early Indian History: Linguistic and textual parameters* in The Indo-Aryans of Ancient South Asia: Language, material culture and ethnicity (Ed) by George Erdosy. Walter de Gruyter. Berlin and New York.

Witzel, Michael 1995b. *Rgvedic History: Poets, Chieftains and Politics*; in The Indo-Aryans of Ancient South Asia The Indo-Aryans of Ancient South Asia:

Language, material culture and ethnicity (Ed) by George Erdosy. Walter de Gruyter. Berlin and New York.

Witzel, Michael. 1999. *Substrate languages in Old Indo-Aryan (Rgvedic, middle and late Vedic)*. Electronic Journal of Vedic Studies 5, no. 1. Wœrkens, Martine van, and Catherine Tihanyi.

Witzel, Michael. 2005. *Katha Aranyaka: Critical Edition with A Translation into German and An Introduction*. Harvard Oriental Series 65. Department of Sanskrit & Indian Studies, Harvard University Press.

Witzel, Michael. 2013. *The Origins of the World Mythologies*. Oxford University Press.

Witzel, Michael. 2016. *Agnihotra Rituals in Nepal* in Homa Variations: The Study of Ritual Change across the Longue Durée (Eds.) Richard K. Payne and Michael Witzel. Oxford University Press.

Witzel, Michael. 2019a. *Beyond the Flight of the Falcon: Early 'Aryans' Within and Outside India* in Which of Us are Aryans. Aleph Book Company

Witzel, M. 2019b. *Early 'Aryans' and their neighbors outside and inside India. J Biosci* 44, 58

Anonymous. *Thus Spake Professor Michael Witzel: A Harvard University Case Study in Prejudice?*

Notes

1. "California Parents for the Equalization of Educational Materials v. Kenneth Noonan" Case S-06-532-FCD-KJM Document 212, pp 13. Retrieved on 3 December 2021 (https://www.govinfo.gov/content/pkg/USCOURTS-caed-2_06-cv-00532/pdf/USCOURTS-caed-2_06-cv-00532-14.pdf).

2. Witzel 2019a:1

3. Witzel 2019a:2

4. See "Swadeshi Indology Conference – 3" for a range of papers on Aryan theories and their contemporary implications. Retrieved on 3 December 2021 (https://infinityfoundationindia.org/si-3/).

5. Witzel cites Khatayat et al (2017: 4) where it suits him, but ignores all other recent archaeological evidence

6. See Sastry, Kalyanasundaram, 2019c

7. Witzel 2019a:5

8. Patton 2005:17

9. See Michael Danino's 2006 paper for an excellent compilation of evidence that counters Witzel's arguments on the horse.

10. J.P. Joshi, 1990.

11. Bökönyi 1997:297

12. Witzel 2019a:5

13. Witzel 2019a:8

14. Witzel 1995a:104

15. Witzel 1995a:105

16. Witzel 1995a:106

17. Ibid

18. Witzel 2016:372

19. Witzel 1995a:113-114

20. Ibid, footnote 74

21. Witzel, 1999

22. Witzel, 1995:320

23. Agarwal, Vishal. "The Aryan Migration Theory: Fabricating Literary Evidence." Retrieved on 3 December 2021 (https://web.archive.org/web/20030618043907/http://vishalagarwal.bharatvani.org/AMT.html). Also see, Elst, 2007. "Petty Professorial Politicking in The Indo-Aryan Controversy : A note on a Harvard professor's assiduous misrepresentation of my position in the Aryan invasion debate." Retrieved on 3 December, 2021.

    (https://www.researchgate.net/publication/289528588_Petty_Professorial_Politicking_in_The_Indo-Aryan_Controversy_A_note_on_a_Harvard_professor%27s_assiduous_misrepresentation_of_my_position_in_the_Aryan_invasion_debate)

24. Cardona, Jain 2003:35

25. Witzel's response on 15 July 2000 on the Indian Civilization List as message no. 453, as cited in Agarwal, Vishal. "The Aryan Migration Theory: Fabricating Literary Evidence." Retrieved on 3 December 2021. (https://web.archive.org/web/20030618043907/http://vishalagarwal.bharatvani.org/AMT.html).
26. Sastry, Kalyanasundaram, 2019c
27. Jamison & Witzel 1992:29
28. Jamison & Witzel 1992:79
29. See Sastry, Kalyanasundaram, 2019b, for a review of Heinz Bechert's dating of Gautama Buddha
30. Jamison & Witzel 1992:3
31. See Malhotra's *Being Different* for some of the fundamental differences
32. Jamison & Witzel 1992:12
33. ibid
34. Jamison & Witzel 1992:14
35. Jamison & Witzel 1992:24
36. Jamison & Witzel 1992:21
37. Jamison & Witzel 1992:46-47
38. Jamison & Witzel 1992:48
39. Jamison & Witzel 1992:64
40. Swaminathan V. 2003. "Panini's Grammar, Sayanacharya's Vedic Bhashyas & Michael Witzel's 'Philology.'" Bharatvani. (https://web.archive.org/web/20040217030827/http://www.bharatvani.org/reviews/philology.html), "Panini's Understanding of Vedic Grammar: A Rejoinder to Professor Michael Witzel and Daniel Baum." Bharatavani. (https://web.archive.org/web/20031230061950/http://www.bharatvani.org/reviews/baumrejoinder.html). Both links retrieved on 3 December 2021.
41. Swaminathan V. 2003. "Alas, Panini was not a German!" Bharatvani. Retrieved on 3 December 2021 (https://web.archive.org/web/20050403200012/www.voi.org/indology/VSPanini.html).
42. See "*Anonymous - Thus Spake Professor Michael Witzel A Harvard University*

Case Study in Prejudice" pp.9 for a compilation of Witzel's attacks in merely one of his works.

43. As quoted in Agarwal, Vishal. "The Aryan Migration Theory: Fabricating Literary Evidence." Retrieved on 3 December 2021 (https://web.archive.org/web/20030618043907/http://vishalagarwal.bharatvani.org/AMT.html).

44. For a list of these errors, see Agarwal, Vishal. "It is Official Now - Romila Thapar Defends the Aryan Invasion Theory!" Retrieved on 3 December 2021

    (https://web.archive.org/web/20070216125524/http://www.india-forum.com/articles/60/1).

45. Witzel, Thapar 2006

46. "Outcome Unknown." Hinduism Today. Retrieved on 3 December 2021. (https://www.hinduismtoday.com/magazine/april-may-june-2006/2006-04-outcome-unknown-on-california-texts/)

47. Ibid

48. "Bhagwan Singh versus Michael Witzel!" Retrieved on 3 December 2021

    (https://ontogenyphylogenyepigenetcs.wordpress.com/2009/07/22/bhagwan-singh-versus-michael-witzel/).

49. Witzel, 2013

50. Malhotra & Neelakandan, 2011.

FOUR

Devdutt Pattanaik
Deconstructing Devduttology

Subhodeep Mukhopadhyay

Introduction

Devdutt Pattanaik is a prolific writer who has produced a vast amount of literature on various religious and social issues, especially pertaining to India and Hinduism. In his own words, he writes on the "relevance of mythology in modern times, especially in areas of management, governance and leadership."[1] He has authored over fifty books, many of which are bestsellers, and has written over a thousand columns for various websites like *Mid-Day, The Times of India, DailyO, Scroll* amongst others. He was a speaker at the first TED[2] conference in India held in November 2009 and his talk is available in thirty-one languages; and has been viewed over 2.3 million times.[3] Pattanaik has consulted for Star TV Network on popular Hindi serials like *Mahabharata, Devon Ke Dev...Mahadev* and *Siya Ke Ram,* helping provide "a different take" on the stories.[4] *Devlok with Devdutt Pattanaik* is a very popular series on Indian mythology which airs on EPIC channel and Netflix.

Pattanaik is considered a modern-day authority on Hinduism and his followers accept his views as being grounded in authentic Indian tradition. His book *Indian Culture, Art and Heritage,* published by Pearson, is recommended as reading material for Civil Service aspirants in India.[5] Pattanaik has received effusive praise for his work on Indian mythology from prominent personalities across disciplines such as humanities, films, and science, including writer Ashwin Sanghi, Hindi film actress Sonam Kapoor as well as psychologist Urmi Chanda-Vaz.

Through his TV programs, Pattanaik tries to attract young people and is confident that his work will be able to "procure eyeballs of younger audience as they'll relate to it big time."[6] Pattanaik is very active on Twitter, with more than 7.4 lakh followers, and his Tweets are well-received and often shared.[7] As is evident, Pattanaik is a very influential figure today in both mainstream and social media and is considered an expert in the interpretation of Indian tradition through the lens of mythology. His works impact the views of millions of Hindus both in India and abroad, while shaping global discourse about India, Hinduism and dharma. At the same time, his work has been criticized by Misra (2017) and Malhotra (2018), as well as practitioners of Hinduism for numerous factual errors, for distorting important philosophical ideas and for portraying Hinduism in a poor light.[8] He has also been criticized for his derogatory and insulting remarks towards his detractors, including women, using abusive terms like 'idiots' and 'bitches'; he accuses them of being Hindutva trolls, and has publicly shamed a woman by insisting that she is into 'slapping', 'insulting' and 'BDSM'.[9] Bhattacharjee (2019) finds it difficult to reconcile his rabid misogynist comments with his feminist credentials (albeit self-proclaimed), especially as an author who has penned books like *Devi* and *Laksmi*.[10]

In this essay, I explore some of the important ideas and themes that percolate his myriad works and examine his positions on various issues related to Hinduism and India. I have analyzed his scholarship from two perspectives. In the first level of examination, I illustrate how some of his claims on Indian traditions, in general, and Hinduism in particular, as well as Indian history, are problematic and at times, downright incorrect. Given that Pattanaik is viewed as an insider authority on Hinduism and his views end up providing millions of Hindus a false and pessimistic understanding about Hindu dharma and India's past, I have countered his questionable claims by citing evidence from traditional sources themselves. At a structural level, I have analyzed his positions together, in order to create a complete picture of his world view, and shown how Pattanaik uses a combination of Postmodernism, mythology and colonial categories in his scholarship. While I have no problems with Post-modernism as a Western social construct being applied to Western societies, I find a postmodern interpretation of Hinduism to be misleading and problematic on many fronts as I will show later. It is not only fundamentally opposed to how insiders view their own traditions, but also undermines the very ethos of unity and congruence that percolates through various Indic communities, howsoever distinct they may outwardly appear to be. Thus, rather than bringing together what appear to be disparate streams of thoughts, which is the essence of Hinduism; his scholarship, as I will demonstrate, accentuates differences, creates sharp binaries and promotes divisiveness in the guise of providing contemporary interpretations of Hindu ideas.

Dharma

Dharma has been an integral part of Indian spiritual systems from time immemorial and the idea of dharma, as that universal ideal which sustains or upholds civilization has been in vogue in India since ancient times.

> "Dharma sustains the society, Dharma maintains the social order, Dharma ensures the well-being and progress of humanity." – *Mahabharata Karna Parva* 69.58[11]

Hinduism is therefore, *sanatana dharma*, or the primordial dharma of more than a billion people worldwide. In Hinduism, dharma has a range of well-accepted contextual meanings like righteousness, piety, practices, customary observance like *yajnas*, prescribed conduct, duty, or the nature of things.[12] Some of the common characteristics of dharma in the human context are truthfulness, to be free from anger, sharing wealth with others, forgiveness, purity, absence of enmity, straightforwardness, patience, piety or self-control, honesty, sanctity, sense-control, reason, knowledge or learning, non-violence, and compassion.[13] It would not be wrong to say that dharma has been the fountainhead and guiding principle of Indian civilization for millennia, and has informed people of their social and ethical duties, and roles and responsibilities vis-à-vis nature and other creatures, in order to ensure a sustainable civilization.

> "Dharma is that which sustains and ensures progress and welfare of all

in this world and eternal Bliss in the other world."—Madhavacharya[14]

It has been dharma that has bound together disparate streams of thoughts, myriad *sampradayas* and diverse people together in Bharata. In the last couple of centuries, and especially the last few decades, dharma has unfortunately been incorrectly translated as religion, an error which has been time and again pointed out by many scholars like Malhotra (2011) and Paranjape (2021).[15] In fact, the Hindi translation of the Preamble to the Constitution rejects the equivalence of dharma and religion and translates secularism as *pantha-nirapekshata* or religiously-neutral and not as dharmically-neutral.[16] Pattanaik (2015), however, does not accept the standard range of traditional meanings of the term dharma; nor does he view dharma as religion.

He instead provides a radically different purport and import to the term, ostensibly to simplify the idea behind the word. He says:

> "Dharma has been made out to be a complicated word. That way you can call anything dharma... Dharma is potential. The best of what anything or anyone can do." [17]

Let us consider his first statement. Contrary to his assertion, dharma is indeed a complicated concept, and traditional scholars have studied it with utmost seriousness. It is a technical philosophical term with reasonably well-defined and contextual range of connotations and denotations. Even the *Mahabharata* prefers to leave it as *that* ideal or principle, without venturing into specifics:

> "It is most difficult to define Dharma. It has been explained to be that which helps the upliftment of living beings. Therefore, that which ensures the welfare of living beings is surely Dharma. The learned rishis have declared that which sustains is Dharma." – *Mahabharata Shanti Parva* 109.9-10 [18]

Again, unlike his second claim, people do not call everything dharma, since the scope and sources of dharma has been well-delineated in the tradition.

> "Puranas including the Brahma purana and others, Nyaya including Tarkashastra, Mimamsa which involves discussion about the content of Vedas, Dharmashastras including the Manu and other Smrtis, Angas including the Shad Vedangas, and Vedas (four of them)—these are the fourteen vidyasthanas and dharma-sthanas."—*Yajnavalkya Smriti* 1.3[19]

In other words, the roots of dharma are the *Vedas*.

> "Veda is the source of dharma and the tradition and practice of those that know it (the Veda)." – *Gautama Dharmasutra* 1.1.1-2[20]

> "For those greatly interested seekers of Dharma, the Vedas (Shrutis) are the highest authorities." – *Manu Smriti* 2.3[21]

Any new definition of dharma or shade of meaning or expansion in meaning, must be based on pre-existing tradition and cite references from the texts. That has been the standard practice among various sampradayas. Pattanaik, however, does not explain how he arrived at the definition of dharma as 'potential' or which Vedic sources he consulted, in coming up with this specific meaning. 'Potential' is not a standard definition and is not found in any of the major Sanskrit dictionaries. Therefore, while he accuses ordinary Hindus of hijacking the term and reinterpreting it as commandments so as to "control (or oppress?) sections of the population", by which he probably means Muslims and Dalits, he himself, indulges in a similar re-interpretive exercise.

The implications of this definition are manifold. A *mujahideen* terrorist may claim that by resorting to violence, he is fulfilling his potential as a terrorist and is therefore, more Dharmic than those who preach non-violence. By the same logic, even infamous iconoclasts like Mahmud Ghazni (11th century CE) or Aurangzeb (17th century CE) would have been able to justify their temple destruction. By destroying false gods, they were fulfilling their potential as ideal Muslims and therefore more Dharmic than those who created and revered the *murtis*. Clearly such a premise is problematic and goes against the traditional understanding of the term. Pattanaik (2015) further says:

> "Neither violence, nor non-violence is dharma. For dharma is a thought, not an action." [22]

This is a rather strange idea which again does not find support in tradition, and leads to some uncomfortable conclusions. Dharma should indeed be seen as transcending both the binaries of violence and non-violence, and thought and action, but at the same time it does require them to flourish. The entire *Bhagavad Gita* is premised on the fact that Arjuna as a Kshatriya had grave misgivings about his duty to fight the enemy, and Krishna exhorts him to wage war against the enemies. In this context, violence against the enemies is a Kshatriya's duty, and Krishna explicitly says so:

> "Considering your specific duty as a kshatriya, you should know that there is no better engagement for you than fighting on religious principles; and so there is no need for hesitation." – *Bhagavad Gita* 2.31[23]

At the same time, there is ample space for non-violence as well. One of the important characteristics of dharma listed by both Yajnavalkya and Manu in their dharmashastras is *ahmisa* or non-harm.[24] In other words, defending dharma is as important as preserving dharma. If one were to take Pattanaik's position that dharma and violence are not related, one could potentially rationalize any kind of violence, whether against living creatures or cultures or societies. One could in fact, justify the slaughter of animals for food, saying that it is outside the purview of dharma, and in an Indian context, perhaps also make a pernicious case for beef-eating. Pattanaik's incorrect view of dharma therefore, negatively impacts Hindus on all fronts. By insisting that dharma is neither about violence nor non-violence, but a thought, Pattanaik is actually weakening Hinduism by propagating a world-negating and escapist ideology, which goes against the very spirit of pragmatics and realism as espoused by all great leaders like Krishna, Janaka, Kautilya, Adi Shankaracharya and Swami Vivekananda. Pattanaik (2015) then adds:

> "In case of humans, dharma is the seed of thought that determines what will sprout as action. It is not what you do that is dharma; it is why you do it that is dharma."[25]

In this instance, Pattanaik seems to conflate dharma, which he refers to as seed, with the cycle of *karma* and *vasana* (or *samskara*).[26] Parthasarathy (2017) in his commentary of *Bhagavad Gita* describes vasana as "the seed of human personality" which manifests as thoughts, desires and actions. The root of all actions originates in a person's vasanas, which are his innate tendencies. The vasanas in turn, are results of previous actions, and present vasanas go on to create further actions. The karma-vasana cycle goes on unceasingly similar to a tree-seed or hen-egg cycle.[27] The entire purpose of *yoga*, *sadhana* and knowledge is to break this cycle of vasana/ samskara and karma. Bryant (2009) explains how samskaras and actions tend to reinforce each other, perpetuating a vicious cycle or virtuous cycle, depending on whether the actions are dharmic or adharmic. One's motives are the result of past experiences, and these motives prompt action, producing samskaras which further perpetuate the cycle of action and become increasingly reinforced. This is similar to how bad habits like smoking become reinforced with each puff of the cigarette. By changing the motivation, it is possible break this cycle, which is the entire purport of Yoga.[28] Pattanaik, however, equates these well-established concepts of karma and vasana with dharma, and provides a rather novel definition of dharma.

Instead of going into a detailed bottom-up exploration of Indian knowledge systems in general, and Hindu philosophy in particular, Pattanaik seems content to tread the surface and keep his analysis perfunctory. Such cursory perusal serves his purpose, as his target audience, the English-speaking urban Hindu elites tend to have superficial knowledge of Hindu *darshanas* and *sampradayas*. They have neither the time, nor the wherewithal nor the inclination to explore deep philosophical concepts. For them, Pattanaik is a guru of Hinduism, who offers them glib feel-good sound bites on Hindu ideas, in a language they know and using idioms they can relate to, while at the same time not shying away from exposing, to all intents and purposes, alleged evils of Hindu and Indian society. It is especially among the elite and corporate crowd, that Pattanaik is able to legitimize his standing as a "management guru." He spares no effort to include Indian philosophical terms alongwith business management jargon, thereby coming across as a profound modern-age philosopher. For Jayaraman (2013), Pattanaik is therefore, someone who "fuses scriptural knowledge with modern day management principles to evoke a very Indian approach to business and its role in society."[29] However, more often than not, Pattanaik trivializes profound philosophical concepts and reduces complex personalities and heroes to uni-dimensional caricatures. In a discussion with Singh (2016) on Indian approaches to leadership and power, Pattanaik agrees with the view that Lord Rama's "obsession with rules dehumanized him". He uses Rama and Sita's relationship to illustrate cost-benefit analysis and says:

> "That Ram always follows the rule makes him dependable. You know what to expect from him. That's a good quality too. It also means that around him, there will be Sitas who will suffer."[30]

This is a poor characterization of not only the personality of Rama, who is uniformly considered an exemplar of righteousness and virtue across India, but also a demeaning portrayal of Sita as a passive eternally-suffering wife. If one were to ask ordinary Indians, who they consider to be the embodiment of dharma, and the personification of purity and self-sacrifice, more often than not, the answer will be Lord Rama and Sita. Yet, in Pattanaik's scholarship Rama and Sita are reduced to props in a business management and leadership case study. Even Raghavendra (2018), who has commended Pattanaik's domain expertise and admired the fact that he is "well-informed on the most esoteric aspects" of Hinduism, finds Pattanaik's discomfort with the idea of dharma as a social ethic, and its avoidance, very perplexing. He writes that dharma as a contextual ethical notion can be used to interrogate the moral questions of a society, and can also be seen as a mechanism to bind society as a whole; but Pattanaik with "self-improvement as his only objective, declines to address the issue." He concludes:

> "Pattanaik's HRD-driven approach with self-improvement as the agenda consistently sidesteps what seems to me to be the most interesting aspects of mythology, which would be better presented by someone with a background in anthropology."[31]

Truth and Knowledge

As important as dharma is the idea of Truth, and Indian rishis, philosophers and scholars throughout the ages continue to remain obsessed with the constructs of truth and knowledge. The Brihadaranyaka Upanishad says:

> "Nothing is higher than dharma. The weak overcomes the stronger by dharma, as over a king. Truly that dharma is the Truth (Satya)."
> - Brihadaryanaka Upanishad 1.4.14[32]

In Hindu texts–whether *Vedas*, or their commentaries, or the *tantra* and *agamas* – 'truth' is the principal backbone against which the entire cosmos revolves, and against which everything else is to be evaluated. The concept of 'truth' is one of the central tenets of each and every school of Indian thought without any exception. So much so, that many of the pithy sayings in Indian tradition are associated with the idea of truth. The national motto of India is *"satyameva jayate"*, which means Truth alone triumphs. The *Taittiriya Upanishad* tells us: *"satyam vada, dharmam chara"*, which means "Speak the truth and abide by dharma." Although there are many different schools of thoughts within Hinduism, almost all of them, including the Tantric schools[33] accept an Ultimate Truth which is beyond space, time and causation.

Hindu thought is very clear on technical definitions of Sanskrit terms, and hence, concepts like 'truth' and 'reality' are quite well defined in the *astika* schools, and non-standard interpretations not rooted in Vedic thoughts are classified as *nastika* and not accepted as Hindu thought. For example, *Advaita Vedanta* classifies reality into various categories, but accepts only one Ultimate Truth. The first category is *sat* or that which is eternally real. This is the *paramarthika satta* or *Brahman*. Another category is known as *asat* or that which is eternally non-real. The classic example given in traditions is that of a sky-flower or hare with a horn. The third category is *mithya*, which refers to that which is perceived to be real at first, but later on rejected when the Ultimate Truth is realized. This is again of two types – *vyavaharika* and *pratibhasika*.

Vyavaharika is related to the world around us, while *pratibhasika* is a category of personal errors, like mistaking a rope for a snake.[34]

Related to Truth is the idea of what constitutes knowledge and how to attain such knowledge. Almost all dharmic schools, including the non-Vedic *nastika sampradayas* like Jainas and Bauddhas, accept ignorance as the root cause of all misery and removal of ignorance as the greatest aim of life. This requires right knowledge, and how that knowledge is acquired, varies from school to school. *Pramana shastra* or epistemology of Indian knowledge systems supports a wide variety of valid means of knowledge (*pramana*) like *pratyaksha* (perception), *anumana* (inference), *upamana* (comparison and analogy) and *shabda* (testimony of authority figures).[35] Thus, while the *Charvaka* school accepts only perception, the *Vishishtadvaita* and *Dvaita* Vedanta schools accept pratyaksha, anumana and shabda as valid means of knowledge. There is nothing ambiguous or wishy-washy about these definitions in dharmic traditions. Scholars, philosophers, grammarians and etymologists, have discussed, debated and argued on practically each syllable of every known technical Sanskrit word for millennia. Each term has a range of accepted meanings across different sampradayas, and one simply cannot super-impose their own meanings or interpretation on them, and pass them off as an insider view.

However, as a self-styled mythologist, Pattanaik (2006) dismisses the traditional understanding of truth and reality, and argues that there are many types of truth – subjective, objective, logical, intuitive, cultural, universal, evidence-based and faith-based truths.[36] Pattanaik (2017) views 'truth' as a political battleground, where different stakeholders like rationalists, secularists, atheists, traditionalists, supremacists, scientists and shamans, fight with each other for power and try to propagate their own versions of what they believe to be the truth.

> "When truth becomes singular and definitive, truth invariably becomes territory – a battlefield. The warriors here are not just religious radicals, but also politicians fighting to make India or America or Britain great again, and of course, academicians and activists and journalists, armed with facts."[37]

He conceptually seems to understand and appreciates the differences between the Advaita view of *sat*, as truth independent of any frame of reference, and *mithya* as a delusion or limited and distorted view of reality. The ancient Hindu rishis, he says, made use of mithya as a window to understand the truth of sat.[38] Unlike them, however, Pattanaik (2018) prefers to make use of post-modern and post-structural models of thinking to understand and make sense of societies, cultures and religions. He sees truth as a continuous spectrum, something fluid, and not something absolute. On one end of the spectrum is fact, which is everybody's truth, and on the other end is fiction or nobody's truth. In the middle is myth which he defines as "somebody's truth" or "subjective truth."[39] He believes that facts, rather than truth, are more important for knowledge production.[40] Dharmically speaking, he assigns more importance to the idea of pratyakasha pramana, than *sat*, a view similar to that held by the ancient school of materialists *Charvakas* who were well-known for their animosity towards the followers of the Vedas. Dasgupta (1951) in his analysis of pre-Buddha *nastika* philosophies shows how the Charvakas not only rejected the validity of inferences (anumana) as an epistemic category, but also the very existence of an eternal Self.[41] What this means, is that, in the Charvaka worldview, anything can be interpreted in any way, without recourse to any totalizing principle, and therefore we would not be wrong in locating Pattanaik in the nastika philosophical camp. His views on Hinduism are etic, or from the perspective of an outsider, and not emic.

His understanding of India's past is colored by this view and he understands *itihasa* as being neither history, nor fantasy but as cultural memoirs, and hence, the same as myth. It is the story which matters and not the facts, and these stories help produce "a map into the culture's mind over time and space", thereby facilitating one's understanding of the culture.[42] Here also his interpretation of the term varies from that of tradition since the word itihasa itself is another technical term and related to the idea of *purusharthas* or the four aims of human life accorded primacy in Hinduism—*dharma*, *artha* (all-round prosperity), *kama* (all-round pleasure and love) and *moksha* (self-actualization).

Itihasa specifically refers to the re-telling of the past in such a way, so as to help the flowering of the purusharthas.[43] While he comes across as being critical of Western categories and assumptions of normativity, as in Pattanaik (2003)[44], he often uses the same categories to interrogate Hinduism. He (2006) says:

> "Ideas such as rebirth, heaven and hell, angels and demons, fate and freewill, sin, Satan and salvation are religious myths."[45]

Almost all the categories and conceptual binaries used by Pattanaik are derived from monotheistic Abrahamic faiths. The idea of Salvation lies at the very heart of Christianity, and is the basis of massive global missionary programs to convert people. Christians of all denominations believe that all humans are born sinners and therefore, forever condemned. However, there is 'Good News' – a way out of what they call "Eternal Damnation." Since Jesus died on the Cross and took upon himself the sins of mankind, by accepting Jesus as their savior and becoming a Christian, a person can redeem himself. It is thus the duty of every Christian to help facilitate salvation by showing them the true way of the Christ.[46] Similarly, the idea of Satan does not exist in Hinduism, because Satan pre-supposes the existence of a transcendent all-mighty Creator God. Again, 'free will' is a not a universal idea but a theological term in Christianity and the shrill debates and polemic among Roman Catholics, Orthodox Church and Protestants on what constitutes free will is well documented. Even within the Protestant fold, Calvin, Luther and Arminius could not reach a consensus on the definition and scope of the concept.[47]

The term 'myth' is a politically loaded term and has traditionally been used by the West to pejoratively refer to the non-West's self-understanding of its past, especially in the context of religion and history. Therefore, *Ramayana* and *Mahabharata* were considered mythical in the same way as Greek and Norse mythology, but the historicity of Jesus was never called into question. Hegel (1827) for example famously dismissed Hinduism as a "religion of phantasy" (*die Religion der Phantasie*)[48] while characterizing Christianity as a rational religion and

Jesus as a rationalist philosopher.⁴⁹ Jung (1949) saw myths as a necessary construct to make sense of the world. They were the "original revelations of the preconscious psyche" and a vital aspect of human life. Myths were in a sense the psychic life of the primitive tribe and mythology its living religion.⁵⁰ Graves (1968) defines myths as those heroic or religious stories which were "so foreign to a student's experience that he cannot believe them to be true."⁵¹ Leach and Fried (1984) define 'myth' as a story of a previous age which are meant to explain "the cosmological and supernatural traditions of a people, their gods, heroes, cultural traits, religious beliefs, etc."⁵² Thury and Devinney (2017) in their seminal work, *Introduction to Mythology*, considered a standard introductory text on the subject, place everything from ancient Greek, Egyptian and Norse legends, to the Ramayana, to native American legends to *Star Trek* as well as *Harry Potter*, under the ambit of mythology. They say:

> "Mythology allows you to take a journey into an exciting and mysterious world. In your travels, you can expect to encounter gods, heroes, monsters, exotic countries, and amazing adventures."⁵³

Mythology may therefore, be seen as the culture, belief and religion of the ancient past; it served the same purpose to the people of a past period, as contemporary faith and belief does for the present-day society. Treating Hinduism or Indian past through the lens of mythology essentially means that Pattanaik does not see continuity between the past and the present. Hindu past becomes the "other" to be studied through the prism of mythology in the present post-modern world. While modernity may have its own contemporary myths, the West has in essence transcended the myths of their primitive past, while traditional societies like India still cling to them and consider it their living tradition. In this sense, unlike the progressive West built on secular ideals and Judeo-Christian ethics, Hinduism is frozen in a state of stagnant apathy and unchanging moral degeneracy. Pattanaik conveniently positions himself as an insider in this cultural milieu in order to liberate Hindus from the shackles of Hinduism itself. He uses this vantage point to perpetuate a sanitized and West-friendly version of Hinduism de-rooted from tradition, while continuing to build his career as a leadership coach and expert in the "Indian approach to management."[54]

While Hindu leaders themselves, often refer to itihasas and puranas as myths, Christian theologians and serious practitioners outright reject all attempts to categorize their past as myths. Hardon (1998), an American Jesuit (Catholic) priest categorically stated: "Christianity is not mythology."[55] Carl Henry, a prominent American evangelical (Protestant) Christian theologian was very clear that "Judeo-Christian revelation has nothing in common with the category of myth" (quoted in Mohler (2009)).[56] In fact, in Christianity the study of ideas like Heaven and Hell, the resurrection of the dead, the Last Judgment and end of times is an important academic discipline in itself called Eschatology. The search for archaeological sites associated with Jesus is a serious endeavor and there is a large amount of academic literature, as well as popular programs on National Geographic and History channels on the "historicity" of Jesus.[57] Hindu deities, on the other hand, are considered mythical and dismissed casually as ancient aliens.[58]

It is this lens of religious myth that Pattanaik uses to deconstruct, analyze and explain Hinduism to his millions of readers and followers. As is evident, his basic views on truth, reality, knowledge, epistemology and religio-spiritual categories are alien and often opposed to the traditional Hindu understanding of itself. Therefore, one should be wary of associating with him any expertise in either Hinduism or Indian knowledge systems.

Nationhood and India

Pattanaik does not accept the idea of nationhood, and considers ideas like sovereignty and nation state as myths and in this context, the independence movement, symbolism of national flags and national anthems are but tools to reinforce the myth of a nation state. He says (2006):

> "Ideas such as sovereignty, nation state, human rights, women's rights, animal rights and gay rights are secular myths." [59]

Pattanaik explains that there are two views about India and Hinduism. One view is that Hinduism and India are both rather recent colonial era fabrications. The other is the traditional view that both Hinduism and India, have existed in some form for many millennia. He says (2017):

> "A large number of scholars ... write tomes informing us that Hinduism and India did not exist before the modern era, and that these are unifying constructions of colonial and post-colonial forces. This confuses the average Hindu who has spent all his life performing the ancient sankalpa ritual before any ceremony ... Why can't the two views coexist?" [60]

In a free society like India, people are free to have an opinion on any matter, subject to reasonable restrictions, including the view that Hinduism and India are colonial constructs. However, for someone who is considered an authority on Hinduism and India, it is quite reasonable to expect that he or she should take an unequivocal and categorical stand on the matter. The onus is on them to state without any hesitation or ambiguity that while many theories may exist, the existence of both India and Hinduism, in some form, *is not a topic up for debate*. The concept of India as a civilizational state is an ancient idea, accepted by both Indians as well as people to the East and West of India.[61] For Indians, India (or Bharata or Hindustan) has always been a sacred *bhumi*, a unifying force, and their association with it has been enriched with a deeply embodied physical recognition of the geography and its resources. As I will discuss later, many rituals and pilgrimages are tied to some specific sacred geography. For someone who is considered an expert on Hinduism, to not acknowledge or take a stand on this, is a pointer to his lack of deeper understanding of the matter. Pattanaik either sits on the fence, or openly admits that he does not subscribe to a single idea of India, since India being a diverse and extremely complicated society cannot have one over-arching grand narrative. He says (2015):

> "I kept hearing the concept of the idea of India. I am very very uncomfortable with the definitive article 'the.' ... When we are talking of the idea of India, and the shifting idea of India, we are essentially

assuming that there is a definite idea of India and there is a shift to another definite idea of India. But if we were to look at it differently and say there are many ideas of India and some ideas amplify themselves at different points of time, the same thing looks very different."[62]

A single idea of India for him is simply a ploy to garner power and exercise control. It is an unrealistic imaginative ideal as well as a hegemonic tool, and he does not view with favor those who perpetuate such ideas.

"When somebody imagines one idea of India, they are really not scientific, they are poets with a control freak trait."[63]

This kind of posture towards nationhood is characteristic of much of Leftist and India-centric post-modern thought, and is also reflected in the views of eminent scholars like Romila Thapar, Nivedita Menon, and many other prominent Indian social scientists.[64] They subscribe to the view that since nation and nationalism are recent developments in world history and a result of specific institutional, technological and economic forces during the industrial age, India is therefore an imagined entity and essentially a British project. It is at best a nebulous idea and each community or subaltern group has its own idea of India. This is one of the usual canards raised by many scholars to challenge the antiquity of India as an unified geopolitical entity.

While it is true that India as a nation state may not have existed until recently, that does not mean that India as a civilizational state, subsuming clans, tribes and kingdoms, never existed. When Darius I, in 515 BCE referred to India as the land of the Hind, he, as well as the Indians whom he referred to, had a very good idea of whom Darius was talking about. When Megasthanes (350 BCE) talked about "Indica", and came to India, it was not some imaginary amorphous South Asia that he visited, but a real land with well-defined borders, cultures and practices. Indians had their own traditional categories of *rajya, rashtra* and *desha* to denote various levels of citizenship, and well-known terms of self-identity like

Bharatavarsha and *Aryavarta*.[65] Apart from this, Indians had their own models of civilizational unity, such as sacred geography as encapsulated in the pan-India *tirtha-sthala* (pilgrimage sites) of *Kumbha Mela, Shakti Pithas* and *Jyotirlingas*, and those mentioned in *Ramayana* and *Mahabharata*. Even today across India, when Hindus perform the *jala shuddhi* or water purification ritual, they invoke the seven pan-Indian rivers Ganga, Yamuna, Narmada, Godavari, Sindhu, Saraswati and Kaveri.[66] In other words, from ancient times, Indians had a reasonably clear idea of India's civilizational spread and understood dharma as the unifying principle which bound diverse people, languages, societies and cultures together. Diversity and multiplicity in India is civilizationally bound by the Hindu thread – it is neither chaotic nor a synthetically unified diversity as Pattnaik projects.

It is problematic therefore, when a public intellectual of his stature deliberately chooses to ignore all these conceptions of self-identity. More importantly, India today is a sovereign state with its own Constitution, judiciary and rule of law, and based on democratic ideals. To characterize India as an 'idea' is not only utterly irresponsible but reeks of nefarious intent, because if there is no India in the first place, there cannot be any unifying Indian meta-narrative. India for Pattanaik (2017) is therefore a hodgepodge of different sub-cultures, many of which are incompatible with each other and hence easy to fragment:

> "Indian culture is like a masala box. The dominant spices we identify as Hindu, but not all of them came into being here, or at the same time. Some came into being following indigenous challenges, such as the rise of Buddhism, which introduced ideas of monastic orders. Others came into being following foreign challenges, such as the arrival of the Greeks who introduced the idea of stone temples enshrining stone images of heroes and gods, very different from the portable imageless rituals of Vedic culture, or the river and mountain and tree gods of local tribes. Some spices refuse to be identified as Hindu, but do not mind being called Indian. Some spices insist on being identified as non-Indian. Then there are spices that are best called global, as they are found everywhere."[67]

Constantly harping on diversity, pluralism and multiculturalism in order to question the legitimacy of the state is a typical postmodern posture. Such arguments do not hold water since the same postmodernists do not attempt to analyze American, British, French or Chinese metanarratives, which have in fact become increasingly stronger, especially in a post-Brexit era. Branding and identity are an important aspect of any social group. Every nation, corporate entity, sports team, or even a local library has a distinct identity as a group. Members may come from different backgrounds, but within the organization, have to abide by certain minimum common requirements. In the corporate world, for example, grand narratives are absolutely essential. Would it not be absurd if the company leadership suddenly start insisting that they are postmodernists and do not see any distinction between themselves and their competitors?

Of course, India is a diverse country, with different people, languages, food and practices. Similarly, China is too. Yet China has always had a very distinct identity as a world civilization from ancient times. Today, China has massive programs to propagate its grand narrative, which is based on ancient Confucian thought combined with Taoism, Buddhism and its own kind of modernity. Mandarin has played a very important role in unifying such a large country and in instilling national pride among all Chinese. Every Chinese learns about the greatness and glory of his civilization from ancient to modern times. Not only is this narrative popularized internally within China, but also promoted globally through a large network of Confucius Institutes.[68]

Hindu Hegemony

For Pattanaik (2021), Hinduism is essentially a modern elitist upper-caste hegemonic enterprise which has used violence and intimidation to dominate other castes and communities. The term Hindu, he says, was a foreign term, first used as a self-identifier in the 14th century by Vijayanagar kings to differentiate themselves from foreign Turkish invaders. Although it gained currency across India, it remained an elitist enterprise which had no room for either the untouchables or the tribal communities of India.[69] He says:

> "Poets like Kabir and Chaitanya used the word Hindu loosely to refer to followers of Vedas who saw brahmins as the priests. But did this term apply to the 'untouchables' who were told they were impure by everyone, even new converts to Islam? Does this apply to the tribal communities of India? Did anyone ask them?"[70]

Here too, Pattanaik seems to confuse the concept of Hindu identity and the term 'Hindu'. While the earliest epigraphic evidence of the word Hindu as a self-identifier belongs to the second millennia CE, it does not necessarily mean that Hindus had no idea about their spiritual identity prior to that. The earliest reference to the term Hindu, in fact, appears in the *Zend Avesta*, the book of the ancient Iranians. It refers to a place called *Hapta Hindu*, or land of seven rivers, identical with the Vedic land of *Sapta Sindhavas*, and the connotation is geographical[71] as well as doctrinal.[72] By the time of Darius I in the 5th century BCE, the word was understood to mean the people to the west and east of Indus River, and who followed specific customs and rituals. Sharma (2002) argues that 'Sindhu' as a word acquired different semantic meanings as it traveled to the west and east of India. During the Islamic rule, the Arabic and Persian world was quite clear about the distinction between 'Hind' as a geographical term and 'Hindu' as a religious term.[73] As Elst (2013) points out, when the Muslims invaded India, they used the term Hindu to specifically mean anyone who was a resident of India but not Abrahamic – including so-called savarnas, Jains, Buddhists, low-castes and tribals.[74] This is the same definition which has been officially accepted by the Indian state during the drafting of the Constitution under the leadership of Dr. B.R. Ambedkar, and is reflected in various laws.[75] In other words, the concept of Hindu identity has been well-understood across the board for a very long time, and to insist that Hinduism was an elitist upper-caste fabrication and that people were not consulted while this definition was being constructed is disingenuous to say the least.

Pattanaik (2015) builds upon his thesis by insisting that Hindus are a violent community. In his readings of Jain scriptures, he sees a tension between the Jains' self-view and the views of militant Hindus who consider Jains as a sect of Hinduism. The Jains, he says, have never been able to reconcile to the violent nature of Hinduism:

> "...people simply assume that 'ahimsa' is a Hindu idea, when, in fact, it is a Jain idea and there is a vast amount of literature that shows us how animals were sacrificed during Vedic yagnas, but with the rise of monastic orders like Buddhism, this practice was frowned upon and eventually many brahmins – not all – adopted vegetarianism and saw non-violence as a virtue."[76]

Violence is thus, endemic to Hinduism according to him and he points out (2021) that there are numerous instances of Hindus fighting each other – battle between castes, over cattle, land and women. He also gives an example of India invading foreign lands – the invasion of Malaysia by the naval fleet of the Tamil Chola Empire in 1068 CE, which happened "less than 50 years after Mahmood of Ghazni raided the Somnath temple."[77] He traces this to the Vedas and says that Vedic scriptures "are very clear that violence is a necessary component of existence, if one chooses to be part of existence."[78] Pattanaik (2016) sees caste as playing a major role in the Hindu propensity for violence, inequality and discrimination. The question he asks is if caste is an essential requirement of Hinduism and whether it is traceable to *Vedas, Bhagavad Gita* and *Manusmriti*.[79] Elsewhere, he says (2011) that it is this Vedic conception of caste which has hugely magnified hierarchy and inequality. The Brahmins, Kshatriyas and Vaishyas dominated other members of society on religious, political and economic grounds. He argues that "the idea of human diversity and hierarchy is rooted in hymns that speak of varna" and that the core idea of caste was: "no sharing of women and food with members of other castes."[80]

Pattanaik (2018) attributes the present-day caste system to the chariot-riding Aryan warriors who, in collaboration with mantra-chanting divine mediums, asserted dominance over a large group of people. He blames Brahmins for making the system rigid and it was they who set-up the infrastructure to marginalize and discriminate against ritually unclean people. This system by the Brahmins "dehumanised people, denied them human dignity, and access to common resources like water and education."[81] Hinduism for Pattanaik is therefore, a melting pot of all evils which has ever afflicted mankind since the beginning of human race. It is remarkable how his characterization of Hinduism as an elitist, and inherently discriminatory supremacist project, is no different from that of 11th century CE Muslim historian Albiruni who described Hindus as "haughty, foolishly vain, self-conceited"[82], or of modern Dalit intellectual and Christian sympathizer, Kancha Ilaiah Shepherd who describes Hinduism as being "anti-scientific and anti-nationalistic" and bats for a post-Hindu India.[83] In fact, Pattanaik's views on caste and Hinduism are no different from colonial Indologists who located every possible vice in Hinduism, and conveniently traced it to the Vedas and the so-called chariot-borne invading Aryans. As will be discussed later, Pattanaik relies heavily on the discredited colonial-era Aryan Invasion/ Migration Theory and in the colonial-era construction of caste, to arrive at his characterization of Hinduism as a tool of caste supremacy and Brahminical hegemony.

Characterizing Hinduism as being inherently violent, racist and oppressive, and blaming it all on upper-castes in general or Brahmins in particular, conveniently allows one to whitewash the crimes of foreign invaders. For example, the brutal Islamic invasion of India and centuries of persecution, torture and discrimination of Hindus during the Islamic period can now be viewed in a sympathetic light. The implication is that since Hindus had ostensibly persecuted Jains and Buddhists, and even colonized south-east Asia, they should not complain when they are invaded. This is of course, a spurious argument because of the fundamental differences in the very nature, scale and frequency of the two events. There is little evidence to suggest that Hindus carried out genocides of Buddhists or Jains in the same way that Muslims did of Hindus, Buddhists and Jains; the latter is well-documented in Islamic texts starting from the time of Mahmud Ghazni. Moreover, unlike Muslim invaders, who conquered new lands, to bring them under the pale of Islam, Indian military intervention in foreign lands (a very rare occurrence), were usually for economic purposes, like capturing the lucrative sea route of Malacca Strait.

In all this, Pattanaik's disdain for Hinduism shines forth brightly and it is therefore, quite surprising that someone with such a deep-seated animosity towards Hindu dharma is considered an insider authority on Hinduism!

Passport to Distort

Postmodernism, as a cultural phenomenon emerged primarily as a reaction against the philosophical assumptions of modernity in Western intellectual thought. Many of the ideas associated with Postmodernism are in fact an outright rejection of ideas usually associated with the Enlightenment movement in Europe as well as its derivatives like Marxism and Liberalism. Foucault (1977) argued that 'truth' and 'power' were intricately linked, and that, 'truth' is neither a universal ideal, nor the outcome of liberation. Truth is in fact, produced by power and shaped by different "knowledge regimes" in which certain things are assumed to be true. Every society has its own "general politics" of truth, which informs them what is sanctioned and what is not, and thus, there can be no truth without power.[84] Lyotard (1979) characterized the post-modern era as one which has no sympathy for quintessential enlightenment and modern values like 'reason' and 'truth' and dubs them as totalizing metanarratives. Postmodernism therefore, attacks the very idea of monolithic universals and instead encourages multiplicity of interpretations in the form of little narratives.[85] Butler (2002) says that post-modernists were heavily influenced by the works of Derrida and his central thesis of deconstruction, and believe that relationship between language and the world was not as trustworthy as they have been made out to be traditionally, and that we often tend to privilege "transcendental signifiers" like God or reality to organize our discourse.[86]

Pattanaik uses these ideas of truth, power and metanarratives in his analysis of Hinduism, India and India's past. He incorrectly applies the postmodern critique of the Western universals, which is in essence a critique of culture and society, onto the spiritual domain, and labels spiritual universals and truths as myths. A postmodern analysis of Hinduism is problematic, as it is in direct opposition to the Dharmic worldview, on multiple fronts. Traditionally dharmic knowledge systems can be understood through two categories of texts: *shruti* and *smriti*. Shruti is *apaurusheya*, or knowledge which is non-contingent upon humans, and hence considered spiritual truths. Rishis are considered *mantra drashta*, enlightened beings who "saw" the truth and expressed them in the form of poetry.[87] Postmodernism categorically rejects the notion of any absolute truth, and hence, denies the legitimacy of the shruti texts. More importantly it denies Brahman, the most fundamental truth of Hindu philosophical systems. It not only rejects logic and reasoning (anumana and upamana), but argues that traditional authority (*shabda*) is false, as well as, corrupt and hence, must be rejected, thereby repudiating standardized means of knowledge accepted as valid practices in Indian knowledge systems. What this means is that, everything that is quintessentially Hindu and Indian is rejected by Postmodernism. At the same time, it allows one to interpret texts in myriad ways without recourse to tradition, since the latter is seen as a totalizing hegemonic tool of oppression. This perhaps explains Pattanaik's outlandish and often incorrect interpretation of Hindu sources.

Interpretation of Hindu texts has traditionally been a serious academic endeavor. Only a qualified person belonging to a specific sampradaya, who has undergone systematic training under his *guru* is considered eligible to interpret texts and write commentaries. Not everybody has the *adhikara* or necessary qualification to interpret the *Shastras*, since the subject matter in question is highly technical and requires decades of arduous training. Moreover, any new interpretation should strictly abide by the basic framework of *pramana shastra*. All schools of thought, irrespective of their positions, are based on this epistemology, since it enables one to understand the similarities and differences between two sampradayas by providing a common meeting ground. However, Postmodernism not only denies the importance of adhikara but also does away with the need for pramana shastra (epistemology) itself. Hence, anyone can interpret Hindu texts in whichever way they desire, without being held accountable for mistranslations and misreading. As a postmodern thinker and self-proclaimed mythologist, Pattanaik perhaps feels that he has the license to undertake radical re-interpretation of standard terms and concepts, including precise technical terms, with no recourse to the pre-existing knowledge *parampara* of various sampradayas.

Another problematic issue is that Pattanaik (2013) maps many Western constructs onto Hinduism, ostensibly to highlight differences between Indian and Western thought, but ends up evaluating Hinduism using Abrahamic categories. For example, he equates the idea of the Abrahamic "promised land" to the Hindu ideas of *svarga*, *kailasha* and *vaikuntha*.[88] This is a controversial proposition, because the very notion of a promised land, which can be either a physical place or an imaginary place (heaven), pre-supposes the existence of one God, one Prophet, and one Holy Book. It is inherently discriminatory since it is a place meant only for the "chosen people" and worship of other divinities or idolatry is a punishable offence.[89] The entire premise is that humans do not have any agency and need to be saved by some super-human personality. In Hinduism, there is no concept of any one exclusive God who demands submission of people and designates certain groups as chosen people. *Svarga* for example, is not a physical location to which people can travel at will or under the commandment of some deity or prophet. It is a subtle plane of existence within the cosmos, and *Jivas* who strictly abide by their dharma*s*, reside there temporarily. Once their accrued karma is used up, they return to the mortal plane.[90] Inherent in this, is the idea of reincarnation, which again is something categorically rejected by Abrahamic faiths.

Mapping Western categories onto a dharmic framework is therefore, prone to irreconcilable errors, as it not only creates surface level confusion, but also generates deep-rooted misconceptions and prejudices. Pattanaik (2020) says:

> "Hindus were seen as divided and there was a need for a philosophy to unite everyone... Advaita Vedanta of Adi Shankara seemed the right fit as it transcended Hinduism's polytheistic paganism."[91]

Let us focus on the phrase "polytheistic paganism." Not only are both categories, polytheism and paganism, Judeo-Christian in origin as well as connotation, they are also deeply derogatory, and have been contested by many practitioners as well as academicians alike. Bowersock, Brown, and Grabar (1999) insist that pagan has been a standard "all-embracing, pejorative term for polytheists" and often has the "overtones of the inferior and the commonplace".[92] Lamb (2011) points out how even now Western monotheists denigrate polytheists as ignorant and often equate them with "evil and demonism."[93] Pattanaik does not hesitate to use these disparaging terms, and in fact, seems to build upon his thesis that Hinduism is a rather recent invention of upper-caste Hindus, and an elitist project foisted upon the rest of Indians. Not only is Hinduism seen as an artificial construct, the motivation behind its creation is understood as being purely political.

An important idea which percolates much of Pattanaik's work is his animosity for Hindutva. He (2015) is critical of contemporary Hindu-right politics and equates Hindutva with "militant Brahminism."[94] He (2017) characterizes proponents of Hindutva, as crackpot figures that argue that mythical figures like Shiva, Rama and Krishna were real historical figures, and insist that India was always an advanced civilization "privy to advanced technology such as plastic surgery and even the aeroplane." Hindutva for him, is an inherently discriminatory, intolerant and majoritarian enterprise which considers "secularism as minority appeasement" and sees "doctrines of social justice and gender equality (as) threatening traditional Hindu family values."[95] Hindutva, he says (2021) is a racist and patriarchal system which admires Hitler and Zionists, and wants to impose Hindi across India.[96] At the same time, he points out that Hinduism is not to be confused with Hindutva. He says that Hindutva:

> "...is political in nature, and has a distinct tendency to bristle with rage at even the slightest criticism, howsoever valid, of what are seen as Hindu customs and beliefs."[97]

Publicly Pattanaik insists that Hindutva is a sociopolitical movement while Hinduism is a spiritual movement. But then, what is one to make of the following two statements from an essay (2020) on his views of *Advaita Vedanta*?

> "Advaita Vedanta is the de facto philosophy followed by Hindutva. The reason for this is not spiritual. It is political."
>
> "The idea of Advaita Vedanta being the foundation of Hinduism is relatively new, with origins in writings of the 19th and 20th century Hindu thinkers like Dayanand Saraswati, Vivekananda and Sarvepalli Radhakrishnan."[98]

On the one hand, he equates Advaita and Hinduism, and on the other, he associates Advaita with Hindutva. What this means is that despite all his protests to the contrary, he sees Hindutva as being essentially the same as Hinduism. His criticism of Hindutva as a bigoted, unscientific, and supremacist ideology is therefore equally applicable to Hinduism, as seen in the previous section. By equating Advaita Vedanta and Hindutva, Pattanaik reduces an ancient and sophisticated philosophical tradition followed by millions of Hindus to a contemporary socio-political movement. Moreover, his view that Advaita – by which he presumably means Adi Shankaracharya's interpretation – is the foundation of Hinduism is incorrect. Advaita is one of the many streams thriving in the Hindu ecosystem, and non-dualism is also seen in numerous sampradayas including different post-Shankara Vedanta schools, Kashmir Shaivism as well as many Tantric schools.[99]

Pattanaik's depiction of Hinduism as a spiritual system in perpetual war with nastika sampradayas like Jainas and Buaddhas, as well as being in a constant state of tension because of inter-sect rivalries, is another problematic thesis. Pattanaik deliberately exaggerates the so-called sectarian divide between the dualists and Advaitins, between followers of Bhakti and monastic traditions, and between Sringeri and Kanchi Mutt, and portrays them as major internecine conflicts.[100] Here I am reminded of the first scene of the Tamil movie *Dasavatharam* where Kamal Haasan intentionally exaggerates and plays up the schism between the Shaivites and Vaishnavites, by painting it as a bitter fight to death. Highlighting alleged sectarian divides only helps bolster Pattanaik's thesis that there is no unifying theme in Hinduism. This is not to say that there are no doctrinal differences and that there wasn't the occasional physical conflict. There are and always will be differences between different sampradayas, and it is in fact this diversity of thought that has propelled India's unmatched advancements in diverse domains like philosophies, arts, math and sciences. Unlike in the West, where the relationship between science and religion has been a subject of bitter and acrimonious debate, in Indian knowledge systems, all sciences and arts (*shastras*) are seen as varied manifestations of the fundamental principle of the unity of Brahman. There is neither perpetual war nor vicious antagonism nor a state of studied indifference between the spiritual domain and the domain of logic, reasoning and sciences. Brahman as the Universal Principle is beyond polarities, and every new domain is accepted and welcomed as yet another manifestation, as long as it abides by dharmic principles. For a self-proclaimed expert on Hinduism to not even acknowledge this, and portray the various sects, which adore and worship and follow different aspects of the same ultimate Brahman, as only fighting polarities, betrays his intent. Moreover, by and large, philosophical differences between sampradayas have been traditionally resolved through academic discussions and scholarship. As Kapoor (2005) points out, the intense debates between different groups like *Naiyayikas,* Buddhists and Jainas on epistemological and ontological questions, continued for a staggering period of over twelve centuries![101]

More importantly, from time to time, there have been great rishis and scholars that unified disparate ideas and myriad streams of thoughts into an organic whole without subsuming their individuality. Traditionally it was Vyasa, who is believed to have compiled, organized and standardized the four Vedas from the disparate oral tradition of the rishis and rishikas spread over a large geography and accumulated over centuries and millennia prior to him. Similarly, as Ram (1995) argues, it was Vijnanabhikshu who in the 15th century CE developed a system of thought which seamlessly blended apparently disparate systems like Vedanta, Yoga, and *Samkhya* philosophies into his system of *avibhagadvaita* (Integral Non-dualism).[102] In other words, unlike what Pattanaik suggests, there were more attempts to understand, harmonize, integrate and synthesize wherever possible, purportedly disparate systems, under the broad umbrella of Hinduism, rather than to ameliorate and weaponize dissimilarities.

Another major theme that permeates Pattanaik's scholarship is violence. He is obsessed with conflicts and wars among castes, sects and different groups in India and in his endeavor to show Vedic Hindus (whom he views as descendants of Aryans) as being violent. He literally tortures literary texts to glean non-existent invasions and conquests. Hindu narratives, according to him (2006), retain memories of conflicts between the nomadic invasion-loving Indo-European herdsmen, settled agriculturists, and animist hunter-gatherers of the forest, and he cites the example of Kadru and Vinata from the *Mahabharata* as an example of such a war. His readings of southern Indian folklore suggest that they retain the memories of migration of the *Nagas* from the north after their forest homes were destroyed by migrating Aryas.[103] Pattanaik (2019) is not sure whether to characterize the movement of Brahmins from areas near Saraswati, Ganga, Godavari and Narmada rivers to southern India, as an immigration or invasion. He wonders whether the story of Agastya moving from Kailash to southern India refers to Vedic migration or invasion, while sparing no thought as to why the texts across the canon would fail to mention either.[104]

Incidentally, this obsession with invasions also neatly ties into what Malhotra (2018) refers to as the "Invasion Theory of India" which is widely accepted by many Indologists and social scientists. A legacy of colonial scholarship and its assumptions of teleological historicism, this theory posits that India is a passive entity without any agency, which from time to time undergoes significant historical change under the influence of invasions and immigrations.[105] Thus, the Aryans brought to India Sanskrit language and its associated culture, the ancient Greeks brought philosophy, mathematics and astronomy, the Mughals gave India art, architecture and composite culture, while the British gave India modernity, science, technology and railways. The implication is that if Mughals and British colonialists are to be considered outsiders, then so were the Vedic Aryans or Hindus. At the same time, every significant positive change or major shift in Indian society post-Aryans has been on account of external impetus or invasions, while all social evils in India are attributable to the inherently discriminatory and rigid practices of Brahminical Hinduism.

In fact, Pattanaik (2019) subscribes to the idea that everybody in India is an immigrant:

> "Recent genetic studies have shown that everyone in India is a migrant. If we are all migrants, to whom then does any land belong? On what basis? Does it belong to those who came first, the mool-nivasis as some aboriginal tribal groups have now started identifying themselves?" [106]

This is such an outlandish and unscientific assertion, that one is rendered dumbstruck. According to the "Out of Africa" model of early human migration, which is the currently the dominant model of early migration of anatomically modern humans (Homo sapiens), all modern non-African populations are substantially descended from people who migrated out of Africa starting 100,000 years ago (Nei, 1995)[107], with the last wave being about 70,000–50,000 years old. However, since then, the Indian subcontinent has remained continuously populated for *at least 50,000 years* (Pugach et al. 2013).[108] Surely if a land has been peopled for such a long time and where its natives have lived for thousands of generations, calling everyone a migrant is a stretch. Of course, there have been multiple waves of *small migrations* both out of and into India, a phenomenon that continues till today – but that is something which is not specific to India, and happens all across the world.

Pattanaik's works are therefore, replete with all these categories of errors and debatable positions, and this is particularly troublesome since consumers of his knowledge consider him an expert and figure of authority. They tend to accept his views on Hinduism as authentic without seeing the necessity of undertaking further due diligence. In his analysis of Pattanaik's scholarship, Misra (2017) points out a large number of specific mis-readings, incorrect translations and misinterpretations.[109]

He says that Pattanaik often gets basic facts wrong during his retelling of Purana and Itihasa episodes and assigns motives which are not there in the original texts. He also invents etymologies of many Sanskrit words and ascribes new meanings to standard Sanskrit terms. Pattanaik loves to read sex, violence, lesbian, gay, bisexual and transgender themes in Hindu texts even when nothing of this sort exists. Seeing two *gopis* together in a picture, Pattanaik concluded that they are lesbians, although as Misra points out there is nothing in our tradition to suggest lesbianism in such a context.

In fact, Pattanaik (2021) appears to consider the entire institution of marriage a patriarchal ploy denying married women the right to choose men outside their marriages; he uses itihasas, puranas and other texts to somehow justify his positions. Demure and domesticated wives such as Anasuya and Arundhati are praised, he says, whereas adulterous wives like Ahalya are punished, and for Pattanaik this is yet another example of patriarchal domination.[110] Pattanaik narrates an incident from the Bhil version of *Mahabharata*, where Radha has an affair with a handsome bangle-seller, who eventually turns out to be Krishna himself. From the absence of any anger on Krishna's part, he concludes that Krishna accepted and endorsed infidelity. Similarly, from the story of Vasuki and Arjuna, he argues that at no point does Arjuna expect fidelity from his wife.[111] In other words, Pattanaik sees the Brahmanical version of the epics as being essentially patriarchal, and unwilling to accept the sovereignty of women's desire independent of the institution of marriage. As a postmodern intellectual, Pattanaik challenges what Vorster (2016) refers to as the "old idea of heterosexual official marriages" and in its stead encourages "new forms of civil relationships". The idea of 'sanctity' in marriage is deemed irrelevant and marriage is seen "as a social construct that is fully determined by various historic and contemporary cultural situations."[112]

Pattanaik distorts well-established philosophical ideas and misrepresents them as socio-political issues. For example, as Misra (2017) points out, Pattanaik mis-translates critical philosophical words like *brahman*, *adhyatma* and *adhidaiva* by relating them to mind and body. He incorrectly translates *brahmana* as expanding the mind, an interpretation not found in any known Sanskrit dictionary or *nirukti*, and in twenty-eight instances in *My Gita* (2015) uses the word in this erroneous sense.[113] Misra is perplexed at how Pattanaik ignores well-established traditional interpretations, and is quite critical of Pattanik's questionable interpretation of well-established concepts:

> "The book—categorised as 'non-fiction/philosophy' on its back cover by Rupa Publications—is replete with errors. Its interpretations display a lack of basic knowledge of Sanskrit. The philosophical elements are a hodgepodge (or 'masala-mix') of terms, ideas, and concepts drawn from various kinds of sources, including probably the author's own imagination, and presented as if they are based on Hindu texts. The work falls short when it comes to both nuanced details as well as the big picture. Consequently, one of the core texts of Hindu philosophy has been trivialised to a deficient caricature."[114]

Aryans and Invasions

Regarding the origin of Indo-European languages and ancient Indian history, Pattanaik (2017) accepts the Aryan Migration Theory (AMT) as a "scientific theory" explaining the origin of Sanskrit. Pattanaik points out that the AMT is viewed negatively among the Hindutva circle, as they consider it a newer version of "the old discarded colonial Aryan Invasion Theory (AIT)."[115] He (2019) subscribes to the view that the so-called Vedic Aryans as a distinct group of migrants who spoke proto-Indo European languages and brought Vedic culture to India, after Harappan cities had collapsed.

> "DNA studies are now showing that Harappans did not have genes of steppe pastoralists (Aryans). But these Aryan genes are found in about 30 per cent of the Indian population. This means the Aryans came after Harappan cities had collapsed. They did not invade Harappa, but many Aryan men, who came in waves, over centuries, certainly did migrate and marry Harappan women. More accurately, Aryan men married women whose ancestors built Harappan cities, and who followed Harappan customs."[116]

Pattanaik (2011) concedes that AIT is based on the Western template of a violent conflict where the winner always overwhelms the loser, yet he believes that "any alternate theory, howsoever rational, as a result, sounds defensive and apologetic, and so is invalidated even before it is presented."[117] He (2017) insists, that proponents of Hindutva prefer the Out of India Theory (OIT) according to which, Indo-European languages spread out of India to the whole world, and their speakers the Vedic Aryans were "100 per cent Indian with no foreign contamination."[118] According to him, proponents of Hindutva believe, that all that is good in the world, including plastic surgery are products of the Vedic civilization, while all social evils like casteism originated from dark-complexioned non-Aryans. He dubs the OIT as a Hindutva supremacist ideology which claims that Indian-ness originated in the Vedas alone,[119] and as Right-wing propaganda as ludicrous as flat-earth theory in America.[120]

Discussing the various positions held by scholars in the Aryan Migration theory versus Out of India Theory debate is beyond the scope of this essay. Rather, we will try to see how much Pattanaik's positions differ from that of the Hindu tradition he claims to represent. None of the Itihasas, Puranas or Shastras, refer to any specific Aryan race, or have any memory of a distant foreign homeland from where the Aryans supposedly came to India. This absence has been pointed out time and again by many prominent historians since the colonial times when these racial theories first started developing, along with Hindu spiritual giants like Sri Aurobindo and Swami Vivekananda, in the previous century. Sri Aurobindo insisted that the difference between Aryan and un-Aryan was "a cultural rather than a racial difference."[121] Swami Vivekananda dubbed the entire scholarship about Aryans coming from some foreign land and invading India as "fanciful ideas" and "pure nonsense."[122] Using a *Nyaya* framework, the present author (2019) has demonstrated how traditional authority figures (*aptas*) such as Swami Vivekananda, Sri Aurobindo, and Sri Sri Ravi Shankar have categorically rejected the Aryan invasion/migration theory.[123] A detailed analysis by Sastry and Kalyanasundaram (2019), of thirteen different Sanskrit sources to understand the context and nature of the occurrences of the terms *arya* and *dravida* in Sanskrit literature, not only demonstrates the complete absence of any Aryan invasion/migration event in literary records, but also reinforces the traditional understanding of the term arya as a person of "cultural refinement and noble standing."[124] Moreover, genetics may inform us about the makeup of certain individuals or populations and the migrations of certain people, but it cannot tell us the language spoken by the migrants or about the spread of languages. The relation between genetics and linguistics is no different from the relation between nasal index/skull-measurement based anthropology and race science a century ago.

Pattanaik trivializes the entire scholarship under the broad umbrella of Out of India Theory/Indigenous Aryan theory, by labeling all its supporters as proponents of Hindutva, and by characterizing them as fringe elements and chauvinists who believe in plastic surgery and nuclear wars in ancient India. He summarily dismisses the scholarship of numerous serious Indian, as well as Western scholars who have proposed different models for decades, without even a modicum of investigation, thereby demonstrating his own vested interests and intolerance towards alternate viewpoints. As early as 1930, Lachhmi Dhar had provided a linguistic model for an Out of India Theory. Sethna (1992) as well as Kenoyer (1997) theorized that Indo-European languages were spoken in a large area spanning north-western Indian subcontinent in the east and Caspian Sea to the west, and from there it spread to Europe.[125] Elst (1996) proposed a linguistic model explaining how Proto-Indo European languages developed in India, and how "other Indo-European languages left India at various stages, some of them preserving particular Proto-Indo-European linguistic features that were not preserved in Vedic."[126] Apart from this, scholars like Nicholas Kazanas, Igor Tonoyan-Belyayev and Aleksandr Semenenko have also contributed significantly to OIT scholarship.[127]

Shrikant Talageri's comprehensive model explaining the origins of Aryan culture within India, and the spread of Indo-European languages in various waves, is yet to be challenged by any mainstream proponent of AIT. Based on an extensive investigation of the *Rig Veda*, *Avesta* and archaeological evidence in terms of Mitanni inscription, Talageri provides a dateable model which reconciles dispersal of IE-languages as well as physical migration of tribes mentioned in Vedas and Puranas like *Anu* and *Druhyu*.[128] His two books *The Rigveda, A Historical Analysis* (2000) and *The Veda and the Avesta, the Final Evidence* (2008), along with his articles in various websites provide a comprehensive linguistic model explaining the OIT, and challenging the AIT/AMT. But Pattanaik, dismisses his entire scholarship and wonders whether Talageri knows Sanskrit or not.[129] Dismissing counter-theories without even bothering to examine them, and then indulging in polemics against opponents is but a single example of Pattanaik's questionable scholarship.

Hindu tradition is essentially indifferent to the question of Aryan invasion. Since the entire construct of Aryan race and Proto-Indo-European homeland was a product of 19th century European Indology, Sanskrit works produced before such time, have no reference to AIT/AMT. Vedic knowledge is considered *apaurusheya* and not contingent upon human inputs, and hence, unconcerned about issues like AIT/OIT. However, given that AIT was proposed and did develop into a full-fledged model in Western academia, many academic and spiritual teachers like Swami Vivekananda and Sri Aurobindo defended their tradition by categorically rejecting the theory.[130] In this respect also, Pattanaik's position is diametrically opposite to Hindu tradition that he claims to represent.

Conclusion

As is evident, Pattanaik's understanding of Hinduism is significantly different from that of most of the well-known sampradayas, and practitioners of faith may find his view incorrect, bizarre and often controversial. His scholarship is replete with what any serious and unbiased researcher, would consider blatant falsehoods and gross misrepresentations. In terms of traditional Indian categories, Pattanaik may be classified as a 'Charvaka'. As noted earlier, historically Charvakas were bitterly opposed to the Vedic system as well as other *shramanic* sects. Therefore, a Charvaka claiming to represent and popularize

Hinduism, is as ludicrous and dangerous, as a Pakistani coach advising Indian cricket players on how to win the World Cup. By systematically sabotaging from inside that which they are supposed to represent they cause irreparable harm. Pattanaik is a very influential and powerful figure in the postmodern camp, and his characterization of Hinduism as a problem-ridden system with inbuilt discrimination, casteism, patriarchy, misogyny and racism is readily accepted by his millions of followers who do not doubt his academic credibility. His creative output in terms of popular books, TV programs, YouTube videos and sketches, inform the views of a large section of Hindus and non-Hindus alike, both in India and abroad.

As noted by Gerbner (1969), long-term exposure to extremely negative portrayal of a society, make people interpret social realities in a way which is closer to how they are portrayed in the media.[131] Nabi & Riddle (2008) based on a study on the impact of different personality traits on perceptions of violence, concluded that people across the board are susceptible to either cultivation regarding personal vulnerability to crime or to cultivation regarding societal violence perceptions.[132] Pattanaik's view of Hinduism as a violent and divisive system, therefore, becomes accepted as an authentic representation of Hindu dharma. In fact, it is likely that prolonged and consistent media exposure to the same biased ideas over and over again, may end up mainstreaming such views, as noted by Griffin (2012); as pointed out by Gerbner (1998) people then suddenly start finding resonance or similarities between their lives and what they see on screen.[133] Hinduism is perceived as being even more brutal, militant, divisive and patriarchal; and Hindus end up suffering from a greater sense of anxiety, pessimism, an inferiority complex and become more vehement in criticizing their native traditions.

Pattanaik's prejudiced deconstruction of Hinduism, Indian civilization and Indian nation state, ostensibly in the guise of academic freedom, not only feeds into academia, but also impacts the general populace through media, judiciary, civil services and the executive. Laws or policies enacted based on such questionable Western models of state and societies have real-life social and economic impact – often negatively impacting family structures, marriages, and relationship between different groups. The fact that Postmodernism rejects grand narratives and by extension ideas like sovereignty and nation-states, is another challenge because the very legitimacy of India as a nation-state is challenged. India is seen as a battleground of different subalterns fighting against the hegemonic state, and each myriad group has its own idea of India. India is thus, not a single unified entity with minimum common principles and shared past as behooves a nation, but as a marketplace of competing identities, ideologies, narratives and histories. As Appiah (1992) points out, Postmodernism emerged as a response to Eurocentric hegemony attitudes masquerading as universalism, and not as a response to universalism per se.[134] It opposed the universality assumed by the white, male, heterosexual, Western viewpoint, and is therefore, a Western solution to a Western problem, which uses a Western map of categories. It is an etic perspective when it pertains to Hinduism, and Pattanaik is no different from a Western trained anthropologist or sociologist analyzing India and Hinduism. Malhotra (2016) says in this regard:

> "Postmodernism has provided academic respectability to a whole generation of bright Indians to deconstruct their own nationality and civilization. The self-flagellation is made fashionable by association with West-based, 'successful' Indian scholars, and is encouraged through funding and career paths. India is to be replaced by a large number of 'sub-nations' according to this trendy theory."[135]

It is necessary for those with a dharmic inclination to not only understand why his interpretations of Hindu texts are radically different from traditional interpretations, but also, how such views have negative real-world implications. In the Hindu tradition, Ravana is often depicted as an extraordinarily brilliant but flawed figure. Ravana was a great devotee of Shiva, a scholar par excellence, and a great performer of *yajna*s, and in that sense, he was a Dharmic individual. Yet, because he ultimately followed the path of *adharma*, he lost the battle against Lord Rama. Today, in Hindu thought, Ravana is the embodiment of adharma and everything that is undesirable. If dharma is to be accepted as the absolute gold standard that defines Hinduism, then it is clear, that Devdutt

Pattanaik's scholarship promotes adharma in the guise of glorifying dharma. Just as Ravana kidnapped Sita and carried her away to Lanka, in the same way, Pattanaik has hijacked traditional discourses on Hinduism and popularized a flawed postmodern and Left-liberal compliant domesticated *avatar* of Hinduism. Many of the core ideas of Pattanaik are opposed to dharma and need to be brought to light systematically and with determination, in the same way as Sita was rescued from Lanka. In this essay, I have performed an initial *purvapaksha* of Devdutt Pattanaik's scholarship, identified issues where his views differ significantly from that of the tradition that he claims to represent and responded to some of his more bizarre and controversial claims. His scholarship must be understood for what it is – a nastika view of Hinduism masquerading as an insider astika view. It is imperative that traditional scholars of Hinduism and Sanskrit studies, understand and respond to his work and counter his misinterpretations and distortions.

Bibliography

Appiah, Kwame A. 1992. *In My Father's House: Africa in the Philosophy of Culture*. New York: Oxford University Press.

Badrinath, Chaturvedi. 2019. "What the Iranian scholar Albiruni said about Hindus, echoed centuries later by Vivekananda." Scroll. Retrieved April 30, 2022 (https://scroll.in/article/938208/what-the-iranian-scholar-albiruni-said-about-hindus-echoed-centuries-later-by-vivekananda).

Bhattacharjee, K. 2019. "From 'Devi' to 'Chup Chudail': Devdutt Pattanaik's fall from grace with obnoxious tweets involving women." OpIndia. Retrieved April 30, 2022 (https://www.opindia.com/2019/10/devdutt-pattanaik-abuse-against-women-on-twitter/).

Bowersock, G.W., Peter Brown, and Oleg Grabar. 1999. *Late Antiquity: A Guide to the Postclassical World*. Cambridge, Massachusetts, and London, England: Harvard University Press.

Bryant, Edwin. 2001. *The Quest for the Origins of Vedic Culture*. New York: Oxford University Press.

Bryant, Edwin F. 2009. *The Yoga Sutras of Patanjali*. Berkeley, California: North Point Press.

Butler, Christopher. 2002. *Postmodernism: A Very Short Introduction.* Oxford: Oxford University Press.

Chaudhuri, Roma. 2012. *Ten Schools of Vedanta.* Kolkata: Rabindra Bharati University.

Dasgupta, Surendranath. 1932. *A History of Indian Philosophy Vol. I.* London: Cambridge University Press.

DevduttMyth. 2018. "Devdutt Pattaniak explains the difference between Mythology & Fiction." YouTube. Retrieved October 18, 2021 (https://www.youtube.com/watch?v=I2Jk70YOCaA).

Dundes, Alan. 1984. *Sacred Narrative: Readings in the Theory of Myth.* Berkeley, Los Angeles, London: University of California Press.

Elst, Koenraad. 2013. "Buddha was every inch a Hindu." Bharata Bharati. Retrieved April 30, 2022 (https://bharatabharati.in/2013/08/10/buddha-was-every-inch-a-hindu-koenraad-elst/).

Elst, Koenraad 2019. "The unique place of Shrikant Talageri's contribution to the Indo-European Homeland debate." in *Genetics and the Aryan Debate: "Early Indians" Tony Joseph's Latest Assault.* Delhi: Voice of India.

Foucault, Michel. 1980. *Power/knowledge: Selected Interviews and Other Writings, 1972-1977.* New York: Pantheon Books.

Gerbner, George. 1969. "Toward" cultural indicators": The analysis of mass mediated public message systems." *AV communication review* 137-148.

Gerbner, George. 1998. "Cultivation analysis: An overview." *Mass communication and society* 1(3-4):175-194.

Graham, Billy. 2010. "Have You Heard the Good News of Salvation?" Billy Graham Evangelistic Association. Retrieved April 30, 2022 (https://billygraham.org/story/have-you-heard-the-good-news-of-salvation/).

Graves, Robert 1968. "New Larousse Encyclopedia of Mythology (trans. Richard Aldington and Delano Ames)." Pp. v-viii in *Introduction.* London: Hamlyn.

Griffin, Emory. 2012. *A First Look at Communication Theory.* 8th ed. New York: McGraw-Hill.

Hardon, John A. 1998. "The Resurrection of Jesus." The Real Presence Association. Retrieved April 30, 2022 (http://www.therealpresence.org/archives/Prayer/Prayer_029.htm).

HISTORY. 2016. "Ancient Aliens: The Mighty Shiva (Season 11, Episode 15)." YouTube. Retrieved April 30, 2022 (https://www.youtube.com/watch?v=NFxJeu7x9Uk).

Ilaiah, Kancha. 2009. *Post-Hindu India: A Discourse in Dalit-Bahujan, Socio-Spiritual and Scientific Revolution.* New Delhi: SAGE India.

IPPAI SPEAKS. 2015. "Mr. Devdutt Pattanaik, Author, Mythologist." YouTube. Retrieved October 18, 2021 (https://www.youtube.com/watch?v=jAm8Q0TyHFo).

Islampurkar, Vaman S. 1893. *The Parasara Dharma Samhita Or Parasara Smriti with the Commentary of Sayana Madhavacharya: Vol I, Part I.* Bombay: Government Central Book Depot.

Jackson, A.V. W. 1922. "The Persian Dominions in Northern India Down to the Time of Alexander's Invasion." Pp. 319-344 in *Ancient India*, edited by E. J. Rapson. Cambridge, U.K: Cambridge University Press.

Jayaraman, Gayatri. 2013. "Devdutt Pattanaik on how to be the ideal manager by understanding gods." India Today. Retrieved April 30, 2022 (https://www.indiatoday.in/india/north/story/devdutt-pattanaik-how-to-be-the-ideal-manager-understanding-gods-india-today-158479-2013-04-11).

Kapoor, Kapil. 2005. *Dimensions of Panini Grammar: The Indian Grammatical System.* New Delhi: D.K. Print World Ltd.

Lamb, Ramdas. 2011. "Polytheism and Monotheism: A Hindu Perspective." HuffPost. Retrieved April 30, 2022 (https://www.huffpost.com/entry/polytheism-and-monotheism_b_841905).

Leach, Maria and Jerome Fried. 1984. *Funk & Wagnalls Standard Dictionary of Folklore, Mythology, and Legend.* New York: Harper & Row.

Lokeswarananda, Swami. 1989. *Studies on the Tantras.* Kolkata: Ramkrishna Mission Institute of Culture.

Lyotard, Jean-François. 1984. *The Postmodern Condition: A Report on Knowledge.* Manchester: Manchester University Press.

Malhotra, Rajiv. 2011. "Dharma Is Not The Same As Religion." Huffpost. Retrieved April 30, 2022 (https://www.huffpost.com/entry/dharma-religion_b_875314).

Malhotra, Rajiv. 2016. *The Battle for Sanskrit*. Noida: HarperCollins Publishers India.

Malhotra, Rajiv. 2018. "Weaving India's MAHAKATHA (Grand Narrative) for the 21st Century." rajivmalhotra.com. Retrieved October 18, 2021 (https://rajivmalhotra.com/wp-content/uploads/2018/04/Weaving-Indias-MAHAKATHA-Grand-Narrative-for-the-21st-Century_RML-20Mar2018.docx-1.pdf).

Mishra, Rambhavan and Lalbihari Mishra. 2017. *Nitya Karm Puja Prakasha*. Kolkata: Gita Press Gorakhpur.

Misra, Nityanand. 2017a. "Not Just His Gita, It's Pattanaik's Own Fantasy World." Swarajya. Retrieved November 28, 2019 (https://swarajyamag.com/culture/not-just-his-gita-its-pattanaiks-own-fantasy-world).

Misra, Nityanand. 2017b. "Notes to the review of Devdutt Pattanaik's 'My Gita'." Academia. Retrieved April 30, 2022 (https://www.academia.edu/31277814/Notes_to_the_review_of_Devdutt_Pattanaik_s_My_Gita_).

Molher Jr., R. A. 2009. "The Mythology of Star Wars: The Faith versus the Force." Albert Nohler. Retrieved April 30, 2022 (https://albertmohler.com/2009/07/16/the-mythology-of-star-wars-the-faith-versus-the-force).

Mukhopadhyay, Subhodeep. 2019. "Yogic Perceptions of Aryan-Dravidian Controversy." *Proceedings of Swadeshi Indology Conference Series* Studies in Tamil Civilization(Fount of Culture):245-260.

Nabi, Robin L. and Karyn Riddle. 2008. "Personality traits, television viewing, and the cultivation effect." *Journal of Broadcasting & Electronic Media* 52(3):327-348.

National Geographic. 2017. "Experience the Tomb of Christ Like Never Before." YouTube. Retrieved April 30, 2022 (https://www.youtube.com/watch?v=t9GU_e6Pn28).

Nei, Masatoshi. 1995. "Genetic support for the out-of-Africa theory of human evolution." *Proceedings of the National Academy of Sciences of the United States of America* 92(15):6720-6722. (https://www.ncbi.nlm.nih.gov/pmc/articles/PMC41400/pdf/pnas01491-0076.pdf).

Paranjape, Makarand R. 2021. "Dharma is not the same as religion." The New Indian Express. Retrieved April 30, 2022 (https://www.newindianexpress.com/opinions/columns/2021/jul/24/dharma-is-not-the-same-as-religion-2334479.html).

Parthasarathy, A. 2017. *Bhagavad Gita*. 3rd ed. Mumbai: A. Parthasarathy.

Pattanaik, Devdutt. 2003. *Indian Mythology: Tales, Symbols, and Rituals from the Heart of the Subcontinent*. Rochester, Vermont: Inner Traditions.

Pattanaik, Devdutt. 2006a. *myth = mithya*. New Delhi: Penguin.

Pattanaik, Devdutt. 2006b. "Myth as History." devdutt.com. Retrieved December 5, 2019 (https://devdutt.com/articles/myth-as-history/).

Pattanaik, Devdutt. 2011a. "Passport Caste." devdutt.com. Retrieved February 15, 2020 (https://devdutt.com/articles/passport-caste/).

Pattanaik, Devdutt. 2011b. "Politics of Origin." Devdutt. Retrieved November 26, 2019 (https://devdutt.com/articles/politics-of-origin/).

Pattanaik, Devdutt. 2015a. "Devdutt Pattanaik on the rise of non-violent terrorism." DailyO. Retrieved November 27, 2019 (https://www.dailyo.in/politics/devdutt-pattanaik-non-violent-terrorism-hindutva-jainism-hindus-gandhi-ahimsa-militant/story/1/6156.html).

Pattanaik, Devdutt. 2015b. "Cow slaughter and dharma." DailyO. Retrieved November 29, 2019 (https://www.dailyo.in/politics/maharashtra-beef-ban-cow-slaughter-and-dharma-devendra-fadnavis/story/1/2389.html).

Pattanaik, Devdutt. 2016. "Beyond Hinduism: Is caste a religious or a regional problem?" Scroll. Retrieved November 26, 2019 (https://scroll.in/article/802759/beyond-hinduism-is-caste-a-religious-or-a-regional-problem).

Pattanaik, Devdutt. 2017a. "A plea for 'alternative facts': When truth is singular it becomes a territory and thus, a battlefield." The Times of India Blogs. Retrieved November 27, 2019 (https://timesofindia.indiatimes.com/blogs/toi-edit-page/a-plea-for-alternative-facts-when-truth-is-singular-it-becomes-a-territory-and-thus-a-battlefield/).

Pattanaik, Devdutt. 2017b. "Devdutt Pattanaik: Itihasa is not fantasy." Mid-Day. Retrieved December 5, 2019 (https://www.mid-day.com/articles/devdutt-pattanaik-itihasa-is-not-fantasy/18305159).

Pattanaik, Devdutt. 2017c. "Is Hinduism the same as Hindutva?" Devdutt. Retrieved November 27, 2019 (https://devdutt.com/articles/is-hinduism-the-same-as-hindutva/).

Pattanaik, Devdutt. 2017d. "How Sanskrit evolved in India." Devdutt. Retrieved November 26, 2019 (https://devdutt.com/articles/how-sanskrit-evolved-in-india/).

Pattanaik, Devdutt. 2017e. "Did arrival of Muslim invaders a thousand years ago destroy Hindu culture?" DailyO. Retrieved December 3, 2019 (https://www.dailyo.in/variety/muslim-invaders-hinduism-india-bharat-islam-christanity/story/1/17529.html).

Pattanaik, Devdutt. 2018. "Were Hindus always casteist?" DailyO. Retrieved November 27, 2019 (https://www.dailyo.in/variety/hindus-caste-devdutt-pattanaik-brahmins-kshatriyas-vaishyas-shudras/story/1/21555.html).

Pattanaik, Devdutt. 2019a. "Vedantic attachment and Islamic idolatry." The Hindu. Retrieved November 27, 2019 (https://www.thehindu.com/opinion/op-ed/vedantic-attachment-and-islamic-idolatry/article30069843.ece).

Pattanaik, Devdutt. 2019b. "Harappan and Aryan roots of Rig Veda." Mid-day. Retrieved November 29, 2019 (https://www.mid-day.com/articles/harappan-and-aryan-roots-of-rig-veda/21729187).

Pattanaik, Devdutt. 2020. "What They Don't Tell You About Advaita." devdutt,com. Retrieved June 9, 2021 (https://devdutt.com/articles/what-they-dont-tell-you-about-advaita/).

Pattanaik, Devdutt. 2021a. "Hindutva: A Sampradaya, Not a Parampara." devdutt.com. Retrieved June 9, 2021 (https://devdutt.com/articles/hindutva-a-sampradaya-not-a-parampara/).

Pattanaik, Devdutt. 2021b. "Were Hindus Ever Invaders?" devdutt.com. Retrieved June 9, 2021 (https://devdutt.com/articles/were-hindus-ever-invaders/).

Pattanaik, Devdutt. 2021c. "Can the Ramayana Be Feminist?" devdutt.com.

Retrieved June 9, 2021 (https://devdutt.com/articles/can-the-ramayana-be-feminist/).

Pattanaik, Devdutt. 2021d. "Does the Mahabharata Respect Women's Desire?" devdutt.com. Retrieved June 9, 2021 (https://devdutt.com/articles/does-the-mahabharata-respect-womens-desire/).

Pugach, Irina, Frederick Delfina, Ellen Gunnarsdóttir, Manfred Kayser, and Mark Stoneking. 2013. "Genome-wide data substantiate Holocene geneflow from India to Australia." *Proceedings of the National Academy of Sciences* 110(5):1803-1808. (https://www.pnas.org/doi/full/10.1073/pnas.1211927110).

Raghavendra, M.K. 2018. "The problem with Devdutt Pattanaik's approach to mythology, with self-improvement as the agenda." Firstpost. Retrieved April 30, 2022 (https://www.firstpost.com/living/the-problem-with-devdutt-pattanaiks-approach-to-mythology-with-self-improvement-as-the-agenda-4378531.html).

Rajiv Malhotra Official. 2018. "Demolishing Devdutt Pattanaik Point by Point in Detail." YouTube. Retrieved October 18, 2021 (https://www.youtube.com/watch?v=vtkMFLuOa3M).

Rajiv Malhotra Official. 2019. "Decolonizing Romila Thapar: Nation & Nationalism - 1/5." Rajiv Malhotra Official. Retrieved October 18, 2021 (https://www.youtube.com/watch?v=s-VD_nnsVqE).

Ram, Kanshi. 1995. *Integral Non-Dualism: A Critical Exposition of Vijnanabhiksu's System of Philosophy*. Delhi: Motilal Banarsidass Publishers.

Samim Asgor Ali Photographer. 2016. "Prof. Nivedita Menon's Lecture on Nationalism at JNU Alternative Classroom (HD)." YouTube. Retrieved March 31, 2022 (https://www.youtube.com/watch?v=0eOYTp5Do2c).

Sastry, Manogna and Megh Kalyansundaram. 2019. "The A of ABC of Indian chronology: Dimensions of the Aryan problem revisited in 2017." *Proceedings from the Swadeshi Indology Conference Series* Studies in Tamil Civilisation(Land of Dharma):87-130.

Satprakashananda, Swami. 1974. *Methods of Knowledge*. Kolkata: Advaita Ashrama.

Sen, Debarati S. 2013. "Devdutt Patnaik roped for Mahabharat." The Times of India. Retrieved April 30, 2022 (https://timesofindia.indiatimes.com/tv/news/hindi/Renowned-author-Devdutt-is-all-set-to-make-his-off-screen-TV-debut-with-Mahabharat-/articleshow/22255263.cms).

Sharma, Arvind. 2002. "On Hindu, Hindustān, Hinduism and Hindutva." *Numen* 49(1):1-36.

Signoracci, Gino. 2017. *Hegel on Indian Philosophy: Spinozism, Romanticism, Eurocentrism.* New Mexico: University of New Mexico. (https://digitalrepository.unm.edu/cgi/viewcontent.cgi?article=1022&context=phil_etds).

Singh, Pooja. 2016. "Devdutt Pattanaik's business lessons from mythology." Mint. Retrieved April 30, 2022 (https://www.livemint.com/news/business-of-life/devdutt-pattanaik-s-business-lessons-from-mythology-1541246780620.html).

Srinivasan, Madhumitha. 2021. "India in a nutshell." The Hindu. Retrieved April 30, 2022 (https://www.thehindu.com/education/india-in-a-nutshell/article34734361.ece).

Stewart, Don. 2018. "What Are the Major Protestant Theological Systems: Calvinism, Arminianism, Lutheranism, and Anglicanism?" Blue Letter Bible. Retrieved April 30, 2022 (https://www.blueletterbible.org/Comm/stewart_don/faq/bible-basics/question20-what-are-the-major-protestant-theological-systems.cfm).

Stewart, Jon. 2022. *An Introduction to Hegel's Lectures on the Philosophy of Religion: The Issue of Religious Content in the Enlightenment and Romanticism.* Oxford University Press: Oxford.

Talageri, Shrikant. 2019. *Genetics and the Aryan debate: "Early Indians" Tony Joseph's Latest Assault.* New Delhi: Voice of India.

TEDIndia. 2009. "East vs. West -- the myths that mystify." TED. Retrieved April 30, 2022 (https://www.ted.com/talks/devdutt_pattanaik_east_vs_west_the_myths_that_mystify).

TEDx Talks. 2013. "The Indian approach to business: Devdutt Pattanaik at TEDxGateway 2013." YouTube. Retrieved October 18, 2021 (https://www.youtube.com/watch?v=KcrUs8FAt40).

The Wire. 2017. "Romila Thapar on nationalism and the role of public intellectuals." YouTube. Retrieved April 30, 2022 (https://www.youtube.com/watch?v=kV7hfUhNIHk).

Thury, Eva M. and Margaret K. Devinney. 2017. *Introduction to Mythology: Contemporary Approaches to Classical and World Myths.* New York, Oxford: Oxford University Press.

Vorster, Jakobus M. 2016. "Marriage and family in view of the doctrine of the covenant." *HTS Teologiese Studies/Theological Studies* 72(3):1-8.

Yadav, Sangeeta. 2017. "God of small screen." The Pioneer. Retrieved April 30, 2022 (https://www.dailypioneer.com/2017/sunday-edition/god-of-small-screen.html).

Zavada, Jack. 2014. "The Promised Land in the Bible Was God's Gift to Israel." Learn Religions. Retrieved April 30, 2022 (https://www.learnreligions.com/what-is-the-promised-land-699948).

Notes

1. "Devdutt Pattanaik." devdutt.com. Retrieved April 30, 2022 (https://devdutt.com/about).
2. TED (Technology, Entertainment, Design) is an American media company that organizes free online talks by experts in various domains under the slogan "ideas worth spreading." See: "TED Ideas worth spreading." ted.com. Retrieved April 30, 2022 (https://www.ted.com).
3. (TEDIndia 2009)
4. (Yadav 2017)
5. (Srinivasan 2021)
6. (Sen 2013)
7. "Devdutt Pattanaik@devduttmyth." Twitter. Retrieved April 30, 2022 (https://twitter.com/devduttmyth).
8. See: (Misra 2017a) and (Rajiv Malhotra Official 2018)
9. "So easy to fool idiots. Don't know difference between 'invention' and 'popularising'. Did your mother feed these @TIinExile bitches while menstruating ??????". Twitter. Retrieved April 30, 2022 (https://i0.wp.

com/www.opindia.com/wp-content/uploads/2020/02/fgf.jpg). Original Tweet has been deleted by the author.

"For her abuse is like 🌶 as she is into slapping insulting and BDSM. I support her perversion." Twitter. Retrieved April 30, 2022 (https://twitter.com/devduttmyth/status/1230117081569517569).

"She will swallow the pea and the pee as part of BDSM." Twitter. Retrieved April 30, 2022 (https://twitter.com/onlinecolloquy/status/1223726656197660674/photo/1). Original Tweet has been deleted by the author.

10. (Bhattacharjee 2019)

11. dhāraṇād dharma ityāhurdharmo dhārayate prajāḥ
    | yat syād dhāraṇasaṃyuktaṃ sa dharma iti niścayaḥ ||

12. The meaning of dharma is narrower in spiritual systems of the Bauddhas and the Jainas, but they make use of the same nomenclature and epistemology as the parent system from which they evolved.

13. dhṛtiḥ kṣamā damo'steyaṃ śaucamindriyanigrahaḥ |
    dhīrvidyā satyamakrodho daśakaṃ dharmalakṣaṇam || - *Manusmriti* 6.92
    ahiṃsā satyamasteyaṃ śaucamindriyanigraḥ |
    dānaṃ damo dayā kṣāntiḥ sarveṣāṃ dharmasādhanam ||
    - *Yajnavalkyasmriti* 1.122

14. abhyudaya-niśreyase sādhanasattvena dhārayati iti dharmaḥ ı
    See: (Islampurkar 1893:63)

15. See: (Malhotra 2011) and (Paranjape 2021)

16. "Bharat ka Samvidhan." Government of India – Legislative Department. Retrieved April 30, 2022 (https://legislative.gov.in/sites/default/files/Hindi.pdf).

17. (Pattanaik 2015b)

18. tādṛśo'yamanupraśno yatra dharmaḥ sudurlabhaḥ ı
    duṣkaraḥ pratisaṃkhyātuṃ tatkenātra vyavasyati ıı
    prabhavārthāya bhūtānāṃ dharmapravacanaṃ kṛtam ı
    yaḥ syātprabhavasaṃyuktaḥ sa dharma iti niścayaḥ ıı

19. purāṇanyāyamīmāṃsādharmaśāstrāṅgamiśritāḥ ı
    vedāḥ sthānāni vidyānāṃ dharmasya ca caturdaśa ıı

20. vedo dharmamūlam tadvidām ca śmṛtiśīle |
21. dharmajijñāsānāṃ pramāṇaṃ paramaṃ śrutiḥ ||
22. (Pattanaik 2015b)
23. svadharmamapi cāvekṣya na vikampitumarhasi |
    dharmyāddhi yuddhācchreyo'nyatkṣatriyasya na vidyate ||
24. ahiṃsā satyaṃ asteyaṃ śaucaṃ indriyanigrahaḥ |
    dānaṃ damo dayā kṣāntiḥ sarveṣāṃ dharmasādhanam ||
25. (Pattanaik 2015b)
26. In the Yoga Sutra, the author has used vasana with samaskara. See: (Bryant 2009:423-424)
27. (Parthasarathy 2017:201-205)
28. See: Yoga Sutra 4.11 (Bryant 2009:423-424)
29. (Jayaraman 2013)
30. (Singh 2016)
31. (Raghavendra 2018)
32. tasmāddharmātparaṃ nāsti | athō abalīyān balīyāṃsamāśaṃsate dharmēṇa | yathā rājñaivam | yō vai sa dharmaḥ satyaṃ vai tat |
33. From a lay practitioner's standpoint, there is hardly any difference between Vedic, Paurnaik and Tantrik streams. He sees them as one integrated system. A typical *Nitya Karma Paddhati/ Puja* book anywhere in India, typically contains mantras and rituals from a variety of different sources. For example, the section of *Japa Vidhi* (rules for performing *Japa*) refers to *Nrisimha Purana, Yamala* (Tantric texts), *Acharabhushana* as well as Dharmashastra texts while enumerating the necessary japa practices (Mishra and Mishra 2017:44-46). Agama texts are the basis of temple construction – they describe in details eligible locations, image types, permissible materials, sacred dimensions and a host of other things.
34. (Chaudhuri 2012:28)
35. See: (Satprakashananda 1974:35-39) for a detailed discussion on the different pramanas accepted by various schools of Indian thought.
36. (Pattanaik 2006a:xiii)
37. (Pattanaik 2017a)

38. (Pattanaik 2006a:xiii-xxiv)
39. (DevduttMyth 2018)
40. (Pattanaik 2017a)
41. (Dasgupta 1932:79)
42. (Pattanaik 2017b)
43. dharmārthakāmamokṣāṇāmupadeśasamanvitam pūrvavṛttaṃ kathā-yuktamitihāsaṃ pracakṣate |
44. (Pattanaik 2003:1-2)
45. (Pattanaik 2006a:xiv)
46. (Graham 2010)
47. For an easily accessible overview of Calvinism, Arminianism and Lutherism, and their positions on free will, see (Stewart 2018)
48. (Signoracci 2017:104)
49. See Chapter 6 "Hegel's Philosophical Interpretation of Christianity" of (Stewart 2022)
50. Quoted in (Dundes 1984:248)
51. (Graves 1968:v)
52. (Leach and Fried 1984:778)
53. (Thury and Devinney 2017:3)
54. "Business Sutra: By Devdutt." devdutt.com. Retrieved April 30, 2022 (https://devdutt.com/books/business-sutra).
55. (Hardon 1998)
56. (Molher Jr. 2009)
57. (National Geographic 2017)
58. (HISTORY 2016)
59. (Pattanaik 2006a:xii-xxv)
60. (Pattanaik 2017a)
61. (Sharma 2002:4)
62. (IPPAI SPEAKS 2015:00:13:40)

63. (IPPAI SPEAKS 2015:00:13:40)
64. See: (The Wire 2017) 00:25:25 onwards. Also: (Samim Asgor Ali Photographer 2016)
65. (Rajiv Malhotra Official 2019)
66. gaṅge ca yamune caiva godāvari sarasvati ı narmade sindhu kāveri jale'smin samnidhim kuru ıı
67. (Pattanaik 2017e)
68. (Malhotra 2018:7-8)
69. (Pattanaik 2021a)
70. (Pattanaik 2021a)
71. (Jackson 1922:324-325)
72. Thompson (1999) mentioned in (Sharma 2002:2)
73. (Sharma 2002:4)
74. (Elst 2013)
75. See: "Hindu Marriage Act, 1955." India Code: Digital Repository of All Central and State Acts. Retrieved April 30, 2022 (https://www.indiacode.nic.in/show-data?actid=AC_CEN_3_20_00004_195525_1517807318992&orderno=2).
76. (Pattanaik 2015a)
77. (Pattanaik 2021b)
78. (Pattanaik 2015b)
79. (Pattanaik 2016)
80. (Pattanaik 2011a)
81. (Pattanaik 2018)
82. (Badrinath 2019)
83. See: (Ilaiah 2009)
84. (Foucault 1980:131)
85. (Lyotard 1984)
86. (Butler 2002:18-21)

87. Smritis are texts which contextualize spiritual truth according to time, place and customs.
88. (TEDx Talks 2013)
89. (Zavada 2014)
90. te taṃ bhuktvā svargalokaṃ viśālaṃ kṣīṇe puṇye martyalokaṃ viśanti (Gita 9.21)
91. (Pattanaik 2020)
92. (Bowersock, Brown, and Grabar 1999:625)
93. (Lamb 2011)
94. (Pattanaik 2015a)
95. (Pattanaik 2017c)
96. (Pattanaik 2021a)
97. (Pattanaik 2017c)
98. (Pattanaik 2020)
99. (Lokeswarananda 1989:42-44, 76, 163)
100. (Pattanaik 2020)
101. (Kapoor 2005:1)
102. (Ram 1995:157)
103. (Pattanaik 2006b)
104. "When Brahmins in South India claim roots to families who once lived near Saraswati, Ganga (Kashi), Godavari or Narmada, does it mean they are immigrants to South India, or invaders? Does the story of Agastya moving from Kailas to South refer to Vedic migration or invasion?" Twitter. Retrieved October 18, 2021 (https://twitter.com/devduttmyth/status/1169959879517147137).
105. (Malhotra 2018b:66-67)
106. (Pattanaik 2019a)
107. (Nei 1995:6720)
108. (Pugach et al. 2013:1803)
109. (Rajiv Malhotra Official 2018)

110. (Pattanaik 2021c)

111. (Pattanaik 2021d)

112. (Vorster 2016:1)

113. (Misra 2017b:5-6)

114. (Misra 2017a)

115. (Pattanaik 2017d)

116. (Pattanaik 2019b)

117. (Pattanaik 2011b)

118. (Pattanaik 2017d)

119. (Pattanaik 2017d)

120. "The Aryan problem for Indians. No matter what scientific papers say: https://thequint.com/voices/opinion/genomic-study-vedic-aryan-migration-dravidian-languages-sanskrit LW will refer to Aryan migration as 'invasion' and 'conquest' RW will insist Out of India is truth, like Flat Earth theory in America. Let us accept this reality and be at peace." Twitter. Retrieved October 18, 2021 (https://twitter.com/devduttmyth/status/982098173257658368).

121. (Bryant 2001:55)

122. (Bryant 2001:56)

123. See: (Mukhopadhyay 2019)

124. See: (Sastry and Kalyansundaram 2019:101-103) for more details. The authors have analyzed Ṛg Veda, Sāma Veda, Rāmāyaṇa, Mahābhārata, Brahmapurāṇa, Skandapurāṇa, Garudapurāṇa, Nātyaśāstra, Arthaśāstra, Manusmṛti, Abhijñānaśākuntalam, Kumārasaṃbhavam, and Raghuvaṃśam. They have also demonstrated that there are no references to the word drāviḍa in any of the three books of the Tolkāppiyam—the Ezhuttadikaram, the Solladikaram and the Poruladikaram—the oldest surviving work on Tamil grammar, literature and linguistics.

125. (Bryant 2001:140-142)

126. (Bryant 2001:146)

127. (Elst 2019)

128. (Talageri 2019)

129. "Somebody asked me if Shrikant Talageri knows Sanskrit? I assumed he does since he quotes Rig Veda a lot. Doesn't matter really. But does he? In all videos he speaks only English. If someone can forward me a video of him speaking Sanskrit would love to forward on Whatsapp." Twitter Retrieved April 30, 2022 (https://twitter.com/devduttmyth/status/1185791457405235205).

130. See (Mukhopadhyay 2019) where I have summarized the positions of Sri Aurobindo and Swami Vivekananda on the Aryan question.

131. See: (Gerbner 1969)

132. (Nabi and Riddle 2008:237)

133. See: (Griffin 2012) and (Gerbner 1998:180)

134. (Appiah 1992:58)

135. (Malhotra 2016:179)

FIVE

Irfan Habib
Hoodwinking History

Manogna Sastry

Introduction

The series of essays in this collection have, at their core, individuals who have played significant roles in shaping contemporary narratives of post-Independent India. An important factor in selecting them has been their brazen attempts to rewrite Bhārata's civilizational history, through not only etic lenses, but methods driven primarily by distortion, obfuscation, and effacement. One hopes this essay, and others in the collection, actively contribute to efforts of decolonization of the contemporary Indian mind and potentially have positive consequences for national institutions and narratives alike, especially since at the heart of the issue lies our collective identity.

Irfan Habib is particularly important in this series for his role in deeply entrenching the Marxist lens in historical revisionism, and a modus operandi characterized by 1) concealment and inversion of historical facts; 2) creation of new narratives and false historical accounts to perpetuate agendas; and 3) the use of obfuscation to counter any challenge posed to his work. Habib has played a starring role in executing the above through control of influential institutions and publications, the building of Marxist school of thought in premier Indian academic centers including the Indian Council for Historical Research (ICHR) and Indian History Congress (IHC) to institutionalize anti-Hindu narratives, and his unforgettable role in falsifying the historicity of the

Ayodhya temple. The current essay aims to validate each of these special choreographies with successive arguments.

Habib has authored several works, including books from the series *People's History of India,* funded by ICHR for several years, which has focused on *The Indus Civilization, The Vedic Age, Mauryan India* and *Indian Economy.* His other noteworthy books include *The National Movement: Studies in Ideology and History, An Atlas of Ancient Indian History* (jointly authored with Faiz Habib), *Medieval India: The Study of a Civilisation, Agrarian System of Mughal India, 1556-1707, Essays in Indian History: Towards a Marxist Perception* and *An Atlas of the Mughal Empire,* where much of his work has focused on the economic history of India during the medieval period under the Mughals. Habib has often been hailed as one of the most important Marxist historians of India and in the article, the author considers some of his key observations on a range of issues—nationalism, using caste studies to vilify Hinduism wholesale, re-writing historical events from the perspective of absolving invaders of all blame while redirecting it towards Dharmic concepts and rulers and creating hegemony at academic institutions to perpetuate divisive and false historical accounts.

Turning National Institutes into Fiefdoms

Political independence of India from Britain in 1947, is an important milestone in her several millennia old history. It marked a moment brimming with opportunities to craft and engineer India's rise in Asia and the world once again, for the progress of humanity. Therefore, the creation and functioning of its national institutions in the following decades assume a greater import considering the magnitude of service they were expected to render in nation building, especially at the level of recognizing our collective identity. Against this backdrop, the directions through which these institutions have been taken by a handful of individuals to the detriment of the collective deserves serious study and consideration. One such important center, and the role of this essay's protagonist in it, is the Indian Council for Historical Research. Irfan Habib has been a nominated member of the ICHR for five terms and its chairman for two, from 1986-93. He stands in proud company of fellow Marxist historians including the first chairman of ICHR, Professor R.S. Sharma, who changed the syllabus at Patna University to one based on the Marxist lens during the several years he headed the institution.

Established through an Administrative Order of the Ministry of Education of the Government of India, ICHR primarily receives aid from the ministry for the stated aim "to promote and give directions to historical research and to encourage and foster objective and scientific writing of history," and the first of its objectives is "to foster objective and scientific writing of history such as to inculcate an informed appreciation of the country's national and cultural heritage."[1] ICHR's primary role lies in providing grants and funds for various symposiums and workshops, along with its publication department, including its peer reviewed journal *Indian Historical Review*. The advisory committee for the journal, disbanded in 2015, comprised historians of the likes of Irfan Habib and Romila Thapar and played a major role in reviewing the articles that appeared in the journal. Despite worthy aims and objectives, what the country's premier historical institute has found itself used for has been anything, but honorable.

Communists in India have been seen to use professions, careers, ministries, and institutes, over several decades across the nation to imprint their ideologies. This spread institutionalized itself, especially since the time of Saiyid Nurul Hasan, appointed as the Union Minister of State for Education by Indira Gandhi in 1972, who gave the Left one of its strongest academic platforms – the Jawaharlal Nehru University.[2] The consequences of this narrative's stranglehold on academia and public discourse have been disastrous for the country as a whole and innumerable individuals alike.[3] Arun Shourie, in his very readable book *Eminent Historians*, describes the work by the ICHR as "planning to do in some undefined future what they had themselves been actually doing for decades – that is, write history to a purpose."[4] Shourie highlights, how the historians who laid siege to premier institutes of India for decades, peddling theories to undermine true accounts of the history of the land, not only furthered their careers and reputations in the process, but more importantly, shaped public discourse based on lies, misrepresentations and obfuscation for decades.

Among Habib's many achievements must be counted the 'Foreword' he wrote for the plagiarized work submitted by Tasneem Ahmad, who passed off the English translation of *Arif Qandhari's Tarikh-i-Akbari* by Dr. Parmatma Saran, written in 1970s for the ICHR volumes, as his own thesis for a PhD in 1992 from the Rajasthan University. While Habib received fulsome praise from Dr. Ahmad, the fact-finding committee instituted to examine the plagiarism charges ruled the following: "The Committee was provided with sixty-odd pages of type-script of the translation of Tarikh-i-Akbari done by Professor P. Saran. These pages were recovered from the file dealing with the translation assigned to Professor P. Saran. These pages were compared with that published by one of the members of the ICHR, Shri Tasneem Ahmad, and the Committee found overwhelming similarity between Professor P. Saran's translation and Shri Ahmad's book. The Committee felt that the similarity could not be accidental and the element of plagiarism cannot be ruled out."[5] Such is the work to which Professor Habib lends his stamp of approval through the 'Foreword'. Professor D.K. Chakrabarti's remarks, "Since the coming of this group to power, the world of Indian historical studies has been largely criminalized," are true literally, metaphorically and in every possible way indeed.[6]

Shourie's book documents the amount of grants and money spent on the various projects of ICHR, including the Medieval Sources Project, where Irfan Habib's *Akhbarat-e-Aurangzeb* is due with money already spent on it since decades but remains incomplete. ICHR's *Towards Freedom* project, as part of the institute's Special Research Projects must be amongst the costliest national mistakes, running since 1972, that is, as old as ICHR itself. The project's aim was to produce a set of nine volumes, with Habib writing on the 'Dictionary of Social, Economic and Administrative Terms in Indian/South Asian Inscriptions' project, which was started in 1989 with the mandate to bring out nine volumes in fifteen years. As of 2015, Rs. 42 lakh had been spent on the single volume, with each year's review of ICHR revealing astonishing lack of oversight for the project, funded by tax-payer money. Consider the following response, in 2015, by the then chairperson of ICHR, Professor Sudershan Rao, to queries on the status of the project: "I don't know how it's shaping up. There's just no update," Professor Rao said.[7] Habib's record in particular, receives the following update, "If the annual reports are to be believed, he has been promising to submit his manuscript since 2006-07. It went on until, interestingly, the 2011-12 and 2012-13 annual reports certified he was making "satisfactory progress"! The Aligarh Muslim University professor is yet to submit a single volume. When *Mail Today* enquired about the stage of Professor Habib's work, ICHR informed that "Habib saab has excused himself from this project,"[8] such has been the lack of accountability and hold of Habib and his clique over ICHR. Shourie hits the nail on the head when he outlines what exactly has been at stake at such premier institutes of our country for decades—not only financial irregularities and corruption, but more importantly, "...the real crime of these eminences does not lie in the loss they have inflicted in terms of money. It lies in the condition to which they have reduced institutions. It lies in their dereliction – because of which projects that were important for our country have languished. It lies even more in the use to which they have put those institutions."[9]

Witness #70 for the Sunni Waqf Board

Irfan Habib's role in the 'Ayodhya dispute'[10] from misleading petitioners of the case, to misusing national institutions, fabricating smokescreens, maligning stellar professional reputations and careers, can be seen as following the maxim *suppressio veri suggestio falsi*. Habib is in the distinguished company of his peers who have been 'advisers' to the Babri Masjid Action Committee (BAMC), building and providing it with the case to fight, even appearing as Witness #70 for the Sunni Waqf Board, while standing under the umbrella of being an objective and independent historian and passing himself off as the expert on the BAMC panel. With the final Supreme Court judgment pronounced in 2019, giving a clear victory to the historical fact of the disputed site having been the seat of a temple, the damage done by the false case built by the historians of ilk of Irfan Habib and Romila Thapar lies not only to a petitioner of the case, i.e. the Sunni Waqf Board, but to the entire country, exposing how, for decades, these historians brazenly perpetuated astonishing falsehoods without facing the consequences. They have couched their work at ICHR in the lofty labels of defending 'rationality' and 'truth', while openly acting in opposition to it, as validated by the above instance. ICHR's historians have leveraged their institutional position and clout to even discuss and attempt the passing of resolutions regarding the Babri Masjid's demolition case on international platforms such as the World Archaeology Conference, which held special sessions on it during the World Archaeological Congress in Croatia on the "Destruction and Conservation of Cultural Properties".[11]

The judgment by the Constitution Bench of the Supreme Court of India in December 2019 laid open for the entire country the truth—that a handful of 'learned' and 'experienced' historians, fully aware of the consequences of their false narratives, had been peddling lies to the entire nation. The Supreme Court of India ruled in favor of building a temple at the site believed to be the birthplace of Lord Srīrāma in Ayodhya, where the historical place had, at its base, enough evidence discovered by the Archaeological Survey of India (ASI) pointing to the existence of a prior temple upon which the Babri Masjid had been built.[12] While the country displayed a remarkably calm acceptance of the verdict, certain historians led by Irfan Habib, who had built profitable careers based on their own lies, continue to this day, to perpetuate false narratives. The Aligarh Historians Society, under Habib's presidentship, categorically refused to accept the findings of the ASI in 2010 itself, when the Allahabad High Court had accepted the ASI report. In his interview to *The Frontline* following the SC verdict in 2019, Habib characterized the archaeological evidence presented as 'dubious', and continues to perpetuate statements which have been conclusively proved otherwise. Habib states: "As for archaeology, the Supreme Court should surely have looked into the credentials of the Archaeological Survey officials, who could not distinguish Babri Masjid as a mosque. It is always designated "disputed structure", while imagining a fifty-pillar temple, without finding a single pillar or a strong enough base on which a pillar could have stood, nor any blocks that must have formed its walls and roof."[13] The archaeological evidence of pillars and much more seems not to exist, only in Habib's world. The judgment reports lists all the evidence collected over the years, including the Commissioner's report in 1950 which details the dozen and more Kasauti pillars which held the now demolished mosque carved with Hindu symbols including lotus flowers, Tandava nritya, varaha and so on.[14]

Habib further comments that the Babri Masjid, believed to have been constructed in the 16th century CE, is older than the *Skanda Purāṇa*, a text whose earliest redactions are attributed to several centuries prior, at least around 8th century CE and has references to the significant role played by Ayodhya in Srīrāma's life.[15] With history based on untruths and where openly falsities are presented as 'facts', only monumental blunders arise. The tragedy in this situation though, is that an entire nation bears the resulting responsibility to clean up such deeply entrenched lies. Dr. K.K. Muhammed's first-hand account, in his autobiography, *Naanemba Bhaarateeya*, through the proximity he had in his former role as Regional Director (North) of the Archaeological Survey of India, speaks of the extent to which 'Habib and co', created false narratives, whitewashed historical truths and prevented peaceful resolution of the matter for decades. The book details the extent to which Habib had a hegemonical hold over Aligarh Muslim University, where Dr. Muhammed was once his student, including, the former's acts of scuttling career progressions of those who opposed him.

Irfan Habib also has the distinction of being amongst the most vocal and unrelenting voices, opposing the archaeological results of Professor B.B. Lal's team of the excavations at Ayodhya, against the backdrop of the dispute for the land demolished at the erstwhile Babri Masjid. Habib's notorious work in this matter includes claiming to have carbon-dated the artefacts excavated at the Ayodhya site and concluding them to be of recent vintage, only to have his entire work discredited by the Archaeological Survey of India.[16] The eminent historian and expert Meenakshi Jain, also notes the role played by Habib on one of the key inscriptions found during the excavation. In *The Battle for Rama*, Dr. Jain details how the 'Treta ka Thakur' inscription, which Habib vociferously claimed was stolen from the Lucknow Museum and placed at Ayodhya in 1992, is distinct from the 'Vishnu-Hari' inscription recovered from the demolished site at Ayodhya. Spinning imaginary tales to obfuscate the evidence contrary to his claims, Habib wrote in 2002, with all the authority of his 'expertise', and total lack of any evidence to explain his analysis, that the inscription found at the site in Ayodhya was "brought from somewhere else."[17] Changing initial claims, as is usually wont of Leftist historians—in 2006, Habib claimed that the inscription had been taken from Lucknow museum, where it had been moved, having originally been discovered by the colonial archaeologist A. Fuhrer at 'Treta ka Thakur' temple in Ayodhya. Despite evidence being presented that the two inscriptions are different,[18] in the words of Dr. Jain, "Thus far neither Dr. Roy, nor Professor Prasad, nor Professor Irfan Habib have responded to the publication of the photograph of the Treta Ka Thakur inscription, which falsifies the arguments they have been persistently advocating for over two decades."[19] In fact, Habib continues to brazenly attribute the 2019 judgment to victory of "judicial fancy."[20]

More Historical Revisionism

Irfan Habib's work, *The Formation of India*, is a fine example of an agenda-driven exercise of history writing, where the exploits of invaders such as Mohammed Ghazni are soft pedalled. Consider his statement on Ghazni and the period,

> "Even when Alberuni was writing his book a new wave of cultural diffusion into India was under way. It had its violent side, which the scientist recognized as he spoke of 'the wonderful exploits' of Mahmud of Ghazni [1000-30] 'by which the Hindus became like atoms of dust scattered in all directions and like the tale of old in the mouth of the people'. But the expansion of knowledge proceeded. Alberuni goes on to tell us that when at Lahore, in his conversations with Hindu scholars, he himself began to expound the principles of science and logic (derived from the Hellenistic-Arabic tradition) 'they flocked together round me from all parts, wondering and most eager to learn from me.'60."[21]

As long as the expansion of knowledge is seemingly present, violent exploits by invaders can be seen in favorable light—this is the potential take-away from Habib's writing, in line with Indian Marxist historical analysis. Habib, like his peers including Romila Thapar, perpetuates the myth of invasions being either harmless or worse, in the case of Islamic invasions, even benign, based on false attributions to contributions and exchanges between the Islamic invaders and the Hindus of the land. The downplaying of the territorial unity of the erstwhile Bhārata and the invasions it suffered is a signature of Habib's work and indeed, the invasion narrative traces its roots to the Aryan Invasion/Migration Myth which has been elevated to the status of gospel truth for more than a century now, with beneficiaries ranging from colonial imperialists to agenda driven Marxists such as the protagonist of this essay. Habib's remarks on this, such as,

> "Within the limits so set, cultural affinities had developed which led people to distinguish those in India from the rest of the world. Many of these affinities appear as aspects of the Hindu tradition. That the caste system and Brahmanical ideas and rituals were important among the culturally shared elements is undeniable. But it can be shown (as I have tried to do in a couple of essays) that the concept of India as a country is stronger in writers like Amir Khusrau (d.1325) or Abu'l Fazl (d.1603), writing in Persian, than in any identifiable preceding writer in Sanskrit. This is surely because the cultural affinities were not exclusively religious. Tara Chand, in his *Influence of Islam on Indian Culture*, observed that extensive political structures like the Delhi Sultanate and the Mughal Empire helped to generate larger political allegiances, and so made the consciousness of the country's unity still stronger. Even in the eighteenth century, when he had lost all power, the Mughal emperor was seen as the natural sovereign of Hindustan".[22]

not only betray the attempt at portraying the Islamic invaders as being among the front runners of creating the idea of India as a country, but also demonstrate a treacherous denial of the existence of Bhārata as a culturally and integrally unified (as against synthetic) whole since millennia prior to the invasions.

An important Marxist exercise in India has involved co-opting itself into the Indian Independence movement. The basis for this is seen in Habib's work. "It is inherent in the unity of past and present that Marxist historiography must continuously turn to fresh aspects to explore and re-explore and fresh questions to answer."[23] Habib's work *Note Towards a Marxist Perception of Indian History,* builds a clear picture of the Marxist attempt at co-opting various national movements and using them to deflect attention away from historical facts and towards entities the Communists wish to vilify. From R.P. Dutt, D.D. Kosambi, E.M.S. Namboodripad to R.S. Sharma, Romila Thapar and Habib himself—the doyens of history, retain the focus on targeting forces that showcase Bhārata and her dharmic identity in the most disempowering light. Habib in this essay identifies "some major problems of Indian history" to include the following: caste, repression of women, peasant revolts, while the key movement co-opted, is the national freedom struggle. "Just like gender inequality, the caste system is not linked to any particular mode of production but has subsisted under different modes of production in India. The main beneficiaries have not been the Brahman priests, who in time, became its codifiers and interpreters, but the ruling classes to whatever ethnic group religion or caste they belonged," writes Habib, bringing in the class struggle angle.[24] While the Vijayanagara Empire is associated with pinnacles of development and prosperity, Habib tries to draw attention to a stray occurrence and uses it to present a forced argument, in line with features of Indian Marxist historiography which focusses heavily on peasant revolts, real and exaggerated, throughout centuries, to feed into caste discourse. Relying on the work of Y. Subbarayalu and N. Karashima of the Vijayanagara Empire in the 15th century, Habib argues that peasant revolts took place in the empire but were overshadowed by "caste or religious colouring or ambitions of the leaders from higher groups"[25] and that more research needs to unearth material from these angles.

As seen in his analysis, Habib begins with a random and singular data point, uses it as the basis to read a conclusion which his own 'evidence' doesn't suggest. The connection to caste and exploitation by higher groups must be established at any cost, even if it is by attribution of motive, despite the absence of any evidence to indicate thus, as a fundamental requisite of Marxist analysis of Indian history. What is not alluded to, even slightly or remotely, is the association between the Communists and the British in the pre-Independence era, which Shourie meticulously documents in his work *The Only Fatherland*. Habib's work also bears another quintessential Communist signature, i.e, the complete absence of Indian traditional sources or accounts to understand India.

The Leftists, as seen explicitly in Habib's work, wish to co-opt themselves in favorable light into the freedom struggle movement as well. Habib writes the following: "the partial, self-righteous acknowledgement of the need to revisit the abuse that they had hurled at leaders like Gandhiji, and to revise the Marxist assessment of the national freedom movement – however, this need not mean that the Communists or the other Left groups were incorrect in all the basic positions they took, for example in 1942."[26] Shourie highlights this important point in his book as well, that the Left in India has been recasting the freedom struggle as movement of 'common heritage' to which they have contributed enormously. Habib remarks that the reality of the Left's participation in the freedom movement, which consisted of doing everything possible to hinder the efforts of those sacrificing on ground:

> "An overwhelming preoccupation with the "errors" of the Left,' Irfan Habib writes – collaborating with the British; submitting reports to them about the sterling work communists were doing to sabotage the Quit India Movement; insisting that the freedom movement be subordinated to the interests of the Soviet Union; supporting the Muslim League in its demand that the country be partitioned: just errors, and that too within quotation marks – 'as in the volume edited by Professor Bipan Chandra, is unfortunate, since by this very preoccupation, it belittles the achievements of the Left during the National Movement and its contributions to it. After all, the creation of the organized Kisan Movement and the trade unions was mainly the

handiwork of the Communists and their allies; and that cannot be forgotten.' Even the 'bourgeois-democratic values' of the national movement – 'such as secularism, women's rights, national unity, freedom of the press, and parliamentary democracy' – can be put to good use today, Irfan Habib points out, "These can form the initial points for a people's front, in which all classes may be united as can carry forward the cause of democracy and socialism."[27]

This unification of all economic classes during the Indian freedom movement is important in Habib's scheme of history, for it is a line of thought that can be conveniently extended to new groups every decade. Consider his editorial remarks in 2017, where he uses the airbrushed role of the Left in the freedom struggle as an example of how nationalism in India used to be more "relaxed" and that "rigid nationalism" was a fringe concept which cast "Muslims, communists and foreigners (mostly from the West)" as aggressors and to this list, secular liberals have now been added.[28] The incorporation of the freedom movement into the Communist framework is more important against the backdrop of the Karachi Resolution of 1931, which Habib highlights as one significant to the religious minorities of the country:

> "The real answer to the Simon Commission was, therefore, the Karachi Resolution of March 1931, in which the Congress spelt out the political, social and economic contours of the future free India in which the state would ensure 'fundamental rights' to all. The Indian state, it was pledged, would observe 'neutrality in regard to all religions', and the cultures and languages of 'the different linguistic areas' would be protected."[29]

While Habib lays the outline for the Marxist embracing of the freedom movement and its role as a temporary unifying force, he denies the same role to other players and forces, as seen in his quote: "While we did borrow the idea of nationalism from the West, like we did with many other ideas and institutions, we borrowed them after a serious churning during the freedom struggle itself. Unfortunately RSS stayed away from that exercise, and thus always felt uneasy with the inclusive nationalism we had practiced all these years."[30] One should note the tone where, with mere theorizing and in the absence of any evidence, not only has the freedom struggle been airbrushed to include the Left prominently and favorably in it, but also painted as something *always* practiced. This is a departure from his own earlier statement.

Studying the Communist methods of reinterpretation of historical facts is, indeed a fascinating albeit disturbing act, for one marvels at how easy it is to distort historical truths. Habib's defense of how one could potentially review the Communists' role in the freedom struggle despite the movement being a unifying factor across regions and groups, is the following: "In hindsight it is possible to argue that for the success of the anti-colonial struggle, a multi-class alliance was always necessary; and much rested perhaps not so much on the necessity of such an alliance as on the mutual concessions among the antagonistic classes that such an alliance required. There is also the allowance that has to be made for levels of mass consciousness."[31] Thus, the unity seen in the country during the freedom movement is explained away as a multi-class alliance mutually giving concessions to each other. The subterranean Indian Marxist trope remains that Bhārata never had true and integral unity it was always a disparate set of players temporarily united.

Habib on Indus Valley Civilization

One of Irfan Habib's major writings as an 'eminent historian', is on the Indus Valley Civilization (IVC), including a monograph (2002) which forms the second volume in the *A People's History of India* series. Since historical materialism is one of the core elements of Marxist historiography, where the relationships between society (viewed as various classes) and its means of material production are studied to understand the economic and other aspects of the system, one finds in Habib's work conclusions drawn from focus on material developments such as for instance, particular kind of pottery, forming the basis for analysis. Habib's 2002 work stands on very little solid ground today than ever before, for not only has the debate on IVC extended unto becoming the Sarasvati-Sindhu civilization, but the results from domains such as archaeology, geo-hydrology and so on have pushed back against the chronology used by Habib to frame his arguments. Detailed analysis of the Marxist historiographical methods, particularly applied to ancient India and in particular the Indus Valley Civilization, is a separate work, which must begin with engagement with the first principles laid down by D.D. Kosambi in his *Introduction to the Study of Indian History*, including understanding the Marxist periodization scheme based on slavery and feudalism and its inability to be applied to India resulting in the elevation of 'caste' as the de-facto mechanism to study. While this analysis is beyond the scope of this essay, what we do consider below are a few major assertions made by Habib which have important consequences for the collective Indian identity.

Gregory Possehl's *The Indus Age: The Beginnings* forms the basis for the chronological template primarily used by Habib for IVC. Habib dates the IVC to 1500 BC by linking it with, despite his own admission of little evidence, with its apparent predecessor the Helmand civilization, based on IVC beads unearthed in Mesopotamia.[32] It is indeed telling, that even if we were to set aside the published research of the past two decades, at the time of Habib's writing, the research on dating IVC sites at Dholavira, Rakhigarhi, Lothal and so on, based on remarkable excavations and carbon dating the unearthed materials, seems to be a lesser standard of evidence than resorting to analysis of IVC material found in Mesopotamia.

Having maintained that there is no evidence of writing in IVC[33], Habib's research thesis changes to being mere heresy or superstition, "... we must not forget the factors of ideology and superstition. Towns could also be centers of religious cults and places of pilgrimage. Temples dedicated to gods could rival rulers' palaces. Religious faith often bound people in allegiance to rulers, who might be priest-kings or even (as in Egypt) 'god-kings', closely allied with the priesthoods. By the nature of their occupation, the priests dealt with marks and symbols, representing deities, royalty and rituals. Special marks could also be put on goods to indicate ownership or identity of the producer. It is possibly out of such marks that some of the early systems of writing developed."[34] The other potential influence could be from south western Iran, maintains Habib, and that the "earlier" Proto-Elamite script could have shaped writing in IVC due to its geographical proximity.³⁵ Not once does Habib even consider the possibility that the arrow of influence, if present, could be from IVC to Iran instead of the other way, especially considering how much the upper limits of the range of dates for IVC have been pushed farther based on physical evidence.

Although some historians of the colonial era have been given to changing their positions attributing linkages between Sumerian and IVC, for instance, John Marshall, the pre-Independence head of ASI at the time of the excavation of the 'Priest-King', dropped the initial Indo-Sumerian civilization label in favor of Indus Valley Civilization, Habib continues to harp on speculative associations between the two. Habib remarks that "The Indus civilization cannot at first sight be admired for any great art," but the Priest-King statue unearthed at Mohenjo-Daro must have connections to Mesopotamia, "The surprising features of the figure are the cut of the beard and the trefoil ornament of the robe thrown over one shoulder, since both of these recall the fashions of Mesopotamia. If it is a portrait, the subject is most likely to have been a merchant familiar with Mesopotamia, and the designation commonly given, 'Priest-King', may be misleading. There is no justification at all for the title 'Yogi', which is based on nothing more tangible than the seemingly half- closed eyes."³⁶ The 'Pasupati' seal excavated at Mohenjo-Daro too is subject to similar analysis; Habib sees associations with Elamite culture again, with the figure the bull-deity in Proto-Elamite representations instead of any association with Shiva as Pashupati and anything to do with yoga.³⁷ Habib's work on IVC heavily follows the thread of analysis of colonial archaeologists such as Stuart Piggott and Mortimer Wheeler, with the latter's attribution of end of IVC to 'Aryan Invasion' thoroughly discredited.

Despite the lack of tangible evidence for any of the above assertions, Habib ably demonstrates why one can always safely rely on a Marxist historian to spot discrimination, even in situations where the objective data on hand could have multiple explanations. Analyzing the genetic traits unearthed from the burial grounds of the IVC sites, he admits that the profusion of the 'Mother Goddess' clay images discovered leads to the assumption that a matrilineal system was perhaps in vogue at the time, but "...even if such a system existed, women still remained underprivileged. Dental studies of the Harappa skeletons show that, compared with the men, the women (from childhood onwards) were less well cared for, and ate much less meat. From Nausharo, comes a clay figurine of a woman grinding grain with a roller on a flat stone (Figure 2.22). The wide occurrence of spindle-whorls in the Indus houses suggests that hand-spinning too was done by women at home. Both kinds of labor, given the absence of rotary hand-mills and spinning wheels, were especially strenuous."[38] One wonders how many Harappa skeletons he studied to come to this conclusion and his method in ruling out any other normal cause.

While an extensive discussion on the various aspects of IVC, especially the evolution of the debate with recent research, is beyond the scope of this essay, what is relevant is to consider Habib's work especially concerning the *Rig Veda* and IVC. Habib maintains that, since the *Rig Veda* is primarily a religious text, one must compare it with the religious elements of IVC, to consider if the Harappans were Rig Vedic people or not.

Habib summarizes that the IVC deities, as seen through their seals and amulets, were primarily zoomorphic, with the one-horned hump-less (mythical) bull being the most significant. In contrast, Habib maintains that the Rig Vedic gods are anthropomorphic. The IVC seals do not show any cow, horse or camel, while the *Rig Veda* does not consider the mythical unicorn or assign any sanctity to animals like the elephant, rhinoceros or tiger. Habib also maintains that the *Rig Veda* has no prominent female deity nor a goddess who has the body of a tiger, as seen on an Indus seal. Also, the *Rig Veda* identifies with the cremation of the dead while the IVC shows burial of the dead.

In each of the above assertions, it is interesting to study Habib's dismissal of challenges and counters to his arguments without considering the merit. The Pasupati seal, as mentioned earlier, fails to be identified with either Shiva/Pusan of the *Rig Veda*, in Habib's reading, because more specious association with the "posture of the hooved bull-deity on Proto-Elamite seals from Susa, c. 3000-2750 BC, and has, therefore, no kinship with any yogic tradition" deserves primacy.[39] Habib does not consider 'the dancing girl' figurine to be associated with Usha of the *Rig Veda*, and only spotlights the argument that no prominent female deities are mentioned in RV and hence there is no connection.

Habib also dismisses the evidence of the fire altars found at IVC sites such as Kalibangan and Lothal as being connected with rituals of *Rig Veda*, on the basis that the altars were "local phenomena" which were not found in Harappa and Monhenjo Daro and that instead, "the Indus civilization could have on its own generated a cult of fire." The dismissals of any challenges to his position continues with Habib remarking that even the presence of Indus river basin names in *Rig Veda* amounts to little, for, the general idea that even if languages change, river names are usually retained do not hold true because Habib's neighborhood apparently has exceptions to this general idea and hence, the "Aryan forms" of the river names that have existed continuously since the times of IVC are not a proof that the two were in fact the same.[40]

Habib's chronology dates the *Rig Veda*, even the oldest parts of the text, to a period not earlier than 1500 BC. The basis for Habib's range are not any evidentiary material related to the text itself from Sanskrit scholars, but the dating of tablets found in Turkey, which contain words used by the Mittani tribe. Habib maintains that the language spoken by the Mittani and that of the *Rig Veda* would have been close in time and hence uses the former, with no substantial evidence apart from the bias for primacy to outsider sources, to date the latter and insists that "a date for the Rigveda outside the range of 2000-800 bc most improbable."[41] Further, Habib uses the *Avesta* to date the *Rig Veda*, despite many challenges to this assertion being a part of the domain literature at the time of Habib's publication, "The *Rigveda*'s linguistic proximity (in both vocabulary and grammar) to the Avesta, the earliest Old Iranian text, provides yet another indicator of its date. Various kinds of evidence, such as the relationship of the Old Avestan with the language of the Achaemenid inscriptions, the occurrence of Iranian names in Mesopotamian inscriptions, the extent of linguistic changes in the Young Avesta, and the geography of the Avesta, all help to date the Old Avesta to no earlier than 1300 bc, and probably close to 1000 bc. Given this range of dates for the *Avesta* and its kinship with the *Rigveda*, no part of the *Rigveda* itself is likely to be earlier than 1500 bc."[42] All the scientific evidence one finds – archaeological, geological, geo-hydrological – which has unearthed the Sarasvati river civilization, its presence in the *Rig Veda*, the unscientific nature of comparative linguistics forming the basis for absolute chronologies seem to matter little in Habib's scheme of research. Sastry, Kalyanasundaram's 2017 presentation and paper on these dimensions of the Aryan problem offer counters to several of the above arguments and is referred to for an in depth analysis. Sastry and Kalyanasundaram also highlight a crucial point in their paper, "Whether posited as an invasion by or migration of Aryans, these variant forms—of an into-India hypothesis (supposed movement into India around the second millennium BCE)—are underpinned by one constant: the consequence that the earliest forms of Vedic culture and Sanskrit are not indigenous to India."[43]

Habib's work, while falling short of openly endorsing the discredited Aryan Invasion/Migration Theory, still stays true to its ideological course and introduces clever back door entry points for the implications of AI/MT. Speculating on the end of the IVC, Habib again resorts to comparisons with the end of the Helmand cities Shahr-i Sokhta and Mundigak, around 2000 BC, and the destruction of the Kot-Diji culture, "with such violence as to leave traces in the archaeological record. Similar traces of arson are found also at the Kulli-culture site of Nal and the Indus border settlement of Dabar-kot. The inference, then, seems irresistible: that there were invasions from the west which overwhelmed, first, the Helmand cities, then, the late Kot-Diji culture and, finally, the Indus civilization."[44] Holding on to contrived explanations for some of the positions in which the skeletons of Mohenjo-Daro were found, Habib suggests that they could have been victims of violence "from invaders or marauders" and even though the inference has been criticized in the domain literature, Habib believes there's no convincing alternative explanations. Never mind that no indigenous text mentions or records any such invasion or violence, or even such large scale migration from Central Asian Steppes or other places, for in Habib's scheme, what is important is speculation on events outside the actual geographical locus being considered. Further, Habib writes that "With the large number of calibrated carbon dates now available, the end of the Indus civilization in its main parts cannot be put later than 1900 BC; and this date is more than 400 years too early for the earliest elements in the *Rigveda*, the earliest Vedic composition (see Note 2.2). That the intruders, or some of them, were pre-Vedic Aryans', that is, speakers of some form of proto-Aryan speech (out of which the language of the Rigveda developed later), is not impossible, but cannot be proved.)."[45] In order to understand in detail the implications of the theorizing of the above resorted to by Habib, Sastry and Kalyanasundaram's papers on Bhāratīya chronology are highly recommended.[46]

Conclusion

Marxism as a tradition, has associated itself very strongly with features of science, especially in terms of the economic impact of technology on society, politics, philosophies and ethics alike. The historical materialism that lies at the heart of Marxist historiography is claimed as a scientific way of looking at history. The Left in India particularly, has so deeply entrenched the idea that their historiography is 'scientific' that the proof of burden has been shifted to those who challenge their narratives instead of Marxist claims themselves being subject to scrutiny. Yet, if one were to objectively consider the method and consequently theorizations of many Indian Marxist historians, especially that of this essay's kingpin, scientific is perhaps one of the last adjectives that would ever characterize his work.

Irfan Habib's role in treating national institutions such as the ICHR as 'fiefdoms' and the Ayodhya temple case demonstrate all the hubris of a person who thinks he is beyond scientific evidence. The continuous denial of material evidence of the temple underneath the demolished mosques, the misrepresentation of biographical details about Srīrāma, sending the petitioners on a wild goose chase by claiming that the Treta ka Thakur and Vishnu-Hari inscriptions are the same, and finally refusing to accept the Supreme Court judgment itself and labelling it as judicial fallacy all point to a refusal to consider objective proofs and reason in a scientific manner. Habib's work on IVC, and especially in his role, along with those such as Romila Thapar, in perpetuating discredited theories which have a tremendous impact on our collective historical identity, through their influence in having them adopted as published learning material from national institutes such as ICHR, for generations of students, needs to be jettisoned for good.

Bibliography

Agrahari, Amit. 2020. *Azad, Ahmed, Hasan and more – HRD Ministry has remained in the hands of secularists since forever.* https://tfipost.com/2020/01/azad-ahmed-hasan-and-more-hrd-ministry-has-remained-in-the-hands-of-secularists-since-forever/ Accessed on 23 November 2021.

Balakrishna, Sandeep. *Tarikh-i-Habibi: The Dénouement of Irfan Habib*. The Dharma Dispatch. https://www.dharmadispatch.in/history/tarikh-i-habibi-the-dnouement-of-irfan-habib. Accessed on 21 November 2021.

Chakrabarti, D.K. 2012. *Romila Thapar and the Study of Ancient India: History as propaganda*. FOLKS Magazine (Ed) NS Rajaram. https://bharatabharati.in/2012/06/07/2-romila-thapar-and-the-study-of-ancient-india-history-as-propaganda-dilip-kumar-chakrabarti/ Accessed on 23 November 2021.

Chakrabarti, D.K. 2020. *Nationalism in the Study of Ancient Indian History*. Delhi: Aryan Books International.

Dasgupta, Surajit. 2015. *A History of "Tolerance"*. https://swarajyamag.com/magazine/a-history-of-tolerance Accessed on 23 November 2021.

Gupta, Shantanu. 2020. *Indira Gandhi vs Morarji Desai: How JNU was at the centre of battle to capture academia.*

https://theprint.in/pageturner/excerpt/indira-gandhi-vs-morarji-desai-how-jnu-was-at-the-centre-of-battle-to-capture-academia/350831/ Accessed on 23 November 2021.

Habib, Irfan. 1988. *Problems of Marxist Historiography* Social Scientist Vol. 16, No. 12, 3-13.

Habib, Irfan. 1997a. *The Formation of India – Notes on the History of an Idea.* Social Scientist Vol25, Nos. 7-8.

Habib, Irfan. 1997b. *Civil Disobedience 1930-3.1* Social Scientist Vol. 25, No. 9/10. 43-66.

Habib, Irfan. 1999. *The Envisioning of a Nation: A Defence of the Idea of India.* Social Scientist Vol. 27, No. 9/10,18-29.

Habib, Irfan. 2010. *Note Towards a Marxist Interpretation of Indian History.* The Marxist, XXVI 4, 37-48.

Habib, Irfan. 2002. *The Indus Valley Civilization.* Volume 2 of A People's History of India New Delhi: Tulika books.

Habib, Irfan. 2017a. (Ed.) *Indian Nationalism.* New Delhi: Aleph Book Company.

Habib, Irfan. 2017b. *The RSS's Reliance on Lal-Bal-Pal to Justify Its Own Cultural Nationalism Fails to Recognise The Trio's Inclusive Politics* in The Caravan. https://caravanmagazine.in/vantage/rss-lal-bal-pal-cultural-nationalism. Accessed on 23 November 2021.

Habib, Irfan. *The Nation that is India.* The Little Magazine Volume III, Issue 2 – In Bad Faith. http://www.littlemag.com/faith/irfanhabib.html. Accessed on 23 November 2021.

Jain, Meenakshi. 2017. *The Battle for Rama.* Delhi: Aryan Books International.

Kumar, Utpal. 2015. *Indian Council of Historic Rot: How ICHR's 'special research projects' are dragging on for years and bleeding taxpayers of crores.*

https://www.dailymail.co.uk/indiahome/indianews/article-3164359/Indian-Council-Historic-Rot-ICHR-s-special-research-projects-dragging-years-bleeding-taxpayers-crores.html. Accessed on 23 November 2021.

Muhammed, K.K. (Tr. Narasinga Rao B). 2019. *Naanemba Bhaarateeya*. Vamshi Publications.

Rajalakshmi, T.K. 2019. *'A simple piece of judicial fancy' an interview with Professor Irfan Habib* in Frontline December 6, 2019 https://frontline.thehindu.com/cover-story/a-simple-piece-of-judicial-fancy/article30015505.ece. Accessed on 21 November 2021.

Rao, Nandini. 1995. *Politics and the World Archaeological Congress.* Trabeojos de Prehistoria 52 no 1, 5-11.

Sastry, Manogna & Kalyanasundaram, Megh. 2019. *The A of ABC of Indian chronology*: Dimensions of the Aryan problem revisited in 2017* Land Of Dharma (Proceedings of the Swadeshi Indology Conference Series) Edited by: Dr. Shrinivas Tilak and Dr. Sharda Narayanan. 3-71.

Shourie, Arun. 1993. *The Buckling State.* Ayodhya and The Future India (Ed) Jitendra Bajaj. Centre for Policy Studies, Madras. South Asia Books. https://www.cpsindia.org/index.php/pub/155-ayodhya-and-the-future-india/contents/chapter-2/117-chapter-2. Accessed on 21 November 2021.

Shourie, Arun. 1999. *Eminent Historians – Their Technology, Their Line, Their Fraud.* Harper Collins India .

Shourie, Arun. 2014. *The Only Fatherland – Communists, Quit India and the Soviet Union.* Harper Collins Publishers India.

https://bharatabharati.in/2012/06/07/2-romila-thapar-and-the-study-of-ancient-india-history-as-propaganda-dilip-kumar-chakrabarti/ Accessed on 23 November 2021.

Notes

1. "Aims and Objectives" of Indian Council of Historical Research. Retrieved on 23 November 2021. (http://ichr.ac.in/content/innerpage/aims---objectives.php)
2. See several accounts of this episode including:
   - Chakrabarti 2020: 3-20, 293-31
   - "Indira Gandhi vs Morarji Desai: How was JNU was at the centre of battle to capture academia" .The Print. Retrieved November 23, 2021 (https://theprint.in/pageturner/excerpt/indira-gandhi-vs-morarji-desai-how-jnu-was-at-the-centre-of-battle-to-capture-academia/350831/).
   - "Azad, Ahmed, Hasan and more – HRD ministry has remained in the hands of secularists forever" TFIPost. Retrieved November 23, 2021 (https://tfipost.com/2020/01/azad-ahmed-hasan-and-more-hrd-ministry-has-remained-in-the-hands-of-secularists-since-forever/)
3. See accounts of Dr. Krishna Sharma and Dr. Manana Devahuti, cited by Madhu

Kishwar in "A History of Tolerance." Swarajya. Retrieved on 23 November 2021. (https://swarajyamag.com/magazine/a-history-of-tolerance)

4. Shourie 2015:4
5. See account of entire episode in Shourie 2015:22-25
6. Chakrabarti 2012
7. "Indian Council of Historic Rot: How ICHR's 'special research projects' are dragging on for years and bleeding taxpayers of crores." Mail Online India. Retrieved November 23, 2021 (https://www.dailymail.co.uk/indiahome/indianews/article-3164359/Indian-Council-Historic-Rot-ICHR-s-special-research-projects-dragging-years-bleeding-taxpayers-crores.html).
8. ibid
9. Shourie 2015:4
10. The dispute centered around the birthplace of Srīrāma in Ayodhya where once a historically attested temple stood and was raised to the ground to build the Babri mosque and subsequent demolition of it in 1992, leading to a land title case, which examined archaeological evidence at the site and the final verdict decided in favour of rebuilding a Hindu temple.
11. See "Ayodhya Committee WB9." World Archaeological Bulletin. Retrieved on 21 November 2021 (https://worldarch.org/world-archaeological-bulletin/ayodhya-committee-wb9/), and Rao 1995:5-11 for some accounts (To change to standard format)
12. See the final 2019 Supreme Court of India Judgment on the matter for all the evidence considered by the court: "Civil Appeal Nos 10866-10867 of 2010." Supreme Court of India. Retrieved on 21 November 2021 (https://www.sci.gov.in/pdf/JUD_2.pdf).
13. "A Simple Piece of Judicial Fancy." Frontline. Retrieved on 21 November 2021. (https://frontline.thehindu.com/cover-story/a-simple-piece-of-judicial-fancy/article30015505.ece)
14. See pp 81-82 of the Supreme Court of India Judgement "Civil Appeal Nos 10866-10867 of 2010." Supreme Court of India. Retrieved on 21 November 2021 (https://www.sci.gov.in/pdf/JUD_2.pdf).
15. Habib comments, "Lord Rama was indeed believed to have been born in Ayodhya, but not at any particular site. "Ram-janma" is mentioned only in the Skanda Purana, again without any precise indication of the place, though it was compiled much later than the construction of the Babri Masjid," in "A

Simple Piece of Judicial Fancy." Frontline. Retrieved on 21 November 2021. (https://frontline.thehindu.com/cover-story/a-simple-piece-of-judicial-fancy/article30015505.ece))

16. Shourie 1993
17. Jain, 2017:109
18. Jain 2017:103-115
19. Jain 2017:112
20. "A Simple Piece of Judicial Fancy." Frontline. Retrieved on 21 November 2021. (https://frontline.thehindu.com/cover-story/a-simple-piece-of-judicial-fancy/article30015505.ece))
21. Habib 1997a:6
22. "Irfan Habib." Little Magazine. Retrieved on 23 November 2021. (http://www.littlemag.com/faith/irfanhabib.html pp.1)
23. Habib 1988:3
24. Habib 2010:46
25. ibid
26. Habib 1988:10
27. Shourie 1999
28. Habib 2017: ix
29. "Irfan Habib." Little Magazine. Retrieved on 23 November 2021. (http://www.littlemag.com/faith/irfanhabib.html pp.1)
30. "The RSS's reliance on Lal-Bal-Pal to justify its own cultural nationalism fails to recognise the trio's inclusive politics." The Caravan. Retrieved on 23 November 2021 (https://caravanmagazine.in/vantage/rss-lal-bal-pal-cultural-nationalism)
31. Habib 2010
32. Habib 2002:15
33. Habib 2002:13
34. Habib 2002:2
35. Habib 2002:50
36. Habib 2002:52
37. Habib 2002:54
38. Habib 2002:58

39. Habib 2002:72
40. Habib 2002:73
41. ibid
42. ibid
43. Sastry, Kalyanasundaram, 2019, pp. 87. Also see Slide 5 for the assets and issues at stake in the presentation "Aryan Problem from the perspective of Textual Evidence and Linguistics." Retrieved on 23 November, 2021. (https://www.academia.edu/40037600/Aryan_problem_from_the_perspective_of_Textual_Evidence_and_Linguistics_Aug_02_2019_)
44. Habib 2002:64
45. Ibid
46. See the works at "Bhāratīya Chronology." Retrieved on 23 November 2021. (https://independent.academia.edu/bharatiyachronology)

SIX

Shashi Tharoor
The Quintessential Macaulay Putra

Divya Reddy

Public Persona

Shashi Tharoor is a well-known Indian politician, award-winning author, and former international diplomat. He is currently (2021) serving as the Member of Parliament (Indian National Congress) of the Lok Sabha from Thiruvananthapuram, Kerala. He was formerly the Under-Secretary General of the United Nations and contested for the post of Secretary-General in 2006. He has also served as the Minister of External Affairs and Human Resource Development in the Indian government. He is a globally recognized orator and an acclaimed author with over twenty best-selling works of fiction and non-fiction. He has authored hundreds of columns and articles in publications such as *The New York Times, The Washington Post, Time Magazine, Newsweek* and *The Times of India.* His writing focuses on Indian history and culture, Hinduism, politics, society, and foreign policy.

Tharoor's career is the quintessential dream of a typical English-speaking Indian and remains an inspiration for many an Indian. Having graduated from the prestigious St. Stephen's College, Delhi; obtaining a Ph.D. from Tufts University at the age of twenty-two, serving the United Nations for nearly three decades and to becoming a full-fledged Indian politician and a popular author, Shashi Tharoor has had a highly successful career, by most popular parameters. The English-speaking urban population of India, Non-Resident Indians, and the larger Indian diaspora constitute his wide audience. He enjoys a massive following on social media with more than eight million followers on Twitter and remains an influential personality in the media today.

Some of his best-selling books are *Inglorious Empire: What the British did to India*, *An Era of Darkness: The British Empire in India*, *The Great Indian Novel*, *India Shastra: Reflections on the Nation in our Time*, *Why I am a Hindu*, *The Hindu Way* (excerpted from the bestseller *Why I am a Hindu*) and the latest *The Battle of Belonging: On Nationalism, Patriotism, And What It Means to be Indian*. Tharoor is also celebrated for his mastery over English and is popular for using unique English words in his everyday parlance. His recent book *Tharoorosaurus* is a testament to his popularity in the world of English vocabulary and lexicon.[1] For an average modern Indian, who views mastery over English as the most important mark of intellectual credibility, Tharoor is viewed as an intellectual giant par excellence.

In academia, popular media and for most aspirational urban Indians, Tharoor is seen as a modern and perhaps the most eloquent interpreter of Hinduism for the twenty-first century. Through his books, Tharoor explains what he believes is the essence of Hinduism and counters the 'narrow-minded' narratives by the 'Hindu Right' popularly referred to as the 'Hindutvavadis.'[2] He also claims to have written books focusing on Hinduism to counter the growing "intolerance"[3] by the 'Hindu Right'. Although Tharoor has written extensively on various issues ranging from international affairs to politics to Indian history, the focus of this essay are his positions on *dharma*.

Tharoor – An Intellectual Ravana?

With his impeccable credentials, one might wonder what makes Tharoor an 'Intellectual Ravana'. Ravana was an intellectual giant, his strength and valor matchless. Through rigorous *tapasyā*[4], he had obtained enormous blessings and scholarship which made him unconquerable. However, Ravana used all these powers for adharmic deeds which were harmful for mankind, and he was later vanquished by the forces of dharma.

Tharoor uses his eloquence and impressive public persona to propagate his views on dharma and India. However, his position on dharma is counter-productive to the unity and integrity of India, as I will demonstrate in this essay. Tharoor's work on Hinduism is majorly an assortment of theories drawn from colonial Indologists and historians whose aim was to conjure a history of India which denies the indigenous origin of the country's mainstream culture, instead giving credit to foreign invaders while devaluing India's cultural heritage by trivializing her contribution towards the betterment of humanity at large. There are also many instances where Tharoor has taken extensive liberties in his interpretation of Sanskrit words and Hindu ideas, leading to manipulated and loaded narratives as we shall examine in the later part of the essay.

Tharoor claims to interpret Hinduism through the prism of a pluralistic, liberal Hindu as we shall discuss below. Given his wide popularity, his work influences the civilizational idea of India and subverts the native cultural identity for the modern Indian. However, a true understanding of something seminal like Hinduism needs to be broad-based and reflect fidelity to the tradition's own self-perceptions, while not being colored by subjective prejudices. A factual and unbiased analysis of his books, articles, and thoughts is therefore very much the need of the hour in order to counter some of the biases implicit in his works. While Tharoor probably deserves a book-length critique, a brief, albeit concise, highlight of some fundamental issues in the Tharoor narratives is presented in this essay, which one hopes, will encourage the readers not to take his books and narratives at face value, but to delve deeper and understand the underlying motives behind such narratives.

Pūrva-pakṣa: Positions held by Tharoor

This section attempts to summarize Tharoor's views and understanding of Hinduism.

Tharoor's "anything-goes" Hinduism

Tharoor's work on Hinduism primarily focuses on the pluralistic and flexible nature of Hinduism. He acknowledges the fact that he is neither a 'Sanskritist' nor a scholar of Hinduism, and therefore his work is not a scholarly exposition. Tharoor also makes it clear that he presents a layman's view of Hinduism, that is, his personal understanding of the faith after his "attentive" reading and understanding of the scriptures, academic texts and learnings from great thinkers of the religion.[5] However, despite his proclamations about his non-scholarly work, his books are considered to be the 'new-age' authority on Hinduism, especially in urban India. His works serve as a 'handbook' on Hinduism for many modern Hindus, making it all the more important to factually counter his erroneous positions. For instance, at a marriage ceremony, the *Bhagavad Gita* was replaced by Tharoor's book *Why I am a Hindu*, and the groom's mother shared this 'proud revolutionary' moment on social media. She was also quoted saying that Tharoor's book was a 'more meaningful and relevant text.'[6]

Tharoor claims to be a passionate follower of Swami Vivekananda and credits notable personalities like Dr. Sarvepalli Radhakrishnan, Ananda Coomaraswamy, Ramakrishna Paramahamsa, Paramahansa Yogananda, A.L. Basham, R.C. Zaehner, Raimon Panikkar and Dr. Karan Singh, for his wisdom on Hinduism.[7] He also credits his contemporary fellow 'intellectual Ravana', Devdutt Pattanaik, for guiding him on his book *Why I am a Hindu*.[8] Tharoor argues that Hinduism is a religion with no boundaries or barriers of entry, or fundamentals, or defined rituals or prescribed books or a specific place of worship.[9] He emphasizes the fact that it is a faith that accommodates every belief and therefore there is no need to choose some and reject others.[10] He also points out that Hinduism is a faith without dogma and consequently there is no particular framework from which one can deviate. Hindus can choose from a variety of rituals, deities, customs and practices as per their needs and wishes. An inherent trait of every true Hindu is therefore, to accept and tolerate every worldview. In short Tharoor believes that every way of life is the Hindu way[11].

Hinduism seemingly embraces myriad forms of beliefs and worship and thus Tharoor wholeheartedly agrees with India's first Prime Minister, Jawaharlal Nehru, who had famously said that 'being a Hindu means all things to all men'.[12] Tharoor concludes by saying: "As a Hindu I subscribe to a creed that is free of the restrictive dogmas of holy writ, one that refuses to be shackled to the limitations of a single volume of holy revelation."[13]

Tharoor on Hinduism's Perspective on Other Faiths

Tharoor asserts that Hinduism stands for 'universal tolerance and acceptance' as emphasized by Swami Vivekananda[14]. It is therefore, important for every adherent of the faith to tolerate and accept every other religion as their own irrespective of how the other faith treats Hinduism.[15]

> "Hindu legends have the gods manifesting themselves in so many shapes and forms that the notion of one agreed image of God would be preposterous. Thus one can imagine God as a pot bellied man with an elephant head, and also as a ten-armed woman with a beatific smile; and since both forms are equally valid to the worshipper, why not also imagine God as a bleeding man on a cross? All are acceptable to the Hindu; the reverence accorded to each representation of the unknowable God by worshippers of other faiths is enough to prompt similar respect from the Hindu. Acceptance is always the name of the game." (Tharoor 2019:47-48)

He extols Hinduism for its resilience against foreign invaders and credits its strength to the doctrinal openness and flexibility.[16] Surprisingly, he does not touch upon the ideas of *Kshatriya* dharma[17] that are integral to Hinduism and majorly responsible for victories in war over millennia and perhaps India's very survival.

Tharoor writes and talks a lot on the idea of tolerance which he defines as indulging the other, however hostile they may be. As an Indian parliamentarian, Tharoor's choice of words such as 'indulge' in the context of Hindus and 'tolerance' seem rather surprising, given that millions of Hindus have laid down their lives fighting nearly thousand years of foreign invasions only to protect the country's political, economic, and cultural sovereignty.

> "Tolerance, after all, implies that you have the truth, but will generously indulge another who does not; you will, in an act of tolerance, allow him the right to be wrong." (Tharoor 2019:18)

Thus, as per Tharoor, it is perfectly acceptable for an artist, a filmmaker, an actor or an author to interpret Hinduism in whichever way they deem fit. To counter or defend such interpretations, which many within the Hindu tradition may perceive as distortions, is for Tharoor, no less than an act of intolerance and against the ethos of Hinduism. Tharoor feels a book needs to be respected, even if it derides a Hindu Goddess, for a book is a sacred item. Therefore, as far as Tharoor is concerned, those who had protested against Wendy Doniger's (a contemporary 'Intellectual Ravana')[18] book on Hinduism and dubbed the book as being anti-Hindu are intolerant bigots[19].

Tharoor is also a strong critic of the Rashtriya Swayamsevak Sangh (the RSS) and its ideologues. He alleges that the proponents of Hindutva ignore the concept of tolerance embedded in Hinduism. He criticizes the RSS for its idea of India as a 'khichdi' as opposed to his 'thali' theory. Below is an excerpt from his article where he is critical of the current RSS chief Mohan Bhagwat's idea of India:

> "The first idea assumes that there are various kinds of Indians, with very different views of their own identity, including religious assumptions that differ markedly from each other. Yet, we all belong together and share a common allegiance to India. I have described this for many years now, in various speeches and writings, as my "thali" theory of Indian nationalism. Like a thali, we are a collection of different items in different bowls; since we are in different dishes we don't necessarily flow into each other, but we belong together on the same platter and combine on your palate to give you a satisfying repast.
>
> Bhagwat's idea of India is not that of my thali. It is, instead, a khichdi theory of nationalism: We are one dish, with many ingredients all mixed up and cooked together. Thus for him, all true Indians are Hindus; there might be a "Muslim Hindu" here and a "Christian Hindu" there, but they must acknowledge that they are part of the mixed khichdi and have no identity separate from it. Their diversity, in other words, is subordinate to their common role as a part of the larger unity." (Tharoor 2018a)

In fact, Tharoor views invasions as a necessary evil which allowed Hindus to borrow culturally from the invaders and thereby enrich itself. He does not agree with the view that Hinduism suffered a great deal on account of Muslim invasions, and therefore, feels that notions of retaliation or civilizational anger of the Hindus are not only against secular ideals but also unnecessary.

> "Hinduism has survived the Aryans, the Mughals, the British; it has taken from each—language, art, food, learning—and outlasted them all. Muslim invaders destroyed Hindu temples, putting mosques in their place, but this did not make India a Muslim land, nor did Hinduism suffer a fatal blow." (Tharoor 2019:227)

It is striking that Tharoor fails to acknowledge that one-third of 'Bharat' was indeed Islamicized and that led to the ultimate creation of two independent nations, Pakistan and Bangladesh, while leaving behind eternal socio-political conflict in several places of the country that continue to drain our resources to this day. Again, Tharoor seems to be deliberately underplaying the extent of the loss of Bharat's geography over the years. It is hard to believe that a scholar of his stature is not aware of India's original geography prior to foreign invasions.

Tharoor on Religious Conversion

Tharoor quotes Swami Vivekananda and Mahatma Gandhi, to point out that religious conversion is unwarranted. But for a Hindu like himself, he feels that every individual's spiritual needs are different, and if some wish to find **salvation** (emphasis added) through a different faith, that is entirely their prerogative. He also feels that a self-confident faith like Hinduism, secure in its own broad-minded liberality, has no need of violence in its defence. He insists that religious conversion is not a threat to society and is a non-violent activity. Tharoor feels every Indian is entitled to change his faith if he is not happy in his current one, be it for spiritual or materialistic gains and therefore religious proselytizing is not an anti-national activity. Conversion, according to Tharoor, is just merely trying a different item on the spiritual menu. Hinduism, being the most tolerant faith, must also allow its adherents to freely convert to another faith without any apprehensions. Tharoor argues that preventing religious conversion is also against Indian nationalism and the ethos of dharma.[20]

Tharoor's Use of Aryan Invasion Theory

Tharoor insists that the Aryan Invasion/Migration Theory (AI/MT) stands true despite the "controversy" created around it by the Hindutvavadis (adherents of the Hindutva ideology/Hindu "extremists"). He writes that the Indo-Aryan people migrated to northern India from the Central Asian Steppes some time before 1500 BCE and authored the foundational texts of Hinduism, the Vedas. However, the *Rig Veda* consists of references to the northern Indian flora and fauna. Tharoor links these references to Aryan Invasion/Migration Theory by explaining that the references could suggest that while the Aryans came from elsewhere, they only composed the Vedas after having created a settled civilization in the Indo-Gangetic plains. He also claims to have enough genetic research to prove the Aryan Invasion /Migration Theory theory[21], citing a Martin P. Richards and et al's paper '*A Genetic Chronology for the Indian Subcontinents Points to Heavily Sex-biased Dispersals*'. With this theory, Tharoor feels that if Islam or Christianity can be labeled as religions having its origins outside India, so is Hinduism or Vedic religion for it was brought into India by the Aryans, thus putting forth the classic insidious consequence of Aryan Invasion/Migration Theory.

Tharoor insists that migrations have always been a permanent feature of Indian history and therefore it is no surprise that the Aryans also migrated into the subcontinent and founded Hinduism.[22] While he resorts to citing seemingly scientific papers to bolster his case, he doesn't accord the same respect to studying and negating the opponent's position, but only merely casting it aside. Tharoor also quotes the *Puranas* to substantiate his interpretations:

> "In the Puranas there is the story of a debate between the rishis Vasistha and Vishwamitra on whether the Vedic religion could be universalized or whether it was intended for the Aryan people alone." (Tharoor 2019:116)

Tharoor does not bother to provide any proof for his above claims. It is ironic that Tharoor claims to be an ardent follower of Swami Vivekananda but ignores Swami Vivekananda's take on Aryan Invasion/Migration Theory:

> "There is not one word in our scriptures, not one, to prove that the Aryans ever came from anywhere outside India...The whole of India is Aryan, nothing else." (Vivekananda 1958:293)

Tharoor selectively quotes Swami Vivekananda, prompting one to question the integrity and credibility of Tharoor's interpretation of not only the sage's work, but of his other sources as well. One knows of "Cafeteria Christians" (a non-scriptural term used to refer to the practice of choosing for oneself the parts of the Bible to either accept or reject)[23] but one might as well coin 'Cafeteria Hindu' to describe Tharoor, due to his selective use of data, inferences, whitewashing historical facts and causes—one can pick and choose one's use of rationality in his world.

Tharoor's Chronology of Hinduism

Tharoor's chronology is based on the Aryan Invasion/Migration Theory[24] as noted above and accordingly, he believes that the Aryans migrated to India sometime before 1500 BCE and thereafter composed the Veda-s. The four Vedas are believed to have been created between 1500 BCE and 500 BCE. He also believes that the first eight *Upaniṣad-s* to have been written between the eighth century BCE to the fourth century BCE, which is congruent to the age of Buddha. The next three *Upaniṣad-s* are post-Buddhist and date from 300 BCE to 200 CE and that the remaining ninety-seven *Upaniṣad-s* belong to the Puranic period i.e., second century CE to the tenth century CE. He believes the Smriti-s were composed between 300 BCE and 200 CE, *Rāmāyaṇa* around 200 BCE to 200 CE and the *Mahābhārata* between 400 BCE and 400 CE. He dates the *Purāṇa-s* to 250 CE and 1000 CE.[25]

This artificial chronology that was created by colonial scholars to serve various purposes, has been challenged and countered time and again over the last century. Yet, it continues to hold sway over academia, and the Western baselining of Indian history still continues in several forums. While, many Indian scholars have begun to challenge the dates and chronological structures framed by colonial Indologists, the silver lining is that, there are increasingly vibrant discussions in public space and awareness amongst the younger generations, as to the logical fallacies in their narrative.

Tharoor's Interpretation of the Veda-s, Itihāsa, Purāṇa-s and Smriti-s

Tharoor's work analyzing Hinduism's important texts is replete with serious misinterpretations and factual errors. Tharoor believes that Hinduism is not absolved of gender bias and quotes *Manusmriti* and excerpts from the *Anuśāsana Parva* of *Mahābhārata* to substantiate his claims on misogyny.[26]

Firstly, *Manusmriti* does not define Hinduism. There are few modern Hindus who wake up in the morning and read the *Manusmriti* to guide their actions, because, fundamentally, smriti-s are codified laws which are context, time and place driven and not eternal truths or the last word. *Manusmriti* cannot be compared to the Bible/Quran which transcend time, place and context. Moreover, Manu's code is explicit in stating that it is not universal. It calls for updates, amendments and rewrites in order to suit different circumstances. Tharoor also refers to the *Manusmriti* as the 'Hindu Law' even though it has never been enforced as the divine and all-encompassing law of all Hindus.[27] It was the British who referred to the *Manusmriti* as the 'Hindu law' to show that they were ruling in accordance with the laws of the Hindus, albeit with colonial motives.[28]

Indian spiritual texts have traps for the uninitiated, therefore it is of prime importance to rely on a Guru or the one who has the *adhikāra* to interpret the esoteric texts.[29] Tharoor neither has the adhikāra nor has he made any attempt whatsoever to learn from the right people and his ignorance shines through his misinterpretations.

Tharoor insists that *soma* or *soma-rasa* means alcohol, and that it was the favorite beverage of the Vedic deities and was offered in most of the sacrifices performed in honor of Rig Vedic gods like Indra, Agni, Varuna, and others. This is again one of his grossly mistranslated and misinterpreted terms.[30] The term 'soma' has multiple meanings and interpretations in the Rig Veda based on the context it has been used for. The pressing of the drink from the eponymous plant represents an act of "purifying the mind". Soma represents the 'moon', and also sometimes Vishnu and even Śiva (Somanātha).[31] Tharoor points out that though the cow was sacred in Vedic times, it was this belief that allowed for beef to be consumed. He also (without proof from the tradition)[32] insists that there are references in the Rig Veda, and in the Dharmaśāstra-s literature, that *Taittiriya Brahmana ('Verily, the cow is food') and the Vajasaneyi Brahmana* that support the contention of beef being eaten at the time. He quotes the Leftist historian D.N. Jha to assert that *Rig Veda* is full of allusions to the slaughter and consumption of cows.[33] Tharoor claims that the adoption of vegetarianism by Hindus, especially Brahmins, is a Jain contribution.[34]

Contrary to his claims on the cow in the Rig Veda, the venerated animal was elevated to the status of divinity in the Rig Veda itself. In book VI the hymn XXVII attributed to Riṣi Bhardvaja, it extols the virtue of the cow. In *Atharva Veda* (Book X, Hymn 10), the cow is formally designated as Vishnu, and "all that the Sun surveys."

> "Tilam na dhaanyam, pashuvah na Gaavah" (Sesame is not a cereal, cow is not an animal). (Swamy 2010:215)

The *Yajur Veda* and the Atharva Veda also lay emphasis on vegetarianism.[35] It is amply clear from the Vedic verses that the cow was highly revered in the Vedic society, and that vegetarianism has always been regarded as an ideal way of life. However, a dharmic society has always been accommodative of every individual's temperament, lifestyle, tastes and preferences albeit with certain conditions. Tharoor's guile lies in proclaiming a laundry list of incorrect interpretations of the Hindu canon while beginning his works with the caveat that he has no scholarly expertise, cleverly instead citing discredited theories from fellow intellectual Ravana-s.

Tharoor on Hindutva

Tharoor believes Hindutva to be a hindrance to globalization,

> "The Hindutva ("Hinduness") movement in India is part of the backlash against cosmopolitanism, multiculturalism, and secularism in the name of cultural rootedness, religious or ethnic identity and nationalist authenticity." (Tharoor 2018b)

It is obvious to the discerning researcher that Tharoor has not understood the difference between globalization and Westernization. He has also not understood the importance of protecting cultural differences and identity. Tharoor equates Hindutva with Islamic fanaticism and 'white' nationalist Christian fundamentalism, another example of his sweeping brush strokes without any basis in reality or fact.[36] Tharoor believes that the Hindutva ideology has nothing to do with Hinduism, although it claims to represent the faith,[37] and views Hindutva as a narrow-minded, violent, intolerant and bigoted movement consequently distorting the philosophy of Hinduism. He also insists that Hindutva is contradictory to Indian nationalism, for the Indian nationalist movement rejected the belief of religion in shaping a political identity, thereby establishing a dichotomy between Indian Nationalism and Hindu Nationalism.[38] On the contrary, the Hindutva inspiration was the emotional spearhead for the first major nationalist struggle—the Swadeshi movement, in which Sri Aurobindo was the prime mover—the movement that followed the partition of Bengal in 1905.[39] Tharoor says that the Hindutva project seeks to reinvent Hindu identity with a new belief structure and new vocabulary:

> "Hindutvavadis seek to make Hinduism more like the semitic religions, by picking fewer sacred books, notably the Gita, to focus on fewer gods, notably Shiva, Rama and Krishna, with Ganesh and various forms of Devi, to standardize religious practices around specific festivals, rituals and gatherings, that would provide a greater sense of community." (Tharoor 2018b)

Tharoor alleges that Hindutva prefers uniformity over the accommodative, inclusionist, flexible and agglomerative ethos of Hinduism. Tharoor equates the idea of a 'Hindu *Rashtra*' with 'Hindu Pakistan' and vehemently opposes the former.[40] His understanding of the concept of a Rashtra is to merely imply to the 'nation-state' in the Western sense.[41] He further harps on the global media such as *The New York Times*, *The Washington Post* (the arbiters of journalistic truth to most colonized Indian liberals) and television shows by John Oliver to point out the growing intolerance and hate crimes against minorities (Muslims and Christians) arising mainly out of the Hindutva ideology.[42]

Tharoor reinforces Nehru's arguments on science and religion, which were influenced by 19th century Marxism:

> "India's first prime minister, Jawaharlal Nehru, argued that unlike religion – which tends to produce "intolerance, credulity and superstition, emotionalism and irrationalism" and "a temper of a dependent, unfree person" – a scientific temper "is the temper of a free man."" (Tharoor 2018g)

It is evident that his interpretation of Hinduism is through the Biblical lens legitimized by the Western institutions. He follows the framework of the colonial Indologists, just that he is a brown sahib.[43]

Tharoor questions Hindu customs

Tharoor claims that he cannot be comfortable with the tenets of any faith other than Hinduism for its intellectual fit[44]. Indeed, it would be interesting to see if Tharoor is brave enough to subject other religions to the same open scrutiny. Tharoor categorizes the caste system as a 'Hindu Custom.' He feels that the problems of casteism have been cited as legitimizing discrimination in some of Hinduism's sacred texts.[45] It is unfortunate that Tharoor who claims to have "attentively" read the scriptures, cannot acknowledge the excesses sometimes carried out in the name of caste but the lack of sanction for such discrimination in the Hindu tradition. He represents the colonized camp of Indians who believe that the caste system is intrinsic to Hinduism despite the glaring evidence of the forced imposition of this system by the British to cripple a flourishing India. Proving the foreign origins of the caste system is beyond the scope of this essay, however, it is worth highlighting Tharoor's recklessness in explaining the tenets of a faith he claims to respect so dearly. There is ample evidence by well-meaning scholars on India, of the foreign origins of the caste system, its systematic imposition, distortion and misinterpretation of the profound Varna-ashrama dharma. Rajiv Malhotra's *Breaking India* (2011) extensively writes on the birth of the caste system in India, and it is telling that intellectuals of Tharoor's kind refuse to engage and address such material.

Analyzing Tharoor's Work

Tharoor's key views on Hinduism considered above demonstrate important themes in his work as shown through the enumeration of the following points:

- Hinduism is the most tolerant and inclusive faith with no boundaries and barriers of entry and needs to retain this openness despite receiving no reciprocal mutual respect.
- The Kśatriyata/action-oriented approach towards adharma needs to be subdued as it does not fit the infinitely open, flexible and tolerable themes of Hinduism. The Kśatriyata spirit of dharma is the root for violence and must be shunned as emphasized by our great Gurus like Swami Vivekananda, Mahatma Gandhi.
- The ideology of Hindutva is contradictory to Hinduism

Some unanswered questions raised by Tharoor have been:

1. What makes Hinduism flexible and open?
2. How 'elastic' is Hinduism?
3. Does Hinduism have no boundaries at all? Can any book be thought of as the sacred text? Can anything and everything be part of Hinduism?

Implications of Tharoor's Work

- anything-goes Hinduism, myth of sameness[46], relativism, hostile

forces making way into the system, confused Hindu and a faith that is prone to disintegration
- gateway for digestion eventually leading to extinction[47]
- serves as a narrative for the Breaking India forces
- passivity/complacency toward defending dharma, which leads to adharma

Tharoor takes the liberty to distort and misinterpret the notion of 'liberalism' and 'pluralism' inherent in Hinduism to convince a Hindu into cowardice and inaction. For an average 'Macaulayized' English-speaking Hindu youth, who has no deep moorings in Hindu thinking, it is easy to get swayed by his eloquence, public persona and his well-articulated writings. He positions himself as an insider and leads Hindus on a self-implosive trajectory. If Tharoor had genuinely wanted to discuss Hinduism's openness and flexibility, there would have been clarity in his explanations of many of Hinduism's vaunted characteristics. Other than deliberate misplaced characterizations, the genuine reader, looking for logical and plausible explanations will most likely feel cheated after reading Tharoor. He instead throughout his work contrives to establish the myth of sameness.

Before one delves into deconstructing the metaphysics of Tharoor's work, one should understand a few terms from Rajiv Malhotra's vocabulary that will be of vital importance to us in the subsequent sections.

History-Centrism: The Abrahamic religions (according to most interpretations) deny the existence of any infinite human potential that, in effect, could make every human a potential prophet. They consider that 'God' only sends a few prophets with the message containing critical spiritual knowledge. To abandon the history through which this prophetic knowledge has been passed down, or to lose the exact account of these historically transmitted canons would be catastrophic.[48] As Tharoor points out, the fixated nature of the Abrahamic faiths on one God, one book and so on, is precisely because of this history-centric nature, which he fails to articulate.

Non History-Centrism: The spiritual traditions based on self-realization hold that humans are born with infinite potential and their essence is 'divinity' (*sat-chit-ananda*). Hence, if all historical records and knowledge were to vanish or become corrupted or inaccessible to humans for whatever reason, new self-realized living masters would be able to teach us the highest truths based on their own enlightenment. Even though these masters are very rare, they have existed throughout history in many cultures. The result is that (i) knowledge of history is not necessary to be a religious person, and (ii) no culture has a monopoly on religious truth, although different cultures may have used or misused this knowledge in different ways.[49] The flexible and open nature of Hinduism is because 'dharmic' traditions are non-history centric.

Integral and Synthetic Unities: The dharmic traditions are steeped in the metaphysics of the non-separation of all reality, physical and non-physical, from the divine – what is referred to henceforth as 'integral unity.'[50] This approach is the opposite in Western religions, which start with the assumption of separateness – of matter, life and the divine. The spiritual goal in the Judeo-Christian faiths is to achieve unity or synthesis where none existed before. Such a worldview may achieve unity but it is a tentative unity, tenuous and artificial at best. Moreover, force and domination are often used to achieve it. This is referred to as 'synthetic unity.'[51]

The above terms help us in understanding the basic metaphysics of the Abrahamic and the dharmic faiths. The worldview and the societies of both the dharmic and Abrahamic faiths are built on these underlying principles. Apart from understanding the philosophy of different religions, these principles can be applied to understand and solve global social problems. Based on the above concepts, we find that India needs to be analyzed through the dharmic lens, that is, a lens constituting themes such as the Integral Unity and Non-history centrism. Tharoor, however, uses the Western or the Abrahamic lens to analyze Hinduism, and that is at the root of his flawed assessment.

Tharoor applies the constructs of synthetic unity to explain Hinduism and India. For instance, he insists on the 'thali' theory of Indian

Nationalism.[52] He first emphasizes the intrinsic cleavages present in India such as the 'Aryans', 'Dravidians', 'foreign imported religions' and then he tries to create an artificial or synthetic unity among the identities with contradicting views.

> "Dharma philosophers would argue that for systems lacking wholeness which is built-in, any attempts at unification are necessarily imperfect with irreconcilable schisms and enduring fault lines." (Malhotra 2011:102)

While Tharoor is right in understanding Hinduism as a faith that does not have a rigid entity with dogmas enforced by a centralized authority equivalent to a church, nor a single founder, linear history, 'one truth' and so forth, it is his muddled understanding of Hinduism's clear distinction between valid and invalid religious claims which is the cause of concern. The traditional Hindu teachings make a clear distinction between dharma and adharma, *sat* (truth) and *asat* (falsity), *daivika* and *asuric*, and so on.[53] Hinduism has certain definitive boundaries that are non-negotiable, for instance the concepts of karma and reincarnation are fundamental to explaining the philosophy of Hinduism. The Vedas form the basis of dharma, and are fundamental to an *astika*.

As the title of one of Tharoor's books *The Hindu Way* suggests, indeed Hindus have a definitive way and not 'every way' is a 'Hindu Way' as the content of the book seems to suggest. The quote below is from Tharoor's book *The Hindu Way* and substantiates our analysis of his thesis:

> "Indeed the term "the Hindu way" is in itself a fallacy as there is no one Hindu way." (Tharoor 2019:64)

When Tharoor makes an audacious statement as above notwithstanding the fact that he is paving the way for 'anything goes' Hinduism. (Or is that his intent?) In the realm of pop culture or 'new age spirituality' it is fashionable to interpret Hinduism as infinitely elastic or as vaguely as one pleases. If every way of life counts as the 'Hindu Way', then the natural question of what defines a Hindu arises.

Rajiv Malhotra uses the term 'open architecture' to explain the flexible, hard to define quality of Hinduism. The term 'open architecture' refers to a framework that can be populated by a range of ideas, practices, symbols, rituals, and so on. He draws an analogy between Hinduism and the functioning of the internet, as explained in the book *Indra's Net*:

> "The internet is not infinitely open but only relatively so: its boundaries are defined by what it rejects-for example, viruses or abusive elements. Despite these rejections, the internet has abundant flexibility for the future. Similarly, Hinduism does not comprise all conceivable kinds of spirituality and religious claims, because it must exclude those that would destroy its underlying principles of integral unity, openness and flexibility." (Malhotra 2016:20)

Swami Vivekananda defined Hinduism with three essential features—belief in God, in the Vedas as revelation, and in the system of karma and transmigration. While Tharoor represents Hinduism as a faith that is infinitely open to embracing everything unconditionally—such extremism is counter-productive because the survival of the entire system is compromised.

As stated above, just as the Internet is hostile to viruses or abusive elements that would hamper its productivity, Hinduism must also be guarded against elements that would threaten its philosophical unity. Tharoor fails to identify such elements (perhaps deliberately?) and draw a definitive boundary against what is not Hinduism.

Hinduism cannot be accurately defined and explained without differentiating dharma from religion. Tharoor applies the Abrahamic lens to Hinduism leaving the reader confused and muddled, because the term 'religion' has a definitive set of qualities associated with it which cannot be applied to dharma.[54] Without clearly defining what dharma stands for, it is only counter-productive to explain Hinduism. Tharoor also harps on the Nehruvian idea of separating religion and science, influenced by Marxism.[55] The tenets of a religion are irreconcilable with science, but that is not the case with dharma, as it is explained in detail in *Being Different*. A non-religious society may still be ethical without belief in God, but an a-dharmic society loses its ethical compass and falls into corruption and decadence.[56]

As discussed earlier, the terms 'integral unity' and the metaphor of 'Indra's net' succinctly explains the underlying philosophical unity of Hinduism. Although the Hindu dharma provides great flexibility as well as enormous freedom to adapt and evolve, at the same time, the dharma has a boundary and excludes hostile elements that do not reflect this unity.

If all religions were the same as Tharoor portrays them to be, then what good is it to remain a Hindu?

Tharoor, a Facilitator of Cultural Appropriation?

When Hinduism is loosely defined, without definitive boundary markers, Tharoor is opening up for digestion.[57] The term 'digestion' in this context essentially means that the predator religion separates the desirable elements of a particular faith, then 'scrubs' the elements to remove the dharmic context in order to make it more acceptable to appropriate to the predator faith, thereby making the predator religion more robust and stronger. For eg: Christian Yoga[58]. The threat of such a process is that, it may eventually lead to extinction of a weaker civilization, because the predator religion keeps becoming stronger and what is left of a civilization after the predator is done with it, is waste material to be removed and destroyed. For example, as in the case of pagans of Europe, many of their rituals were appropriated by Christianity eventually leading to the extinction of the faith.[59]

When Tharoor extensively talks about the tolerant aspect of Hinduism and insists that Hindus must tolerate and accept other religions as their own, what he fails is to advocate a level playing field for all religions to exhibit 'mutual respect' rather than just Hindus tolerating the other. In fact, the concept of 'mutual respect' does not appropriate and digest, instead acknowledges the contributions, differences, diversity and gives necessary credit where it is due. Therefore, instead of modifying Yoga to Christian Yoga to make it more palatable to its adherents, the Abrahamics can simply and respectfully acknowledge that Yoga is central to Hinduism and is beneficial to oneself and society. However, because of the very missionizing and evangelical nature of Abrahamic religions, they will refuse to follow this path and go down the route of creating non-existent connections to try and fit into their system. While Hindus like Tharoor cheer on quoting the flexible nature of Hinduism only to later learn that the original system of Yoga has ceased to exist. Tharoor, who claims to be a champion of Pluralism and Liberalism ought to promote 'mutual respect' than mere 'tolerance.' By that lens, one naturally wonders if works like those of Tharoor's are that of a confused and shallow understanding or a deliberately aimed dubious scholarship

This is especially relevant in an environment of aggressive religious conversions by the Abrahamic religions. The history of brutal invasions and conquests by the Abrahamic faiths cannot be ignored in this context. Religious conversion is the pinnacle of religious intolerance. The term 'mutual respect' would be more appropriate in the inter-faith dialogue today.[60] Let us analyze the term 'tolerance':

> "Tolerance' implies control over those who do not conform to our norms by allowing them some though not all, of the rights and privileges we enjoy. A religion which involves the worship of 'false gods' and whose adherents are referred to as 'heathens' can be tolerated, but it cannot be respected. Tolerance is a patronizing posture, whereas respect implies that we consider the other to be equally legitimate—a position which some religions routinely deny to others, instead declaring these 'others' to be 'idol worshippers' or 'infidels' and the like." (Malhotra 2011:16)

However, the flexibility and the openness of Hinduism does not mean that it is not worthy of expecting the same respect and acceptance from other religions. There is a fine line between accepting and submitting, which Tharoor fails to highlight. Religious conversions are one such example of Hindus being deprived of mutual respect.

As mentioned earlier, the pluralistic inherent unity and acceptance of dharmic faiths need to be reciprocated with mutual respect, which is a two-way path. When mutual respect is compromised, whenever it is under siege, dharma needs to be defended or protected, for that is the true essence of dharma. This fact has been constantly emphasized in our puranas, ītihāsa and the Bhagavad Gita. However, it is evident through the work of Tharoor that he constantly tries to subdue this Kṣatriya spirit of the Hindus. This is one of the major reasons why Tharoor's work is against the ethos of Hindu philosophy, as not only is his interpretation in contradiction to the fundamental ethos of dharma, but also mentally conditions a Hindu to become submissive and slavish.

Tharoor, capitalizing on the broad-minded philosophy of Hinduism, aims to convince a Hindu that all religions are the same and every path leads to the same God, therefore it is perfectly alright to convert to another faith or just accept the exclusive nature of the Abrahamic religions. But he fails to highlight the fact that every path is indeed different despite leading to the same destination, and that one path may help you reach your destination faster. If Tharoor is genuinely concerned about religious violence, he ought to understand the root cause of these tensions.

Hinduism and Hindutva

Diversity and difference are inherent traits of Hinduism. Most Hindus have grown up experiencing life as a rich diversity of ideas and practices passed down from their ancestors. So vast is the sense of openness among the majority Hindus that they feel no natural urge to draw boundaries between themselves and others. This attitude of the Hindus was fine until the Abrahamic religions went around the world with their ambitious conquests, invasions, suppression, religious conversion, oppression, all in the name of religion.[61] Therefore, it is vital for Hindus to understand the nuances of fighting adharma, for Hinduism is all about adhering to dharma. As the profound adage goes—'*dharmo rakṣati rakṣitaḥ.*' This is when the Kṣatra dharma of Hinduism gained momentum, what we call *Hindutva* today. When Tharoor alleges that Hindutva is a project to make Hinduism more like the Semitic faiths, or to make India a Hindu Pakistan, it is important to note that it is impossible for a non-history-centric faith like Hinduism with integral unity and open architecture as its philosophical foundations to be converted to a Semitic faith. Unless, the core tenets of the faith are altered, then Hinduism ceases to exist, and it becomes another Abrahamic faith. It is also important to note that Hindutva is based on the philosophical tenets of Vedanta expounded in Kśatra dharma. It is therefore paramount to understand what role Hindutva can play in the twenty-first century in defending the country against threats. Therefore, separating Hindutva from Hinduism makes no sense.

> "The spiritual tradition of Sanatana Dharma, which we call Hinduism includes the code of Raj Dharma and Kshatra Dharma that is needed to defend the nation. This is part of the Hindutva. This dharma is needed to defend the society against hostile forces seeking to destroy the society, especially its spiritual foundation. It is the Kshatra Dharma popularly referred to as Hindutva today that protected and defeated the tyrant foreign forces, especially the Islamic invasions." (Swamy 2010:47)

Tharoor absolutely blames Hindutva ideology for apparent religious violence in India. But what he ought to understand is that history-centric religions[62], as mentioned/explained above, have inherent religious conflicts. Global terrorism perpetrated by Islamic fundamentalists, the Jihadists who seek to establish Dar al-Islam and aggressive evangelical activities carried out by missionaries in the economically weaker countries, is a testament to the internal tensions arising out of history-centrism. *Non-History Centric* faiths offer the only viable spiritual alternative to the religious conflicts that are inherent among *History-Centric* religions.

Tharoor on Mahatma Gandhi

Tharoor selectively quotes Mahatma Gandhi, while ignoring Gandhi's assertion on the usage of Sanskrit non-translatables, celebration of cultural differences, the need to decolonize our lifestyle and so on. He also loosely translates Gandhi's principle of 'ahimsa' to mean 'non-violence'. It is to be noted that Gandhi's notion of ahimsa is not the same as the Western idea of pacifism, as explained by Rajiv Malhotra:

> "'Himsa' means harm and 'ahimsa' means non-harming. To achieve ahimsa requires activity and confrontation. To challenge the world's mightiest empire, one that caused himsa on a large scale, required great strength. Paradoxically, it takes a fighter to actualize ahimsa. Gandhi was such a fighter." (Malhotra 2011:348)

'Ahimsa' is one of the most commonly misinterpreted terms. It is often mistranslated into English as 'non-violence.' For the likes of Tharoor, whose aim is to subdue the Kshatriya spirit of Hindus and sow the seeds of passivity, distorting the essence of 'ahimsa' fits the bill. As per the Hindu view, taking appropriate, punitive action against adharma is an act of ahimsa, and an intrinsic part of the Kshatriya dharma whereas inactivity is an act of himsa.[63]

> "The devastation of cultures is an important kind of himsa which is not often acknowledged in typical accounts of non-violence. For example, when the United Nations drafted its laws on genocide, they eliminated the phrases which described cultural genocide. In the officially defined UN law, cultural genocide is not prohibited. Gandhi fully understood this kind of violence and often talked about it. Cultural genocide is the systematic and complete elimination or suppression of the native religion, language, dress, way of life, customs, and/or symbols of one people by another." (Malhotra 2011:349)

The Question of Religious Conversion

When Tharoor argues, that if some people wish to find 'salvation' through another faith, that is entirely their prerogative. One can deduce that he assumes 'salvation' to be an equivalent of 'moksha.' This is another classic example of Tharoor's muddled understanding or rather the misinterpretations and mistranslations of Hinduism's core components. 'Salvation' in Christian theology refers to a solution to the problem of Eternal Damnation caused by the Original Sin. The dharma traditions do not have the problem of 'Original Sin' to begin with, among many other irreconcilable differences with the Abrahamic religions. Therefore, for Tharoor to make his case by equating 'Salvation' to the Hindu concept of 'Moksha' is irresponsible and factually wrong. It seems like Tharoor has neither understood the concept of Salvation nor of Moksha.

Tharoor also questions why a secure faith like Hinduism should worry about conversions. Religious conversion essentially stands for exclusivity. That is, to convince the adherent of a particular faith that his/her faith is simply not good enough.

To paraphrase it in Tharoor's own terms—to convert to a religion that says his/her way is the only way, we are reducing the number of paths to reach the Ultimate. For someone like Tharoor, who is one of the strongest proponents of Pluralism, as we have noted in his work so far, it is an irony that he supports an act of reducing diversity.

When Tharoor says it is one's individual freedom to convert, it is also important to point out that, it is every individual's right to know what he/she is getting into, just like the terms and conditions of an organization that one would agree to, to opt for their product/service.[64] However, going by the data of mass conversions happening in India in contemporary times, it is mostly through deception.[65] For instance, one must be educated enough to distinguish between Hindu good news and Christian good news.[66] Freedom to proselytize also comes with a moral responsibility. One cannot have unlimited freedom. That would be a level playing field. No other form of conversion can ever be justified, for it is a gruesome violation of human rights, to exploit the vulnerable status of an individual be it due to innocence/poverty/personal problems and so on. It is the pinnacle of religious intolerance that is against achieving world peace. The issue of religious proselytization highlights the fact that Abrahamic faiths are unable to accept the differences of other paths to God and live-in harmony. This goes against the norms of peaceful co-existence. It is ironical that Tharoor lectures a faith with no history of religious conversion on 'tolerance' and acceptance of other religions.

Sanskrit 'Mis-translations'

> "Indian scholars have not been able to form themselves into a great and independent school of learning is due to two causes: the miserable scantiness of the mastery in Sanskrit provided by our universities,

crippling to all but born scholars, and our lack of sturdy independence which makes us over-ready to defer to European [and Western] authority." (Aurobindo 1972)

Tharoor's work is replete with mistranslations of Sanskrit terms that do not have English equivalents. Consequently, some of the profound concepts of Hinduism stand distorted or misinterpreted. He takes on the authority of explaining Hinduism to a layman and bears the responsibility of presenting the philosophy of Hinduism accurately sans distortion. It makes one question if it is an attempt by Tharoor to make Hinduism appear the same as Abrahamic religions or is this how colonized he is, though he sees himself as an anti-colonial intellectual. The non-translatable nature of certain Sanskrit terms and the issue with mistranslations is well-established by Rajiv Malhotra and Satyanarayana Dasa Babaji in the book *Sanskrit Non-Translatables: The Importance of Sanskritizing English*.

> "Sanskrit has certain properties which reveal the inherently contextual and unique nature of dharmic philosophy from which it arose. With Sanskrit, there is also another deeper source of non-translatability: Among its primary sounds, there are layers of connections and interrelationships forged by common underlying vibrations. The complete meaning is thus a composite of the collection, not unlike an algebraic formula. Therefore, great harm is done when a foreign culture, especially a colonial one, imposes its own simplistic, and often incorrect, translations of Sanskrit. Even greater harm is done when the natives of a colonized culture adopt these foreign translations – a process that is often gradual and subtle, and achieved with rewards of upward social mobility offered by the dominant culture." (Malhotra and Babaji 2020:xxxv)

However, such translations of certain Sanskrit terms to their near English equivalents, are usually loaded with the Western philosophical or cultural narrative that suits Tharoor's agenda of diluting or distorting the essence of dharmic traditions to merge them with the Abrahamic faiths.

The open and flexible nature of Hinduism makes it prone to 'digestion' (as mentioned earlier). One of the ways of protecting philosophical unity and marking distinct boundaries for Hinduism and to protect it from further disintegration and distortion, is to retain some Sanskrit terms that have no English equivalents. Below are some of his key mistranslations:

Sanskrit Term	Tharoor's English Equivalent
Brahmā, Viśnu, Īśvara	Holy Trinity
Mokṣa, mukti	Salvation
Paramātmā	Supreme Soul
Soma-rasa	Alcohol
Hanumān	Monkey-God
Māyā	Illusion

The Battle of *Idiocy*

Tharoor's recent book *The Battle of Belonging*, seems like another desperate attempt to substantiate his theories formulated through previous books. This book seems like a compilation of all his previous books and the numerous articles he has published in the public domain. The book is largely a critique on the recent major decisions by the Bharatiya Janata Party (BJP) concerning the Citizenship (Amendment) Act, 2019, abrogation of Article 370, construction of Ram Mandir, and so on. It, however, claims to explore topics of nationalism, patriotism, secularism, and Pluralism in India. The astonishing fact of this book is the number of contradictory and hypocritical statements and the amount of liberty taken in distorting facts. Let's examine a few of these instances from the book.

While he dedicates chapters to explain the history and origin of nationalism as a Western import, he seems to have no qualms with secularism, which is also a Western construct designed for a purely Abrahamic society. His principle of secularism, Pluralism, and Liberalism lies in Hindus forgoing their sentiments for places of worship or animals such as the cow, which is worshipped as an incarnate of the divine for millennia, simultaneously making way for the Abrahamic faiths to hold on to their rigid exclusivist religious sentiments. Tharoor believes that if a Muslim does not want to recite 'Vande Mataram' only because it consists of a hymn to goddess Durga, it is perfectly permissible. At the same time, it is unacceptable for a Hindu to assert his religious preferences. Tharoor on justifying the aversion of Muslims to recite the 'Vande Mataram' quotes the following:

> "The core of [V]ande Mataram is a hymn to goddess Durga: this is so plain that there can be no debate about it...no Mussulman can be expected patriotically to worship the ten-handed deity as "Swadesh"...." (Tharoor 2020:265)

Conclusion

Tharoor's recent books seem to be an elaborate attempt to distort Hinduism and usurp the high ground regarding its narrative in popular imagination. The rising political power of the unapologetically Hindu political groups, however limited, is challenging the decades old power structures. The well-nurtured establishment and the controllers of India's self-narrative in academia and mainstream need Tharoor's articulation to wrest the narrative. The books are seriously well-written, well-presented and will mislead uninformed naïve readers, especially those eager to know the Hindu story. He has managed to get enough credibility as an insider by masquerading as a patriotic Hindu through his books, especially the ones critiquing and questioning the British rule in India. Much of his critique is nothing new and has always been in the public domain by some serious and well-meaning historians of India.

A careful reading of Tharoor's work will help one deduce that not only does he aspire to create a class of subservient and submissive Hindus, but also strives to instil a sense of shame by deliberately misinterpreting the sacred scriptures to bring out issues such as misogyny, superstitions, animal cruelty, alcoholism and so forth. Young Hindu readers, especially those who are reading these books in their attempts to address yearnings for identity, who are subconsciously seeking to understand their place in the world, will be manipulated and their Hindu identities weakened. Reading the books will confuse and, in some cases, even cause damage to the sense of self-worth. This probably is Tharoor's goal and he is mostly successful.

As already indicated, a few thousand words of this essay might not possibly suffice. Tharoor's work does require deeper critique. However, I have presented some key arguments in our *purvapaksha* of Tharoor, which will help the serious reader deconstruct Tharoor for themselves and enable a deeper understanding of the methods and motives.

Bibliography

Aurobindo, Sri. 1972. *The Harmony of Virtue: Early Cultural Writings*. Pondicherry, Pondicherry: Sri Aurobindo Ashram Trust.

Dr. Shashi Tharoor Official. 2020. "Dr Shashi Tharoor with Karan Thapar on #Tharoorsaurus and beyond." YouTube. Retrieved October 18, 2021 (https://www.youtube.com/watch?v=ZXTUgSu59MA).

Malhotra, Rajiv. 2002a. "The Axis Of Neocolonialism." rajivmalhotra.com. Retrieved October 18, 2021 (https://rajivmalhotra.com/library/articles/axis-neocolonialism/).

Malhotra, Rajiv. 2002b. "The Root Of India-Pakistan Conflicts." rajivmalhotra.com. Retrieved October 18, 2021 (https://rajivmalhotra.com/library/articles/root-india-pakistan-conflicts/).

Malhotra, Rajiv. 2004. "Myth Of Hindu Sameness." rajivmalhotra.com. Retrieved October 18, 2021 (https://rajivmalhotra.com/library/articles/myth-hindu-sameness/).

Malhotra, Rajiv. 2006. "Follow Up On Manusmriti To My Article In Outlook India." rajivmalhotra.com. Retrieved October 18, 2021 (https://rajivmalhotra.com/library/articles/follow-manusmriti-article-outlook-india/).

Malhotra, Raijv. 2011. *Being Different*. Noida: Harper Collins.

Malhotra, Rajiv. 2012a. "The Tiger And The Deer: Is Dharma Being Digested Into The West?" rajivmalhotra.com. Retrieved October 18, 2021 (https://rajivmalhotra.com/library/articles/tiger-deer-dharma-digested-west/).

Malhotra, Rajiv. 2012b. "Dharma Is Not The Same As Religion." rajivmalhotra.com. Retrieved October 18, 2021 (https://rajivmalhotra.com/library/articles/dharma-religion/).

Malhotra, Rajiv. 2012c. "Hindu Good News." rajivmalhotra.com. Retrieved October 18, 2021 (https://rajivmalhotra.com/library/articles/hindu-good-news/).

Malhotra, Rajiv. 2016. *Indra's Net*. New Delhi: HarperCollins.

Malhotra, Rajiv and Satyanarayana D. Babaji. 2020. *Sanskrit Non-Translatables: The Importance of Sanskritizing English*. New Delhi: Amaryllis.

Rajiv Malhotra Official. 2016. "Rajiv Malhotra & Dr Swamy talk on Christian Missionaries Religion Conversion Tactics." YouTube. Retrieved October 18, 2021 (https://www.youtube.com/watch?v=liKAbE7beNI).

Rajiv Malhotra Official. 2017. "Discussing the Digestion of Yoga with a White Hindu." YouTube. Retrieved October 18, 2021 (https://www.youtube.com/watch?v=SNpVBfgzPmo).

Rajiv Malhotra Official. 2019. "Rajya is Strong, Where is the Rashtra?" YouTube. Retrieved October 18, 2021 (https://www.youtube.com/watch?v=SnkbmERdyBg).

Rajiv Malhotra Official. 2020. "How Christianity Overtook Europe." YouTube. (https://www.youtube.com/watch?v=yKkZeiwlkeU).

Rajiv Malhotra Official. 2020. "Western Influence on Indian Social Sciences | Come Carpentier with Rajiv Malhotra." YouTube. Retrieved October 18, 2021 (https://www.youtube.com/watch?v=luYdq8yYRc0).

Swamy, Subramanian. 2010. *Hindutva and National Renaissance*. New Delhi: Har-Anand Publications.

Tharoor, Shashi. 2018. *Why I am a Hindu*. New Delhi.

Tharoor, Shashi. 2018a. "Mohan Bhagwat's idea of India is not a thali of identities but a khichdi: Shashi Tharoor." shashitharoor.in. Retrieved October 18, 2021 (https://shashitharoor.in/writings_my_essays_details/125).

Tharoor, Shashi. 2018b. "Shashi Tharoor: All the reasons I'm proud—and not—to be Hindu." shashitharoor.in. Retrieved October 18, 2021 (https://shashitharoor.in/writings_my_essays_details/33).

Tharoor, Shashi. 2018c. "Hindu religion is about Hinduism not Hindutva: Shashi Tharoor." shashitharoor.in. Retrieved October 18, 2021 (https://shashitharoor.in/writings_my_essays_details/36).

Tharoor, Shashi. 2018d. "Tharoor's New Book Asks: Will Constitutionalism Tame Hindutva?" shashitharoor.in. Retrieved October 18, 2021 (https://shashitharoor.in/writings_my_essays_details/42).

Tharoor, Shashi. 2018e. "Shashi Tharoor: A 'Hindu Pakistan' wouldn't be Hindu at all, but a Sanghi Hindutva state." shashitharoor.in. Retrieved October 18, 2021 (https://shashitharoor.in/writings_my_essays_details/105).

Tharoor, Shashi. 2018f. "Global perception of India has taken a beating." shashitharoor.in. Retrieved October 8, 2021 (https://shashitharoor.in/writings_my_essays_details/100).

Tharoor, Shashi. 2018g. "India's War on Science." shashitharoor.in. Retrieved October 18, 2021 (https://shashitharoor.in/writings_my_essays_details/86).

Tharoor, Shashi. 2019. *The Hindu Way*. New Delhi: Aleph Book Company.

Tharoor, Shashi. 2020. *The Battle of Belonging: On Nationalism, Patriotism, And What It Means to be Indian*. New Delhi: Aleph Book Company.

Vivekananda, Swami. 1958. *The Complete Works of Swami Vivekananda, Vol-3*. Kolkata: Advaita Ashrama.

Notes

1. (Dr. Shashi Tharoor Official 2020)
2. (Tharoor 2019:xi)
3. (Tharoor 2018:Preface, Acknowledgement, para. 1)
4. "Tapasya, Tapasyā, Tāpasya: 30 definitions." Wisdomlib. Retrieved October 18, 2021 (https://www.wisdomlib.org/definition/tapasya).
5. (Tharoor 2019:xii-xiii)
6. "Hi @ShashiTharoor This is Rohini mohandas, Coimbatore, ex-landmark. Wanted to share this image from my son's wedding last month. For the customary kashi yatra ritual, where groom carries Bhagavad Gita (tradition) I thought your book would be a more meaningful, relevant text."

Twitter. Retrieved October 18, 2021 (https://twitter.com/rohinimdas/status/1329451316985335809).

7. (Tharoor 2018:Paart 1 - My Hinduism, para. 1)
8. Refer to chapter 2 for a detailed analysis on Devdutt Pattanaik's scholarship.
9. "We knew of Hinduism as a religion without fundamentals: no founder or prophet, no organized church, no compulsory beliefs or rites of worship, no uniform conception of the 'good life', no single sacred book." (Tharoor 2019:3-4)
10. (Tharoor 2019:14)
11. (Tharoor 2019): See sections on My Truth, A Faith without Dogma
12. (Tharoor 2019:15)
13. (Tharoor 2019:9)
14. (Tharoor 2019:17)
15. As per Tharoor, acceptance is the key for Hindus while he gives a free pass to a Muslim for not wanting to chant Vande Matarm as it consists of a hymn to Goddess Durga (see section 'The Battle of Idiocy').
16. (Tharoor 2019:157)
17. "A Hidden Gem from Mahabharata, Shri Krishna's Excellent Definition of a Kshatriya." Satchitananda. Retrieved October 18, 2021 (https://tfipost.com/2017/12/shri-krishna-defines-kshatriya-01/).
18. Refer to chapter 10 of this volume for a detailed critique on Wendy Doniger's scholarship.
19. (Tharoor 2019:233-234,239)
20. (Tharoor 2019:247-256)
21. There are dozens of papers in the *Population Genetics* research area, proving that the data and proof are insufficient to make such wide ranging conclusions. In general AIT per se has been critiqued and challenged from various other data sources, not limited to geology, archaeology, archaeogenetics, and archaeoastronomy. To make a sweeping conclusion based on one claim, is a bit far-fetched.
22. (Tharoor 2019:230-232)

23. "Cafeteria Christianity." Conservapedia. Retrieved October 18, 2021 (https://www.conservapedia.com/Cafeteria_Christianity).

24. AIT has been well-established as a baseless and a fabricated theory. Therefore Tharoor's entire chronology that stands on the AIT theory is baseless and falls flat. See Rajiv Malhotra's Breaking India (2010) for more on the invention of AIT. Also see- Sastry, Manogna and Megh Kalyansundaram. 2019. "The A of ABC of Indian chronology: Dimensions of the Aryan problem revisited in 2017." Proceedings from the Swadeshi Indology

    Conference Series Studies in Tamil Civilisation (Land of Dharma):87-130.

25. (Tharoor 2019:73-74)

26. (Tharoor 2019:70)

27. (Tharoor 2019:75)

28. (Malhotra 2006)

29. "The Big Scandal of Indology." Medium. Retrieved October 18, 2021 (https://subhashkak.medium.com/the-big-scandal-of-indology-2994f178f0d9).

30. (Tharoor 2019:236)

31. "The Secret of the Veda." Medium. Retrieved October 18, 2021 (https://subhashkak.medium.com/the-secret-of-the-veda-3efcfbae26af).

32. Kane, Vaman Pandurang. 1930. *History of Dharmasastra.*

33. (Tharoor 2019:245-246)

34. (Tharoor 2019:153)

35. "There was no 'Vedic beef-eating'. Here's what Vedas say on killing cows." DailyO. Retrieved October 18, 2021 (https://www.dailyo.in/politics/beef-cow-slaughter-dadri-murder-vedas-bhagavad-gita-hindutva-hinduism/story/1/7111.html).

    Yasmintsarvāni bhutānyātmaivābhūdvijānatah tatra ko mohah kah śokah ekatvamanupasyatah -*Yajurveda 40.7*

    "Those who see all beings as souls do not feel infatuation or anguish at their sight for they experience oneness with them"

    Brīhimattam yavamattamatho māśamatho tilam Eśa vām bhāgo nihito ratnadheyāya dantau mā hinsiśtam pitaram mātaram ca -*Atharvaveda 6.140.2*

"O teeth! You eat rice, you eat barley, you eat gram and you eat sesame. These are specifically meant for you. Do not kill those who are capable of being fathers and mothers."

36. (Tharoor 2018b)
37. (Tharoor 2018c)
38. (Tharoor 2018d)
39. (Swamy 2010:36)
40. (Tharoor 2018e)
41. (Rajiv Malhotra Official 2019)
42. (Tharoor 2018f)
43. (Malhotra 2002a)
44. (Tharoor 2019:8)
45. (Tharoor 2019:104)
46. (Malhotra 2004)
47. (Malhotra 2012a)
48. (Malhotra 2004)
49. (Malhotra 2004)
50. (Malhotra 2011:101)
51. (Malhotra 2011:101)
52. (Tharoor 2018a)
53. Kane, Pandurang Vaman. 1930. History of Dharmaśāstra.
54. (Malhotra 2012b)
55. (Rajiv Malhotra Official 2020)
56. The post-Independence political history of India is a testament to this fact
57. (Malhotra 2011:36)
58. (Rajiv Malhotra Official 2017)
59. (Malhotra 2012a)
60. (Malhotra 2011:25)
61. (Malhotra 2002b)

62. On analyzing any histories of World Violence, Wars- a vast majority over the past 2000 years are triggered by the Christian or Islamic needs of expansionism. (Rajiv Malhotra Official 2020)

63. (Malhotra and Babaji 2020:122-123)

64. (Rajiv Malhotra Official 2016)

65. "Joshua Project in Action – Strategies Used for Conversion to Christianity." madhukishwar.blogspot.com. Retrieved October 18, 2021 (http://madhukishwar.blogspot.com/2018/02/joshua-project-in-action-strategies.html).

66. (Malhotra 2012c)

SEVEN

Audrey Truschke
Truschke-nāma or The Tales of Truschke

Subhodeep Mukhopadhyay & Manogna Sastry

Introduction

Audrey Truschke, a well-known public intellectual, academic and social media activist, is an Associate Professor of early modern and modern Indian history at Rutgers University. She has authored three books, *Culture of Encounters* (2016, Columbia University Press), *Aurangzeb: The Life and Legacy of India's Most Controversial King* (2017, Stanford University Press) and *The Language of History: Sanskrit Narratives of Indo-Muslim Rule* (2021, Columbia University Press).[1] Her works on Mughal history have been widely cited, including, in the *Oxford Research Encyclopedia of Asian History*.[2] She is also a vocal political commentator and, as a prominent South Asian scholar activist, she ostensibly espouses progressive and inclusive politics, in order to counter Right-wing forces, especially 'Hindu supremacy.'[3] A member of the American Institute of Pakistan Studies,[4] she is a key driver in the polemical *Hindutva Harassment Field Manual*, which claims to be "a resource guide" to help deal with "Hindutva attack."[5] A popular figure in the Left-Liberal literary scene in India (Jaipur Literature Festival), as well as in Pakistan (Lahore Literary Festival), Truschke is a frequent commentator on various socio-political issues in many Left-leaning platforms, like *The Caravan*,[6] *Scroll*[7] and *The Wire*[8]. Her current areas of research include developing a single volume history of India, and investigation of US-based Hindu Right-wing movement.[9] A recipient of numerous literary awards and grants, she has been lauded for her "invaluable contribution to the field of South Asian studies."[10]

While Truschke has received praise for her scholarship and activism, she has also earned the ire of academics and non-specialists alike, on both sides of the political spectrum, for her provocative and often controversial statements which are more akin to polemics than unbiased scholarship. For example, Robert Goldman, Professor of Sanskrit at the Department of South and Southeast Asian Studies at the University of California, Berkeley, refers to her interpretation of Hindu epic *Rāmayaṇa* as "extremely disturbing", "inappropriate" and "vulgar."[11] In 2021, the Hindu American Foundation filed a lawsuit in US District Court for the District of Columbia against Audrey Truschke (among others) for defamation – a purported fight-back against "coordinated attacks against Hindu Americans in the public space" by the defendants.[12] She has received the support of Indian American Muslim council,[13] a group with ties to radical Islam, and sympathy for Kashmir separatism and Taliban government in Afghanistan.[14] She is on the advisory board of Students Against Hindutva Ideology (SAHI)[15] which is associated with Stand With Kashmir,[16] a group with links to the Islamist organization Jamaat-e-Islami, through its American proxy, the Islamic Circle of North America.[17] There have also been serious national security concerns that through her scholarship and activism, which purports to paint India as a Hindu majoritarian state with scant regards for human rights, she is actually serving the interest of the Pakistan 'deep-state' in India, a charge which she has denied.[18]

Truschke is therefore, an important public intellectual, whose work has consequences for studies on India and her past, especially in the university setting. She has received many accolades and grants for her contribution to South Asian cultural and intellectual history. For example, in 2021 she won one of the twenty-five National Endowment for the Humanities (NEH) Public Scholars grants in the US – such grants are intended to "support well-researched books in the humanities aimed at a broad public audience."[19] At the same time, there are allegations that through her scholarship and activism she perpetuates blatant Hinduphobia. Truschke, however, dismisses the concerns of her critiques as 'trolling', and insists that it is she who is the victim – she claims to have received vicious threats and abuse, including anti-Semitic slurs on her various social media profiles, as well as, being targeted by Hindus for belonging to "the wrong colour and the wrong sex."[20]

In other words, Truschke is a polarizing figure in the area of South Asian studies, Hinduism and politics. In this essay, we offer a clear-eyed perspective on the public debate over Truschke and her scholarship. We analyze in-depth, some of her key positions on Mughal history, Aurangzeb, Hinduism, Hindutva and modern India. We show how she is part of a larger ecosystem of academics and activists who are uncomfortable with the idea of a strong Indian state as well as the Dharmic underpinnings of Indian society.

Revisionism and Negationism

Revisiting historical sources with a fresh perspective and incorporating newer evidence, like DNA or public release of archived documents or fresh archaeological discovery, to better understand the past, is an essential part of the discipline of history. By and large, such research can have a positive impact, often leading to a re-interpretation of historical accounts and challenging established views held by scholars. Revisionism, an idea which has its roots in Marxist thoughts, has proven useful in challenging mainstream narratives and popular misconceptions – for example, in the studies about indigenous people in former colonies like America and Australia.[21] However, when politically motivated or taken to an extreme, revisionism often seems to border on 'negationism', where its proponents employ methods ranging from casting doubt on the authenticity of genuine documents, deliberately mistranslating texts and deriving questionable conclusions. For example, politically-motivated revisionists have looked for various ways to deny horrific events like Armenian genocide,[22] genocide of Native Americans in North America[23] and the Jewish holocaust.[24] In India, revisionism has unfortunately been the bedrock of Leftist interpretation of history for the last few decades, and, as some scholars have pointed out, a systematic attempt has been made to 'doctor' history textbooks and pervert India's historical narrative.[25]

As shown in this essay, Truschke not only carries forward this tradition of negationism but also propagates an alternate history of India where the religious persecutors are shown as blameless and often benevolent, and victims of persecution are blamed for the ills facing society today. She goes all out in denying the inherent violence of India's Islamic rule, a position no different from that of an influential section of Indian intelligentsia which is constantly trying to wipe out "from Hindu memory the history of their persecution by the swordsmen of Islam."[26] Truschke instead, sees realpolitik motivation behind many of the actions of Muslim rulers like temple destruction, iconoclasm and religion-specific taxation.[27] Not only does she dismiss all claims of religious excesses of Muslim rulers as figments of Hindutva imagination, she in fact, blames modern Hindu politicians of propagating this falsehood of Mughal tyranny, so as to persecute Muslims in present-day India. She also insists that not only did Muslim rulers not destroy many Hindu temples, but also that they picked up the practices of temple destruction from Hindus themselves. In the rest of this essay, we will examine her assertions and provide responses to, and challenge some of her bizarre claims.

Temple Destruction

According to Truschke, the view that Muslim rulers destroyed numerous Hindu temples, especially for religious reasons, is a pernicious myth. She makes two claims in this regard:

1. That the actual number of temples destroyed during Aurangzeb's reign is probably a few dozens in number – "There are numerous gaping holes in the proposition that Aurangzeb razed temples because he hated Hindus, however. Most glaringly, Aurangzeb counted thousands of Hindu temples within his domains and yet destroyed, at most, a few dozen."[28] She bases her thesis primarily on the work of Richard Eaton and concurs with his view that "the evidence is almost always fragmentary, incomplete, or even contradictory."[29]

2. That temple desecration was a well-known political practice among Hindu kings and Muslims merely continued this old custom.[30]

Truschke sets the stage by insisting that it is a fool's errand to focus on the number of temples destroyed in pre-colonial India. According to her, Aurangzeb was an even-handed ruler who occasionally carried out targeted destruction of certain temples which he deemed to be involved in seditious or immoral activities, and that this number was not more than a few dozens. Not only is there no evidence of large-scale temple destruction under Aurangzeb's rule, she insists that Aurangzeb granted Mughal state protection to Hindu and Jain temples which dotted his kingdom. The false view of large-scale religiously sanctioned temple destruction, she says, has its roots in colonial-era scholarship "where positing timeless Hindu-Muslim animosity embodied the British strategy of divide and conquer."[31]

Her views, however, contradict that of a very important Persian work *Maasir-i Alamgiri*, a chronicle of the life and times of Aurangzeb. Written by Muhammad Saqi Mustaid Khan, it was completed in 1710, three years after the death of Aurangzeb, at the behest of Aurangzeb's secretary Inayetullah Khan Kashmiri, who made the state archives and records available to the author to complete his work.[32] This work details many temple destructions carried out during Aurangzeb's reign. For example, in the list below from the year 1680, the author, provides very specific dates, location and the exact number of temples destroyed in each of these regions.

- 24th January, 1680 (2nd of Muharram, 1091 AH) – 3 temples on the banks of Udaisagar lake to be razed.[33]
- 29th January, 1680 (7th of Muharram, 1091 AH) – Destruction of the temple situated in the palace of Rana, and 172 more in the neighboring districts[34]
- 22nd February 1680 (1st Safar, 1091 AH) – Destruction of 63 temples at Chitor[35]

The dates and locations in these instances are too specific to be the figments of someone's imagination. Truschke, however, dismisses the credibility of the entire work, and claims that the author "has a noted tendency to exaggerate the number of temples" and that he changes facts to suit his taste and hence his work must be cited with "extreme caution."[36] She, however, does not give any reason or evidence in support of why she thinks thus. As is evident from the data presented above, there is nothing fragmentary, incomplete or contradictory in the information provided, as Truschke would have us believe. We see clear evidence of systematic temple destruction and not the "dark curtain drawn across an unknown past" as she so poetically writes.[37] It is hard to believe that the author Khan, who not only had royal patronage but also access to the state archives, made up stories, especially such very specific incidents with places, dates and numbers. As Sarkar points out, while the Mughal era writings were often replete with fulsome, and often, nauseating praise of their rulers, it was, however, "more a defect of manner than one of fact."[38]

What this means is that, in a span of two months, under Aurangzeb, two hundred and thirty-eight (238) temples were destroyed in just a handful of localities, which is far greater than the few dozen temple destruction in four decades, as Truschke posits. The interesting thing to be noted is that, while Truschke summarily dismisses the book, she also picks up from the very same book, a statement describing the 1670 destruction of Mathura's Keshava Deva Temple as "a rare and impossible event that came into being seemingly from nowhere."[39] From this single statement, she reaches the conclusion that temple destructions were rather rare and unusual in Aurangzeb's India. It is clear that Truschke selectively chooses evidence which suits her narrative of a benevolent Aurangzeb, and ignores all evidences which go against her thesis.

She cites Eaton's work on temple destruction to buttress her claim that "the number of confirmed temple destructions during Aurangzeb's rule at just over a dozen, with fewer tied to the emperor's direct commands."[40] Therefore, it is important to examine Eaton's work, since Truschke considers him "the leading authority on the subject."[41] Eaton in his paper, *Temple desecration and Indo-Muslim states,* provides a list of eighty instances of temple desecration by Islamic emperors, sultans, governors, commanders and crown princes, between 1192 to 1760, a period of over five hundred years, of which five temple desecrations have been attributed to Aurangzeb directly.[42] This low number has been accepted as sacrosanct by many historians and popular writers who parrot this figure without seeing the need for any further investigation.[43] Translated in terms of rate, this would mean that Muslim rulers destroyed one temple every seven years. This is a far cry from thousands of temple destructions recorded by Muslim biographers themselves, as well as, the cultural memory of Hindus and their understanding of the land's Islamic past (as well as present).

This idea can be illustrated by a couple of recent examples. In Pakistan since the 1990s, over a period of thirty years, 408 temples were destroyed to make way for commercial properties and houses,[44] which works out to around ninety temples destruction in seven years. Similarly, in Bangladesh, over a period of eight years from 2013 to 2021, there were more than 1,670 cases of Hindu temple vandalism and desecration.[45] There is no reason to suggest that Muslims today are more extreme in temple destruction than medieval Muslim kings. Therefore, the view that there were very few actual temple desecrations must be examined closely – why is there such a huge gap between their thesis and that of the lived reality of Hindus engaging with Muslims for centuries?

One reason for this mismatch, as Elst suggests, is that the figure eighty is not exhaustive. Each item on the list, he says, may not necessarily refer to one temple – for example in Benares (which is listed as item six in Eaton's list), contemporary Muslim sources indicate that almost one thousand temples were destroyed by Muhammad Ghori's army in 1194. Therefore, the eighty instances "still amount to thousands of individual temples forcibly replaced by mosques."[46]

Another reason for the mismatch could be on account of differing interpretation of Persian verses by various historians. Jadunath Sarkar whose *History of Aurangzib* (5 Vols., 1912-1958) is still considered one of the most authoritative works on Aurangzeb, translates one of the passages from *Maasir-I-'Alamgiri* for 8th April 1669, as:

> "...in the provinces of Tatta, Multan and especially at Benares, the Brahman misbelievers used to teach their false books in their established schools, and that admirers and students both Hindu and Muslim, used to come from great distances to these misguided men in order to acquire this vile learning. His Majesty, eager to establish Islam, issued orders to the governors of all provinces to demolish the schools and temples of the infidels and with utmost urgency put down the teaching and the public practice of the religion of these misbelievers." (Sarkar 1947:51-52)

Truschke as well as Eaton, however, choose to translate the same passage differently. Truschke writes:

> "In Thatta, Multan, and especially at Benares, deviant Brahmins were teaching false books at their established schools. Curious seekers— Hindu and Muslim alike— traveled great distances to gain depraved knowledge from them." (Truschke 2017:Ch. 6, Destroyer of Temples, para. 13)

Eaton translates the rest of the text as:

> "Orders respecting Islamic affairs were issued to the governors of all the provinces that the schools and places of worship of the irreligious be subject to demolition and that with the utmost urgency the manner of teaching and the public practices of the sects of these misbelievers be suppressed." (Eaton 2001:74)

Sarkar prefers the usage "Brahman misbelievers" whereas, Truschke refers to them as "deviant Brahmins", thereby shifting the sense of the passage away from a religious one, and bringing in a casteist angle. Eaton claims that the royal order in question did not state that temples and schools ought to be demolished outright, but rather be subject to demolition, which according to him implies that local authorities would have undertaken an investigation before proceeding.[47] In other words, even if an order demanded the razing down of all temples, the number of temples actually destroyed could have been much lower than the total number of temples in existence once investigations were completed, a view which Truschke accepts and endorses since according to her, Aurangzeb targeted "specific Hindu temples while leaving the vast majority untouched."[48]

One may also note, the use of the word 'irreligious' instead of 'infidel' which Sarkar uses. 'Infidel' is a pejorative term used by certain religions to describe the "Other", those who do not abide by their faith. For a Muslim, a Hindu is an infidel because he does not accept Allah as the one and only God and Mohammed as the last prophet. 'Irreligious' on the other hand, is a non-controversial term which simply means someone who does not subscribe to a religion and includes atheists, scientists and agnostics, and has nothing to do with the concept of 'Chosen People'. Eaton also prefers to use the word 'sect' instead of 'religion', and thereby establish that rather than being an imperial order to destroy all schools and temples, the order "was targeted at investigating those institutions where a certain kind of teaching had been taking place."[49] What is to be noted further is that, that this entire thesis of investigation is conjectural, with no actual evidence from any cited investigation. Instead of a blind acceptance of Eaton's claims, the burden of proof lies with him to supply evidence, without which his number must be rejected. It is additionally telling of Truschke's research abilities, that instead of probing the basis of Eaton's work, she eagerly grounds her entire work on such shaky material and her thesis collapses for want of evidence.

Evidence from contemporary sources of large-scale temple destruction during the Islamic period is in fact so profuse, that one is left flabbergasted at the blatant misrepresentation of facts by Truschke and her mentor, Eaton. Historian Sitaram Goel in his analysis of eighty historical works spanning a period of more than twelve hundred years, lists 154 localities in the Indian subcontinent, where temples were destroyed by sixty-one kings, sixty-three military commanders and fourteen Sufis.[50] It is reasonable to expect that each locality had a number of temples, especially those in the heartland or major socio-economic regions. For example, even in the outlying and very sparsely populated

Gilgit and Baltistan region, 15th century Shia-Sufi preacher Shamsuddin Araki organized the demolition of more than eighty temples.[51] In other words, as per Islamic sources themselves, more temples were destroyed in one of the least populated areas in a very short period of time, than what Truschke and Eaton would have us believe is the total number of temples razed by Muslim rulers during six centuries of Islamic rule. Extrapolating based on the Gilgit and Baltistan data cited earlier, the true number of temples destroyed would probably have been, at least two orders of magnitude more than what is acceptable in the Marxist circles. Goel, for example, published a list of two thousand Hindu, Buddhist and Jain temples which were demolished and Muslim monuments built on their sites.[52]

Truschke dismisses a contemporary source which lists a large number of temple destruction as unreliable, but then picks a single line from the very same source and uses it to buttress her thesis that temple desecration was an anomaly rather than the norm. Instead of examining all available facts and arriving at a conclusion, she cherry-picks and chooses ideas, and even phrases, which suit her narrative and uses the work of Eaton to support her claim. The assertion that most temples located within Mughal domain "still stood at the end of Aurangzeb's reign"[53] does not point to Mughal magnanimity, but rather, if true, implies that the temples survived *despite* a discriminatory Mughal reign.

The second part of the equation considers iconoclasm as a preexisting Indian custom and that Muslim rulers merely continued it as part of statecraft and political administration, which we study below.

Iconoclasm

Truschke maintains that temples in India were widely understood to be political in nature and hence, they were subject to "politically motivated destructions."[54] From 7th century CE, Hindu kings, she says, regularly looted and defiled images of Durga, Ganesha, Vishnu and other deities. They destroyed each other's temples and "even commissioned Sanskrit poetry to celebrate and memorialize such actions."[55] This became the basis of the Muslim practice of iconoclasm, which did not necessarily have religious motivation. Aurangzeb's demolition of Hindu temples like the Keshava Deva temple in Mathura in 1670, must be seen in this light. The Gyanvapi mosque which was built in its place by recycling the existing temple's stones for purpose of convenience, was meant as a stern warning to his political opponents.

> "Indo-Muslim rulers, such as Aurangzeb, followed suit in considering Hindu temples legitimate targets of punitive state action. ... Mosques were erected on the former sites of both the Vishvanatha and Keshava Deva Temples, although they were built under different circumstances. The Gyanvapi Masjid still stands today in Benares with part of the ruined temple's wall incorporated into the building. This reuse may have been a religiously clothed statement about the dire consequences of opposing Mughal authority." (Truschke 2017:Ch. 6, Destroyer of Temples, para. 7,8,9,10)

She wonders why Aurangzeb targeted certain temples and left others intact, and surmises that it was probably an action against errant Brahmins, whom she refers to as 'charlatans.' Truschke maintains that Aurangzeb (and in general, Mughal rulers) feared that Brahmins were misrepresenting Hinduism to lower castes, deceiving common Hindus about their own religion, misguiding Muslims and teaching false books at their schools and in temples.[56] In other words, the very idea of Islamic iconoclasm, or religiously motivated idol destruction is false, and that it was the deceit and fraudulent practices of Brahmins, which made Aurangzeb do what he did.

Her thesis on Islamic iconoclasm speaks more about herself, than it tells one about Aurangzeb. Her characterization of Brahmins as being greedy and arrogant, charlatans, who preyed upon ordinary folks, as well charges against Brahmins themselves, which incidentally are not backed by any evidence, reveal her innate Brahminphobia. Based on the opinion of one French traveler Jean de Thevenot, and her belief of how she thinks Aurangzeb may have felt vis-à-vis the "dubious practices" of Brahmins, she cleverly puts the entire blame of temple destruction on Hindus themselves. This is a classic example of victim-blaming where the affected party is held partially, if not entirely responsible for the harm that befell them. This is no different from anti-Semitic imagery in Europe which portrayed Jews as being greedy, cunning and scheming.[57] She cites an example of how Benares was teeming with greedy Brahmins looking to make quick money–how is this pejorative characterization any different from early Jewish ghetto portrayal being likened to rats swarming in a sewer?[58]

Even if one makes allowances for her personal views on Hinduism, the primary issue is that she has not presented a single piece of evidence to back up her claim that Aurangzeb's motives in destroying temples had anything to do with 'scheming' Brahmins deceiving common Hindus, and of Aurangzeb ordering Mughal officials to investigate such matters. It is rather difficult to imagine Aurangzeb, a self-confessed pious Muslim, being so distressed at the plight of common Hindus being hoodwinked by their own (the Brahmins) being taught wrong Hinduism and deviant practices, that he ordered the destruction of temples to save Hindus from themselves. Such theorization by Truschke only reveals her abysmal research abilities.

Let us consider the evidence provided by her on Hindu kings destroying each other's temples and how, later Muslim rulers merely adopted the said practice as part of state policy. Scholar Girish Shahane, a regular contributor to far-Left web portal *Scroll*, a vocal critic of the Hindu Right[59] and Modi,[60] and a supporter of Aryan Migration Theory[61] like Truschke, lambasts her for basing her entire thesis on exactly one example, which upon further investigation turns out to be "a fictive incident created by misunderstanding a bit of verse."[62] Moreover, as Shahane points out, Hindu kings did take away deities, especially those considered powerful, but instead of destroying them, they had them consecrated and installed within their own kingdoms, "the precise opposite of the idol smashing of Islamic iconoclasm."[63] Elst also points out the same. When early 9th century Pandyan king Shrimara Shrivallabha invaded Sri Lanka and took away the statue of the Buddha, the deity itself was not touched, but rather preserved. In fact, the Lankan army was later able to retrieve and restore the idol.[64] Equating this with Islamic iconoclasm is an example of shoddy scholarship on the part of Truschke. Elst writes:

"In Islamic iconoclasm, the whole idea was not to preserve but to destroy the idols; and more fundamentally, to destroy the religion embodied in the idols. ... it artfully blurs the distinction between looting, i.e. carrying away as a prized good, done by a victorious king who shared the idolatrous tradition of his defeated opponent and continued it; and destruction, i.e. an act of contempt and hate for the idolatrous religion and meant to terminate it." (Elst 2011:27)

Moreover, there is no evidence to show that Islamic iconoclasm was a continuation of an earlier Hindu practice. Goel in his work, lists numerous instances of Muslims justifying iconoclasm with reference to the Prophet's example, but was not able to locate a single example of anyone claiming that their actions were based on a Hindu precedent. In fact, the sixth sultan of the Shah Miri dynasty of Kashmir from 1389 to 1413, Sikandar Shah Miri, was epithetized 'Butshikan', which literally means "idol-breaker."[65] As Shahane points out, Truschke's portrayal of Aurangzeb as a misunderstood personality, is full of holes, and he suggests that the latter "was a bigot not just by our standards but by those of his predecessors and peers."[66]

Incidentally, this also sheds light on one of her other major claims, regarding the attack and looting of the Somnath temple by Mahmud of Ghazni in 1025. How is it that an event that is alleged to be cataclysmic in modern Hindutva debates has not been touched upon by contemporary Brahmin thinkers, she wonders and remarkably concludes:

"Perhaps the event was unremarkable to local Brahmins who were accustomed to temple raids from Indian kings across the board."[67]

As demonstrated, there is scant evidence of the alleged Hindu iconoclasm; hence, it is very unlikely that Brahmins were already accustomed to temple raids by Indian kings. The fact that Hindus did not write about certain events does not mean that the incident did not happen. Quite a few Muslim historians have waxed eloquent about Ghaznivids and Mahmud's raid of Somnath.[68] It is more likely, that the few survivors and the victims of horrific Ghaznavid attacks, were not in a position to sit and write Sanskrit prose. Below is an excerpt of a typical fort takeover from *Tarikhu-s Subuktigin*, a history of the house of Ghazni up to 451 H., 1059 CE:

> "The Brahmans and other higher men were slain, and their women and children were carried away captive and all the treasure which was found was divided amongst the army."[69]

It seems to be the standard practice of historians to ignore the mountains of Islamic literary evidence, contemporary as well as otherwise, which unapologetically and often gleefully describe the pillaging, and plunder and gruesome death of the 'infidels'. Instead, historians demand evidence from Hindus, who are clearly the victims as per Islamic records. This brings us to a large issue of Truschke's views on Hinduism and Hindutva, especially, given her stated anti-Hindutva activism.

Truschke on Hindutva and AI/MT

Audrey Trsuchke is a vocal critic of 'Hindutva', which she characterizes as a violent and fascist ideology, based on ideas of Nazi-sympathizers.[70] She defines Hindutva or Hindu Nationalism as "a political ideology that advocates Hindu supremacy, specifically over Muslims."[71] Proponents of Hindutva, she says, claim that ancient India had internet, aeronautics and modern medicine. Their thesis, that this golden age of scientific progress came to a halt with Muslim invasion is nothing short of a political ploy to demonize Muslims.[72] Supporters of Hindutva are inherently misogynistic and she claims that she has been subjected to virulent attacks by Hindu nationalists.[73] Further she says that she has evidence that Hindu nationalist groups recruit and attempt to radicalize students on US university campuses.[74]

Hindutva ideologues, according to her, reject cultural change as a desirable process and instead embrace the position that India and Indians possess a timeless and unchanging essence. In other words, they posit a flat history without change, and react to anything contradictory as a major threat. She finds it shocking that Hindutva supporters reject the "ironclad linguistic evidence" (which she does not cite with sources as in any scholarly exchange) of an Aryan migration into India some 4000 to 3500 years ago.[75] With regards to pre-modern Indian history, Hindu nationalists are determined to purge Mughals and their heritage from the Indian psyche. Thus, on the one hand, there is a frenzy of renaming cities and streets, while on the other hand, Mughal monuments are being neglected. History books are being rewritten so as to remove all references to the Mughals.[76] Hindu nationalists are busy rewriting Mughal history by inventing atrocities, so that they can justify "the oppression and violence they wield against Muslim communities today."[77] In this dystopian India – she refers to it, as Modi's India – where the Hindu nationalist state is busy with its 'anti-Muslim exertions', scholarly debate has taken a backseat and instead, dishonesty and academic hooliganism rules the roost.[78]

> "When Hindu nationalists are not marginalising the Mughals, they villainise these long-dead kings as proxies for modern-day Indian Muslims." (Truschke 2018a)

According to her, another myth perpetuated by Hindutva ideologues is the phenomenon of 'love jihad', which is yet another weapon in the arsenal of the Hindu Right to target Indian Muslims. Trsuchke says:

> "It underlines their vicious Islamophobia, investment in controlling female sexuality, and a preference for religious segregation. It also speaks to their projected fragility and desire to maintain social dominance, including by inventing a persecution story." (Truschke 2021)

There are a number of issues, factual and otherwise, with her statements and positions. First of course, is her disparaging characterization of India as 'Modi's India'. India does not belong to Narendra Modi, or the Bharatiya Janata Party (BJP) or to those who are vehemently opposed to Modi and his policies. It is a land of Indians, and whether she likes it or not, Indians which include Hindus, Muslims and Christians alike have decided, not once but twice, to give BJP the opportunity to form a government at the Center under the leadership of Narendra Modi, in a democratic, independently-monitored electoral exercise. Truschke represents the quintessential colonial Western thinking, which assumes imaginary authority and non-existent *locus standi* on anything related to democracy and finds situations which go against their ideologies, even when backed by people's mandates, to be dismissed with aspersions and strange accusations. By referring to India as 'Modi's India', she is accusing the entire nation of being proponents of her understanding of Hindutva, which is that of anti-science, anti-reason, misogynist, fascist and racist individuals baying for the blood of Muslims.

This characterization allows her the opportunity to paint all her critics with the same brush stroke – Hindutva 'trolls'. Anyone who opposes her views or criticizes her scholarship must be an adherent of Hindutva, and hence, to be disparaged at a personal level and dubbed a 'troll'. It does not matter if the person does not subscribe to her definition of Hindutva or if they are *bona fide* scholars providing genuine critique. Truschke trivializes India's immense contribution to Indian science and technology by sensationalizing the absurd and making it appear as if a few bizarre claims constitute the bulk of Indian science. By associating science in India with Hindutva, she is perhaps trying to make the case, that since supporters of Hindutva are anti-science, whatever science India has is of foreign origin, that India never had any scientific prowess and that current Indian science is an area dominated by crackpot theorists. This is an absurd claim, and there is enough literature on India's immense contribution to mathematics, medicine, mind sciences, astronomy and other areas.[79] Truschke's wholesale dismissals and accusations though, manage to achieve with their shrill tone and absurd claims, the need to engage in any rational and intellectual exchange with scholarship which proves her claims wrong.

Instead, Truschke uses her academic credentials and strident charging, to wade into commentaries on issues related to India about which she knows very little but has the need to make clamoring statements such as for instance, on 'love jihad'.[80] She incorrectly, but conveniently defines it as a phenomena where "Hindu girls are claimed to be at risk of corruption and Hinduism itself at risk of extinction due to interreligious marriages that result in forced conversions to Islam."[81]

Most practitioners of Hinduism understand 'love jihad' as a strategy where Muslim men pretending to be Hindus, entrap Hindu women into a relationship or abduct them and then force them to convert to Islam. Truschke of course, deigns not to touch upon this point of pretension and entrapment, and instead obfuscates the issue by painting the entire matter as Hindu opposition to interreligious marriage. 'Love jihad' is neither a product of someone's imagination nor a Hindutva problem nor a solely Indian problem. In 2014, the Akal Takht, the highest temporal seat of Sikhism in UK, expressed grave concern over reports of Sikh girls falling victim to Pakistani youths attempting to seduce and convert them to Islam as part of 'jihadi' efforts.[82] In 2017, Mathews Gregorios, the Bishop of the Syrian Independent Orthodox Church, announced that 'love jihad' was a reality and Christian youth ought to stand up and fight this evil.[83] In the same year, Ladakhi officials said that there were reports of young Buddhist girls, lured into marriage by Muslims pretending to be Buddhists.[84] As recent as 2021, Mar Joseph Kallarangatt, Bishop of Palai, openly accused a section of the Muslim community of targeting Christians through 'love jihad'.[85] Whether 'love jihad' actually exists or not, and to what extent, is a matter for the police and the courts to investigate, however, it is clear that Christians, Buddhist, Sikhs and Hindus alike, do see 'love jihad' as a cultural threat. What is clearly apparent, meanwhile, through the issue, is Truschke's need to wade into every issue related to Hinduism, whether she has any understanding or not, and expressly manifest her Hinduphobia.

It comes as no surprise, that Truschke off-hand dismisses an entire school of thought called the "Out of India" theory (to be discussed later), and dubs their proponents, which incidentally include many European and American scholars, as Hindu Nationalists resorting "to specious arguments and even fraud"[86]. Among several of the damaging consequences of colonial scholarship in India, the perpetuation of the Aryan invasion/migration theories (AI/MT) particularly stands out. The theory has gone through several stages – from being a tool to create false identities for people, to using the same to fester divisions among Indians. One of the most interesting aspects of it is also the manner in which it reveals biases in scholarship, especially seen in the case of

Truschke's work. AI/MT has been discredited conclusively through the works of several scholars, from different fields such as linguistics and various branches of archaeology. But, Truschke, in her typical research style of making assertions without any basis, claims that the theory needs no bolstering and attributes it to "scholarly consensus."[87] Instead of addressing specific questions which challenge her beliefs in the validity of AI/MT, such as, the absence of even a mention of any invasion/migration in the huge corpus of texts of India, or the archaeological excavations at Sanauli, Rakhigarh and numerous other IVC sites, or the findings of the Sarasvati river paleo channels and their implications for the chronology of India, or the numerous reports from peer reviewed, scientific findings of Archaeological Survey of India and individual researchers; Truschke, in her quintessential manner, resorts to bashing up Hindutva and accusing Hindus of "rewriting history."[88] The arrogance and lack of self-awareness in her article is so glaring, that one wonders at her *adhikāra*[89] in calling herself a scholar, while her entire defense of her beliefs in AI/MT contains one paltry reference to a 1991 paper by John Hawley and quoting from Tony Joseph's work.[90] What serves Truschke's agenda well though, is the use of AI/MT to perpetuate the Marxist lens of Indian history, rooted in deep Hinduphobia.

Truschke on Hinduism

Truschke does not consider many Sanskrit texts, including the Upaniṣad-s and Purāṇa-s as "Hindu scriptures."[91] She also insists that the *Rāmāyaṇa* and *Mahābhārata* are not Hindu texts per se. During Akbar's reign, all eighteen books of *Mahābhārata* were translated to Persian. However, the translation team, which apparently also included many Brahmins of repute, did not consider the *Mahābhārata* a Hindu work, but rather a "purported history (*tarikh* in Persian) of pre-Islamic India."[92] In fact, the Persian adaptation of *Razmnamah* played an important role "in the politico-cultural fashioning of Akbar's court, whereby the Mughals developed a new type of Indo-Persian imperial aesthetic."[93] The Persian translators (which also included Brahmins) did not apparently consider even the *Rāmāyaṇa* as a Hindu religious text, but rather as an epic romance with "martial narratives" and "love sagas."[94] The *Bhagavad*

Gītā, in the same vein is "hardly uniquely Hindu"[95] but rather a text which attempts to address the moral dilemma of a war "by way of a philosophically dense discourse."[96]

> "Few if any saw it as the central, unique text of Hinduism." (Truschke 2015:4)

This depiction reflects Truschke's lack of understanding and intentional ignoring of copius literature from the canon by practicing Hindus. For example, in the Vedanta school of Hindu philosophy, there is a concept of *prasthānatrayī*, which refers to three canonical texts with epistemic authority – the Upaniṣad-s, the Brahma Sūtra-s and the *Bhagavad Gītā*. It may be noted that Vedanta is perhaps the most prominent school of Hinduism, and Vedantic traditions have led to the development or heavily influenced many spiritual movements and *sampradayas* all across India, including Vaiṣṇava, Śaiva and Śakti traditions.[97]

> "The Hindu religious sects, the common faith of the Indian populace, looked to Vedanta philosophy for the theoretical foundations for their theology. The influence of Vedanta is prominent in the sacred literatures of Hinduism, such as the various Puranas, Samhitas, Agamas and Tantras ..." (Nakamura 2004:3)

By classifying two out of three of these sources, namely, the Upaniṣad-s and the *Bhagavad Gītā* as not being Hindu, Truschke is clearly denying the legitimacy of Vedanta and by extension, Hinduism.

Regarding the antiquity of Hinduism, Truschke says that the word 'Hinduism' has been in use only for a few hundred years and is a Western idea.[98] The term 'Hindu' itself is a Perso-Arabic invention used in India for a thousand years, and mostly in a geographic rather than a religious sense.[99] She remarks that sometimes the term was used in a narrow sense and limited to upper classes, especially Brahmins.[100] If Hinduism is to be judged by the concept of a Holy Book, then the oldest layers of the Veda-s are not more than 3500 years old, she says.[101] However, in terms of practices, she says that "most Hindus worship different gods now than Vedic people did 3,500 years ago, and in quite different ways."[102] If the

Bhagavad Gītā is to be considered the primary book of the Hindus, then Hinduism is not more than two thousand years old,[103] while 'Bhakti' came only in the post-Christian era.

What her statements seem to indicate is the view that Hinduism is neither a religion nor is it ancient. It is a rather, a recent artificial construct of Western origin, and the *Rāmāyaṇa* and the *Mahābhārata* were Indian cultural artefacts appropriated by Hindus. She is careful to avoid the use of the words 'Hindu' and 'philosophy' together, and instead refers to 'dharma' and 'karma' as "Indian philosophical concepts."[104] By highlighting the fact that Indo-Persian thinkers also included Brahmins, Truschke tries to peddle the idea that this was a view that even Brahmins of the Mughal era accepted and endorsed. The implications are two-fold: If a practicing Hindu were to criticize the Mughal socio-political order, this would be akin to denigrating the *Mahābhārata* (and by extension Hinduism), since the epic was an important part of Mughal rule. The second is that the Mughals are as Indian as anyone else in India, given that their rule was premised on the *Mahābhārata*. Thus, a criticism of Mughal rule is a criticism of the *Mahabharata* and hence, of Indian-ness.

There is of course nothing new in this thesis of Neo-Hinduism, espoused by many in the Left-Liberal establishment, where Hinduism is claimed to have no coherent self-understanding of its distinctiveness or similarity to other religious traditions. Neo-Hinduism was constructed artificially by trying to forcefully integrate pre-existing native traditions, many of which are inherently irreconcilable.[105] Hinduism is denigrated as some kind of fragmented and incoherent admixture of ideas, without any central authority or ecclesiastical structure or scared texts.[106] Therefore, for Truschke, the Veda-s are replete with "animal sacrifice, sexual practices, spells" and merely an inducement to sleep, given the large number of hymns present in them.[107] *Indra's Net* by Rajiv Malhotra offers a systematic rejoinder to such views by articulating Hindu dharma's innate self-understanding which is coherent as well as multi-dimensional, and premised on a unified open architecture which allows continuous evolution.[108]

Hindutva = Hinduism?

An objective analysis of Truschke's work reveals that there have been instances where Truschke points out that 'Hindutva' and 'Hinduism' are not the same. The "Dismantling Global Hindutva" conference held from September 10-12, 2021 and endorsed by Audrey Truschke,[109] clearly says that Hindutva is not Hinduism.[110] According to the *Hindutva Harassment Field Manual* that she helped develop, proponents of Hindutva often hide their narrow, biased and extremist politics by claiming to represent Hinduism. Such a move causes great harm to the inherent diversity of Hinduism, and many within the Hindu fold oppose such a view:

> "Hindutva and Hinduism are distinct. Hindutva is a narrow political ideology whereas Hinduism is a broad-based religious tradition. Many Hindus oppose Hindutva ideology, both in India and in the US-based diaspora, and it is offensive to conflate the two".[111]

Thus, it would appear that Truschke is perhaps sympathetic to Hinduism, but inimical to Hindu Nationalism. A clearer examination though, summarizes some of the key takeaways of Truschke's views on Hinduism and Hindutva, based on the preceding sections:

- Hinduism is neither a genuine religion, nor is it old – historically it was a geographic identifier and perhaps in a narrow sense a religious identifier of upper classes, especially Brahmins.
- Hindutva is an anti-science, misogynist, fascist, racist and supremacist ideology advocating Hindu supremacy over Muslims.

In other words, she is sympathetic to neither Hinduism nor Hindutva. Consider for instance, her claims that 'Hindutva Rama' is different from 'devotional Rama', more aggressive than standard depictions, and then extending this to associate Rama with Hindu supremacy and slaughter of Muslims.

> "In August 2020, the BJP and other Hindu nationalist groups celebrated breaking ground for a new temple to the Hindutva Ram, known popularly as Ram Mandir, in Ayodhya ... The new Ram Mandir in Ayodhya celebrates this violent exercise of Hindu supremacy, in which a modern myth about the past can justify the mass slaughter of Muslims." (Truschke 2020:para. 17)

These are rather bizarre and serious claims, where she seems to question the very independence of the Indian judiciary. While it is true that Hindu deities have many different iconographies, Hindu practitioners do not distinguish between 'Hindutva Rama' and 'devotional Rama'. This is clearly an attempt to obfuscate her disdain for the Hindu deity by throwing a 'Hindutva' versus 'devotional' red herring. Moreover, by associating Ram Mandir with Hindu supremacy and slaughter of Muslims, it is evident that she does not see any difference between 'Hinduism' and 'Hindutva', although she may publicly say otherwise. Again, one of the positions held by the "Dismantling Global Hindutva Conference" was that Hindutva was merely "political Hinduism, not a distortion of an older tradition but a continuation of it."[112] In fact, Truschke seems to associate the (largely Hindu) Indian diaspora with Hindutva. She writes:

> "In US society, Hindutva hate is pretty mild. That's because the Indian diaspora is still a minority here. Indian Americans form about 1% of all Americans – that's not a huge number, but that's obviously not insignificant". (Prakash 2021)

The above statements show that her attacks on Hindutva are in fact attacks on Hinduism. Thus, when she says Hindutva proponents are primitive, racist and misogynist, these charges are equally applicable to all Hindus. She is neither the first Hinduphobic scholar, nor will she be the last. Truschke in fact, denies the very existence of Hinduphobia and says there is no evidence to support either Hinduphobia or that Hindus faced persecution under foreign rule. Considering the very poor evidences she presents to bolster any of her theses, it appears farcical when Truschke claims to work only with evidence and thus, dismisses any Hinduphobia:

"I think the charges lack substance, I don't think that there's any evidence behind them. And as academics, we work in a world of evidence." (Venkataramakrishnan 2021)

One of her counter-arguments is since nobody can claim to speak on behalf of all Hindus, the entire idea of a Hindu identity is contentious.[113] And if there is no Hindu identity, then how can there be Hinduphobia? *Academic Hinduphobia* by Rajiv Malhotra provides a good framework to understand the evolution of such Hinduphobic scholarship in Western academia. Setting aside any consideration for the actual victims, Truschke in fact, milks the matter to play the victim card and alleges that educated outspoken women (like her?) are abused. She also uses this opportunity to associate Hindutva, and by extension Hinduism, with Talibanism,[114] an extremist Islamic fundamentalist and militant ideology. She truly has the ability to relate anything under the sun to Hindutva and cast herself as the victim.

Truschke on the Ayodhya Judgment

Truschke has authored an article on the Supreme Court of India's judgment following the 'Ram Janmabhoomi' case at Ayodhya. Showing scant understanding of the independence of the Indian judiciary or of the history of the case, Truschke casts serious aspersions on the judges of India's Supreme Court when she paints them as participants in what she sees as a Hindutva rewriting and remarks that the judgment is devoid of "history before the nineteenth century" and "misstates the precolonial past."[115] Despite a link to the actual judgment copy in her article, it is astonishing that Truschke has not even followed the case enough to understand the evidences unearthed and the careful arguments presented over the years at various stages, at both the Allahabad High Court and the Supreme Court of India.

Despite an academic background and supposed knowledge of Hinduism and Sanskrit (e.g. of the significance of the *avatāra, garbha griha* and *parikrama*), for she has no obvious *locus standi* or expertise to comment on the matter, Truschke charges that Lord Rāma is not even a historical figure to begin with and the onus falls on the Hindus to first show his historical existence in a court of law – "It criticises the Muslim plaintiffs for failing to provide "evidence of the offering of namaz in the mosque, over this period [1528-1856/7]."[116] Yet, in over nine hundred pages, the judgment never asks either of the two Hindu defendants for proof that Ram's birth constituted a historical event." What Truschke seems to not have read in those 900 pages, are entire sections considering verses from various sources including the *Skanda Purana* and *Ayodhya Mahatmya* which build on the association of the place under dispute in Ayodhya with the birth of Lord Rama.[117] Truschke's scholarship in pre-modernity is further called into doubt, while making her scorn for Hinduism and its practitioners obvious, when she remarks that most Hindus "did not much care about Ram's birthplace, an apathy indicated by the sheer lack of attention to this issue in premodern texts."[118]

Truschke's analysis in the article is at times infantile, exemplified with her pointing at one place that the Supreme Court judgment mentions the Hindus 299 times in its text while speaking of the Muslims relatively lesser 174 times. Even as she comes up with such silly barometers for what constitutes judicial fairness, she remarks that the court has not defined either group, which apparently shocks her deeply. Truschke attempts to school the Indian Supreme Court on Oriental prejudice and legality, "The assumption of a static, homogenous group of "the Hindus" reeks of the Orientalist prejudice that Indians and India exist outside of historical change. For the court, this fiction of timelessness served the bid to make a relatively recent article of faith—Ram's precise birthplace—a legal basis for action."[119] The SC judgment nowhere paints a picture of treating the Hindus as a static group outside of historical change. In fact, it has sections considering evidence, from various sources including foreigners traveling to India and accounts of invaders, of relevant material before 1528, from 1528-1858, 1859-1947, and post-Independence. It becomes clear that Truschke's issue is not with whether or not the SC has defined Hindus or Muslims, but with the fact that history of Hindus and India, as defined by a group of biased and motivated distortionists such as herself, increasingly no longer find currency today.

The Supreme Court judgment considers evidence unearthed by the Archaeological Survey of India and consequently presented in its 2003 report and while doing so, accords lesser significance to the 1991 report by R.S. Sharma et al, as newer material evidence was absent in forming the conclusions of the historians' work in 1991. The unearthing of the pillars of a previously existing Hindu temple, the machinations of the Leftist historians to try and pass the evidence off as belonging to a Buddhist place – none of these are considered by Truschke, and instead, she disparages the ASI as an organization whose work has little standing within and outside the country, with an additional lesson on what constitutes historical method. Instead of the admission that the material evidence unearthed clearly points to the existence of a temple, as what is expected in an unmotivated and honest scholarship, Truschke accuses the Hindus, of 'sophistry'. "But Hindutva ideologues think differently. They commonly brandish some new piece of evidence favorable to a preconceived idea, regardless of its source or merit, as invalidating all prior academic work. This is a fine tactic as sophistry, but it carries no intellectual weight."[120] Truschke's work further shows that she has not even understood the concept of an avatāra,[121] but tries, very unsuccessfully, to frame the arguments against a backdrop of historicity. Rehashing notions from colonial scholarship, despite seemingly claiming to criticize it, she perpetuates the ideas of the *Rāmayana*, at best, being an imaginary work and thus, "by modern legal standards, the Hindu claimants have no compelling evidence regarding Ram's life and birthplace."[122]

Truschke and Mistranslating Sanskrit Intentionally

Audrey Truschke has a long record of translating words from Sanskrit to present a colorful tone of passages from key Hindu texts, and in some case, even manufacturing what she wants to read into a text. Despite her claimed expertise in Sanskrit, the numerous examples of Truschke's translations call into question not only her ability, but demonstrate a prejudiced gaze. Consider for instance, the 2018 episode of Truschke 'translating' passages from the *Ramayana* to attribute to devi Sita, lines which were a complete fabrication and not present in the original Vālmīki text. Referring to supposed lines 6.102-106, Truschke claims to use Robert Goldman's translation and says Sita, "loosely" called Bhagawan Rama a "misogynist pig and uncouth"; when challenged by many to produce the exact lines from the text to back up her claims, Truschke cited Goldman's translation.[123]

When a concerned reader reached out to the Sanskritist Robert Goldman himself with Truschke's claims, Goldman wrote back clearly refuting any such interpretation of the text in his work and said, "I find it extremely disturbing but perhaps not unexpected to learn that AT (Audrey Trushcke) has used such inappropriate language and passed it off as coming from Valmiki. Neither the great poet nor we used anything like such a vulgar diction and certainly Sita would never have used such language to her husband even in the midst of emotional distress. Nowhere in our translation of the passage do we use words such as you mention AT as using."[124] What Truschke had done, was 'translate' the text in ways that suited her agenda and attributed it to the authority of Goldman's work for credibility. Despite Dr. Goldman's clear rebuttal, neither did Truschke issue a withdrawal of her statements, nor a correction. Nityananda Misra, the Sanskritist, has also provided a detailed analysis of the episode.[125] Truschke's tweets remain on her account to this day.

Instead, Truschke's response was a sinuous attempt at portraying herself as a victim of hatred and abuse from Hindus for apparently writing about the truth. Writing in *The Wire*, Truschke does not address specifically the origin of her translations or her sleight of hand in passing off her own translations as that of Dr. Goldman's. Instead, she comes across as being proud of the controversy, and shockingly, and one wonders at her delusions, tries to compare the situation to the original in the text and she being in a place similar to devi Sītā!

> "I did not and do not endorse Sita's criticism of Rama, but many – including Professor Goldman – thought they glimpsed my own views within the translation. Upon seeing such blunt language, many got angry. In this sense, however, perhaps my translation was at least

partially successful. In Valmiki's *Ramayana*, Sita's words at the agnipariksha evoke anger, sparking a strong reaction from Lakshmana (6.104.20). The difference is that Lakshmana directed his wrath at Rama (briefly, before he calmed down), whereas, in the last few days, my critics have villainised the interpreter of the story, namely, me." (Truschke 2018b)

Truschke's frequent resorts to victimhood has become such a predictable part of her *modus operandi*, that it begs the question if it is a part of a strategy to garner more reportage and eye-balls. [126]

Hinduism and Hinduphobia

Having considered the above material, an interesting question to ponder upon is, why is Audrey Truschke Hinduphobic? What drives her rabid Hinduphobia disguised as objective scholarship? Some have posited that her deep-seated hatred of Hinduism could stem from her loyalty towards her family which is closely associated with a Christian missionary organization, First Baptist Church of Monterey[127] (which once had an allied movement "To Win India For Christ"[128]), or her close ties with Pakistan, an Islamic nation with constituitionally sanctioned discrimination against Hindus.[129] It could also be the influence of her mentor, Sheldon Pollock, whose Neo-Orientalist school is perhaps, the most important Left-wing, post-Marxist, post-modernist school today that influences almost all discourse about India both within the country and around the world.[130] Whatever be the reasons, we are now in a better position to understand many of her statements on Hinduism, India and politics in general.

In a 2017 tweet (now deleted), Truschke expresses her shock at the "forceful inclusion" of Sikhism in Hinduism.[131] She also does not consider "tribal religions" as part of Hinduism.[132] As shown earlier, she insists that the term 'Hindu' was historically a term with regional connotations and religious in a very narrow sense. She insists that Indian groups target minorities and Dalits under the charge of "forced religious conversion."[133] In effect, Hinduism for her is an elitist enterprise of a few upper castes only, and Sikhs, tribals and Dalits are not part of it. She, of course, is not alone in making such claims, as she is in the hallowed company of firebrand Christian activist Kancha Ilaiah Shepherd. Being entitled to one's opinions is a fundamental right in India but does not necessarily mean that one is correct, logical or rational. There are many people who still believe in ideas like Immaculate Conception or flat earth, and they have every right to do so. The legal definition of Hinduism, however, is very concise and unambiguous. A Hindu is:

- One who is a Hindu by religion in any of its forms or developments, including a Virashaiva, Lingayat, Brahmo Samaji, Prarthana Samaji as well as Arya Samaji
- One who is Buddhist, Jain or Sikh by religion
- Anyone else who is not a Muslim, Christian, Parsi or Jew by religion[134]

Conclusion

The article has considered a few important themes which constitute the main body of Audrey Truschke's work, while focusing on specifics of her research methodology. The key features of her *modus operandi* that emerge, as shown, include her proclivity to back her research with little verifiable and factual evidence, and tendency to actively blur the lines between objective scholarship and her manifest Hinduphobia. She cherry-picks data to suit her thesis, and shows a complete lack of objective and professional engagement with scholars whose work challenges her own, and frequently casts herself as a victim in situations which expose her lack of knowledge and bias.

Considering the nature of the scholarship that emerges in this profile, subjecting Truschke's work to a rigorous examination to check the veracity of her translations of Sanskrit texts becomes an important potential line of further study. The instance of her mistranslations and even outright fabrications of the verses from the *Rāmāyaṇa* raises important questions regarding the veracity of most of her work. *Sanskrit Non-Translatables* makes an excellent case for the need to retain words from the language as is,[135] to retain fidelity and prevent digestion and distortion of Hindu concepts. This paradigm becomes especially important while studying the work of scholars such as Truschke, whose work is riddled with poor evidence and careless mistranslations.

Truschke's missionary zeal in criticising scholars who do not subscribe to her ideologies, as seen in the recent exchange between her and the historian Vikram Sampath, regarding the latter's book on Savarkar, is another instance of her overreaching activities. Truschke's claim of over seventy-five signatories to a letter criticizing Sampath was shown to be fake, with many supposed signatories, such as Ramchandra Guha, saying they have not even seen the letter, let alone sign it.[136] The Delhi High Court's intervention, asking Twitter to delete the defamatory tweets[137] and the author's recourse to judicial actions point to interesting pushback against Truschke's endless propaganda.

In Indian socio-moral and ethical thought, it is the concept of 'dharma' that distinguishes civilization and human evolution from barbarism and anarchy. The *Brihadaranyaka Upanishad* says that nothing is higher than dharma and that dharma and truth are the same.[138] Dharma manifests in many ways, through steadiness, forgiveness, self-control, purity, discernment, knowledge and truthfulness at all times.[139] By implication 'adharma' is associated with untruthfulness and falsehood all things which are harmful for humanity and detrimental to the progress of human civilization. Rama is thus a representation of all that is dharmic while Ravana represents the side of adharma. Ravana may have been an intellectual giant and a great spiritual person, but his propensity to tread the path of adharma is what eventually lead to his downfall. Similar to Ravana, Truschke is an influential public intellectual who has decided to follow the path of adharma in academia. We hope that she be held accountable for her inflammatory, and irresponsible remarks and her propaganda under the guise of scholarship.

Bibliography

An-Na'im, Abdullahi A. 2008. *Islam and the Secular State: Negotiating the Future of Shari'a*. Cambridge, Massachusetts, and London, England: Harvard University Press. (https://eltearabszak.hu/wp-content/uploads/2019/01/

Abdullahi-Ahmed-An-Na-im-Islam-and-the-Secular-State_-Negotiating-the-Future-of-Sharia.pdf).

Baird, Benjamin. 2021. "Exposed: Indian American Muslim Council's 20-Year Love Affair with the Taliban." Retrieved February 15, 2022 (https://www.meforum.org/62722/indian-american-muslim-council-loves-taliban).

Bose, Joydeep. 2021. "Bangladesh: 'Over 3,600 attacks' on Hindus since 2013, rights groups concerned." Retrieved February 15, 2022 (https://www.hindustantimes.com/world-news/bangladesh-over-3-600-attacks-on-hindus-since-2013-rights-groups-concerned-101634868827734.html).

Chaubey, Santosh. 2021. "In 'Secular' Pakistan of Jinnah's Dreams, Stories of Temple Destruction Scream. Data Proves Them Right." Retrieved February 15, 2022 (https://www.news18.com/news/world/in-secular-pakistan-of-jinnahs-dreams-stories-of-temple-destruction-screams-4055888.html).

Eaton, Richard M. 2001. "Temple Desecration and Indi-Muslim States." *Frontline*, January 5, pp. 70-77. (http://www.columbia.edu/itc/mealac/pritchett/00islamlinks/txt_eaton_temples2.pdf).

Elst, Koenraad. 2011. "Ayodhya's Three History Debates." *Journal of Indian History and Culture* 13-55.

Elst, Koenraad. 2014. *Negationism in India: concealing the record of Islam*. New Delhi: Voice of India.

Fani, Aria. 2019. "Culture of Encounters: Sanskrit at the Mughal Court, Audrey Truschke, New York: Columbia University Press, 2016, ISBN 9780231173629 (hbk), xiii + 362 pp." *Iranian Studies* 52(1-2):231-237.

Financial Express. 2004. "Redefining The Hindu Rate Of Growth." Retrieved February 15, 2022 (https://www.financialexpress.com/archive/redefining-the-hindu-rate-of-growth/104268/).

Goel, Sita R. 2012. *Hindu Temples: What Happened to Them, Vol.2: The Islamic Evidence*. New Delhi: Voice of India.

Hindu American Foundation. 2021. "Hindus for Human Rights & Indian American Muslim Council leaders, Rutgers Professor Audrey Truschke sued for defamation and conspiracy against HAF." Retrieved February 15, 2022 (https://www.hinduamerican.org/press/haf-defamation-lawsuit-iamc-hfhr-truschke).

Hindustan Times. 2014. "'Love jihad': UK Sikh girls' exploitation worries Takht." Retrieved February 15, 2022 (https://www.hindustantimes.com/

punjab/love-jihad-uk-sikh-girls-exploitation-worries-takht/story-6awkCCoAHZDu627o9FIfrN.html).

Hovannisian, Richard G. 2015. "Denial of the Armenian Genocide 100 Years Later: The New Practitioners and Their Trade." *Genocide Studies International* 9(2):228-247.

Jha, D.N. 2018. "Monumental Absence: The destruction of ancient Buddhist sites." Retrieved February 15, 2022 (https://caravanmagazine.in/reviews-and-essays/dn-jha-destruction-buddhist-sites).

Kanga, Surabhi. 2021. "The Hindu Right cannot debate me because it rejects critical thought: Audrey Truschke." Retrieved February 15, 2022 (https://caravanmagazine.in/history/hindu-right-cannot-debate-me-audrey-truschke).

Lee, Martha. 2020. "Stand With Kashmir not an innocent hashtag, it supports violent Islamists and terrorists." Retrieved February 15, 2022 (https://theprint.in/opinion/stand-with-kashmir-not-innocent-supports-violent-islamists-terrorists/429425/).

Lerner, Lawrence. 2021. "Audrey Truschke Wins NEH Grant to Write Sweeping History of South Asia." Retrieved February 15, 2022 (https://sasn.rutgers.edu/news-events/news/audrey-truschke-wins-neh-grant-write-sweeping-history-south-asia).

Malhotra, Rajiv. 2016. *Indra's Net: Defending Hinduism's Philosophical Unity*. HarperCollins: Noida.

Malhotra, Rajiv and Satyanarayana D. Babaji. 2020. *Sanskrit Non-Translatables: The Importance of Sanskritizing English*. Noida: Amaryllis.

Malhotra, Rajiv and Aravindan Neelakandan. 2011. *Breaking India: Western Interventions in Dravidian and Dalit Faultlines*. New Delhi: Amaryllis.

Mishra, Abhinandan. 2021. "Pak GHQ influencing some US academics to tar India." Retrieved February 15, 2022 (https://www.sundayguardianlive.com/news/pak-ghq-influencing-us-academics-tar-india).

Nair, Naveen. 2017. "The BJP and the Church find common ground on 'Love Jihad' in Kerala." Retrieved February 15, 2022 (https://www.hindustantimes.com/india-news/the-bjp-and-the-church-find-common-ground-on-love-jihad-in-kerala/story-krCpAE2YLaxTLxLZuXAnhJ.html).

Nakamura, Hajime. 2004. *A History of Early Vedānta Philosophy, Part 2*. Delhi: Motilal Banarsidass.

Pandit, M.S. 2017. "Ladakh tense over Muslim-Buddhist 'love jihad' marriage." Retrieved February 15, 2022 (https://timesofindia.indiatimes.com/india/ladakh-tense-over-muslim-buddhist-love-jihad-marriage/articleshow/60471076.cms).

Prakash, Priyali. 2021. "'Targeted by hate': Audrey Truschke on why she helped write a 'Hindutva Harassment Field Manual'." Retrieved February 15, 2022 (https://scroll.in/article/999710/targeted-by-hate-audrey-truschke-on-why-she-helped-write-a-hindutva-harassment-field-manual).

Rajagopal, Raju and Sunita Viswanath. 2021. "Audrey Truschke and the Blitzkrieg from the Hindu Right." Retrieved February 15, 2022 (https://iamc.com/audrey-truschke-and-the-blitzkrieg-from-the-hindu-right/).

Rajiv Malhotra Official. 2019. "False Translation Feeds Audrey Truschke's Hinduphobia." YouTube. Retrieved March 15, 2022 (https://www.youtube.com/watch?v=9BMXVgqrMJY).

Rutgers University. n.d. "Audrey Truschke." Retrieved February 15, 2022 (https://sasn.rutgers.edu/about-us/faculty-staff/audrey-truschke).

Sarkar, Jadunath. 1947. *Maasir-I-'Alamgiri: A History Of The Emperor Aurangzib-'Alamgir (Reign 1658-1707 A.D.) of Saqi Mustad Khan.* Calcutta: Royal Asiatic Society of Bengal.

Sastry, Manogna and Megh Kalyanasundaram. 2022. "A response to Tony Joseph's article dated Dec 30 2021 in 'The Quint'." Retrieved March 15, 2022 (https://www.academia.edu/66835366/A_response_to_Tony_Josephs_article_dated_Dec_30_2021_in_The_Quint).

Shahane, Girish. 2017. "Aurangzeb was a bigot not just by our standards but also by those of his predecessors and peers." Retrieved February 15, 2022 (https://scroll.in/article/856178/aurangzeb-was-a-bigot-not-just-by-our-standards-but-by-those-of-his-predecessors-and-peers).

Shahane, Girish. 2018. "All Modi has to show for on the world stage are minor victories and major mistakes." Retrieved February 15, 2022 (https://qz.com/india/1262687/indian-foreign-policy-is-blighted-by-modis-incompetence/).

Shahane, Girish. 2019a. "From Israel to Ayodhya, how Might becomes Right in politics and law." Retrieved February 15, 2022 (https://scroll.in/article/944377/from-israel-to-ayodhya-how-might-becomes-right-in-politics-and-law).

Shahane, Girish. 2019b. "Why Hindutva supporters love to hate the discredited Aryan Invasion Theory." Retrieved February 15, 2022 (https://scroll.in/

article/937043/why-hindutva-supporters-love-to-hate-the-discredited-aryan-invasion-theory).

Shourie, Arun. 2014. *Eminent Historians: Their Technology, Their Line, Their Fraud*. HarperCollins: New Delhi.

Sify News. 2021. "Audrey Truschke's anti-India stance due to disruptions in family business of conversions?" Retrieved February 15, 2022 (https://www.sify.com/news/audrey-truschkes-anti-india-stance-due-to-disruptions-in-family-business-of-conversions-news-national-vjkqktajjbfbj.html).

Singh, Shreeya. 2020. "Narendra Modi's Treatment of Muslims in India." Retrieved February 15, 2022 (https://www.teenvogue.com/story/students-against-hindutva-protests-modi-muslims).

The Hindu. 2019. "Pakistan's parliament blocks bill allowing non-Muslims to become country's PM, President." Retrieved February 15, 2022 (https://www.thehindu.com/news/international/pakistans-parliament-blocks-bill-allowing-non-muslims-to-become-countrys-pm-president/article29593495.ece).

Truschke, Audrey. 2011. "The Mughal Book of War: A Persian Translation of the Sanskrit Mahabharata." *Comparative Studies of South Asia, Africa and the Middle East* 31(2):506-520.

Truschke, Audrey. 2015. "Indo-Persian Translations: A Disruptive Past." Seminar 671. Retrieved January 31, 2022 (https://www.audreytruschke.com/s/Truschke_Indo_Persian_Translations_A_Disruptive_Past.pdf).

Truschke, Audrey. 2017. *Aurangzeb: The Life and Legacy of India's Most Controversial King*. Stanford: Stanford University Press.

Truschke, Audrey. 2018a. "Mughal Lite." Open. Retrieved January 31, 2022 (https://www.audreytruschke.com/s/Truschke-Mughal-Lite-2018.pdf).

Truschke, Audrey. 2018b. "The Many Criticisms of Rama and the 'Anger' of the Hindu Right." Retrieved March 15, 2022 (https://thewire.in/religion/the-many-criticisms-of-rama-and-the-anger-of-the-hindu-right).

Truschke, Audrey. 2019. "The Ayodhya verdict is a cornerstone of the Hindu Rashtra." Retrieved March 15, 2022 (https://caravanmagazine.in/religion/ayodhya-babri-masjid-ram-mandir-supreme-court-audrey-truschke).

Truschke, Audrey. 2020. "Hindutva's Dangerous Rewriting of History." *South Asia Multidisciplinary Academic Journal (SAMAJ)* 24/25. (journals.openedition.org/samaj/6636).

Truschke, Audrey. 2021. "Audrey Truschke: What the myth of 'love jihad' tells us about the Hindu Right." Retrieved February 15, 2022 (https://scroll.in/article/1006000/audrey-truschke-what-the-myth-of-love-jihad-tells-us-about-the-hindu-right).

Truschke, Audrey. 2021. *The Language of History: Sanskrit Narratives of Muslim Pasts*. New Delhi: Penguin Random House India.

Unnikrishnan, Hiran. 2021. "Bishop warns Christians in Kerala against 'love and narcotics jihad'." Retrieved February 15, 2022 (https://www.thehindu.com/news/national/kerala/bishop-warns-christians-in-kerala-against-love-and-narcotics-jihad/article36377244.ece).

Vardhan, Anand. 2018. "The Unscholarly Dishonesty of Audrey Truschke." Retrieved February 15, 2022 (https://www.newslaundry.com/2018/04/30/the-unscholarly-dishonesty-of-audrey-truschke).

Venkataramakrishnan, Rohan. 2021. "Interview: Audrey Truschke on Sanskrit histories of the Mughal era and Hindutva trolls." Retrieved February 15, 2022 (https://scroll.in/article/990717/interview-audrey-truschke-on-sanskrit-histories-of-the-mughal-era-and-hindutva-trolls).

Whitt, Laurelyn and Alan W. Clarke. 2019. *North American Genocides: Indigenous Nations, Settler Colonialism, and International Law*. Cambridge: Cambridge University Press.

Wistrich, Robert S. 2012. "Negationism, Antisemitism, and Anti-Zionism." *Holocaust Denial: The Politics of Perfidy* 257-268.

Notes

1. (Rutgers University n.d.)

2. See: "The Mughal Empire." Oxford Research Encyclopedias: Asian History. Retrieved on February 15, 2022 (https://doi.org/10.1093/acrefore/9780190277727.013.357).

3. See: "Hindutva's threat to academic freedom." Religion News Service. Retrieved on February 15, 2022 (https://religionnews.com/2021/07/07/hindutvas-threat-to-academic-freedom).

4. See: "AIPS Member Publishes Book." American Institute of Pakistan Studies. Retrieved on February 15, 2022 (http://www.pakistanstudies-aips.org/content/aips-member-publishes-book-0).

5. See: "Identifying an Attack." Hindutva Harassment Field Manual. Retrieved on February 15, 2022 (https://www.hindutvaharassmentfieldmanual.org/targets).

6. See: "AUDREY TRUSCHKE." The Caravan. Retrieved on February 15, 2022 (https://caravanmagazine.in/author/1128).

7. See: "Stories written by Audrey Truschke." Scroll.in. Retrieved on February 15, 2022 (https://scroll.in/author/10495)

8. See: "Audrey Truschke." The Wire. Retrieved on February 15, 2022 (https://thewire.in/author/audrey-truschke).

9. (Rutgers University n.d.)

10. (Fani 2019)

11. (Vardhan 2018)

12. (Hindu American Foundation 2021)

13. (Rajagopal and Viswanath 2021)

14. (Baird 2021)

15. See: "About Us." SAHI. Retrieved on February 15, 2022 (https://www.studentsagainsthindutvaideology.org/about-us).

16. (Singh 2020)

17. (Lee 2020)

18. (Mishra 2021)

19. (Lerner 2021)

20. (Kanga 2021)

21. In Marxism, revisionism is used pejoratively to describe deviations from Marx's core ideas. In a political context, the term has abusive connotations especially when it pertains to relations between two communist regimes. See: "revisionism." Oxford Reference. Retrieved on February 15, 2022 (https://www.oxfordreference.com/view/10.1093/oi/authority.20110810105729649).

22. The Armenian genocide was the state sanctioned destruction of the (Christian) Armenian people and identity through robbery, rape, and ethnic cleansing in the (Muslim) Turkish Ottoman Empire in 1915 during World War I. See: (Hovannisian 2015) to understand how this genocide

has been systematically denied for almost a century using sophisticated research methods and critical-thinking techniques.

23. See: (Whitt and Clarke 2019)
24. See: (Wistrich 2012)
25. For a comprehensive treatment of this subject see: (Shourie 2014)
26. From the cover of (Elst 2014). The book has a detailed treatment on how many Indian historians, journalists and politicians confidently deny that there ever was a Hindu-Muslim conflict, and ridicule the very idea of Hindu persecution during India's Islamic rule.
27. See: (Truschke 2017:Ch. 6, Destroyer of Temples)
28. (Truschke 2017:Ch. 6, Protector of Temples, para. 3)
29. (Truschke 2017:Ch. 6, Destroyer of Temples, para. 3)
30. (Truschke 2017:Ch. 6, Destroyer of Temples, para. 7)
31. (Truschke 2017:Ch. 6, Protector of Temples, para. 3,4,5)
32. (Sarkar 1947:v)
33. (Sarkar 1947:116)
34. (Sarkar 1947:116-117)
35. (Sarkar 1947:117)
36. (Truschke 2017:Ch. 6, Destroyer of Temples, para. 4)
37. (Truschke 2017:Ch. 6, Destroyer of Temples, para. 3)
38. (Sarkar 1947:iv)
39. (Truschke 2017:Ch. 6, Destroyer of Temples, para. 4)
40. (Truschke 2017:Ch. 6, Destroyer of Temples, para. 3)
41. (Truschke 2017:Ch. 6, Destroyer of Temples, para. 3)
42. (Eaton 2001:73)
43. For example see: (An-Na'im 2008:146). See also (Jha 2018): "They. relentlessly propagate canard that 60,000 Hindu temples were demolished during Muslim rule, though there is hardly any credible evidence for the destruction of more than 80 of them."
44. (Chaubey 2021)

45. This was accompanied by arson targeting houses, shops and businesses of Hindus, sexual assault and rapes, and murder of Hindus (Bose 2021).
46. (Elst 2011:24-25)
47. (Eaton 2001:74)
48. (Truschke 2017:Ch. 6, Destroyer of Temples, para. 5)
49. (Eaton 2001:74-75)
50. (Goel 2012:Ch. 8, para. 1)
51. (Elst 2011:24-25)
52. (Goel 2012:Appendix 4 - Questionnaire for the Marxist Professors, II, para. 15)
53. (Truschke 2017:Ch. 6, Destroyer of Temples, para. 2)
54. (Truschke 2017:Ch. 6, Destroyer of Temples, para. 7)
55. (Truschke 2017:Ch. 6, Destroyer of Temples, para. 7)
56. (Truschke 2017:Ch. 6, Destroyer of Temples, para. 13, 14, 15)
57. Who can forget Shylock the greedy and vengeful moneylender in William Shakespeare's play The Merchant of Venice (c. 1600 CE)?
58. See: "Antisemitism Explained." Philadelphia Holocaust Remembrance Foundation/Horwitz-Wasserman Holocaust Memorial Plaza. Retrieved on February 15, 2022 (https://www.philaholocaustmemorial.org/antisemitism-explained).
59. (Shahane 2019a)
60. (Shahane 2018)
61. (Shahane 2019b)
62. (Shahane 2017)
63. (Shahane 2017)
64. (Elst 2011:26)
65. See: "Explained: A short history of Kashmir before the Mughals." The Indian Express. Retrieved on February 15, 2022 (https://indianexpress.com/article/explained/explained-a-short-history-of-kashmir-before-the-mughals-5886523).

66. (Shahane 2017)

67. (Truschke 2021:Ch. 1, Brahmin Silence As the Exception, para. 1)

68. See: Asaru-l Bilad of Zakari'ya Al Kazwini (b. in Kazwin, Persia; written c. 1270 CE), Tarikh-i Alfi. Maulânâ Ahmad et al., eds 1582 CE and Kamilu-t Tawarikh of Ibn Asir (b. 555 H., 1160 CE)

69. See: "Tarikhu-s Subuktigin of Abu-l Fazl al Baihaki (b. 388 H., 995 CE; d. 470 H., 1077 CE). A history of Ghaznivites up to 451 H. (1059 CE)." Infinity Foundation. Retrieved on February 15, 2022 (https://www.infinityfoundation.com/mandala/h_es/h_es_tarikhu_frameset.htm).

70. (Kanga 2021)

71. (Truschke 2020)

72. (Truschke 2020)

73. (Kanga 2021)

74. (Kanga 2021)

75. (Truschke 2020)

76. (Truschke 2018a)

77. (Kanga 2021)

78. (Truschke 2018a)

79. IIT Bombay, India's premier technology and research institute has a full online course on the development of mathematics in India from ancient times to the present. See: "Mathematics in India – From Vedic Period to Modern Times." NPTEL. Retrieved on February 15, 2022 (https://nptel.ac.in/courses/111/101/111101080).

Infinity Foundation has published fourteen volumes on the history of Indian science and technology by authors who are experts in their respective fields, and covering domains like the prowess of Indian society in the fields of agriculture, architecture, iron smelting and refining, zinc metallurgy, animal husbandry, water management, hydraulic engineering, bead technology, and various allied technologies. See: "History of Indian Science and Technology | Infinity Foundation Series." Amazon. Retrieved on February 15, 2022 (https://www.amazon.com/History-of-Indian-Science-and-Technology-%257C-Infinity-Foundation-Series-12-book-series/dp/B08NCXRBC8).

80. The term jihad refers to religious war undertaken by Muslims as their belief or duty. See: "jihad." Merriam Webster. Retrieved on March 15, 2022 (https://www.merriam-webster.com/dictionary/jihad).

81. (Truschke 2021)

82. (Hindustan Times 2014)

83. (Nair 2017)

84. (Pandit 2017)

85. (Unnikrishnan 2021)

86. (Truschke 2020)

87. See: "Scholars discarded the Aryan Invasion Theory before I was born. Hindu nationalists alone keep beating that dead horse. Why? Their own politics and hang-ups. The Aryan Migration Theory is scholarly consensus; the evidence is extraordinarily strong." Twitter. Retrieved on March 15, 2022 (https://twitter.com/AudreyTruschke/status/1477625885616488454).

88. (Truschke 2020)

89. For the full range of meanings see: "adhikāra." Kosha.Sanskrit.Today. Retrieved on March 15, 2022 (https://kosha.sanskrit.today/word/sa/adhikAraH?q=adhik%C4%81ra).

90. (Sastry and Kalyanasundaram 2022)

91. (Truschke 2015:1)

92. (Truschke 2015:4)

93. (Truschke 2011:507)

94. (Truschke 2015:4)

95. (Truschke 2015:6)

96. (Truschke 2011:513)

97. For the full range of meanings see: "sampradāya." Kosha.Sanskrit.Today. Retrieved on March 15, 2022 (https://kosha.sanskrit.today/word/sa/sampradAya?q=samprad%C4%81ya).

98. "If you want to know: How long have people been using the word "Hinduism"? The answer is: With spelling variants, a few hundred years, max. It's a Western idea." Twitter. Retrieved on February 15, 2022 (https://twitter.com/AudreyTruschke/status/1169669344546172928).

99. "If you want to loosen up on precise vocabulary and ask: How long have people been using the world "Hindu"? The answer is: A thousand years, maybe a tad more. It's a Perso-Arabic invention. Also, the Perso-Arabic "Hindu" sometimes meant Indian, more geographic than religious." Twitter. Retrieved on February 15, 2022 (https://twitter.com/AudreyTruschke/status/1169669653670612994).

100. (Venkataramakrishnan 2021)

101. "If you want to ask: How long have people relied upon a Hindu holy book? The answer is: What book are we talking about? Vedas? Gita? Ramayana? We oldest layer of the Vedas gives you 3,500 years at the utmost. But how many modern Hindus read the Vedas, or do Vedic sacrifices?" Twitter. Retrieved on February 15, 2022 (https://twitter.com/AudreyTruschke/status/1169670319327580160).

102. "Most Hindus worship different gods now than Vedic people did 3,500 years ago, and in quite different ways. Bhakti didn't even come about until the CE era. The four aims of Hindu life? Originally, there were only 3 (moksha was added later)." Twitter. Retrieved on February 15, 2022 (https://twitter.com/AudreyTruschke/status/1169671961930338304).

103. "We could go with the Gita as a core Hindu holy book, but then date-wise we're only going back 2,000 years roughly. For the Ramayana... If you go for stuff like shadow Sita, Lakshmana rekha, etc... you're in the 2nd millennium CE before a lot of that stuff comes up." Twitter. Retrieved on February 15, 2022 (https://twitter.com/AudreyTruschke/status/1169671082653167616).

104. (Truschke 2011:514)

105. "Another common charge in the campaign to de-legitimize Hinduism is that it had no self-defined and conscious understanding of its own distinctiveness from other religions. The foundation of neo-Hinduism is said to have been built by distorting prior traditions, which themselves had no unity and were a mishmash of irreconcilable texts and local customs." (Malhotra 2016:36)

106. "Since there is no central authority or ecclesiastical structure in Hinduism, no closed canon or 'Bible' of sacred texts, and since there are no 'creeds' to which members of the faith must subscribe, Westerners tend to denigrate it as random, fragmented, chaotic and without unity." (Malhotra 2016:36)

107. "Honestly, when scholars start telling people, including modern Hindus, what's actually in the Vedas, responses sort of go back and

forth between people falling asleep (lots of hymns in there) and being utterly shocked at animal sacrifice, sexual practices, spells, etc." Twitter. Retrieved on February 15, 2022 (https://twitter.com/AudreyTruschke/status/1169670603957329920).

108. See (Malhotra 2016:29-43) where the Rajiv Malhotra summarize the eight basic assumptions or myths underlying the theory of 'neo-Hinduism', with a brief response to each.

109. "Dismantling Hindutva conference September 10-12, virtual, cosponsored by 45+ centers / departments at 40+ universities (including Rutgers). Do consider attending to learn more about the threat and power of #Hindutva in our world." Twitter. Retrieved on February 15, 2022 (https://twitter.com/audreytruschke/status/1426677197855760387).

110. See: "Hindutva is not Hinduism." Dismantling Global Hindutva. Retrieved on February 15, 2022 (https://dismantlinghindutva.com/resources/hindutva-is-not-hinduism).

111. See: "What is Hindutva?" Hindutva Harassment Field Manual. Retrieved on February 15, 2022 (https://www.hindutvaharassmentfieldmanual.org/defininghindutva).

112. "I take Hindutva as political Hinduism, not a distortion of an older tradition but a continuation of it." Twitter. Retrieved on February 15, 2022 (https://twitter.com/dghconference/status/1436394578970546187).

113. "If you're looking to understand this, a couple of thoughts -- Religious identities are not fixed. When Hindus speak and act, as Hindus, they are contributing to defining their tradition and identity. But nobody speaks for all Hindus. Hence, the identity is often contested." Twitter. Retrieved on February 15, 2022 (https://twitter.com/AudreyTruschke/status/1451584684631236611).

114. See: "There is a special place in hell for those using the horrific Taliban takeover of Afghanistan—and what it means for women's rights—to abuse outspoken, educated women. Hindutvavadis — I'm looking at you." Twitter. Retrieved on February 15, 2022 (https://twitter.com/audreytruschke/status/1427293023159869449).

115. (Truschke 2019)

116. (Truschke 2019)

117. See: "IN THE SUPREME COURT OF INDIA CIVIL APPELLATE JURISDICTION Civil Appeal Nos 10866-10867 of 2010." Supreme Court of India. Retrieved on March 15, 2022 (https://www.sci.gov.in/pdf/JUD_2.pdf).

118. (Truschke 2019)

119. (Truschke 2019)

120. (Truschke 2019)

121. For the full range of meanings see: "avatāra." Kosha.Sanskrit.Today. Retrieved on March 15, 2022 (https://kosha.sanskrit.today/word/en/avataara?q=avat%C4%81ra).

122. (Truschke 2019)

123. See: "Re #RamayanaGate over here, let me correct the reference for Sita's agnipariksa to 6.102-106; criticism from Sita in 6.104. Given here in the English translation of Goldman. Note, especially, vv. 5, 7, and 14." Twitter. Retrieved on March 15, 2022 (https://twitter.com/AudreyTruschke/status/987371326884151296).

124. See: "The Scholar Whom Audrey Truschke Cites Finds Her Tweet 'Shocking'." Swarajya. Retrieved on March 15, 2022 (https://swarajyamag.com/culture/the-scholar-whom-audrey-truschke-cites-finds-her-tweet-shocking).

125. (Rajiv Malhotra Official 2019). Also see: "Lost And Failed In Translation: Audrey Truschke." Swarajya. Retrieved on March 15, 2022 (https://swarajyamag.com/ideas/lost-and-failed-in-translation-audrey-truschke).

126. See: "The secret to Audrey Truschke's success (no, it's not her scholarship)." DailyO. Retrieved on March 15, 2022 (https://www.dailyo.in/voices/audrey-truschke-historian-aurangzeb-william-dalrymple-hindus/story/1/25995.html).

127. See: "What we Believe." First Baptist Church of Monterey. Retrieved on February 15, 2022 (https://www.fbcmonterey.org/what-we-believe).

128. (Sify News 2021)

129. (The Hindu 2019)

130. See: "Vakyartha Sadas." Infinity Foundation India. Retrieved on February 15, 2022 (https://infinityfoundationindia.org/vakyartha-sadas).

131. See: "I shouldn't be shocked at this, but I am nonetheless that 21st-century folks maintain the forceful inclusion of #Sikhs in #Hinduism." Twitter. Retrieved on February 15, 2022 (https://drive.google.com/file/d/1iVZiOFL4khOSeGRAWI7_Q9kg5V8OoC_a).

132. See: "Early Hindutva ideologues especially liked Hitler's treatment of Jews. They saw it as a useful model for how to treat Indian Muslims. Think about that, and let that seep in for a bit." Twitter. Retrieved on March 15, 2022 (https://twitter.com/audreytruschke/status/1085147401319403520).

133. See: "How #Indian groups and laws use the charge of 'forced religious conversion' to target #minorities and #Dalits." Twitter. Retrieved on February 15, 2022 (https://drive.google.com/file/d/1jeJN0yYo8jvcP0jwIWCaMUStbKJVdXSS).

134. The below four Acts very clearly define the scope of Hinduism.

 - "The Hindu Marriage Act, 1955." High Court of Punjab and Haryana. Retrieved October 16, 2021 (https://highcourtchd.gov.in/hclscc/subpages/pdf_files/4.pdf).

 - "The Hindu Adoption and Maintenance Act, 1956." Tripura Commission for Women. Retrieved October 16, 2021 (http://tcw.nic.in/Acts/Hindu%20adoption%20and%20Maintenance%20Act.pdf).

 - "Hindu Minority and Guardianship Act, 1956." National Commission for Protection of Child Rights. Retrieved October 16, 2021 (http://www.ncpcr.gov.in/view_file.php?fid=423).

 - "The Hindu Succession Act, 1956 (HSA)." National Commission for Women. Retrieved October 16, 2021 (http://ncwapps.nic.in/acts/TheHinduSuccessionAct1956.pdf).

135. The theory of Sanskrit Non-Translatables (SNT) first introduced in the book, *Being Different* and later developed into a complete thesis in *Sanskrit Non-Translatables : The Importance of Sanskritizing English*, suggested that Western scholars and Westernized Indians often translate and map dharmic concepts and perspectives onto Western frameworks. This is problematic since Dharmic traditions are compromised and many elements atrophy when the Western substitutes become acceptable, although they may not accurately represent the original Indian idea. This inadequate translation of vocabulary facilitates the cultural digestion of dharma into the West and during this process, often carried out under the guise of modernity

many crucial distinctions and understandings are lost, and important, productive and visionary dimension of dharma are eradicated and relegated to antiquity. The SNT book takes these ideas forward and launches a new movement using Sanskrit Non-Translatables as a device for protecting key ideas from getting distorted, plagiarized, or allowed to become obsolete. See: (Malhotra and Babaji 2020)

136. See: "Ram Guha, Sanjay Raut distance themselves as 'Concerned Scholars' after a letter purportedly signed by them against Vikram Sampath goes viral." OpIndia. Retrieved on March 15, 2022 (https://www.opindia.com/2022/02/ramchandra-guha-sanjay-raut-vikram-sampath-letter-audrey-truschke-did-not-sign).

137. See: "Delhi HC bars 3 historians from publishing defamatory material on Vikram Sampath." Times of India. Retrieved on March 15, 2022 (https://timesofindia.indiatimes.com/life-style/books/features/delhi-hc-bars-3-historians-from-publishing-defamatory-material-on-vikram-sampath/articleshow/89698944.cms).

138. dharmaḥ tasmāddharmāt paraṃ nāsty atho abalīyān balīyāṁsamāśaṁsate dharmeṇa yathā rājñaivam ǀ

yo vai sa dharmaḥ satyaṃ vai tat tasmātsatyaṃ vadantamāhur dharmaṃ vadatīti dharmaṃ vā vadantaṁ satyaṃ vadatīty etaddhyevaitadubhayaṃ bhavati ǁ

Nothing is higher than dharma. The weak overcomes the stronger by dharma, as over a king. Truly that dharma is the Truth (Satya); Therefore, when a man speaks the Truth, they say, "He speaks the Dharma"; and if he speaks Dharma, they say, "He speaks the Truth!" For both are one. — Brihadaranyaka Upanishad, 1.4.xiv

139. dhṛtiḥ kṣamā damo'steyaṃ śaucamindriyanigrahaḥ ǀ

dhīrvidyā satyamakrodho daśakaṃ dharmalakṣaṇam ǁ

(1) Steadiness (2) Forgiveness, (3) Self-control, (4) Abstention from unrighteous appropriation, (5) Purity, (6) Control of the Sense-organs, (7) Discrimination, (8) Knowledge, (9) Truthfulness, and (10) Absence of anger,- these are the ten-fold forms of duty. — Manusmriti 6.92

EIGHT

Ramachandra Guha
Anarchic #Fiberal[1]Distorian[2]

T.N. Sudarshan and Divya Reddy

*'If you can't dazzle them with brilliance, **baffle** them with bullshit.'*–W.C. Fields
Your good name, Sir – Anonymous Reporter[3]

Intellectual swaraj (self-rule) is as fundamental to the long-term success of a civilization as in the political and financial arenas. Therefore, it is important to ask whose way of representing knowledge will be in control? It is the representation system that defines the metaphors and terminologies and most importantly, grants privileges by determining who controls this marketplace of ideas. – (Malhotra 2002)

1 The Neo-Colonial Nation (Un)Builder

Ramachandra Guha is a self-styled 'contemporary' historian (albeit, very much post-truth, mostly fact-free and opinionated), who is considered popular for his elaborations on 'Nehruvian'ism', M.K. Gandhi, cricket history, environment, politics and economics. He has produced books on a variety of subjects, ranging from biographies, politics, to environmental issues. Some of his bestselling books are *India after Gandhi: The History of the World's Largest Democracy, Democrats and Dissenters*. He is also a columnist for *The Telegraph, The Hindustan Times* and the Hindi daily, *Amar Ujala*. His articles appear in national newspapers such as *The Hindu*. He is also a regular contributor to various academic journals, Guha has also written for *The Caravan* and *Outlook* magazines. Guha held a visiting position, the Philippe Roman Chair in History and International Affairs at the London School of Economics and Political Science (LSE) between 2011 and 2012. Due to his large body of work, covering a wide range of fields he is considered to be a significant figure in Indian historical studies. He was conferred the Honorary Foreign Member prize for the year 2019 by the American Historical Association (AHA). He is the third Indian historian to be recognized by the association, joining the ranks of Romila Thapar and Jadunath Sarkar, who received the honor in 2009 and 1952 respectively. He was also the recipient of the Padma Bhushan in 2009, India's third-highest civilian award. He is quite popular on social media (Twitter) with over two million followers.

Guha positions himself as a liberal Indian, focused on interpreting the modern history of India post 1947. He admonishes the concept of a nation state, let alone, a civilizational state, and denies the existence of any significant common factor that can unite the people of one geographical territory. His views, in our opinion, are generally divisive in nature and pose a threat to the integrity of India as we shall examine in this essay. Serious practitioners of Hinduism may take offense at the perceived *Hinduphobic* nature of his work. He likens the concept of Hindutva and Nationalism to the virulent nature of Islamic supremacy.[4] Guha claims to be a Gandhian, and selectively quotes Gandhi (and everyone else) to propagate his Hinduphobic agenda. We attempt to provide a limited deconstruction and factual analysis of a few of his writings (books, essays and lectures), those that he has widely shared in the public space. The essay is structured to unearth the implicit message in much of Guha's work. See sections titled 'Message to Reader' as we expose the underlying intent.

As we shall see, his elaboration and his views on Hinduism and Hindutva, nationhood, Gandhi, Nehru, caste, cow slaughter, the concept of secularism are indeed interesting to analyze, as much of it follows the tropes and boundaries of his neo-colonial masters. The principal agenda as becomes apparent is his legitimization of the Western lens to view

Indian history, his strict *"good and dutiful schoolboy"* adherence to the notion of Western Universalism and the Western gaze on India.[5]

Rajiv Malhotra, in his hard-hitting essay on neo-colonialism describes the role of history in nation building as also its unbuilding. Guha is a classic example of a **nation-(un)builder.**

> "History writing has been used both to build nations and to dismantle them. ...History has never been an objective reporting of a set of empirical facts. It's a present day (re)conception and filtering of data pertaining to the past, to build a narrative that is consistent with the myths of the dominant culture. ... While each rich and powerful civilization emphasizes its indigenous cohesiveness and continuity, and with scholarship under control of those loyal to it, the reverse is the trend among the economically weak civilizations such as India. In the case of Indian civilization, the scholars' emphasis has been on how there might not even be such a historical entity as India or Hinduism, and how its civilization was entirely brought by foreigners into India. This intellectual breakup of Indic Traditions into historical layers of cultural imports, each with a nexus in some other part of the world, is the intellectual equivalent of the political breakup of India. That so many Indian have sold out to this project is certainly noteworthy, and is a major untold story of our times. In the long run, it is tempting for the West to assimilate this last remaining non-Western knowledge system, and breaking it into digestible modules facilitates this. However, the havoc that such a potential breakup would unleash would also be of catastrophic global proportions. Furthermore, the future positive harvests that this civilization is capable of giving to the world would end." (Malhotra 2002)

Rajiv Malhotra's essay explains the origins of neo-colonialism, shows that many Indians are themselves perpetuating neo-colonialism today and finally links this phenomenon with Western control from above the glass ceiling.

Applying Malhotra's deconstruction and analysis, Guha's deep seated 'brown shame' causes him to play the role of the guilt-ridden sepoy to the hilt, aimed at impressing both his sepoy peers (see the book: *A Functioning Anarchy*, a book of essays celebrating Guha) and his masters in Western ivory towers.

> "Sparked by Guha's wide-ranging and important work, a functioning anarchy is a collection of essays by historians, social scientists, ecologists and journalists."[6]

David Gilmour, contributor of an essay[7], titles it as *"The many Rams in Ramachandra Guha."* It could well have been titled as *"The many Ravanas in Ramachandra Guha."*

2 The #FiberalDistorian Spin on Important Personalities

Some of Guha's most insidious work are his biographies and commentaries, his *own* opinions of people. Mostly, he plays the role of a 'good cop' by criticizing both the Left and the Right. Importantly, he does not take any *dharma* driven positions, but all the while adopts a prominent Hinduphobic and anti-national stance as noted in the examples below. The endless Hinduphobic hate speech is amplified through contemporary channels such as blogs and social media. Readers are encouraged to peruse his writings at *ramachandraguha.in* and his Twitter timeline (*@Ram_Guha*). Guha positions himself as a liberal and as a patriot sans nationalism. He claims to criticize the extremes of both the Left and the Right, the bigotry of the Sangh Parivar, corruption of the Congress and also Marxism.[8] He claims to be influenced by the patriotism of Shivarama Karantha and Mahasweta Devi.[9]

2.1 On Mahatma Gandhi

Gandhi, according to Guha is the greatest reformer of Hinduism, which until the period of Gandhi was orthodox, heterodox, superstitious and ridden with caste and women issues. Guha feels that Gandhi started off as a xenophobe which was reflected in his 1920s movement, and later took a U-Turn, after Rabindranath Tagore wrote a letter to Gandhi rebuking his xenophobic ways. Thereafter, Gandhi set on a course of self-correction and stopped demonizing Western ideas.[10] According to Guha, Gandhi was inspired by a Jain poet and thinker called Raychandbhai who he had met in Bombay in 1891. Guha insists that it was Raychandbhai who convinced Gandhi that 'moksha' or liberation, is not hastened on worshipping mythological figures like 'Krishna' or 'Rama'. Guha points out that, while Gandhi seriously read and identified with the *Bhagavad Gita*, he ignored the Bhakti elements of the *Gita* that emphasized the veneration of avatar Krishna.[11]

Message to Reader[12]**:** Ignore Bhakti. Ignore temples. Ignore Itihasa and Purana. All for your own good.

'Gandhi' (as a genre) is used by Guha effectively (multiple books, papers, articles, thousands of pages on Gandhi) to push in all manner of anti-*Sanatana* attacks, mostly amplifying tropes from Western scholarship. Themes and dialectic inspired by Marxism, Postmodernism, anarchist theories and the like, as can be clearly seen in the following examples. The abhorrent mis-use of "Gandhi" as the mascot to delegitimize the idea of a sanatana civilization, and as a prop for pushing as "contemporary" intervention in polity and public discourse is a consistent feature of Guha's work.[13] Just as the "Western" has become a versatile genre in Hollywood, Gandhi as a genre has become equally versatile in the hands of Guha, used as a backdrop, metaphor for all manner of contemporary (mostly insidious) messaging.

> "With characteristic originality, Gandhi ignored or finessed the element of bhakti in the Gita—as in its call to venerate the avatar Krishna—in favour of an action-oriented understanding of its message."[14]

Unlike the conventional or traditional Hindu as Guha points out, where religious devotion is expressed through the scrupulous observance of rituals and intense adoration of a personal or family God or a deep knowledge of the scriptures. Guha insists that Gandhi's faith consisted of commitment to truth, chastity, non-violence, and, especially, service.[15]

Message to Reader: Hinduism is not committed to truth, chastity, non-violence and service.

As Jordens writes, 'no school of sect [within Hinduism] did ever elevate the activity of service itself into one that caused the realisation of moksha'—which is what Gandhi did.[16]

Message to Reader: Hinduism has to learn about "service" from Christianity, among many other things.

Guha wonders if Gandhi called himself a Hindu or a 'sanatani' despite his rubbing shoulders with the orthodoxy.

> "Was this out of sentimental attachment to an ancestral faith, or for tactical reasons, since positioning himself as an outsider would make it harder to persuade other Hindus of his arguments? Be that as it may, aspects of Gandhi's faith resonate closely with spiritual (or intellectual) traditions that are other than 'Hindu'. The stress on ethical conduct brings him close to Buddhism, while the avowal of non-violence and non-possession is clearly drawn from Jainism. The exaltation of service is far more Christian than Hindu. The emphasis on the dignity of the individual echoes Enlightenment ideas of human rights."[17]

Message to Reader: Sanatana Dharma has to be reformed and there is a distinct lack of human rights. Sanatana Dharma desperately needs enlightenment.

Guha believes that Gandhi's faith synthesized various experiences that he derived from living in the West, being mentored by a certain Jain friend, and having close Christian or Buddhist friends. Guha also insists that Gandhi's fight against untouchability was not inspired[18] by **dharma** as defined by "Brahmins" and the "Shrutis" and "Smritis" but, in truth, renunciation, passion-lessness, and ahimsa. It is important to note the use of English words and Christian concepts by Guha and not any Sanskrit words for the equivalent dharma concepts like *satya, aparigraha* etc.

Message to Reader: Hindus have to learn about their own religion from others (like Gandhi did), as Hindus themselves do not know much about it. Sanatana Dharma encourages fratricide. Sanatana Dharma has **many** truths. It is upto the person (as an individual) to **look** for it (importantly in a postmodern sense—it can be whatever the person wants to look for).

As per Guha, Gandhi believed that every religion was an unstable mixture of truth and error and he rejected the idea of one privileged path to God.[19]

Message to Reader: There is nothing different about Sanatana Dharma (so why even have it), it is just like any other religion. All conceptions of God are likely the same. Sanatana Dharma is unstable like any other human conception.

2.2 On Pt. Jawaharlal Nehru

(Pt) Nehru is another of Guha's important genres. Guha describes Nehru as a Westernized Brahmin, one of the greatest leaders India has ever seen.[20] He emphasizes most critically on (Pt) Nehru's pivotal role in the formation of modern India post 1947. Guha extols Nehru for upholding the secular and pluralistic values of India and for constantly reinforcing those values through his efficient administration, thereby preventing communal conflicts and holding the society in harmony.[21] According to Guha, Nehru was a brave man, who fought religious chauvinists, a selfless man who had endured years in jail to win freedom and above all he was a good man.[22] He helped harmonize the masses with the classes. Guha describes Nehru as the perfect bond between the world and India as he served as India's representative to the great Western democracies and also as their representative to India.[23] Much of Guha's "Nehru" genre serves to whitewash and extol Nehru in an unashamed attempt to impress and be in the good books of the Nehru dynasty which remains close to power in India.

The Western nations certainly look upon him as such and expect him to guarantee India's support for them, which is why they are so upset when Nehru takes an anti-Western or neutral line. They feel they are being let down by one of themselves.[24]

Guha sympathizes with Nehru for having to take on the onus of putting together a country that was desperately divided and very poor.[25] Adult suffrage, a federal polity, mixed economy, non-alignment in foreign policy, cultural pluralism and the secular state, Guha feels that all these decisions were collectively made by the leaders, first generation India's nation-builders and Nehru cannot be entirely blamed for the results of those policies. According to Guha, instead of asking why the Indian state chose to be secular rather than theocratic, we should ask why Nehru did so.[26]

What Gandhi meant was that as a person of decency and charm, a patriot of integrity and commitment, Nehru more closely approximated the moral virtues that men of faith often profess but less often practise.[27]

That, Nehru was quintessentially a politician, is presented to the readers as a virtue. He whitewashes Nehru's choice of socialistic model for India by blaming it on 'Bombay plan' and on a group of industrialists.[28] According to Guha, Nehru's economic policies have not been altogether unsuccessful. He insists that Nehru's policies have built a decent industrial base, helped assure self-sufficiency in food, and have created a pool of technically skilled manpower that has fueled the recent software boom (a brilliant illustration of retroactive credit-taking).[29] Given that Nehru was the first prime minister of independent India, Guha predicts that Nehru's mistakes would any day compare smaller to anyone else in his shoes. For Guha, Nehru was the best Prime Minister India ever had and definitely better than Patel or Bose.[30]

Message to Reader: Nehru's contribution to India was far superior than that of either Subhash Chandra Bose or Sardar Patel.

Guha believes that Nehru was the epitome of liberalism in the sense that he had transcended the boundaries of 'race, religion, caste, class, gender and geography.' As a testament, Guha points out the fact that Nehru was befriended by Muslims and also trusted and respected by women.[31]

Message to Reader: Nehru was also a 'Mahatma', perhaps even a bigger one than the original. A true Brahmin is one who gives up the duties of his varna, and in this way achieves greatness, and indeed Nehru was an exemplar of this.

Guha extols Nehru for sowing the seeds of nationalism and uniting Indians, irrespective of their cultural differences. Guha also praises Nehru for giving special consideration to Muslims to make them feel Indian.[32]

Comment: Guha ignores Nehru's grave blunders that cost India dearly, such as his adamancy in retaining Article 370 that gave special status to Jammu and Kashmir and the creation of Pakistan-occupied

Kashmir (PoK), all of which consequently laid the grounds for the Kashmir Hindu genocide. Unfortunately, none of these blunders make it to the Left-liberal narrative when discussing Nehru's tenure despite his debacles haunting India to this day.

2.3 On Lal Bahadur Shastri

Recent works and discourse (a movie even—*The Tashkent Files*), which discuss Shastri, give us insights into the life and times of Shastri. Guha's creativity in history writing is on display in his description of Shastri's demise.

> "In the first weeks of 1966 Shastri died of a heart attack in the city of Tashkent, which was then part of the Soviet Union. The Indian prime minister had gone there, at the invitation of the Soviets, to forge a peace treaty with Pakistan's Ayub Khan. There has been some speculation about whether Shastri died of natural causes—speculation that continues because the Government of India has (typically) refused to release the official report on his death. But perhaps there was no hanky-panky—**perhaps it was just that his traditional apparel did him in, with a dhoti and kurta inadequate protection against the harsh cold of an Uzbek winter.**
>
> Shastri was only sixty-three when he died. **The question one must ask is not how he died**, but what if he had lived another five or ten years?" (Emphasis ours) (Guha 2010)

Guha's imaginative "shifting" of goalposts, and speculative whitewashing of Congress' failure in investigating the mysterious death of one of India's beloved prime ministers is amply evident from his above quote.

3 #Fiberal Distorian Positions on *Videshi Siddhanta*

3.1 Subalternism

Guha feels Hinduism is ridden with gender hierarchies and all manner of caste issues.[33] B.R. Ambedkar and Nehru played a pivotal role in reforming the 'Hindu personal laws' which granted women equal rights and opportunities which until then was strictly denied to women and always treated them as un-equals.[34] He equates Hinduism and Islam as one and the same when it comes to treating women and the unfair treatment that both the religions entail. Furthering the dichotomy of the subaltern lens, he creates his divide based on upper caste, lower caste, city dwellers, village dwellers, Brahmin, Dalit, Hindu and Muslim. He feels the discrimination against women and lower castes is not at all the fault of the white colonizers, but rather the product of Indian traditions and customs.[35]

3.2 Colonialism

Guha is of the strong view that British colonialism, despite the vile motive, helped India advance from a primitive civilization, which was once ridden with orthodoxy and social issues, to a modern country.[36] He believes that India is an amalgamation of cultures and religions and had no prior indigenous civilization that was significant enough to be proud of or worthy enough to be spoken about.[37] Guha's narrative on British colonialism is that of an apologetic India suffering from the Stockholm syndrome. Guha ignores the fact that Britain owes India an astronomical sum of financial reparations. He is oblivious to how the concocted history of India by British Indologists threatens the sovereignty and integrity of India to this day. Guha is also deafeningly silent about the centuries of Islamic pillage and the invasions and the violent conversion of hundreds of millions to Islam. South Asia is now home to more than seven hundred million Islamic adherents, all former Hindus, products of violent conversion and Islamic colonization. But, for Guha, Islamic colonization did not happen. Period. It seems like for Guha, ideological loyalty is more important than the nation. See linked readings for Guha's repertoire on Islam.

3.3 Nationalism

Guha is a strong critique of 19th century European nationalism which he thinks served as the template nationalism for countries like Israel and Pakistan. He describes this nationalism as one that is based on a common language, common religion and a common enemy.[38] He equates this nationalism with Hindu Rashtra and contradicts it with the pluralistic and inclusive nature of Indian civilization and the Constitution. Thereby, terming the idea of a 'rashtra' as unconstitutional, fascist and chauvinistic. Guha feels a new modern nation called India was formed post 1947.[39] Guha says that the idea of a plural and inclusive India has three enemies.

1) Hindu fundamentalism (where he refers to the idea of a Hindu Rashtra)
2) The threat posed by the communist party of India (Maoist)
3) This challenge goes back to the idea of founding the nation. This is the notion that the Indian Union is an artificial cobbling together of many rival nationalities that must, in time, break up into its constituent parts.[40]

Guha insists that the reassertion of religious orthodoxy in all faiths that includes Muslims, Christians, Sikhs, Jains (note the deliberate splitting of the *dharmic* faiths) and Hindus is a challenge to the idea of a united India. But he points out that the religious reassertion of the Hindus is the most dangerous of all because of the numbers that are the majority in the population.[41]

> "The threat to India from Hindutva bigotry was at its most intense from about 1989 to about 2004. When judged by political (and social) influence the threat appears to have receded, although the terrorist activities, recently exposed, of sundry sadhvis and swamis suggest that one should not be too sanguine on this score." (Guha 2016:Chapter 1, Section III, Paragraph 1)

Guha feels that in addition to the above three challenges there are new materialistic challenges: inequality, corruption, and environmental degradation. According to him, the disparity in incomes and inequality of wealth in the upper castes (Brahmins and Banias in particular) go to better schools and better hospitals, and are massively over-represented in the professional and entrepreneurial classes. In economic as well as social terms, Hindus, Sikhs and Christians are significantly better off than Muslims.[42]

3.4 Marx-ism

Unsurprisingly, Guha feels Marx was **right** on the 'history of class struggles' theory.

For sometimes, caste and religion serve as more important markers of social identity than class. But the basic premise is accurate; namely, that social conflict is a major motive force in human history. Shared interests and identities bring different individuals together on a common platform, to struggle against groups composed of individuals whose identities are, or seem to be, different from theirs. Hence the struggles of workers vs capitalists, Dalits vs Suvarnas, peasants vs landlords, women vs men, and (more regrettably) Hindu vs Muslim, which have all been such a visible feature of life in modern India.[43]

Guha in his article in *The Hindustan Times* titled *'Three Things Karl Marx Mostly Got Right'*, insists that Karl Marx's analysis on British colonialism in India, is one of the things that he got right, referring to Marx's assertions that the British helped India get rid of caste and gender hierarchies that were prevalent in Indian society.

Guha fervently believes that it is the British conquest that provoked thinking, reflective Indians to demand equal rights for women and Dalits, and to seek to replace absolutist and authoritarian forms of government with modern democracy.[44] He also feels that reformers like Rammohan Roy, Jyotiba and Savitri Phule, Tarabai Shinde, Gopal Krishna Gokhale and 20th century thinkers like Gandhi, Ambedkar, Nehru, Periyar, Kamaladevi Chattopadhyay brought in a Constitution that helped India prepare for the challenges of the modern world, which until then the tradition or heritage had (not even) remotely prepared us. Guha also feels that the British, despite their vilest motives in conquering India, were an unconscious tool of history, compelling the best and the bravest Indians to correct what was flawed in their society and politics.[45]

Analysing Guha as a #FiberalDistorian

Guha's lenses of analysis and tropes are unabashedly *videshi* in nature. The combination of brown shame and of existential realities, the desire to be part of the establishment (popularly known as the Lutyens cabal), makes Guha a leading and effective wielder of the "vocabularies", "theoretical frameworks", "analytic lenses" originating in the deep Abrahamic culture of the West. As is acknowledged (see Rajiv Malhotra's *Being Different* for an initial treatment), even the secular, modern and postmodern formulations are but reactions and modifications deriving from the deeper stable Abrahamic sub-structures—the nature of man, the nature of society, the nature of life and the relationship of Man with Nature and with the Universe.

As seen in the few examples in the preceding subsections, the deep (antithetical to the idea of dharma) understandings of such a large library of adharmic ideas enables Guha to effectively use them to serve the agenda of the West via Nation (Un)building, The intellectual weaponization of the poisons in the aforementioned "library" – are put to use for dismantling the (sanatana) civilizational basis of India.

4 Vicious Hatred of Hindutva

Guha views Hindutva as one of the major challenges to the idea of India. He describes Hindutva as an ideology born out of a combination of two narratives. One is that of the *'victim nation syndrome'* in the sense that Hindus have been unfairly victimized down the ages and the unforgotten memories of Hindus persecuted at the hands of foreigners. The second is that of the *'chosen nation syndrome'* where the ideologues insist that the Vedas are the oldest holy books, the *Upanishads* and the *Bhagavad Gita*, the most profound philosophical texts. The Hindutva ideologues also insist that the ancient Hindus were the first greatest scientists, supporting their claims with their astonishing talents in astronomy and their invention of the number 'zero'. Guha feels that Hindutva is a nationalist ideology that is at once paranoid and triumphalist.[46] He also feels that the *Hindutvavadis* insist that Hindus alone were the original inhabitants of Bharat and views other faiths as the latecomers or interlopers, therefore he views this ideology as one ridden with chauvinism, bigotry and fundamentalism. He brands the ideology as deeply xenophobic.[47] Guha also criticizes the Rashtriya Swayamsevak Sangh for calling out the Western powers that demean and defeat India mainly through NGOs and human rights groups. He calls this as an irrational fear arising out of the past foreign invasions. He also feels that the Hindutvavadis view the independent-minded intellectuals (such as himself) as the 'unholy western trinity of Marx, Mill and Macaulay'.[48]

He equates 'Akhand Bharat' (which he thinks the Hindutvavadis lay claim to) with the Biblical territories that Zionists think they were chosen to inhabit. He insists that the minority in India particularly Muslims (who by the way were Hindu only a few generations ago) are always living in constant fear from the Hindutvavadis.[49] He equates Hindutva with Hindu fundamentalism (a fundamentalism which exhorts that all are divine and all paths to divinity are valid) and finds it a conceptual and ideological challenge and threat to Hinduism and India. Guha also insists that given the antiquity of Indian culture it is difficult to distinguish native from foreign influences and therefore he believes there should be no place for chauvinism.[50]

Message to Reader: Hinduism is a hodgepodge of various influences over centuries, with nothing original or unique to offer. There is no point in being Hindu you rather be something else or nothing at all.

Be it the loot and plunder of thousands of ancient temples under the Islamic rule, or the British imperialism for over two hundred years or the creation of Pakistan by brute force, Guha feels that it is unnecessary for a certain section of the society (that he refers to as Hindutvavadis) to discuss or reflect upon it even to this day.[51]

Message to Reader: Grow up Hindus and smell the modern Western coffee. Forget all these needless trifles of the past and move on.[52]

Guha wields the 'Western lens' effortlessly and convincingly, uses it to analyze Hindutva, and fits it into a framework devised by Western historians. Let us contrast this with some of the original proponents of Hindutva such as V.D. Savarkar, Swami Vivekananda, Sri Aurobindo and the likes.

"Hindutva is a concept that reflects the broad spiritual ethos of India, an ethos fostered by many great rishis, yogis and sanyasis, and their diverse teachings but in one spiritual vision. The word 'Hindutva' was popularized in the mid-nineteenth century meaning "Hinduness". In the context of the Hindu political struggle against British colonial rule, Sri Aurobindo gave the clearest exposition of national renaissance emanating from and founded in Sanatana Dharma, thus giving content and root meaning to Hindutva. Veer Savarkar gave it political currency. Hindutva basically conforms to Vedanta as propounded by Swami Vivekananda, and also as re-interpreted by Gandhi, Golwalkar and Upadhyaya. The Hindutva inspiration was the emotional spearhead for the first major nationalist struggle–the Swadeshi Movement. Hindutva is a multi-facet concept of identity, socio-constitutional order, modernity, our civilization's history, economic philosophy and governance." (Swamy 2010:34)

While Guha extensively talks about how India survived Balkanization post 1947, despite initial skepticism by world leaders such as Winston Churchill, he does not cogently explain what kept India united and undivided for at least eight prior millennia (and possibly much more) and what will also keep it united and coherent in the future, as the nation of modern India.

From a study of nations that remain united and contrasted with those which have disintegrated, it seems that the crucial element for national integrity is the concept of 'who we are', the sense of collective co-identity, that people within a geo-political boundary accept. Ramchandra Guha also ought to know that the India of today would not have been in existence had the past attempts to divide and eliminate Hindus succeeded. Over the last eight centuries or more, there have been incessant attempts to divide the Hindu community into castes and races, by targeted persecution, and by religious conversion, attempts if had they been successful, would have made the Islamic faith easily the single largest community in India. The religious tax 'jazia' was one such instrument to widen the caste gulf. Therefore, it is important to note that, it is the web of spiritual ethos of Hinduism that is holding together the diverse faiths of this land as one pluralistic, inclusive country. Enough has been written (especially by many whose work and ideas Guha should be well aware of, S. Balagangadhara, S.L. Bhyrappa and many more). They have spent lifetimes analyzing the fundamental issues of "religion" and the various reasons why sanatana Hinduism is far more than "religion" and needs to be treated and understood far more differently. Guha's flippant reductionism on matters spiritual and Hindu (which is the default mode of Western scholarship) serves its petty purpose, that of virtue signaling to his masters, that he is being an obedient and effective tool to subvert the civilizational narrative of India.

Only Hindu-ness, any form of Hindutva can be the basis and foundation for any sort of universal peace and harmony. It is the only way. It makes it all the more important to articulate and propound Hindutva for peace and harmony.[53]

Guha is also a strong critique of preserving any so-called cultural unity of India. However, what he fails to understand or rather deliberately whitewashes is the fact that it is the culture of this land that held together the people for millennia and continues to do so. It is the spawning of Hindu-ness of this land that has led to the acceptance and seamless assimilation of various faiths and cultures as one. Therefore, it becomes a fundamental duty to protect the unique and profound cultural identity of this land, the Hindu-ness or Hindutva.

> "I venture to say that there is no country that can rival the Indian Peninsula with respect to the unity of its culture. It has not only a geographical unity, but it has over and above all a deeper and much more fundamental unity–the indubitable cultural unity that cover the land from end to end."[54]

Hindutva, in fact aims to solve the identity crisis of the minorities which is not only causing a divide amongst them but also causing alienation from the Hindus and from the nation. The identity crises caused by a millennium of invasion, violent Islamic conversion of hundreds of millions, Christian conversion, colonial plunder and its excesses, the post-Independence Nehruvian deracination, reservation driven meritocracy murdering quota kingdoms, vicious and debilitating babu-dom, vote-bank politics and a hundred other deep cuts.

Such a **healing** Hindutva, will at an intellectual level, threaten the status quo of multi-century Western frameworks of history, sociology, anthropology, various genres of Indology, postmodern anarchy theories and much of the rest. Tens of thousands of scholars, millions of pages of rhetoric and theorizing, wonderfully concocted analytic frameworks, celebrated texts, self-congratulatory awards, the shallowness of the socio-political influence, the elaborate infrastructure of reward, fame, power, all of it would stand exposed.

The role of the sepoy is to **prevent the possibility** of any such eventuality. With ears close to the ground and armed with an arsenal of diversionary tactics, doggedness, a vicious single mindedness, the sepoy defends the territory and protects his masters at all costs.

5 #FiberalDistorian: Methods to the Madness

One of the best ways to understand the workings of an Intellectual Ravana is to attempt to understand the operating methods and style. This is also considered to be part of the process of *purvapaksha*, as seen in the Indian tradition. Its modern contextual application has been very ably demonstrated by Rajiv Malhotra in much of his work, where he engages in deep analyses of methods used by scholars. What are the features of Guha's thinking? What are his possible goals? What does he aim to achieve with his brand of critique? Who is his primary audience? Whom does he hope to influence? These kinds of questions generally help uncover the motives and the methods of scholarship. It is a contrasting feature that Guha admires Ambedkar, Gandhi and Nehru all at the same time, who indeed have contrasting ideologies. His creative and selective usage of facts to fit narratives which again are fluid is another notable feature. In essence, we highlight some of the common characteristic markers we have uncovered across Guha's work:

- Tends to be relentless about the need to create foundations of *"Western Universalism."*
- There is simply no engagement with **dharma vocabulary** in any manner, however superficial.
- Following from the above, there is the resulting reinforcement of Western categories and the tendency for all analysis and rhetoric to derive from within this tiring lens.

- Beholden to the Western idea of history, as a self-styled "contemporary historian", the current affairs rhetoric of Guha is also given the "history" treatment. Unrelated and unessential trivia are weirdly juxtaposed, as intellectual props.

- Beholden to the painfully shallow Western conceptualization of environmentalism, ecology, nature protection, Guha has penned multiple books, narratives on these themes which make for tiresome reading. A dutiful brown sepoy, doing his master's bidding, ignores the bounties from the traditional knowledge systems, various sampradaya, practices and the deeper planes of meaning and understanding that Vedic perspectives allow.

- Guha takes his role as an anthropologist of his "own" people very seriously as noted in his work so far. His commentary on Indians as some sort of **other** is truly his own. No other modern Indian writer in the public space is as pompous and as disdainful of his fellow citizens.

- A rather elaborate and comical charade is that of Guha masquerading as a scientist. A chair at the Indian Institute of Science, serves to rub it in. Creative use of the "covering fire" of comment and opinion by famous scientists (obviously beholden to Western authority structures and approval), are used by Guha to push, more vigorously, the anti-tradition narrative. Some of the civilizationally-aware Hindu 'Twitterati' have even called it the *Guha-Venki (Nobel Prize winning Venki Ramakrishnan, President of the Royal Society)* Hinduphobic circus.

6 #FiberalDistorian – Some Swadeshi Deconstruction

A brief attempt at examining Guha using a dharma lens is presented. Some of the questions that could be asked are:

- Is the writing causing *Dharma*?
- Are the forces, causes of *Adharma* identified?
- Whose side is he on?
- Is the writing provoking any Dharmic action in the reader?

Firstly, he does not articulate the pluralism of India, the origins of the pluralism nor any sort of analysis of India's deep strengths. Prof. R. Vaidyanathan's thesis on caste as the basis of social capital and irrepressible entrepreneurship, highlights the fact that it was the colonial interests which destroyed the economic status of the *jatis* what we refer to as backward classes.[55] Guha's rhetoric on India's strengths, its vigorous social groupings, uses the same unoriginal rigid lens of caste.

For a scholar of sociology who has been plodding on for decades one is challenged to identify even one original conceptual insight or any incisive data driven analysis in all of Guha's voluminous output. It is possible that the deep aversion to the idea of India as a civilizational nation, forces Guha into intellectual positions of no return. To make things simple for the reader, we provide highlights of the deconstructive exercise.

General Observations

- Ramachandra Guha, is one of the **strongest proponents of Colonial Indology** along with other colonized historians in India. During colonial times, Indology was started as the study of Indian history, cultures, languages, and literature. In contemporary times, it is also called South Asian Studies. Guha uses Western categories and experiences to investigate India, especially Hinduism.

- He has become part of the ecosystem developed over the last 250 years, a relentless assault on the sanatana civilization through systematic study using flawed methods and misinterpretation. This has resulted in many conflicts within India and it is feeding the "Breaking India" forces. Some problems created include the Aryan/Dravidian divide, casteism, basic issues of dignity, povertarianism (the institutional *making of poverty and its alleviation*), minority-ism, pseudo-secularism, break up of families, human rights degradation, environmental disasters, etc.

- Guha has also been in the forefront of **delineating Hindutva from Hinduism** and is also a strong critique of the Hindutva ideology and the organizations such as the RSS and Vishwa Hindu Parishad. India is secular and plural because of its civilizational ethos of acceptance of difference. This was the ethos of Hindutva based on the philosophy of Vedanta. Guha denies the very existence of such an ethos.

- Guha abhors, deeply despises this notion of a civilizational India.
- ***Deconstructing Guha's "Fiberalism".*** See the notes section for liberalism gobbledygook.[56]
- Guha plays the quintessential "good cop" when he wears the "liberalism" hat. *The Liberal is caught between the narratives of Caste (of the Left) and Religion (of the Right).*
- Guha effectively shepherds and curates, the narrative of fiberals. He tends to be the first among the cabal to partake from the glorious "pool" of Western enlightenment: new theories, new tropes, new vocabulary.
- Positioned as a thought leader and as an ideal to be aspired for, the ecosystem facilitates this transition. (*See new book, positioning Guha as an aspirational role-model, a senior citizen among the nation un-builders*)
- He is the self-appointed *Thekedar* of liberalism, intellectualism and other assorted -isms.
- Guha selectively usurps the *"Brahminical"* label, applies it to himself and positions critiques from the mainstream using well-rehearsed "good-cop-bad-cop" routines.
- As is evident from earlier discussion, Guha seems to be a no-holds barred apologist for Islam. For further details, one may read his book *The Enemies of the Idea of India*.

Deconstructing the 'Distorian':

- There are many examples of whitewash/willful distortion and manipulation of contemporary narrative (*example: "Inside every thinking Indian there is a Gandhian and a Marxist struggling for supremacy"*)

- As is evident from the earlier sections discussing Guha's narrative on personalities such as Nehru, Gandhi, groups like the RSS, his interpretations are loaded with subtle manipulations, and littered with the manufacturing of nefarious intent.
- Readers are encouraged to read Guha's discussions on the issue of Kashmiri Pandits, the Constitutional (Amendment) Act, 2019 legislation and others.
- The interested reader can also peruse Guha's critique of Hindus and Hindu identity in general.
- What is especially important to note in the *Distorian's* arsenal of Guha is the selective use of quotes and facts. They usually derive from well-known reliable sources but the full picture is almost always not given as examined in the sections above. In writings related to history and opinion making, all the facts are as a rule, not laid in front of the reader.
- As a *Distorian*, Guha, as expected uses little to no traditional/native sources of history. All *local itihasa, sthala purana* are ignored, at best they are used as caricatures or as props to distract the reader.
- In general, the delineations of "Western Indology" are adhered to and the main tropes are amplified with new context and flowery rhetoric. The claims to credibility are almost always based on "western" sources or a Western approved sepoy source.
- Guha makes emotional appeals based on vigorous pleas to some woolly "ideals" based on *Western siddhanta*.
- He camouflages nation un-building poison in many of his shallow writings on cricket, environment and contemporary commentary.
- He has become prolific in new media, despite the heavy crossfire from the awakened nationalists. New media has far more traffic than traditional channels. It remains to be seen how effective the Distorian strategies are, despite the fact that the major social media channels themselves are heavily Left leaning.

- Many of his recent pieces are baffling with weird hard positions (See Guha's recent (since 2019) positions on cow protection in the Constitution, Sabarimala issue , the CAA issue)

7 Summary: #FiberalDistorianRavana

As a takeaway for Dharmics, below is a succinct summary of why we think that Guha should be classified as a Ravana is provided. (A twelve-point summary is also made available in the Notes section as a powerful mnemonic to unravel the Guha genre and the Ravana prototype that he represents).[57]

Guha's unabashed disdain for any sort of dharma driven dialectic, especially when seen in roles of a public intellectual, is amply clear from his work examined so far. Guha uses the colonized lenses (hermeneutics), in the analysis and dissemination of the (non) idea of a civilization nation. His flippant and dismissive use of dharma categories and an established ignorance of the Sanskrit knowledge systems is glaring across his work. All of his work, unfortunately creates an intellectual trajectory for a deep irreversible colonization. More sadly, all of his work aims to affect the Hindu psyche, provoke shame and cause irreparable confusion of identity. His work reflects an unconcealed attempt to abort ideas and the thought of any sort of harmonious overarching national identity. Guha's work is an elaborate and multi-pronged approach to instil an inferiority complex and self-doubt, and to corrode any civilizational basis, among generations of readers. His indiscriminate manipulation of historical events and use of false contexts to help build corrosive narratives is a testament to this fact. He has become a senior amongst the nation (un)builders and is now a living repository and curator of all manner of anti-Hindu and anti-national intellectual tropes. He is now far more dangerous than ever.

The modus of Breaking India 2.0 (See Rajiv Malhotra's recent book, *AI and the Future of Power*)[58], which is already in progress and is AI powered, will use data sets and text written by the likes of Guha to train the sentiment, concept labeling, matching, language understanding algorithms. The impact of Guha's work will be amplified by the bots and algorithms trained by his *text*. Hindus and the wider Indian community are minimally aware of these deep threats and the technologies that are being built to usurp any India narrative. Guha, is a recognized master in 'Breaking India' by *Breaking Dharma*–a multi-step methodical approach to excavate fault lines, curate them and then contemporarize them. Guha sometimes even weaponizes them in the grand fiberal nation unbuilding project. Being opposed to any Indian Grand Narrative, Guha celebrates the dissolution of the civilizational narrative at the altar of Western globalism.

Bibliography

Guha, Ramachandra. 2001. "The Absent Liberal: An Essay on Politics and Intellectual Life." *Economic and Political Weekly* 8.

Guha, Ramachandra. 2004. "REFORMING THE HINDUS, The Hindu." ramachandraguha.in. Retrieved October 9, 2021 (https://ramachandraguha.in/archives/reforming-the-hindus.html).

Guha, Ramachandra. 2008. "MYTHS AND BORDERS, The Hindu." ramachandraguha.in. Retrieved October 9, 2021 (https://ramachandraguha.in/archives/myths-and-borders.html).

Guha, Ramachandra. 2009. "CHAUVINISTS OF THE WORLD, UNITE!, Hindustan Times." ramachandraguha.in. Retrieved October 9, 2021 (https://ramachandraguha.in/archives/chauvinists-of-the-world-unite.html).

Guha, Ramachandra. 2010. "IF SHASTRI HAD LIVED - India's history took an unexpected turn in Tashkent." The Telegraph. Retrieved October 9, 2021 (https://www.telegraphindia.com/opinion/if-shastri-had-lived-india-s-history-took-an-unexpected-turn-in-tashkent/cid/532935).

Guha, Ramachandra. 2011. *The Enemies of the Idea of India*. Kottayam: DC Books.

Guha, Ramachandra. 2014. "Paranoia and Triumphalism, The Telegraph." ramachandraguha.in. Retrieved October 9, 2021 (https://ramachandraguha.in/archives/paranoia-and-triumphalism-the-telegraph.html).

Guha, Ramachandra. 2016. *Patriots and Partisans*. Gurgaon: Penguin.

Guha, Ramachandra. 2018. "Three Things Karl Marx Got Mostly Right,

Hindustan Times." ramachandraguha.in. Retrieved October 9, 2021 (https://ramachandraguha.in/archives/three-things-karl-marx-got-mostly-right-hindustan-times.html).

Malhotra, Rajiv. 2002. "The Axis Of Neocolonialism." Rajiv Malhotra: Infinity Foundation. (https://rajivmalhotra.com/library/articles/axis-neocolonialism/).

Malhotra, Rajiv. 2021. *Artificial Intelligence and the Future of Power: 5 Battlegrounds*. New Delhi: Rupa Publications India.

Swamy, Subramanian. 2010. *Hindutva and National Renaissance*. New Delhi: Hindustan Publishing Corporation.

Vaidyanathan, R. 2019. *Caste As Social Capital*. Chennai: Westland.

Notes

1. See: "Fiberal." Urban Dictionary. Retrieved October 9, 2021 (https://www.urbandictionary.com/define.php?term=fiberal).
2. See: "Distorian." Urban Dictionary. Retrieved October 9, 2021 (https://www.urbandictionary.com/define.php?term=distorian)
3. Guha's pompous self-image gets a reality check. See: "Your Good Name Sir?? And the likes of Ram Guha think that common Indians know them Watch till end." Twitter. Retrieved April 4, 2022 (https://twitter.com/rose_k01/status/12076389926041600001).
4. See: "Ramachandra Guha: Drawing parallels between Islamism and Hindutva." Hindustan Times. Retrieved April 4, 2022 (https://communalism.blogspot.com/2016/02/ramachandra-guha-drawing-parallels.html).
5. (Malhotra 2011:307-310)
6. See: "A Functioning Anarchy? Essays for Ramachandra Guha." Penguin. Retrieved October 9, 2021 (https://penguin.co.in/book/the-language-of-history/).
7. See: "Ecology, cricket, Marx, history — The many Rams in Ramachandra Guha." ThePrint. Retrieved October 9, 2021 (https://theprint.in/pageturner/excerpt/ecology-cricket-marx-history-the-many-rams-in-ramachandra-guha/648772).
8. (Guha 2016:Chapter 3, Section III, Paragraph 7)
9. (Guha 2016:Preface, Section 8, Paragraph 14, 16)

10. (Guha 2014)
11. (Guha 2016:Chapter 3, Section III, Paragraph 2)
12. The *"Message to the Reader"* is the apparent subliminal (or in some cases, direct) message that Guha is communicating to the reader. This is our reading of Guha's text.
13. This could well be an interesting topic of dissertation.
14. (Guha 2016:Chapter 6, Section III, Paragraph 10)
15. (Guha 2016:Chapter 6, Section III, Paragraph 16, 17)
16. "Be that as it may, aspects of Gandhi's faith resonate closely with spiritual (or intellectual) traditions that are other than 'Hindu'. The stress on ethical conduct brings him close to Buddhism, while the avowal of non-violence and non-possession is clearly drawn from Jainism. The exaltation of service is far more Christian than Hindu. The emphasis on the dignity of the individual echoes Enlightenment ideas of human rights." (Guha 2016:Chapter 6, Section III, Paragraph 18)
17. (Guha 2016:Chapter 6, Section 3, Paragraph 20, 21)
18. "Thus in his battle against Untouchability, Gandhi was moved, inspired and directed not by 'the dharma of the law-books and Brahmans, but the dharma that rests on ahimsa, truth, renunciation, passionlessness, and an equal love for all God's creatures ... Both Yudhisthira and Gandhi, notes R.C. Zaehner, saw themselves as failures for being unable to prevent fratricidal warfare, between Pandavas and Kauravas in the one case, and between Hindus and Muslims in the other. Yet 'both were yet triumphant, for both had been true to themselves, to conscience, to Truth, to the sanatana dharma as they saw it in themselves, and therefore to God." (Guha 2016:Chapter 6, Section IV, Paragraph 3, 4) (Guha 2011)
19. "First, Gandhi rejected the idea that there was one privileged path to God. Second, he believed that all religious traditions were an unstable mixture of truth and error." (Guha 2016:Chapter 6, Section V, Paragraph 2)
20. (Guha 2016:Chapter 7, Section VI, Paragraph 6)
21. (Guha 2016:Chapter 7, Section V, Paragraph 5)
22. (Guha 2016:Chapter 7, Section II, Paragraph 4)
23. (Guha 2016:Chapter 7, Section II, Paragraph 11)
24. (Guha 2016:Chapter 7, Section II, Paragraph 11)
25. (Guha 2016:Chapter 7, Section VII, Paragraph 6)

26. (Guha 2016:Chapter 7, Section IV, Paragraph 3, 4)
27. (Guha 2016:Chapter 7, Section I, Paragraph 5)
28. (Guha 2016:Chapter 7, Section IV, Paragraph 5)
29. (Guha 2016:Chapter 7, Section V, Paragraph 4)
30. "Nehru's contribution to the building of modern India is immense. He made mistakes, to be sure, but other people in his place would most likely have made bigger ones. As a historian, I am quite clear that India was very fortunate to have him as prime minister for that crucial first decade after Independence. His record was unquestionably better than that of those who succeeded him. It was better than that of those who came to rule the other ex-colonial countries of Asia and Africa. And, so far as one can judge these matters, it was probably better than what might have been if some other Indian, say Patel or Bose, had happened to become prime minister in 1947." (Guha 2016:Chapter 7, Section VI, Paragraph 1)
31. "Like the Mahatma, he transcended the divisions of race and religion, caste and class, gender and geography. He was a Hindu who was befriended by Muslims, but also a Brahmin who did not observe the rules of caste, a north Indian who would not impose Hindi on the south, a man who could be trusted and respected by women." (Guha 2016:Chapter 7, Section V, Paragraph 10)
32. "To this end he encouraged a nationalism that would make Indians feel that they were Indians instead of feeling that they were Tamils or Punjabis or Dogras or Assamese or Brahmans or Kshatriyas or this or that caste, as they are apt. He gave special consideration to the Muslims so as to induce them to feel Indian." (Guha 2016:Chapter 7, Section VI, Paragraph 4)
33. (Guha 2018)
34. (Guha 2004)
35. (Guha 2018)
36. (Guha 2018)
37. (Guha 2009)
38. (Guha 2011:Section 1, Paragraph 6)
39. (Guha 2008)
40. (Guha 2016:Chapter 1, Section VI, Paragraph 1)
41. (Guha 2016:Chapter 1, Section II, Paragraph 10)
42. (Guha 2016:Chapter 1, Section VI, Paragraph 1)

43. (Guha 2018)
44. (Guha 2018)
45. (Guha 2018)
46. (Guha 2014)
47. (Guha 2009)
48. (Guha 2009)
49. (Guha 2016:Chapter 1, Section II, Paragraph 2)
50. (Guha 2014)
51. (Guha 2014)
52. (Guha 2014)
53. In the Abrahamic sense, even one who believes in God but does not accept Jesus or Muhammad as intermediary is considered a non-believer and therefore a sinner or a Kafir. These two major religions simply do not accept pluralism. This is what makes both Christianity and Islam exclusive, definitionally Hinduism pluralistic and tolerant, and therefore Hindutva naturally inclusive.
54. Dr. B.R. Ambedkar in 1916 paper titled "Castes in India: Their Mechanism, Genesis, and Development" See: "Dr. Babasaheb Ambedkar: Writings and Speeches, Vol. 1." 1979. Retrieved on October 18, 2021 (http://www.columbia.edu/itc/mealac/pritchett/00ambedkar/txt_ambedkar_castes.html).
55. (Vaidyanathan 2019)
56. (Guha 2001) This essay explores the rise and decline of liberal thought in modern India. It argues that Indian liberalism is a sensibility rather than a theory, a product of empirical engagement rather than an elaboration of principles laid down in canonical texts. Where liberals dominated the intellectual landscape in the 1950s and 1960s, more recently they have become an endangered species. Liberals have been squeezed out by the identity politics of the Left, which holds that caste is and should be the fundamental axis of Indian society, and by the identity politics of the Right, which assigns a hegemonic role to religion.
57. Twelve-point summary as a powerful mnemonic to unravel the Guha genre and the Ravana prototype:
    1. Guha's unabashed disdain for any sort of dharma driven dialectic, especially so for a public intellectual.

2. Guha's use of colonized lenses (hermeneutics), in the analysis and dissemination of the (non) idea of a civilizational nation.
3. Guha's flippant and dismissive use of dharma categories and an established ignorance of the Sanskrit knowledge systems.
4. All of his work, sadly, creates an intellectual trajectory for a deep irreversible colonization.
5. More sadly, all of his work aims to affect the Hindu psyche, provoke shame and cause irreparable confusion of identity.
6. There is an unconcealed attempt to abort ideas and the thought of any sort of harmonious overarching National identity.
7. An elaborate and multi-pronged approach to instil an inferiority complex and self-doubt, and to corrode any civilizational basis, among generations of readers.
8. The indiscriminate manipulation of historical events and use of false contexts to help build corrosive narratives.
9. He has become a senior citizen amongst the nation (un)builders and is now a living repository and curator of all manner of anti-Hindu and anti-national intellectual tropes. He is now (2021) far more dangerous than ever.
10. The modus of Breaking India 2.0 (See Rajiv Malhotra's recent book, *AI and the Future of Power*), which is already in progress and is AI powered, will use data sets and text written by the likes of Guha to train the sentiment, concept labeling, matching, language understanding algorithms. The impact of Guha's work will be amplified by the bots and algorithms trained by his ***text***. Hindus and the wider Indian community are minimally aware of these deep threats and the technologies that are being built to usurp any India narrative.
11. A recognized master in 'Breaking India' by *Breaking Dharma*–a multi-step methodical approach to excavate fault-lines, curate them and then contemporarize them. Guha sometimes even weaponizes them in the grand fiberal nation unbuilding project.
12. Being opposed to any Indian Grand narrative, Guha celebrates the dissolution of the civilizational narrative at the altar of western globalism.

58. (Malhotra 2021)

NINE

Kancha Ilaiah
Bharat Vikhander

Sharda Narayanan &
Subhodeep Mukhopadhyay

The mother of all parasitic cultures is the culture of Brahmanism
– *Kancha Ilaiah*[1]

Introduction

Kancha Ilaiah Shepherd is a noted Indian writer, academician and a self-described 'Shudra intellectual'.[2] The author of influential books like, *Why I am not a Hindu* and *Post-Hindu India*, he is considered an important Indian social thinker and is referred to as the "Good Shepherd."[3] He was Associate Professor in the Department of Political Science at Osmania University till 2012, when he retired and then served as Director of the Centre for Social Exclusion and Inclusive Policy at Maulana Azad National Urdu University (MANUU) in Hyderabad.[4] Currently, he provides leadership and guidance to an organization called Telangana Mass and Social Organizations (T-MASS), an alliance of Dalit and Marxist (communist) social justice and activism groups whose aim is to dismantle Hindutva forces through a "socio-cultural revolutionary movement."[5]

In academic circles, Ilaiah is regarded as a pre-eminent social scientist following "a long and illustrious line of dissenters and critics" of the Hindu social order and a key player in the fight against "violent Hindutva assertion."[6] He is quite well-known in rural areas and in government institutions, his work having influenced numerous Dalit intellectuals and students including school students.[7] Ilaiah is also famous internationally and has been instrumental in internationalizing Dalit issues and bringing it to the attention of the international mainstream. In a written testimony submitted to the UK Parliament, the Christian Solidarity Network, a Right-wing Christian evangelical organization, cited Ilaiah's testimony at a US Congress hearing, on how anti-conversion laws in India perpetuate Dalit slavery by obstructing their freedom to leave the Hindu religion[8]. He has been referred to as one of "India's most prominent political journalists" by an Arizona Republican Congressman on the floor of the United States House of Representatives.[9] In one his poems he writes that he is willing to lay down his life for the abused although he knows very well that he is not Jesus Christ and will not be resurrected.[10]

Kancha Ilaiah Shepherd is, therefore, a very prominent voice in the Dalit intellectual and activism space, recognized both in India and abroad, and hence, it is important that we understand and analyze his works systematically and with the dignity, that a public figure of his stature demands.

At the same time, it would not be wrong to say that his writings have often courted controversies and his critics have complained that in the guise of being an outspoken advocate for marginalized and minority communities, he has specifically targeted Hinduism in general and Brahmins along with other so-called upper castes in particular. For example, he explicitly calls for civil war to exterminate Brahmins globally in order to make Indian society more energetic and explains in-depth how a civil war is a "necessary evil" for every society to rejuvenate itself.[11] During his tenure as Associate Professor at Osmania University he had been advised by the then Registrar, to desist from writing in a way "that tended to accentuate prejudices or inflame hatred among various sections of people."[12] He has been accused of promoting social unrest and enmity, of targeting Hinduism and criminal cases have been filed against him in the states of Andhra Pradesh and Telangana.[13] Ilaiah is also against big businesses as he feels they are controlled by the Hindu Baniya capitalists whom he refers to as social smugglers.[14]

Ilaiah uses the term Dalitbahujan to refer to people of Scheduled Castes (SC) as well as the Other Backward Castes (OBC), and optionally also the Scheduled Tribes as suggested by Kanshi Ram, the founder of the Bahujan Samaj Party.[15] On the one hand, Ilaiah says that his aim is to play a positive role in empowering Dalitbahujan forces in India in all spheres of life[16]. On the other hand, he seems to spew venom against certain Hindu communities, provoke tensions, clashes between different groups in India, and incite violence in the name of 'academic' freedom. The question before us is, does he live up to his lofty goals of providing emancipation to the underclass? Is he really intent in bringing about national integration and reforms though his criticisms of India and Hinduism? Or is he bent upon fomenting divisiveness, hatred and social unrest through his writing and radical activism?

The following essay delves into these issues. The authors offer a critique of Ilaiah's writing on Hinduism, based on his books, essays, commentaries and lectures. They analyze his scholarship methodologies, his epistemic practices, his ideological leanings and his positions on various socio-cultural issues. They look at not only what he says, but also, delve deep to understand his thoughts and actions in order to understand what informs his views on India and Hinduism. They respond to some of his specific criticisms of Hinduism and Hindu communities.

Purvapaksha of Ilaiah's Work

Ilaiah characterizes Hinduism as being inherently violent with no space for either debate or discourse. This is in stark contrast to Christianity which he feels has an ethic of sacrifice: "Christ's crucifixion is a symbol of sacrifice, it is not a killing symbol."[17] In fact, he insists that Hinduism is not a religion at all, since it does not have a holy book, but is rather a 'cult' which encourages vegetarianism, nudity and sexual perversion.[18] He admits:

> "Yes, I hate Hinduism... I am angry at the Hindu gods...We do not trust the Brahmin leaders. We cannot trust the sadhus and sanyasis who are going naked at the Kumbh Mela... Why do Hindu leaders say only vegetarianism is divine?" (Ilaiah 2000)

He depicts Brahmins as being greedy and gluttonous militants that have not only not contributed to nation building, but also threatened freedom of speech in India.[19] For Ilaiah, nationhood begins with eating beef, and he considers vegetarianism, which he associates with Hinduism, as 'anti-nationalism'. He encourages Indians to eat frog meat and beef in order to sharpen their knowledge of global economics and feels that the Indian "vegetarians brains are not working."[20] For him, cows are a foreign Aryan animal and hence a favorite of the fair-skinned upper castes while buffaloes are Dravidian animals.

> "...the buffalo is a Dravidian animal, whereas the cow is an Aryan animal. The buffalo is a black animal and we are black people. We low caste people represent the rights of the buffaloes." (Ilaiah 2000)

He categorically rejects reforming Hindu culture, which he sees as a foreign 'Aryan' culture foisted on India by the 'cunning' Brahmins, the representative of the Aryans.

> "Brahmins are basically Aryans who came from outside. They brought the cow along with them... All Brahmins in India have been consumers in the history of India. They were never the producers." (Ilaiah 2000)

Ilaiah accepts only Christianity and Islam as being *bona fide* religions since they were "constructed by prophets who sacrificed and struggled in life for people's liberation."[21] He says that there are three types of God – an abstract eternal God, prophets who became Gods and human-Gods. The abstract, shapeless eternal God is the most democratic and is seen in both Christianity and Islam. This God treats humans as superior to all other beings, and other creatures have been created as food for humans. In the second category, Jesus Christ is the greatest example of a Prophet who became a God. According to Ilaiah, Jesus was the first to clearly state the necessity of separating religion and state, and thus, Christian countries are naturally democratic. In the third category, are Hindu deities like Shiva and Vishnu, the Gods imagined as humans, who promote casteism, inequality, misogyny and counter-democracy.[22]

Hinduism according to Ilaiah, is an artificial construct and hegemonic tool crafted by the upper castes to subjugate and oppress the Dalitbahujans. He finds it shocking when the Dalitbahujan communities are classified as Hindus. Speaking on their behalf, he says that, as a community they had never even heard of the word Hindu – "not as a word, nor as the name of a culture, nor as the name of a religion", and that culturally they are similar to Muslims and Christians, rather than Brahmins and Baniyas whose culture he finds alien and, in fact, plain offensive: "the very sight of its saffron-tilak is a harassment to us."[23] He compares Hinduism to the Klu Klux Klan in America, an American white supremacist terrorist hate group, and says that Hindus rape nuns, destroy churches and distribute weapons.[24]

Ilaiah is a strong proponent of English-medium education for Dalitbahujans as he feels that it is the only way to defeat Sanskrit and Brahminical Sanskritic culture in the modern, post globalized world. According to him, upper castes established a pan-Indian connectivity through Sanskritic names; however, Dalitbahujans have neither pan-Indian identities nor connectivity and must therefore, embrace English in all aspects of their lives including even in their names.

> "The farming communities can become Mr and Mrs Tiller, Dalits can have names like Mr and Ms Cobbler, Tanner, Shoemaker. Thus pot makers can have names like Potter, Iron and gold smiths can become Smith. Thus the marginalized communities could all have English names – from Washerman to Fisherman." (Ilaiah 2016)

Ilaiah is a proponent of caste-based reservation in the private sector, and feels that institutions of national importance like IITs (Indian Institutes of Technology) and IIMs (Indian Institutes of Management) must be shut down as they teach discrimination against Dalitbahujan communities.[25] He wants his community to be able to freely embrace global religions like Christianity and Islam.[26]

According to Ilaiah, Hinduism is a "spiritually fascist system" and it is not at all coincidental that Hindus and Nazi Germany share the same swastika symbol.[27] He therefore, endorses the conversion of Dalitbahujan to Christianity, which he says is "happening in a big way."[28]

> "Our spiritual potentials were never released ... They are rebelling against the Hindu order, Hindu spiritual life and quite a lot of them think of Christianity as an alternative." (Ilaiah 2005)

Ilaiah sees caste as a tool of oppression in the hands of upper castes and therefore, advocates a caste-based census to assist policy-making. Such data-driven policies, he feels, will radically alter the very idea of democracy in India. He cites an interesting Biblical parallel of a census two thousand years ago which led to the birth of Jesus in a shepherd's shed.

> "The 'Telangana All family Census 2014' reminded me of Joseph and Mary (the parents of Jesus Christ) travelling to Bethlehem from Nazareth to get counted in their own place. According to the Bible (Luke 2:1-7), "Joseph and Mary's trip to Bethlehem is undertaken in order to satisfy an imperial command that all individuals return to their ancestral towns... Since Mary was pregnant with Jesus at the time the command had to be carried out." (Ilaiah 2021)

Ilaiah feels that there is a need of Bible education in India in order that people can read about God and the notion that all men are born equal. Without this kind of reform, Indians will continue to wallow in depression, poverty, hunger and uncivilized ways of life. He sees English education as a means of salvation as it will allow children to learn about the world and the word of God. Therefore, it is imperative that the Western church help Indians get English education. Each church could sponsor one school itself, he says. He warns that unless such a thing happens urgently, hunger will only increase in India and consequently "huge riots may take place in Indian context breaking the whole society into pieces."[29] He appears to imply that Christianity alone can offer a true English-knowing Universal God, and Dalitbahujan masses must therefore shun the primitive rituals associated with the worship of regional gods.[30]

> "O Brahmins of Bharath and the World, you want to crucify me
> Knowing that I can't resurrect, as I am not Jesus Christ.
> But, I will follow that Star, as I am an Indian shepherd.
> I will not destroy your temples; but, I will destroy all our shackles,
> As I follow only the God of Equality.
> .....
> I am now Ilaiah Shepherd, Kancha Ilaiah Shepherd." (Ilaiah 2016)

Examining Ilaiah's Research Principles

As a teacher of social sciences, I am bound to take up critical writing because, unless there is critical writing, social science does not mean anything – Kancha Ilaiah.[31]

Research in general, entails the process of finding answers to specific questions in a structured, organized and systematic way. Social research, in particular, is meant to produce new knowledge or to improve upon existing knowledge on societies using a collection of well-defined methods and methodologies.[32] In the context of Ilaiah's profound statement on the importance of critical analysis, we therefore, examine not only his scholarship but also his research methodology and methods.

A key requirement of research, whether quantitative or qualitative, is to provide evidence of claims. In this regard, Ilaiah fails miserably, as, throughout his vast corpus of work he makes a large number of unsubstantiated and unverifiable claims, and sweeping over-generalizations on Hinduism, caste, society, economics, which the authors of this paper, will discuss in-depth in the next few sections. In his book, *Why I am not a Hindu*, he admits that his work has autobiographical underpinnings, with inputs from a few Dalit intellectuals. In addition, a number of his upper caste friends had also given him insights into the "socioeconomic life processes in their castes and families."[33]

Ilaiah claims that Harappa is a pre-Aryan indigenous name that has nothing to do with Vedic Sanskrit; rather it is closely linked to South Indian term *appa*. He further claims that Harappa is associated with the Old Testament based on his linguistic analysis which goes as follows:

- Har*appa* ends with *appa*
- *appa* is associated with *ayya*
- Words like Mesaiah and Jeremaiah are actually Mess-*ayya* and Jerem-*ayya*
- Ergo: Harappa is associated with Old Testament

Solely on the basis of superficial similarities in name endings he establishes a fantastic linkage between the Harappan civilization and the Bible! If superficial linguistic similarity is what one is looking for, then why not consider the name Harappa to be closely linked to the *bona fide* Punjabi word *hadippa*, which means, among many things 'hooray' or 'yippee'? There is no need to go all the way to southern India to discover etymological similarities, given that Harappa is located in Punjab (Pakistan)! But Ilaiah doesn't just stop there and continues: "Joseph tells the migration to South first reached Karnataka crossing the Western plains."[34] If his reference is to Joseph, the son of Jacob and Rachel, in the Bible's Book of Genesis, then this is indeed a hitherto unknown and singularly specific Biblical reference to a southern Indian state Karnataka.[35]

Elsewhere Ilaiah claims that a Brahmin never gives away extra rice to others.[36] This is such a bizarre claim that one is left flabbergasted. Is it based on any context that he himself experienced? Is it verified through the experience of a large number of other people and their experiences? Is it based on some specific instance where the person happened to be Brahmin? Is it in the context wherein the Brahmins in consideration were not in receipt of any other benefits from the government, etc.? He does not provide any of the contextual information needed to arrive at a reasonable sociological or political inference.

In another example, he postulates that Kshatriyas are a hybrid caste that emerged from the cross-breeding of white-skinned Aryans with the dark-skinned Dravidian Dalitbahujans.[37] In the same vein, he continues that the Vedic deity Indra was responsible for the genocide of the Harappans, who were of Dravidian racial stock.

> "Indra is the original Aryan leader who led the mass extermination of the Indus valley based Adi-Dravidians, who were also Adi-Dalitbahujans." (Ilaiah 2002:73)

It must be noted, that his entire thesis is based on obsolete colonial era racial Aryan invasion theory, which even its strongest proponents like Romila Thapar have given up on.[38] While modern Aryan theorists talk about migrations and frame the question in linguistic terms, Ilaiah still uses the older racial constructs. It seems that he has not kept himself up-to-date with the latest theories within his own domain. He posits a Dravidian origin of the Harappan civilization and says:

> "Harappa! We are all your descendants
> You shepherded the first civilization
> ....
> You were God's Own Man.
> Brahma came and burnt all your civilization
> Indra damaged it beyond reparation
> Agni and Vayu became their weapons of destruction"[39]

He further writes that the descendants of the Harappans escaped to southern India and became 'Ayyappans';[40] a rather audacious association between two material culture separated by thousands of kilometers and a few millennia.[41] He makes several such fantastic and often derogatory statements about other Hindu deities as well. During his childhood he imbibed from his mother, her portrayal of Saraswati, the Hindu Goddess of learning, as a devil who kills Shudra children, and admits that he often had nightmares about Saraswati in the guise of a female ghost in a white sari and blouse, haunting him in his sleep.[42] This becomes the chief source of his latter interpretation of Saraswati as an illiterate luxury-loving deity without any agency or free-will who spent her life as a courtesan to Brahma.[43] He writes disparagingly:

> "The source of education, Saraswati, did not write any book as the Brahmins did not allow women to write their texts. Nowhere does she

speak even about the need to give education to women. How is it that the source of education is herself an illiterate woman?" (Ilaiah 2002:74)

Ilaiah trivializes the prominent role played by women seers, philosophers and scholars in the development of the Vedic corpus. Not only did women have access to education, they were also encouraged to "study the scriptures and were given *Upanayana Samskara* (initiation into learning)." The *Rig Veda* has hymns composed by twenty-seven women seers like Ghosha, Apala, Vishwavara and others.[44] In the Upanishadic period Gargi and Maitreyi are prominent female scholars mentioned in the Sanskrit texts. Gargi was not only knowledgeable in Vedas and Upanishads, she even participated in scholarly debates with male-philosophers of her time.[45] The entire Hindu idea of worshipping the divine feminine is premised on the fact that women and men had the same potential when it came to spiritual evolution and achieving enlightenment, and therefore for Ilaiah to say that women were not allowed to compose Vedic texts is disingenuous and dishonest. It is in the Abrahamic traditions where women were denied the most basic rights till modern times. Not a single author of any of the books in the Bible, be it the Catholic Bible or the Protestant Bible, were women.[46] In fact, women were not even considered proper humans till late into the modern era and in fact, there were debates on whether women possessed souls and whether they were even humans.[47]

He describes Vishnu as an offspring of Brahmin and Kshatriya parents who was given godly status in order to contain a Kshatriya revolt against Brahminical hegemony. He further claims that Brahmins created Shiva and Parvati to control tribals. According to Ilaiah, Brahmins later created Krishna and even wrote the *Bhagavad Gita* with the sole purpose of quelling a Dalitbahujan rebellion and to implement Manu's law in northern India. He compares Goddess Lakshmi to a masseuse who forever presses the feet of Vishnu.[48] He also claims that Goddess Lakshmi reports to Vishnu all instances of Dalitbahujan men or women acquiring wealth or revolting against the caste system; immediately thereafter, Vishnu rushes off to handle such people.[49]

It is unknown as to how Ilaiah is privy to information about hitherto unknown Dalitbahujan rebellions a few millennia ago or what his sources are on what Goddess Lakshmi reports to Vishnu. Nowhere does Ilaiah cite a single reference, textual or otherwise. Some of Ilaiah's views on Hindu deities are based on the discredited theory by archaeologist, Sir Mortimer Wheeler who had blamed the collapse of the Harappan civilization[50] on the invading Aryan hordes and had declared rather grandly: "Indra stands accused."[51] Ilaiah paints a one-dimensional and very negative image of Hindu deities. He seems to be unaware that almost every Hindu deity has myriad representation across the length and breadth of the country, and that different forms have different origin and achievement stories.[52] For example, in the *Ashta Lakshmi* pantheon[53], Lakshmi manifests in eight different forms where she is seated on a lotus and *not* pressing the feet of Vishnu. Similarly, while Saraswati holds the book and 'veena' in some manifestations, as 'Mahasaraswati' she can as easily wield the bow, arrow and trident[54], and hence' characterizing Saraswati as a delicate, passive, agency-less deity reeks of some underlying motive – one that is most certainly not honest scholarship. Ilaiah, perhaps, feels that he does not need to provide any evidence for his pronouncements, however bizarre, divisive or prejudicial, because he will not be held accountable for his statements.

> "...Hinduism has never been a humane philosophy. It is the most brutal religious school that the history of religions has witnessed." (Ilaiah 2002:114)

He freely misrepresents fundamental Hindu concepts regarding life and death, with no distinction between popular superstitions, cultural practices, Vedic rituals or philosophical explanations.

> "Brahmanism looked upon every dead body as a potential ghost, and it was believed that with the burning of the body, the ghost also gets destroyed." (Ilaiah 2009:65)

Poetic composition allows artistic freedom for the poet to conjure anything. But serious research writing requires substantiation with proper referencing and evidences – something which Ilaiah completely lacks. Most people, with even a passing familiarity with Indian cultural history and Hindu symbolism would exercise caution in their comments for fear of exposing their own ignorance; not so Ilaiah, who blithely plunges to any depth of misrepresentation, no matter how low. Given his personal animosity towards Hinduism and so-called upper caste Hindus, as noted earlier (see section: *Purvapaksha of Ilaiah's Work*), one could very well question as to what extent his research is impartial, and honest – the key ethical requirements of academic integrity. What is more worrying is that, his book *Why I am not a Hindu* has been cited over four hundred times by different scholars in their works, including, in the widely read and definitive book on colonial and postcolonial studies, *Colonialism/Postcolonialism (The New Critical Idiom)* by Ania Loomba – a book which has been described internationally as "exactly the sort of book teachers want their students to read."[55] Incidentally, this also highlights another important aspect of social sciences scholarship in India in general – that those without any depth in understanding Hindu texts, pass of unscholarly and prejudiced writing as scholarship. Not only that, this kind of vitriolic and inflammatory polemic masquerading as scholarship, is then also given legitimacy by being cited as authoritative work.

The Bharat Vikhander[56]

Identity, Separatism and Civil War

As mentioned earlier, Ilaiah uses the term Dalitbahujan to refer to SCs and OBCs, a rather large pan-Indian community with cultural, economic and knowledge system commonalities "which mesh them together like threads in a cloth."[57] According to a National Sample Survey Organisation (NSSO) survey, SCs comprise 20%, ST's 9% while OBCs comprise 41% of Indian population.[58] Dalit-bahujans, therefore, constitute 61% of Indian population. According to Ilaiah, these seventy-eight crore Dalitbahujans are not Hindu by either birth or culture, and forcibly labeling them as Hindus is yet another example of a state-sponsored and state-sanctioned Hindutva supremacy.[59]

"I do not know how I can relate to the Hindu culture that is being projected through all kinds of advertising agencies. The government and the state themselves have become big advertising agencies. Moreover the Sangh Parivar harasses us every day by calling us Hindus." (Ilaiah 2002:x-xi)

If we exclude Muslims, Christians, Buddhists, Jains, Sikhs and others who make up roughly 20% of India, we are then left with the so-called forward caste Hindus, who constitute merely 10% of India's population. It is this 10% of Indians that Ilaiah takes a strong exception to, castigating them at every juncture.

"The Brahmins continue being semi-naked while performing these yagnas and kratus. This reflects their primitive brains and body culture." (Ilaiah 2018b)

Ilaiah is not alone in insisting that Dalits are not Hindus. Quite a few politicians, public intellectuals as well as academicians, including those associated with prominent institutions like Harvard and Columbia, insist that the idea of a Hindu majority India is a faulty one. Hindu majoritarianism is a false construct of 'savarna' Hindus who "have taken for granted the status of Adivasi and Dalits as being Hindu."[60] The Chief Minister of Jharkhand, an elected representative, observed that Hindu religion was separate from Adivasi (tribal) religion.[61] In fact, there is an entire thesis, that modern Hinduism is itself, a sham and an artificial construct made up by Swami Vivekananda and others during the British era, and that, the contours of contemporary Hinduism were bequeathed to us by our colonial masters as explained by Rajiv Malhotra in his book *Indra's Net: Defending Hinduism's Philosophical Unity*.[62]

Setting aside such personal views of public intellectuals and leaders, one questions as to what is the legal position of Hindus as defined in an Indian context? Legally, the definition of Hinduism is very crisp, unambiguous and consistent as can be seen in various codified Hindu Laws and the Constitution, itself chaired by B.R. Ambedkar.

a. One who is a Hindu by religion in any of its forms or developments, including a Virashaiva, Lingayat, Brahmo Samaji, Prarthana Samaji as well as Arya Samaji
b. One who is Buddhist, Jain or Sikh by religion
c. Anyone else who is not a Muslim, Christian, Parsi or Jew by religion[63]

In other words, all Dalitbahujans are Hindus, except those, who have converted to other religions like Christianity or Islam. And this definition happens to be a major problem since it quite obviously renders the opinions of Ilaiah and his ilk irrelevant. It is hard to believe that an intellectual of the stature of Kancha Ilaiah, is unaware of how the state legally defines Hindus. Moreover, this has nothing to do with either Hindutva or what Ilaiah imagines the Sangh Parivar[64] want him to believe. What then are his intentions?

If one is to summarize his work so far, Ilaiah detests Hinduism, as well as the so-called forward caste of Brahminical Hindus. Nor does he intend to reform Hinduism in any way. Rather he makes ad hominem attacks on Hindu communities and vilifies them to no end. He accuses Hindus of killing wantonly, raping women, and burning alive hundreds and thousands of people and hence, feels that a violent uprising is justified.

> "Social upheavals with a vision of change to establish better human relations and equality as an essential goal of human beings are necessary evils." (Ilaiah 2009:238)

He concludes by going so far as to justify why a civil war against Brahminism (used interchangeably with Hinduism) is required and how it can serve as a harbinger of new knowledge and eventual equality of all Indians.

Moreover, Hinduism, according to him, is against collective economic activity. He makes the charge that Hindus use socially useful products, but are unaware as to how they are produced – they consider such products as a product of prayer.[65] A civil war will lead to a revolutionary transformation of the poor into rich and vice versa and bring about social, economic and scientific development.[66]

Ilaiah's Strategy

What is it that will help in this endeavor of rebellion/revolution? Ilaiah is categorical that it is Christianity alone, which can grant the disenfranchized the right to equality, and the process can begin with the reading of the Bible. It was the Bible which was the "harbinger of civil wars to achieve socio-spiritual equality in the West."[67] Therefore, it is Bible reading among Dalitbahujans and the knowledge of the universal ethic of monotheism inherent in Christianity will bring about dignity to the Indian masses.[68]

Ilaiah's agenda now starts becoming clear. Based on the plethora of evidence furnished thus far, it seems that he wants to Christianize India through the following steps:

a. First by positioning himself as a champion of the Dalitbahujan communities, declaring that they are not Hindus and by alienating them from their Indic roots

b. Second, by developing 'atrocity literature' to target Hinduism and attack Hindus, especially Brahmins, and to incite people and provoke violence against Hindu groups through his writings, international support and activism

c. Third, encouraging civil war to wipe out the so-called Brahminical forward castes, whom he sees as violent, barbaric, racist and discriminatory groups

d. Fourth, by offering Christianity as an alternative and encouraging Bible reading among the Dalitbahujans

e. Final: Post-Hindu Christian India

It is no wonder, that he believes that a "believer in God of Equality is a better nationalist, than those who worship gods that breed inequality."[69] Could one not conclude that, according to him, therefore, only Christians are true nationalists, while so-called Hindu nationalists are nothing but fascists and militants?

It is to be noted that calling for the genocide of Brahmins, a minority community which makes up less than three percent of India[70], has become exceedingly common, and normalized through mass media and academia. Starting with the Islamic invasion of India, all the way to modern India, this trend has continued, and if nothing else, has become especially exacerbated in recent times. Ilaiah is therefore, not alone in calling for an extermination of Brahmins; he is in the hallowed company of famous personalities like the Christian missionary Francis Xavier and Dravidian ideologue E.V. Ramasamy Naicker.[71] In the words of the former:

> "There are in these parts among the pagans a class of men called Brahmins. They are as perverse and wicked a set as can anywhere be found, and to whom applies the Psalm which says: 'From an unholy race, and wicked and crafty men, deliver me, Lord.' If it were not for the Brahmins, we should have all the heathens embracing our faith." (Sharan 1991:97)

Ilaiah's caricature of Brahmins is equally problematic. Discerning readers may observe interesting parallels between his controversial views on Brahmins and the systematic buildup of animosity towards Jews in Europe culminating in the Nazi Holocaust. In the words of Koenraad Elst:

> "Read e.g. Kancha Ilaiah's book Why *I Am Not a Hindu* (Calcutta 1996), sponsored by the Rajiv Gandhi Foundation, with its anti-Brahmin cartoons: move the hairlocks of the Brahmin villains from the back of the head to just in front of their ears, and you get exact replicas of the anti-Semitic cartoons from the Nazi paper *Der Stürmer*." (Elst 2007:12)

Ilaiah's Ideological Position

What is the ideological basis of Ilaiah's work? What is the intellectual framework which informs his academic positions? What are his conceptual assumptions?

A study of Ilaiah's work reveals, that he is obsessed with the ideas of the 'white-skinned' invading Aryan race and the dark-skinned Dravidian who is the 'son of the soil'. Most of the divisive hate speeches popular in India revolve around the controversial racist Aryan Invasion Theory (AIT), subsequently moderated to an equally controversial linguistic Aryan Migration Theory (AMT).

> "The Brahmans.....Once they occupied India after the Aryan invasion, they never left this land." (Ilaiah 2009:186)

As shown earlier, Ilaiah considers cows as foreign animals, Aryan in origin, and white in color, whereas, buffaloes are indigenous, and the favorite animal of the dark-skinned natives of India. Perhaps he is unaware that aurochs, the ancestors of modern cows originated almost *two million years ago in India*, and spread westwards all the way to Europe. Around nine thousand years ago, domestication of cow took place in the Indian subcontinent, much earlier than any supposed Aryan invasion in 1500 BCE.[72] Cows may be white or brown or black or any color in between, and their presence in India has nothing to do with any invasion, Aryan or otherwise.

Much has been written by various scholars challenging each and every aspect of the contentious and problematic Aryan theory. Discoveries in archaeology, genetics, hydrology, linguistics and other disciplines have robustly contested these racial theories and exposed the grave problems inherent in their positions. In his seminal book *Breaking India*, Rajiv Malhotra traces the evolution of this theory, from the invention of the Aryan race all the way to Nazism. He also delves into the parallel development of the Dravidian thesis – from the invention of the Dravidian race to modern Christian Dravidianism. Malhotra illustrates how imperial evangelism shaped Indian ethnology and the evolution of race science to classify Indians to castes and groups.[73] Manogna Sastry and Megh Kalyanasundaram, have studied the so-called Aryan-Dravidian schism, in detail, and shown how these were colonial tools meant to provide "a revised historical account and new theories of the very origin of the land's culture."[74]

Renowned archaeologist B.B. Lal, based on his extensive archaeological discoveries and research, demonstrates the cultural continuity of Indians from Harappan times to present, the absence of any evidence of invasion, and insists that Aryan invasion or migration is a myth.[75] Genetic studies indicate that there has been no significant external genetic influence in India since 3000 BCE, significantly predating any supposed Aryan invasion in 1500 BCE.[76] Similarly, there are no literary accounts in Hindu scriptures of any exotic racial group known as Brahmins bringing Vedas into this land from some foreign land, nor is there any racial connotation anywhere in our central literature.[77] In fact, there is an entire field of scholarship, referred to as 'Out of India theory', which proposes that, by and large, all Indians are indigenous to India and that Indo-European languages, including Sanskrit, originated in India and spread out to other locations.[78] Ilaiah, however, does not appear to be interested in conducting an open-minded well-rounded academic inquiry on the Aryan question.

He appears to be driven more by political and religious zeal rather than academic interest. It is no wonder that he ascribes all manner of evils to Hinduism.

> "While they continue their murderous activities, the priests perform special pujas for money so that murderers can keep murdering and rapists can keep raping women again and again." (Ilaiah 2009:192)

Such prejudicial views can hardly qualify as scholarship. In fact, some of Ilaiah's statements are downright libelous and malicious as shown above. If unsubstantiated claims and defamatory sentences like these are supposed to be examples of Ilaiah's critical thinking, it is but a reflection of the sad plight of social sciences research in India. So deep is his hatred for Hinduism and an imagined Hindu *rashtra*, that Ilaiah even dismisses genuine science coming out of India.

> "It is because of Hindu casteism that India has remained a land barren of scientific discoveries throughout modern history. It has survived on modern science begged and borrowed from other countries, and the Brahmanic intellectuals are solely responsible for this status of the nation." (Ilaiah 2009:xii)

This view is the exact opposite of all known knowledge of scientific achievements of India and discounts India's stupendous advancements in astronomy, mathematics, medicine, surgery, Ayurveda, music, metallurgy and architecture over the centuries. Much of this indigenous knowledge was often, way ahead of its times and far more advanced than the rest of the civilized world. For example, more than two thousand years ago Panini, the ancient Sanskritist par excellence, made several discoveries in the fields of phonetics, phonology, and morphology many of which remained more advanced than the west until the mid-20th century.[79] Or that more than two thousand years ago, the physician Sushruta was performing cataract surgeries.[80] In fact, the West has routinely, without acknowledgement, appropriated (and continues to do so) knowledge of Indian models of mind, into the cutting edge of western cognitive sciences.[81] Infinity Foundation has published fourteen volumes on the history of Indian science and technology covering areas like animal husbandry, water management, iron and zinc technologies and other areas, written by top experts in the fields.[82] Ilaiah ought to study these books, and clear his misconceptions about the history of indigenous science and technology.

Shepherd of Hindu Hatred: Allegations and Responses

Claim: Hinduism promotes Inequality

Ilaiah's work is replete with factual errors and misrepresentations, especially in the context of Hindu texts. For example, he traces what he calls Hinduism's "spiritual fascism" and propensity for inequality to the *Purusha Suktam* in the Rig Veda.[83] The *Purusha suktam* describes the divine, figuratively, and says that Brahmanas or priests came out of his mouth, the Kshatriyas or kings and warriors from the shoulders, the vaishyas or tradesmen from his thighs and the Shudras or laborers from his feet. Ilaiah often uses this hymn to showcase inequality and discrimination in Hinduism. Perhaps, he is not aware or chooses to ignore the fact, that in Hinduism, the feet is not considered inferior or derogatory in any way. Rather, it is celebrated – the concept of "lotus feet" is integral and perhaps unique to Hinduism.[84] The very names of revered saints are referred to by alluding to their lotus feet.[85] *Pada puja* is done by offering sandal paste and flowers to a revered person's feet and even his sandals are taken as emblems in case the person is not present. There are popular hymns like *Guru Paduka Stotram* and the *Paduka Sahasram* which glorify the feet.[86] In the Ramayana, Bharata acting as Lord Rama's regent during the long years of exile placed the sandals on the throne as the royal emblem, not Rama's weapon, crown or scepter.[87] In other words, reverence for the feet is an ancient tradition traceable to the Vedic age, and the *Purusha sukta* in that vein is simply a metaphorical description of a society with its priests, kings, warriors, tradesmen and laborers, and not an exhortation to racially discriminate certain groups.

The next example is from the *Bhagavad Gita*. Even those who have not read the *Gita,* are perhaps familiar with 47th verse of the second chapter which goes: "You have a right to perform your prescribed duty, but you are not entitled to the fruits of action."[88] But Ilaiah gives this celebrated verse an altogether different twist or interpretation. He concludes from a foreign translation of the *Gita*, that, this verse establishes an ideology which says that Dalitbahujans must work but they must not aspire to enjoy the fruits of that work, which would accrue to the upper castes.[89] This example, incidentally, highlights a major problem of Hindu scripture translations, which are not grounded in tradition, and make use of academic lenses; Postmodernism for example, thereby resulting in numerous instances of what practitioners would deem as misinterpretation or mistranslations. This verse simply states that each individual should perform his duty with integrity and sincerity, irrespective of whether the act brings him rewards or any loss. If the rewards come, it is good to enjoy them; but in case there are no benefits, one must not give in to despondency, but instead should continue to cheerfully perform one's duty. It has nothing to do with any particular strata of society or the relation between different groups. The verse has to be taken to discuss the connection of a person's efforts and his own gains, not between two different individuals, leave alone two different castes. To interpret this in the manner cited, is pure slander based on falsehood, to build prejudice among new readers and to garner support for his own hate speech. If one is interested in reading about the *Gita*, why not choose any of the traditional translations and commentaries by either Chinmaya Mission or Ramakrishna Mission or Gita Press?

Claim: Hinduism promotes Racism

Ilaiah interprets the *Mahabharata* as the fight between Dalitbahujans, represented by the Kauravas, and the Brahminical forces, represented by the Pandavas.[90] As usual there is no substantiation, whatsoever, for his grand pronouncements. Perhaps, he is unaware that the Kauravas and Pandavas were cousins belonging to the same clan, and thus, it would follow that Dalitbahujans and Brahmins also belong to the same racial stock and not to different racial groups as he wants everyone to believe! Ilaiah looks at the *Ramayana* through a seemingly post-modern social justice lens, adding everything from racism, to patriarchy to Hindutva supremacy and nationalism, to the mix, as illustrated in the following allusion to Lord Hanuman.

> "It is common knowledge that Hanuman was a South Indian Dalit who joined the imperial army of Rama to fight against the south Indian nationalist ruler – Ravana. Hanuman worked day in and day out in the interest of 'Ramarajya' (anti-dalitbahujan and anti-women kingdom), yet his place in the administration was always marginal and subservient." (Ilaiah 2002:58-59)

The above lines abound in errors – Hanuman is, by no means, accorded a marginal role, being the only deity from *Ramrajya* to continue being widely worshipped till date. It is well known that Lord Hanuman was an erudite scholar proficient in the *Vedas* and *Vedangas*, and also a staunch proponent of the dharmic way of life.[91] If he were indeed, a southern Indian Dalit, nobody seemed to mind (even to this day), since northern India is dotted with innumerable Hanuman temples. Hanuman is the resident deity even today, of most indigenous Indian gymnasiums and 'akhadas'. His deep friendship and devotion to Lord Rama began well before he joined the imperial army. As to Ravana being a south Indian nationalist leader, it is based on false propaganda by E.V. Ramasamy, who presented a distorted account of classical literature to stir up hatred against Sanskrit and Brahmins among the populace.[92] In most such cases, Ilaiah repeats popular notions of Left liberals, Western neo-orientalists and Dravidian separatists with no attempt at any verification with facts or original research. Many of these notions are also obsolete in academia but Ilaiah freely uses them to develop his agenda, and somehow reaches the conclusion that *Ramayana* was written after *Mahabharata*.[93]

Claim: Hinduism promotes White-ness

Ilaiah makes another claim that Hindu ethos is prejudiced against the color black and shows a favorable bias towards the color white.[94] He cites Devi Saraswati's swan and raiment being pure white and cows venerated as they are white, while the black buffalo is blacklisted. A cursory study of Vedic literature shows that, in addition to white cows, there were red, black and spotted cows as well.[95] He is perhaps unaware, that the god Yama riding a black buffalo is regarded as Dharmaraja, the ultimate dispenser of justice.[96] Lord Ganesha's pet mouse is black, as also crows, which are considered the representatives of one's own ancestors (yes, even those of Brahmins). There does not seem to be any notions of superiority or inferiority based on color, supposedly echoing the varied complexion of the people of India. Lord Krishna is known to be very dark in color, represented with blue in art so that the eyes and other features are visible, and so is Lord Rama for that matter.

Claim: Hinduism promotes Discrimination

Unlike Abrahamic traditions and their concept of God's chosen people, Hinduism considers all life as being important – human life as well as animal, flora, fauna and insects. Having said that, we must accept that discrimination in some form of other did and still does exist in Indian society, as it does the world over, and Hindu gurus have never shied away from this fact. Throughout the ages, social reformers from all strata of society have tried to reform Hinduism from within. However, it must be noted that such discrimination, if any, was not sanctioned by the 'shastras', in the way, the Quran sanctions *jihad* against the *kafirs*.[97] Let us recall Adi Shankaracharya's unequivocal rejection of social exclusions which he felt were not in line with Advaita's tenets of inclusion and universalism. He says:

> "....I am that which pervades as a witness in the bodies of all living beings right from Brahma to the tiny ant. One who has the deep conviction that 'I am That, not any of the objects of perception', he is a Guru, whether a Chandala or a Brahmana..." (Venkataraman 2014:107)

Jaina, Bauddha, Siddha, Saiva, Yoga, Sankhya and Vaishnava are only a few of the myriad traditions that flourished within the folds of *Sanatana Dharma* in various periods in India, each with many smaller variations within themselves. Caste has never been a predominant feature of Indian thought; rather, philosophical inquiry has always taken the highest precedence. In Tamil Saiva devotional literature of the revered Nāyanār-s, the saints devoted to Lord Siva, came from all walks of life.[98] In the Vaishnava tradition, Sri Ramanuja is known to have brought a large number of people – irrespective of their social strata – to the Vaishnavite fold.[99]

In the *Pañcatantra* story of the greedy holy man Devasharma, who is cheated of his gold coins by a rogue who comes to win his trust in the garb of a disciple, the unsuspecting guru utters these words while initiating him as his disciple:

> "Whether he be a śūdra or any other, a caṇḍāla or a sannyāsī, once he is initiated with the Śiva-mantra, smeared with sacred ash, he becomes as auspicious as Śiva Himself." (Kale 2012:29)

This shows that the sannyasi (whom Ilaiah reviles as a rapacious Brahmin burden on society) had no caste. Whoever wanted to adopt a lifestyle of prayer, meditation and study, was free to do so. Buddhist, Christian, Jain and other religions have the concept of monkhood, but Ilaiah displays great rancor when it comes to Hindu sannyasis.

The story of Satyakama and Jabala in the *Chandogya Upanishad* illustrates the Hindu ideals of equality of man, the strength and value of truth, the importance of practical knowledge, hard work and the importance of spiritual knowledge. The fact that Satyakama was the son of unknown parentage, did not stop him from being accepted by his teacher. After completing his basic education, his teacher, in order to test his suitability for higher learning, gave him five hundred cows, asking him to take them to the forest and return when they had multiplied to a thousand. Not only did Satyakama complete his assignment and more, he went on to become a celebrated rishi in his own right.[100] This story illustrates how Hindu thought has time and again, urged humanity to overcome petty social discrimination and to aim at the loftier ideals of life. It disproves Ilaiah's oft-repeated accusation that 'Brahminism' has no practical knowledge and is 'non-productive'.[101]

In the traditional system of education, a prince and a pauper all lived in the same manner, sharing domestic and farm work, as in the case of Sri Krishna and Sudama in their teacher's hermitage during student years. This tradition of education for all, continued till the pre-modern period before the advent of the British. It is apparent, that youngsters learnt about the ways of the world and practical matters before they undertook kingly, priestly or commercial offices. In many farms, people from a wide variety of castes shared the manual work. In his book, *The Beautiful Tree*, Dharampal provides data from early 19th century British survey records on Indian education which completely negates Ilaiah's claims that upper-caste Hindus denied Dalitbahujans the right to education. For example, in Madras Presidency the percentage of Dalitbahujan students in indigenous educational institutions in different regions were as follows[102]:

- Tamil speaking regions – 70 to 84%
- Malayalam speaking regions – 54%
- Kannada speaking regions – 63%
- Oriya speaking regions – 64%
- Telugu speaking regions – 35 to 41%

In Bengal Presidency, comprising modern-day West Bengal, Bihar, Bangladesh and Assam, British records indicate that a large number of students from 'Dom' and 'Chandal'[103] communities, whom social scientists classify as "untouchables", studied alongside students of so-called forward castes.[104] One wonders where is the large-scale discrimination against Shudras by Goddess Saraswati that Ilaiah talks about.

Claim: Hinduism promotes Backwardness

Ilaiah is quite critical of the backward and primitive practice of idol worship among Hindus.[105] It must be understood that *murti-puja* in Hinduism does not mean idol-worship; the deity is consecrated and regarded a living person through prāna-pratiṣṭhā.[106] Hence, He or She is a divine manifestation who allows the worshipper *darshan* and the opportunity to perform rituals to aid in their spiritual progress. Devotees offer food items to the deities as a gesture of love and reverence, just as one offers food to a loved one. While a modest quantity is offered to the deity, a large amount is distributed to all devotees who visit the temple, rich or poor. It is a routine feature of every temple during festivals, that the peasants and poor people line up to savor temple *prasada*. All temples have "*annadana*" or feeding the poor arrangements; in fact, temples have numerous social, educational and charitable activities on which Ilaiah is absolutely silent.

Ilaiah riles at the 'madi' concept of purity and hygiene followed by many Brahmins, especially in southern India, in the cooking and storing of food.[107] 'Madi' requires people to bathe before starting cooking and to wear washed clothes. The previous day's food is to be consumed or removed from the vicinity of the fresh cooking and the stove is to be wiped clean. The reasons for these rules were ostensibly for better shelf-life and to avoid food spoilage, an important concern in a tropical climate. In a sense, this is no different from modern norms and rules of food storage that help in preserving nutrients better and offer more health benefits. One would think that people would laud, emulate the older generations for following such stringent hygiene and cleanliness norms! Ilaiah, however, freely mocks the entire practice, and sees evidence of racism in them. Most of his allegations are in fact, obsolete and irrelevant for the past hundred years. To make this concept of previous centuries appear like a current practice is plain maliciousness on the part of the writer.

People have complete freedom to choose their diet as long as it adheres to the food safety factors, cultural norms and value systems of their nation.[108] But Ilaiah's views of vegetarianism and consumption of meat especially beef, seem to be driven by acute 'Hinduphobia' rather than, being based on evidence driven science. For example, studies have shown clear linkages between rising meat consumption, climate change and pandemics.[109] On the other hand, a global shift towards a plant-based diet could increase longevity by ten percent or more, and also decrease greenhouse gas emissions by as much seventy percent.[110] Yet, as shown earlier, Ilaiah keeps on insisting on a beef-based diet for everybody despite well-documented health and environmental risks.

Hinduism Problem: Christianity Solution

For Ilaiah, Hinduism is the reason behind numerous social ills that ails society Indian today especially with regards to the plight of Dalit-bahujans and women. We have discussed many of his claims that Hinduism is inherently racist, and that violence towards Dalits is embedded in the DNA of Hinduism, and will not repeat them here. Regarding women, similarly, he makes a number of strange observations. For example, he makes a curious statement that while wife-beating is common across India, upper caste women, unlike Dalitbahujan women, lack agency and have to passively accept all sorts of ill-treatment at the hand of patriarchal Hindu males.[111] He refers to 'Sati' as if it is a common existing practice for Hindu women to die along with their husbands.[112] For him, therefore, **Hinduism is the problem and Christianity is the solution** and he asks of Hindu gods:

> "If the God believed by a person doesn't have democratic values, where will this person get those democratic values from? In fact, shouldn't they explain why they create such Gods who are violent, undemocratic and anti-women?" (Ilaiah 2015)

It is surprising (or perhaps not), that Ilaiah finds a worldview that promotes mutual respect among different cultures problematic, whereas those like Abrahamic faiths, which, at best preach tolerance, is perfectly acceptable to him.[113] A system which prompts yoga and mental wellbeing, sustainable living, holistic health-care, vegetarianism, eco-feminism, feminine divine and diversity of spiritual paths is equally problematic for Ilaiah.

The essay will now examine the second part/premise of the equation. Is Christianity really a solution to all alleged evils of Hinduism? To answer this, some additional questions must be asked[114]:

- Is the Church qualified to 'cure' Indian society?
- What is the track-record of Christianity in solving social evils in Third world countries in the past?
- Does Christianity have a superior human rights track record compared to Hinduism?

Ilaiah clearly seems to believe that Christianity and its Abrahamic God is a solution to all of Hinduism's alleged evils. To understand if Christianity is indeed the answer, let us take a look at the condition of converted Christians in India. Assuming they converted to Christianity, in order to escape the shackles of caste discrimination and untouchability, surely they must now be living a life of dignity at par with all other converted Christians irrespective of their earlier castes. Unfortunately, the reality is quite different. A well-known Jesuit, practicing lawyer and Dalit-Christian activist admits:

> "...the Catholic Church says there is no caste bias but caste discrimination is rampant in the Church ... There are hardly any inter-caste marriages among converted Christians. Until recently, Church-run magazines carried matrimonial advertisements containing specific caste references." (Natarajan 2010)

Syrian Christians are said to take ritual baths after physical contact with lower castes.[115] Inter caste marriage is not common among Indian Christians: a Syrian Christians from Kerala will not marry a Dalit

Christian, and will sometimes prefer to get married to a higher class Hindu instead.[116] Converted Christians belonging to influential castes routinely lobby to allow only the person belonging to their caste being appointed as bishop in their diocese, and Dalit and upper caste converts cannot bury their dead in the same cemeteries.[117] In many churches, Dalits have separate cemeteries and funeral carts and are denied the use of the common road leading to the church, and this problem is present in both the Protestant and Catholic Church.[118] Evidently, Christianity is not a solution to the "problem" of caste at least.

One should now explore this question from a global perspective. Rajiv Malhotra in a rejoinder to Kancha Ilaiah makes a very valid point, that if Christianity were indeed the solution then why is it that there are so many problems in Latin America and among African-Americans in the US.[119] We would like to build upon this thesis.

In terms of rape statistics (number of rapes per 100,000), all the top ten countries are Christian majority nations, including USA, Australia and Sweden, and some relatively recently Christianized nations like South Africa, Nicaragua and Botswana.[120] In the US, which for Ilaiah is the bastion of human rights, and where he gives testimonies against India, African-American women face greater domestic violence than white women.[121] In USA, blacks receive twenty percent longer sentences than whites for committing the same crime.[122] In the UK, according to the British Institute of Human Rights, one in four women experience domestic abuse and one in five sexual assault during their lifetime.[123] In terms of violent crimes, the countries with the highest murder rates are mostly from South America, Caribbean and Africa – countries where natives were converted with missionary zeal.[124] Some of the recently converted countries still continue to be mired in poverty and backwardness. Clearly, Christianity has not solved crime against women, or racial discrimination or other social evils. We wish that Ilaiah and his cabal of Hinduphobic academicians reflect on these hard facts.

Ilaiah of course, paints a rosy picture of Christianity, portraying it as a religion of enlightened superior values, beyond superstitions and prejudices, and one where God treats every human being with equal compassion. He blithely claims that Christianity gives enormous dignity to labor and that from a spiritual standpoint all animals have equal rights[125], glossing over the very important point, that in Christianity, animals do not have souls, and hence, there is no question of spirituality. In fact, throughout the existence of Christian faith there have been shrill debates whether women have souls.[126] Unsurprisingly, therefore, Ilaiah remains silent on many of Christianity's problems. For example, there is no discussion on Indian evangelists claiming to miraculously cure chronic illnesses with prayers.[127] He is silent on Biblical stories like demon pigs being possessed by heretic souls[128], or of forty-two young boys being mauled by two bears in the name of the Lord[129], or how God raises an army of bones[130], and numerous other such stories which the Church accepts as literal truth since the Bible is the word of God. Ilaiah does not talk about the innumerable Church abuse cases including sexual crimes and pedophilia across the globe[131], including India.[132] While Ilaiah has no qualms in characterizing Hindus and their Gods as violent, he is absolutely silent on violence and genocides in the Bible, whether the Old Testament or the New Testament.[133] It would be interesting to find out his reaction and response to Richard Dawkin's description of the Abrahamic God as[134]:

> "... the most unpleasant character in all fiction: jealous and proud of it; a petty, unjust, unforgiving control-freak; a vindictive, bloodthirsty ethnic cleanser; a misogynistic, homophobic, racist, infanticidal, genocidal, filicidal, pestilential, megalomaniacal, sadomasochistic, capriciously malevolent bully."

It is also evident that Ilaiah suffers from a delusion of grandeur. Just as the great prophet-God-like Jesus was referred to as Good Shepherd[135], Ilaiah too changed his name and added the suffix 'Shepherd' to his name. He can now become the great Messiah of the Dalitbahujans, delivering them from the brutality and backwardness of Hinduism by showing them the path of true deliverance in Christendom, and heralding the dawn of a new post-Hindu Christian era.

A Breaking India Sepoy

Kancha Ilaiah is one of the most influential Indian foot-soldiers of the 'Breaking India' forces – nexuses of academic, religious and activist groups, intent upon stirring up separatism and social divisiveness in order to weaken India as a civilization and as a nation state. He is a favorite among mainstream media houses and social sciences academia for his controversial and often pejorative comments against Hindus and Hinduism, as well as for his cries to the "victims" of oppression, the Dalitbahujans, to violently revolt against the Indian nation state, whose representatives are the forward caste Brahminical forces. In India, he portrays himself as a Left-liberal intellectual and a champion of the underclass, yet paradoxically in the West he collaborates with Right-wing forces and Church groups, and freely gives testimonies against what he describes as India's abject human rights situation. Rajiv Malhotra explains this kind of hypocritical behavior very succinctly:

> "Pro-India perceptions are ignored and the Indian legacy of supporting the rights of down-trodden are dismissed derisively. Worldviews that emphasize conflicts are encouraged. Ideologues give open call to racial civil wars, which are published by prestigious academic publishing houses of the West. US governmental monitoring mechanisms focus on India with distorting lenses and quote and requote their own reports to project a savage imagery of India as a dark frontier region ripe for Western intervention." (Malhotra and Neelakandan 2011:173)

In other words, Ilaiah is a classic sepoy, similar to Indian sepoys used by the British to fight against Indians during the colonial era. In the world-view of Ilaiah, everything about Hinduism and so-called forward caste Hindus are bad. For Ilaiah, Hindus are oppressors, racists, violent criminals, patriarchal misogynists, murderers, rapists, smugglers and everything evil imaginable, and in Christianity's egalitarianism he sees a solution to all of India's ills. This kind of divisive and separatist perspective is in fact, encouraged in the field of Dalit studies, both in India as well as in the Western academia. Postmodernism and subalternism provide academic respectability to such racist and prejudicial studies, many of which are directly against the interest of the nation. Ilaiah of course, chooses not to mention the significant cooperation among so-called caste Hindus and Dalitbahujans in the development of much of Hindu sacred literature. There is no mention that a large part of Bhakti literature was contributed by Dalits.[136] Instead, like a typical formulaic 'Breaking India' activist he sees India as a patient afflicted with diseases like caste, untouchability, sati and patriarchy, and the Bible and Church as a miracle cure.

Conclusion

Social issues like discrimination, consumerist greed, and exploitation are universal in nature and India is no exception. If anybody says that India does not have any issues, they are living in denial. Our gurus and leaders throughout the ages recognized it, and reformed Indian society from within, one evil at a time. Post-Independence, affirmative action to assist the underprivileged, became a founding principle of our constitution. As a belief system, Hinduism has undergone numerous reforms from ancient times up to the recent past, and all of this happened without the intervention of any foreign power claiming to be the dispensers of human rights. But modern human rights activists are not interested in reforming Hinduism. They have a deep seated hatred for the Hindu identity itself and have garnered huge amount of international support in their activism against Hinduism.

Ilaiah belongs to this camp of self-proclaimed revolutionary social warriors who see Hinduism itself as the evil plaguing India. The solution he envisages for India is Christianity. He wants a Christian India without Hindus and Hinduism, and masks his racist activities as social justice activism in support of the underclass. According to him, Hindus must pay, now and in the future as well, for what he sees as the crimes of their forefathers. If generations need to pay for sins of their fathers, would Ilaiah, based on the principle of parity, agree that Christians have to account for the cultural genocide they have unleashed world over – whether it was the brutal colonization of the Americas, or the Spanish inquisition, or the Goa Inquisition or the Rwandan genocide?

Every society has traditions and norms that have evolved through practical experience of trial and error. An excessive sense of victimhood can rob the youth of confidence and constructive energy, leading to anger and unreasonable expectations. Politicians, social scientists and social leaders have a responsibility to inspire right values in younger generations in order for them to grow into successful, well-adjusted citizens of the modern world. As a Shepherd, he should guide the nation for the betterment of humanity, but not so for him. He is but one, of a large group of individuals engaged deeply in undermining dharma and the national integrity of India. There are probably thousands like him, if not millions, funded and fed by the larger global Hinduphobic ecosystem, working round-the-clock like a well-oiled machine, intent on destabilizing India and fomenting discord among communities.[137] The authors hope that this critique of Kancha Ilaiah's scholarship goes some way in raising awareness amongst dharma-minded individuals and also to humanity at large.

Bibliography

Devi, Naorem J. and Kambhampati Subrahmanyam. 2014. "Women in the Rig Vedic age." *International Journal of Yoga - Philosophy, Psychology and Parapsychology* 2(1):1-3. (https://www.ijoyppp.org/text.asp?2014/2/1/1/157985).

Dharampal. 2000. *The Beautiful Tree: Indigenous Indian Education in the Eighteenth Century*. Mapusa, Goa: Other India Press.

Elst, Koenraad. 2007. *Asterisk in Bhāropīyasthān: Minor Writings on the Aryan Invasion Debate*. Delhi: Voice of India.

Fleischer, Manfred P. 1981. ""Are Women Human?"-The Debate of 1595 between Valens Acidalius and Simon Gediccus." *The Sixteenth Century Journal* 12(2):107-120. (https://www.jstor.org/stable/2539503).

Ilaiah, Kancha. 1997. "The State of Dalit Mobilization: An Interview with Kancha Ilaiah." www.oocities.org. Retrieved October 11, 2021 (http://www.oocities.org/indiafas/India/state_of_mobalization.htm).

Ilaiah, Kancha. 2000a. "The Rediff Interview/Dr Kancha Ilaiah." www.rediff.

com. Retrieved October 16, 2021 (https://www.rediff.com/news/2001/jan/17inter.htm).

Ilaiah, Kancha. 2000b. "The attempt to censor my writings." www.rediff.com. Retrieved October 16, 2021 (https://www.rediff.com/news/2000/may/24ap.htm).

Ilaiah, Kancha. 2002. *Why I am not a Hindu*. Kolkata: Samya.

Ilaiah, Kancha. 2005. "Interview with Dr Kancha Ilaiah - Leading Dalit Rights Campaigner in India." Christian Today. Retrieved October 11, 2021 (https://www.christiantoday.com/article/interview.with.dr.kancha.ilaiah.leading.dalit.rights.campaigner.in.india/4495.htm).

Ilaiah, Kancha. 2009. *Post-Hindu India*. New Delhi, London, California & Singapore: Sage Publications.

Ilaiah, Kancha. 2015. "Case filed against social scientist Kancha Ilaiah for asking, 'Is God a democrat?'." scroll.in. Retrieved October 16, 2021 (https://scroll.in/article/731416/case-filed-against-social-scientist-kancha-ilaiah-for-asking-is-god-a-democrat).

Ilaiah, Kancha. 2016. "The violence of caste: Why I have changed my name to Kancha Ilaiah Shepherd." Scroll.in. Retrieved October 10, 2021 (https://scroll.in/article/808890/kancha-ilaiah-explains-why-he-decided-to-add-shepherd-to-his-name).

Ilaiah, Kancha. 2018a. "T-MASS: A New Experiment In Ambedkarite-Marxist Alliance." www.kanchailaiah.com. Retrieved October 11, 2021 (https://www.kanchailaiah.com/2018/02/01/t-mass-a-new-experiment-in-ambedkarite-marxist-alliance/).

Ilaiah, Kancha. 2018b. "How Brahmins ensured India never progressed." www.kanchailaiah.com. Retrieved October 12, 2021 (http://www.kanchailaiah.com/2018/09/09/how-brahmins-ensured-india-never-progressed/).

Ilaiah, Kancha. 2018c. ""Saraswathi would kill our children if they are sent to school": From the memoirs of Kancha Ilaiah Shepherd." caravanmagazine.in. Retrieved October 28, 2021 (https://caravanmagazine.in/education/kancha-ilaiah-shephard-memoirs).

Ilaiah, Kancha. 2019a. "Freedom to Eat." caravanmagazine.in. Retrieved November 25, 2021 (https://caravanmagazine.in/reportage/fight-beef-democratic-right).

Ilaiah, Kancha. 2019b. "The Untold Story of Harappa in the words of Kanch Ilaiah." sabrangindia.in. Retrieved October 28, 2021 (https://sabrangindia.in/article/untold-story-harappa-words-kanch-ilaiah).

Ilaiah, Kancha. 2020. "Early India, Goats and Brahmins | Kancha Ilaiah Shepherd." mainstreamweekly.net. Retrieved October 20, 2021 (https://www.mainstreamweekly.net/article9591.html).

Ilaiah, Kancha. 2021. "Upper caste networks of political parties are resisting caste census. But not for long." theprint.in. Retrieved October 16, 2021 (https://theprint.in/opinion/upper-caste-networks-of-political-parties-are-resisting-caste-census-but-not-for-long/726540/).

Jha, Ganganath. 1942. *Chandogya Upanishad with Shankara Bhashya*. Poona: Oriental Book Agency.

Kale, M.R. 2012. *Pancatantra of Visnusarma*. Delhi: Motilal Banarsidass.

Malhotra, Rajiv. 2011. "Tolerance Isn't Good Enough: The Need for Mutual Respect In Interfaith Relations." Huffpost. Retrieved October 16, 2021 (https://www.huffpost.com/entry/hypocrisy-of-tolerance_b_792739).

Malhotra, Rajiv. 2013. *Being Different*. Delhi: HarperCollins.

Malhotra, Rajiv. 2014. *Bharat Vikhandan*. New Delhi: Harper Hindi.

Malhotra, Rajiv. 2016. *Indra's Net: Defending Hinduism's Philosophical Unity*. Noida, Uttar Pradesh: HarperCollins Publishers India.

Malhotra, Rajiv and Aravindan Neelakandan. 2011. *Breaking India: Western Interventions in Dravidian and Dalit Faultlines*. New Delhi: Amaryllis.

Manoharan, Karthick R. 2020. "Freedom from God: Periyar and Religion." *Religions* 11(10).

Narayanan, Sharda. 2019. "Introduction: Vedic Tradition has no Racism." *Studies in Tamil Civilization*.

Natarajan, Swaminathan. 2010. "Indian Dalits find no refuge from caste in Christianity." bbc.com. Retrieved October 28, 2021 (https://www.bbc.com/news/world-south-asia-11229170).

Neuman, W. L. 2006. *Social Research Methods*. 6th ed. New Delhi: Pearson Education.

O'Malley, Charles D. 1970. *The History of Medical Education: An International Symposium Held February 5-9 , 1968*. University of California Press.

Rajiv Malhotra Official. 2016. "Rajiv Malhotra's Rejoinder to Kancha Ilaiah's Breaking India Activities." YouTube. Retrieved October 13, 2021 (https://www.youtube.com/watch?v=yMRw4TF7CAk).

Rajiv Malhotra Official. 2017. "India's (Unacknowledged) Contributions to Mind Sciences: Rajiv Malhotra." YouTube. Retrieved October 29, 2021 (https://www.youtube.com/watch?v=ZyApm_PJ-W8).

Rajiv Malhotra Official. 2018. "SABARIMALA: Deities & Judges." YouTube. Retrieved November 26, 2021 (https://www.youtube.com/watch?v=D5bjycdVfXw).

Sastry, Manogna and Megh Kalyanasundaram. 2019. "The A of ABC of Indian chronology: Dimensions of the Aryan problem revisited in 2017." *Studies in Tamil Civilization: Land of Dharma* 87-130.

Sharan, Ishwar. 1991. *The Myth of Saint Thomas and the Mylapore Shiva Temple*. 2019th ed. Delhi: Voice of India.

Venkataraman, Nochur. 2014. *Ātmatīrtham: Life and Teachings of Sri Sankarāchārya*. Chennai: Rishi Prakasana Sabha, Nikaya Trust.

Notes

1. (Ilaiah 2009:26)
2. (Ilaiah 2019a)
3. "Good Shepherd: Dalit thinker Kancha Ilaiah on name, caste." Hindustan Times. Retrieved October 16, 2021 (https://www.hindustantimes.com/india/we-need-a-new-god-says-dalit-thinker-kancha-ilaiah/story-ooWKO6iUKLAXv7qFqEW4ML.html).
4. "About Ilaiah Shepherd." kanchailaiah.com. Retrieved October 16, 2021 (https://www.kanchailaiah.com/about/).
5. (Ilaiah 2018a)
6. "Taking aim at the messenger: on the attack on Kancha Ilaiah." The Hindu. Retrieved October 16, 2021 (https://www.thehindu.com/opinion/op-ed/taking-aim-at-the-messenger/article19797679.ece).

7. How a caste reference in his 2009 book has come back to haunt Kancha Ilaiah." Retrieved 10-Oct-2021 (https://www.hindustantimes.com/india-news/how-a-caste-reference-in-his-2009-book-has-come-back-to-haunt-kancha-ilaiah/story-q7EbiFUWXbW902JDn5u1MI.html).

8. "Written evidence submitted by Christian Solidarity Worldwide." UK Parliament. Retrieved October 16, 2021 (https://publications.parliament.uk/pa/cm200506/cmselect/cmfaff/574/574we20.htm).

9. "In US Congress, Concern Over Gauri Lankesh Murder, Threat To Kancha Ilaiah." NDTV. Retrieved October 16, 2021 (https://www.ndtv.com/india-news/in-us-congress-concern-on-gauri-lankesh-murder-threat-to-kancha-ilaiah-1763322).

10. See his poem "O Bharatiya Brahmins." in (Ilaiah 2016)

11. (Ilaiah 2009:238)

12. (Ilaiah 2000b)

13. "Yet another FIR against Kancha Ilaiah, woman from Prakasam district files complaint." The News Minute. Retrieved October 16, 2021 (https://www.thenewsminute.com/article/yet-another-fir-against-kancha-ilaiah-woman-prakasam-district-files-complaint-69913).

14. (Ilaiah 2009:Chapter 9)

15. (Ilaiah 2002:viii-viix)

16. (Ilaiah 2009:xxvi)

17. (Ilaiah 1997)

18. Ilaiah says: "...Kamasutra – was meant to control the Shudra/Dalit masses– particularly women." See: "The Shudra Kings And Brahmins: A Mirror Image Of History." www.kanchailaiah.com. Retrieved October 16, 2021 (https://www.kanchailaiah.com/2021/08/25/the-shudra-kings-and-brahmins-a-mirror-image-of-history/).

19. (Ilaiah 2016)

20. "Vegetarianism is anti-nationalism, says Kancha Ilaiah." The Times of India. Retrieved October 16, 2021 (https://timesofindia.indiatimes.com/city/lucknow/vegetarianism-is-anti-nationalism-says-kancha-ilaiah/articleshow/51833906.cms).

21. (Ilaiah 2000a)

22. (Ilaiah 2015)
23. (Ilaiah 2002:xi)
24. (Ilaiah 2005)
25. "Institutes like IITs and IIMs should be closed down." DNA India. Retrieved October 16, 2021 (https://www.dnaindia.com/india/report-institutes-like-iits-and-iims-should-be-closed-down-1023204).
26. (Ilaiah 2000a)
27. It is a misconception that Hitler used the Swastika as the Nazi symbol, which is based on the Hakenkreuz or Hooked Cross, a Christain symbol. See: "World Hindu Council of America Initiative Urges New York Senate to Differentiate Between Swastika and the Nazi Hakenkreuz." India New England News. Retrieved October 16, 2021 (https://indianewengland.com/2020/07/world-hindu-council-of-america-initiative-urges-new-york-senate-to-differentiate-between-swastika-and-the-nazi-hakenkreuz/).
28. (Ilaiah 2005)
29. (Ilaiah 2005)
30. (Ilaiah 2016)
31. (Ilaiah 2000b)
32. Methodology and methods are interdependent but distinct ideas. While methodology deals with assumptions, principles and ethics, methods have more to do with specific techniques for data gathering, analysis and reporting. See (Neuman 2006:2)
33. (Ilaiah 2002:vi)
34. (Ilaiah 2020)
35. The only two explicit reference to India in the Bible are in Esther 1:1: and Esther 8:9.

    See: "Esther 1:1." BibleGateway. Retrieved October 28, 2021 (https://www.biblegateway.com/verse/en/Esther%201:1) and "Esther 8:9." BibleGateway. Retrieved October 28, 2021 (https://www.biblegateway.com/verse/en/Esther%208:9)
36. (Ilaiah 2002:97)
37. (Ilaiah 2002:76)

38. "Romila Thapar: 'Who were the Aryans?' is a less important question than what it meant to be 'Aryan'." Scroll.in. Retrieved October 16, 2021 (https://scroll.in/article/912945/romila-thapar-who-were-the-aryans-is-a-less-important-question-than-what-it-meant-to-be-aryan).
39. (Ilaiah 2019b)
40. Ayyappan is a Hindu deity worshipped predominantly in southern India. The most prominent Ayyappan temple is at Sabarimala in Kerala, which in 2018 became the site of a heated and deeply divisive dispute between Hindu practitioners and traditionalists on the one hand and social justice activists on the other hand. For more details watch the video (Rajiv Malhotra Official 2018)
41. (Ilaiah 2019b)
42. (Ilaiah 2018c)
43. (Ilaiah 2002:75-76)
44. (Devi and Subrahmanyam 2014)
45. (O'Malley 1970:331)
46. "Were there any female authors in the Bible?" Grunge. Retrieved June 22, 2022 (https://www.grunge.com/595583/most-impactful-women-of-the-bible/).
47. See: (Fleischer 1981)
48. "Brahminical gods under caste scrutiny." bangaloremirror.indiatimes.com. Retrieved October 28, 2021 (https://bangaloremirror.indiatimes.com/opinion/views/brahminical-gods-under-caste-scrutiny/articleshow/52625856.cms).
49. (Ilaiah 2002:77-78)
50. Modern studies suggest that a number of factors may have contributed to the collapse of the large urban centres of Harappan civilization:
    - *Climate change* – See for example: Marris, Emma. 2014. "Two-hundred-year drought doomed Indus Valley Civilization." Nature. Retrieved October 16, 2021 (https://www.nature.com/articles/nature.2014.14800#b1).
    - *Drying up of the Ghaggar-Hakra River* – See for example: "An Ancient Civilization, Upended by Climate Change." The New York

- Times. Retrieved October 16, 2021 (https://green.blogs.nytimes.com/2012/05/29/an-ancient-civilization-upended-by-climate-change).
- *Earthquakes* – See for example: Prasad, Manika and Amos Nur. 2001. "Tectonic Activity during the Harappan Civilization." Retrieved October 16, 2021 (https://www.researchgate.net/publication/253859373_Tectonic_Activity_during_the_Harappan_Civilization).
- *Infectious diseases like leprosy and tuberculosis* – See for example: Schug et al. 2013. "Infection, Disease, and Biosocial Processes at the End of the Indus Civilization." Retrieved October 16, 2021 (https://www.ncbi.nlm.nih.gov/pmc/articles/PMC3866234).

51. Elst, Koenraad. 1999. *Update on the Aryan Invasion Debate*. Retrieved October 16, 2021 (https://voibooks.bitbucket.io/ait/ch47).

52. Hindu mantra texts are replete with different dhyana shlokas for different rupas of the same deity, and also how a deity is conceptualized and its associated iconography has been continuously evolving over the ages.

53. "Ashtalakshmi." Retrieved October 16, 2021 (https://www.artofliving.org/in-en/ashtalakshmi).

54. *ghaṇṭāśūlahalāni śaṅkha musalē chakraṃ dhanuḥ sāyakaṃ hastābjairdhadatīṃ ghanāntavilasachChītāṃśutulyaprabhāṃ | gaurīdēhasamudbhavāṃ trijagatām ādhārabhūtāṃ mahā pūrvāmatra sarasvatī manubhajē śumbhādidaityārdinīṃ ||* - Dhyana Shloka: Devi Mahatmyam Ch 5

    For original Devanagari text see: "devImAhAtmyam: pa~nchamodhyAyaH." sanskrit.safire.com. Retrieved October 28, 2021 (http://sanskrit.safire.com/pdf/DURGA700color.pdf).

55. "Colonialism/Postcolonialism." Retrieved October 16, 2021 (https://www.routledge.com/ColonialismPostcolonialism/Loomba/p/book/9781138807181).

56. This is a play on the Sanskrit word *vikhandan*, taken from the Hindi translation of *Breaking India* called *Bharat Vikhandan*. Vikhander is used here in the sense of one who breaks or destroys. See: (Malhotra 2014)

57. (Ilaiah 2002:viii-viix)

58. "OBCs form 41% of population: Survey." Retrieved October 16, 2021 (https://timesofindia.indiatimes.com/india/OBCs-form-41-of-population-Survey/articleshow/2328117.cms).

59. (Ilaiah 2002:x-xi)

60. "Adivasis are not Hindus. Lazy colonial census gave them the label." Retrieved October 16, 2021 (https://theprint.in/opinion/adivasis-are-not-hindus-lazy-colonial-census-gave-them-the-label/618051).

61. "Hemant Soren at Harvard conference: Tribals were never Hindus, need Sarna code." Retrieved October 16, 2021 (https://timesofindia.indiatimes.com/city/ranchi/soren-at-harvard-conference-tribals-were-never-hindus-need-sarna-code/articleshow/81140892.cms).

62. (Malhotra 2016)

63. The below four Acts very clearly define the scope of Hinduism.
    - "The Hindu Marriage Act, 1955." High Court of Punjab and Haryana. Retrieved October 16, 2021 (https://highcourtchd.gov.in/hclscc/subpages/pdf_files/4.pdf).
    - "The Hindu Adoption and Maintenance Act, 1956." Tripura Commission for Women. Retrieved October 16, 2021 (http://tcw.nic.in/Acts/Hindu%20adoption%20and%20Maintenance%20Act.pdf).
    - "Hindu Minority and Guardianship Act, 1956." National Commission for Protection of Child Rights. Retrieved October 16, 2021 (http://www.ncpcr.gov.in/view_file.php?fid=423).
    - "The Hindu Succession Act, 1956 (HSA)." National Commission for Women. Retrieved October 16, 2021 (http://ncwapps.nic.in/acts/TheHinduSuccessionAct1956.pdf).

64. See *Introduction* of (Ilaiah 2002:x-xii)

65. (Ilaiah 2002:110)

66. (Ilaiah 2009:237)

67. (Ilaiah 2009:239)

68. "Why did Hinduism create the images of many Gods as against the universal ethic of mono-theism?" (Ilaiah 2002:71)

69. (Ilaiah 2016)

70. (Ilaiah 2009:182)

71. "If you see a snake and a Brahmin, kill the Brahmin first" – E V Ramaswamy Quoted from Barnett, Marguerite Ross. 2015. *The Politics of Cultural Nationalism in South India.* Princeton University Press. PP 71.

72. "Indians and Cows: A Complicated Bond." The New Indian Express. Retrieved October 16, 2021 (https://www.newindianexpress.com/magazine/voices/2021/jul/11/indians-and-cowsa-complicated-bond-2327432.html).

   See also: "Aurochs genetics, a cornerstone of European biodiversity." pp 8. rewildingeurope.com. Retrieved October 28, 2021 (https://rewildingeurope.com/wp-content/uploads/2016/01/Aurochs-genetics_summary_final.pdfhttps://www.newindianexpress.com/magazine/voices/2021/jul/11/indians-and-cowsa-complicated-bond-2327432.html).

73. (Malhotra and Neelakandan 2011)

74. (Sastry and Kalyanasundaram 2019:88)

75. "No evidence for warfare or invasion; Aryan migration too is a myth: B B Lal." NewsGram. Retrieved October 16, 2021 (https://www.newsgram.com/no-evidence-for-warfare-or-invasion-aryan-migration-too-is-a-myth-b-b-lal).

76. See: Sengupta et al. (2005). "Polarity and Temporality of High-Resolution Y-Chromosome Distributions in India Identify Both Indigenous and Exogenous Expansions and Reveal Minor Genetic Influence of Central Asian Pastoralists." Retrieved October 16, 2021 (https://www.ncbi.nlm.nih.gov/pmc/articles/PMC1380230/).

   See also: Underhill et al. (2009). "Separating the post-Glacial coancestry of European and Asian Y chromosomes within haplogroup R1a." Retrieved October 16, 2021 (https://www.ncbi.nlm.nih.gov/pmc/articles/PMC2987245/).

   See also: Tamang and Thangaraj (2012). "Genomic view on the peopling of India." Retrieved October 16, 2021 (https://www.ncbi.nlm.nih.gov/pmc/articles/PMC3514343/)

77. (Narayanan 2019:19)

78. Trautmann, Thomas. 2005. *The Aryan Debate. Oxford University Press* See also: *Bryant, Edwin. 2001. The Quest for the Origins of Vedic Culture: The Indo-Aryan Migration Debate. Oxford University Press.*

79. Staal, Frits. 1988. *Universals studies in Indian logic and linguistics. University of Chicago Press. pp. 47.*

80. Finger, Stanley. 2001. *Origins of Neuroscience: A History of Explorations Into Brain Function*, Oxford University Press, 66.

81. (Rajiv Malhotra Official 2017)
82. "FAQ: What is HIST series?" Infinity Foundation. Retrieved October 16, 2021 (https://infinityfoundation.com/faq/)
83. (Ilaiah 2009:188)
84. For example in the popular the Guru stotram we see the following lines:

    tsarvaśrutiśiroratnavirājita padāmbujaḥ | vedāntāmbujasūryoyaḥ tasmai śrīgurave namaḥ ||
    Salutation to the noble Guru, whose lotus feet are radiant with (the luster of) the crest jewel of all Srutis and who is the sun that causes the Vedanta Lotus (knowledge) to blossom.
    Another example is from the Bhāgavatam:
    gurv-arthe tyakta-rājyo vyacarad anuvanaṁ padma-padbhyāṁ priyāyāḥ pāṇi-sparśākṣamābhyāṁ mṛjita-patha rujo yo harīndrānujābhyām
    To keep the promise of His father intact, Lord Rāmacandra immediately gave up the position of king and, accompanied by His wife, mother Sītā, wandered from one forest to another on His lotus feet, which were so delicate that they were unable to bear even the touch of Sītā's palms. (Śrīmad-Bhāgavatam 9.10.4)

85. For example, Adi Shankara's teacher Govinda Bhagavatpada; in modern times, Srila Prabhupada, the founder of ISKCON.
86. For a detailed commentary on Paduka Puja and its spiritual significance see: "Sandals' Splendor – Glory of Guru Padukas." chinmayamission.com. Retrieved October 28, 2021 (https://www.chinmayamission.com/sandals-splendor-glory-guru-padukas/).
87. "Valmiki Ramayana: Ayodhya Kanda 113." sanskritdocuments.org. Retrieved October 28, 2021 (https://sanskritdocuments.org/sites/valmikiramayan/ayodhya/sarga113/ayodhya_113_frame.htm).
88. *karmaṇyevādhikāraste mā phaleṣu kadācana mā karma-phala-heturbhūrmā te saṅgo 'stvakarmaṇi |* (Bhagavad Gita 2.47)

    You have a right to perform your prescribed duty, but you are not entitled to the fruits of action. Never consider yourself the cause of the results of your activities, and never be attached to not doing your duty.

89. (Ilaiah 2002:28)
90. (Ilaiah 2002:85)

91. In the *Hanuman Chalisa,* Hanuman is described to as *gyana-guna-sagara,* or ocean of wisdom and virtue. See: "Significance of Hanuman Chalisa." www.artofliving.org. Retrieved November 15, 2021 (https://www.artofliving.org/in-en/hanuman/hanuman-chalisa-lyrics-meaning).

   Hanuman is a knower of nine vyakaranas and is said to have learnt the shastras from Surya. See commentary of Swami Sivananda: "Hanuman." www.dlshq.org. Retrieved November 15, 2021 (https://www.dlshq.org/religions/hanuman/).

92. See (Manoharan 2020) on Periyar EV Ramasamy's appropriation of Ravana as a Dravidian hero who fights hegemonic Brahminical nationalistic narratives that celebrated Rama as an ideal.

93. (Ilaiah 2002:81)

94. (Ilaiah 2009:101)

95. *tvam etad adhārayaḥ kṛṣṇāsu rohiṇīṣu ca | paruṣṇīṣu ruśat payaḥ ||* - Rg Veda 8.93.13

    English Translation - "It is you that keep this bright milk in the black, red, and spotted cows."

    "Rig Veda 8.93.13." www.wisdomlib.org. Retrieved October 28, 2021 (https://www.wisdomlib.org/hinduism/book/rig-veda-english-translation/d/doc837112.html).

96. "Yama: Hindu God." britannica.com. Retrieved October 28, 2021 (https://www.britannica.com/topic/Yama-Hindu-god).

97. There are more than one hundred references to *jihad* in the Koran. Some verses are explicit in their description of what all *jihad* entails. See: "164 Jihad Verses in the Koran." answering-islam.org. Retrieved October 28, 2021 (https://https://answering-islam.org/Quran/Themes/jihad_passages.html).

98. "63 Nayanmargal." pradosham.com. Retrieved October 28, 2021 (http://www.pradosham.com/nayanmargal.php).

99. Madabhushini Narasimhacharya. *Sri Ramanuja.* Sahitya Akademi, 2004. p. 11.

100. (Jha 1942:189-198)

101. (Ilaiah 2002:24)

102. (Dharampal 2000:29-30)

103. Traditionally these communities were involved in the disposal of corpses.

104. (Dharampal 2000:54)

105. (Ilaiah 2009:191)

106. See (Malhotra 2013:284-287) for a detailed explanation.

107. (Ilaiah 2009:73)

108. For example, pork is banned in Muslim countries. Horse-meat is banned in the US and UK.

109. Emissions from livestock make up fifteen percent of global emissions (carbon dioxide, methane and nitrous oxide). See: "Rising meat consumption, climate change and pandemics: Untangling the multilevel connections." orfonline.org. Retrieved October 28, 2021 (https://www.orfonline.org/expert-speak/rising-meat-consumption-climate-change-and-pandemics-untangling-the-multilevel-connections-68346).

110. "A Vegan Diet: Eating for the Environment." pcrm.org. Retrieved October 28, 2021 (www.pcrm.org/good-nutrition/vegan-diet-environmen).

111. (Ilaiah 2002:40)

112. (Ilaiah 2002:16)

113. "Religious tolerance was advocated in Europe after centuries of wars between opposing denominations of Christianity, each claiming to be "the one true church" and persecuting followers of "false religions." Tolerance was a political "deal" arranged between enemies to quell the violence (a kind of cease-fire) without yielding any ground. Since it was not based on genuine respect for difference, it inevitably broke down.... I found that while most practitioners of dharma religions (Hinduism, Buddhism, Jainism and Sikhism) readily espouse mutual respect, there is considerable resistance from the Abrahamic faiths.... The idea of "mutual respect" poses a real challenge to Christianity, which insists that salvation is only possible by grace transmitted exclusively through Jesus. Indeed, Lutheran teaching stresses this exclusivity!" (Malhotra 2011)

114. Based on the list of questions in (Malhotra and Neelakandan 2011:188)

115. Prasad, Rajendra. 2009. *A Historical Developmental Study of Classical Indian Philosophy of Morals*, Concept Publishing Company, 12.

116. George, Sobin. 2012. "Dalit Christians in India: Discrimination, Development Deficit and the Question for Group-Specific Policies" Indian Institute of Dalit Studies, Working Paper Series, Vol VI, No. 02

117. (Natarajan 2010)

118. "Discrimination within the Church." The Hindu. Retrieved October 16, 2021 (https://www.thehindu.com/news/national/tamil-nadu/Discrimination-within-the-Church/article14388130.ece).

119. (Rajiv Malhotra Official 2016)

120. "Statistics: Crime: Sexual Violence." Unodc.org. Retrieved October 16, 2021 (http://www.unodc.org/documents/data-and-analysis/statistics/crime/CTS12_Sexual_violence.xls). Incidentally these numbers are way higher than those of India.

121. "Violence Against Women in the United States: Statistics." National Organization for Women. Retrieved October 16, 2021 (https://now.org/resource/violence-against-women-in-the-united-states-statistic).

122. "Black men sentenced to more time for committing the exact same crime as a white person, study finds." The Washington Post. Retrieved October 16, 2021 (https://www.washingtonpost.com/news/wonk/wp/2017/11/16/black-men-sentenced-to-more-time-for-committing-the-exact-same-crime-as-a-white-person-study-finds).

123. "Violence Against Women." The British Institute of Human Rights. Retrieved October 16, 2021 (https://www.bihr.org.uk/vaw).

124. "Countries by murder rate – ranked." The Facts Institute. Retrieved October 16, 2021 (https://www.factsinstitute.com/ranking/countries-by-murder-rate).

125. (Ilaiah 2009:105)

126. "Living Philosophy: Essay/Discussion Questions." Oxford University Press. Retrieved October 16, 2021 (https://global.oup.com/us/companion.websites/9780190628703/sr/ch16/essay/)

127. "Controversial 'miracle man' passes away in Vasai." Hindustan Times. Retrieved October 16, 2021 (https://www.hindustantimes.com/mumbai-news/controversial-miracle-man-passes-away-in-vasai/story-7ffxk1zATKeY2xQaZSOKQM.html).

128. "Matthew 8:28." BibleGateway. Retrieved October 28, 2021 (https://www.biblegateway.com/verse/en/Matthew%208:28https://www.biblegateway.com/verse/en/Esther 1:1)

129. "2 Kings 2:24." BibleGateway. Retrieved October 28, 2021 (https://www.biblegateway.com/verse/en/2%20Kings%202:24https://www.biblegateway.com/verse/en/Esther 1:1)

130. "Ezekiel 37:5." BibleGateway. Retrieved October 28, 2021 (https://www.biblegateway.com/verse/en/Ezekiel%2037:5https://www.biblegateway.com/verse/en/Esther 1:1)

131. "Timeline of the Crisis." BishopAccountability.org. Retrieved October 16, 2021 (https://www.bishop-accountability.org/timeline-of-the-crisis).

132. "Abuse, Cover-Ups and Silence: Why India's Catholic Church Needs a Reformation." The Wire. Retrieved October 16, 2021 (https://thewire.in/religion/abuse-cover-ups-and-silence-why-indias-catholic-church-needs-a-reformation).

133. "Violence in the New Testament." Bible Odyssey. Retrieved October 16, 2021 (https://www.bibleodyssey.org/en/passages/related-articles/violence-in-the-new-testament).

134. Amarasingam, A. (2010). 1. Introduction: What Is The New Atheism?. In *Religion and the new atheism* (pp. 1-8). Brill.

135. (Ilaiah 2009:122)

136. (Malhotra and Neelakandan 2011:178-179)

137. See (Malhotra and Neelakandan 2011) for details on how this Hinduphobic and anti-India ecosystem thrives and prospers with the tacit support of certain influential individuals and their foot-soldiers in academia, activism and different walks of life.

TEN

Wendy Doniger
Quest for Eroticism

H.R. Meera

Wendy Doniger is an American Indologist who is into Sanskrit studies and Indian textual traditions. Holding the Mircea Eliade Distinguished Service Professor of History of Religions at the University of Chicago, she has numerous works connected with various aspects of Hinduism to her name. Her academic activity has spanned over forty years with several tomes in different genres, including interpretive works on religion (works like *Asceticism and Eroticism in the Mythology of Siva* and *The Hindus: An Alternative History*), translations (works such as *The Rig Veda: An Anthology, The Laws of Manu* and *Vatsyayana Kamasutra*) and edited volumes (such as *Karma and Rebirth in Classical Indian Traditions* and *The Norton Anthology of World Religions*). She is one of the most influential academicians in the field, having authored many articles in academic journals, while furthering her reach amongst the masses through her articles in various magazines and newspapers.

Doniger has an ardent following among a certain section of the academia where her work has been hailed for its "path-breaking" approach, whereas it has received severe criticism from another quarter, which considers her writing to be disrespectful of Hinduism. Some traditional scholars prefer to ignore her writing, in the belief that it is highly academic in nature, with limited readership and therefore unlikely to negatively impact *Sanātana dharma*. However, it needs to be recognized that she wields a great influence – both in the academia and on the general public – through her writings and the students she has trained, who produce similar oeuvre on a large scale. One needs to recognize that the trickle-down effect from the academia to the popular narrative, to the culture of a population, needs to be critiqued and refuted at the top, if we are to not lose the narrative down the stream.

In this essay, we attempt to look at the primary ideas that crisscross her various works through a meta-analysis of her methods of analyses, frameworks of analyzes and the manner of expression. We do this by mainly critiquing one of her latest books and citing parallel observations from her other writings.

The book under consideration is, *Against Dharma Dissent in the Ancient Indian Sciences of Sex and Politics* published from Yale University Press in 2016. This is a work that juxtaposes three texts (mainly): *Manusmṛti*, *Arthaśāstra*, and *Kāmasūtra*, and discusses the element of *dharma*, or "the lack thereof", as handled in the three works.

If the entire book is to be summarized in a short paragraph, it is aimed at building a narrative that the two texts, *Arthaśāstra* (AS) and *Kāmasūtra* (KS), are essentially subaltern texts that have sneaked in adhārmic content and have broken the stranglehold of *dharma* that is imposed by *Manusmṛti* (MS). True, they too talk about the *puruṣārtha*-s but according to the author, that is mere "window-dressing." The entire book is about "fleshing out" this idea. The present essay focuses on critiquing this work for the prejudicial stances that are taken by the author with regard to the various topics but more importantly, this aims at highlighting the modus operandi of scholars such as Prof. Doniger. In order to refute all of the contentious points that are made in the work, one would require to key in a tome, rather than attempt to handle it in a chapter of a book and hence, the present essay deals in the various categories via which the mischief is attempted in Doniger's book. As many examples as can be handled in this essay will be provided. Keeping in mind the limited length, a select set of statements made with regard to AS will be dealt with as exemplars.

An Overview of the Book

This is a book with six chapters and an epilogue, notes and bibliography. At the beginning, a "relevant" timeline of events is given. The **first**

chapter deals with the three *puruṣārtha*-s – *dharma, artha* and *kāma*. Here, a fix on time and space is attempted as to when *puruṣārtha*-s were arrived at as three in number, and these three *śāstra*-s are corresponding to the three Aims of Life. There is a discussion on the history of the three texts (i.e which influenced which) and the ranking of the three aims. It is here, that the first glimpse of what is to come in the book is discussed – the "intertextuality" and the "hidden transcript" of *adharma* that is to be found in AS and KS.

The **second chapter** discusses the closeness of AS and KS. The basic premise is that KS derived a lot from AS. Structural similarities and similarities of content are cited and commenting on how both out-Machiavelli Machiavelli.

The **third and fourth** go into details of the *adharma* that is found as an undercurrent in the two texts. The fifth chapter discusses how these two texts have "found a technique" to sneak in the *adharma,* even as they overtly talk of *dharma*. The **sixth** chapter deals with the history and the philosophy of the Cārvāka-s and the Lokāyatika-s and how essentially AS and KS are Cārvāka texts, kept alive through the centuries in a rather covert manner.

The **Epilogue** talks of the how the two texts have "lived on" touching upon the effect of the two texts through the ages till the current era, where the current wave of nationalism and the current government in power are accused of subverting science.

The analysis of this piece of writing of Doniger's is done under several heads and we propose to infer the general scheme of the modus operandi. The following sub-headings touch upon some of the issues handled in the text. Rather than providing rebuttal to all the issues raised (which will take us off at tangents to the central aim of the essay), we attempt mainly to highlight the issues which may be taken up for response in a later work while analyzing the underlying method of building a narrative.

Historicity and Dating

Throughout the work, the dating of works considered differs considerably from the traditional dates. For instance, the *Rāmāyaṇa* is dated between

200 BCE and 200 CE, after the reign of Aśoka, MS placed at 100 CE, AS at 200 CE and KS at 300 CE. Also, she makes a clear distinction that Kautilya (*sic*) who composed AS lived in a different time period from Candragupta Maurya, whose Chief Counselor Cāṇakya (or Kauṭalya) is supposed to have been. The general direction of the assumed dates is in keeping with the latest possible dates to push all the works to this side of the Common Era as possible.[1]

While our focus in this critique is not with regard to dates, it is important to note that there are issues with Doniger's understanding of Indian chronology, as has been pointed out in a detailed critique of Doniger (2009) by Agarwal (2015): for instance, her dates for *Ṛgveda* is 1700-1500 BCE on p.103 while on another (p.121) it is supposed to be from 1200 BCE. Also, expectably, there is an assumption about the Aryan Invasion Theory (Agarwal 2015: Chapter 4), and what is more, she considers no new archaeological evidence from the Sindhu-Sarasvatī sites: while many urban settlements of Harappan (i.e. Sindhu-Sarasvatī) civilization have been discovered in the last thirty years, she names only Harappa and Mohenjodaro as the only two cities discovered (Doniger 2009: 67).

It is interesting to note the "relevant" events mentioned in the timeline (Doniger 2016a) has some considerable gaps. For instance, from the Ghaznavid invasions of 10th century to the beginning of the Mughal empire, there is a void. Neither is there any mention of the Maratha rule in Delhi after the Mughals were ousted. Some points during the colonial rule, followed by 1947 and jumping to the final event with the Bharatiya Janata Party and Narendra Modi getting elected to the Center in 2014. The choice of events and their relevance itself is an interesting study.

With regard to the very dates, problematic assertions there are not a few. For instance, she claims "*Shastras* had been composed from about the sixth century CE," whereas we can easily think of multiple *śāstra* works in the BCE. Pāṇini's Vyākaraṇaśāstra (*Aṣṭādhyāyī*) is dated easily at 5th century BCE. In fact, the endnote 'graciously' cedes that this work "might be as old as 4th c BCE" without even mentioning that Pāṇini himself refers to a great tradition which was already in vogue. This also incidentally reveals one of the typical tactics—currently seen much in the mainstream media—**Claim Big, Retract Small.**[2]

For the period between the fall of the Mauryan Empire in 2nd century BCE and the beginning of the Gupta Empire in 4th century CE, it is claimed that "India experienced a vivid influx of other cultures." Does that mean that there was no stable governance then? The impression given is that there was cultural exchange only then and not earlier. This can be contested.

The purpose of this paper is not to focus on the chronology and historical issues and hence we are merely drawing attention to some issues related to AS/KS/MS and moving on. For instance, she writes, "The *Arthashastra* is about a century older than the *Kamasutra* and gives no evidence of knowledge of any *Kamasutra*." While KS showing similarities to AS merely places AS earlier than KS, there does not seem to be any reason given to why it is placed only one hundred years earlier.

She makes the following assertions:

"... Manu is the only one of the three authors whose night job was as a mythological figure: Manu is recognized by many texts as the son of the Creator and was (by his own testimony in his *dharma-shastra*) present at the original creation; he is also the ancestor of all humans (who are called *manava*, after him). His authority is therefore of a very different nature from that of our other two authors." Doniger (2016a: 8)

"The brilliant chief counselor who helped the Mauryan emperor Chandragupta win and maintain a great empire, beginning in the fourth century BCE. And indeed, there may have been some sort of rudimentary *Arthashastra* at the time of the Mauryas, now lost to us. But the actual text of our *Arthashastra* first began to be compiled in the middle of the first century CE ..." Doniger (2016a: 11)

There are multiple problems in the two sets of assertions above:

1. That the Cāṇakya/Kauṭalya, the Mauryan counselor and Kauṭalya the author of AS are assumed to be different.
2. That there "may have been some sort of rudimentary" AS during

the Mauryan era. There is no reason cited. The many past masters who have been mentioned in AS are completely neglected, indeed even practically called figments of Kauṭalya's imagination.

3. That the AS she refers to – which is AS in its present form – was probably compiled in 1st century CE. Reason? None given.
4. That the AS survived to 20th century CE since it was "probably handed down and frequently recopied within court and government archives" but the "rudimentary" AS was not. Why? No reason given.
5. That MS came directly in its final form while AS went through various iterations.
6. That Manu, the son of the Creator, the ancestor of all humans and the author of MS is essentially the same person while the author of the "rudimentary" AS and "our AS" are different. Also, note the derisive tone while referring to Manu. This is consistently seen throughout the book.

The general "method" while debating the authorship of texts, as we can see, is to assume multiple persons and layers when it suits her (as in the case of AS) and assuming otherwise elsewhere (as in the case of MS). Logical fallacies abound in the reasoning here.

Should These Texts be Compared at all?

On the one hand, it *is* a useful exercise to see how a politico-socio-economical manual like AS considers the nuances of *dharma* spelt out in a *dharmaśāstra* book like MS. One might say that MS contains generic instructions on guarding *dharma,* while a specialized text like AS contextualizes that for its specific field. On the other hand, blindly comparing different fields – whose purposes (and hence, methodologies too) are completely different – is not only useless, but misleading as well.

Throughout the book, AS and KS are invariably pitted against MS (sometimes against the *Mahābhārata*) and sometimes against each other. The structural similarities of the two texts, AS and KS, are repeatedly stressed and this has been also used, in a way, to underscore the joint "adhārmic-ness" of both, supposedly going against the *dharma* that is espoused by MS. The problem comes from the neat one-to-one mapping she wants to make with MS-AS-KS and *dharma-artha-kāma*. More on this in the next section.

The following paragraphs analyze some of her contentious claims:

On the *Puruṣārtha*-s

She claims that "*moksha* is not part of the worldly realm of the *shastras*" (2016a: 10) whereas we see that even in many of the so-called "secular" *śāstra*-s, there is an element that would direct us towards *mokṣa*. The first statements of many *śāstra* works are, in fact, proclaiming that their ultimate purpose is to lead to *mokṣa*. She also claims that amongst the three Aims of Life, *artha* and *kāma* are entirely this worldly, and *dharma* too is primarily this-worldly while working "within the shadow of the other world." (2016a: 10)

The primary reason why the *puruṣārtha*-s are listed in the specific order – as *dharma, artha, kāma* and *mokṣa* – is that *artha* and *kāma* are to be pursued within the limits of *dharma* and *mokṣa*. (Rangapriya Swamiji and Chayapati 2019: 68) Which is why, *kāma* also figures in the list of the Six Enemies – *ariṣaḍvarga* – of *kāma, krodha, lobha, moha, mada* and *mātsarya*. Which is also why Gītācārya says "*dharmāviruddho bhūteṣu kāmo'smi bharatarṣabha*" (Bhagavadgītā 7.11).

The word *dharma* is often translated as "religion." This is perhaps the single most harmful translation and here, separating the other-worldliness of *dharma* from this-worldliness of it and *artha* and *kāma* gives a completely skewed view of the intricate relationship amongst them. She also divides *dharma* as communal, and *artha* and *kāma* as individual. What then of *svadharma*, the *dharma* practised by an individual in his/her unique set of circumstances? What of the aspirations of a nation or an entire community? We can see that this 'communal' versus 'individual' divide is quite artificial.

She equates each of the three texts – MS, AS, and KS – to each of the three *puruṣārtha*-s, *dharma, artha* and *kāma*, which in itself is problematic as there is no such watertight compartmentalization possible. *Dharma* encompasses a whole lot more than how she portrays it and *kāma* is the generic "desire" which cannot be reduced to the sensual pleasure only. She also equates MS to Brahmins, AS to kings and KS for all four classes, rather than taking each of those texts as belonging to the realm that they were meant for – MS as a *dharmaśāstra* text listing out rules, AS as a *śāstra* discussing all aspects of statecraft and KS as a *śāstra* discussing all aspects of one particular type of *kāma*. The neat one-to-one mapping contemplated here and trying to brand the two supposedly standing for *artha* and *kāma* as providing a subaltern view is simply not a tenable claim.

What's in a Name?

She consistently refers to Kauṭalya as Kautilya (*sic*) in order to help her interpret his name as "crooked." Her derision with regard to Manu is evident from the very beginning. Both Kauṭalya and Vātsyāyana are compared to Machiavelli and indeed, it is mentioned multiple times, about how much less crooked Machiavelli was when compared to the authors of AS or KS...or rather, she cites two others – Nathan Tarcov and Max Weber – of saying that, while commenting that Kauṭalya makes Machiavelli look like Mother Teresa. Well, Hitchins showed how Machiavellian Mother Teresa was and so that is a nice conclusion, is it not?[3]

On the Tradition of Citing Pūrvapakṣa

> "Kautilya and Vatsyayana, both evidently fairly liberal Brahmins (Kautilya far more legalistic than Vatsyayana), largely ignored or evaded, rather than challenged, the power of the more traditional Brahmins, who often appear in both the *Arthashastra* and the *Kamasutra* as anonymous "scholars" or "teachers" (*acharyas*)... But Kautilya and Vatsyayana almost always cite such "scholars" only in order to disagree with them, often to mock them." Doniger (2016a: 22)

When an academic discussion and disagreement is interpreted/portrayed as above, it is an attack on the very basis of the intellectual tradition of India (comprising both, discussion and disagreement). When specific scholars are mentioned, she questions the very existence of those and when it is attributed to "*kecit*" or "*ācārya*-s", it is criticized as anonymous. It is a valid practice in Indian tradition, that when one cited a certain *pakṣa* to disagree, the people presenting that *pakṣa* are not named out of propriety, lest it be treated as an ad hominem attack.

This is a deliberate feigning of ignorance to the tradition in order to paint this as a mocking of tradition, leading to undermining of the tradition itself through one of its valuable works.

On Translations

This is where the "magic" is done, if we go by her earlier works too. Deliberate (or may be, merely ignorant) mistranslations of various quotes and individual words are the key to building a thesis which vilify the most revered of symbols/traditions.

Even though there is a note at the beginning of the book that words like *dharma*, *adharma*, *artha*, *kāma*, and *mokṣa* are not translated because they are "the stars of this drama", the author has been creative in coining terms around one key word – *dharma*. Hence, we come across expressions like "ethical dharma" (would there be "unethical dharma"?), "social dharma", and "theological dharma." (2016a: 61)

The very usage of such terms raises questions about what exactly is meant by *dharma* itself. The section on non-translatables in Malhotra (2011) is an eye-opener for many a Hindu. Doniger's tactic here, however, is much more insidious – in that, she assumes one particular meaning of '*dharma*' (which would be applicable only in certain contexts) and uses the word '*dharma*' to mean just that one thing, while tacking on other concepts such as 'ethical', 'social' etc. The tacit assumption of a narrower and stripped-of-the-context meaning of a potent word like '*dharma*' does even greater harm than directly mistranslating it, because it is fixing the word ('*dharma*') itself with that narrow concept and vilifying it.

There is, of course, the method of stripping a verse of its context and producing it as an "evidence" to bolster her argument. Take for instance, she claims "...Prince Rama criticizes his father for giving in to his young wife's sexual blackmail and putting her son on the throne..." while giving the translation of the original as "When I reflect on the disaster and my father's change of heart, it seems to me that kama is a more potent force than either artha or dharma (2.47.8-10)." (Doniger 2016a:14).

The original verses read:

anāthaś ca hi vṛddhaś ca mayā caiva vinā kṛtaḥ |
kiṁ kariṣyati kāmātmā kaikeyyā vaśamāgataḥ ||
idaṁ vyasanam ālokya rājñaś ca mativibhramam |
kāma evārthadharmābhyāṁ garīyān iti me matiḥ || (2.47.8-9)[4]

"[My father] is now without anyone to look after him and he is old. Neither am I near him now. He is now, at the mercy of Kaikeyī, having been indulgent towards her. Seeing this plight of the king and his infatuation, I think *kāma* is a bigger force than *dharma* or *artha*."

(Translation ours)

When one reads the context in which these words appear, it is when Rāma, Lakṣmaṇa and Sītā are spending their first night in the forest and Rāma is trying to persuade Lakṣmaṇa to return to Ayodhyā by first, picturing his father's piteous state, then by picturing Kaikeyī's feeling victorious, having achieved her objective and then the grief of Kausalyā and Sumitrā. The interpretation of "*kāmātmā kaikeyyā vaśam āgataḥ*" as "giving in to young wife's sexual blackmail" is ludicrous, and translating "*mativibhramam*" as "change of heart" rather than "delusional" is simply wrong; but stripping it of the context is the bigger problem. The traditional *ṭīkā*-s have interpreted "*kāmātmā*" as "someone who was strongly desirous of doing *paṭṭābhiṣeka* of Rāma"[5] while other traditional scholars have interpreted the *kāma* of Daśaratha as "indulgence", but portraying him as a lustful king who was sexually blackmailed by Kaikeyī, is a travesty.

A full reading of the *sarga* conveys to us that Rāma's primary motive is to persuade Lakṣmaṇa to return to Ayodhyā (else, why would Vālmīki have said in an earlier verse – *imāḥ saumitraye rāmo vyājahāra kathāḥ śubhāḥ* (2.47.5) - "Rāma said these good words to Saumitri"? How would criticism of his father, and an even harsher criticism of Kaikeyī be deemed *śubhāḥ kathāḥ*?) and to that end, he made an emotional and persuasive argument. Suppressing that context and saying "This reversal of the usual order is a powerful way of saying that his father's values were entirely upside down," (Doniger 2016a: 14) is a very twisted conclusion, where Rāma's own opinion regarding his father's decision, at worst, is that he is under a fit of infatuation. It is **not** that his father's values were upside down. Had the latter indeed been the case, would Daśaratha decide on Rāma's coronation at all? There are many questions indeed that can be raised against such a translation as we see in Doniger (2016a), but we merely point out a sample and move on. It is interesting to see that stripping the context is a favorite weapon used by another Indologist too.[6]

Apart from this brand of mischief, she follows the "usual" path of translating the names of some texts and persons, making them sound utterly ridiculous. For instance, *Pañcatantra* is called the "book of beast fables." "The Arthashastra is generally attributed to Kautilya ("Crookedness"), also called Vishnugupta ("Protected by the god Vishnu") and Chanakya ("Chick-pea")."[7]

It is indeed amusing that while she gets her effects through these various "innovative translations", she discusses – in great detail – translating 'Carvakas' and 'Lokayatikas' as 'materialists/skeptics/hedonists' in the sixth chapter.[8]

While Doniger has translated several texts of the Hindu tradition, not many in academia have actually critiqued her understanding itself, of the source language viz. Sanskrit. Witzel comments on her translation of various texts such as the *Ṛgveda, Jaiminīya Brāhmaṇa* and *Manu Smṛti*.[9] While the scathing critique written by Witzel charges Doniger's writing of flaws "not just in translation" but in interpretations as well, with usage of colloquialisms[10], and with leaving out difficult sentences (to name a few), it is interesting that all the content of this critique is no longer found anywhere on the web – even the web archive. The details of that criticism can now be found only in Rajiv Malhotra's essay on "Wendy's Child Syndrome" and the work *Invading the Sacred* which reproduces that essay and websites that cite from that source. It is interesting that Witzel criticizes Doniger on lack of both philological method and common sense while translating a word (Ramaswamy *et al* 2007: 482). Agarwal (2015) points out several flawed translations such as, *āsakti* being translated as 'addiction' instead of 'Attachment, devotion, fondness; intentness, application' (Apte 2000).

Misinterpretations

Since her avowed aim is to "prove" the *adhārmic* nature of AS and KS, the mentions of *dharma* in those texts are taken to be as mere lip-service or window-dressing. What is said by the authors themselves explicitly, is being denied here. She superimposes her own interpretations again and again. This is in fact, a cruder version of the sophisticated 3D Philology that Pollock puts forth.

Even where Vātsyāyana explicitly talks of how he is describing ways to commit adultery, not to encourage it but to be aware of it, she laughs it off, saying that it is a clever ruse to be a subaltern, *adhārmic* text while living in a "dharmic" world. This is again perhaps the Freudian framework that she is so fond of, rearing its head here – she sees what she herself does.

While a majority of her direct quotes from modern authors consist of excerpts from her ideological kinsfolk, she does quote here and there from other sources. However, interpreting the words so as to suit her ideological proclivities is not uncommon. For instance, she quotes S.K. De (1969: 98)

> "It's worth noting that, generally speaking, while the *dharmashastra* was always anxious to note and reprimand transgression, and enjoined *sadachara* [proper behavior] as determinant of conduct, the idea of sense enjoyment and desire for wealth in accordance with the *shastras* of *artha* and *kama* remained more or less unaffected." and interprets it as "Many of the ideas in these texts were antinomian or transgressive, challenging the dharma tradition and often amounting to a tacit incitement to adharma". Doniger (2016: 21) (*spelling and italics as in Doniger – not as in De*)

A normal reading of the same quote of De would be to take it as – yes, *dharmaśāstra*-s reprimanded transgression and were on the stricter side but people did enjoy *artha* and *kāma* in accordance with those guiding texts.[11] And there is nothing wrong in wanting *artha* and *kāma* but it is well to have some fear of *dharma* – would be the import. Giving an overview of KS, the same De writes in the previous page (1969: 97): "... the impression that is given by Vātsyāyana's work as a whole is that social life, if it gained in material prosperity and aesthetic culture, was still controlled in the main by the ideas of the Dharma-codes."

De goes on to list how KS explains what kind of union is allowed and what is not, and how Vātsyāyana discusses union with lower caste women and even widows; and the circumstances thereof. Is it not evident, that she has again plucked a quote that would suit her theory instead of considering the full context and faithfully reflecting what De has to say on the matter?

The kinds of misinterpretations that she has done are varied and many stem from seeing the text through lens that are not meant to be used. For instance, just as she is trying to conclude that AS and KS are essentially adharmic texts, she has also spoken this about the *Bhagavadgītā* in Drexel University:

> "The Bhagavad Gita is not as nice a book as some Americans think," she said, in a lecture titled "The Complicity of God in the Destruction of the Human Race."
>
> Throughout the Mahabharata, the enormous Hindu epic of which the Gita is a small part, Krishna goads human beings into all sorts of murderous and self-destructive behaviors such as war in order to relieve "mother Earth" of its burdensome human population and the many demons disguised as humans.
>
> "The Gita is a dishonest book; it justifies war," Doniger told the audience of about 150, and later acknowledged: "I'm a pacifist. I don't believe in 'good' wars."
>
> Several in the audience objected to her reading of the Gita, but she made no apologies and "begged" her listeners to plunge deeper into the Upanishads and other great literature of Hinduism.
>
> O'Reilly (2000) as cited in Malhotra (2001)

One only has to see the kinds of interpretations that have come from her protégés and students, to see the importance of having to address the source of misinterpretations since they all have invariably drawn 'inspiration' from her. For instance, compare the translation of the term *paśukarmaratah*[12] in *Devībhāgavata* by Doniger (1975) "he made love in the manner of a mere beast" and by Courtright (1985: 37) "made love to his daughter Sati in the manner of a mere beast" – the phrase "to his daughter Sati" coming straight from his imagination, when there is no hint of incestuous rape or even rape in the text. This is a great example of *śiṣyād icchet parājayam*.[13]

Loaded Wording

The examples in this section would probably be the best samples of propaganda writing, for the kind of overt and covert messaging that is given by the usage of certain expressions. In the following instances, the italics are ours, highlighting this.

The following statements give a sense of the kind of emphasis that she means to give in order to prove her agenda (*italics ours*)(*words within [ ] added by us for clarity*):

> "... the hidden transcript...[was] designed to challenge the *stranglehold of dharma*..." (2016a: 22)

> "...Kautilya to maintain power, Vatsyayana to facilitate pleasure, in both cases *without letting dharma get in their way*." (2016a: 22)

> "...Machiavelli himself is *not nearly as Machiavellian* as they [viz. Kauṭilya and Vātsyāyana] are." (2016a: 25)

> "Kautilya makes *Machiavelli look like Mother Teresa*." (2016a: 25)

> "More precisely, their prose chapters, containing down-to-earth, *often undharmic instructions*, are capped at the ends by one or two verses that often express dharmic exhortations, contradicting the point of the preceding prose." (2016a: 28)

Similar provocative wordings can be found in her other writings and even reviews of other books. For instance, the blurb on the back cover for the Courtright (1985) (which comes from the Foreword for the book) she characterizes Ganeśa as

> "Ganesa has everything that is fascinating to anyone who is interested in religion or India or both: charm, mystery, popularity, *sexual problems, moral ambivalence,* political importance, the works." (Courtright 1985: vii) (*italics ours*)

Imposing Foreign Frameworks

As can be seen in one of the samples cited in the previous section, the concept of "hidden transcripts" is read into the ancient texts. So is the concept of the subaltern view. The reference here is to Scott's theory of a "public transcript" of the open, public interactions of the dominating being separate from the embedded, "hidden transcript" of the critical discourse that goes on amongst the dominated, the oppressed. What needs to be noted here is that Scott is a social scientist who has theorized that the dominated groups criticize the oppressors through what he calls "hidden transcript", which cannot be understood if one analyzes only the "public transcript" of their overt actions and acquiescence. By imposing this alien framework[14] on ancient texts whose time and space, text and context form a complex matrix, none of which have been attempted to be understood in the frameworks that are meant for them, is akin to force-fitting an iron frame to a delicate but brittle filigree work.

On the nature of the text itself, Doniger claims that AS is actually several works bound together by a compiler who divided them into chapters and added the terminal "brahmanical" verses. This is a favorite theory of an old core which had layers added, later improvements and is in keeping with the linear theory of evolution where subsequent modifications are improvements over the previous, "rudimentary" work.

On why neither AS nor KS were easily available, she claims "They were relatively neglected by the scribal traditions all those years because they were dangerous texts, adharmic texts." (Doniger 2016a: 163). There can be so many causes for a text becoming unavailable that it is practically foolhardy to assert its "adhārmic" nature. If that was indeed the criterion for the non-availability of the texts, one could claim that even Bhāsa's plays – which were known only by name and were not discovered until 1912 (Macdonell 1913: 186) – were "adhārmic." When *arthaśāstra* as a field has been spoken of negatively in the context of Duṣyanta refusing to accept Śakuntalā in the play of Kālidāsa (*Śākuntala* 5.25)[15], one could jump to the conclusion that *arthaśāstra* as a field is adhārmic but the words there are to be taken in the context of the play and can be seen as a caution, rather than a general assertion.

The notorious approach Doniger has popularized is to superimpose the Freudian framework on to Indian texts. The description given by an article in *BBC* based on an interview with her in 2002 sums her work up best: "All her special works have revolved around the subject of sex in Sanskrit texts."[16] It even talks about her would-be *pièce de résistance* – a translation of *Kāmasūtra*. Her *Redeeming the Kamasutra* has been published in 2016. Indeed, seeing eroticism in any text that she picks up seems to be her favorite *leitmotif*.[17] For instance, in O'Flaherty (1969) she relies on Levi-Strauss's theorization of Structuralism to 'reconcile' the *tapas* and *kāma* in Lord Śiva, with regard to whom she consistently translates *liṅga* as 'phallus'.[18] She takes up many traditional texts like *purāṇa*-s, *kāvya*-s etc to weave theories around Lord Śiva to portray different aspects of eroticism – such as portrayal of Śiva as an 'ithyphallic ascetic' (Doniger 1975: 9), "Incest of Śiva", "Apparent Lust of an Ascetic" and "Erotic Powers of an Ascetic."[19] To establish that Kāma gains greater power over Śiva after he has been burnt down has been pieced together using various texts like *Pārvatīpariṇaya, Mattavilāsa-prahasana* etc.[20]

Influence

We can see her influence on various academicians who have produced literature of this type and this has also led to the trickle-down effect that we have spoken of earlier. Thanks to this approach we have several 'interpretations' of ideas that are sacred to the Hindus finding their way into places such as museums and encyclopedias[21] and such interpretations are getting mainstreamed both in Western society as well as Indian. Revered figures in Indian heritage such as Ramakrishna Paramahamsa have been 'analyzed' by her students and associates, while she herself has written about our gods like Lord Śiva and Lord Kṛṣṇa and the *Mahābhārata*.[22] Doniger's student, Jeffrey Kripal, in his book *Kali's Child* based on his PhD dissertation[23], makes a study of Ramakrishna Paramahamsa and brings in conclusions about sodomy and homosexuality to name a few faulty and extremely offensive conclusions. As also, any objections the Hindu 'insiders' might have to such interpretations are countered at various levels

1. The ones that are responding are not in the academia and are not 'learned' to respond to the interpretations.[24]

2. Bringing in and cultivating young academicians who are technically 'insiders' but are actually nurtured on only these frameworks so that this work can be carried on and get a legitimacy through the diverse ethnicities of the students involved.[25]

3. Those that criticize her arguments are labeled as supporting the violent, Hindu Right-wing ideology[26] with herself as the scientific-minded fighting the obscurantists.[27]

To add to all of this, it would not hurt to add a victim-card for themselves.[28]

Project of Desacralizing

One of the major projects that have been taken up by Indologists in general has been with regard to Tantra-śāstra, taking it apart to desacralize it, and equating it to only sex.

In a very revealing article in the *Swarajya* online magazine, Malhotra (2015) interviews Stuart Sovatsky, who is an American Indologist and Tantra practitioner initiated by a *guru*. To briefly cite his views, he argues that there is almost no necessity of using psychoanalytic techniques on dhārmic *vidyā*-s and hence what Doniger and others who frequently use this technique are causing distortions. Differentiating psychiatric disorders from the feelings generated by *bhakti* or meditation has been his area and he promotes usage of dhārmic perspectives in therapy and counselling. He argues that if Freud indeed was a "tantrik guru", devout and mature, and learned in *ars erotica* of India (instead of the Judeo-Christain one that it is now), it would have been a different and respectful lens revealing the tantric depths and the hypothetical book of Doniger based on such an analysis would have indeed been "an alternative history" appreciated by all (implying that the current lens applied is inappropriate).

In her review of the work *Kiss of the Yogini*, Doniger (2004) writes in very positive terms the views of 'Whites' on Tantra. As Malhotra points out, Tantra has been equated to sex alone in the work, and the review does not question the presuppositions. And just as she connects the present-day BJP-led NDA government at the Center with the alleged undermining of science by that government to her thesis in Doniger (2016), she labels those who consider Tantra to be a spiritual practice as a hard-line Right-winger of India (Rampersad 2007: 75). The Foreword also conveniently brings in Schweder's theory about native societies not owning their own culture. Politicizing a non-political topic seems to be an attempt to easily ward off any opposition that the assumptions and arguments might stir up. It is interesting to note, however, that Tantra which forms the core of Tibetan Buddhism is left alone, as it has greater implications in the liberal world thanks to the acceptance and clout that the Dalai Lama enjoys, whereas Tantra as related to Hinduism is targeted (even while they share several concepts[29]). She writes and accuses Hindus of being hypocritical ('overcoding' here, being a euphemism for 'duplicity' or 'whitewashing').

> "A system of 'overcoding' permitted high-caste, conformist householder practitioners to have it both ways, to lead a double life by living conventionally while experimenting in secret with Tantric identities. Such people might put on a public face of Hindu orthodoxy." Doniger (2004)

She does acknowledge that the book has some assumptions which cannot be proved and that there is an arbitrariness in assuming parts of the text to be literal or metaphorical[30] but bats for ignoring these anyway because "The argument ...has a political importance that eclipses reservations of this kind..."

As Malhotra sums up succinctly, the 'legacy' of Wendy Doniger is

(i) project their own obsessions tinged by the "prudish and male chauvinistic myths of Abrahamic religions" on to the 'other' viz. Hinduism in this case

(ii) mapping of Hindu Goddess on to Mother Mary – "to preserve cultural supremacy and continuity of identity" or for Hinduphobic agenda such as portraying the Hindu Goddess as symbolizing female violence or male oppression

(iii) projecting the zero-sum game of Abrahamic God versus Satan and the Western myth which is male-dominated where the female has to fight for a position, on to Hinduism. Consequently, self-assured Hindu women rooted in their tradition are shunned even as those wanting to tow the line of Western establishment are preferred and propped up to bolster the White Woman's Burden. The implications of these are serious, in that, it delegitimizes the actual *adhikārin*-s, the true insiders, relegating them to position of 'native informants' or are brought under the tutelage of those who belong to this school of thought. The deeper tradition is compromised by highlighting the understanding only with regard to lower *cakra*-s and ignoring the higher levels of interpretations which would legitimize the tradition. The so-called knowledge production will involve superimposing pieces of texts on to contemporary theories and narratives peppering it with their own imagination and bits and pieces from other Indic traditions, and all this is served up wrapped in jargon. (Rampersad 2007: 104-105).

Conclusion

After the many and extensive attempts of individuals like Rajiv Malhotra to apprise the public to the kind of scholarship that is being produced in the Western academic in the 1990s and 2000s, many commoners have shown a lot of opposition to her works and are taking cognizance of this type of literature. While Malhotra confronted her arguments and narrations – which is desirable – much of it has been dismissed as the reactions by non-academicians.[31] The legal route has been taken in another case. Her book *Hindus: An Alternative History* published by Penguin was sought to be banned by Dinanath Batra which was resolved in a settlement with the publisher withdrawing the book in India. However, it returned via a different publisher.[32] Hence, this one too is not a very effective one. There have been instances where Doniger was attacked in person.[33] This is the least effective one and in fact, this has played into Doniger's hands, as she – and indeed the media – used this as a weapon to both lionize her work and paint the Hindus who opposed it as 'intolerant' and 'violent'.

The rebuttals have come from professionals trained in other fields, who are practising Hindus – who have, in Taleb's terminology, "skin in the game."[34] While they have been ignored, claiming that they are not from the academia, the credentials of the academicians who are engaging in 'interpreting' Hinduism are questionable, as evidenced by their lack of expertise in the fields they are pulling their frameworks from[35] as also their methodologies questioned for their arbitrariness.[36]

It is notable that even with all the flaws, most scholars do not break rank as can be evidenced by the mutual back-patting, support[37], citation and awards that are exchanged[38] with the media providing the ambient background score.

While there have been a few reviews pointing out the flaws in various aspects of her writings, it is necessary to produce detailed critiques basing them in the traditional texts and frameworks by trained insiders, in order to set the narrative right. This is the only way forward in order to level the playing field and bring back balance.

Bibliography

Agarwal, Vishal. (2015). *The New Stereotypes of Hindus in Western Indology.* California, US: CreateSpace Independent Publishing Platform.

Apte, Vaman Shivaram. (2000, 1891[1]). The Student's Sanskrit English Dictionary. Delhi: Motilal Banarsidass.

Bagchi, P.C. (1969, 1937[1]). "Evolution of the Tantras." In Bhattacharyya (1969). pp 211-226.

Banerjee, Aditi. (2007). "Whistleblowers, Witch Hunters and Victims." In Ramaswamy *et al.* pp 249-340.

Basham, A.L. (1986, 1954[1]). *The Wonder That Was India.* Delhi: Rupa Publications.

Bhagavadgītā. See Radhakrishnan.

Bhattacharyya, Haridas. (Ed.) (1969, 1937[1]). *The Cultural Heritage of India. Vol 4: The Religions.* Calcutta: The Ramakrishna Mission Institute of Culture.

Bohtlingk, Otto. (1991). *Sanskrit Worterbuch.* Delhi: Motilal Banarsidass.

Courtright, Paul. (1985). *Ganeśa: Lord of Obstacles, Lord of Beginnings.* London: Oxford University Press.

De, Sushil Kumar. (1969). *Ancient Indian Erotics and Erotic Literature.* Calcutta: Firma K.L. Mukhopadhyay.

Devadhar, C.V. (Ed.) (1972). *Abhijñāna Śākuntalam of Kālidāsa.* Delhi: Motilal Banarsidass.

Doniger, Wendy. (1975). *Hindu Myths: A Sourcebook Translated from Sanskrit.* UK: Penguin.

Doniger, Wendy. (1976). *The Origins of Evil in Hindu Mythology.* Berkeley: University of California Press.

Doniger, Wendy. (1980). *Women, Androgynes, and Other Mythical Beasts.* Chicago: University of Chicago Press.

Doniger, Wendy. (1981). *The Rig Veda: An Anthology.* UK: Penguin.

Doniger, Wendy. (1985). *Tales of Sex and Violence: Folklore, Sacrifice, and Danger in the Jaiminiya Brahmana.* Chicago: University of Chicago Press.

Doniger, Wendy. (1993). *Purana Perennis: Reciprocity and Transformation in Hindu and Jaina Texts.* Albany: SUNY Press.

Doniger, Wendy. (1999). "When a Lingam is Just a Good Cigar: Psychoanalysis and Hindu Sexual Fantasies." In Vaidyanathan and Kripal. pp 279-303.

Doniger, Wendy. (2000). *Laws of Manu.* New Delhi: Penguin Books India.

Doniger, Wendy. (2004). "Tantric bodies." Review of Kiss of the Yogini: Tantric Sex in its South Asian Contexts, by David White. Published in *The Times Literary Supplement* 20 May 2004. Reproduced in https://gaudiyadiscussions.gaudiya.com/topic_2049.html. Accessed on 30 Apr 2020.

Doniger, Wendy. (2009). *The Hindus: An Alternative History.* New York: Penguin Press.

Doniger, Wendy. (2016a). *Against Dharma: Dissent in the Ancient Indian Sciences of Sex and Politics.* New Haven, Connecticut: Yale University Press.

Doniger, Wendy. (2016b). *Redeeming the Kamasutra.* New York: Oxford University Press.

Doniger, Wendy., and Kakar, Sudhir. (2002). *Vatsyayana Kamasutra.* New York: Oxford University Press.

Gita Press Edition. (1960)(Samvat 2017). *Śrīmadvālmīkīya Rāmāyaṇa* (with Hindi Translation). Gorakhpur: Gita Press.

Hegde, Manjushree. (2018). *Reclaiming Rāmāyaṇa: Disentangling the Discourses.* Chennai: Infinity Foundation India.

Hitchens, Christopher and Ali, Tariq. (1994). *Hell's Angel: Mother Teresa of Calcutta.* Documentary. BBC Channel 4.

Hitopadeśa. See Parab.

Kale, M.R. (1981, 1923[1]). *Kumārasambhava of Kālidāsa.* Delhi: Motilal Banarsidass.

Kannan, K.S. (Ed.) (2017). *Western Indology and Its Quest for Power.* Chennai: Infinity Foundation India.

Kannan, K.S. and Meera, H. R. (2017). "Sanskrit: The Phoenix Phenomenon." In Kannan (2017). pp 203-231.

Kazanas, Nicholas. (2001). "Indo-European Deities and the Rgveda." *Journal of Indo-European Studies.* Vol. 29. No.s 3-4. pp 257-293.

Kripal, Jeffrey J. (1998). *Kali's Child: The Mystical and the Erotic in the Life and teaching of Ramakrishna.* Chicago: University of Chicago Press.

Kumārasambhava. See Kale.

Macdonell, A.A. (1913). "Three Plays of Bhasa in the Trivandrum Sanskrit Series." *Journal of the Royal Asiatic Society.* Vol. 45. Issue 1. pp 186-190.

Mahesh, B. (2015). "Doniger's Hindus Returns, 20 Months after its Withdrawal." *Pune Mirror.* 8 December 2015. https://punemirror.indiatimes.com/news/india/Donigers-Hindus-returns-20-months-after-its-withdrawal/articleshow/50080603.cms. Accessed on 14 June 2020.

Malhotra, Rajiv (2001). "RISA Lila I – Wendy's Child Syndrome." Originally published on Sulekha.com. Currently available at https://rajivmalhotra.com/library/articles/risa-lila-1-wendys-child-syndrome/. Accessed on 30 April, 2020.

Malhotra, Rajiv. (2004). " Wendy, Tantra, BJP: What does scholarship have to do with anything these days?". *Post on Abhinava Forum.* 27 May 2004. http://www.svabhinava.org/friends/RajivMalhotra/DeSpiritualizingTantra-frame.php. Accessed on 10 June 2020.

Malhotra, Rajiv. (2011). *Being Different.* New Delhi: Harper Collins Publishers India.

Malhotra, Rajiv. (2015). " 'Oh, Doctor!' Wendy Doniger On The Couch (A Tantric-Psychoanalysis)." *Swarajya.* 30 Sep 2015. https://swarajyamag.com/culture/oh-doctor-wendy-doniger-on-the-couch-a-tantric-psychoanalysis. Accessed on 12 June 2020.

Misra, Nityanand. (2017). "Not Just His Gita, It's Pattanaik's Own Fantasy World." Swarajya. https://swarajyamag.com/culture/not-just-his-gita-its-pattanaiks-own-fantasy-world. Accessed on November 28, 2019.

O'Flaherty, Wendy Doniger. (1969). "Asceticism and Sexuality in the Mythology of Śiva. Part I." *History of Religions.* Vol. 8. No. 4. pp 300-337.

O'Flaherty, Wendy Doniger. (1975). *Mysticism and Eroticism in the Mythology of Śiva.* Delhi: Oxford University Press.

O'Flaherty, Wendy Doniger. (Ed.) (1980). Karma and Rebirth in Classical Indian Traditions. Berkeley: University of California Press.

Parab, Kāśīnāth Pāndurang. (1955). *The Hitopadeśa of Nārāyaṇ Paṇḍit.* Bombay: Nirnaya Sagar Press.

Pollock, Sheldon. (2016). *A Rasa Reader.* New York: Columbia University Press.

Radhakrishnan, S. (Ed.) (Tr.) (1948). *The Bhagavadgītā.* London: George Allen and Unwin Ltd.

Ramaswamy, Krishnan., de Nicolas, Anotnio., and Banerjee, Aditi. (Ed.s) (2007). *Invading the Sacred.* New Delhi: Rupa. Co.

Rāmāyaṇa.　　　See Gita Press.
　　　　　　　　See Shastri.
　　　　　　　　See Vaidya.

Rampersad, Pandita Indrani. (2007). "De-Siritualizing Tantra." In Ramaswamy et al (2007). Pp 96-107.

Rangapriya Swamiji and Chayapati (2019). *Śrīraṅga Vacanāmṛta – Selection of Quotes by Śrīraṅga Mahāguru* (in Kannada). Bangalore: Ashtanga Yoga Vijnana Mandiram.

Rothstein, Edward. (2005). "The Scholar Who Irked Hindu Puritans." *The New York Times*. 31 Jan 2005. https://www.nytimes.com/2005/01/31/books/the-scholar-who-irked-the-hindu-puritans.html. Accessed on 10 June 2020.

Śākuntala. See Devadhar.

Shastri, Shrinivasa Katti Mudholakara. (Ed.) (1991, 1920[1]). *Rāmāyaṇa of Vālmīki* with the commentaries *Tilaka* of Rāma, *Rāmāyaṇaśiromaṇi* of Śivasahāya and *Bhūṣaṇa* of Govinda. Vol. 2. Delhi: Parimal Publications.

Taleb, Nicholas. (2018). *Skin in the Game: Hidden Asymmetries of Daily Life*. London: Penguin Books Limited.

Taylor, McComas. (2011). "Mythology Wars: The Indian Diaspora, "Wendy's Children" and the Struggle for the Hindu Past." *Asian Studies Review*. Vol. 35, Issue – 2. Pp 149-168. https://doi.org/10.1080/10357823.2011.575206

Vaidya, P.L. (Ed.) (1962). *The Ayodhyākāṇḍa*. (Critical Edition). Baroda: Oriental Research Institute.

Vaidyanathan, T.G. and Kripal, Jeffrey J. (1999). *Vishnu on Freud's Desk*. Delhi: Oxford University Press.

Vedantam, Shankar (n.d.). "Wrath Over a Hindu God." *Who Owns Native Culture?*. https://web.williams.edu/AnthSoc/native/courtright.htm. Accessed on 10 June 2020.

Woodward, Hiriam W. (1991). *Asian Art in The Walters Art Gallery: A Selection*. Baltimore: The Trustees of the Walters Art Gallery.

Notes

1. Agarwal (2015: Ch.7) brings out the late dating of the Āraṇyaka-s, Upaniṣad-s, Śrauta-sūtra-s. Chapter 10 of the same book lists out the issues with the dates of the *Rāmāyaṇa* and the *Mahābhārata*.
2. We see similar tactics in other 'stalwarts' of Western Indology, like Prof. Sheldon Pollock (see Kannan and Meera (2017: 225-226)).
3. See Hitchens and Ali (1994).
4. In the Shastri Edition of the *Rāmāyaṇa* this is 2.53.8-9.

5. *Rāmāyaṇaśiromaṇi-ṭīkā* on 2.53.8 (Shastri 1920); Gita Press edition too translates it as *unkī kāmanā mana mein hī rahgayī tathā kaikeyī ke vaśa mein paḍa gaye hai* (1950: 333).

6 See Hegde (2018: 55).

7. Indeed, this tactic of translating the names of the works too – until an insider reader cannot even recognize it while the non-native, outsider will never be able to familiarize oneself with the text – seems to be another standard tactic. See, for instance, Pollock (2016) where *Nāṭyaśāstra* is *The Treatise on Drama*, *Kāvyādarśa* is *The Looking Glass on Poetry* and so on.

8. This is comparable to the tactic "selective playing-up and playing-down" of Pollock that has been highlighted in Kannan and Meera (2017: 225)

9. Prof. Michael Witzel published these on the web which were later made available at The University of Liverpool website (no longer accessible now):

    http://listserv.liv.ac.uk/cgi-bin/wa?A2=ind9511&L=indology&P=R1031

    http://listserv.liv.ac.uk/cgi-bin/wa?A2=ind9511&L=indology&P=R1167

    http://listserv.liv.ac.uk/cgi-bin/wa?A2=ind9511&L=indology&P=R1167

    And also available on https://rajivmalhotra.com/library/articles/risa-lila-1-wendys-child-syndrome/

10. "balls of cow shit, balls of shit", "balls of Indra"

11. Cf. Basham (1986: 217-218) who clearly argues in that in ancient India "worldly wealth was looked on as morally desirable" and that the householder was "encouraged to build up the family fortunes." His portrayal of economic life in the past clearly agrees with the traditional view of the desirability of the *artha* and *kāma* but without transgressing the boundaries of *dharma*.

12. This word (as well as the word *prāṇikriyā*) means "copulation" ("Begattung." See Bohtlingk). This merely refers to the base functions of a human being, quite in keeping with the famous *sūkti*:

    āhāra-nidrā-bhaya-maithunaṁ ca sāmānyam etat paśubhir narāṇām |

    dharmo hi teṣām adhiko viśeṣo dharmeṇa hīnāḥ paśubhis samānāḥ ||
    Hitopadeśa 0.25

    (Eating, sleeping, fear and mating are common to both humans and animals; *dharma* is the speciality in them [=humans]; those who are devoid of *dharma* are equivalent to animals)(*Translation ours*).

It is hence referring only to mating, and in the context, it only refers to Dakṣa mating with his own wife. "...in the manner of a beast" is not warranted in the least.

13. Meaning: One should expect to be defeated by the disciple.

    Indeed, the appreciation expressed for Courtright by Doniger as insightful with regard to his interpretation of the *daṇḍa* held by the *brahmacārin* viz. "From a psychoanalytical perspective, this ritual move may be read as a symbolic castration, in that his ascetic/guardian staff protects him while he remains celibate" (Courtright 1985: 101) can only bring to our mind what a normal Hindu is up against, when we think of the psychological damage it will wreak on our younger generation if exposed to such perverted interpretations.

14. This is again not a new phenomenon as other "Indologists" too have indulged in this exercise. Whether this is just a quest for "something new" for the sake of it, irrespective of how appropriate it is or not, or if this is a deliberate attempt to look at native cultures in a lens that the modern (mostly Western) academia has developed discarding the perspectives of the native cultures themselves – one cannot say easily.

15. *parātisandhānam adhīyate yair vidyeti te santu kilāptavācaḥ* ||

    "while they, forsooth, who make the deception of others their study, calling it a science, are to be considered as worthy of trust!" (*Translation Devadhar*)

16. http://web.archive.org/web/20020911134952/

    http://www.bbc.co.uk/asianlife/tv/network_east_late/biogs/wendy_doniger.shtml

17. A very pointed critique comes from Prof. Kazanas (2001: 283) about Doniger (1980) that she seems to see only erotic functions. This has continued in her later works as well.

18. The glossary of the work (Doniger(1975: 324) gives only the meaning "The phallus, particularly of Śiva" for the word liṅga, whereas, the Sanskrit English dictionary itself lists "a mark , spot , sign , token , badge , emblem , characteristic" as the first amongst 19 meanings.

19. These are all a few of the headings in various chapters of Doniger (1975).

20. That Śiva himself grants permission and power to Kāma after the gods beseech Him to when Śiva has been won over by the tapas of Pārvatī and

the marriage has just taken place (See *Kumārasambhava* 7.92-93) has been twisted to say that Kāma's strength corresponds to Śiva's new 'weakness' (Doniger 1975: 163) rather than see this as Kāma being given a legitimate status as it is deserved in a householder's life.

21. The comparison between Lord Gaṇeśa's trunk to a phallus that has been provided in Woodward (1991: 20) which details of the 'art objects' from Asia in Walters Art Gallery, can be traced to Courtright's work on Gaṇeśa which was initially of interest only in academia. (Courtright 1985). Courtright gets a glowing foreword by Doniger.

22. For instance, her 'interpretation' of an incident narrated in the *Mahābhārata* of an impalement on a stake involves homosexual violation, castration and a super penis. Doniger (1999: 290-291),

23. Kripal (1998)

24. Rampersad (2007:105); Banerjee (2007:322);

25. Malhotra (2001)

26. Rampersad (2007:75); Doniger (2004): "Right-wing Hindu groups, in India and in the diaspora, have increasingly asserted their wish, indeed their right, to control scholarship about Hinduism. They have transformed the soft-core interpretation of Tantra from one among others to the only acceptable view."

27. Ramaswamy (2007: 498): "[Doniger] compares India to Monotheistic, Mal-God cultures, there is "in general an inverse ration between the worship of goddesses and the granting of rights to human women." Doniger does not produce any evidence to substantiate this sweeping statement which she has made, for instance, in *The Washinton Post*, January 20, 2007.

Also see Banerjee (2007: 315).

28. This has been highlighted after comparing articles that came out in Doniger's defence by Rothstein (2005) and WaPo and UChicago Magazine. (Ramaswamy 2007: 364).

29. "There are common elements as well as common bases in the Brāhmaṇical and Buddhist Tantras..." (Bagchi 1969: 220)

30. "...is there any reason to assume that the physically possible act of drinking menstrual blood was done other than that it could be done?" (Doniger 2004)

31. It is very revealing to study the chapter "Character Assassination" in Ramaswamy *et al* (2007) to know the arrogant manner in which Doniger has brushed off attempts to have a meaningful dialogue with a serious, well-read Hindu insider like Rajiv Malhotra – the communique devolving into ad hominem attacks – the same, for instance, that she has used for reviewing the work of Campbell (Banerjee 2007: 306). And again, true to the liberal ilk which liberally uses the victim card, she has made claims of reverse discrimination (Banerjee 2007: 308)

32. Mahesh (2015).

33. See Rothstein (2005).

34. Taleb (2018).

35. For instance, Doniger is not trained in psychology, her translations in Sanskrit have been questioned by Sanskritists like Witzel; Kripal's knowledge of Bengali (and consequently Doniger's expertise in the same, as she was his guide) has been questioned seeing his interpretation of the Bengali original; neither is Kripal trained in psychological theories that he has applied to the case study of Ramakrishna Paramahamsa; Courtright's knowledge of Indian texts have been questioned (Ramaswamy *et al* 2007); Pattanaik (a student of Doniger) has come under critique for his dubious and faulty knowledge of Sanskrit (Mishra 2017).

36. Doniger's arbitrary assumptions with regard to AS have been highlighted in an earlier section. Elsewhere she herself points out the arbitrariness of Courtright's assumptions, while avowedly ignoring it for a 'bigger' purpose (Doniger 2004; Ramaswamy 2007: 191). Such instances are numerous.

37. See Taylor (2011), Vedantam (n.d)

38. For instance, see Banerjee (2007: 336).

Acknowledgments

This book is the result of significant support from several individuals from its perception to final outcome. We begin by thanking the contributors for their valuable time and dedication to this project. Each one of them deserves special credit for their in-depth research, attention to detail, and selfless effort in ensuring that the essays are of the highest academic standards while also keeping in mind a general readership.

Subhodeep Mukhopadhyay, Manogna Sastry, and Divya Reddy were responsible for internal review, editing, and co-ordination with the authors to ensure smooth and efficient completion of the book. They took overall ownership for the quality of the manuscript. Shalini Puthiyedham helped with internal review and editing during the initial stages of the book and provided valuable feedback. Dr. Madhura Ganguli provided excellent inputs on a tight schedule during the final round of editing.

We would also like to thank Shri Sankrant Sanu and Ms. Sanjana Roy Choudhury for their valuable editorial inputs.

It is thanks to the combined efforts of the wonderful team at Infinity Foundation India that the book became possible after it was first conceptualized at their 2019 retreat in Rishikesh, Uttarakhand.

We would like to thank our mentor, Shri Rajiv Malhotra, whose work has inspired us to take up such endeavors. We thank him for his constant guidance, support, and key inputs that always remain invaluable.

Finally, we would like to thank all our donors, supporters, and well-wishers for helping us achieve important milestones in the *Dharmakshetra*. In particular, the following have made significant contributions towards funding this book: Sashi Kejriwal, Mahesh Krishnamurthy, Laxman Prajapat, Hariharan Raghavan and Shasta Foundation.

About the Authors

Dr. K.S. Kannan is the Sant Rajinder Singh Ji Maharaj Chair Professor at IIT-Madras, Chennai. He is the Director of Swadeshi Indology Conference Series, and is the Chief Editor of the series of volumes of the Proceedings of the Conferences. He is also a Member of Indian Institute of Advanced Study, Shimla (nominated by MHRD). A former Professor at Jain University, Bangalore., and former Director, Karnataka Samskrit University, Bangalore, he has taught Sanskrit for more than four decades. He is the recipient of several awards such as the "International Merit Award" for his paper on Machine Translation; the title "Vidyānidhi" was conferred on him by HH Rangapriya Swamiji; and DLitt (*Honoris Causa*) was awarded by Rashtriya Sanskrit Vidya Peetha, Tirupati. His publications include over 30 books (authored/edited) on various subjects covering Vyākaraṇa, Kāvya, Nāṭaka, Āyurveda, and Indology, to name some, and several book chapters, journal articles and invited articles. He has presented numerous papers at national and international conferences, and has delivered invited talks at many prestigious institutions. He is also on the Academic Committees, Board of Studies etc. of various prestigious organisations such as Kavi Kula Guru Kalidasa University, Ramtek, and Veda Vijnana Gurukula, Chennenahalli.

Dr. Sharada Narayanan completed her Ph D (Sanskrit) on *Vakyapadiya* of Bhartrhari from JNU, New Delhi after Samskrita Sahitya exams at Sri Chamarajendra Sanskrit College in Bangalore, M.Sc (Physics) and M.A (Sanskrit) from Bangalore University. Currently teaching Indian Philosophy and Aesthetics in Chennai, she has published and presented papers at various conferences including WSC at Edinburgh, Bangkok and Vancouver. Her published books are on the topics of *Vakyapadiya, Sastradipika (Mimamsa), Gitagovinda of Jayadeva* and *Tirumurai (Tamil)*. She is currently working on a critical study of the *Slokavarttika* of Kumarila Bhatta.

Dr. H.R. Meera is an engineer by qualification, and has worked in India and abroad as a software engineer. Shifting her field of work, she earned an MA in Sanskrit, and got a PhD degree in interdisciplinary studies (Cognitive Linguistics and Alaṅkāra-śāstra) from National Institute of Advanced Studies, Bangalore. She has translated, along with Prof. K.S.Kannan, *Being Different* (of Sri Rajiv Malhotra) into Kannada as *Vibhinnate* (2013). She was involved in the organising of Swadeshi Indology Conferences, and is the Senior Editor for the said Conference Proceedings. She is also the Editor of the volume *Karṇāṭaka Śāstrīya Saṅgīta - Past, Present, and Future*, the Proceedings of the Fifth SI Conference (on Karnatic Classical Music), held in Bangalore (2019). Apart from this, she was invited as a Visiting Professor at the Indian Institute of Advanced Study, Shimla, to deliver three lectures; they are to appear in the form of a monograph from the same institute. A trained Karnatic classical vocalist, she has given public performances, and has presented relevant Sanskrit texts set to music in various lectures and Aṣṭāvadhāna-s.

Manogna Sastry is a Master of Science from the Indian Institute of Astrophysics, with a strong background in theoretical physics and mathematics. She is currently the Team Leader, Research, at Infinity Foundation India, and has served as the Chief Operations Officer and Research Associate at Centre for Fundamental Research and Creative Education for several years previously. Her research interests span major domains including astrophysics, Indology, civilisational studies, consciousness studies, work on Sri Aurobindo, sustainability and education. She has presented at several conferences and published papers in peer-reviewed journals, which can be accessed here: https://independent.academia.edu/ManognaSastry. Manogna is also a passionate sustainability practitioner and environmentalist.

Subhodeep Mukhopadhyay is a civilization studies researcher whose writings on culture, economics and philosophy have appeared in newspapers, magazines and academic journals. His scholarly contributions have provided insights on dharma-religion encounters and on the sociocultural impact of technology. He is the Editor of the *Intellectual Kshatriya* research platform and serves as a Trustee for Infinity Foundation India. Subhodeep is a student of Sanskrit and Vedanta in the traditional mode and a recipient of the *Foundation for Indian Civilization Studies* award 2017. He is a B.Tech in Computer Engineering, MBA (Finance) and MA in Journalism and Mass Communication. For more information, please visit his website: www.subhodeepmukhopadhyay.com

T. N. (Therani Nadathur) Sudarshan is a Computer Scientist by profession, expertise in the fields of AI and related technologies. Apart from technology consulting for start-ups, he is also actively involved with research initiatives at Infinity Foundation. His research and practical interests in the extant civilizational encounter  have been to formalise and enable the reification of the dharma dialectic and its related semantics in the socio-cultural space.

Anurag Sharma is an engineer by training and holds Bachelor's and Master's degrees from the Indian Institute of Technology, Bombay. After a successful career as a research scientist and analyst, Anurag joined Infinity Foundation India, where he is involved in various research activities in the area of civilizational studies. He has a keen interest in the research areas related to ancient Indian history, science, technology and Hindu philosophy. In his spare time, he enjoys travelling and reading.

 **Divya Reddy** is an engineer and a post-graduate in Management who joined Infinity Foundation India as a researcher and host of the 'Youth Asks Series.' At IFI, she is actively involved in consolidating the youth to carry forward the vision and mission of the organization.

Her research interests encompass studying ancient Indian history, science, technology, philosophy, and its relevance in the contemporary world. Her writings have appeared on the *Intellectual Kshatriya* platform of IF.

BOOKS BY INFINITY FOUNDATION

HISTORY OF INDIAN SCIENCE AND TECHNOLOGY

SWADESHI INDOLOGY JOURNALS

For more details, visit: https://www.rajivmalhotra.com/books

GARUDA PRAKASHAN BOOKS

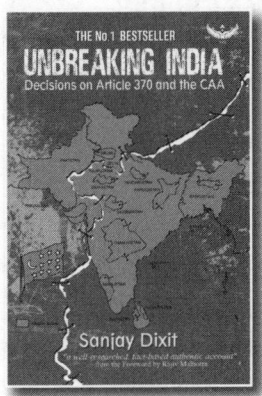

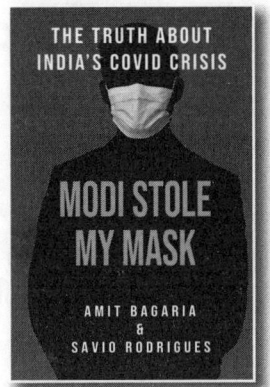

THE GARUDA CLUB
BE THE CHANGE

GET OUR BEST BOOKS EVERY MONTH at a 40% DISCOUNT

- Our best Book shipped free every month
- Best-selling Authors
- Game changing Scholarship

GRPR.IN/GC
Scan Me

*T&C apply.

Register:
Please register your book purchase at **grpr.in/register** to stay in touch and get informed about future books!

To order:
www.garudabooks.com

Follow us:

Website: www.garudabooks.com

www.facebook.com/garudaprakashan/
@garudaprakashan
@garudabooks
/garudabooks

Contact:
Email: contact@garudabooks.com

International queries:
Email: international@garudabooks.com

Walking with the Saints

Dedication

*In Loving Memory of my dear parents
who taught me so much*

Walking with the Saints

by Jenny Child
with a Foreword by The Very Rev. Dr. Robert Willis,
Dean of Canterbury

First published in 2011 by
the columba press
55A Spruce Avenue, Stillorgan Industrial Park,
Blackrock, Co Dublin

Designed by Emer O Boyle
The cover photograph is of St Anselm's Chapel, Canterbury Cathedral
and appears by the kind permission of
Cathedral Enterprises Ltd, 25 Burgate, Canterbury CT1 2HA
Origination by The Columba Press
Printed in Ireland by Gemini International Ltd

ISBN 978 1 85607 758 3

By the Same Author:

Celtic Prayers and Reflections
with a foreword by David Adam
The Columba Press, 2008
ISBN: 978 1 85607 592 3

Lord, Hear Our Prayer
with a foreword by The Most Rev. Rowan Williams
The Columba Press, 2011
ISBN: 978 1 85607 725 5

Copyright © 2011, Jenny Child

Foreword

Throughout the church's history the Christian year has been made holy by the commemoration of saints on different days. Some of the days are well known to us and illustrate a story from the gospels. The nativity of Jesus on Christmas Day sanctifies 25 December as a day of thanksgiving for the incarnation, and the annunciation of the Blessed Virgin Mary on 25 March has been a major festival for most of the church's history. It is the same with the days commemorating the major apostles and evangelists and these festivals give a richness and colour to the year as it preceeds through the seasons. Now in this very well researched book, *Walking with the Saints,* Jenny Child has given us a complete year of saints in which every day commemorates a different name as saints from the different centuries are remembered. There is a wonderful blending of the regular calender of Roman usage with that of the Celtic Church but the saints are not just confined to the British Isles or even Europe. There is an international quality about this collection which makes it not just of historic interest but also of a tapestry of different cultures and spirituality.

It is a great pleasure to write a commendation at the beginning of this interesting and lovely book and I am sure people will find their own pilgrimage helped by *Walking with the Saints.*

Robert Willis
Dean of Canterbury

Introduction

As I walked on the Holy Island of Lindisfarne, I knew that I was following in the footsteps of St Aidan and St Cuthbert who lived there on that beautiful tidal island in Northumbria just south of the Scottish border. I felt moved to write a book to encourage people to 'walk with the saints' in their daily pilgrimage.

In addition to the familiar Biblical saints, I have included lesser known ones as well as some who have been martyred for their faith in our own time. As Brian Wren, the hymn writer says 'there are big saints and little saints'.

I am privileged to work and worship in a holy place – Canterbury Cathedral. Here saints such as Alphege, Dunstan, Anselm and Thomas Becket lived their lives in service to God and humanity. Many people who visit, remark that there is something special about the place. The cathedral, like all holy places, has been sanctified by the prayers and praise of those who have lived and worshipped here through the ages.

Perhaps the best description of a saint comes from a small boy. When asked by his Sunday School teacher 'What is a saint?', he replied, looking at the stained glass window above him, 'A person through whom the light shines.' An apt description.

May God give us grace to follow the saints and to be inspired by their example.

Jenny Child

1 January

The Naming and Circumcision of Jesus

The celebration of this feast is threefold. Firstly, the naming of the infant Jesus according to the angel's words to Mary (Luke 1: 31). Secondly, the sign of the covenant between God and Abraham and his chosen people. Thirdly, the first shedding of Christ's blood.

Lord God, your Son was circumcised in accordance with the law at the beginning of his earthly life. As we begin this New Year, help us to put the past behind us, to use the present wisely and to commit the future into your hands.

2 January

Seraphim of Sarov

Born at Kursk in 1759, the son of a builder, Seraphim became a monk at Sarov in 1779. A year later he fell ill and was confined to bed for three years during which time he had visions of the Virgin Mary and apostles. Ordained a priest in 1793, he then became a hermit living in a wooden hut two hours' walk from his monastery. His life was austere and he spent some years in silence. Nevertheless, he befriended the wild animals which lived in the forest. Inspired by another vision to give up his solitary lifestyle, he decided to offer hospitality to all who came to seek his advice. In his latter years, he greeted everyone with the Easter greeting, 'My joy, Christ is risen.' He died 14 January 1833 and was canonised by the Russian Church in 1903.

Risen Lord, your servant, Seraphim daily experienced the joy of your resurrection. Help us to live as Easter people with "Alleluia" as our song.

3 January

Genevieve

Born at Nanterre, Genevieve became a nun at the age of fifteen. She is reputed to have encouraged Parisians to avert the coming of Attila the Hun by prayer and fasting, so it is not surprising that she was adopted as the patron saint of Paris. She built a church dedicated to St Denys (patron saint of France). When she died miracles took place at her tomb. The people of Paris sought her help in times of national crisis, particularly in 1129 when the city was hit by an epidemic of Ergotism (a poison caused by eating infected rye). Several churches in both France and England are dedicated to her. She is sometimes depicted holding a candle.

God, our refuge, you called Genevieve to encourage her people when in danger. May we turn to you, knowing that nothing can snatch us from your care.

4 January

Elizabeth Seton

Elizabeth Seton was born into a wealthy family in New York on 28 August 1774. When she was nineteen she married a rich businessman, William Magee Seton. During the marriage they had five children. Soon after he was declared bankrupt, her husband died in 1803. Although brought up in the Episcopal Church, she became a Roman Catholic in 1805. This caused a rift in the family. She gave up a life of ease in order to obey God's calling in her life. She founded the Sisters of Charity of New York in Emmitsburg, Maryland to care for poor children. This was the cause to which she devoted her life until she died of tuberculosis at the age of forty-six. In 1975 Pope Paul VI canonised her, making her the first American to be declared a saint.

God of compassion, you called Elizabeth Seton to care for children living in poverty. Give us a generous spirit willing to share with those in need.

5 January

Simeon Stylites

The son of a shepherd born in 390 AD, Simeon practised harsh acts of penance in order to seek forgiveness for his sins. He fasted until he became unconscious and sometimes chained himself to a rock. He spent years of his life perched on the top of pillars. Yet in spite of his extreme behaviour, his preaching was compassionate and showed no trace of fanaticism. When he died in 459 AD, he was buried in Antioch.

Lord God, may we know that salvation is a gift freely given through the death of your Son, not earned by our deeds.

6 January

Epiphany

In the Book of Common Prayer this feast was called 'The Manifestation of Christ to the Gentiles'. This acknowledges the fact that the good news was for everyone, not just for Jews. We know little of the Magi (Wise Men) except that they brought gold, frankincense and myrrh to the child Jesus. People in northern Europe celebrated the Nativity of Christ on 25 December, while those to the east had their festivities on 6 January. The western church adopted the 'twelve days of Christmas' and so 'Twelfth Night' was celebrated on the eve of the Epiphany. By the fifth century the church had a tradition that this was the day on which the Magi arrived to see the infant Christ. This date is the day on which Orthodox Churches celebrate the birth of Christ.

God of majesty, you led the Magi by a star so that the infant Christ might be revealed to all nations. Give to us a glimpse of your eternal glory and open our hearts to the whole human family.

7 January

Kentigerna

Born in Ireland, Kentigerna's father Cellach was the prince of Leinster. She married an Irish prince and had a son Fillan. When her husband died, she decided to leave Ireland and became a nun in Scotland. She died on Inchcailleach in Loch Lomond c.733 AD. A church dedicated to her was built here, the ruins of which remain to this day.

Faithful God, you inspired Kentigerna to renounce a life of royal privilege in order to live in simplicity. Help us to be willing to sacrifice possessions if you call us to do this.

8 January

Gudule, Patron Saint of Brussels

The daughter of Amalberga who was a niece of the emperor Pepin, Gudule was born c.648 AD. Her cousin, Gertrude of Nivelles educated her. However, when her cousin died, Gudule lived in Brabant and devoted her time to prayer and fasting. Each day she would walk two miles from her home to the church at Moorsel to attend the service. When she died in 712 AD, she was buried in her hometown of Hamme. Her remains were then moved to Moorsel and later to Brussels in 978 AD. Finally interred in 1047, in what is now Brussels cathedral, her relics were scattered by the Calvinists in 1579. Gudule is usually depicted carrying a candle or lamp which she would have used on her way to worship.

Give us, O Lord, faithfulness in worshipping you like Gudule, that we may come into your presence regularly and joyfully.

9 January

Hadrian (Adrian) of Canterbury

Born in Africa, Hadrian became a monk and later an abbot of a monastery in Naples. When Deusdedit, the Archbishop of Canterbury died in 664 AD and Wighard, the archbishop-elect in 665 AD, the pope wanted to appoint Hadrian to the See of Canterbury. Hadrian declined but suggested Theodore of Tarsus as a possible candidate. Subsequently, Hadrian was made the abbot of St Augustine's monastery in Canterbury. He laboured there for over forty years teaching students from England and Ireland. When he died in c.709/10 AD, Hadrian was buried in the monastery of SS Peter and Paul in Canterbury.

God of wisdom, your servant, Hadrian laboured faithfully for many years teaching his students. We pray for those who teach that they may always be aware of their great responsibility to those committed to their care.

10 January

William Laud, Archbishop of Canterbury

Born in Reading, Berkshire in 1573, Laud was educated at Reading School and then at St John's College, Oxford. He was ordained in 1601 and was supportive of High Church liturgy and was deeply opposed to the Puritans. Laud held various positions before being consecrated Bishop of St David's Wales in 1622, Bishop of Bath and Wells in 1626 and Bishop of London two years later. He was prominent in government and a keen supporter of King Charles I who appointed him Archbishop of Canterbury in 1633. The Puritans, who held the balance of power, accused him of being a papist because of his High Church leanings. He tried to get all sections of the church to conform including the Presbyterians in Scotland which resulted in the Bishops' Wars. Parliament accused him of treason in 1640 and this lead to his imprisonment in the Tower of London. He was beheaded on 10 January, 1645.

Lord God, help us to be brave to stand up for what we believe in, that strengthened by your grace we may be faithful witnesses to your name.

11 January

Mary Slessor, Missionary in West Africa

In 1848, Mary was born in Aberdeen to working class parents. When she was eleven years old they moved to Dundee seeking to obtain work. Sadly her father was an alcoholic, but Mary's mother made sure that she attended church. It was during these years that Mary developed a real passion for Africa, as she heard missionaries telling of their experiences. In 1875 she went as a teacher to the mission in Calabar, Nigeria, where she endeared herself to the native people as she could speak their language and showed her care for them by ministering to their needs. She adopted unwanted children, particularly twins who were usually killed because of superstition. Mary intervened in disputes and helped the Okoyong people, amongst whom she later settled. She received the Order of St John of Jerusalem in 1913. However, she was very weak from recurring bouts of illness and died in 1915 of a fever. Given a state funeral, she was buried in Nigeria.

Merciful God, you called your servant, Mary Slessor, to show your love to those around her. Fill our hearts with that love that we may seek to care for others as she did.

12 January

Benedict Biscop, Abbot of Wearmouth

Born of a Northumbrian family in 628 AD, Benedict was a servant to King Oswiu till 653 AD. Before he became a monk he travelled with Wilfred (the Elder) to Rome. On his return journey, he spent several months at the monastery at Lerins situated on an island off the south coast of France. While there he decided to become a monk and later was the founder and first abbot of Wearmouth. This first trip whet Benedict's appetite for travel as well as giving him the opportunity to search for beautiful treasures for the English church. Twelve years after his first journey, he accompanied Prince Alchfrith, the king's son to Rome. In 669 AD he was made the abbot of the monastery of SS Peter and Paul at Canterbury. King Egfrith of Northumbria gave him land at Wearmouth in 674 AD to establish his own monastery. Benedict sought far and wide in Europe for skilled craftsmen to build this and later another monastery at Jarrow. On his fifth trip abroad he returned home with relics and precious books and paintings. His final journey to Rome was in 685 AD. Four years later he died after encouraging his monks to keep his library in good repair and to live according to the Rule of St Benedict.

Creative God, help us like Benedict Biscop to appreciate beautiful things and recognise that you are the source of their inspiration.

13 January

Kentigern (Mungo)

He may have been the son of the pagan king of Gododdin, a part of Scotland now called Lothian. His mother was cast adrift in a coracle which was washed ashore in Culross. It was here that she gave birth to her son who was probably illegimate. Kentigern was educated in a nearby monastery by St Serf. He was ordained by an Irish bishop and later built a church near the Molendinar Burn (this area was to become the site of Glasgow). In 543 AD, he was consecrated bishop of Cumbria. However, as he was persecuted by the local king, he fled to Wales where he spent many years in exile. When Riderch Hael became king he asked Kentigern to return to Strathclyde and become its first bishop. He lived at Dumfries and Glasgow where he is said to have been buried in the cathedral when he died in 612 AD. The Coat of Arms of the City of Glasgow shows a fish and a ring, commemorating one of his miracles. He was affectionately called 'Mungo' (dear friend).

We give thanks, O God, for those who like Mungo spread the light of the gospel not only with words but by the example of their lives.

14 January

Sava of Serbia

Sava was born in Bulgaria in 1173, the son of a prince. He became a monk at Mount Athos in 1191, where his father joined him in 1197. Some years later he returned to Serbia where the country was in turmoil because of his brothers' feuding. He enabled the Serbian Orthodox Church to free itself of the jurisdiction of the Greek Orthodox Archbishop of Ohrid. Sava was consecrated the first archbishop of the Serbian Orthodox Church in 1219 by Germanus, the exiled patriarch. He felt his ministry was to evangelise the Serbs. In 1230 he travelled to the Holy Land on pilgrimage and while there he built a monastery dedicated to St John of Jerusalem. Sava encouraged Serbian literature as well as arranging the translation of several Greek works. He died of pneumonia at his birthplace of Tirnovo, Bulgaria in 1235. Recognised as the founder of the independent Serbian Orthodox Church, he is also venerated as the patron saint of education and medicine.

O God, you called Sava to preach the good news to his own people. Empower all evangelists to tell of your saving grace for all people that they might teach your gospel fearlessly and faithfully.

15 January

Ita

She was possibly born near Waterford, Ireland about 475-80 AD. Even as a child she wanted to spend time in prayer. When she moved to Limerick, she founded a convent where she spent much time in prayer and fasting with special devotion to the Holy Trinity. This dedication probably came from a dream which she had as a young girl when an angel offered her three stones. These stones signified the gifts of the Father, the Son and the Holy Spirit. Ita is supposed to have taught several Irish saints including Brendan, to whom she may have given a triad of doctrines. She told him that God loved three things – a pure heart, a simple lifestyle and generous love. It was Ita who first introduced the concept of the saints as 'soul-friends'. This idea came to Ireland from Egypt and North Africa. Tradition has it that she wrote an Irish lullaby to the infant Jesus. Ita spent a great deal of time in solitude but was also a wise counsellor and many came to her seeking advice. She died about 570 AD and there are many churches dedicated to her. Ita is one of the two leading female saints of Ireland along with Brigid.

Merciful Father, we give thanks for all the saints of the Celtic Church, particularly Ita. Give us wisdom to listen and motivation to act.

16 January

Fursey

Bede, the author of the *Ecclesiastical History of the English People*, says that Fursey was born near Lough Corrib, Galway at the end of the sixth century. He was of noble birth and would have had access to sacred writings as well as having the opportunity to observe monastic discipline. He journeyed with Foillan from Ireland to East Anglia in England where he converted the Roman fort of Burgh Castle into a monastery. When King Sigebert, the king of this region, was killed by the pagan King Penda of Mercia, Fursey travelled to France and established a monastery at Lagny-sur-Marne. He died at Mezerolles in 650 AD and was buried at Peronne in Picardy. This monastery later became a hostel for pilgrims travelling to the Holy Land. Bede also recounts Fursey's visions of the afterlife (one of the earliest reported).

Lord God, you allowed Fursey to glimpse your glory. Keep our feet planted firmly on the earth so that we can be used in your service, but may our hearts be fixed on heaven and our eternal home.

17 January

Anthony of Egypt

Anthony was born at Coma in Egypt about 251 AD. While still a young man he sold all his possessions and lived in complete solitude for twenty years. Later he encouraged like-minded Christians during the persecution by the Roman Emperor, Maximinus. Plato and Origen influenced his philosophy of life. Many people regarded him as a worker of miracles as he healed many, both humans and animals. The legend of St Anthony can be seen on the backs of the choir stalls in Carlisle Cathedral in the north of England. He died in 356 AD and was buried according to his wishes, in an unknown place. However, his remains were found in 561 AD and were moved to Alexandria in Egypt.

God of peace, you called your servant Anthony to forsake everything to live a life of solitude in the desert. Help us to make space in our lives to meditate in quiet contemplation and just to be still and know that you are God.

18 January

Prisca

Prisca was a Christian girl who lived in Rome in the early centuries of the Roman Empire. When only thirteen, she was accused of being a Christian and ordered by the emperor to sacrifice to idols. This she refused to do and so she was beaten and thrown into prison. During the night she sang hymns of praise to God, and had a vision of angels. The next day she refused to deny her faith and was thrown to the lions, which sat meekly beside her and did not attack. Finally, she suffered a cruel death by hooks tearing at her flesh and was then beheaded.

O God, be with those who today are still tortured and face death for their Christian faith like Prisca. May we, with them know that ours is an eternal destiny in heaven.

19 January

Wulfstan, Bishop of Worcester

Wulfstan was born to Anglo-Saxon parents in about 1008 at Long Itchington in Warwickshire in England. Ordained in 1038, he was offered a wealthy parish but declined this to become a Benedictine monk at Worcester. Several years later he was made prior and began reforms there. In 1062 he was consecrated Bishop of Worcester where he proved himself to be a caring pastor. He seems to have been the first English bishop to have visited his diocese in an organised manner. Wulfstan achieved the abolition of the slave trade between Bristol and Ireland by his preaching. He was later appointed the suffragan bishop at Canterbury. He is said to have died at the age of eighty-seven while washing the feet of a dozen poor men (he did this daily). This was in 1095 and he was buried in the Crypt of Worcester Cathedral (his shrine is now destroyed). Many people were healed by coming to his tomb.

Merciful God, you called Wulfstan to be a bishop of your Church. Bless all church leaders and help them to be faithful pastors of your people.

20 January

Sebastian

He may have been a Roman soldier and was probably born in Milan, Italy. After seeking to alleviate the suffering of some Christians during the persecution by the Emperor Diocletian, that same emperor ordered him to be killed by arrows. He recovered from this when his wounds were tended by the widow of a martyr. Finally the emperor ordered him to be clubbed to death. The earliest image of him is a mosaic in a Ravenna church. He is the patron saint of archers and many people sought his help in time of plague.

Almighty God, your servant Sebastian, encouraged your followers even when they were faced with death. Help us to be a support to those faced with problems.

21 January

Agnes, Child-Martyr

Agnes lived in Rome and at an early age had consecrated her virginity to God. She refused an arranged marriage and was willing to die for her faith. During the Diocletian persecution she was condemned to death by fire. The flames went out, and so she was killed by the sword. Her name is similar to the Latin word for a lamb (*agnus*) and so she is often depicted with a lamb, or with an angel protecting her. It is thought that she died about 304 AD and her feast day has been celebrated ever since.

God of grace, your child Agnes, sought to live a pure life for you even when faced with death. May we too seek to follow the example of our blessed Saviour, the Lamb of God, in the living of our lives.

22 January

Vincent of Saragossa, Deacon, First Spanish Martyr

Born in Saragossa in Aragon late in the third century, he was ordained a deacon by Valerian, who was his bishop. Both he and the bishop were persecuted by Diocletian and Maximian. Vincent was an eloquent speaker and proclaimed the gospel with such passion that the governor ordered his immediate death. After being imprisoned and starved, his final torture came when he was placed on the rack, then burnt. He died in 304 AD and his relics are claimed by various places from Valencia to Paris. Vincent is often depicted as a deacon holding a palm branch. There are six churches in England dedicated to him.

Almighty God, give us a steadfast faith like Vincent's, that we may have the courage to defend what we believe in and to live it daily.

23 January

John the Almsgiver

Born in Cyprus, John married and his wife had several children. The children all died young and his wife also died. He became patriarch of Alexandria and lived a very simple life giving most of his possessions, even his bedding, to the poor. He founded many hospitals and hostels. John's generosity was extended to everyone he met, regardless of their race or creed. He sought in worship to offer the best he could to God showing his 'worth-ship'. After he died in Cyprus he was buried in Constantinople. His mortal remains were later given by a Turkish sultan to King Matthias of Hungary who arranged for their interment at Bratislava in 1632. He was the patron of the Knights of Malta.

Give us a spirit of generosity, O God, that like John the Almsgiver, we may be willing to share, not only our possessions but also our time.

24 January

Francis de Sales, Bishop of Geneva

Born in 1567 in the castle at Sales in Savoy, Francis was educated in Paris and Padua where he studied theology, philosophy and rhetoric. He was ordained a priest in 1593 and from this time he preached vehemently against Calvinism. Six years later he was appointed Bishop-Coadjutor of Geneva and when he was made the Bishop in 1602, he administered the diocese from Annecy. Roman Catholic worship was outlawed in Geneva until 1799. His writing of the *Introduction to the Devout Life* proved to be very popular and was translated into several languages. As well as being a brilliant preacher he showed great care for the poor. He died at Lyons on 28 December 1622.

Lord, inspire all bishops to live diligent and devout lives like Francis de Sales, that people may be drawn to the faith of Christ because of their example.

25 January

Dwyn, Welsh Virgin

Dwyn was born sometime during the fifth century in Wales. She was the daughter of the Welsh king, Brychan Brycheiniog of Brechon. She felt a particular care for the sick as well as for young people. In fact, she is the Welsh patron of lovers. She herself prayed that she would never want to marry and so she became a nun. Dwyn founded a convent at Llanddwyn, just off the coast of Anglesey. Both Llanddwyn and Porthdwyn in Wales are named in her honour. The former was a rich religious site as many made offerings there, believing that the movement of fish in the water could foretell the future. Many people invoked her prayers for the healing of their animals, even after the Reformation. The ruins of Llanddwyn chapel, a sixteenth century Tudor church at the site of the priory can still be seen, as well as a Latin cross dedicated to St Dwyn. One of her favourite sayings was 'Nothing wins hearts like cheerfulness'. She died in 460 AD.

Creator God, help us to care for all creatures and to seek their welfare as Dwyn, your servant did. May we have a firm resolve to save all animals from unnecessary pain and cruelty.

26 January

Conan, Bishop

Little is known of Conan's early life though he is thought to have been an abbot of a monastery. He may have taught Fiacre who was an Irish hermit. Once he was consecrated a bishop, Conan spent the rest of his life working in the Hebrides and the Isle of Man where several places are named after him. Although he is occasionally referred to as the first Bishop of Sodor, this name is a Viking word meaning 'southern islands' as different from the Shetland and Orkney Islands described as 'northern islands '. Conan died in 648 AD.

God our Shepherd, we pray for bishops seeking to lead your people in remote places as Conan did. Give them the strength and courage they need.

27 January

Angela Merici,
Founder of the Ursuline Order

Angela Merici was born in 1474 near Lake Garda in Italy. Her parents died early in her life and she became a Franciscan tertiary. Several friends joined her and they taught poor girls. They gave themselves to this work under the patronage of Ursula, although they did not take any vows, nor did they wear special clothing. Church authorities did not acknowledge this organisation until 1565, as they would not recognise any orders that were not enclosed. Today many describe her Order as the 'oldest and most considerable teaching' order of women in the Roman Catholic Church. She died in 1540 and was canonised in 1807.

Lord, you taught the poor and had compassion on them. Bless all teachers seeking to improve the lives of needy children by improving their education.

28 January

Thomas Aquinas

Born in Rocca Secca near Aquino, Italy about 1225, Thomas was educated from an early age at the monastery of Monte Cassino (founded by St Benedict). Later he studied at the university at Naples for five years. He was drawn to the simple lives of the Dominican friars who went about begging alms. His family were horrified at this and as a result they imprisoned Thomas for over a year. Nevertheless, he joined the Dominicans in 1244. He spent the rest of his short life studying and lecturing in Paris and in Italy. He was a deep thinker and wrote several theological works as well as commentaries on the Creed, the Lord's Prayer and the Hail Mary. He died in 1274 while on his way to the Council of Lyons in France. Canonised in 1323, his remains were later moved to Saint-Sernin, Toulouse in 1368. His final resting place is the Jacobins' church in Toulouse where his relics were placed in 1974.

God of wisdom, you inspired Thomas Aquinas to enrich the church with learning and holiness. Bless those who study your Word, that they may find your truth revealed and may they help others to understand its mysteries.

29 January

Gildas

Possibly born in Scotland c.500 AD, he became a monk at Llaniltud in southern Wales. Prior to this he may have been married and then widowed. He visited Ireland and some Irish monks became his followers. In his famous work, *De excidio Britanniae*, written c.540 AD he condemned both secular rulers and the clergy for their decadence and blamed them for the victory of the Anglo-Saxon invaders. Gildas lived as a hermit on Flatholm Island in the Bristol Channel before later moving to Brittany where he founded another island monastery. It was here that he died c.570 AD.

Steadfast God, give us like Gildas, courage to stand up for what we believe to be right, but may our comments be tempered with love.

30 January

Bathild

Bathild was born in England. She was sold into slavery and was taken to Neustria (western part of the kingdom of the Franks). There she was employed in the king's household and later married King Clovis II in 649 AD. They had three sons, Clotaire III, Childeric II, and Thierry III – all of whom became kings. When King Clovis died in 657 AD, Bathild acted as regent until the young Clotaire was old enough to rule. She founded a Benedictine convent at Chelles and also St Denis monastery at Corbie. After Clotaire became king, she retired to her convent at Chelles where she died in 680 AD.

Almighty God, give grace to Christian kings and queens that they may rule with justice and integrity.

31 January

John Bosco, Priest and Founder of the Salesians

The son of a peasant family, John was born in Piedmont in the Turin region of Italy in 1815. His father died while he was still very young and his mother struggled in extreme poverty. He was ordained in 1841 and worked among the poor and those in prison. Even politicians who were opposed to the church, admired his tireless work with homeless young people. He set up evening classes and industrial schools which others later sought to emulate. Bosco tried to instil in children a real love of beauty and nature. He founded a religious order in 1859 which was called the Pious Society of St Francis de Sales, better known as the Salesians. By the time of his death in 1888, this order was firmly established in several countries.

Loving God, we remember those who labour in extreme poverty with limited resources. Encourage those, who like John Bosco, seek to minister to them.

1 February

Brigid,
Abbess of Kildare

Also known as Bride, Brigid is thought to have been born to humble parents near Kildare in Ireland and may have been baptised by St Patrick. Brigid lived a life showing compassion and caring to those around her. In some ways her image fused with that of the Virgin Mary. Some believe that she may have been consecrated a bishop by Bishop Ibor. This story was probably spread by those who wanted to increase the importance of the abbey at Kildare. Brigid is the patron saint of poets, healers and blacksmiths. Her symbol shows a cow lying at her feet. This is reminiscent of her time when she was a milkmaid in a convent. She died c.525 AD and her tunic is kept in St Donatians church in Bruges, Belgium.

God of compassion, may we, like Brigid, show gentleness in our dealings with others that we may be Christ to all those we meet.

2 February

Presentation of Christ in the Temple

The Jewish law required a woman who had given birth to a male child to be 'cleansed' forty days after this event. Until this ceremony took place, she was not allowed to touch anything considered holy, nor to enter the sanctuary. When Mary and Joseph took the Baby Jesus to the Temple, Simeon, a faithful servant of God prophesied that he would be the 'light to enlighten the nations'. Anna, the prophetess who spent all her time, since early widowhood, in the Temple, gave thanks to God when she saw the child. The use of candles at this feast, also called Candlemas, proclaims Christ, the Light of the World. This day marks the end of the Church's celebration of the Christmas season.

Heavenly Father, your Son was presented in the Temple to fulfil the law. Grant that we may offer pure and holy lives to you.

3 February

Anskar, Archbishop of Hamburg

Anskar was born near Amiens in France and became a monk at Picardy. He then moved to Westphalia (the region between the rivers Rhine and Weser, north of the Ruhr River). The Danish King Harold, who had become a Christian while living in exile, asked Anskar to return to Denmark with him. After spending time in Sweden, Anskar was consecrated Bishop of Hamburg in 832 AD. In 845 AD the Vikings raided Hamburg. Anskar was appointed Archbishop of Hamburg and Bremen. He lived a life of humility and deprivation (even wearing a hair-shirt next to his skin). Anskar showed great kindness to the poor. He evangelised the Danes and was made their patron saint. In 865 AD Archbishop Anskar died at Bremen where he was buried.

God of power and glory, you called your servant Anskar, to bring the good news to the Nordic peoples. Bless all those who preach your word in obedience to your command to go into all the world spreading the gospel. We pray for the people of Denmark that inspired by the example of Anskar, they may seek to please you.

4 February

Gilbert of Sempringham

Gilbert was born c.1083, the son of a Norman knight and an Anglo-Saxon mother. Due to some physical disability he was unable to follow his father's profession and so went to Paris to study. Although not yet ordained, he cared for the parishes of Sempringham and West Torrington in Lincolnshire. The income which he received from these he gave to the poor. He became a clerk in the Bishop of Lincoln's household in 1122. After ordination, he returned to his parish where he set aside a house in which holy women lived. In 1163 the Gilbertines (the Order of monks which he had founded) helped Thomas Becket, the Archbishop of Canterbury to escape to Europe. In so doing they incurred the wrath of King Henry II, whose ill-chosen words led to the murder of the archbishop in his own Cathedral at Canterbury. Gilbert lived till he was almost ninety and died in 1189. During his life he founded many monasteries as well as hospitals for lepers and orphanages.

May we like Gilbert use our income wisely and generously, O Lord, to help those in genuine need.

5 February

Agatha

Little is known of her early life but it is thought that Agatha was born in Catania in Sicily. She wished to remain a virgin but was tortured by a spurned suitor who used the rack, rods and fire to try to make her renounce her faith. Her breasts were cut off as part of this persecution which happened while Quintinian was consul. She died c.251 AD. Agatha is the patron saint of bell founders and bakers as well as those suffering from breast cancer.

Unchanging God, we pray for those who face torture and even death for their Christian faith. May they have the strength and courage to face any ordeal.

6 February

Martyrs of Japan, 1597

Francis Xavier was the first Christian missionary to visit Japan in 1549. Almost fifty years later there were 2,000 believers. When Hideyoshi, the Japanese ruler, came to power, he decided there were too many Christians and ordered them to be persecuted. In 1597, twenty-six people were murdered for their faith: Paul Miki, a Japanese priest, several Franciscans and Japanese lay people as well as a Korean. They all suffered the cruelty of having their left ears cut off, before being crucified at Nagasaki. This persecution continued for another thirty-five years, during which time many sacrificed their lives for their faith.

'The blood of the martyrs is the seed of the church'. Lord, we give thanks for all those in every age who have laid down their lives for their faith.

7 February

Ronan,
Bishop of Kilmaronen

No details of the date of Ronan's birth are available, nor indeed of his death. He was the bishop of Kilmaronen in Lennox in Scotland. Sir Walter Scott's novel *Innerleithen* made St Ronan's well a popular site in Peeblesshire. Legend has is that when Ronan moved to the valley to live, he drove out the Devil. This event is celebrated every July with a week of festivities when a schoolboy is chosen to represent St Ronan and given a bishop's staff (crozier) to drive out the Devil.

Draw near to us, Lord, when we are tempted and give us strength not to yield to temptation.

8 February

Jerome Emiliani

The son of a wealthy Italian family, Jerome was born in 1481 in Venice. His father died when Jerome was a teenager and he ran away from home at the age of fifteen. After living a riotous life, he joined the Venetian army in 1506 and was appointed commander of Castelnuovo (Treviso). He was taken prisoner during a siege but managed to escape from the dungeon. Jerome was ordained priest in 1518 and worked tirelessly to relieve people's suffering. He housed orphans in his own home as well as tending the sick. At night he walked the streets to bury those who had died of the plague by the roadside. Not surprisingly, he caught the plague himself, but when he recovered in 1531, he founded hospitals, orphanages and a shelter for repentant prostitutes. A small group of monks assisted him in this ministry and so began the Order of Somaschi (Company of Servants of the Poor). He died in 1537 after a life of service to the poor. He is the patron saint of orphans and abandoned children.

Lord God, we pray for those who spend their lives caring for others. Strengthen their resolve to minister to these little ones who are committed to their care.

9 February

Teilo

Possibly born at Penally in Wales in the sixth century, Teilo spent most of his working life as a monk and later as a bishop, in the steep valleys of Llandeilo Fawr. This area now forms one of the most remote parts of the Brecon Beacons National Park. The Gospels of Chad, kept by a church in Wales, show entries indicating that Teilo was venerated in the ninth century. When Teilo died at Llandeilo Fawr, three towns claimed his body – Llandeilo, Penally and Llandaff. His tomb is in Llandaff Cathedral and oaths were taken on it. Several churches are dedicated to him in Carmarthenshire, Glamorgan and Pembrokeshire in Wales. His feast day is celebrated in Wales and Brittany.

God of eternity, we praise your name for all your saints, who like Teilo, have served you throughout the ages.

10 February

Scholastica, Abbess of Plombariola

The sister of Benedict and the first nun to live according to his Rule, Scholastica was born at Nursia, Italy c.480 AD. Her convent was in Plombariola near Monte Cassino. She and her brother met each year for spiritual counsel and prayer. On the last visit which was three days before her death, Scholastica begged Benedict to stay longer. A severe thunderstorm managed to keep him with her longer than he had planned. She died c.543 AD and was buried in the tomb Benedict had prepared for himself. She is the patron saint of Benedictine convents.

God of wisdom and knowledge, bless those who teach and make them aware of the great responsibility that is theirs that they may love and nurture their students.

11 February

Gobnet

Gobnet was born in County Clare in Ireland in the fifth century. She escaped to the Aran Islands to avoid a family quarrel. While she was there she had a vision showing her that this was not to be her final resting place. She was to seek out a place where she would see nine white deer grazing and so she settled near Dungarvan, where she saw white deer. Gobnet founded the church at Kilgobnet near Dungarvan and later moved to Ballyvourney where she established a convent according to the guidance of St Abban. In art she is often depicted with bees as she was a keen apiarist.

God of peace, be with those, who like Gobnet, have left home because of friction and misunderstanding. May they know that you are ever constant and that you are always with them.

12 February

Ethilwald, Bishop of Lindisfarne

Northumbrian born, Ethilwald became a monk at Melrose, Scotland where he was later appointed prior and then abbot. When Edfrith, bishop of Lindisfarne and the scribe of the Lindisfarne Gospels, died, Ethilwald (Ethelwald) was chosen to succeed him. He was supportive of Edfrith's work and arranged for a hermit called Billfrith to make a binding adorned with precious stones for the Lindisfarne Gospels (this binding is now lost). The pages of the book were probably stitched by Bishop Ethilwald himself. He died in 740 AD, and when Viking raids caused the monks of Lindisfarne to take the body of St Cuthbert and flee, Ethilwald's remains accompanied them. A stone cross bearing his name was removed from Lindisfarne to Durham, where St Cuthbert's relics are also buried.

Creator God, you inspire beauty and creativity, bless those who use their artistic skills to bring glory to your name and delight to the eye.

13 February

Modomnoc

Possibly a member of the royal household of the O'Neill family in Ireland, Modomnoc was born in the sixth century. He studied in the monastery founded by St David at Menevia in Pembrokeshire, Wales. Here one of his duties was looking after the bees. It is said that when a swarm of bees settled on the ship in which he was travelling he knew that it was time to return to his native Ireland. So bee-keeping was introduced to Ireland as he took the swarm and made hives for them when he decided to live in Tibberaghny, Co Kilkenny, Ireland. Some writers claim that he may have been Bishop of Ossory.

We thank you, O God, for the signs you give us of your guidance. Make us astute to be aware of your leading.

14 February

Cyril and Methodius

These two brothers were born in Thessalonica and both showed an ability to speak several languages from an early age. They were both ordained and travelled to Constantinople (modern day Istanbul). The emperor sent them to preach the gospel in Moravia. Cyril and Methodius invented the Glagolithic alphabet (the forerunner of the Cyrillic (Russian) alphabet). They were known as the 'Apostles to the Slavs' because they established Slavonic literature. Cyril became a monk shortly before his death. Methodius was consecrated Archbishop of Sirmium and returned to Moravia where he was a great advocate of ecumenism. Pope John Paul II made them patrons of Europe. Today both the Christian Churches in the West and the East celebrate these two missionaries.

God of every nation, you gave your servants Cyril and Methodius the ability to preach the gospel to the Slavs in their own language. Bless all those who translate the scriptures into many languages and dialects that they may be guided by your Holy Spirit.

15 February

Sigfrid, Apostle of Sweden

Possibly of English birth, Sigfrid became a monk at Glastonbury. He was sent by King Ethelred to King Olaf Trggvason, king of Norway to evangelise the Norwegians and the Swedes. Two companions, who were also destined to become bishops, accompanied Sigfrid on this missionary journey in the eleventh century. He baptised the king of Sweden and built a church at Vaxjo where he was the bishop. Here he was assisted by his nephews, all of whom were later murdered. Sigfrid, seeking to put his faith into action, asked the king to show mercy and to spare the lives of the murderers. He died at Vaxjo in 1045 and is especially venerated throughout Scandinavia.

Lord God, be with all missionaries who leave their homes and native lands to share the good news of the gospel.

16 February

Juliana,
Virgin and Martyr

Little is known of her early life. Legend tells that she had a verbal battle with the Devil when he tried to persuade her to marry. She finally met her end at Cumae or Naples. Pope Gregory the Great asked Fortunatus, the bishop of Naples for her relics so that they could be placed in an oratory built by a wealthy woman on her property and dedicated to Juliana. Her life has been celebrated in England since the time of Bede, the great church historian.

Ever present God, when we feel Satan subtly tempting us from the path you would have us follow, may we call upon your name in our time of need.

17 February

Janani Luwum,
Archbishop of Uganda and Martyr

Born in 1922 at Acholi, Uganda, Janani's first job was as a goatherd. He showed a great aptitude for learning when given the opportunity. He became a teacher and was converted to Christianity in 1948. A year later he began study at Buwalasi Theological college and was ordained in 1956. He was consecrated Bishop of Northern Uganda in 1969 and he became Archbishop of Uganda in 1974. Three years prior to this Idi Amin had seized power in a military coup. His regime was harsh and undemocratic. Janani Luwum and some bishops sent a letter to the president protesting the virtual sanctioning of murder by government officials. On 16 February 1977, Archbishop Luwum and two government officers were supposedly 'killed' in a car accident. Their bullet-ridden bodies proved that they had been murdered at the instigation of Idi Amin. A statue of Archbishop Luwum can be seen with other twentieth century martyrs on the west front of Westminster Abbey in London.

We give thanks, O Lord, for your servant Janani Luwum's life, for his shining witness even in the face of death and the assurance that evil will never overcome your light and goodness.

18 February

Colman, Bishop of Lindisfarne

Although born in Ireland, Colman trained on Iona where he became a monk. Later he was consecrated Bishop of Lindisfarne (Holy Island), a position he held from 661 AD to 664 AD. At the Synod of Whitby in 664 AD, the dating of Easter and the style of the monks' tonsures were discussed. King Oswiu declared that the Roman usage should be adopted rather than the older way of the Celtic Church. As a result of this decision, Colman left Lindisfarne in Northumbria with thirty monks and returned to Iona. He later settled on the Isle of Inishbofin with those of Irish descent. The English monks settled in County Mayo. Colman died c.676 AD.

Holy God, we give thanks for those who have formed part of our Christian heritage. May we value it and treasure the examples of these early saints.

19 February

Odran

The *Life of Patrick* written by Jocelyn, describes Odran as the driver of St Patrick's cart. Odran knew that there were many who wished Patrick dead and so he prevailed upon Patrick to drive the horses pulling the cart while he pretended to be the saint. Subsequently, they were ambushed and Odran was killed by those who lay in wait to kill Patrick. As they thrust their spears into Odran, Patrick saw angels bearing his faithful servant's soul to heaven.

Your faithfulness is great, O God, and new every morning. We pause to reflect on the lives of the 'little saints', so often the unsung heroes in the scheme of things.

20 February

Saints and Martyrs of Africa

Over the centuries many Christians have lived and died in Africa for their faith. Charles de Foucald in the Sahara, Peter Masiza the holy man of the Transkei, Thomas Bako in Nigeria, Yowa Kanamuzey in Rwanda, Andrew Kaguru in Kenya and countless others have died the martyrs' death.

Loving God, we pray for the people of Kenya as they suffer upheaval and bloodshed. We praise your name for those in the present day as well as in the past who have given their lives for the sake of the gospel.

21 February

Peter Damian

Born in Ravenna, Italy in 1007, Peter's parents both died in his early childhood. Consequently he was educated by his brother and later became a teacher. He then decided to enter a monastery and for some time lived a simple life as a hermit. Appointed abbot of a monastery in 1043, he showed kindness and energy in his ministry but could not abide laziness. In 1057 he was consecrated Bishop of Ostia in Italy and undertook several diplomatic missions while in this office. However, he sought the life of a monk and was relieved of his episcopal duties by Nicholas II. In his old age he enjoyed wood-carving and died in 1072 while on a journey to Rome.

Lord our God, help us to seek a simple lifestyle and to be content with what we have, rather than being lured by materialism.

22 February

Margaret of Cortona

The daughter of a farmer, Margaret was born in Tuscany, Italy c.1247. Her mother died early in life and her father remarried, but unfortunately her stepmother mistreated her. For some nine years she was the mistress of a knight and had a son. The knight was murdered and she and her son were cared for by two women recommended by the Franciscan friars. Margaret showed her penance publicly for her past life and later spent her time nursing the poor and the sick. She is reputed to have cured people miraculously. In 1297 she died and was buried in Cortona.

God of wholeness and healing, we ask that you will bless those involved in nursing the sick and tending to the needs of the poor.

23 February

Polycarp, Bishop of Smyrna

Polycarp was a bishop and martyr of the second century. He stood firm in his Christian belief against the heresies of the day. Polycarp was a disciple of St John the apostle and was made bishop of Smyrna. He was known for his wisdom and holiness. Blamed for the death of a youth at a pagan festival, he was captured and ordered to renounce his faith in Christ. He said that he would not deny his Saviour, and so, Polycarp was killed by a sword wielded by an official and then his body was burnt. He probably died c.155 AD or some years later.

God of truth, you gave Polycarp grace not only to live out his faith but also courage to die for it. We pray for Christians who are persecuted that they may know you are with them always, even to the end of the world.

24 February

Montanus, Lucius and Companions

These were amongst the earliest Christian martyrs. They were imprisoned in Carthage for their faith during the persecution begun by the Emperor Valerian. Montanus had a vision while in prison which showed stains on his chest. He had quarrelled with a fellow Christian called Julian and had not forgiven him. Lucius told him that these stains showed that he had not forgiven Julian. When after many months' imprisonment, they all confessed to being Christians they were executed. Lucius who was in poor health was the first to die. Montanus addressed the crowd, berating those who had denied their Christian faith as well as exhorting the believers to stand firm and not waver in their allegiance to Christ.

Our Father, help us to forgive those with whom we have quarrelled, knowing that unless we forgive others, you will not forgive us.

25 February

Caesarius of Nazianzen

He lived in the fourth century in what is today known as Turkey. His father was Bishop of Nazianzen. Gregory, the brother of Caesarius, wanted to be a priest, but Caesarius had his mind set on becoming a doctor. He completed his studies in medicine at Constantinople where he became a trusted physician. In fact, the Emperor Constantius wanted him to be his doctor. A court official named Julian, who had renounced his Christian faith, tried to tempt Caesarius to do the same by offering bribes and flattery. In 368 AD Caesarius almost lost his life in an earthquake and he took this as a sign from God that he should live a life of prayer. As a result he gave everything he owned to the poor and devoted himself to a quiet, prayerful life. He died in 369 AD.

Save us, Lord, from being lured from following your path by the flattering words of others, that like, Caesarius, we may remain true to our calling.

26 February

Porphyrius

Born in the fifth century, Porphyrius was the son of wealthy parents. At the age of twenty-five, he left home in Thessalonica in Greece to travel to Egypt, where he entered a monastery. Five years later he made a journey to the Holy Land, for he had a great desire to visit the places where Jesus had actually spent time while on earth. During his travels he saw how the poor suffered and so, he sold everything he possessed and gave the money to those in need. He was ordained a priest at the age of forty and was later consecrated Bishop of Gaza. Although he had many enemies who opposed him, he spent much time ministering to the Christians there, dying in 420 AD.

God of peace, we pray for the people of the Holy Land in the conflicts and warfare they suffer. Give all factions a willingness to listen to each other, and to show tolerance and justice to all who live in this place where our Saviour lived and walked.

27 February

George Herbert, Priest, Poet

George was born in 1593 to a wealthy aristocratic family in Pembroke in Wales. He studied at Cambridge in 1614 and later as a fellow of Trinity College. Herbert became a public orator and then a member of parliament. Ordained deacon in 1626, he married three years later and became a priest in 1630. As vicar of Bemerton near Salisbury, he ministered to those in his care during his short life. He wrote *The Country Parson*, a treatise about the life of a priest, as well as composing poetry. The words of his hymn 'Seven whole days not one in seven, I will praise Thee', are still popular today. He died in 1633.

King of glory, you opened the eyes of your servant, George Herbert, to the glory of your creation, may we, like him, seek to praise you 'seven whole days, not one in seven'.

28 February

Oswald, Bishop of Worcester

Born of Danish parents, there is little known of Oswald's early life. However, he was made a canon of Winchester before becoming a Benedictine monk. Educated in France, he was ordained a priest about 958 AD. He was appointed Bishop of Worcester in 961 AD and Archbishop of York in 972 AD. In both of these positions, he proved himself to be an able administrator as well as a builder of churches and monasteries. It was while he was washing the feet of twelve men one day that he died at Worcester in 992 AD. A shrine was built for him there about 1086.

Lord God, we pray for those in administrative positions in the church. May they never lose sight of the truth of your Word and may they be ready to take on the servant role.

29 February

Cassian

Probably born in Romania c. 360 AD, he became a monk in Bethlehem but later travelled with a friend to Egypt to study monasticism there. He was ordained deacon in Constantinople c.400 AD. Cassian was greatly influenced by John Chrysostom and became a staunch supporter of him. When John Chrysostom was deposed at the Synod of the Oak, Cassian and other followers went with him to Italy where Cassian pleaded John's cause with the pope. Quite possibly Cassian was ordained priest in Marseilles where he also founded two monasteries. The monastic movement needed leadership there as it was being attacked by some Christian, as well as pagan, forces. Cassian, with his knowledge of Egyptian monastic tradition, was able through his writing to help provide some cohesion. Cassian was adamant that the monastic life was apostolic in origin and was patterned on the early church depicted in the Acts of the Apostles. He wrote several treatises and with the works of Augustine and Gregory, these provided the monastic guide used throughout the Middle Ages and later. He died in 433 AD.

Risen Lord, give us grace to follow your saints in faith and hope and love.

1 March

David, Patron Saint of Wales

Details of St David's early life are scarce except for the fact that he was born in the sixth century in Wales. He became a monk and his monastery is thought to have been at Menevia (St David's) in Pembrokeshire in Wales. David lived an austere life of fasting and praying and doing good deeds. His mother was St Non. He was consecrated Bishop of Menevia and died sometime between 589 AD and 601 AD. In 1275 his relics were placed in St David's Cathedral. This site became a place of pilgrimage even visited by William the Conqueror and Henry II. In fact two visits to St David's were equivalent to one visit to Rome. David is usually shown standing on a hill with a dove on his shoulder. The Welsh spelling of his name is Dafydd, hence the description of any Welshman as 'Taffy'. He is the patron saint of Wales.

Almighty God, you called your servant David to be a faithful shepherd of the Welsh people. We pray that you will inspire all bishops to be caring pastors of your flock. Bless the people of Wales that they may seek to emulate David's example.

2 March

Chad,
Bishop of Lichfield and Missionary

Chad was the brother of Cedd, whom he succeeded as abbot of Lastingham in Yorkshire. Aidan of Lindisfarne sent him to be educated in Ireland. King Oswiu arranged Chad's consecration as bishop of the see of Northumbria while Wilfrid, the candidate chosen for Deira by the sub-king Alcfrith was in Gaul seeking consecration. On his return, Wilfrid, a great opponent of the Celtic church, challenged the validity of Chad's consecration. Chad, a meek and devout man, stood down from his position leaving Wilfrid Bishop of York. Theodore, Archbishop of Canterbury, reconsecrated Chad as there had been some irregularities in his first consecration, and so, the see of Lichfield was established. Chad lived humbly and simply, walking barefoot everywhere. Archbishop Theodore had so little success in persuading Chad to ride on horseback that the archbishop once lifted him physically onto a horse and set him on his way. When Chad died in 672 AD, several cases of healing took place at his tomb. A shrine for his relics was later built in Lichfield cathedral.

Holy God, you called Chad to minister to his own people – the fledging English nation. May we seek to emulate his gentleness and humility in our own lives.

3 March

Non,
Mother of St David

Non is thought to have been a nun near Dyfed in Wales. She may have been seduced by Prince Sant or she may have been married to Sant, becoming a nun when he died. In any case she was the daughter of a chieftain and seems to have lived in Cornwall at Altarnon for some time. She died in Brittany and is buried at Finistere. There is a chapel and a well dedicated to her at St David's in Wales. Several churches in Cornwall, Devon and Wales are named for her.

God our Father, you called Non to be the mother of St David, bless all mothers as they care for their children and be with those who will never hold their own child in their arms.

4 March

Casimir of Poland

Son of the Polish king, Casimir was born at Cracow (modern day Krakow) in 1458. The people of Hungary wanted him to become their king and so his father sent an army with the thirteen-year-old prince. The army refused to fight as the soldiers had not been paid. The king blamed Casimir and exiled him to Dobzki Castle. Casimir said that he would not fight any Christian country, nor would he marry as he desired a life of celibacy. In 1484 he died of tuberculosis and was buried at Vilna where miracles of healing began to take place. He was adopted as the patron saint of the Lithuanians in the struggles against the Russians.

Lord, look with pity on your war-torn world still fighting today as in centuries past. Give the leaders of all nations a desire to solve conflict by diplomatic means rather than resorting to war and bloodshed.

5 March

Piran

Piran was born either in Ireland or Wales and lived in Cornwall where the town of Perranporth is named after him. His oratory and retreat were completely buried by sand during the Middle Ages. The site was excavated in the sixteenth century and again in the nineteenth century when three skeltons were found. A Celtic cross stands as a memorial to mark the spot. Piran was especially venerated in Wales and Brittany and also at Exeter in England. He died c.480 AD. St Piran is the patron saint of tin-miners as well as being the national saint of Cornwall.

We give thanks, O God, for those who have laid the foundations for our Christian heritage in this land. May we be faithful stewards of all that they have left us.

6 March

Baldred

During the eight century Baldred lived the life of a hermit at Tyningham in Northumbria. Later he moved to the rugged Bass Rock just off the east coast of Scotland. This island is now a bird sanctuary. A legend tells that he prayed that a jagged reef which impeded the passage between the mainland and Bass Rock be removed. This is said to have happened and is called St Baldred's Rock. It is thought that his remains now rest in Durham Cathedral.

Give us determination, like Baldred, to ask for obstacles in the way of the gospel to be removed. If they remain unchanged give us the courage to persevere in your strength.

7 March

Perpetua, Felicity and their Companions

Perpetua was a young mother, of noble birth, who was arrested with other African believers during the persecution of Christians by the Emperor Septimus Severus in the third century. Felicity, who was Perpetua's slave, and was pregnant, accompanied her. The other companions were Saturas, who was possibly a priest, Saturninus and Revocatus, the husband of Felicity. It seems that most of them were new Christians who were baptised in prison. While in prison Felicity gave birth to a daughter and Perpetua had several visions there. They were all sentenced to die while the Games were being staged. So they shared a last Eucharist (*Agape*) together. When the wild beasts mauled them, they were not instantly killed by the first attacks. They exchanged the Kiss of Peace and were then killed by the sword. They died in 203 AD in Carthage. Rather than suppressing Christianity, the believers were encouraged to hold fast to their faith even to death.

O God, our help in ages past, we pray for all those faced with the daily reality of being put to death for their faith. Give them the courage of these early martyrs who gave their lives joyfully witnessing to their Lord.

8 March

Duthac

Duthac was born in Scotland and educated in Ireland. He returned to Scotland and was consecrated bishop and spent most of his ministry working in Ross. Duthac died in 1065 in Tayne where he was buried. Seven years after his death, his incorrupt body was placed in a shrine where miracles were reported to have taken place. His relics were translated to a more beautiful shrine at St Duthus Collegiate church between 1370 and 1458. They disappeared at the time of the Reformation in 1560. Duthac was greatly venerated in his native Scotland and churches were dedicated to him at Arduthie, Kilduich and Kilduthie.

We thank you, O God, for our forebears in the faith who established the gospel in the British Isles. May we treasure their legacy and may we also remain firm in the faith of Christ.

9 March

Constantine, A Cornish King

Cornish tradition says that Constantine was converted by Petroc and that after his wife died he became a monk and founded churches in Devon and Cornwall. There are two places called Constantine in Cornwall – one near Padstow, the other in south-west Cornwall where the monastery continued until the eleventh century. He is thought to have spent time on Iona with St Columba and was probably martyred on one of the missionary journeys from there to Kintyre in 576 AD. The churches at Milton Abbot and Dunsford in Devon claim him as their patron.

Holy God, we give thanks for all those missionaries, like Constantine, who have given their lives for the sake of the gospel.

10 March

Kessog

The son of the royal family of Munster, Kessog was born in Cashel, Co Tipperary, Ireland in the sixth century. He travelled to Scotland where he became a monk and was later appointed bishop of the region around Loch Lomond. Robert the Bruce gave him land at Luss for his monastery. Kessog, however, lived on Monk's Island in the middle of the loch. He is thought to have been murdered at Bandry where a cairn once marked the site. Scots shouted his name in battle before they adopted St Andrew as their patron saint.

Lord God, you still call each one, as you did Kessog to dare to follow you with a spirit of adventure. Give us courage to be guided by your hand.

11 March

Oengus the Culdee

Irish born in Ulster, Oengus studied at the monastery of Clonenagh in County Laois. Oengus was the author of the earliest Irish martyrology. He spent several years living the austere life of a hermit before entering the monastery of Tallacht near Dublin. Here he spent his time doing menial tasks until the abbot, Maelruain realised who he was, as he observed him teaching an unsuccessful student. He then asked Oengus to help him compile the Tallacht martyrology which he did as well as completing the *Féilire,* which he had begun some years earlier. He died c.824 AD.

Lord, you inspire all that is good and beautiful. We give thanks for those, like Oengus, who have compiled books and manuscripts at which we still marvel today.

12 March

Paul Aurelian

Also known as St Pol, Paul Aurelian came from Wales to Brittany to live in the sixth century. He may have lived as a hermit for a time before he was consecrated a bishop. He is said to have died at the great age of 104 and his body was interred at Fleury in France c.960 AD where it remained until 1562. His head and an arm bone are supposedly in the cathedral of Saint Pol-de-Leon. Aurelian may have been confused with the Welsh Paulinus (not the Paulinus of York).

Help us to use our lives to your glory, whether they be long or short, O Lord. Give us grace to shine as lights in a dark world.

13 March

Gerald of Mayo

Of English descent, Gerald became a monk at Lindisfarne (Holy Island). He probably went to Inishbofin in Galway, Ireland with some other monks from Lindisfarne after the Synod of Whitby in 664 AD had ruled that the Roman usage be adopted in lieu of the traditions of the Celtic Church. These mainly concerned the dating of Easter and the style of tonsure worn by the monks. At this time Gerald was appointed the abbot of the English monks who settled in Mayo. He encouraged study and education and died c.732 AD.

Almighty God, heal the divisions of the Christian church, we pray. May love and tolerance abound rather than hate and bigotry.

14 March

Matilda

The wife of King Henry I of Germany, Matilda was born at Engern in Westphalia c.895 AD. She was educated at the monastery of Erfurt. Henry's first marriage to a young widow had been declared invalid and so, he married Matilda in 909 AD, and gave her 'Walhausen' (the place of their marriage) for a dowry. They had five children – Otto, Henry, Bruno, Gerberga and Hedwig. Matilda's husband, Henry, became Duke of Saxony when his father died in 912 AD. Four years later when King Conrad of Germany died, Henry was asked to be king. During Henry's reign of seventeen years, Matilda proved herself to be a generous and devout woman always seeking to care for the poor. On the death of her husband, however, Matilda wanted her second son, Henry (her favourite) to ascend the throne rather than her first-born, Otto. Subsequently, Otto was elected as the rightful heir. Needless to say, Matilda's actions caused friction between the two brothers who then accused her of causing the monarchy's financial difficulties because of her over zealous generosity. Matilda built many churches as well as founding monasteries before her death in 968 AD.

Bounteous God, you shower us with so many gifts. May we be ready and willing to share what we have with those who have so little of this world's goods.

15 March

Longinus

According to tradition this is the name given to the soldier who pierced Christ's side at the Crucifixion. Many legends have sprung up about his life. He is thought to have suffered from incipient blindness (the early stages of loss of sight) and was cured by Christ's blood. Longinus was arrested for refusing to sacrifice to idols. At his trial he smashed some idols and the governor became possessed by evil spirits. Longinus's prophecy that the governor would become sane again came true after the soldier's death. The lance thought to be the one which pierced Jesus's side was found at Antioch during the First Crusade.

Give courage, O God, to those who have to 'put their lives on the line' for their faith, that strengthened by your Spirit they may dare everything they have for your sake.

16 March

Finian Lobhar, The Leper

The son of Conal, chieftain of ancient Fingal, Finian was born at Bregia in Leinster, Ireland. He may have founded a church and a monastery at Innisfallen. Ordained by Bishop Fatlad, he spent several years at Clonmore monastery in county Wexford. He was then made the first abbot of Swords Abbey near Dublin which was founded by St Columba c.560 AD. Finian may have established the monastery at Ardfinnan in Co Tipperary. He healed many people but may have contracted leprosy himself. This would explain why he was called 'The Leper'. He spent the last thirty years of his life at Clonmore and died there c.650 AD.

God of compassion, have mercy on those who try to minister to the sick in remote places where there are few medical supplies. Give them strength and perseverance.

17 March

Patrick, Patron Saint of Ireland

Patrick was born in Britain c.390 AD. His father was a deacon and his grandfather a priest. As a young man he was taken by brigands to Ireland where he was a slave for several years. Somehow he found his way back to his family in Britain. He trained for the priesthood and sometime later was made a bishop. Patrick returned to Ireland and made Armagh his base (possibly because of its strong king). He proved to be a humble and caring pastor to his people and wrote some of the earliest British literature including *St Patrick's Breastplate*. There is some doubt as to where he is buried though he died c.461. He is usually depicted as a bishop walking on snakes (from the legend which says that he drove all the snakes from Ireland).

Unchanging God, you called your servant Patrick to be the apostle to the Irish. Bless the people of Ireland and rekindle that fire of faith in us as we travel on our earthly pilgrimage.

18 March

Cyril,
Bishop of Jerusalem

Cyril was born probably in Caesarea c.315 AD and was educated in Jerusalem. He later instructed those adults preparing for baptism. Consecrated bishop c.349 AD, he was later charged with selling church property to help the poor. When he was accused of heresy in 357 AD, he was sent into exile by the emperor, so almost half of his time as bishop was spent away from the people committed to his care. He died c.386 AD. During his lifetime he made changes to the liturgy for the observance of Holy Week and Easter which laid the foundation for that which is used today.

Lord, you lead your people like a shepherd, we pray for all those who hold positions of leadership and responsibility in your church, that they may ever be conscious that this authority comes from you.

19 March

Joseph, Husband of the Blessed Virgin Mary

The scriptures tell us that he was a carpenter but few other details concerning him are known. The gospels recount his dreams, first that he was to marry Mary, even though she was pregnant and he felt he would have to break their engagement. Again warned by God in a dream, he fled from King Herod's wrath into Egypt with Mary and the Christ Child. Many male children perished in the massacre of the Holy Innocents instigated by Herod. Tradition seems to imply that Joseph was quite old when he married, although there is no evidence to confirm this. Joseph is the patron of several occupations and institutions, particularly hospitals and many churches are dedicated to him.

Almighty God, you chose Joseph to be the guardian of your Son and the husband of blessed Mary. Give us his willing obedience to follow your commands and to trust you.

20 March

Cuthbert, Bishop of Lindisfarne

The son of a wealthy Northumbrian family, Cuthbert was born c.634 AD. On the night that St Aidan died, Cuthbert was tending the sheep on the Lammermuir hills when he saw a bright light and had a vision of Aidan's soul being transported to heaven. In 651 AD Cuthbert decided to become a monk at Melrose where Boisil the prior was noted for his holiness of life. Cuthbert himself was appointed prior there some ten years later. After the Synod of Whitby in 664 AD, as prior of Lindisfarne he tried to smooth relations between those in favour of the Celtic usage and those who wanted the Roman rite. Cuthbert always desired the life of a hermit and spent time on St Cuthbert's Island opposite Lindisfarne (Holy Island). Today, at low tide, pilgrims still walk across the sands to visit this special place. Cuthbert later moved to Inner Farne, a group of islands some distance off the Northumbrian coast where he found the greater solitude which he craved. However, fame of his humility and holiness spread and King Egfrith and Archbishop Theodore of Canterbury prevailed upon him to be bishop of Hexham. Eata, bishop of Lindisfarne, moved to Hexham so that Cuthbert could be the bishop of Lindisfarne. Many stories exist of Cuthbert's rapport with animals. A specially lovely one tells how after spending a night standing in the sea praying, as he came to the shore his feet were dried by otters which then received his blessing.

Cuthbert died on Inner Farne on 20 March 687 AD and was buried on Lindisfarne. It seems appropriate that today the Farne Islands are a wildlife sanctuary for birds and seals. After the Viking raids, the monks began an arduous journey, taking Cuthbert's body with them as they left the Holy Island of Lindisfarne. They finally reached their permanent home in 995 AD where Durham Cathedral now stands. St Cuthbert's relics were translated to a shrine there in 999 AD. Cuthbert's body remained incorrupt for centuries – a sign of his sanctity. He remains one of Britain's best loved saints with over one hundred and thirty churches, in England alone, dedicated to him.

Loving God, you called your servant Cuthbert from caring for sheep to be a shepherd of your flock. Help us to follow his example by bringing those who are lost, home to your fold.

21 March

Enda of Aran

Enda was born in Meath, Ireland and became a soldier and the king of Oriel. His sister, Fanchea, an abbess, sought to persuade him to lay down his arms and marry. There is a legend which says that the girl Fanchea had chosen for him had just died in her convent. Subsequently, Enda decided to become a monk at St Ninian's monastery at Whithorn in Galloway, Scotland. He later returned to Ireland where his brother-in-law, the King of Cashel, gave him land on the Aran Islands. Here Enda founded the monastery of Killeaney on Aran Mor, which was one of the first monasteries in Ireland. Enda was in fact the first person to really establish monasticism in Ireland along with St Finnian of Clonard. He spent most of his life on the Aran Islands and was buried there c.530 AD.

God of contemplation, help us to pause in the busyness of our lives to just be still and know your presence with us.

22 March

Basil of Ancyra

Little is known of his early life. However, Basil was a priest in Ancyra (Ankara), Byzantium, in modern Turkey, during the fourth century. He opposed the pagans and those who promoted Arianism (a heresy which denies the divinity of Christ). Basil spoke out in defence of Bishop Marcellus when the Arians tried to oust him from his position. In 362 AD, under the orders of the Emperor Julian the Apostate, Basil was arrested and tortured and finally executed on 22 March. Many other Christians lost their lives during this persecution.

God of hope, we pray for all Christians who live with the daily threat of imminent danger. Strengthen them with the assurance that you are always with them.

23 March

Ethilwald of Farne

He became a monk at Ripon where he was ordained a priest. Later in 687 AD he moved to Inner Farne (off the Northumbrian coast) where he lived as a hermit in the hut built by St Cuthbert. It is said that his prayers prevented some Lindisfarne (Holy Island) monks from being shipwrecked after they had visited him. Ethilwald died in 699 AD and was buried on Lindisfarne Holy Island with Cuthbert and Edbert who were both bishops. His remains were finally placed in Durham Cathedral.

Lord God, we remember those whom you have called to spend their lives in quietness and contemplation. May we be strengthened by their prayers for the world and all its peoples.

24 March

Dunchad,
Abbot of Iona

A member of the Conall Gulban family, Dunchad was born in Ireland. He became a monk and sometime later was appointed abbot of Killochuir in southeast Ulster. Bishop Egbert persuaded Dunchad, while he was abbot of Iona, to encourage the monastery there to adopt the Roman dating of Easter, as well as changing the style of tonsure worn by the monks. This Roman usage, in lieu of that of the Celtic Church, had been agreed upon at the Synod of Whitby in 664 AD. Dunchad died in 716 AD and is the patron saint of Irish sailors.

God of love, we pray for all those involved in peace negotiations, that like Dunchad, they may seek to bring harmony and tolerance rather than discord and fighting.

25 March

The Annunciation

This feast marks the momentous occasion when the angel, Gabriel, visited the Blessed Virgin Mary to tell her that she would bear God's own Son – Jesus Christ, the Saviour of the world. The Christian Church has celebrated this day since the fourth century. Jesus embodied perfect humanity and entire divinity. Mary was acknowledged as *Theotokos* (the God-bearer) translated in the western church as the Mother of God. This day is often referred to as 'Lady Day', particularly in England.

God of grace, we give thanks for Mary's unwavering obedience to do your will. May we, like her, gladly allow you to use us for your glory.

26 March

Liudger, Bishop of Munster

Liudger was educated by Gregory, a friend of Boniface, missionary and Archbishop of Mainz, at Utrecht and then at York by Alcuin, the famous scholar. Liudger was involved in the Anglo-Saxon mission to Europe. He rebuilt churches and destroyed pagan shrines. Ordained priest in 777 AD, he built several churches. In 784 AD when the Saxon invasion was launched under Widekund, many churches were destroyed and priests driven from their positions. While this was happening, Liudger spent two years in Rome and at Monte Cassino in Italy. During this time he decided to build a Benedictine monastery. This he later achieved at Werden in Germany. Liudger was consecrated bishop of Munster c.804 AD. He was a gentle pastor who achieved much for Christianity by his patient persuasion. Liudger died at Werden in 809 AD after a long illness and was buried there.

Almighty God, you inspire all that is good and worthwhile, bless those who seek to build churches to your glory. May they never forget that Christ himself is the sure and only foundation of our faith.

27 March

Rupert, Bishop

Rupert may have been of Irish or Frankish descent. He founded St Peter's monastery at Salzburg, Austria as well as the convent at Nonnberg where his sister was the abbess. After his consecration as bishop of Worms and Salzburg, he preached the gospel far and wide in the Danube region and later at Regensburg in Bavaria. He is often depicted in art carrying a barrel of salt because he developed the salt-mines near Salzburg. He died c.710 AD.

Lord God, you have called us to be 'the salt of the earth', may we enhance your world by living for you.

28 March

Alkelda

Also known as Athilda, she was the patron of the church at Middleham in Yorkshire as well as at Giggleswick (West Riding). King Richard III established a college in Middleham dedicated to Christ, the Blessed Virgin Mary and St Alkelda. Local tradition has it that Alkelda was a Saxon princess who became a nun. She was strangled by some Viking women c.800 AD. Alkelda was buried in the church at Middleham.

Loving God, help us to remain true to our calling no matter what the cost to us may be.

29 March

Woolos (Gwynllyw)

Woolos was a chieftain in south-east Wales and his wife Gwyladys was one of the twenty-four children of Brychan. They lived a life of violence before their son Cadoc showed them the Christian way of life. Woolos and Gwladys moved near Newport in Gwent and lived an austere life. However, each night in summer or winter they bathed in the river Usk and then went for a long walk naked. Cadoc disapproved of this behaviour and persuaded his parents to live apart. Gwladys moved to Pencanau in Bassaleg. Woolos devoted himself to a life of prayer c.480 AD. He built his 'cell' on Stow Hill, Newport (the site of the present St Woolos' Cathedral). As he lay dying he is thought to have been visited by St Dyfrig.

Creator God, may we seek to follow the example of your Son Jesus Christ in the way in which we live. Grant that our behaviour may bring glory to your name.

30 March

Osburga, Abbess

Osburga was the abbess of a convent founded by King Canute at Coventry. When she died c.1018, miracles are said to have taken place at her tomb. The people of Coventry wanted to honour her and so her feast day was established in 1410.

Lord God, bless those who seek to live holy lives, that knowing they are saved by your grace, they may rejoice with all Christians.

31 March

John Donne, Priest, Poet

Born c.1571, John Donne was brought up as a Roman Catholic and was the great-great nephew of Thomas More. Like many young people, he was sceptical about religion. However, during his studies at Oxford and Cambridge, he found his faith in the Church of England. After much soul-searching, he was ordained and later became Dean of St Paul's Cathedral in London. He showed compassion and understanding to those testing their vocations to the priesthood. Donne was much loved by the people of London who flocked to hear him preach. He wrote several love poems to his wife, as well as religious ones, which became very popular in the twentieth century. John Donne died in 1631.

God of all beauty and creativity, we give thanks for the poetry and the life of John Donne. May we take the time to pause in our busy lives just to see and appreciate the diversity of this world which you have made and may we guard its fragility.

1 April

Gilbert of Caithness

His father, a lord, owned vast estates in Scotland. Gilbert was appointed Archdeacon of Moray, a violent and difficult area. In 1223 Adam, the bishop, was murdered and Gilbert filled this position. He built the cathedral at Dornoch as well as some hospices. His episcopacy of twenty years was peaceful and he was able to bring order to this troublesome region. He died in 1245 and was declared patron saint of both cathedral and diocese.

God of harmony, we pray for all church leaders working in the ecumenical movement, that a spirit of peace and tolerance may prevail between all Christians.

2 April

Francis of Paola

Born in 1416 Francis entered a Franciscan priory when only thirteen years old and then went on a pilgrimage to Rome and Assisi. Later he became a hermit and lived in a cave where he was joined by several others attracted by his simple lifestyle. As a result he founded the Minim Friars in 1464. During his life he is said to have performed miracles as well as prophesying. Louis XI, the French king, asked for him to come to him as the king lay dying. Francis himself died at Tours in France in 1507.

Lord God, help us to 'unclutter' our lives that we may seek to live simply without setting too much store on possessions.

3 April

Richard of Chichester

In 1197 Richard was born at Droitwich, the son of a yeoman farmer. He studied at Oxford, Paris and Bologna later becoming chancellor to his former tutor, Edmund Rich who was Archbishop of Canterbury. Ordained in 1242 Richard was given charge of Deal and Charing in Kent, until he was reappointed chancellor to Archbishop Boniface. He was consecrated bishop at Lyons in France in 1245 and when he returned to England as Bishop of Chichester, he found that diocese in a sorry state. Richard proved to be a caring pastor as well as working hard to bring some order to his diocese. He is best remembered for the prayer which he wrote '… O most merciful Redeemer, Friend and Brother, may I know thee more clearly, love thee more dearly and follow thee more nearly, day by day.'

Jesus, our Redeemer, our Friend and our Brother may we, like Richard, seek to know you better and to serve you more faithfully day by day.

4 April

Isidore of Seville

Born c.560 AD of a noble family of Seville, Spain, Isidore received much of his education from his brother Leander who was a monk. Some years after becoming a priest, Isidore was consecrated Archbishop of Seville, succeeding his brother in this office. He continued Leander's work of organising the church in Spain as well as seeking to convert the Visigoths. A notable scholar, he wrote several books, his most famous, *Etymologies* was a type of encyclopaedia covering many subjects. His works were very popular in the Middle Ages, and indeed, Gregory the Great dubbed him 'Schoolmaster of the Middle Ages'. He died in 636 AD.

Lord, you are the source of all knowledge, bless those who seek to inspire us to learn new things that can be used for the good of humanity.

5 April

Derfel

According to tradition he was one of the knights of King Arthur. Born in Wales in sixth century he became a soldier and distinguished himself at the battle of Camlan in 537 AD. Later he became a monk and possibly abbot at Bardsey. He founded a monastery at Llanderfel in the county of Gwynedd where there was a wooden statue of him riding a horse and holding a staff. People trusted him implicitly and many came on pilgrimage bringing cows or horses or money to him. Many years later, at the Reformation Thomas Cromwell's agent destroyed the statue at Smithfield by having it burnt.

Thank you, O God, for those we can trust, those who set an example for us to follow.

6 April

Brychan

Brychan may have been a legendary Welsh king who is thought to have fathered a large number of children. These are mainly venerated in Devon and Cornwall in England. A sixteenth century stained glass window in St Neot, Cornwall shows Brychan holding ten children in his arms.

Give patience and wisdom to all parents as they seek to rear their children and guide them to show love and care to those little ones committed to them.

7 April

Goran

He may have been the same person as Vuron the hermit, who is said to have lived south of Bodmin. The cave where he lived and the well from which he drew water still exist at Gorran in Cornwall where he is the patron saint.

Be with those, gracious God, who feel called to live a life of solitude that they may find you and serve you.

8 April

Julia Billiart

Born to a family of peasant farmers in 1751 in Picardy, France, Julia Billiart suffered a debilitating illness as a result of shock, when a gun was fired at her father. The priest in her hometown was replaced in 1790 by one who supported the French Revolution. Julia sought to hide fugitive priests and because of this she had to flee from house to house during the Reign of Terror. Befriended by Frances Blin de Bourdon, Viscountess de Gezaincourt, she met Father Joseph Varin who inspired her to rise from her bed-ridden state. In faith she did so and found that she was completely cured. Julia became the co-founder of the Institute of Notre Dame of Namur (an organisation formed to care for the spiritual welfare of poor children). She died in 1816.

God of compassion, be with all who seek to help children in poverty that they may show your love and care.

9 April

Dietrich Bonhoeffer, Lutheran Pastor and Martyr

Dietrich Bonhoeffer was born into an academic family in 1906 and was later ordained in the Lutheran Church. Karl Barth had a profound influence on his theology and Dietrich lectured in Spain and the USA arriving back in Berlin in 1931. He opposed Nazism and was a leader of the Confessing Church which sought to stand against Hitler's regime. Arrested in 1943 by the Nazis he was murdered by the Nazi police in Flossenburg concentration camp in 1945.

Give us courage to stand firm in our faith and for what is right as your servant Dietrich did.

10 April

Hedda of Peterborough

Abbot of a community of some eighty monks, Hedda was killed in 870 AD by the same Danes who slew King Edmund of East Anglia. During the Middle Ages the Hedda Stone was erected over Hedda's grave and those of his fellow monks. Candles were placed in the holes gouged out of the stone.

Lord, you call all Christians to shine as lights in a dark world. May we like Hedda live a life of service to you and to others.

11 April

George Augustus Selwyn, Bishop of New Zealand

George Selwyn was born in 1809 and was educated at Cambridge. When ordained he was appointed curate at Windsor. In 1841 he was consecrated the first Bishop of New Zealand where he worked for twenty-seven years. During the Maori Wars he supported the rights of the Maori people against the white settlers and so his life was endangered from both sides. He taught himself to navigate and as a result of his travels he was able to establish congregations in the Melanesian Islands. The Constitution for the New Zealand church which he drew up greatly influenced the churches in the Anglican Communion. In 1868, having been persuaded to return to England he became Bishop of Lichfield where he died in 1878.

Encourage those who work for justice for native peoples that fairness and mutual trust may prevail, O Lord. We pray for the people of New Zealand that they may be sustained by your Holy Spirit.

12 April

Zeno, Bishop of Verona

Zeno was born in Africa and received a good classical education. Consecrated Bishop of Verona in 362 AD, he lived a life of poverty and spent much time training priests for his diocese. He gained a reputation for his hard work both as a pastor and as a builder of churches and founder of several convents. Zeno was a bishop for about ten years. Tradition says that he built the first basilica in Verona on the site of the present day cathedral. He died in 371 AD.

Creator God, you inspire all that is good in our lives. Help us to build for your kingdom and for the good of humanity.

13 April

Guinoch

Guinoch was born in Scotland and is thought to have been an advisor to King Kenneth II. His prayers and counsels supported both church and state in Scotland. He died in 838 AD.

Almighty God, we pray for those who like Guinoch have the responsibility of advising those in positions of authority. May they seek your guidance and work for the welfare of all.

14 April

Caradoc

Caradoc's Welsh parents were comfortably off. As he grew up Caradoc played the harp at the court of Rhys ap Tewdwr (prince of South Wales 1077-1093). After falling out of favour by losing the prince's greyhounds, Caradoc journeyed to Llandaff where he became a hermit at St Kyned's church in Gower. After a time he was ordained priest at Menevia and, with his companions, moved to an island off the coast of Pembrokeshire. However, the Vikings harassed this settlement prompting another move to St Isells, Haroldston where Caradoc died in 1124. He requested that he should be buried in the cathedral at St David's.

Lord God, help us all to realise we are only pilgrims on the earth. Save us from being too attached to worldly possessions.

15 April

Ruadhan

Possibly descended from the royal Munster line, Ruadhan was born in Ireland and educated at Clonard. He founded a monastery at Lothra, Co Tipperary near Terryglass which consisted of one hundred and fifty monks. The Irish secular rulers were cursed by him but it is thought that King Diarmait continued to reside at Tara, the seat of the High Kings. A bell bears Ruadhan's name and is in the British Museum. Ruadhan died c.584 AD.

Give wisdom, Almighty God, to those who seek to advise others, that they may always be honest in their dealings and not push their own agenda but work for a fair and just society.

16 April

Magnus

The son of a Viking ruler of the Orkneys, Magnus was born c. 1075. When he became a Christian he gave up his buccaneering exploits. King Magnus Barefoot captured him, forcing him to plunder the west coast of Britain. He escaped to Scotland and remained there until the Norwegian king died. Magnus returned to the Orkneys where he jointly ruled with his cousin Haakon for a time. He was later murdered by Haakon and his supporters and died praying for those who killed him. Buried in Kirkwall cathedral where miracles occurred at his tomb, he is the major saint of the Orkneys and Shetland Islands and northern Scotland.

Lord of the saints, we think of those who have given their lives for their Christian faith and especially the saints and martyrs of our own time and give thanks for their courage.

17 April

Donan

Irish born, Donan became a monk on Iona while Columba was abbot there. He established a monastery on the island of Eigg in the Inner Hebrides off the coast of Scotland. During the celebration of Mass one night, robbers forced the monks into their refectory and burnt them alive. Over fifty died in this raid. Several Scottish churches are dedicated to him.

May those who inflict cruelty on their fellow human beings be brought to justice and seek your forgiveness, O Lord.

18 April

Deicola

In the seventh century Deicola was born in Ireland and later became abbot of the monastery at Bosham after leaving St Fursey's abbey at Burgcastle in East Anglia. While preaching in Sussex 681-86 AD Wilfrid met Deicola and his monks. Little is known of Deicola who shares his feast day with another Irish monk of the same name who was a follower of Columbanus.

Lord, may each one of us see ourselves as pilgrims on a journey, companions on the road and may we be given grace to go where you want us to go.

19 April

Alphege, Archbishop of Canterbury

Alphege was born in 954 AD and later entered the monastery at Deerhurst, near Worcester. He founded the abbey at Bath and was appointed abbot by Dunstan. Consecrated bishop of Winchester in 984 AD he became Archbishop of Canterbury in 1006. During this time there were continual Viking raids and King Aethelred sought to buy peace while Alphege tried to win them by the power of the gospel. However, when another raid took place in 1011, Canterbury was sacked and the cathedral set on fire. The monks were murdered and Alphege was taken prisoner. He refused to ask his people to pay the ransom for his release. Finally, after seven months he was pelted to death at Greenwich with ox bones by the Danes in 1012. His body was sold to the people of London and was buried in St Paul's Cathedral. In 1023 his remains were interred at Canterbury Cathedral. Alphege was a faithful pastor who stayed at Canterbury, even in the face of death, to support his people.

Heavenly Father, we pray for all those who have responsibility for your flock. May they like Alphege seek to protect and encourage your servants.

20 April

Caedwalla,
Anglo Saxon King

King of Wessex from 658 AD to 688 AD, he was descended from Ceawlin and became king by conquest. He was a successful though violent ruler. Caedwalla was baptised by Pope Sergius on Easter Eve 689 AD. Immediately after this he became ill and died and was buried in the crypt of St Peter's Rome. He was the first of four Anglo Saxon kings to die in Rome.

Lord, we pray for all those preparing for baptism that they may seek to fulfil the promises they will make.

21 April

Anselm,
Archbishop of Canterbury

Anselm was born at Aosta, Italy c.1033, the son of a rich family from Lombardy. At the age of fifteen Anselm wanted to enter a monastery but his father refused to give his consent. After his mother's death his father made his life unbearable, so Anselm left home. Hearing of the fame of Lanfranc, he visited the monastery at Bec in France. He became a monk and later was abbot there. Bec monastery owned land in England and so it was necessary for Anselm to visit this property. His patient manner and care endeared him to the English people, and so, when Lanfranc, Archbishop of Canterbury died, the clergy wanted him to be archbishop. Anselm, who desired a life of prayer, against his better judgement, was consecrated Archbishop of Canterbury in 1093. Once in office he was harassed by the king and had to go into exile. As archbishop he showed great care for those around him including animals. He was a brilliant scholar and theologian. Anselm died on Palm Sunday 1109 while one of the monks read the Gospel to him.

Almighty God, we give thanks for those, like Anselm, who have inspired and still inspire the lives of others.

22 April

Theodore of Sykeon

His mother was an innkeeper at Sykeon and she and her daughters were prostitutes. His father, who worked in a circus had little to do with Theodore's upbringing. In spite of all this, his mother had him baptised. Her ambition was to see him employed in the service of the emperor of Constantinople. However, she abandoned this plan after St George appeared to her in a dream. The appointment of a new cook, Stephen, at the inn saw a change in Theodore's mother's circumstances. Not only was Stephen an excellent cook thus increasing the profitability of the inn, but more importantly, he was a devout man who encouraged Theodore to pursue Christian things. After almost dying from the Plague, Theodore became a hermit at Arkea and was devoted to the cult of St George. He later became bishop of Anastasiopolis in Galatia. During this time many miracles are reputed to have taken place. Theodore died in 613 AD and was buried in Constantinople.

God of eternity, you use the most unlikely people to fulfil your will on this earthly pilgrimage. May each one of us be ready to follow where you lead us.

23 April

George

George may have been a soldier. The legend about him slaying the dragon became popular when William Caxton printed the book *The Golden Legend*. The dragon's anger was daily appeased by the sacrifice of two sheep. When this supply ceased humans were offered instead. In fact, the king's daughter presented herself as a bride to be sacrificed but was rescued by George. During the Crusades, he was adopted as the protector of the army. In England, where he is the patron saint, the Order of the Garter was founded by Edward III and the chapel of St George was built at Windsor Castle. He was persecuted during the reigns of Diocletian and Maximian and died at Lydda c.303 AD.

God of compassion, instil in us a willingness to stand up for the rights of the poor that justice may be done and fairness may come to society. Bless the people of England that they may value their Christian heritage.

24 April

Egbert,
Monk of Lindisfarne

Born in Northumbria of noble parents, Egbert studied in Ireland and became a monk on Lindisfarne (Holy Island). When he caught the plague he vowed that if spared he would go into voluntary exile for life. He recovered and inspired several Anglo-Saxon missionaries to go to Europe to spread the gospel. Egbert wanted to join them but had a vision in which he felt called to go to Iona. There he encouraged the community to accept the Roman dating of Easter. He died in 729 AD.

Loving God, we pray for those who are involved in bringing peace and reconciliation to tense situations that they may seek your blessing in all that they undertake.

25 April

Mark

Mark was Jewish and is thought to have been a cousin of Barnabas. He accompanied Paul and Barnabas on their first missionary journey. He later went with Barnabas to Cyprus and to Rome with Paul. Mark also paid another visit to Rome with Peter. Mark's gospel is thought to have been the earliest and may have been written while he was in Rome. Probably based on the preaching of St Peter it was no doubt written from Mark's own memory of events.

Lord God, we give thanks for your inspired word, for those who have written it and translated it into so many different languages. May we read it and obey it more faithfully in our daily pilgrimage.

26 April

Riquier (Richarius)

Born at Celles near Amiens in France. While still a young man, Riquier protected some Irish missionaries from harassment by the local population. They explained the Christian faith to him and he was converted from paganism. After his ordination as a priest he spent several years in England before returning to France where he founded a monastery at Celles. Seeking a life of contemplation he resigned his position as abbot and became a hermit at Forest-Moutier where he died c.645 AD.

We think of those, O God, who feel called to a life of contemplation. May each one of us draw near to you in the silence of our own hearts and feel your peace.

27 April

Zita, Virgin

Zita's parents were devout Christians and her sister became a nun. When Zita was twelve years old she became a servant at Lucca in the house of a wool and silk-weaving merchant. She did her duties well and also spent much time in prayer at night and attended early Mass in the parish church. Zita shared her food with the hungry and cared for the poor. When she became the housekeeper she was able to spend more time with those less fortunate as well as praying fervently for criminals sentenced to death. After forty-eight years of faithful service to the same family she died in 1278.

God of compassion, your loving hands are always stretched out to those in need. Stir our cold hearts that we, like Zita, may be instruments of your care to all who suffer.

28 April

Peter Chanel, Missionary & Martyr in the South Pacific

His parents were peasants when Peter was born near Cras, France in 1803. Educated by his parish priest, he showed brilliance as well as holiness. After ordination he became the priest in the parish of Crozet which was in a very rundown state. After three years of Chanel's ministry it began to show signs of growth. He joined the Marist missionary congregation in 1831 hoping to work overseas. However, he spent five years lecturing in Belley till he was sent in 1836 to minister to some islands in the Pacific Ocean near Fiji. He and a companion won the trust of the people by healing the sick as well as preaching the gospel. The son of a chief asked to be baptised but this request enraged his father and subsequently, Peter Chanel was clubbed to death in 1841. His sacrifice was not in vain as the whole island became Christian a year later.

Creator God, we pray for the peoples of the South Pacific that they may remain faithful to their calling and seek, like Peter Chanel, to spread the good news of your kingdom to their neighbours.

29 April

Endellion

Little is known of her life but Endellion was probably the daughter of St Brychan and may have been born in the sixth century. The town of St Endellion in Cornwall is named after her and part of her tomb is still in existence. There are two wells bearing her name and she may have lived at Tregony where a chapel is dedicated to her. Legend has it that the lord of Tregony killed a cow which had strayed onto his land. Endellion's godfather caused the lord to be slain but she brought him back to life. At Lundy Island off the coast of Devon another chapel was dedicated to her.

We give thanks O God, for your saints in every age. May we like them seek to follow your example as we walk this earthly pilgrimage.

30 April

Pandita Mary Ramabai, Translator of the Scriptures

Her father, a Brahmin intellectual believed that girls should be educated as well as boys and so after Pandita's birth in 1858, as she grew, her father taught her and her mother to read and write Sanskrit. No doubt her father's view, including his opposition to the traditional social structure, led her to become a social reformer. Pandita especially espoused the plight of Indian women and travelled all over India, and even visited England and the USA, to bring this problem to the attention of the public. A poet and author she wrote many books including *The High Caste Hindu Woman*. She died in 1922.

God of justice, be with those who seek to promote fairness and equality for all peoples whatever their race, religion or background.

1 May

Asaph

Possibly a descendant of Coel Godebog, Asaph was a disciple of Kentigern (Mungo). He worked mainly in Flintshire at Lllanasa until becoming Bishop of Llanelwy where he remained until his death in the early seventh century. No doubt he had a profound effect on the local inhabitants who changed the name of their town to St Asaph. There are also several churches and wells dedicated to him, and a fair took place on his feast day each year.

As we remember Asaph this day we pray that all bishops and leaders of your church may be faithful witnesses to the gospel and lead your people with a shepherd's care.

2 May

Gennys

There is little factual information about his life. However, Gennys is the patron of the town of St Gennys in Cornwall. He has been confused with Genesius of Arles in France whose feast day is celebrated on 25 August.

We know so little of many of your saints, nevertheless they are known to you, O Lord. Help us to know that we are surrounded by a cloud of witnesses – of big saints and little saints who have served you faithfully in many different places.

3 May

Glywys (Gluvias)

A monk of Welsh origin, Glwys is thought to have been the nephew of St Petroc and is the patron of St Gluvias in Cornwall. His dates of birth and death are unknown but he is celebrated in Cornwall on 3 May.

For all your saints we praise you living Lord. Help us to follow your example as we walk this earthly pilgrimage.

4 May

Godehard (Gothard), Bishop of Hildesheim

Born in Bavaria, Godehard was educated by the canons of the Benedictine abbey of Nieder-Altaich. He came to the notice of Archbishop Frederick of Salzburg who took him to Rome and made him provost of canons at the tender age of nineteen. After he was ordained priest, he became Abbot of Nieder-Altaich and later in 1022 he was consecrated Bishop of Hildesheim. Although at this time aged sixty, Godehard carried out his work of building and restoring churches as well as promoting education with tireless energy. He also founded a hospice. He died in 1038.

Give patience and endurance to those who minister to the sick and dying that the love of Christ may shine forth in all their actions.

5 May

Hydroc

Probably a fifth century Cornish saint, possibly a hermit. The National Trust property of Lanhydrock is named after him. The church of St Hydroc Lanhydrock dates back to the fifteenth century and there is an ancient cross at St Hydroc's church Trebyan.

O Lord, we give thanks for the saints of the Celtic church may we seek to preserve our Christian heritage.

6 May

Edbert (Eadbert), Bishop of Lindisfarne

The Venerable Bede describes him as a 'priest of great biblical learning, famous for his generosity'. Each year he gave a tenth of everything he owned to the poor. He was Bishop of Lindisfarne from 688 AD to 698 AD and during this time he arranged for the wooden church built by Finan to be roofed with lead. Like St Cuthbert, his predecessor, he spent time on St Cuthbert's Isle just off the Holy Island of Lindisfarne especially during Lent. Edbert died suddenly on 5 May 698 AD and after this miracles began to take place at his tomb.

God of pilgrimage, as we walk in the footsteps of your saints may we be inspired by their example.

7 May

John of Beverley

John was born in Humberside and studied at Canterbury under the tutelage of Adrian, abbot of St Augustine's. Later he became a monk at Hilda's double monastery at Whitby. He was consecrated Bishop of Hexham in 687 AD. In this position he proved himself to be a caring pastor particularly to the poor and disabled. It was John who ordained The Venerable Bede as a deacon and later priest. In 705 AD he became Bishop of York. He founded a monastery at Beverley in 717 AD and spent four years there before his death in 721 AD. Both Bede and Alcuin of York recorded his miracles.

Lord, lead us in the way of your saints that encouraged by their lives we may seek to follow in the way you call us to go.

8 May

Odger

Born in the eighth century, Odger became a deacon and a monk. He travelled to Rome with the Northumbrian saints Wiro and Plechelm and also helped them in their missionary work in Holland. He and his companions built a church and monastery at Odilienberg and it is here that Odger is buried.

Heavenly Father, bless your servants who leave their native land in order to preach the gospel to the corners of the earth. May we each in our place live out the Christian life to your glory.

9 May

Pachomius, Abbot

He is thought to have been born c.292 A.D. At the age of twenty he was conscripted for the army of the emperor. When he and his fellow soldiers were being transported down the River Nile in dreadful conditions, the Christians at Latopolis (Esneh) showed them great kindness. This compassion moved Pachomius to be baptised and he later sought out a hermit in the desert and became his disciple. One day while visiting the desert area near Tabennisi, he felt moved to build a monastery there. He himself refused ordination but founded several monasteries. During an epidemic, he died in 348 AD.

Help us, Lord, to realise that you have no hands but our hands to do your work today. May the light of Christ shine in our lives.

10 May

Conleth

Nothing is known of his early life, but Conleth was an Irish monk who became a bishop ministering in Co Kildare in Ireland. He spent time as a hermit at Old Connell and was a skilled artisan of metalwork. Brigid asked him to make the communion vessels for Kildare and he is also thought to have fashioned a crozier (crook) for St Finbar of Termon Barry. Conleth died c.520 AD.

God of creativity, you lavish your gifts upon us, may we, like Conleth, use our talents to bring glory to your name.

11 May

Tudy

Tudy who was born in the sixth century became a monk and later abbot. He founded monasteries in Brittany as well as doing missionary work among the local inhabitants. There are several places named for him including Ile-Tudy. The parish of St Tudy in Cornwall is certainly dedicated to him.

Lord God, you call every Christian to be a missionary in his or her daily life. May each one of us seek to show people Jesus in all that we do or say.

12 May

Pancras of Rome

Pancras died as a martyr when he was about fourteen years old in the fourth century. A church on the Via Aurelia in Rome was his burial place. Some of his relics were sent to Oswiu, King of Northumbria, by Pope Vitalian c.664 AD. A monastery in Rome was dedicated to him as was a church in Canterbury. There are six ancient churches in England named in his memory including the one in north London after which St Pancras Railway Station is named.

The blood of the martyrs is the seed of the church. May we too be willing, if required, to give our lives for your sake, O God.

13 May

Andrew Hubert Fournet

During the French Revolution Andrew Fournet the parish priest at Maille, Poitiers fled to Spain. After five years in exile he became ashamed and returned to France to minister to his flock in secret. He had a couple of narrow escapes from government officers and was in fact caught once. He had not wanted to be a priest, desiring a life of idleness and enjoyment. However, after spending time with an uncle who was in charge of a very poor parish he felt called to offer himself for ordination. When Napoleon allowed the Church to operate openly in France again, Fournet continued his ministry at Maille. He founded a group of teachers known as the Daughters of the Cross which cared for the sick and taught young girls about the Christian faith. He died in 1834.

Give courage to those who risk their lives by being Christians and in preaching the faith. May they know that you are with them no matter what happens to them, O Lord.

14 May

Gemma Galgani

Gemma fervently wanted to be a nun. She was born in 1878 near Lucca, Italy. However, as she suffered bouts of serious illness she was prevented from achieving that goal. During the years 1899-1901 she often received the stigmata (the wounds of Christ) in her own flesh as well as having visions. She also suffered severe attacks by the Devil. Despite these trials, she showed great patience in her life of pain. The name 'Gemma' is still popular with many parents for their daughters.

Lord Jesus, when you walked upon this earth, your hands were always ready to heal. Look in love on all who suffer, especially those who feel hampered in their service to you by the physical and mental problems of their bodies.

15 May

Hallvard

The patron saint of Oslo, Hallvard was born in Husaby, Norway. His youth was spent in Viking pursuits. One day while in a boat on the Drammenfjord, he came across a woman who begged him to save her from her pursuers and to take her into his boat. She had been accused of being a thief but was in fact innocent. When her accusers arrived, Hallvard refused to surrender the woman to them. Subsequently, they were both shot dead by arrows. Hallvard's body, though weighted down, floated on the surface of the fjord. His body was later placed in a shrine in a church in Oslo.

May we like Hallvard, seek to protect the innocent and the vulnerable that your way of justice and righteousness may prevail, O God of love.

16 May

Brendan

Often called 'the Navigator', Brendan was born near Tralee in Ireland c.486 AD. He ministered as a monk and later as an abbot in western Ireland where several places are named after him. He founded a monastery at Clonfert c.559 AD as well as others in Co Galway, Co Clare and Co Kerry. Many Irish monks travelled and Brendan was no exception. The *Navigation of St Brendan* popularised him as a mythical seafarer who set out with other monks to find a promised island in the middle of the Atlantic. Brendan died c.575 AD.

Almighty God, you show your mighty power in the oceans, we pray for those who journey on the seas that they may be protected from harm. Specially be with those who travel to spread the gospel that they may know the assurance of your presence always with them.

17 May

Madron

Details of his early life are non-existent but he may have been born in the sixth century. The town of Madron in Cornwall bears his name. The well and chapel there were visited by pilgrims seeking healing both before and after the Reformation. In 1641 the Bishop of Exeter, Joseph Hall, attested to the validity of a miracle of healing of a young man. Services are still held in the chapel.

'We are pilgrims on a journey.' You call us, Lord, to follow you and to show your love to all those we meet.

18 May

Elgiva

Probably the wife of Edmund king of Wessex (921-946 AD) and the mother of Kings Edwy and Edgar, she founded a nunnery at Shaftesbury in England. According to William of Malmesbury, she was generous, wise and had the gift of prophecy. She became abbess of Wilton and later died in 944 AD.

May we like Elgiva, set aside mean-spiritedness that our lives might overflow with generosity that we might care and share, dear Lord.

19 May

Dunstan,
Archbishop of Canterbury

Born at Baltonsborough near Glastonbury of a noble family, Dunstan joined the household of his uncle Athelm, Archbishop of Canterbury (923-926 AD), and later went to the court of King Athelstan. In 935 AD he was expelled from court on the charge of studying pagan stories and of being a magician. Dunstan almost decided to marry at this time but instead took his monastic vows privately and was ordained by Elphege, Bishop of Winchester. He then returned to Glastonbury, living as a hermit and engaged in painting, metalwork and embroidery, as well as making church bells and was appointed abbot of Glastonbury. In 955 AD his enemies conspired against him and he was banished from court, spending time in exile in Ghent in Belgium. Later King Edgar asked him to return to England making him his chief minister and then appointing him Bishop of Worcester (in 957 AD) and of London two years later. Enthroned as Archbishop of Canterbury in 960 AD, there is a legend that says that during the service a white dove flew down from the roof of the cathedral and settled on his shoulder. Dunstan spent a great deal of energy restoring monastic life on the pattern of the Rule of St Benedict. The form of the Coronation Service used at the crowning of Edgar by Dunstan in 973 AD became the basis of the medieval rite. In his twenty-nine years as archbishop, he led a prayerful life, worked tirelessly for peace, was generous in endowing churches and was a diligent teacher. His influence on the Church was profound. As well as being talented in the illumination of manuscripts, he was also an accomplished musician. Dunstan died in 988 AD and is now buried on the south side of the high altar in Canterbury Cathedral.

God of artistry and beauty we thank you for Dunstan's life, his talents and his pastoral care. We pray for all leaders of your church that they may set an example of godly living that we all may be inspired to follow.

20 May

Ethelbert, King of East Anglia

Ethelbert was murdered by Offa, king of Mercia in 794 AD when he came to visit seeking the hand of Offa's daughter in marriage. He was buried by the River Lugg at Marden and later his remains were reinterred at Hereford where they remained until burnt by the Danes in 1050. There are several churches dedicated to Ethelbert, including Hereford Cathedral where fragments of his shrine remain.

O Lord, stay the hands of those planning treacherous deeds that their consciences may be touched by the power of your Spirit.

21 May

Collen

Virtually nothing is known of Collen except that he was the patron and founder of Llangollen church in Wales and of Colan in Cornwall. There is a legend which says that he may have fought a duel with a Saracen in the presence of the pope. He supposedly delivered the people of the Vale of Llangollen by slaying a fierce female giant who was terrifying them.

God of eternity, details of some of your saints are lost in the mists of time. Nevertheless, help us to follow Collen's example by seeking to protect those who are vulnerable.

22 May

Helen of Carnarvon

Helen was a royal princess and wife of Clemens Maximus, the emperor in Britain, Spain and Gaul (383-388 AD), and is credited with leading a military expedition after her husband's death. Welsh tradition tells that she also arranged the building of roads. She may be the 'Helen' to whom some Welsh churches are dedicated.

Almighty God, we pray for those in powerful positions which affect the lives of others. May they acknowledge that they are answerable to you for the way they use their authority.

23 May

William of Rochester

William was born at Perth in Scotland and became a fisherman. Converted at an early age he devoted his life to good works before going on pilgrimage to the Holy Land in 1201. His companion, however, became his murderer, for a few paltry possessions. People claimed they had been cured after touching the body and so William was buried in Rochester Cathedral. Offerings made at his shrine helped to rebuild the cathedral. The site of St William's hospital near Maidstone in Kent is where he died in 1201. Some celebrate his feast day on 22 April.

Give courage, O Lord, to those who face danger and death because they are Christians. May they know that you will never leave them or forsake them.

24 May

David of Scotland

The youngest son of King Malcolm III of Scotland born c.1085, David was educated for a number of years at the Anglo-Norman court. His marriage to Matilda gave him a strong claim to the earldom of Northumbria. In 1124 he became King of Scotland. After being involved in wars he devoted his efforts to improving Scotland. He sought to dispense justice, made himself available to his subjects and gave generous alms. David died in 1153 and was buried at Dunfermline.

God of justice, may those in positions of authority seek to work for the betterment of the people for whose welfare they are responsible.

25 May

Zenobius of Florence, Bishop

Not a great deal is known of his life, except that he is the patron of Florence and was depicted by early artists of the Renaissance. Noted for his learning, Ambrose recommended him to Pope Damasus whose household Zenobius joined first at Rome and later going on a mission to Constantinople. After this he became bishop of Florence where his preaching and piety became well-known. He died c.390 AD.

God of mercy, may those who lead your church do so with a shepherd's care. By their service to others may they live out the servant role and encourage others to do the same.

26 May

Augustine,
First Archbishop of Canterbury

After becoming a monk, Augustine was later made prior of St Andrew's monastery in Rome. Pope Gregory the Great sent Augustine to England to evangelise the south of the country. Supported by Queen Bertha, who was a Christian, Augustine was received favourably by King Ethelbert. He later built a church (c. 602-3) on the site of the present Canterbury Cathedral.

We give thanks for our Christian heritage. May we value it and learn from those who have served you in every age.

27 May

Julius the Veteran

This Roman soldier, veteran of several military campaigns, when interrogated by the Prefect Maximus, said that he must be faithful to his Christian faith. Maximus respected Julius but still tried to get him to sacrifice to the gods by offering him a financial incentive. Julius refused to comprise his stand and at his execution in 304 AD he said: 'Lord Jesus Christ, I suffer this for your name. I beg you to receive my spirit together with your holy martyrs.'

God of abundance, may we not yield to the lure of this world's riches. Keep us honest in our dealings that we may serve you with a clear conscience.

28 May

Bernard of Aosta

Bernard was an Italian priest who became vicar-general of the Diocese of Aosta. He spent forty-two years there visiting, founding schools and building churches. He also built guesthouses on the mountain passes for travellers. Great and Little St Bernard are named after him. He also established Austin Canon houses to care for Alpine travellers. The dog breed 'St Bernard' (so famous for its role in mountain rescue) is named after him. He died in 1081 aged eighty-five-years-old and was adopted as the patron saint of mountain climbers.

Guide and protect all those involved in mountain rescue, O God. We give thanks for the endurance and loyalty of all dogs which set out to save lives. Be with all who risk their own lives trying to save others.

29 May

Mary Magdelene de Pazzi

Born to a wealthy Florentine family in 1566, Mary became a Carmelite nun, though her parents opposed this choice for their daughter. She had visions and became somewhat of a mystic. Words spoken at these times were recorded in her seven volumes of writings. She was gifted with great insight and could prophesy the future. However, because of this she suffered intense headaches and pain. In 1606 when she knew that she was soon going to die, she called the other sisters together exhorting them to love and serve Jesus alone.

Lord, bless each person in their vocation and ministry that they may seek to live for you and to serve only you.

30 May

Hubert,
Bishop of Maastricht and Liege

Details of Hubert's early life are not known. However, he seems to have been the first to evangelise the Ardennes district of Belgium. He became Bishop of Maastricht in 705 AD. During this time, in 716 AD, he arranged for the relics of his predecessor Lambert to be placed in a church in Liege. Hubert later made this his cathedral. When he died in 727 AD miracles began to take place at his tomb and his relics were moved to Andain (now St Hubert) in 743 AD. There is a story about his conversion. It is said that while he was out hunting on Good Friday he saw an image of the crucified Christ between the antlers of a stag. This is a similar story to that of St Eustace.

As Hubert saw the image of Christ crucified between the stag's antlers, may we ponder that love 'so amazing so divine' that made your Son, O God, willing to die for us all.

31 May

Petronilla

A martyr in the early days of the Roman Empire, little is known of Petronilla's life. It is in the catacomb of the Domitilla family that she is recorded as having died a martyr's death. In 757 AD her remains were moved to a building near St Peter's, Rome which was remodelled to become the Chapel of St Petronilla. This chapel became the burial place of some French kings. When St Peter's was rebuilt in the sixteenth century, her relics were interred near an altar near the cupola. To this day, Mass in St Peter's on 31 May each year is offered for France and attended by French residents in Rome.

Lord, give us the courage to stand firm in the faith of Christ. Grant that if we were ever faced with death because of our Christian belief we would witness to you no matter what the cost.

1 June

Ronan of Brittany

Ronan was a Cornish bishop who died in Brittany. Patron with St Coventin, of the town of Quimper, he was probably a 6th century Irish monk who lived as a hermit in western Brittany. The village of Locronan (where he was buried) is named for him. He was known for his godly life and kind deeds as a bishop. A jealous woman brought a charge of sorcery against him. After his death his remains were removed to Quimper Abbey.

God of truth, we pray for those who are falsely accused by people who are jealous of them. Give them the reassurance that you will never let them down.

2 June

Marcellinus and Peter

Marcellinus, a priest and Peter, an exorcist were martyred in Rome in 304 AD. They were buried in the catacomb of Tiburtius on the Via Lavicana and later a church was built over the spot. Pope Gregory IV sent their relics in 827 AD to the monastery at Seligenstadt where miracles are said to have taken place.

Lord God, we read in the pages of history about the lives of your saints, inspire us by their examples that we might live holy lives to your glory.

3 June

Kevin,
Abbot of Glendalough

Kevin was the founder and first abbot of Glendalough in Co Wicklow just south of Dublin. Set in a beautiful valley with a stream running through it, Kevin chose it as the ideal place to live his life for God. Kevin is thought to have been born into a noble Leinster family which had lost its claim to kingship. Educated by monks, Kevin was ordained a priest. Like-minded companions gathered round him, seeking to live in dedication to God. A story is told that he fed his community for some time with salmon supplied by otters. There is a beautiful legend, that once while the saint had his arms stretched out in prayer, a blackbird laid an egg in his hand. Rather than disturb the bird, he stayed in the same position until the egg was hatched.

As your saints of old were at one with creation, so may we care for the world which you have made. May we ensure that no living thing is treated cruelly or exploited, dear Lord.

4 June

Petroc

A sixth century Cornish abbot and Cornwall's most noted saint, Petroc came from south Wales and founded a monastery at Padstow (Petroc's Stow). He also established other monasteries to which he paid final visits before his death. Petroc spent much of his life as a hermit on Bodmin Moor and when he died he was buried at Padstow. However, through theft and trickery his relics were scattered but some of his remains are contained in a reliquary in the parish church at Bodmin.

So many saints have played a role in bringing the gospel to the British Isles, may we give thanks, O Lord, for their lives and may we emulate their examples.

5 June

Boniface

His parents were land-owning peasants in Devon when he was born c.675 AD. Boniface wrote the first Latin Grammar to be produced in England. Ordained at the age of thirty he became noted as a preacher and teacher. He chose to be a missionary and travelled to Frisia in 716 AD. However, he faced much pagan opposition and returned to England later when given responsibility by Pope Gregory II for Bavaria and Hesse. Boniface was consecrated bishop in 722 AD and made archbishop ten years later. In his eighties, Boniface was killed by some pagans in Frisia while waiting to perform a Confirmation service.

Everlasting God, we pray for those who in our own day minister in difficult and dangerous situations. Give them courage equal to their need.

6 June

Jarlath, Irish monk

Jarlath is thought to have been born to a noble family in Galway, Ireland. He became a disciple of Enda. The monasteries he founded, first at Cluain Fois and later at Tuam, were renowned for their scholarship and learning. Brenda of Clonfert and Colman of Munster may have been taught by him. He was buried at Tuam c.550 AD.

God of all knowledge, enlighten all places of education and learning that your truth may be revealed to those who study.

7 June

Meriasek (Meriadoc)

Although his name is Welsh he was a patron of Camborne (Cornwall) where he founded a church. Meriasek worked in Brittany establishing monasteries as well as becoming bishop of the district near Vannes. His feast is celebrated in Brittany though not elsewhere in France. There are several wells dedicated to him. He is thought to have lived in the sixth century.

Lord, you are our Rock and our Defence, we pray for those who seek to grow churches in today's modern cynical world. May people's hearts be open to the gospel.

8 June

Medard

Born at Salency in Picardy in France c.470 AD, Medard was educated at Saint-Quentin and ordained c.505 AD. Later he became a bishop. He died c.560 AD. Those suffering from toothache often prayed for his help.

God of wholeness and healing, we give thanks for all members of the medical profession as they seek to alleviate suffering and to bring healing to their patients. May your healing hands be stretched out in blessing on those who are sick and those who seek to help them.

9 June

Columba, Abbot of Iona

His name Columcille means 'dove of the Church'. He was born c.521 AD at Gartan in Donegal, Ireland and was of royal blood. Later he became a monk and founded monasteries at Derry (546 AD) and Durrow (c.556 AD) and probably also at Kells. In 565 AD he left his native Ireland with twelve companions. This may have been banishment for a battle which he caused over a book which he had copied and kept without the owner's permission. He and his companions settled on the island of Iona off the south-western coast of Scotland. As abbot of Iona he proved to be an able leader although sometimes he could be severe. Most of his influence was in the Western Islands of Scotland. Columba died in 597 AD and after four Viking raids on Iona, his remains were moved to Dunkeld in 849 AD.

Lord, help us, like Columba to learn from our mistakes and to continue faithfully on the pilgrim way.

10 June

Ithamar,
Bishop of Rochester

A scholarly man, Ithamar was consecrated Bishop of Rochester in Kent in 644 AD by Honorius, Archbishop of Canterbury. He was the first Anglo-Saxon to occupy an English see (diocese). He in fact consecrated the first Anglo-Saxon Archbishop of Canterbury – Deusdedit. Bishop Ithamar died at Rochester c.660 AD. When rebuilding work was taking place at Rochester in 1077, Ithamar's relics were translated to another site in Rochester Cathedral and here miracles of healing were reported to have taken place.

Lord God, you called your servant to be a bishop. We pray for all those who lead the flock of Christ. May they be faithful pastors as they administer your word and sacraments.

11 June

Barnabas

Not one of the Twelve Apostles, Barnabas was of the tribe of Levi, though he was probably born in Cyprus. Barnabas was chosen by the early Christians because he was 'a good man, full of the Holy Spirit'. He spent a year with St Paul in Antioch. After this they made many journeys together preaching and teaching, until there was 'a falling out' over Jewish customs as well as the use of young John Mark in the team. There is uncertainty as to the date of his death.

May we like Barnabas, seek to be filled with your Spirit that we might live for you, O loving God.

12 June

Eskil,
Bishop and Martyr

Eskil, an Englishman, was a relation of Sigfrid of Sweden whom he helped to reconvert the Swedish people. After Anskar (801-865 AD) died the Swedes lapsed into paganism. Eskil was consecrated bishop at Strangnas and is believed to have been its first bishop. When King Inge was murdered, Eskil was stoned to death c.1080, after a pagan altar was destroyed during a violent storm.

Lord, we pray for all who leave their native land to preach the gospel. May they find that your grace is sufficient for them.

13 June

Anthony of Padua

Although Portuguese by birth, Anthony's surname comes from the city of Padua. Born in 1195 he later became a Franciscan monk. He felt called to minister in Morocco where several Franciscans had been martyred. Anthony soon became very ill and on his return journey to Europe, his ship was driven off course to Messina in Sicily. He made his way to Assisi where he attended the general chapter meeting of 1221. After this he was sent to the lonely hermitage of San Paolo and later he was summoned to preach in Lombardy. He seemed to radiate holiness and people were drawn to him as he showed them compassion. With the pope's blessing, Anthony lived in Padua where he had a fruitful ministry. He died at the age of thirty in 1231.

God of compassion, we give thanks for all your servants who like Anthony take the servant role in their loving care of people. May we too seek to show the love of Christ in our lives.

14 June

Dogmael

Dogmael was probably a Welsh monk who worked in Pembrokeshire although there is a church dedicated to him in Anglesey. He may have moved to Brittany to continue his ministry, as there St Dogmael's prayers were sought to help children to walk. He died early in the sixth century.

Lord, you called your servant Dogmael to care for your people. Warm our cold hearts that we too may seek to be Christ to others.

15 June

Trillo

An abbot from the fifth or sixth century, virtually nothing is known of his life. The name of Llandrillo (Denbighshire now Gwynedd) is attributed to him. There is a tiny church dedicated to him at Rhos on Sea. It is so small only about six people can fit inside. There is also a holy well which is over a spring which was used for baptism and is thought to cure rheumatism.

God of compassion, we pray for all those involved in the ministry of healing. Give them wisdom and energy to fulfil their responsibilities with care.

16 June

Ismael

A Welsh bishop in sixth century, Ismael may have been the son of Budic, a prince of Cornouaille who was forced into exile in Dyfed thus prompting a return to Brittany. Teilo may have consecrated Ismael bishop of Menevia, where St David had been bishop. Several churches are dedicated to him in Pembrokeshire and one in Carmarthenshire.

God of power and might, guide all leaders of your church that they may be faithful shepherds of your flock.

17 June

Botolph (Botulf)

East Anglian by birth, Botolph built a monastery in 654 AD on land given by the King of East Anglia. He became abbot of Icanho (maybe Iken in Suffolk). Little is known of his life. His church was destroyed by the Danes. There were sixty-four ancient churches dedicated to Botolph who died in 680 AD.

Inspire and encourage those who set out to build churches to your glory. May they ever be mindful that you desire that we should worship you in spirit and in truth, O God.

18 June

Bernard Mizeki, Martyr

In about 1861, Bernard was born in Portuguese East Africa (Mozambique). When aged twelve or thereabouts he went to live in the slums of Capetown where he worked as a labourer for ten years. When he saw the effects that alcoholism had on people's lives he vowed never to drink alcohol. At night, after work, he attended classes at an Anglican school. During this time he was converted and baptised. He learnt English, French, Dutch and several local African dialects. These skills were put to good use in translating the scriptures. He continued his missionary work in Mashonaland where he built a school and won the affection of the people. Unfortunately, many black African nationalists saw all missionaries as employees of European colonial governments. On 18 June 1896 Bernard was fatally speared. His wife and a helper went to get blankets for him. They said they saw a blinding light on the hill where he lay and heard a rushing sound like many wings. When they reached the spot his body had disappeared. One of the greatest Christian festivals now takes place on the site of his martyrdom.

Give us courage and tenacity to hold onto our faith whatever the cost. Eternal God, may we like your servant, Bernard, be willing to sacrifice our lives for your sake should we be called to do so.

19 June

Sundar Singh

Sundar was born in 1889 in northern India to a wealthy family. He studied Hinduism as well as reading the Koran. He became a Sadhu (a Hindu who forsakes all pleasures) but could not find any peace. Sundar attended a missionary school but rejected the teachings of Jesus and indeed he ripped a Bible apart and burnt it. Three days after this he awoke and said: 'Oh God, if you exist show me the right way, or I will kill myself'. Suddenly there was a brilliant light and he saw the figure of Jesus in the radiance. Then he heard a voice say in Hindi: 'How much longer are you going to search for me? I have come to save you'. Sundar suddenly realised Jesus was alive and fell to his knees and felt peace such as he had never known. He was baptised, much against his family's wishes, and his father disowned him for becoming a Christian. Dressed in a yellow robe, barefoot and with no provisions he wandered from village to village preaching the gospel. He visited Tibet where he endured much hardship. In Nepal he was persecuted by a Buddhist Lama for promoting a 'foreign' religion. Sundar travelled to many countries including Australia, Europe and Israel as well as extensively all over India and Sri Lanka (Ceylon). He visited Tibet every summer, however, in 1929 he was never seen again.

We long to have the bravery to preach Christ and him crucified as Sundar Singh did. O Lord God, give us your strength in our weakness and help us to know that you are with us to the end of the world.

20 June

Alban

Alban is thought to have been a soldier who sheltered a priest who was fleeing persecution. The priest's example had a profound effect on Alban who was converted and baptised. When pursuing soldiers came to arrest the priest, Alban swapped clothes with him to allow him to escape and continue his preaching. Alban refused to offer sacrifice to the emperor and so was beheaded c.250 AD. He was the first British martyr and the town of St Alban's developed around his shrine.

Lord God, we give thanks for Alban, the first British martyr, and his selfless act in offering his life so that the priest could continue with his ministry. Bless the people of Great Britain that inspired by so many saints they may live lives pleasing to you.

21 June

Leufred

Leufred was born in France near Eureux. He later studied at Chartres and although he had planned to be a teacher, he felt drawn to live as a hermit. The Irish monk Sidonius of Rouen had great influence on this decision. Leufred built a monastery and is thought to have been an abbot for forty-eight years. He died in 738 AD.

Heavenly Father, you call some to live a life of seclusion and contemplation and others to live 'in the thick of it' amidst all the temptations and stresses of daily life. May each one in their vocation seek to glorify you in their living.

22 June

Paulinus of Nola, Bishop

French born of a wealthy family from Bordeaux, Paulinus was educated by the poet Ausonius. Later he became a lawyer as well as holding public office. He and his Spanish wife had an affluent lifestyle before becoming Christians. After their conversion they gave much of their wealth to the church. Although married, the Bishop of Barcelona ordained Paulinus a priest. A few friends joined him in a semi-monastic life. About 409 AD he became Bishop of Nola where he remained till his death during Vespers on 22 June 431 AD.

God of grace, may each one of us use our time, talents and money for your service. We must leave behind this world's riches at the end of our earthly journey. Help us to use them wisely now.

23 June

Etheldreda of Ely

The daughter of the king of East Anglia, Etheldreda married Tondberht c.652 AD at a young age and the marriage was never consummated. When he died in 655 AD, she retired to the Isle of Ely which had been her dowry. When married a second time to a fifteen-year-old boy, Etheldreda refused a normal marriage and entered her aunt Ebbe's convent at Coldingham. Etheldreda built a monastery on the site of the present day Ely Cathedral. For seven years she lived a life of penance and prayer. She died in 679 AD.

God of love, we pray for those in unhappy marriages, those going through the trauma of divorce and those who are single but not by choice.

24 June

Bartholomew of Farne,
Monk and Hermit

His parents were Scandinavian but he was born at Whitby. Later he went to Norway where he became a priest. He then returned to England where he entered the monastery at Durham and took the name Bartholomew. After seeing Christ in a vision, he went as a hermit to the island of the Inner Farne where St Cuthbert had spent time. There he remained for forty-two years. Although he did not relate well to other people, he loved his pet bird and spent much time walking on the island singing psalms. He died in 1193.

Draw near, living Lord, to those who find it difficult to relate to people that they may begin to see Christ in others and open their hearts to you.

25 June

Moluag, Abbot

Moluag was born in Northern Ireland c.530 AD and became a monk at Bangor. He spent time in Scotland and founded the island monastery of Lismore c.562 AD. Monks from this monastery established churches in east Scotland, the Isle of Skye and the Outer Hebrides. Moluag is said to have cured some people on Lewis who were suffering from madness.

God of wholeness and healing, look in mercy on those suffering from mental illness. Give patience and wisdom to those who care for them.

26 June

John and Paul, Martyrs

They were Roman martyrs who died c.362 AD. They may have been brothers and were probably soldiers under the Emperor Constantine. Their whole history is rather spurious. There is a beautiful church in Venice dedicated to them and this is where several of the Doges were buried.

We praise your name, O Lord, for all your martyrs who have given their lives rather than deny their faith.

27 June

Richard Fitzralph, Archbishop of Armagh

Richard was a brilliant scholar and had been Chancellor of Oxford University. He taught at Balliol College Oxford in 1325. Richard paid his first visit to the Papal Court at Avignon in France in 1334. After being appointed Dean of Lichfield he returned to England a year later. He was consecrated Archbishop of Armagh in 1346. Born in Dundalk he was known for his pastoral care. Although deeply interested in church history, he nevertheless found time to minister to his people in Dundalk and Drogheda during the Black Death. His writing influenced John Wyclif, particularly regarding use of possessions. He died in 1360 while visiting Avignon for the third time. He was interred in 1370 in St Nicholas's church Dundalk.

God of all knowledge, we pray for all those involved in study at universities and colleges. May they value the opportunity to learn and recognise that you have given them the ability to study and acquire knowledge.

28 June

Austell

Born in the sixth century, Austell was a follower of Mewan. He probably went with him from South Wales to Cornwall and later accompanied him and Samson to Brittany. Austell founded the church in Cornwall at St Austell, the town being named after him. He died at S. Meen in Brittany and is buried there.

Lord, you inspired so many of the early saints to travel long distances and to make hazardous journeys in order to spread the gospel. Give us that same sense of adventure and daring to tell others what you have done for us.

29 June

Peter and Paul

Peter was a fisherman when Jesus called him to follow him and promised that he would be a 'fisher of men'. His wife and his brother Andrew also left their homes to follow Jesus. Peter was originally called 'Simon' but after Peter's acknowledgement that Jesus was the Christ, the Son of God, he was renamed 'Cephas' (Peter). The apostle Peter had a knack for 'putting his foot in it' by making statements which he didn't fulfil. This no doubt makes him one of the best loved biblical saints as we can readily relate to him. He along with James and John were privileged to share many special experiences with Jesus. On the night that Jesus was arrested before he was crucified, Peter denied three times that he knew him. Bitterly disappointed with his denial, Peter was lovingly reconciled to his Lord after Christ's resurrection when Jesus asked him three times did he love him. Receiving the affirmative answer Jesus told him 'to feed his sheep'. Tradition has it that Peter was crucified upside down in deference to his Lord during the time that Nero was emperor.

Saul, as he was known prior to being renamed Paul, was a tent maker by trade and a fanatical opponent of Christians. On the road to Damascus he saw a dazzling light and heard the voice of the Risen Lord speaking to him. When he arose from his knees he found that he was blind and was led into the city where his sight was later restored. A Roman citizen, Paul suffered flogging, imprisonment, shipwreck and starvation for the sake of the Gospel. Tradition says that he was martyred in Rome.

Lord our God, you called Peter and Paul to suffer much for the sake of the gospel and to finally give their lives as martyrs. We thank you for their examples that have inspired so many Christians to go to their death fearless and unafraid.

30 June

Theobald of Provins

His family lived in the Champagne region of France and Theobald was born at Provins (Brie). He was joined by a friend called Walter and they both decided to become hermits rather than join the army. They worked in the surrounding villages to earn their keep. After pilgrimages to Compostela and Rome they settled near Vicenza. After Walter died, the bishop ordained Theobald a priest. He was joined by a small group of followers till his death in 1066. Several medieval churches in England are dedicated to him.

God of pilgrimage, we thank you for those sacred places that are special to each one of us. Help us as we journey through life that we may take time to draw apart from the daily routine.

1 July

Serf (Servanus)

Serf was a Scottish bishop in the sixth century who was born c.500 AD. He ministered in western Fife with his main activity taking place around Culross. He was a contemporary of St Cuthbert. Serf died in 583 AD in Dunning in Perthshire but is buried in Culross.

Lord, you have led your saints in every age, give us grace to follow their examples that we may shine as lights in a dark world.

2 July

Oudoceus

Prior to his birth c.545 AD, Oudoceus's family had moved from Brittany to Wales. During his youth Anglo-Saxon invaders made their way into the western parts of Britain which resulted in the battle of Dyrham in 577 AD. After this the Welsh separated from Devon and Cornwall. Oudoceus was a monk at Llandogo where he became bishop c.580 AD. His endeavours to unite several abbots may have been a precursor to the formation of the see of Llandaff. He died c.615 AD and his shrine remained at Llandaff until 1540.

God of unity and peace, we pray for those who seek to unify situations for the good of others. May we too seek to bring harmony rather than discord to our relations with others.

3 July

Germanus of Man

Germanus, a contemporary of St Patrick, was born c.410 AD in Brittany. He joined Patrick in Ireland c.440 AD and later lived in monasteries in Wales. He met up with Patrick again in Britain c.462 AD and four years later returned to Ireland where he became Bishop of Man. There are various dedications to him. He is often confused with Germanus of Auxerre.

Eternal God, as we travel the road of life may we be mindful of those who have gone before us. Keep us on the narrow way that leads to yourself.

4 July

Elizabeth of Portugal

Named after a relative, Elizabeth of Hungary, she was the daughter of King Peter III of Aragon and was born in 1271. She was married at the tender age of twelve to King Denis of Portugal. Although he was not a good husband, Elizabeth devoted herself to charitable works by founding hospitals and orphanages. Acting as a peacemaker she even diffused the potential for war between Portugal and Castile. After her husband's death in 1324, she went on pilgrimage to Compostela. She lived a simple life as a Franciscan tertiary although she wanted to be a Poor Clare. When she died in 1336 she was buried in the Poor Clare's convent at Coimbra where many miracles are said to have taken place.

Be with those who try to bring peace to this troubled world, O God. May discussions and a willingness to listen to another point of view prevail rather than war and fighting.

5 July

Morwenna

Morwenna was probably born in the sixth century of Irish-Welsh ancestry. A descendant of Brychan whose family lived in North Cornwall, she is the patron saint of Morwenstow in Cornwall. There is a legend that when a church was being built, Morwenna carried a stone on her head to the site. When she put it down to rest, a well sprang up. Where Morwenna finally placed the stone, there the church was constructed although a different site had been chosen.

Living Lord, give us a willingness to change our preconceived ideas that we may do your will.

6 July

Moninne (Monenna)

Also known as 'Darerca' or 'Bline', Moninne became an abbess and foundress of Killeevy, Co Armagh. This foundation consisted of eight virgins and a widow whose son, Luger, later became a bishop. At least one of her community travelled to Whithorn in south-west Scotland to Ninian's foundation with the intention of establishing more monasteries. When she died c.518 AD, many miracles of healing were attributed to her.

You call some to devote their entire lives to prayer and contemplation, O God our Saviour. It is good that some can spend time in prayer unhindered by the worries and stresses of the world. May we feel supported by their intercession for us.

7 July

Sunniva

Sunniva was an Irish princess who became a nun. She and some companions sought to live holy lives. They settled on an uninhabited island called Selje, off the west coast of Norway. Their little community dwelt in caves and lived on fish. A neighbour, Jarl Haakon, heard about them and went to investigate. The nuns fled to the caves asking God to protect them. A massive rock fall blocked the entrances to the caves. Many years later the incorrupt body of Sunniva was discovered. In 1170 her relics were moved to Bergen.

Lord, you have promised to be with us in every circumstance of life. May we trust you that whatever happens to us, you will never forsake us.

8 July

Kilian of Kilmore

Irish born, Kilian set out with eleven companions as missionaries to Germany. They reached Ascaffenburg on the Rhine and then continued to Wurzburg. When Kilian returned from visiting Pope Conon in Rome, he found that King Gozbert had married his brother's widow. Kilian tried to get them to separate but the king had him murdered. He may, with two companions, have been killed in the cathedral at Wurzburg c. 689 AD. He is specially celebrated in Wurzburg, Vienna and Ireland.

May we, like Kilian, be ready to stand up for what we believe to be right, O God of justice. Give us the courage we need to speak up when we see things that are evil.

9 July

Veronica Giuliani

Veronica was born into a wealthy family at Mercatello in 1660. Although her father opposed it she became a Capuchin nun. She showed intense devotion to the Passion of Christ, having visions and receiving the stigmata (the wounds) of Christ in her body. Veronica was in charge of novices for thirty-four years. Not only did she raise the spiritual life of her community, but showed a practical side by installing piped water and enlarging buildings.

God of joy, we thank you for those who, like Veronica, lift our spirits to achieve renewed devotion to serve you.

10 July

Alexander

From the time of the third century, Alexander was one of a group of Roman martyrs later known as the 'seven brothers'. Details of his life are sketchy. However, we do know he was buried in the Jordani cemetery situated on the Salarian Way.

God of all knowing, so many of your saints' deeds are known only to you. Nevertheless, may we seek to be inspired by those who have influenced our own lives.

11 July

Drostan

Scottish born, Drostan was the son of a prince of Demetia (now part of Wales). He was a contemporary of St Finbar. Drostan was appointed abbot and founder of the monastery at Deer in Aberdeenshire. The influence of the monastery at Deer was great. From here several churches on either side of the Moray Firth were established. There are some churches in northeast Scotland dedicated to Drostan. *The Book of Deer* is in Cambridge University library.

We give thanks, Lord, for the vision of those who have built beautiful cathedrals and churches. May we use this legacy left to us for promotion of a living faith and not view these buildings as museums.

12 July

John Gualbert

Although born to a wealthy family in Florence , little is known of his early years. There is one incident recorded that one Good Friday he met the person who had murdered his brother. John refused to take revenge and forgave the penitent murderer. Soon after he became a monk, but saddened by the abuses and excesses of the Church, he eventually set up his own monastery at Vallombrosa near Florence. Hospices inspired by this monastery were established. John was never ordained a priest but was known for his healing and prophecy.

Lord, we pray for those who have lost a loved one in violent circumstances. May they turn to you for consolation and may they by your grace, learn to forgive those who have caused such havoc in their lives.

13 July

Mildred

The daughter of the King of Mercia and Ermenburga, a princess of Kent, Mildred was educated at a convent near Paris. She had escaped to Chelles from an unwanted suitor. After her return to Britain she became a nun at Minster-in-Thanet in Kent. Ermenburga had founded this abbey and Mildred became abbess, prior to 694 AD. Mildred was very even-tempered and showed particular care for children and widows. She died c.700 AD after a long illness and pilgrims starting coming to her tomb. In 1035 her relics were moved to St Augustine's Abbey in Canterbury. The Benedictine nunnery at Minster still exists.

Loving God, we ask that you will make us like Mildred – patient and slow to anger. Give us your power for we cannot achieve these qualities in our own strength.

14 July

John Keble

The son of an Anglican priest, John was born in 1792. He showed early signs of scholastic ability and became a Fellow of Oriel College, Oxford, at the age of nineteen. A collection of his poems, *The Christian Year* published in 1827, won great acclaim and he was elected Professor of Poetry at Oxford in 1831. He was leader of the Tractarian Movement, which opposed the threats to the Church from liberalism in both politics and theology. Keble did not seek a 'high profile' position, becoming a parish priest near Winchester, a position he held until his death in 1836. He wrote many scholarly books and was recognised as a wise counsellor. Keble is probably best remembered for the sermon he preached on 14 July 1833 in Oxford which was seen by some to herald the beginning of the Oxford Movement.

God of wisdom, we give thanks for those who have given us wise counsel as your servant John Keble gave to those who sought his advice.

15 July

Swithun

Chaplain to King Egbert of Wessex, Swithun's birthplace, he was educated at the Old Minster, Winchester. In 852 AD King Ethelwulf appointed Swithun bishop of Winchester. In the succeeding years Wessex became the most important kingdom in England. During this time the first Viking raids in the south of England took place. Swithun built many churches and was noted for his generosity to charitable causes. Prior to his death on 2 July 862 AD, Swithun had requested that he be buried in the cemetery outside the west door of the Old Minster. When Ethelwold became bishop of Winchester in 964 AD, it was decided that Swithun's relics should be translated to a shrine within the cathedral. This took place on 15th July 971 AD. Many miracles were reported there as well as much rain. This was taken as a sign of Swithun's displeasure in having his mortal remains moved. Still today people often say that if it rains on St Swithun's day it will continue for forty days.

God our eternal King, we praise you for those in high places who, like Swithun, still remain humble in spite of their status.

16 July

Plechelm (Pechthelm, Pleghelm)

Plechelm was a missionary in Northumbria in the eighth century. He journeyed with two friends, Wiro and Otger, to Rome on pilgrimage. While there he was consecrated bishop and went to the Meuse valley in the Netherlands to minister. A church and monastery were built at Roermond. Plechelm died at Odilienberg and was buried there for a time. His relics were later moved to Roermond.

Lord, we admire the tenacity of your early saints who travelled great distances to go on pilgrimage. Help us to seek to follow you each day on the pilgrim road.

17 July

Kenelm

Kenelm was born into the royal family of Mercia. He was the son of Coenwulf who was king 796-821 AD. A number of charters were signed by Kenelm, one of which granted him ownership of Glastonbury. Kenelm died probably in battle, before he became king, and was buried at Winchcombe Abbey. Various legends surround Kenelm, one of which classed him as a martyr.

Almighty God, we pray for all Christian kings and queens that they may rule with justice and integrity. May they see their authority as a trust from you.

18 July

Frederick of Utrecht

The grandson of King Radboud, Frederick was born in Friesland c.780 AD. He was taught by members of the clergy at Utrecht. On completion of his studies he was ordained a priest and given the task of converting those who were still pagans in the northern parts of the diocese. When Bishop Ricfried died 815-16 AD, Frederick was consecrated bishop of Utrecht. His wisdom and knowledge were very evident especially during the synod of Mainz in 829 AD. Frederick was murdered c.834-838 AD. The reason for his murder, and the perpetrators of the crime, has never been established. It may have been brought about by some of the area's inhabitants who were violently opposed to Christianity. Frederick was buried in St Salvator's church in Utrecht.

Everlasting God, so many Christians have met and still today meet a violent end. Save us from dying suddenly and unprepared.

19 July

Arsenius

Arsenius was a renowned teacher and deacon. Indeed Pope Damasus recommended him as a tutor for the emperor's children. He was lavished with gifts, money and servants but after living this life of luxury for ten years he sensed God was calling him to a life of prayer and contemplation. He joined the monks in the desert near the Wadi Natrun in Egypt. Arsenius craved silence and spent some years living on a rock called Petra near Memphis. When a relative died who had left him most of his wealth, Arsenius tore the will in two and refused the lure of riches. By the time he died in the desert in 449 AD he had found peace with God.

Creator God, we pray that we may not covet wealth and preferment in this world. Help us to set our hearts on treasure in heaven.

20 July

Wilgefortis

The legendary daughter of a pagan king of Portugal, Wilgefortis vowed to remain a virgin when she was converted to Christianity. Pursued by a suitor she prayed to be ugly and so a beard and moustache grew on her face. It is said that her father had her crucified. There is a statue of her in the chapel of Henry VII in Westminster Abbey.

Lord, help us to be pure in our thoughts and to show forth the fruits of your Spirit in our lives.

21 July

Laurence of Brindisi

Laurence was born into a wealthy Venetian family at Brindisi and became a Franciscan monk at the age of sixteen. He showed great aptitude for learning languages as well as diligently studying the scriptures. Pope Clement VIII recognised his potential and set him the task of the conversion of the Jews. After a life involved in political and military affairs as well as his religious calling, Laurence retired in 1618 to Caserta wishing to spend his life in prayer and contemplation. He died a year later in Lisbon and is buried in the Poor Clares Cemetery at Villafranca.

God of all knowledge, illuminate all those who study the scriptures that they may see your truth revealed to them.

22 July

Wandrille

Wandrille was born c.600AD near Verdun where he grew up and married. Apparently, in 628 AD he and his wife both felt called to monastic vocations and decided to separate. After he trained at Montfaucon-Romain-Moutier he was ordained a priest. He then founded his own monastery at Fontenelle in Normandy. This became known not only for its learning but also its agriculture. After Wandrille died in 668 AD the abbey adopted the Rule of St Benedict as the basis of its life.

Lord, help us to live our lives in service to you and to others that we may shine as lights in a dark world and be faithful witnesses to you.

23 July

Bridget of Sweden (Birgitta)

Bridget was born in 1303 and is the patron saint of Sweden. The daughter of the wealthy governor of Upland, she married at the young age of fourteen. She and her husband had eight children one of whom was to become St Catherine of Sweden. At the age of thirty-two Bridget was commanded to go to court as a lady-in-waiting to Queen Blanche of Namur. During this time she began to experience strange revelations. These did not have any impact on the way the King and Queen lived their lives. However, Bridget became an object of gossip for those at court. She went on pilgrimage to St Olaf's shrine at Trondheim in Norway. Later she visited San Diego de Compostela. Her husband died soon after this and Bridget lived in the monastery at Alvastra. In 1346 she founded a monastery for monks and nuns at Vadstena on Lake Vattern. Three years later she travelled to Rome to obtain approval for her order. She spent the rest of her life in Italy or on pilgrimage. Bridget showed great care for the poor and for pilgrims. She died in 1373 and in 1391 her relics were interred in Vadstena Abbey.

As the heart of your servant Birgitta was touched with compassion to reach out to the poor and to pilgrims, may our hearts, O Lord, be filled with your love for others. We pray for the people of Sweden that, inspired by Birgitta's example, they may serve you faithfully.

24 July

Declan, Bishop

Declan, a prince of the tribe of Decies, was born at Ardmore in Waterford, Ireland. He was probably a bishop in this area and founded the church at Ardmore. Declan may have been educated in Wales or Gaul (France). It is believed that when Patrick was escaping from slavery, Declan's tribe of the Decies may have offered him hospitality.

God of compassion, help us to be willing to offer hospitality to those in need. May we do everything to your glory inspired by your great love.

25 July

Christopher

Possibly a martyr in the third century, little is known of Christopher's life except that he died in Asia Minor. A church in Bithynia was dedicated to him in 452 AD. Legends about him were recorded in Greek and Latin in the eighth century and these were embellished in Germany in the twelfth century. The name Christopher means 'Christ bearer'. A hermit instructed him in the Christian faith and set him the task of helping people cross a river nearby. Tradition has it that one day a child asked to be carried across the river. Christopher is said to have found the child too heavy to carry and was told by the child that he was Jesus Christ bearing the weight of the world's sins. Later Christopher preached in the city of Lycia with great success. He met his death by being beaten with iron rods, shot with arrows and finally he was beheaded. Paintings of him have survived in many English churches. These were painted on the north wall so that these could be seen by all who entered the building. Christopher was the patron of travellers as well as those threatened by water, tempest, plague and sudden death.

Strong and powerful God, may we see Christ in others and be Christ to others.

26 July

Joachim and Ann

Although the Bible does not tell the names of the parents of the Blessed Virgin Mary, by tradition they have been accepted as Joachim and Ann. Joachim is thought to have married Ann at a young age and for a number of years the couple remained childless. Joachim is said to have spent forty days in the desert praying for a child. Ann also grieved being childless and one day when she was praying an angel told her that she would conceive. Ann replied that whether the baby was a boy or a girl she would give the child as a gift to the Lord. It is thought that she was probably about forty when Mary was born.

Lord, you welcomed little children to come to you, we pray for childless couples. May they entrust their future into your loving hands.

27 July

Pantaleon

He was a doctor in the latter part of the third century. Appropriately his name means 'all compassionate'. There is a legend that he was the son of a pagan father and a Christian mother. When he was converted to Christianity he was already a successful doctor with many patients including the Emperor Galerius. In 303 AD during the persecution by Diocletian, he was denounced as a Christian by his colleagues. Arrested and tortured Pantaleon was beheaded c.305 AD.

When you walked the dusty roads of Palestine, you stretched out your hand to heal, O Lord. Give wisdom and compassion to all doctors and members of the medical profession.

28 July

Botvid

Swedish born, Botvid became a Christian while living in England. He returned to his native land to evangelise his fellow countrymen. English missionary monks were already working in Sweden. After the example of St Aidan and St Gregory, he purchased a slave from Finland who he taught and baptised. He gave him his freedom by rowing the slave and a friend across the Baltic Sea. The freed slave stole the boat after murdering both Botvid and the friend.

Be with those, holy God, who have been betrayed treacherously by a friend or someone close to them. May they turn their hearts to you and not seek revenge. Help them to experience the steadfastness of your love.

29 July

Olaf, King of Norway

The son of a Norwegian lord, Harold Grenske, Olaf was born in 995 AD. He turned to war and piracy but after he was converted he went to England. There he fought for Ethelred II against the Danes in 1013. Some years later he returned to Norway where he seized power and became king. His rule brought peace to Norway and Christianity as well. Olaf could be a harsh ruler and Cnut, (Canute) King of England and Denmark, instigated a coup to overthrow him. In 1029 Olaf was exiled and a year later he tried to return. He was defeated and killed at the battle of Stiklestad on 29 July 1030. When he was buried, a spring with healing properties flowed and miracles took place. Olaf is the patron saint of Norway.

Almighty God, we pray for the people of Norway, that beautiful land blessed with magnificent scenery, may they seek to uphold their Christian heritage.

30 July

Tatwin, Archbishop of Canterbury

Tatwin was Archbishop of Canterbury from 731 to 734 AD and is described by Bede as being 'a man noted for his prudence, devotion and learning'. Prior to becoming archbishop he was a priest at the monastery at Bredon in Mercia. King Ethebald probably initiated his promotion. Two of his manuscripts are still in existence – *Riddles* (Enigmata) and four of his Grammar books. He wrote about many subjects including philosophy and the alphabet. Tatwin died in 734 AD and was buried in St Augustine's Abbey at Canterbury.

Inspire all places of education and learning, O God of all wisdom, that those who study may discover new insights into your creation.

31 July

Neot

A Cornish monk and hermit, Neot joined the monastic community at Glastonbury as a young man. Neot became a hermit on Bodmin Moor and founded a monastery there. This is where he was buried c.877 AD. King Alfred sought his counsel during his lifetime. Neot is thought to have been from the royal dynasty of either East Anglia or Wessex. The towns of St Neot in Cornwall and St Neots in Cambridgeshire are named after him.

Help us, Lord, in the 'hub-bub' of daily life to just be still and know that you are God.

1 August

Ethelwold

Born at Winchester c.912 AD, Ethelwold was employed at the court of King Athelstan. However, he became a priest and was ordained by Alphege on the same day as his friend Dunstan. They both ministered at Glastonbury and sought to revive the monastic life. It seems he became disenchanted with Glastonbury and asked to go to the monastery at Cluny in France. (Dunstan was later to become one of the greatest Archbishops of Canterbury). King Edred gave Ethelwold a dilapidated abbey at Abingdon which he restored. In 963 AD he was appointed Bishop of Winchester. He restored and built several monasteries with the support of the king. An able and austere man, Ethelwold worked hard and encouraged his monks to do the same. He died in 984 AD.

We give thanks for those who, inspired by your Holy Spirit, undertake to rebuild and restore the Church's heritage to your glory. May we realise though that here 'we have no continuing city' and seek to set our hearts on treasure in heaven.

2 August

Sidwell

Sidwell was born at Exeter and was murdered by her step-mother. She was buried outside the city and miracles of healing began to take place. Stained glass windows in Exeter Cathedral and All Souls' College, Oxford, depict her with a scythe and beside a well. Her feast is kept by some on 31 July or even 1 August.

Lord, we pray for all who are hurt and abused by members of their families. Give them courage in their suffering and help them to turn to you – the Man of Sorrows.

3 August

Waldef

Northumbrian born c. 1100, Waldef was educated at the Scottish court. When he was about twenty he became an Austin canon at Nostell in Yorkshire. Later he was appointed prior at Kirkham and tried unsuccessfully to unite this priory with Rievaulx. As a result Waldef decided to become a Cistercian monk at Waldron in Bedfordshire but found that the monks opposed him. After some time at Rievaulx, he was made abbot of Melrose in 1149. His predecessor Aildred had a dreadful temper and so Waldef's humility and pastoral care won his community over to him. In 1159 he was elected Bishop of St Andrews, a position he declined because he sensed his death was imminent.

Look in mercy on those who have to live with and labour for difficult people, O God. Give them grace to cope and not retaliate with a harsh word but to be forbearing.

4 August

John Baptist Vianney, The Curé d'Ars

John was ordained in 1814 and four years later he was parish priest of the rundown parish of Ars-en-Dombes. He faithfully continued his ministry there for forty-one years. His patient care and his good example transformed Ars into a thriving Christian community. Many people sought his wise counsel and he became known as the 'humble Cure d'Ars'. By 1855 it is said that those seeking his advice numbered twenty thousand a year. The French government made him a knight of the Legion of Honour. John was amazed and commented: 'Suppose I die, and God says, Away you go. You have already been rewarded.' As a result he refused to have the medal attached to his old cassock. He died in 1859, greatly loved.

Loving God, we thank you for those rare people blessed with the gift of insight and wise counsel. May they like John Baptist Vianney use these gifts to help your servants.

5 August

Oswald,
King of Northumbria

Oswald was the son of Ethelfrith, King of Northumbria. In 616 AD the kingdom was seized by Edwin. Oswald fled to Iona with his brothers and there he became a Christian. When Edwin died in 633 AD, Oswald returned to Northumbria. At the battle of Heavenfield near Hexham, Oswald defeated the tyrant king Cadwalla. Oswald was keen that his kingdom should be Christianised, and so Aidan came from Iona. Lindisfarne (Holy Island) was given by Oswald to Aidan as the site for a monastery. It was near the royal seat at Bamburgh, so it was ideally situated. Oswald supported Aidan's ministry and showed great generosity to the poor. He united both parts of Northumbria – Bernicia and Deira, but unfortunately he only reigned for eight years. He was killed by the pagan king Penda of Mercia in battle in 642 AD. His body was mutilated and various parts attached to stakes. His head was buried in St Cuthbert's coffin at Lindisfarne and today rests in Durham Cathedral.

God of grace, the King of glory, we pray for all Christian rulers that they may exercise discernment in their dealings and be ever mindful that they are answerable to you.

6 August

Justus and Pastor

In the early years of the fourth century, Dacian , one of the emperor's chief persecutors of Christians came to the town of Alcala in Spain. He issued a proclamation that on pain of death all Christians were to renounce their faith. Two school boys named Justus and Pastor refused to give up their faith. Dacian had them viciously flogged but they shouted words of encouragement to each other. This infuriated their tormentors even more. Dacian, shamed by their bravery, still decided that they should be killed, but secretly. They were beheaded outside Alcala when no one was present but their bodies were recovered by Christian friends who buried them where they had died. Today they are considered as the patron saints of Alcala and Madrid.

Holy God, the names of many young children who have faced death and died for their Christian faith, are known only to you. May we ponder their innocent example and seek to live pure lives.

7 August

Cajetan

Born at Vicenza and educated at Padua University, Cajetan proved to be a brilliant scholar. He became a priest in 1516 and founded establishments in Venice, Rome and Vicenza to care for the poor and sick. He sought to reform the corrupt lives of the clergy and was the founder of the Theatine Order. This Order studied the Bible, restored dignity to worship and ministered to the sick.

Lord, we give thanks for those who devote their lives to caring for others. May they be strengthened and encouraged by your Spirit.

8 August

Mary MacKillop

Mary's parents, Alexander and Flora MacKillop, were poor Scottish emigrants who came to Australia to make a better life for themselves. Her father Alexander had studied for the priesthood but had never been ordained. Mary was born on 15 January 1842 at Fitzroy in Melbourne, Australia and was the eldest child. She received her education at private schools as well as from her father. While still a teenager she worked as a nursery governess and a store clerk to help support the family. Mary felt called to the religious life but realised she had to keep working as a teacher for her family's sake. She and her sister moved to Penola in South Australia and founded a free Roman Catholic school for the poor with the support of Father Julian Tennison Woods. Mary also co-founded Australia's first religious order in 1866 – the Sisters of Saint Joseph of the Sacred Heart. Its mission was to provide education for poor children in remote areas. Soon she had another seventeen schools under her jurisdiction. Some of her ideas conflicted with the church's hierarchy and her bishop, who believed some exaggerated stories spread by her educator, told her to surrender control of her schools and her Order. She refused and was excommunicated in 1871. It is thought that this came about because of her part in the exposure of a priest accused of abusing children in a parish north of Adelaide. A year later, her bishop apologised for the baseless allegations against her and returned her to full communion.

Mary spent most of her life caring for the poor and improving conditions for the Aborigines. She died in Sydney on 8 August 1909 where she is buried. Mary was canonised by Pope Benedict XVI on 17 October 2010 – the first Australian born saint. Mary was described as 'very Australian, feisty, a lover of the bush and champion of a "fair go" for the needy'.

God of love, we pray for the people of Australia – that 'wide, brown land' of such diversity. May they be inspired by the compassion and care shown by a real Aussie saint.

9 August

Felim

Born in the sixth century, tradition says that Felim was the father of St Columba. Felim became a hermit living near Kilmore in Co Cavan, Ireland where he later founded a monastery in Tonymore. He is the patron saint of Kilmore diocese. The abbey on Trinity Island in Lough Oughter, not far from the present Church of Ireland cathedral of St Felim, is testament to the early days of Christianity in Cavan.

Lord, we think of those who have withdrawn from the world to live a life of prayer and contemplation. May we too find that quiet space in our busy lives 'to be still and know that you are God'.

10 August

Laurence

Laurence was a deacon in the third century. The very ancient *Depositio Martyrum* attests to his martyrdom. Pope Vitalian sent some of his relics to King Oswiu of Northumbria. There are many churches dedicated to Laurence in Rome, England, Scandinavia and Spain. He died in 258 AD.

Holy God, we give thanks for those who seek to serve as Laurence the deacon did. May our prayer be 'Brother, sister, let me serve you, may I be as Christ to you'.

11 August

Blane

Born on the Isle of Bute, Blane studied in Ireland for a number of years. When he returned home he was ordained a priest and spent time in Scotland. As a bishop he established a monastery on Bute and this is where he was buried in the late sixth century. Dunblane cathedral was built on the site of this monastery.

Give wisdom and dedication to all bishops, priests and deacons, O Lord, that they may faithfully care for your flock.

12 August

Murtagh, Bishop

Traditionally he is considered to have either been converted by the preaching of Patrick or he may have lived at the same time as St Columba. Murtagh was the first Bishop of Killala and established the island monastery on Innismurray in Co Sligo in Ireland. Here are the remains of beehive huts, oratories and other buildings.

Eternal God, we think of those who live in remote places where they have to battle the elements to survive. Give them courage and tenacity to know that you are their refuge and strength.

13 August

Florence Nightingale, Nurse, Social Reformer

Florence was born into a wealthy family in 1820. From an early age she had wanted to become a nurse although this vocation was opposed by her family. Finally, in 1853, she achieved her goal and managed her own private nursing institution in London. Her nursing efforts and those of her colleagues greatly improved conditions and alleviated some suffering for those wounded in the Crimean War. Throughout her life she sought to bring about nursing care reform. The school she founded at St Thomas' Hospital in London helped to consolidate nursing into a recognised profession. She herself suffered many years of ill health and died in 1910.

God of wholeness and healing, we give thanks for people like, Florence Nightingale who worked tirelessly to alleviate suffering and bring healing to many despite being opposed by the social conventions of her day.

14 August

Maximilian Kolbe, Priest

In 1894 Kolbe was born near Lodz. When he was sixteen he became a Franciscan. Soon after this his parents separated and joined different religious orders. Ordained a priest in 1919, he was found to have tuberculosis and returned to Poland where he taught Church History. Kolbe wanted to pursue his militant leanings and started a magazine in Cracow (modern day Krakow). As readership increased the printing press was moved to Grodno. When he became very ill the presses were relocated near Warsaw where he set up a Franciscan community. When Germany invaded Poland in 1939, Kolbe sent the monks home to escape. His monastery continued as a refugee camp for Poles and Jews. He kept on publishing his patriotic magazine which opposed the Third Reich. Maximilian was arrested with four companions and sent to Auschwitz in May 1941. He comforted the other prisoners and sought to exercise his priestly ministry. In 1941 he died instead of another man who was married with young children.

'Greater love has no man than this to lay down his life for his friends'. Lord, we praise you for those who have made the ultimate sacrifice, like Maximilian, to help a fellow human being.

15 August

Arnulf

As a young man, Arnulf was engaged in a successful military career. However, he decided to become a monk at St Medard (Soissons) and lived the life of a hermit until appointed as abbot of a community. In 1081 he was consecrated bishop but was made to flee by an opponent. Subsequently, he established a monastery at Aldenburg in Flanders, where he died in 1087.

Help us, Lord, to come apart and rest awhile in your presence that we may be renewed and refreshed in your service.

16 August

Armel

It is thought that Armel was born in Wales and that he became a monk and then emigrated to Brittany. King Childebert supported him in the founding of two monasteries. He died c.552 AD. His cult spread to various areas in France and also in England where King Henry VII believed he had been saved from shipwreck through Armel's prayers. There is a statue of him in Henry VII's chapel in Westminster Abbey as well as one on the tomb of Cardinal Morton in Canterbury Cathedral. Some hospitals have him as their patron.

God of grace, we thank you for the communion of saints. May we be inspired by the examples of your servants who have gone before us.

17 August

Hyacinth of Cracow

Born of a noble family in 1185, Hyacinth became a Dominican friar and is known as the 'apostle to Poland'. After his education at Prague and Bologna, his uncle, the Bishop of Cracow (modern day Krakow), made him a canon. Together they travelled to Rome where Hyacinth was converted by the preaching of Dominic. He then moved to the community at Santa Sabina to be their friar. He himself preached very effectively in eastern and northern Europe. Hyacinth established various centres of learning. Monks of the order evangelised north as far as Gdansk and east along the Vistula. He died in 1257.

Lord, open our mouths that they may be filled with messages from you. May people see Christ in us by our deeds and by our words.

18 August

Helen

Possibly the daughter of an innkeeper, Helen was born in Bithynia c.250 AD. At the age of twenty she married a Roman general, Constantius Chlorus. In 292 AD he became emperor and divorced Helen. She had borne him a son who was later to become the Emperor Constantine. Helen was converted to Christianity when she was aged about sixty. She devoted the rest of her life to good works, caring for the poor and those in prison. She also generously endowed churches. At the time of her death in 330 AD she was on pilgrimage in the Holy Land.

Good and gracious God, touch our hearts that we may seek to care for those less fortunate and those who are vulnerable.

19 August

Credan

Credan was born in the eighth century and became abbot of Evesham when Offa was king of Mercia (757-796 AD). Little is known of his life and he was viewed with suspicion by Lanfranc and others in the Norman hierarchy. His relics, along with those of others, were burnt in 1077 but they remained intact. Later they are said to have 'shone like gold'.

Lord God, we praise you for all your martyrs who have given up their lives rather than deny their faith. Give us that steadfastness to stand firm in our Christian witness.

20 August

Oswin

The son of Osric, King of Deira in Northumbria, Oswin fled to the kingdom of Wessex in the south of England, when his father was killed by the pagan king Cadwalla in 634 AD. When Oswin's cousin Oswald was killed in battle, Oswin returned to become King of Deira. (Oswald had united Bernicia and Deira to become one kingdom). Oswiu ruled Bernicia but wanted power over both kingdoms. He challenged Oswin to battle. However, Oswin realising that his army was outnumbered, and in order to prevent more slaughter, disbanded his army. Oswin, who had been hiding in the house of his best friend, was betrayed by that friend and put to death on Oswiu's orders. Oswin was generous and caring for both rich and poor and many sought to work in his service. St Aidan, whose ministry Oswin had supported, died just eleven days after him.

Look with compassion on all those who, like Oswin, have been betrayed by a friend. You, dear Lord, have suffered that betrayal by one of your own disciples.

21 August

Pius X

Pius was born to a poor Venetian family in 1835. He was ordained at the age of twenty-three. Consecrated Bishop of Mantua in 1884, he was elected pope in 1903. He set about reforming the Roman Catholic Church and adopted Ephesians 1:10 'to restore all things in Christ' as his motto. Pius encouraged several changes in practice including the admission of children to Holy Communion at the age of seven, improvements to the performance of church music, as well as challenging the church's social conscience. He condemned the extremes of the 'liberal movement' in France. Pius lived a simple life and did not hanker after riches. Indeed, in his will he wrote: 'I was born poor, I have lived poor and I wish to die poor.'

Lord, you made yourself of no account to be born as the Babe of Bethlehem for us. We pray for all church leaders that they may live the servant role and not become proud or arrogant in their positions.

22 August

Sigfrid,
Abbot of Wearmouth

Although, still a deacon, Sigfrid succeeded Eosterwine, the first abbot of Wearmouth monastery. The founder of this community, Benedict Biscop, made this appointment. A diligent scholar, Sigfrid succumbed to a lung disease and died in 688 AD, just two years after Biscop returned from one of his journeys.

Everlasting God, give strength and perseverance to those, who despite illness or disability, still labour on in their various ministries. Help them to know the reality that 'underneath are the everlasting arms'.

23 August

Rose of Lima

In 1586 Rose was born in Peru to a comfortably wealthy Spanish family. Later her family lost money in financial speculation on a mining venture and so they tried to encourage her to marry a wealthy suitor. Rose took a vow to remain a virgin and joined the Third Order of St Dominic. She lived as a hermit in a garden hut where she practised extreme forms of penance for the sins of society. After suffering both mentally and physically, she died in 1617 aged thirty-one. She was the first canonised saint of the New World and became the patron saint of South America.

Bless the many millions who live in South America that they may seek to live their lives according to your commandments, O God.

24 August

Ouen, Bishop

Ouen, born c.600 AD at Sancy, France, was educated at the court of King Clotaire II. He later became chancellor and founded a monastery at Rebais. Ordained late in life, he was appointed Bishop of Rouen in 641 AD. Ouen sent missionaries to evangelise the pagans and founded several monasteries. He sought to stamp out the practice of buying church positions. As well as this he tried to instil holiness of life and a desire for learning into the monks. An advisor to Thierry III, he died in 684 AD near Paris at a place now called Saint-Ouen.

God of righteousness, purify your church, where it is corrupt, purge it, where it is in error correct it. May we, the Body of Christ, be faithful witnesses to your truth.

25 August

Ebba (Ebbe)

When her father Ethelfrith, King of Northumbria, died in 616 AD, Ebba fled to Scotland. Later she entered the monastery at Coldingham near Berwick and after a time became abbess of this double monastery (for monks and nuns). Although noted for her piety, her nuns seemed to have engaged in frivolous pursuits. Ebba was warned by Adomnán the priest, of the lax state of affairs. There doesn't seem to have been much improvement in the nuns' behaviour. Ebba died in 683 AD and the monastery was burnt down three years later. Ebchester and St Abb's are named after her.

Give courage to those who seek to lift the standards of those in positions of trust and authority. Help us, Lord God, to realise that one day each one of us will be called to give account of how we have lived.

26 August

Ninian,
Bishop

Ninian was a British bishop in the fifth century. He has traditionally been known as 'the apostle of the Picts'. His ministry centred around Whithorn and Galloway in Scotland. The monastery at Whithorn was later referred to by Bede as *'ad candidam casam'*. Remains of painted masonry indicate that it was painted white. There are many churches dedicated to him. Ninian was buried at Whithorn where his shrine became a place of pilgrimage until the sixteenth century. He was also revered in Kent and in Denmark.

We thank you, O Lord, for the example of your servant Ninian. Help us to preach the gospel not only with our lips but by our deeds.

27 August

Decuman

Probably born in the sixth century in Pembrokeshire in Wales, Decuman became a monk. He settled in north Somerset near Dunster. Decuman lived as a hermit. He was murdered by an assassin in an unprovoked attack while he was praying. His cult was promoted at Wells and Muchelney and there were churches dedicated to him in Cornwall, Wales and Somerset.

God of eternity, give us grace to live our lives wisely and save us from dying suddenly and unprepared.

28 August

Hermes

This third century Roman martyr died in one of the earliest persecutions. A large basilica was built over his tomb in the cemetery at Basilla on the Old Salarian Way. His relics were finally laid to rest at Renaix (Flanders) in 860 AD and this is still a place of pilgrimage. There are three dedications to him in Cornwall – St Erme, St Ervan and Marazion.

Help us, O God, to walk the way of the saints that finally we may share in a joyful resurrection with all your servants from every age.

29 August

Edwold (Eadwold) of Cerne

A hermit in the ninth century, Edwold may have been the brother of Edmund, King of East Anglia. He settled near Cerne in Dorset and is said to have lived on only bread and water. He is reputed to have performed miracles. A monastery was built on the spot where Edwold died.

We praise your name, loving Father, for those who have served you through the ages, may we seek to follow the path of service.

30 August

Rumon

Possibly born in the sixth century, Rumon, patron of Tavistock, was a monk. Later he may have been consecrated bishop. It is thought that he may have been at Glastonbury and founded a community on the Lizard peninsula in Cornwall. He lived a life of 'abstinence and virtue'. Rumon's shrine was at Tavistock where a fair has been held since 1114 in his honour.

Lead us on our pilgrimage through life that we may always honour you by the way we live, O God.

31 August

Aidan,
First Bishop of Lindisfarne

Aidan was a monk on Iona. He came to England in 635 AD when Oswald, the Christian King of Northumbria, who had been exiled on Iona, requested someone to come and preach the Gospel to his people. Aidan was the first Bishop of Lindisfarne, the island given to him by Oswald and close to the royal palace at Bamburgh. Until Aidan learnt the local language, the king acted as interpreter when he was preaching. Aidan founded churches and monasteries and also paid for the freedom of slaves whom he trained for the church. Bede, often critical of the Celtic saints, praised Aidan for his life of prayer and purity, for his humility and his care for the poor and sick. When King Oswin, Oswald's successor, gave him a horse from the royal stables for his own use, Aidan gave it to a poor man who he thought had need of it. Aidan died at Bamburgh in 651 AD. Bishop Lightfoot of Durham called Aidan 'the apostle to the English'.

God of love, you sent the gentle Aidan to be the first bishop of Lindisfarne and to preach the gospel to Britain. Give us grace to live simply and in humility and help us, like Aidan to show your love for the poor.

1 September

Giles

Giles was born in the early seventh century and founded a monastery at a place called Saint-Gilles in Provence. There is a legend that when King Wamba was hunting a deer, he shot Giles with whom the deer had sought refuge. Giles is the patron of cripples, lepers and nursing mothers (as it was a female deer he had saved). His shrine became a popular site of pilgrimage on the way to Compostela and also the Holy Land. There are countless churches dedicated to him and over twenty hospitals in England alone. Giles died c.710 AD.

Merciful God, you made all things and saw that they were good. Bless those who are involved in saving animals from cruelty and help us all to cherish and care for the creatures you have placed on this earth.

2 September

The Martyrs of New Guinea

James Chalmers, Oliver Tomkins and some companions were sent to New Guinea by the London Missionary Society. They met their death by martyrdom in 1901. Forty years later during the Second World War, the Japanese Imperial Army occupied New Guinea. Christians were persecuted and 333 church workers of all denominations died at the hands of the Japanese. Two Anglican priests, Vivian Redlich and Bernard Moore, stayed with their congregations after the invasion in 1942 but were betrayed and killed. Eight Australians and two Papuan evangelists were among those who were murdered.

We praise you, O God, for the martyrs of New Guinea who were faithful unto death. We pray for the people of New Guinea and the Christian church there. May each one of us be ready to sacrifice our lives for our faith if forced to do so.

3 September

Gregory the Great

Gregory was born c.540 AD into the family of a wealthy Roman senator, and entered the service of the state. However, in 573 AD he sold all his properties and founded seven monasteries, one of which was St Andrew's on the Coelian Hill in Rome where he himself became a monk. Gregory gave generously to the poor and lived an austere life as a monk. No doubt some of the ill health which he suffered later in life stemmed from this time. He felt called to go as a missionary to the Anglo-Saxons in Britain. Upon seeing some slaves with fair complexions for sale and having been told they were Angles, Gregory is reputed to have said 'not Angles but angels'. This mission did not eventuate as Gregory was elected pope. As the Plague was raging he was faced with an immediate crisis. Nevertheless, Gregory arranged for Augustine and some monks to lead a mission to Kent in 597 AD. He died in 604 AD.

We thank you, dear Lord, for Gregory's concern for the British people and that, although unable to go himself made sure that Augustine would go in his place.

4 September

Ultan of Ardbraccan

Virtually nothing is known of his early life. However, he was a brilliant scholar who founded a school and educated poor children. He was skilled in producing illuminated manuscripts. Ultan gathered the writings of St Brigid and compiled *A Life of St Brigid*. He may have been a bishop and apostle to the Desi of Meath.

God of creativity, you give many gifts to your servants. We stare in wonder at the beauty of many of the illuminated manuscripts made throughout the ages. Help us to use our gifts to your glory.

5 September

Bertin

He was a monk at Luxeuil and assisted Omer in evangelising the Pas-de-Calais district in northern France. Appointed abbot at Sithiu, he and Omer built the church in 663 AD which later became the cathedral of St Omer. He died in 698 AD and his relics were finally interred at Saint-Bertin in 1052. His cult spread to England, no doubt through trade between the two countries.

God of the harvest, we pray for all church workers as they seek to live out their faith and spread the good news. May our lives be filled with the love of Christ.

6 September

Cagnoald

St Columban's monastery at Luxueil was noted for its holiness of life. Two brothers who trained there were Faro and Cagnoald. Faro became Bishop of Meaux and Cagnoald Bishop of Laon. When Columban criticised King Theodric's immoral life he was banished in 610 AD. Cagnoald decided to join him and so they worked as missionaries near Lake Constance until Theodric gained jurisdiction over this area. Then they moved further afield to Italy where Columban established the famous monastery at Bobbio. Although Cagnoald had not been exiled, nevertheless he decided to stay with Columban to care for him. When Columban died, Cagnoald took up his bishopric until his own death in 633 AD.

Bless those who are carers for sick or aged or disabled people, loving God. When they are tired give them energy, when they feel discouraged lift their spirits and give them patience and compassion.

7 September

Evurtius

In the fourth century Evurtius was Bishop of Orleans in France. He may have been present at the council of Valencia in 374 AD. Nothing is known of his life – not even the date of his death. His name was added to the calendar of the *Book of Common Prayer* in 1604.

God of the saints, the lives of so many of your servants are lost in the 'mists of time'. Yet you know them and all that they have done in your service for the kingdom of God.

8 September

Ethelburga

A Kentish princess, she was the daughter of Ethelbert, king of Kent. She married Edwin, King of Northumbria. When he was killed in battle she returned to Kent with Bishop Paulinus and founded a nunnery at Lyming, where she remained as abbess till her death in 647 AD.

Almighty God, we pray for all Christian kings, queens and rulers that they may lead their people by example and so fulfil your will that all should live in peace and justice.

9 September

Ciarán of Clonmacnoise

The son of a travelling carpenter, Ciarán was born c.512 AD. When he went to study under the direction of Finnian of Clonard, he took his own milk supply with him – a cow. After becoming a monk, he joined Enda on Aran Island till c.541 AD when he was ordained a priest and went to live on Scattery Island. He then settled at Clonmacnoise where he founded a monastery. This community survived several Viking raids as well as various Irish and Anglo-Norman wars until 1552. Ciarán died c.545 AD aged about thirty-three.

Heavenly Father, we praise your name for those who have remained faithful at their posts through wars and disasters. Give us that same courage and tenacity when needed.

10 September

Finnian of Moville

Thought to be of royal blood, Finnian was educated at Dromore and Whithorn (the monastery founded by Ninian). He later returned to Ireland and established two monasteries – one at Moville c.550 AD and the other at Dromin. As well as being abbot, Finnian was also noted for his scholarly teaching, and indeed, one of his pupils was Columba. He died c.579 AD.

God of all wisdom, we pray for all places of education and learning. Bless all who teach and all who learn.

11 September

Deiniol

Deiniol, a descendent of a Celtic chieftain in northern Britain, founded two monasteries in Wales. According to Bede, one of these Bangor Iscoed became the most famous monastery in Britain with over two thousand monks. Later at the battle of Chester this community was destroyed. Deiniol became the first Bishop of Bangor. There are several churches dedicated to him. Gladstone's renowned library at Hawarden was named after him.

Lead us on the pilgrim way, Holy God, that we may be inspired by the examples of your saints. Help us to run the race looking only to Jesus.

12 September

Eanswyth

Daughter of the king of Kent and granddaughter of Ethelbert, Eanswyth refused an offer of marriage from a prince of Northumbria. She then founded a convent at Folkestone and was its abbess. When destroyed and pillaged by Viking raiders, King Athelstan rebuilt the church though not the convent. Eanswyth died at a young age c.640 AD. In 1095 Black Benedictine monks built a monastery on the same site, but this was later eroded away and fell into the sea. A new church was constructed there in the twelfth century and this is the present parish church of SS Mary and Eanswythe – the probable site where Eanswyth's relics were buried.

Lord, help us to build on a firm foundation that we may remain true servants who will be faithful in all circumstances.

13 September

Eulogius of Alexandria

He was the Greek Patriarch of Alexandria from 580 AD to 607 AD and close friend of Pope Gregory the Great who held him in high esteem. Eulogius opposed those who propagated erroneous doctrine in the church. He was able in invigorate the church in Alexandria at least for a time. Many discourses and commentaries were written by him. However, only sermons and fragments of his writings remain.

Guard your church, O Lord, against those who would destroy the faith of Christians. Help us to stand firm in the knowledge of your truth and to build only on Christ the sure foundation.

14 September

Notburga

Notburga was born into a poor peasant family living in the Tyrol in the mid thirteenth century. When she became a kitchen maid at the age of eighteen, at the court of Count Henry of Rattenberg, she soon noticed how much food was wasted there. She gave this to the poor who came to the castle gates. Count Henry's mother supported her in this task but his wife did not. When Henry's mother died, Notburga was dismissed. She went to work for a farmer near Eben who made sure that his workers laboured hard although she insisted on going to church on Sundays. Ill fortune seemed to dog the steps of Count Henry during this time. His wife died and then a quarrel spread to his lands and he became sure that these misfortunes could be attributed to the unjust dismissal of the kitchen maid. So Notburga was reinstated and lived there till her death in 1313. She is the patron saint of servants.

God of justice, look in love on those who are mistreated by employers and those in authority. May they cast their care on you knowing that you care for them.

15 September

Mirin (Merinus, Meadhran)

Probably born in Ireland in the seventh century, Mirin entered the monastery at Bangor, Co Down. He founded a monastery at Paisley in Scotland and this is where he later died and was buried. Many pilgrims visited his shrine. There is a ruined chapel dedicated to him on Inch Murryn, the largest island in Loch Lomond.

God of our pilgrimage, we give thanks for so many holy places touched by the lives of your saints. Help us to draw aside from the busyness of daily life and to just be still and know that you are God.

16 September

Edith

The illegitimate daughter of King Edgar the Peaceable, Edith was born at Kensing in Kent. Her mother was a nun who Edgar had taken forcibly from her convent at Wilton. The penance imposed on Edgar by Archbishop Dunstan was not to wear his crown for seven years. Edith was not only beautiful but learned and pious. She became a nun at an early age and was abbess of three different communities. However, she remained with her mother at Wilton. In 979 AD she had a dream which warned her that her brother would soon die and this proved correct as he was murdered while visiting his step-mother. Edith was offered the crown but declined it. She built a church at Wilton dedicated to St Denis. This was blessed by St Dunstan who wept during the service knowing that Edith only had three weeks to live. She died in 984 AD.

We thank you, Lord, for warnings given to your saints and still to us today. May we be heedful of what you are trying to say to us.

17 September

Hildegard

Born in Germany in 1098, she entered a convent at the age of fifteen and lived a quiet, pious life for seventeen years. Then she began to see visions. In 1136 she was appointed abbess of Diessenberg. Her community grew in numbers and moved to Rupertsberg near Bingen. Hildegard often chided rulers for their evil deeds. She was a talented woman who wrote hymns and poems, as well as works about medicine and natural history. She was almost eighty when she died.

Almighty God, King of kings and Lord of lords, give courage to those who have to rebuke rulers. May they speak honestly but with compassion and reason to those in authority.

18 September

Joseph of Copertino

Joseph made his entry into the world in 1603 in a humble garden shed near Brindisi. His father had sold the family home to pay off his debts. Unwanted by his mother, who was soon widowed, Joseph had an unhappy childhood. He had a fiery temper but was pious in his religious duties. After spending several months with the Capuchin monks, he caused havoc in the kitchen when chided for forgetting his duties by dropping a stack of plates. Finally, he was dismissed. His mother, who was glad to be rid of him, arranged a job as a servant at the Franciscan community at Grottella. Here he proved to be reliable as well as spiritually minded and was admitted as a novice in 1625. Ordained priest three years later, he lived the austere life of a mystic. Joseph had a great affinity with animals. He died in 1663.

God our Father, your Son gathered the little children to himself and blessed them. We pray for all children who are unloved and unwanted, hold them in your everlasting arms.

19 September

Theodore of Tarsus

Theodore was born in Tarsus c602 AD. Educated in Athens he was appointed Archbishop of Canterbury by the pope. Although only a sub-deacon he was promoted to the archiepiscopal see. He immediately set about visiting virtually the whole of England. Theodore endeavoured to reform the Church in England by dividing areas into dioceses and summoned the Synod of Hertford in 673 AD, the most important church council. It issued canons (laws) which dealt with the rights and responsibilities of clergy and religious communities. This council stated that no bishop could interfere in the diocese of another bishop, that monks should be obedient to their abbot as well as many other matters pertaining to the good ordering of the church. These canons were based on those ratified by the Council of Chalcedon. Theodore was the first Archbishop of Canterbury to have the allegiance of all Anglo-Saxon England given freely and not under duress. Theodore died in 690 AD.

God of harmony, we thank you for your servant Theodore who sought to bring good order to the Church. We pray for those who must make decisions for the wise governance of your Church that they may be guided by your Holy Spirit.

20 September

John Coleridge Patteson, Bishop of Melanesia

John was born in London in 1827 and while still a scholar at Eton was strongly influenced by George Augustus Selwyn. He was a graduate of Balliol College. Patteson trained for the priesthood and when ordained, began his life's ministry in 1855 to the islanders of the South Pacific. He founded the Melanesian Mission and became the first bishop of those islands. He believed in training indigenous clergy so that they, together with lay people, could share the Gospel in a way suited to their own culture. As a result Christianity spread rapidly. His method of organisation was to move amongst his people on the ship the Southern Cross. There were some unscrupulous Europeans 'blackbirders' who were slave-traders. They kidnapped islanders to work in Britain and other colonies. One day when Patteson and his fellow-workers landed on the island of Nukapu, they were mistaken for slave-traders and were brutally murdered by the islanders. John Patteson sacrificed his life for the sake of the gospel in 1871. His body was launched in a canoe which drifted back to the Southern Cross. It was soon discovered that five stab wounds had been made in his chest – one for each of five islanders recently taken and killed by the slave-traders. Bishop John's five wounds were covered with a palm branch tied in five knots. It was the martyr's stigmata.

God of every nation, we pray for the people of Melanesia. Strengthen their faith that they may seek to follow in the steps of your Son Jesus Christ for whom John Patteson gave up his life.

21 September

Matthew, Apostle

Matthew was a tax collector – second only to politicians in their corruption throughout history. He was despised, like his fellow workers, for betraying his own people by working for the Romans. When Jesus called him to follow him, he got up from his table and left everything. Jesus shared a meal with Matthew and his companions and this scandalised the Jews. Matthew affirmed his determination to follow his Lord. As one of the twelve apostles, Matthew was martyred for his faith and this is attested in various ancient sources. His symbol in iconography is a man with wings.

Lord, you called your servant Matthew to leave everything and follow you. Help us not to hanker after riches and save us from the love of money.

22 September

Thomas of Villanova

The son of a miller, Thomas was born at Fuetellana in 1486. After studying arts and theology, he was ordained priest in 1517. He was prior to various communities of monks for twenty five years. Consecrated Bishop of Valencia in 1544, Thomas still continued to live a simple life and spent many hours in prayer. He gave great pastoral care to the sick and to orphans as well as improving their lives by generous donations from his own income. His many sermons had great influence on Spanish literature. He died in 1555.

Give grace to those in positions of authority in the Church, O God, that they may find time to just be with you. May they realise that they neglect their spiritual welfare at their peril.

23 September

Adomnán, Abbot of Iona

Irish born in 627 AD, Adomnán became a monk on Iona when Seghine was abbot. He was a proponent of the Roman (rather than the Celtic) way of calculating Easter. In 697 AD the Roman method was adopted by most of the Church except in his own monasteries. Indeed, this issue was not settled until 716 AD. His principal 'claim to fame' is his writing of the *Life of Columba*. He also completed a work about the Holy Places of Palestine. He died in 704 AD. There are several dedications to him in Ireland, Scotland and the Western Isles. In 727 AD his relics were transferred from Iona to Ireland to help settle a family feud. Vikings desecrated his shrine.

God of all knowledge, we give thanks for those who have written literary masterpieces, especially those which glorify you. May we use the talents you have given us in your service.

24 September

Gerard Sagredo

A Venetian by birth, Gerard became a monk then a prior at San Giorgio Maggiore. He set out on a pilgrimage to Jerusalem, but on his arrival in Hungary, the king asked him to tutor his son. Soon after this he was appointed the first Bishop of Csanad. He not only faced opposition from pagans but also found Christians weak in their faith. When the king died in 1038, the people rebelled against Christianity. In 1046 Gerard was attacked at Buda and stoned and speared with a lance. His body was thrown into the River Danube. No doubt his remains were retrieved as in 1333 some of his relics were sent to Venice and then translated onto the island of Murano.

Be with those, heavenly Father, who still today face a violent death because of their Christian faith. Give them courage to stand firm and not to waver in what they believe.

25 September

Ceolfrith

Ceolfrith was born into the nobility of Northumbria and entered a monastery at Gilling in North Yorkshire. Later he moved to Ripon where he was made a priest. Benedict Biscop asked him to come to Wearmouth where he became prior. He returned to Ripon for a time but came back to Wearmouth from where he founded the monastery at Jarrow. During the Plague most of the monks died – only Ceolfrith and Bede, a boy at the time, were spared. In 689 AD when Biscop died, Ceolfrith was appointed abbot of both Wearmouth and Jarrow. He showed great energy in his work and care for his monks. In 716 AD Ceolfrith died at Langres in Burgundy on his way to Rome.

We praise you, loving God, for those who, despite plague or any other disaster have faithfully sought to minister to your people.

26 September

Nilus of Rossano

His family were Greek but lived in Calabria. While still in his twenties, his mistress and daughter died. Nilus then entered a nearby Greek monastery and lived as a hermit before becoming abbot. A fragile peace existed with threats from the Saracens and mercenary soldiers. Nilus was known for his holy life. He was also a brilliant scholar, well-versed in Greek and Latin, and writer of hymns. In 981 AD, threatened by Saracen armies, he and his community fled to Monte Cassino – the monastery founded by Benedict. Finally, after several moves, in 1004 Nilus visited Grottaferrata near Rome. He had seen in a vision that this was where his community should settle. However, he died in 1005 before this could be achieved by him. Today, this monastery is involved in the conservation of old manuscripts.

Eternal God, guide and direct all those involved in conserving and preserving old manuscripts and documents. As they seek to care for these may they be given wisdom and patience in all that they do.

27 September

Barry (Barnic, Barruc)

Born in the sixth century, Barry is thought to have been a disciple of Cadoc. He lived the life of a hermit and settled on the island now called Barry Island in Glamorgan. One tradition says that he died there and his chapel became a place of pilgrimage. Another tradition says that he may have been buried at Fowey in Cornwall.

We know so little of some of your saints, O Lord, yet they served you and their fellow human beings and remained faithful to you.

28 September

Wenceslas

The son of a duke, Wenceslas was born in Bohemia in 907 AD. His grandmother, a committed Christian, educated him. He became duke in 922 AD and worked for the improvement of his people's lives – both physically and spiritually. His support of a submission to Henry the Fowler, the King of the German Empire, set Wenceslas on a collision course with his brother's pagan followers. Boleslav, his brother, is thought to have arranged his murder. After his death in 929 AD, Wenceslas was buried in St Vitus church in Prague. The Christmas carol *Good King Wenceslas* made him famous in England.

Stay the hands of those who plan some evil deed, O God, our refuge and our strength. May those who have committed crimes seek forgiveness and be willing to accept their punishment.

29 September

Michael and All Angels

Traditionally Michael is known as the receiver of the souls of the departed. When there was war in heaven, Michael and his angels fought against the dragon, who fought back with his angels ... the dragon was defeated and cast out of heaven with his angels ... that ancient serpent, called the Devil or Satan, that deceived the whole world. (Revelation 12: 7-9). The name 'Michael' means 'who is like God'. He is seen as the protector of Christians against the Devil especially at the hour of death.

Gabriel whose name means 'the strength of God' is the messenger who was sent by God to the Virgin Mary announcing that she would bear the Christ. Raphael's name means 'the healing of God' and this role is shown in the Book of Tobit where Tobit's sight is restored by Raphael. In the fifth century a basilica near Rome was built dedicated to Michael. The western church now keeps this feast to Michael and All Angels on 29 September.

Lord of all beings, we give thanks that your holy angels not only serve you in heaven but help and defend us on earth. We praise you for those who may be 'angels unaware'.

30 September

Jerome

Jerome, a monk and later a Doctor of the Church, was born in Dalmatia c341 AD. He was educated by his father and then by Donatus in Rome. His later writings attest to the fact that he studied Rhetoric. In Rome he visited many churches as well as the catacombs (where early Christians met together and were also buried). Converted to the Christian faith, he was baptised prior to the year 366 AD. While still a monk at Trier, Jerome and his friends quarrelled and a scandal resulted. Subsequently, he left there and went to live in Palestine. He became a hermit in the desert for a number of years. Jerome, already fluent in Greek and Latin decided to study Hebrew so he could study the scriptures in the original language. During his life, Jerome made many enemies due to his proud, sarcastic nature. He died in Bethlehem in 420 AD and was buried there until his remains were moved to Rome.

Open the eyes of all who seek to study your Holy Word that your truth may be revealed to all who hunger to know your will, O God.

1 October

Remigius, Bishop of Reims

Remigius was born in Gaul and was appointed bishop of Reims at an early age. He baptised King Clovis I, King of the Franks 481-511 AD, and three thousand of his household. When Clovis's infant son was restored to health and Clovis himself had been victorious in battle, he became a Christian. Remigius built churches and established bishoprics under the auspices of King Clovis. He died in Reims in 533 AD. There are six ancient English churches dedicated to him. English Benedictine monasteries celebrated his feast day as 1 October while in Reims it is on 13 January.

God of bounty, we pray for those who endeavour to 'grow' new churches. Give them wisdom and patience in their efforts.

2 October

Thomas of Hereford

Thomas was born in 1218 to a wealthy influential Norman family that was related to several earls. He was educated by his uncle, the Bishop of Worcester. He then went to Oxford in 1237, but due to student unrest he journeyed with his brother to study in Paris. While at the Council of Lyons in 1245 he was ordained and obtained papal dispensation which allowed him to hold several positions simultaneously. He studied civil and canon law. Soon after his return to Oxford he became Chancellor and sought to assist poor students as well as seeking to suppress violent student demonstrations. Thomas was Chancellor of England for a year. In 1275 he was elected Bishop of Hereford. In this role he lived humbly (wearing a hair-shirt) and showed great pastoral care to his people. He quarrelled with John Pecham, the Archbishop of Canterbury, over similar issues to those which led to the murder of Thomas Becket in 1170. Cantelupe was excommunicated by Pecham who also tried to refuse him Christian burial when he died at Montefiascone in 1282. His heart and some bones were sent back to Hereford where his shrine is still in existence in the cathedral today. Many miracles took place there.

Lord, you said: 'Blessed are the peacemakers'. Bless those who try to 'pour oil on troubled waters'. Give them endurance and perseverance in all that they seek to do.

3 October

Hewald The Black and Hewald The White

These two men were Anglo-Saxon priests who evangelised the Old Saxons. They were martyred c.695 AD. The Venerable Bede states that they gained their nicknames because of their hair colour. They spent many years in exile in Ireland before joining Willibrord on his mission to Frisia. Both were holy men and when the local people felt their gods were threatened by Christianity they killed them. Their bodies were thrown into the River Rhine but were later retrieved and were buried in St Cunibert's church in Cologne.

Still today, Almighty God, your servants face the forces of evil, those who would destroy and tear down any good done in your name. May we turn to you in our hour of need and not try to achieve anything in our own strength.

4 October

Francis of Assisi

The son of a wealthy cloth-merchant in Assisi, Francis was born in 1181. His mother was French. Francis fought in a war between Assisi and Perugia and was taken prisoner for a year. When praying in the semi-derelict church of San Damiano of Assisi and contemplating the Byzantine style crucifix, he heard a voice saying: 'Go and repair my house, which you see is falling down'. Francis sold some cloth belonging to his father to buy materials for these repairs. Obviously, this caused strife in the family and the problem was only settled when Francis renounced his inheritance and began to live a life of poverty. He lived alone for some years before being joined by seven companions. They lived near a leper colony in wattle and daub huts and had no possessions except for a few books. Francis felt called to convert the Saracens and so he went on pilgrimage to the Holy Land. He had a great devotion to Christ's passion and received the stigmata (the five wounds of Christ) in his own body in 1224. Francis died at the age of forty-five. He had a strong rapport with and great love for all animals and was much-loved by the members of his monastic Order.

Creator God, bless all those who seek to alleviate the suffering of animals and to bring healing and wholeness to them. May we appreciate the love of our pets and may we recognise that we hold creation as a trust from you.

5 October

Placid

Placid was born in the sixth century and was educated by Benedict at Subiaco, where he trained as a Benedictine monk. Little is known of his life apart from the fact that he was widely celebrated in Benedictine monasteries where he was venerated as the patron of novices. In 1915 his feast was combined with that of Maurus, by the Benedictine liturgical commission. He died c.540 AD.

Lord, there are 'the big saints and the little saints' through the ages. Help us to learn from their examples that we may live lives that are pleasing to you.

6 October

Bruno

Bruno was educated at Reims and Cologne and became the founder of the Carthusian Order. (An enclosed order of monks and nuns). Bruno was born c.1032. He lectured in theology and grammar at Reims for eighteen years and was then appointed Chancellor of the Diocese of Reims. Bruno tried to curb the excesses of Manasses, the scandalous Archbishop of Reims. He decided to live as a hermit and was encouraged in this endeavour by Hugh, the Bishop of Grenoble, who gave his monks some land. Their form of monasticism was based on that of the early monks of Egypt and Palestine rather than the Rule of St Benedict. He died in 1101 at La Torre.

May those who seek to live in solitude, find the 'pearl of great price' for which they are searching, O Holy Father. May they be drawn by your love that everything they do may be to your glory.

7 October

Osith

Osith was an Anglo-Saxon princess of the tribe of Hwiccas and married Sighere, King of East Saxons (656-675 AD). This marriage may have been to consolidate the position in Essex. A son born of this union was Offa who became king of the East Saxons but abdicated in 709 AD. Osith founded a convent at Chich where she died and was buried.

God of unity, we pray for those preparing for marriage. May they have much joy in their lives together and may they know that you are always with them.

8 October

Iwi

Iwi lived in Northumbria in the seventh century. He was a disciple of Cuthbert of Lindisfarne and sought to follow the Celtic aim of being 'an exile for Christ'. He and some sailors set sail without knowing where they would land. Arriving in Brittany, he lived as a hermit and performed acts of healing till his death. His feast is celebrated at Wilton, Winchester and Worcester and other places in the south-west of England.

Give us the faith to set out trusting you alone, O Lord, when we cannot see the way ahead.

9 October

Denys, Bishop of Paris

Denys may have been born in Italy. He was sent with five other bishops to convert the people living in Gaul. He preached eloquently in Paris and founded a centre on an island in the River Seine. Denys and two companions were killed and thrown into the Seine. When their bodies were recovered from the river they were buried in a tomb over which the abbey of Saint Denys was built. This was later to become the burial place of French kings. He is the patron saint of France.

God of love, we pray for the people of France that they may know the reality of your presence surrounding them and that they may seek a renewed faith for the good of their nation.

10 October

Paulinus, Bishop of York

Pope Gregory the Great sent two groups of monks to England. The first in 597 AD included Augustine. The second in 601 AD had Paulinus in its number. When Edwin, King of Northumbria, sought to marry Ethelburga, a Christian princess from Kent, he promised that he would allow her to worship freely. Paulinus was consecrated bishop and travelled north with Ethelburga as her chaplain. Several years later Edwin and his infant daughter were baptised on Easter Day 627/8 AD. Many nobles and others were baptised later by Paulinus in the River Swale near Yeavering as well as in Yorkshire and Lincoln. When Edwin was killed in the battle of Hatfield Chase in 633 AD, by the pagan king Penda and his Christian ally Cadwallon, Ethelburga returned to Kent accompanied by Paulinus. He acted as bishop of Rochester for his remaining years. He died in 644 AD. Five ancient churches were dedicated to him and he was revered in Canterbury and Rochester.

God of new beginnings, look upon those recently baptised, bless them as they grow that they may seek to live for you and resist all that is evil.

11 October

Kenneth (Canice)

Kenneth was born in Co Derry, Ireland c.525 AD and was taught by Finnian at Clonard and was a friend of Columba. When the plague hit his monastery at Glasnevin, he travelled to Llancarvan in Wales. He later returned to Ireland where he founded several churches. In Scotland his main church was at Inchkenneth near Mull. He was a frequent visitor to Iona where a church and cemetery were dedicated to him. Kenneth spent periods of his life as a hermit and had a close rapport with animals. He died c.600 AD.

Help us, God of eternity, to value our Christian heritage. As we remember those who have gone before us leaving their mark on the places associated with them may we seek to follow in the steps of your saints of old.

12 October

Edwin,
King of Northumbria

Edwin was a prince of the Deira dynasty and was born in 584 AD. He was exiled to Wales and East Anglia from an early age, to escape King Ethelfrith of Northumbria of the rival tribe of Bernicia. Edwin married Cwenburg of Mercia and they had two sons. In 616 AD, supported by the King of East Anglia, Edwin defeated and killed Ethelfrith and so became King of Northumbria. Probably by now a widower, Edwin sought the hand of Ethelburga, a Christian Kentish princess, in marriage. When he promised that Ethelburga would be free to worship as she pleased, his offer of marriage was accepted. Supported by Paulinus, her bishop, Ethelburga made the move north. Edwin was converted and was baptised with his infant daughter on Easter Day 627/8 AD. He was the first Christian King of Northumbria, but sadly was killed at the battle of Hatfield Chase in 633 AD by the pagan king Penda. Edwin was loved by his people and regarded as a model Christian king.

O Lord our Governor, how excellent is your name in all the earth. Guide and bless all Christian kings and queens that they may set an example of true godliness that their subjects will want to emulate.

13 October

Comgan

Thought to be an Irish chieftain and prince of Leinster, Comgan succeeded his father Kelly but was driven out by various neighbouring tribes. Wounded in battle he was sent with his sister and her children, into exile in Scotland. Comgan settled in Lochalsh near the Isle of Skye where he established a monastery. When he died his nephew Fillan buried him on Iona.

Be with those, Lord God, who are in any kind of tense situation. May they know the assurance of your presence with them and may they seek to diffuse the problem with your help.

14 October

Burchard

Although born in Wessex, Burchard was one of several people who joined Boniface in spreading the gospel to Germany. In 732 AD he was made the Bishop of Wurzburg. This was the area in which Killan, the Irish bishop had ministered some fifty years earlier. Burchard enthusiastically set himself the task of building an abbey and a school in Wurzburg. He retired from his position c.753 AD and died just a few months later.

We pray for all who seek to spread your Word to the ends of the earth. Give them patience and endurance, O Father, that they may be encouraged in their labours.

15 October

Tecla

Tecla was an English Benedictine nun at Wimborne in Dorset. The abbess Tetta sent her to assist Boniface in the evangelisation of Germany. Tecla became an abbess at Ochsenfurt and then at Kitzingen. When she died c.790 AD her relics were placed in a shrine at Kitzingen, where they remained until the Peasants War in the sixteenth century.

God of every nation, guide each one of us who genuinely seeks to follow you. May we follow the example of our blessed Lord.

16 October

Hedwig

Bavarian born, c.1174, Hedwig married the young eighteen year old king Henry – the future duke of Silesia. She was the daughter of a count and grew up in the monastery at Kitzingen. Hedwig and Henry had seven children whose quarrels caused them much heartache. She founded several religious institutions including the first convent for women in Silesia. After Henry died in 1238 she became a Cistercian nun. She sought to comfort her daughter and daughter-in-law when their husbands were killed in battle. Hedwig died in 1243.

God of reconciliation, we pray for those who are caught up in family quarrels, for all parents grieving for their children's problems, and for those children involved with their parents' difficulties.

17 October

Ethelred and Ethelbricht

The great grandsons of Ethelbert, King of Kent, their father was Ermenred. Their uncle's son Egbert arranged for them to be murdered in 640 AD. They were buried at Eastry. As penance for his part in their murder, Egbert founded the monastery at Minster, where the princes' sister Ermenburga was the first abbess. Their relics were later removed to Ramsey abbey by Oswald of Worcester.

God of truth and justice, we pray for victims of crime that they may turn to you in their distress. Stay the hands of those bent on doing evil that they may have a change of heart and not commit the crime they intend to do.

18 October

Gwen of Cornwall

The sister of Non (mother of St David), she married Selyf, King of Cornwall. She may have been the daughter of Brychan. The mother of Cybi, she founded the church of St Wenn in north Cornwall. There may have been other churches in Devon and Cornwall dedicated to her name.

Lord, give us grace to walk the narrow way, filled with your Spirit and inspired by the lives of the saints.

19 October

Frideswide

A contemporary of the Venerable Bede, Frideswide's father is thought to have been Dida, the sub-king of Eynsham. He generously endowed churches and Frideswide was the first abbess of a double monastery at Oxford. This was on the site of Christ Church. Fridewide, born c.680 AD, was adopted as patron of Oxford University in the early fifteenth century. However, Cardinal Wolsey suppressed Frideswide's monastery so that he could obtain the income from it for his Cardinal College (now Christ Church). Aethelbald of Mercia wanted to seduce her but Frideswide, wishing to remain a virgin, fled from him. Aethelbald was blinded for a time because of this, but his sight was restored when Frideswide prayed for him. She died at Oxford in 727 AD. In recent times part of her shrine has been reconstructed from remains found in a well at Christ Church.

God our Creator, Redeemer and Sanctifer , help us to live lives pleasing to you in thought and deed and word.

20 October

Acca

Acca was employed in the household of Bosa, the Bishop of York. He met Wilfrid, later Bishop of Ripon, and became his travelling companion on his journeys to Europe. When Wilfrid was dying he named Acca as his successor at Hexham. Acca was appointed both abbot and Bishop of Hexham. While bishop, an accomplished singer himself, Acca asked Maban, a monk from Canterbury, to prepare his cathedral chant. Also a brilliant scholar, Acca gave Bede a great deal of information for his Ecclesiastical History. In 732 AD Acca either retired or was removed from his position. However, when he died in 740 AD he was buried in Hexham Abbey.

We praise your name, Lord God, and give thanks for the gift of music. We think especially of those who are responsible for music in cathedrals and churches. May they always seek to glorify you, not only in their music but in their lives.

21 October

Tuda,
Bishop of Lindisfarne

After the Synod of Whitby in 664 AD which decided to adopt the Roman usage instead of the traditions of the Celtic church, Tuda was appointed bishop of Lindisfarne. He replaced Colman who returned to Ireland unwilling to accept the Roman usage. Obviously, Tuda was to be a peacemaker between the Celtic and Roman factions. Described as 'a good and devout man', Tuda sadly died of the Plague in 664 AD.

Gracious God, we pray for all peacemakers, in families, in nations, those who try to keep peace particularly UN forces. We look to the day, when Christ the Prince of Peace will reign.

22 October

Donatus (Donat, Dino)

An Irish monk of the ninth century, Donatus was later chosen as bishop of Fiesole while on his way back from a pilgrimage to Rome. Under the authority of the pope, he led his troops against the Saracens. Donatus was both a scholar and teacher. He wrote *The Life of Brigid* – a poem which praises Ireland, and which was to become his own epitaph. He founded St Brigid's Hospice for Irish pilgrims who were travelling. Donatus died in 876 AD.

Inspire all who teach that they may seek to present truth and a balanced view of life to their students. May who all learn be eager and receptive to gain knowledge and to use what they have learnt for the welfare of humanity, O Lord.

23 October

Ethelfreda

While very young, she joined the community at Romsey, which had been founded by her father Ethelwold of Wessex. She later became abbess there. She lived to a good age.

God of eternity, whether our lives are short or long may we seek to live for you and for your glory.

24 October

Anthony Claret, Archbishop of Cuba

Anthony, born in northern Spain in 1807, followed his father's occupation as a weaver. He felt called to the priesthood and was ordained in 1835. He journeyed to Rome hoping to join the Jesuits in overseas missionary work. Due to ill health he had to return to Spain where he ministered in Catalonia for ten years. Anthony was appointed bishop of the troubled See of Cuba where he later experienced assassination attempts as well as much opposition. In 1857 he became the confessor of Queen Isabella II of Spain. During the revolution of 1868 he joined the queen in exile and died in 1870 in the Cistercian monastery near Narboone.

Give courage and reassurance to those who minister in dangerous and violent parts of the world. May they know that you are with them even to the end of the world, O Lord.

25 October

Crispin and Crispinian

They were both probably Roman martyrs in the third century but there is little factual information about them. They may have been brothers who were shoemakers who earned their living by this trade while preaching to the people of Gaul. A highly unreliable English tradition states that they fled to Faversham in Kent where they worked at the Swan Inn. Shakespeare mentions them in his play *Henry V*, iv, iii. They probably died in the Diocletian persecution in c.287 AD in Rome. They are the patrons of cobblers, shoemakers and leatherworkers.

Merciful God, we pray for those who have to work at a trade to earn enough income to be able to minister and preach in your name. When they are tired, give them energy, when they are despondent , lift their spirits.

Cedd

Born in Northumbria in the late sixth century Cedd and his three brothers were trained on Lindisfarne by Aidan and Finan. They were all ordained and Chad and Cedd became bishops. When King Peada of Mercia was converted in 653 AD he wanted to share the good news of the gospel with his people. Sigebert, King of the East Saxons also became a Christian and so Oswiu of Northumbria, his overlord, sent Cedd to preach and teach in Essex. Consecrated bishop by Finan of Lindisfarne and after a fruitful mission, Cedd established monasteries at Bradwell-on-Sea and at Tilbury. Cedd was present at the Synod of Whitby in 664 AD and acted as interpreter. King Aethelwald (Oethelwald) gave Cedd some land in North Yorkshire and here he built a monastery at Lastingham where he died of the Plague in 664 AD.

You called your servant Cedd, to preach the gospel. May people see the light of Christ in us and be drawn to him.

27 October

Odran of Iona

Odran may have been abbot of Meath monastery and certainly was one of Columba's companions on Iona. Actually Odran died c.563 AD soon after Columba came to Iona. Columba had a vision of Odran's soul being fought over by angels and devils on its ascent to heaven.

Almighty God, Satan would lull us into thinking that battles between the forces of good and evil are fairy stories. May we know that they are real and that we have to wrestle against all kinds of evil powers daily but we can call on you to come to our aid and to fight for us.

28 October

Simon and Jude

Simon and Jude are included in the list of the Twelve apostles' names in St Matthew's gospel. Simon was called the Zealot, so presumably was a member of that nationalistic group in Judaism prior to Jesus calling him to be his disciple. It would seem that Jude was also known as Thaddaeus (although this may have been a surname). In modern times Jude has been thought of as 'the patron saint of lost causes' or 'of those in desperate straits'. Tradition says that Simon and Jude preached together in Mesopotamia and Syria. They were martyred in Persia (modern day Iran). Simon was cut in two while Jude was stabbed with a halberd.

Lord, you called Simon and Jude to be your witnesses even to death. Inspired by the Holy Spirit poured on them at Pentecost, they remained faithful even as they sacrificed their lives.

29 October

James Hannington, Bishop

James was born into a Congregationalist family in 1847. He became an Anglican before going to Oxford to study. After serving a five year curacy he went with the Church Missionary Society to Uganda. He was invalidated home to England due to ill health. However, in 1884 he was consecrated the first Bishop of Eastern Equatorial Africa and returned to Mombasa. The King of Uganda, who was a Muslim and who hated Christians, was very nervous when he heard of James' approach. There is an old legend that says 'beware of the stranger approaching from the east. This is dangerous and he may overthrow the ruler'. And so, king Mwanga had Hannington seized with his companions, tortured for several days and then butchered to death in 1885. As he lay dying Bishop James Hannington said 'my blood has bought this way into Uganda'. In 1977 the railway and the main roads did run into Uganda. When Archbishop Janani Luwum was martyred for his faith in 1977 he was buried next to Bishop Hannington.

Heavenly Father, you gave your martyr James Hannington the courage to die as a witness to Christ and the Gospel, give us the strength to believe and the courage to profess that same faith for which he died.

30 October

Marcellus, The Centurion

Marcellus was a Roman centurion who died a martyr's death because he refused to deny his Christian faith. While present at the birthday celebrations for the emperors Diocletian and Maximian, he cast off his soldier's belt and announced to all those present: 'I am a soldier of Jesus Christ, the eternal King. From now on I cease to serve your emperors and I despise the worship of your gods.' This outburst was reported to the governor who asked Marcellus to repeat what he had said. He reiterated his former statement and so was put to death by the sword in 298 AD.

'The blood of the martyrs is the seed of the church' we are told. Lord God, give us that same courage to surrender our lives, if ever we are called to do so for the sake of the gospel.

31 October

Begu

Reputed to have seen the death of Hilda, abbess of Whitby, in a vision, Begu was of Anglo-Saxon birth. She became a nun at Hackness in North Yorkshire. When Hilda's relics were removed to Glastonbury, the monks from Whitby wanted to find some more relics. When a tomb was found at Hackness inscribed *'hoc est sepulchrum Begu'*, they saw their chance to take these to Whitby. Miracles then began to occur there.

God of grace, as we seek to follow you, give us strength and perseverance 'to run the race which is set before us looking only to Jesus, the Author and Finisher of our faith.'

1 November

All Saints

The great festival of the Christian Church when lives of all the saints, famous and those known only to God, are celebrated. The time when we particularly give thanks for the communion of saints – that mystic link between the church militant here on earth and the church triumphant in heaven. Egbert of York instituted the feast in England where it was added to the *Martyrology of Bede* as 1 November. There are over 1,200 ancient English churches dedicated to All Saints.

'For all the saints who from their labours rest', we give thanks today for that noble army of men, women and children from every race who have sacrificed their lives rather than comprise or deny their faith. Lord, make us to be numbered with your saints.

2 November

All Souls

The date on which the Church remembers the lives of the faithful departed. A day for reflection, for all Christians to think of those who have influenced and nurtured their faith. Lanfranc's *Monastic Constitutions* propagated this celebration in England. Archbishop Chichele who is buried in Canterbury Cathedral, founded All Souls' College at Oxford.

God our Creator, as we look back on our lives we remember and give thanks for certain individuals who have set us on the right path. They have given their love and encouragement (even when we were wrong) to help us and guide us. May we too be willing to spend time and energy on those who need our assistance.

3 November

Malachy, Archbishop of Armagh

Educated at Armagh in Northern Ireland, where he became a monk, Malachy was born in 1094. He sought to reinstate various liturgical ceremonies as well as introducing Roman chants which had been abandoned because of Viking raids. Malachy was a champion of Gregorian reform as instituted by Pope Gregory. Although given the abbey of Bangor, he refused to accept any income from it. Consecrated Bishop of Connor and Down in 1124, he worked tirelessly to transform his diocese until he was exiled by a neighbouring chieftain. He retired to a monastery until appointed Archbishop of Armagh on the death of the previous incumbent, Cellach, in 1129. Once again, driven from his office by a rival, Malachy bided his time till the papal legate took action. This only caused his authority to be recognised in part of his diocese. On a visit to Rome, Malachy met Bernard of Clairvaux in whose arms he died in 1148.

God of righteousness, look upon those who face jealous rivals or people who would stand in the way of progress for the sake of your kingdom. Encourage them and uplift them when they are frustrated.

4 November

Clether (Cleer)

Clether was probably a Welsh hermit in the sixth century. After moving from Wales to north Cornwall, he settled in the Inny valley. In the fifteenth century his oratory and well were rebuilt near the eleventh century church. Details of his life are very sketchy.

Guide us and lead us in the way you would have us go, dear Father that at journey's end we may hear the words 'well done, good and faithful servant'.

5 November

Kea

It is possible that he journeyed with Fili and Rumon, through Devon and Cornwall founding churches. He is remembered in Landkey (Devon) and Kea (Cornwall) as well as in Brittany. He is thought to have been of noble birth and probably moved to Brittany where he later died.

'Christ is made a sure foundation'. We pray for those involved in building churches, Lord, for architects and planners, for local congregations trying to raise the necessary finance. May all their efforts be to your glory and may they never lose sight of the fact that the church is people not a building.

6 November

William Temple, Archbishop of Canterbury

William Temple was born in 1881 and was baptised in Exeter Cathedral where his father was the bishop. (Frederick his father later became Archbishop of Canterbury, as did his son). William was a brilliant scholar and also excelled as a philosopher and theologian. Once ordained, his abilities were recognised by the Church, and he was made a bishop at the very young age of forty. Within ten years he was Archbishop of York. His ministry was much broader than the Church of England and he worked tirelessly for the ecumenical movement as well as showing great concern for social issues. He was particularly concerned for people's welfare and this led to a debate which created state welfare provision after the Second World War. He died in 1944, just two years after becoming Archbishop of Canterbury.

God of compassion, bless those involved with welfare services that they may show patience and genuine concern for all they come in contact with. Light a flame within our cold hearts that we may be open to the love of Christ and seek to show it to those we meet.

7 November

Willibrord, Archbishop of Utrecht

Yorkshire born, Willibrord was later elected Archbishop of Utrecht. Trained by Wilfrid of Ripon, he went with twelve fellow monks as a missionary to Frisis. This work, supported by Pope Segius, proved to be very productive. In 695 AD he travelled to Rome to be consecrated bishop of Utrecht. He was a great builder of monasteries and churches, the largest of which was in Luxembourg where he died in 739 AD. Willibrord was a joyful, gracious man and when he died he was immediately venerated as a saint. His feast is specially celebrated in the Netherlands and Luxembourg.

Lord, make me a joyful Christian, like Willibrord, so that people might see Christ's light and love shining from me.

8 November

Saints and Martyrs of England

No one knows for sure when Christianity came to England. We do know, however, that British bishops attended the Council of Arles in 314 AD, which would indicate that the Church in England was organised and ordered. Through the ages many Christians from England have shared the gospel at home and abroad, some paying the ultimate price of sacrificing their lives for their faith. As the worldwide Anglican Communion (of over seventy-six million) has expanded to include people from many cultures and ethnic backgrounds, there are particular Christians who have stood out in a sometimes dark world.

We give thanks, gracious God, for the saints of England and for the Christian heritage that their faith has given. We pray for the people of the United Kingdom that they may be inspired by the saints of old to dare new endeavours for you and for your kingdom.

9 November

Theodore

Martyred in the fourth century, Theodore was a soldier. The only concrete fact about his life is his martyrdom. He is reputed to have worked miracles and to have refused to worship idols. Theodore is also thought to have destroyed a pagan temple by fire. His relics may have been dispersed to Venice and Chartres.

Many saints, O Lord, could have as their epitaph 'known only to God'. Nevertheless may we be encouraged to lead lives that are pleasing to you.

10 November

Aed

Born in Ireland, Aed founded monasteries at Meath and Munster. As well as becoming a bishop he was also skilled in medicine. His ruined hermitage at Slieve League in Co Donegal, Ireland is still a place of pilgrimage today. These cliffs at Slieve League are said to be the highest and one of the finest marine cliffs in Europe, dropping down three hundred metres to the Atlantic Ocean. There is magnificent scenery there but it is also a terrifying experience. Aed's feast day is celebrated in Scotland and Ireland.

Lord, we can only wonder at the remote places where some saints lived. Help us to take time just to draw aside from our busy lives and to listen to your voice.

11 November

Martin of Tours

Martin was born in Hungary c.316 AD, the son of a soldier. He followed his father's profession though probably as a conscript. When he became a Christian, he felt he could no longer be a soldier and tried to end his military service. He was imprisoned for this offence but later discharged from the army. While still a soldier, it is said that on seeing a half-naked beggar he sliced his cloak in two giving half to the beggar. He later had a dream in which he saw Christ wearing the cloak. Martin was a follower of Hilary of Poitiers until he decided to live as a solitary monk. In 372 AD he was consecrated Bishop of Tours. Yet he still lived as a simple priest and travelled around his diocese on foot, by donkey or by boat. Martin died, an old man, in 397 AD at Canoes and was buried at Tours. A well loved bishop, in France alone, there are over 4,000 churches dedicated to him.

Almighty God, you touched the heart of your servant Martin, to share what he had. Open our hearts, which are often hard and cold, that by the power of your Spirit we may be moved to share and to care for others.

12 November

Machar of Mull

Irish born in the sixth century, Machar may have been the son of Fiachna, a prince of Ulster, and is thought to have been baptised as a young man by Colman of Kilmacduagh. He accompanied Columba to Iona and ministered on the Isle of Mull and later in Aberdeen. Water from his well was used for baptisms in the cathedral in Aberdeen.

Holy God, be with those preparing for baptism whatever their age, that they may 'continue Christ's faithful servants to their lives' end'.

13 November

Stanislaus Kostka

Of a noble family, Stanislaus was born in 1550 in the castle of Rostkovo, Poland. He studied at the Jesuit College with his brother who bullied him. Unhappy with his life and under pressure from his family, Stanislaus became ill. After he recovered he decided to become a Jesuit and travelled to Rome where he was received into the Society of Jesus aged just seventeen. He was only to live another nine months, however, dying in 1568.

God of healing, we pray for all who are ill, be with them and may they know the reality of your presence surrounding them in their distress. May they turn to you the Great Physician.

14 November

Dyfrig

Thought to have been born in Madley, he later ministered around the Hereford/Gwent area. He became a monk and sometime after this was made a bishop. Dyfrig was one of the most important saints in South Wales and played a major role with his involvement with Romano-British Christianity. He built churches and monasteries and died c.550 AD.

Lord God, we ask that you will guide all leaders of your church. May they seek always to remain true to the gospel and to live out their faith in such a way that others may want to follow you.

15 November

Malo

His main 'claim to fame' is as the 'apostle of Brittany'. Malo may have been born in Wales in the sixteenth/seventeenth century. As a bishop he travelled widely on horseback and sang psalms as he journeyed. Unfortunately, he made enemies where he preached and he was driven out from some towns. He was then sent to Saintes where he remained, until the townsfolk asked him to come back. However, he died before this request could come to fruition.

Lord, be with those who seek to preach the gospel, where people are violently opposed to it. Protect and guide those who preach and give receptive hearts to those who listen.

16 November

Margaret of Scotland

Margaret, born in 1046, received most of her education in Hungary. Her family had been exiled there when the Danish kings occupied the English throne. After the Norman Conquest in 1066, since she was one of the last remaining members of the Anglo-Saxon royal family, she fled to Scotland for safety. Malcolm III, King of Scotland and her protector, married her in 1069. This was a happy marriage and the present British monarchy can trace its ancestry through Matilda, their daughter. Not only beautiful but generous and intelligent, Margaret lived out her faith in prayer and reading. She was buried, at the age of forty-seven, beside her husband in Dunfermline Abbey which she had built. During the Reformation their bodies were moved to Madrid.

Almighty God, we give thanks for all Christian kings and queens who govern their people with justice and integrity and seek to lead by example.

17 November

Hugh of Lincoln

Hugh was born in Burgundy c.1140. In his mid-twenties he entered the Carthusian Grande Charteuse monastery where he was appointed Procurator. King Henry II requested him to take on the role of prior of a monastery at Witham in Somerset. This establishment was failing, but under Hugh's leadership it began to improve greatly. He reluctantly accepted the position of Bishop of Lincoln offered by King Henry. Hugh worked very hard in his diocese – visiting, teaching and rebuilding the cathedral after an earthquake. Hugh could be firm but gentle and was greatly loved. He died in 1200. Hugh is usually depicted with a tame swan which had become a pet.

Creator God, we thank you for the joy which animals give, for the love of our pets who share our lives – our laughter and our tears. May we all work for an end to cruelty to these creatures which you have made.

18 November

Mawes

The town of St Mawes in Cornwall, where he was probably born, is named after him. He may have been a bishop in Brittany. Noted for his teaching, Mawes lived with several companions on an island 'Ile Modez' near to the coast of Leon. Many churches in Brittany are dedicated to him.

Lord, give us grace to follow the saints, to be inspired by their examples and to seek to follow in their steps.

19 November

Hilda, Abbess of Whitby (Hild)

Of royal blood, Hilda was born in 614 AD. She was baptised at the same time as King Edwin, her granduncle by Paulinus in 627-28 AD. When she was in her thirties, Hilda was about to enter the convent of Chelles in East Anglia, when Aidan asked her to return to Northumbria. She was abbess of the community at Hartlepool which was governed by the Rule of St Columbanus. In 657 AD she went to the double monastery at Whitby. Under her leadership this became a real centre of learning and she acquired much literature for the library. She hosted the famous Synod of Whitby in 664 AD which decided to favour the Roman usage over that used by the Celtic church. A woman of great wisdom, many came to seek her advice. During the last six years of her life she was very ill. When the Danes attacked Whitby c.800 AD, her relics were removed to Glastonbury, although Gloucester also laid claim to them. There are several churches dedicated to her. She died in 680 AD. Her feast used to be celebrated on 17 November but has been transferred to 19 November.

Lord of all wisdom, we praise you for the life of your servant Hilda who sought for the good of your Church to reconcile those that were divided. By her holiness and guidance she exercised leadership with grace. She shone as a bright light for you where there was darkness and discord.

20 November

Edmund, King of East Anglia

Born into a Christian Saxon family in 841 AD, Edmund became king of the East Angles c.865 AD. The Vikings fought in battle in 869-70 AD against Edmund who was defeated and imprisoned. Given the opportunity to deny his Christian faith and become a vassal of Ingwar, the Viking invader, Edmund stood firm and refused. So he was killed at Hellesdon in Norfolk in 869 AD and his body was buried in a nearby chapel. In 915 AD when his body was found to be incorrupt, his remains were moved to what is now Bury St Edmunds. In 1020 King Cnut (Canute) ordered that a stone church should be built at Bury as a means of reparation for what the Vikings had done.

Edmund sought to honour you, O Lord, in death as he had in life. When we stand before your judgment seat may we hear the words 'well done, good and faithful servant'.

21 November

Condedus

English born in the seventh century, Condedus settled at Fontaine-Saint-Valery in France and became a monk at Fontenelle for a short period. He then returned to living the life of a hermit on an island called Belcinac situated in the middle of the River Seine. This establishment had been supported by King Thierry III. There were other churches on the island as well. Condedus was buried at Fontenelle. In modern times the level of the Seine has risen and the island is no longer visible.

Lord, you bid us to come apart from the world and rest awhile that we may be renewed by your Spirit. Help us to be still and know that you are God.

22 November

Cecilia

Cecilia lived in the third century but very little is known of her life. After her husband and brother were martyred for their faith, Cecilia buried them. She was then called to answer to the Roman prefect. However, she refused to sacrifice to the gods and was put to death. Her remains were later translated c.820 AD by Pope Pascal I to her own church. In sixteenth century she was adopted as the patron of musicians. In 1584 when the Academy of Music in Rome was founded, she was chosen as its patroness. Naturally, she is usually depicted with some musical instrument.

God of beauty and harmony, bless all musicians that they may always seek to offer the best they can in your service till their music is joined with the music of Heaven.

23 November

Clement

The fourth Bishop of Rome, Clement wrote his Epistle to the Corinthians c.96 AD. This was a significant document explaining how the Church and its clergy functioned as well as being definitive evidence of the martyrdom of Peter and Paul. Supposedly, Clement was sent into exile in the Crimea because he was too diligent in his papal duties. He is said to have been forced to work in the salt-mines where he discovered a miraculous water supply. Clement was martyred by being thrown into the sea with an anchor around his neck. The most famous English church dedicated to him is St Clement Danes in London. He is the patron for the authority responsible for lighthouses and lightships.

Encourage those, loving Father, who may seem over zealous in the performance of their duties thus causing colleagues to be jealous of their diligence in doing things for you. May they not be proud but simply keep on doing the very best for you and for your service.

24 November

Enfleda, Abbess of Whitby

Enfleda was baptised as an infant with her father Edwin, King of Northumbria in 627 AD by Paulinus. Her mother was Ethelburga, a Christian princess from Kent. When her father was killed in battle, Enfleda and her mother fled to Kent. In 642 AD she married Oswiu of Bernicia. It was hoped that the marriage would unite the two sections of Northumbria (Deira and Bernicia) into one kingdom. While she kept Easter according to the Roman usage, her husband calculated the date of Easter in the tradition of the Celtic church. This issue was finally resolved at the Synod of Whitby in 664 AD when the majority of those present voted to accept the Roman usage. When Enfleda's husband died in 670 AD she became a nun at Whitby where she was joined by her daughter, Elfleda. She died c.704 AD.

Help us, Lord God, to aim to be peacemakers in all situations. Give us patience and grace to listen to both sides of the argument and to speak wisely guided by your Spirit.

25 November

Isaac Watts, Hymn Writer

Isaac was born at Southampton in 1674 and attended the local grammar school. He could have gone to university, but decided to choose the academy, favoured by dissenters, at Stoke Newington. After achieving a high academic standard there, he became a pastor in the Independent (Congregationalist) Church in London. However, he suffered continual ill-health, so resigned his position in 1712 and retired to Stoke Newington. Some years later, when the doctrine of the Trinity was being imposed on his fellow dissenting ministers, he vehemently opposed this. He is best remembered for the many hymns he wrote including 'When I Survey the Wondrous Cross' and 'Jesus shall Reign where'er the Sun' to name but a few. He died in 1748.

We praise your name, everlasting God, for the gift of music, and especially those who write hymns to your glory. We give thanks for their creativity and their commitment to use their talents in your service.

26 November

Leonard of Port Maurice

Born in Port Maurizio (Liguria) in 1676, he was educated by the Jesuits in Rome. He became a Franciscan and was ordained in 1703. Placed in charge of the Florentine friary of San Francesco del Monte, he implemented the Franciscans' strict rule about poverty. Many were encouraged to join this community. Leonard was made the Guardian of St Bonaventure's in Rome. Here he ministered to soldiers, prisoners and slaves. He often preached in the open air when he went to Umbria and other areas in 1736. Leonard was posted to Corsica in 1744 in the hope of quelling the violence and disorder, but this strategy failed and he only remained there for six months. He died in Rome in 1750.

Heavenly Father, we bring before you the places in our world that are torn apart through violence and ravaged by war. Bless all efforts at peaceful negotiation that diplomacy may win the day and people may be able to live in security.

27 November

Congar of Congresbury

Congar was one of the Welsh missionaries who evangelised Somerset and Devon in the sixth century. He grew up in the monastery at Congresbury in Somerset. There is a legend which says that when he placed his staff in the ground it took root resulting in the growth of a yew tree. Congar later went back to Wales but died while on pilgrimage to Jerusalem. There are churches dedicated to him both in Brittany and Cornwall.

Each day of our earthly pilgrimage draws us closer to the end of our lives. Lord, help us to use the time you give us wisely and to your glory.

28 November

Juthwara (Aude)

She was probably born in Cornwall and when she died, her relics were translated to Sherborne. Apart from this information, little is known of her life. Juthwara may have died at Lanteglos near Camelford in Cornwall. The church there, St Julitta's may have been Juthwara's. A neighbouring parish of Lancast is dedicated to her sisters.

Creator God, we pray for women in their daily lives, as they often struggle to fulfil their role as a parent as well as trying to earn a living. Be with those who are downtrodden and who feel they have never had the opportunity of realising their full potential.

29 November

Brendan of Birr

Brendan was both a friend and disciple of Columba of Iona. At a synod at Meltown in Meath, Ireland, he spoke eloquently for the lifting of Columba's excommunication. When Brendan died, Columba had a vision while on Iona, of angels receiving Brendan's soul. The monastery at Birr which Brendan had founded is where the Macregol Gospels were written. These are now in the Bodleian Library in Oxford.

God of beauty and creativity, you give each one of us gifts to use. We give thanks for the skill and patience of those who compiled and illuminated manuscripts through the ages and for those who seek to conserve their artistry today.

30 November

Andrew

Andrew was one of the Twelve Apostles and brother of Simon Peter. He was a fisherman at Capernaum when Jesus called him to follow him. Prior to this he had been a disciple of John the Baptist. He is mentioned in all four gospels and specially in bringing the boy to Jesus who offered to share his lunch in the feeding of the five thousand. Also he was approached by the Greeks (John 12 vv 20-22) who wanted to see Jesus. No-one knows where Andrew died, although it was c.60 AD, nor where he is buried. Tradition has it that his relics were moved from Patras to Scotland and so for this reason Andrew became the patron saint of Scotland. St Andrew's cross (blue background with white saltire cross) represents Scotland on the Union Jack.

Lord, we thank you for the life of your servant Andrew and pray for the people of Scotland that they may be inspired by his example. May we all seek, like Andrew, to bring others to Jesus.

1 December

Tudwal

Tudwal was a Welsh bishop in the sixth century. He went to Brittany where he established a monastery at Lan Pabu. It was at the insistence of King Childebert I that Tudwal became a bishop. Three places are named after him on the Lleyn peninsula. There is a ruined chapel at St Tudwal's Island East (Ynys Tudwal) which was originally his hermitage. In Brittany his feast is celebrated on 1 December while in some places it is 30 November or 2 December.

God of history, we praise you for our Christian heritage – for men, women and children who have given their lives for your sake in every age. May we too remain faithful and steadfast in our resolve to follow you, whatever the cost.

2 December

Viviana

When the Roman governor, Apronianus, lost an eye in an accident in 363 AD, he blamed the Christians for this. A former prefect of the city and his wife, Flavian and Dafrosa, who were Christians were singled out for punishment. Flavian's face was burnt with red hot metal and his wife was beheaded. They had two daughters, Viviana and Demetria who were also Christians. When commanded to speak before the governor, Demetria spoke boldly of her faith in Jesus and then collapsed to the ground dead. Viviana, however, had much more torture and suffering to endure, yet she never wavered. She was finally tied to a pillar and scourged with lead-tipped whips.

Be with all young people who are trying to live the Christian life, O God, in a world full of so many temptations and hostile to anything good and pure. Strengthen them and help them to walk the narrow way to their journeys' end.

3 December

Birinus

Sent by Pope Honorius I to continue the evangelisation of Britain, Birinus was appointed the first Bishop of Dorchester in Oxfordshire. He set out to go to the Midlands, but when he reached the West Saxons, he found them living in such a pagan state that he decided to settle amongst them. During his fifteen years as bishop, Birinus baptised many people. Late in life he built a church at Winchester which increased its ecclesiastical importance in the kingdom. He died in 650 AD and his relics were translated to Winchester about forty years later.

Give us concern, O God of love, for those around us who do not know you. May we by our caring and our love witness to your truth and bring light to a dark world.

4 December

Osmund

The son of the count of Seez, Osmund followed William the Conqueror to England. Here he acted as a royal chaplain until promoted to the Chancellorship in 1072. Six years later he was made Bishop of Salisbury. He oversaw the completion and consecration of the cathedral with its own Chapter, which became a model for later English cathedrals. Osmund had a great appreciation of books – both reading, copying and binding them. He was involved in the compilation of the *Domesday Book*. He died in 1099 and was buried in the old cathedral at Old Sarum. In 1457 a new shrine was set up in the Lady Chapel of Salisbury Cathedral, remnants of which are still visible.

Eternal God, we pray for those who seek to conserve treasures from the past. May we appreciate these things made with such skill but may we never lose sight of the fact that all these things will pass away one day. May we lay up treasure in heaven.

5 December

Justinian

Definitive information about him is scarce, but it is thought that he may have been born in the sixth century in Brittany, where he was also ordained. He then lived as a hermit on Ramsey Island off the Welsh coast. Justinian is said to have been attacked by three servants who murdered him by cutting off his head. From the spot where it fell a spring of water gushed forth which had healing properties. The church of Llanstinan near Fishguard in Wales is dedicated to him.

We think of those, O Lord, who have been treacherously betrayed by those close to them. You yourself know the betrayal of someone you called 'friend'. Be with all who suffer because of the cruelty of others and may they know that you walk the way of the world's wounded with them.

6 December

Nicholas

Nicholas was born in the fourth century. He later became bishop of Myra in south-western Turkey. Very little is known of his life. Legend has it that he left three bags of gold as marriage dowries to save some poor girls from prostitution. The pawn-brokers symbol of three bags of gold stems from this legend. He is buried at Bari in Italy. Noted for his generosity, Nicholas is the patron of children, sailors as well as various other groups. The personage of Father Christmas (Santa Claus) is based on Nicholas. Benjamin Britten wrote *Saint Nicholas* to celebrate the life of the saint. There are over 400 churches in England alone dedicated to him.

Give us generous hearts, O God, that like Nicholas, we may bring joy to others and may we help to make the world a better place.

7 December

Diuma

Diuma was born in Ireland. He was sent with three other priests by Finan, Bishop of Lindisfarne, to evangelise Mercia after Peada, the son of the pagan king Penda had converted to Christianity c.652 AD. During the reign of King Oswiu of Northumbria, Diuma was consecrated bishop of the Mercians and Middle Angles by Finan. He died in 658 AD.

God of our pilgrimage, walk with us that inspired by the good example of your saints, we may at last reach your heavenly kingdom.

8 December

Budoc

Budoc was the grandson of the King of Brest. He and his mother were exiled to Cornwall for some years in the sixth century. Later he became a monk in Brittany. He may have lived as recluse on the island of Laurea for some time. When he was made Bishop of Dol he continued in this position for many years. Patron of Budock and Budoc Vean in Cornwall and St Budeaux in Devon, he was also venerated in Pembrokeshire and in Brittany. His relics are at Plourin.

God of truth, help us to give ourselves to you daily, that renewed by your Holy Spirit, we may ever hold fast to the blessed hope of our calling. May we like the saints of old, be welcomed into your place of many mansions.

9 December

Leocadia

She was the daughter of a noble family who lived in Toledo. During the persecution by the Roman emperor Diocletian she was arrested and asked to rescind her faith. Leocadia stood firm, refusing to deny her Lord and so was thrown into prison. She was cruelly tortured and eventually died from her wounds in 304 AD. During the ninth century her relics were moved to Oviedo during the persecutions of Abd ar-Rahman II. A basilica was built there over her remains. After several more moves, her relics were finally translated to Toledo in April 1587 in the presence of Phillip II of Spain. The small town of Leocadia, near Samares, between Braga and Guimaraes in northern Portugal is named after her.

Lord, your service is perfect freedom, be with those who are imprisoned for their faith, for prisoners of conscience. May they know that you are with them and will never let them go.

10 December

Eulalia of Merida

Prudentius and Venantius Fortunatus wrote hymns to honour this Spanish virgin martyr. Bede records her martyrdom in his hymn to Etheldreda. Legend has it that Eulalia was a young girl during the persecutions of Diocletian and that she refused to offer sacrifice to the gods. Refusing to deny her faith, she was burnt alive c.304 AD.

God of grace, give us courage as we walk the narrow way on our earthly pilgrimage that with eyes fixed on Jesus, we may serve you faithfully till our lives' end.

11 December

Damasus

Although born in Rome c.304 AD, Damasus was of Spanish blood. His father was a priest. Damasus became a deacon in the church while Pope Liberius was Bishop of Rome. Later in 366 AD Damasus became pope himself, supported by the Emperor Valentinian. However, some of the clergy wanted Ursinus to fill this office. A power struggle ensued and Ursinus was sent into exile. In 382 AD Damasus commissioned Jerome to revise the old Latin translations of the Bible by producing a *Vulgate* version instead of several existing versions. He made sure that the papal archives were well-preserved. Damasus built churches one of which – SS Marcus and Marcellianus was to be his final resting place when he died in 384 AD.

Almighty God, we pray for those who translate the scriptures into different languages and dialects. Inspire them as they seek to share your Word with others.

12 December

Edburga of Minster

Edburga is thought to have been a princess of Wessex who was a follower of Mildred, the abbess of the convent at Minster-in-Thanet. In 716 AD Edburga was appointed abbess of this establishment. She built a church at Minster into which the relics of Mildred were translated. She was skilled in writing and much about her life is contained in the Letters of Boniface. When Edburga died in 751 AD she was buried in the church at Minster and miracles of healing are reputed to have taken place there.

God of healing and wholeness, look in love and mercy on those who are sick, bless those who care for them. May they know that you are with them in all their trials and tribulations.

13 December

Lucia (Lucy)

Lucia was possibly from a wealthy family in Sicily. She gave her possessions to the poor and vowed to remain a virgin. It is thought that she was put to death by the sword in Syracuse in 304 AD during the reign of the Emperor Diocletian. Her feast is celebrated with much joy in Sweden where it is recognised as a festival of light during the dark days of winter. In Swedish families the youngest daughter, wearing a long white robe and wearing a crown decorated with candles, wakes her parents by bringing coffee and rolls to them. The song 'Santa Lucia' is still popular.

May we like your servant Lucia, shine as lights in a dark world, O Lord of light. May Christ shine through us that all may know that we belong to you.

14 December

Hybald

The Venerable Bede describes Hybald as a holy man. He lived in the seventh century and was an abbot in Lincolnshire where there are four churches dedicated to him. The town of Hibaldstow is named for him. His monastery may have been at Bardney.

God of purity and beauty, help us to live holy lives that are pleasing to you. May we set our minds on all that is good and true so that we may glorify you.

15 December

Offa of Essex

Offa, according to Bede, was greatly loved by his subjects. He was the son of Sighere, King of the East Saxons and Osith, an Anglo-Saxon princess. He became King c.707 AD. However, two years later, he left his wife and all his possessions, abdicated his throne and journeyed to Rome. Shortly after this he entered a monastery and died c.709 AD.

Give wisdom, O God, to all rulers that they may make decisions for the benefit of their people. May they never lose sight of the fact that all authority comes from you.

16 December

Adelaide

The Empress Adelaide lived in the tenth century. Her first husband was murdered by his successor, who then sought to marry Adelaide. She refused and was then imprisoned. Eventually she was freed by King Otto the Great who married her. When he died, Adelaide's daughter-in-law forced her to leave the royal court. Later her son thought better of this treatment of his mother, asked her forgiveness and had Adelaide reinstated at court. However, Adelaide was again forced into exile when he died and she did not return till she was in old age. Despite her hard life, she still remained kind and loving. She died in 999AD in the convent at Seltz in Alsace which she had founded.

Loving God, look with compassion on all those who are treated badly by their families. May your reconciling grace move in hearts that are hard and embittered.

17 December

Begga

A daughter of Pepin, mayor to the palace of three Frankish kings, Begga married the son of Arnulf of Metz. A son, Pepin of Heristal, was born of this union and he began the dynasty of the French kings known as Carolingians. While out hunting in 692 AD her husband was killed and so Begga decided to make a pilgrimage to Rome. She founded seven churches at Adenne on the River Meuse. These were inspired by the seven famous churches in Rome. Begga's sister Gertrude had become a nun early in life and the nuns from her convent joined Begga in the abbey which she had established. Begga died there in 693 AD.

Still today people go on pilgrimage, O Lord, lead them in their search even when they do not know what they are looking for. Our hearts are restless till they find their rest in you.

18 December

Flannan of Killaloe

Born in the seventh century, Flannan was a wandering preacher who, like many Irish monks, kept 'on the move' rather that settling in any one place. The cathedral at Killaloe, where he had been bishop became the resting place for his remains. There is also a Flannan mentioned in Scotland after whom the Flannan Islands (west of Lewis and Harris) are named. They are probably one and the same person.

Omniscient God, you know of every person on this earth, for not even a tiny sparrow can fall without you being aware. May such knowledge comfort us that you are always with us.

19 December

Samthann

She was an Irish nun who founded Clonbroney Abbey near Granard in Co Longford. Thought to have been brought up by Cridan, King of Caibre Cabhra, she became a nun at Ernaide, Co Donegal. Samthann inspired many of the leaders of the reform movement *Célí Dé* (Servants of God) by her simple lifestyle. She was a wise and holy woman. Two of her sayings about going on pilgrimage are 'the distance to heaven is the same from every end of the earth and if a person comes close to God, he cannot be far from home' the other is 'the kingdom of heaven can be reached from every land'. She was greatly loved by her community and died in 739 AD. Some people celebrate her feast day as 18 December.

We give thanks, Almighty Father, for holy men and women who have lived their lives in service to you and to others. Urged on by their example may we run with patience the race that is set before us.

20 December

Dominic of Silos

His parents were Spanish peasants and he spent his early life as a shepherd boy. He was born at Canas in Navarre. Dominic entered the Benedictine monastery of San Millan de Cogolla and quickly rose to the rank of prior. However, King Garcia III of Navarre claimed that some of the monastery estates belonged to him. Dominic disputed this and eventually had to flee into exile to escape the king's persecution. He went with two other monks to the court of King Ferdinand I of Castile who gave him protection as well as appointing him prior of the rundown monastery of San Sebastian, Silos in the diocese of Burgos. Dominic and his companions worked hard and eventually their efforts paid off, with that monastery becoming one of the greatest in the land. Dominic died in his monastery in 1073.

Encourage those, O Lord, who seek to get order out of chaos. May they do this to honour you and not from any sense of pride, that your kingdom on earth may expand and spread.

21 December

Beornwald

Beornwald was a priest in the eighth century. He may have been the founder of the large minster church at Bampton. The celebration of his feast there is mentioned in an early twelfth century charter. His shrine was probably in the north transept of the church and is marked by a brass indent of a bishop in episcopal robes but without a mitre on his head. Since Bampton was not a monastic church it would seem that Beornwald was responsible for an old style secular minster.

'To follow the saints, Lord, let this be our aim.' Surrounded by so great a cloud of witnesses may we fix our eyes firmly on Jesus, the Author and Finisher of our faith.

22 December

Jutta of Diessenberg

German born in the late eleventh century, Jutta was the sister of Meginhard, the Count of Spanheim. She became a nun and gathered together a community of like-minded Christian women and later was made their abbess. Jutta was responsible for the upbringing of a weak, sickly girl, Hildegard of Bingen, who was to become one of Germany's greatest mystics. Jutta nurtured the girl as well as educating her. When Jutta died in 1136, Hildegard became abbess in her place. Hildegard praised Jutta's holiness by saying: 'Jutta was like a river with many tributaries, overflowing with the grace of God.' Her tomb was visited by many people.

Lord of the years, we give thanks for those who have nurtured us and led us to know you. May we seek to guide the young that they may strive to follow you.

23 December

Thorlac of Skalholt

Thorlac was born into a noble family in Iceland in 1133. While still in his early twenties, he entered the priesthood studying in Lincoln and Paris for ten years. When he returned to Iceland in 1161, he lived very simply, caring for others. Some years later he was given a large property where he established a community of Austin canons. He was the abbot there and his mother was the housekeeper. Augustine, Archbishop of Nidaros (Trondheim) consecrated him bishop of Skalholt in 1178. He sought to bring some reforms to the church. In his monastery at Thykkviboer it is quite likely that some of the Icelandic manuscripts, which still exist, were produced. He died in 1193 and was canonised by the Assembly of Iceland in 1198. He is Iceland's first saint.

Lord of every nation, we pray for the people of Iceland, that as a nation inspired by Thorlac's life of service they may be steadfast in their service to you.

24 December

Mochua

Mochua was born in Connacht, Ireland. He entered the army for a time, but while still a young man he became a monk. His main community was at Timahoe, Co Laois. He died c.657 AD at another of his monasteries at Derinish, Co Cavan. There are several other saints called Mochua.

God of grace, you call each one of us by name, you know us as individuals. May we recognise that each one is precious in your sight.

25 December

Alburga

Alburga was the half-sister of Egbert, king of Wessex. When her husband Wolstan, Earl of Wiltshire died, Alburga changed the foundation of canons which her husband had established, into a convent. She then became a nun and died c.810 AD in this same convent.

Lord Jesus, thank you for being willing to set aside your majesty and be born as a tiny baby for us. Help us as we read about some of your saints to feel inspired to follow their examples. May we at the last hear you say to us: 'Well done, good and faithful servant'.

26 December

Stephen,
The First Martyr

Stephen was a deacon and first martyr of the Christian Church. The Acts of the Apostles contain the only information we know of him. He was one of seven deacons, quite possibly a Greek Jew, who was appointed to distribute alms and to care for the needs of the faithful, thus allowing the apostles more freedom to concentrate on preaching. Stephen was well-versed in the scriptures. When he launched an attack on the Jews for resisting the Holy Spirit and for killing Christ the Messiah, as their forebears had murdered the prophets, he was set upon and stoned to death. While they were hurling rocks at him, Stephen saw a vision of Jesus seated at the right hand of God. Stephen died c.35 AD.

Living Lord, you called your servant Stephen, to be a faithful witness even to death. Be with those who still today, and in many different countries, lay down their lives for the sake of the gospel.

27 December

John, The Evangelist

The son of Zebedee, John was one of the inner circle of Jesus' disciples with Peter and James who shared several special occasions. Jesus called John and his brother James 'the sons of thunder'. No doubt the episode when they wanted to call down fire from heaven on the unbelieving Samaritans would account for this nickname. James suffered martyrdom at an early age while John lived to a great age. By tradition John is thought to have written the fourth gospel. Christ committed his mother to John's care when he was dying on the cross. After Jesus' resurrection, John settled in Ephesus. He may have written the *Book of Revelation* while on Patmos. He died in the late first century.

Lord Jesus, you called you servant John to be a close friend in your earthly ministry. Open our eyes and our hearts as we read your Word.

28 December

Holy Innocents

When the Magi (The Wise Men) came to Herod the Great asking where a new King had been born, Herod was determined to do away with all potential rivals. He issued an edict that all baby boys under the age of two in Bethlehem should be slain. And so, the massacre of the Holy Innocents ensued. From the earliest Christian times these children have been considered martyrs – not only did they die for Christ but instead of Christ.

You took the little children in your arms and blessed them when you were on earth, dear Lord. Look in mercy on all children who are cruelly treated and especially those who die for their Christian faith.

29 December

Thomas Becket, Archbishop of Canterbury

Thomas was born in Cheapside in London in 1118 and was the son of a merchant of Norman descent. Educated at Merton Priory and in Paris, Becket entered the service of Theobald, Archbishop of Canterbury, as a clerk. Later he studied Canon Law at Bologna and Auxerre, was ordained deacon and was then appointed Archdeacon of Canterbury. On Theobald's recommendation, King Henry II made him Chancellor in 1155 and for seven years Becket and the king remained close friends. After Theobald's death, Henry appointed Becket, Archbishop of Canterbury in 1162. Becket was reluctant, sensing there could be conflict in this position of divided loyalty to the church and to the king. In 1163 Henry sought the agreement of all bishops to a set of articles that was being compiled, one of which was that clergy accused of a crime should be tried by a secular court and not in an ecclesiastical one. When these articles were made public in the Constitutions of Clarendon in 1164, Becket flatly refused to accept them, and the king demanded that a council of bishops and barons should pass sentence on Becket. Becket fled to France where he was given refuge at Pontigny in Burgundy and later at the Benedictine Abbey at Sens which was under the special protection of the French king. Thomas remained in exile for six years, returning to Canterbury in December 1170 where he was given an enthusiastic welcome by the people. Unfortunately, the reconciliation between Henry II and Becket did not last long. While he was in exile, Prince Henry had been crowned king by the other bishops, in defiance of the rights of the Archbishop of Canterbury. Becket excommunicated these bishops. Henry in a fit of rage demanded: 'Will no-one rid me of this turbulent priest?' Four knights took his words literally and sailed from France to England where they murdered Thomas in Canterbury Cathedral during Vespers late in the day on 29 December 1170. Thomas was buried for a time in the crypt but his body was later removed to a shrine in the Trinity Chapel in 1220. Many miracles of healing took place and this remained a site of pilgrimage until it was destroyed by Henry VIII in 1538. Here a single candle still burns to mark the site of his shrine.

God of truth, your servant Thomas gave his life for what he believed to be right. Give us courage to stand firm in the face of adversity that we may honour you by our lives.

30 December

Egwin,
Bishop of Worcester

He may have been related to Ethelred, King of Mercia. Egwin founded Evesham Abbey and later became Bishop of Worcester in 693 AD. Unfortunately, he had powerful enemies who had the ear of the king and the Archbishop of Canterbury and as a result, he was forced to resign from his see. He was later vindicated of any charge by the pope and returned to his diocese. He died in 717 AD. When the authenticity of some of the Anglo-Saxon saints was questioned by Archbishop Lanfranc and some Normans in the eleventh century, the relics of Egwin were subjected to being taken on a tour of southern England by the monks of Evesham Abbey. This was a fund-raising project to procure money to build a new church and miracles also took place in various places.

Give us the faith to trust you, the ears to hear you and the hearts to love you, O Father, that we may believe in spite of our unbelief.

31 December

Sylvester

Sylvester was the son of a Roman called Rufinus. Little is known of his life but he did become pope. He may have been represented at a synod in Arles in France by some papal legates and at the Council of Nicea in 325 AD. Constantine gave him the Lateran Palace in Rome. Sylvester was a great builder of churches in Rome – probably organising the construction of St Peters, Holy Cross and St Laurence-outside-the-walls as well as others. He died in 335 AD and was buried in a church at the cemetery of Priscilla. Sylvester's relics were later translated to the church of St Silvester in Capite in 761 AD.

God of opportunity and new beginnings, as we stand on the threshold of a new year, give us foresight and energy to dare new things for your kingdom. May we know that your saints are in heaven urging us on till we reach our final goal.

Bibliography

Toulson, Shirley, *The Celtic Year*, Vega Books, 28 October 2002.
Harton, Sibyl, *Stars Appearing*, Hodder & Stoughton, 1954.
Clarke, C.P.S., *Everyman's Book of Saints*, Andrew Mowbray Incorporated, Publishers, 01 December 1968.
Bentley, James, *A Calendar of Saints*, Guild Publishing, 1986.
Farmer, David Hugh, *The Oxford Dictionary of Saints*, Oxford University Press, 22 July 2004.
Exciting Holiness: Holy Persons and Holy Days, John Watson
Jockle, Clemens, *Encyclopaedia of Saints*, Collins & Brown, 31 December 1999.
Butler, Alban, *Butler's Lives of the Saints*, Paraclete Press, 1 December 2005.
Simms, George Otto, *Commemorating Saints & Others of the Irish Church*, Columba Press, 1 January 1998.
Frodsham, Paul, *Cuthbert and the Northumbrian Saints*, Northern Heritage, 20 July 2009.
Bede, *The Ecclesiastical History of the English People*, Oxford University Press, 11 September 2008.